STRATEGIC MANAGEMENT

OF HUMAN RESOURCES

IN HEALTH SERVICES ORGANIZATIONS

STRATEGIC MANAGEMENT

OF HUMAN RESOURCES

IN HEALTH SERVICES ORGANIZATIONS

SECOND EDITION

Myron D. Fottler, Ph.D.
Professor and Director, Ph.D.
Program in Administration—
Health Services
Department of Health Services
Administration
School of Health-Related Professions
University of Alabama at Birmingham
Birmingham, Alabama

S. Robert Hernandez, Dr.P.H.
Professor
Department of Health Services
Administration
School of Health-Related Professions
University of Alabama at Birmingham
Birmingham, Alabama

Charles L. Joiner, Ph.D.
Dean and Professor
School of Health-Related Professions
University of Alabama at Birmingham
Birmingham, Alabama

and Associates

NOTICE TO THE READER

Cover Design by Timothy J. Conners
Publishing Team:
  Senior Acquisitions Editor: William Burgower
  Assistant Editor: Debra M. Flis
  Project Manager: Megan A. Terry
  Production Coordinator: Barbara A. Bullock
  Art and Design Coordinator: Timothy J. Conners

For information, address
Delmar Publishers Inc.
3 Columbia Circle, Box 15015
Albany, NY 12203-5015

Printed in the United States of America
Published simultaneously in Canada
by Nelson Canada,
a division of the Thomson Corporation

2 3 4 5 6 7 8 9 10   XXX   00 99 98 97 96 95 94

Library of Congress Cataloging-in-Publication Data

Strategic management of human resources in health services
  organizations / edited by Myron D. Fottler, S. Robert Hernandez,
  Charles L. Joiner.—2nd ed.
      p.   cm.—(Delmar series in health services administration)
    Includes bibliographical references and index.
    ISBN 0-8273-5676-5
    1. Health facilities—Personnel management.   2. Corporate
  planning.   I. Fottler, Myron D.   II. Hernandez, S. Robert, 1946–
    III. Joiner, Charles L. (Charles Lee)   IV. Series.
    [DNLM: 1. Health Services—organization & administration.
  2. Personnel Management—methods.   W 84.1 S898 1994]
  RA971.35.S87   1994
  362.1′1′0681—dc20
  DNLM/DLC
  for Library of Congress   93-27232
                                                          CIP

INTRODUCTION TO THE SERIES

This Series in Health Services is now in its second decade of providing top quality teaching materials to the health administration/public health field. Each year has witnessed further strengthening of the market position of each of the principal books in the Series, also reflecting the continued excellence of the products. Each author, book editor, and contributor to the Series has helped build what is widely recognized as the top textbook and issues collection of books available in this field today.

But we have achieved only a beginning. Everyone involved in the Series is committed to further expansion of the scope, technical excellence, and usability of the Series. Our goal is to do more for you, the reader. We will add new books in important areas, seek out more excellent authors, and increase the physical attributes of the book to make them easier for you to use.

We thank everyone, the authors and users in particular, who have made this Series so successful and so widely used. And we promise that this second decade will be dedicated to further expansion of the Series and to enhancement of the books it contains to provide still greater value to you, our constituency.

Stephen J. Williams
Series Editor

Delmar Series in Health Services Administration

Stephen J. Williams, Sc.D., Series Editor

Introduction to Health Services, fourth edition
  Stephen J. Williams and Paul R. Torrens, Editors

Health Care Economics, fourth edition
  Paul J. Feldstein

Health Care Management: Organization Design and Behavior, third edition
  Stephen M. Shortell and Arnold D. Kaluzny, Editors

Ambulatory Care, Management, second edition
  Austin Ross, Stephen J. Williams, and Eldon L. Schafer, Editors

Health Politics and Policy, second edition
  Theodor J. Litman and Leonard S. Robins, Editors

Strategic Management of Human Resources in Health Services Organizations, second edition
  Myron D. Fottler, S. Robert Hernandez, and Charles L. Joiner, Editors

Motivating Health Behavior
  John P. Elder, E. Scott Geller, Melbourne F. Hovell, and Joni A. Mayer, Editors

SUPPLEMENTAL READER:

Contemporary Issues in Health Services
  Stephen J. Williams

CONTRIBUTORS

Michael Abelson, Ph.D.
Associate Professor
Department of Management
College of Business Administration
Texas A & M University
College Station, Texas

Barbara Arrington, Ph.D.
Assistant Professor
Department of Health Services
   Administration
St. Louis University Medical Center
St. Louis, Missouri

Charles J. Austin, Ph.D.
Professor and Chairman
Department of Health Services
   Administration
School of Health Related Professions
University of Alabama at Birmingham
Birmingham, Alabama

James W. Begun, Ph.D.
Professor and Ph.D. Program Director
Department of Health Administration
Medical College of Virginia
Virginia Commonwealth University
Richmond, Virginia

John D. Blair, Ph.D.
Professor and Director
Program in Health Organization
   Management
College of Business Administration
Texas Tech University
Lubbock, Texas

Kathryn Dansky, Ph.D.
Assistant Professor
Department of Health Policy and
   Administration
College of Health and Human
   Development
Pennsylvania State University
University Park, Pennsylvania

Carson F. Dye, M.H.A.
Vice President
Human Resources
St. Vincent's Medical Center
Toledo, Ohio

Daniel S. Fogel, Ph.D.
University of Pittsburgh
Katz Graduate School of Business
Special Programs—Europe
Pittsburgh, Pennsylvania

Myron D. Fottler, Ph.D.
Professor and Director
Ph.D. Program in Administration—Health
   Services
Department of Health Services
   Administration
School of Health-Related Professions
University of Alabama at Birmingham
Birmingham, Alabama

Bruce Fried, Ph.D.
Associate Professor
Department of Health Policy and
   Administration
School of Public Health
University of North Carolina at Chapel Hill
Chapel Hill, North Carolina

Cynthia Carter Haddock, Ph.D.
Associate Professor
Department of Health Services
   Administration
Department of Health-Related Professions
University of Alabama at Birmingham
Birmingham, Alabama

S. Robert Hernandez, Dr.P.H.
Professor
Department of Health Services
   Administration
School of Health-Related Professions
University of Alabama at Birmingham
Birmingham, Alabama

John C. Hyde, Ph.D.
Ph.D. Candidate in Administration—Health
　Services
Department of Health Services
　Administration
School of Health Related Professions
University of Alabama at Birmingham
Birmingham, Alabama

James A. Johnson, Ph.D.
Professor and Chairman
Department of Health Administration and
　Policy
College of Health Professions
Medical University of South Carolina
Charleston, South Carolina

Charles L. Joiner, Ph.D.
Professor and Dean
School of Health Related Professions
University of Alabama at Birmingham
Birmingham, Alabama

Kerma N. Jones, M.H.A.
Vice President, Human Resources
InterMountain Health Care Hospital
Salt Lake City, Utah

Richard S. Kurz, Ph.D.
Professor and Chair
Department of Health Services
　Administration
School of Public Health
St. Louis University Medical Center
St. Louis, Missouri

Jacqueline Landau, Ph.D.
Associate Professor
Department of Management
Suffolk University
Boston, Massachusetts

Richard I. Lehr, J.D.
Partner
Lehr, Middlebrooks, and Proctor
Birmingham, Alabama

Donna M. Malvey, M.H.A.
Ph.D. Candidate in Administration—Health
　Services
Department of Health Services
　Administration
School of Health-Related Professions
University of Alabama at Birmingham
Birmingham, Alabama

Gail W. McGee, Ph.D.
Associate Professor
Department of Health Services
　Administration
School of Health Related Professions
University of Alabama at Birmingham
Birmingham, Alabama

Robert A. McLean, Ph.D.
Associate Professor and Director
Masters Programs in Health Services
　Administration
Department of Health Services
　Administration
School of Health Related Professions
University of Alabama at Birmingham
Birmingham, Alabama

Norman Metzger, M.A.
Professor and Executive Consultant for
　Human Resources and Labor Relations
The Mount Sinai Medical Center
New York, New York

Elizabeth W. Michael
Ph.D. Student
College of Business Management
Texas Tech University
Lubbock, Texas

Stephen J. O'Connor, Ph.D.
Associate Professor
School of Business Administration
University of Wisconsin—Milwaukee
Milwaukee, Wisconsin

**Gary Drucker Palestrant, M.H.S.A.,
　C.P.A.**
Research Assistant
Department of Health Administration and
　Policy
College of Health Professions
Medical University of South Carolina
Charleston, South Carolina

E. Jose Proenca, Ph.D.
Assistant Professor
Department of Health and Medical Services
　Administration
Widener University
Chester, Pennsylvania

Grant T. Savage, Ph.D.
Associate Professor
College of Business Administration
Texas Tech University
Lubbock, Texas

Richard M. Shewchuk, Ph.D.
Associate Professor
Department of Health Services
    Administration
School of Health-Related Professions
University of Alabama at Birmingham
Birmingham, Alabama

Gregg L. Smith, J.D.
Associate
Sirote and Permutt, P.C.
Birmingham, Alabama

Howard L. Smith, Ph.D.
Professor and Associate Dean
Anderson Schools of Management
University of New Mexico
Albuquerque, New Mexico

Stephen Strasser, Ph.D.
Associate Professor
Graduate Program in Hospital and Health
    Services Administration
Ohio State University
Columbus, Ohio

John H. Westerman, M.H.A.
Interim President
Association of University Programs in
    Health Administration
Arlington, Virginia

CONTENTS

PART FOUR
HUMAN RESOURCES OUTCOMES   481

FOREWORD

Health services managers' approach to human resources management is a bit like a tribal view of history: They have learned nothing and have forgotten nothing. The health services organization climate of recent years has been competitive and stressed and has not led to hoped for changes. There has not been a voluntary combination of health services organizations into fewer comprehensive health care systems. Acute care managers say that the problem is too many hospitals with too many beds. Clinic managers say the problem is too little primary care and too many underemployed specialists. Practicing physician managers complain that incentives do not inspire rational behavior and that it is difficult to be an effective medical manager without appropriate incentives and a method to hold the physician accountable to an acceptable standard. Problems of the uninsured and inadequate access to services are frequently lamented by patients and providers alike. Yet, like the tribal view of history, we seem to have learned nothing.

Ownership seems exempt from the increasing scrutiny of publicly held companies. Unneeded hotels and schools are sold or converted to more useful purposes. Unneeded hospitals start a fund drive, or better yet, demand public funds for their "unique" position in the health community. No one asks why the voluntary trustee does not bring the same quality of judgment to bear on a health organization problem that the trustee brings to bear in his or her business or personal life. Some physicians may be underutilized by 20% to 70%, depending on their specialty. Yet, their first reaction is to blame some other party for lack of patients.

At this writing, it appears a new attempt will be made at rationalizing the system. Conspicuously absent from the new design team are the past stewards. Early stewards of once-respected delivery systems understood community need and social responsibility. Present stewards excel in blame and whining self-righteousness. Is it any wonder that most responsible parties to the process welcome an effort by the federal government to rationalize the health care delivery system through health care reform legislation?

An academic health center task force on human resources for health states, "Health care reform proposals only address the financing of care; attention to human resources issues is noticeably absent. When universal access to health care is achieved the nation will face a second health care crisis because of shortages and maldistribution of health professionals, especially with regard to primary health care and prevention."

Although it might be expected that educators have a major concern with the production end of human resources, the major portion of health professionals are already in practice. The result is a challenge to provide health care professionals with information concerning the strategic management of human resources in existing health care organizations. Herein lies the relevance of this book.

What are the implications of health care reform for current practitioners? What will be the manpower needs of the populations served? What can we learn from managerial epidemiology? Who will be responsible for designing and implementing appropriate changes in manpower mix? How will we go about retraining? To what extent can we expect ownership failures of the past to redefine, let alone address, new human resources problems?

There is probably little consensus on the answers to these questions. The new realities of multiculturalism are in the process of evolution. Awareness of ethnicity must be translated into action-oriented programs. Undoubtedly, change agents will have to contend with a formidable number of established leaders still engaged in the search for new objectives of blame for the current situation. The threshold of denial is high; the amount of self-pity is substantial; and the needs of those who feel wronged by change represent a bottomless pit of therapeutic need. Yet, this book suggests certain ways to avoid the morass and get on with what must be done. It appears that the effective manager of human resources in 2000 will possess certain characteristics. It is interesting to note that executive job descriptions have historically included the following requirements:

- Relates well to board and professional staff
- Understands technology and relationship to organizational structure
- Has demonstrated ability to recruit a talented management team
- Has a track record of having talented managers work as an effective management team
- Is able to develop a corporate culture that focuses on outcomes and cuts across normative organizational arrangements with emphasis on collaboration and cooperation
- Has a demonstrated track record in the application of continuous quality improvement methods

Yet, those involved in the search process rarely articulate the need for an executive versed in the strategic management of health resources. What might be some of the major characteristics that allow the manager of the year 2000 to excel and still catch the attention of those involved in the executive search process? The sections of this book provide an excellent starting point. The effective manager of 2000 may be described as follows:

- Understands the deployment of human resources systems with an integrated strategic management system. Human resources management should be seen as a vehicle for change, not a barrier to be overcome.

- Is a keen student of human behavior and understands what motivates, how to develop appropriate incentives and how to adapt cutting-edge technology systems to create a corporate culture that thrives on optimizing a diverse work force, and approaches change in an opportunistic manner
- Is able to integrate the human resources process systems into the creation of an environment that makes it fun to come to work and rewarding to achieve implementation of priority organizational programs
- Has an open mind about how to achieve human resources outcomes. The process should be interactive with a penchant for pilot programs and innovation.

It may be that the current lament about our large, slow-to-respond, dinosaur-like corporations will translate to a radically different decentralized approach to human resources management. A passion for neat policy manuals will be replaced by an action-oriented, point-of-service, problem-solving mentality. Large personnel departments with multiple steps of approval will be replaced by general guidelines for cost-center program managers. Personnel resources allocation will be a decision for program managers to make with the full understanding of the consequences—negative operating margins. Health organizations will be a system of managing clinical programs of a human dimension and scale. Organizations will not be viewed as a source of lifetime job security, but as a rich source of entrepreneurial opportunity.

The Accrediting Commission on Education for Health Services Administration (ACEHSA) and the Joint Commission on Accreditation for Health Care Organizations (JCAHO) continue to recognize the role of human resources in their respective standards. Changes under consideration at JCAHO with regard to standards covering the organized medical staff may have implications for human resources management. If JCAHO shifts the medical staff responsibilities to the health care organization and abolishes the medical staff chapter, it may be that other health professionals will lessen their autonomous status and become an institutional responsibility.

The future tends to be bullish on change. Human resources issues will be center stage to many of the changes. This book should be of great value to those coping with health care reform.

John H. Westerman
Interim President
Association of University Programs
on Health Administration (AUPHA)

PREFACE

Several competing management issues and philosophies seem to be working at cross purposes within the health services industry in recent years. On the one hand, there has been growing interest in increasing the participation of employees in decision-making processes and improving their level of psychological involvement and commitment with the organization. This interest is evidenced by the popularity of management texts on so-called Japanese management, the implementation of quality circles and total quality management and the discussions of the value of corporate culture in assisting a health services organization in its quest for performance. These techniques are envisioned as assisting the organization in its quest for high performance.

On the other hand, financial and economic pressures on the organization have caused these same institutions to become concerned about maintaining market share, improving their competitiveness, achieving internal efficiencies, and maximizing reimbursement. The drive for financial performance often forces health institutions to reduce their work force through terminations, to curtail spending on employee development, to postpone compensation increases, and to make other short-term decisions that are not conducive to a quality work life for their employees.

Given this paradoxical situation, we feel there is need for an up-to-date text on the management of human resources within health services organizations and *Strategic Management of Human Resources in Health Services Organizations* is an attempt to address this important gap in the health services management literature. We hope that the book makes a unique contribution by articulating the links that exist among strategy, organizational design and behavior, and human resources management. We believe that a need exists for this articulation, given the labor-intensive nature of the industry and the emphasis being placed on productivity in the increasingly competitive environment fostered by health care reform proposals.

The relationship between strategy and selected organizational systems is described in the first part. Our view of the relationships that exist among strategy, organizational design and behavior, and human resources management are illustrated in the model that is presented in Chapter 1. Subsequent chapters describe the legal and economic environment, processes for formation of strategy within health services organizations, the relationship that should exist between strategy and human resources management, and methods for strategic management of human resources at various stages of the organizational life cycle.

The influence of these strategic choices upon structural and behavioral systems are explicated in Part Two. The effect of these systems on human resources management activities are detailed. This part contains descriptions of the contributions that structural and behavioral systems make to individual and organizational performance. Part Three provides information on the performance of selected human resources functions such as recruitment, selection, training and development, compensation management, and negotiating and administering the labor relations contract. Part Four looks at the assessment of human resources outcomes and present and future challenges.

Topics given increased emphasis in the second edition, include the legal and economic environment, work force diversity, job analysis, and assessment of human resources outcomes. This material is presented in the form of additional chapters. In addition, topics such as total quality management, corporate restructuring, and downsizing are integrated into several of the chapters which were in the first edition.

Our purpose is to describe not only human resources functions within organizations but also to provide a model of major organizational components that shape the human resources options available for health services managers. We hope that this approach will be an important contribution to our industry and will be of interest to practitioners as well as students in health services administration programs who are interested in expanding their understanding of strategic planning, human resources management, and senior management within hospitals, hospital systems, and other health services delivery organizations.

Given the diverse topics covered in our text, we feel that the contributing authors provided the expertise that was necessary for this undertaking. The contributors' expertise in the prescribed areas was essential for the achievement of the objectives of the book.

Myron D. Fottler
S. Robert Hernandez
Charles L. Joiner

ACKNOWLEDGMENTS

We would like to thank a number of persons who contributed to the development of this book. John Hyde and Donna Malvey, Ph.D. candidates in Health Services Administration at University of Alabama at Birmingham, provided valuable research assistance as did Holly McIntyre, a masters student in Health Administration at UAB.

Linda Godwin, Deana Breckenridge, Diane Hyche, and Linda Poole provided typing of various drafts of the chapter manuscripts, administrative support, and assistance for the project. Without their help our other responsibilities could not have been fulfilled.

The opportunity to work with Debra Flis and Bill Burgower at Delmar Publishers has been a pleasure as they labored with us to ensure that we provide the very best manuscript that can be produced. Steve Williams, Series Editor of the Series in Health Services, was extremely helpful in seeing that this manuscript was initiated, after the idea was first proposed at an American Public Health Association meeting long ago. Kelly Ricci of Spectrum Publishers Services did an excellent job in guiding the production of this second edition.

A note of thanks to our wives, Carol, Joy, and Gloria, for their love and support during this publication endeavor. Dr. Hernandez would like to express special thanks to his children, Susan and Robert, for their understanding and patience with the time required for this activity. Dr. Joiner desires to acknowledge his girls, Amy, Rebecca, Laura, and Ashley, for the important place they fill in his life and to express appreciation for their understanding and interest in this project.

Finally, we wish to thank administrative officials at the University of Alabama at Birmingham for providing a conducive work environment that allowed this book to be completed.

Myron D. Fottler
S. Robert Hernandez
Charles L. Joiner

PART ONE

STRATEGY AND ORGANIZATION SYSTEMS

CHAPTER

1

INTEGRATING STRATEGIC MANAGEMENT AND HUMAN RESOURCES

S. Robert Hernandez

Myron D. Fottler

Charles L. Joiner

LEARNING OBJECTIVES

Upon completing this chapter, the reader should be able to . . .

- Describe and discuss the changing health care environment and its impact on human resources.
- Describe and discuss a model for the strategic management of human resources in health services organizations.
- Describe and discuss the structural, behavioral, and human resource systems that impact health care organizational outcomes.

INTRODUCTION

Like most other service industries, the health care industry is very labor intensive. One reason for the reliance on an extensive work force is that it is not possible to produce a "service" and store it for subsequent consumption. The manufacture of the commodity that is purchased and the consumption of that commodity occur simultaneously. Thus, the interaction between consumers and health care professionals is an integral part of the provision of health services. Given the dependence on health care professionals for service delivery, the possibility of heterogeneity of service quality must be recognized, both within an employee as skills and competencies change over time and among employees as different individuals or representatives of different professions provide a service.

The intensive use of labor for service delivery and the possibility of variability in professional practice require that the attention of leaders in the industry be directed toward managing the performance of the persons involved in the delivery of health services. The effective management of people requires that health services executives understand the factors that influence the performance of individuals employed in their organizations. These factors include not only the traditional human resources management activities (i.e., recruitment and selection, training and development, appraisal, compensation, employee relations), but also environmental and other organizational factors that impinge on human resources activities.

The strategic management of human resources is ensuring that qualified, motivated personnel are available to staff the portfolio of business units that will be operated by the organization. This book explains and illustrates the methods and practices that can be used to increase the probability that competent personnel will be available to provide the services delivered by the organization and that these personnel will perform necessary tasks appropriately. Implementing these methods and practices means that requirements for positions must be determined, qualified persons must be recruited and selected, employees must be trained and developed to meet future organizational needs, and adequate rewards must be provided to attract and retain top performers.

Of course, these functions are performed within the context of the overall activities of the organization. They are influenced or constrained by the environment, the mission and strategies that are being pursued, the structure of the organization, and the behavioral systems indigenous to the institution. *To manage human resources strategically, health care executives must understand the relationships that exist among these important organizational components and the human resources functions so that appropriate methods can be selected to accomplish the objectives in service delivery desired by the organization.*

The next section presents an overview of fundamental changes occurring in the health services environment that affect the numbers, types, and roles of health practitioners. This material is followed by a model of the relationships that exist among strategy, selected organizational design features, and human resources management activities.

EFFECT OF ENVIRONMENT ON HEALTH PERSONNEL

In the United States, employment in the health services industry has grown more rapidly than overall employment. In 1900, persons employed in health occupations accounted for 1.2% of the labor force. This proportion increased to 2.1% in 1940, 3.0% in 1960, and 7.6% in 1990 (Freudenheim, 1990; U.S. Department of Labor, Bureaus of Labor Statistics, 1990). Using the restricted standard industrial classification of the U.S. Department of Commerce (sic 80), the health care work force accounted for about 7.5 million workers in 1989 (U.S. Department of Labor, Bureaus of Labor Statistics, 1990). If the health care workers who are affiliated with other industries such as insurance, pharmaceutical companies, and government are added, the total exceeds 9 million—an increase of about 50% since 1980 (Freudenheim, 1990).

In fact, the health care industry is now the nation's third largest employer after government (nonhealth) and retailing. Employment growth in health services has outpaced both overall employment and population growth in the economy. This growth is accentuated by the fourfold increase in the rate of health care personnel per 100,000 population from 518 in 1910 to 2209 in 1980 to 3571 in 1990 (Ginzberg, 1990; Mick & Moscovice, 1993).

Changes in the types and characteristics of health professionals in the twentieth century have been dramatic. Health professions requiring a college education or professional preparation accounted for approximately 200,000 persons in 1900 as compared to 4.9 million in 1990 (Ginzberg, 1990; Kissick, 1968; U.S. Department of Health, Education, and Welfare, 1970). For instance, in 1900, three in five health professionals were physicians. By 1990, rapid growth in other occupations reduced the proportion of physicians to about one in eight professional health workers (Ginzberg, 1990). A further decline is expected as other disciplines experience more rapid rates of growth and as new categories of personnel emerge.

The most rapid growth in the supply of health professionals has occurred in the recently developed occupations of physician assistants, nurse practitioners, multiskilled health practitioners, laboratory technicians, occupational and physical therapists, medical records personnel, radiologic technologists, and so forth. More than two-thirds of all people employed in the health care industry in 1990 were employed as nontraditional allied health or support service personnel (U.S. Bureau of the Census, 1991).

The primary reasons for this growth in these nontraditional health occupations during the twentieth century were the interrelated forces of technological change, specialization, and the emergence of the hospital as the central focus of the health care system. The technological revolution led to the increased use of hospitals, concentration of health care personnel in them, and specialization of health personnel.

Table 1.1 provides an overview of the estimated supply of selected health personnel from 1970 to 1989. Few industries have the diversity of personnel and the wide variation in educational preparation, technical skills, professional responsibilities, and professional values seen in health services. Preparation ranges from 6 to 8 weeks of on-the-job training for nursing assistants to more than 10 years of postbaccalaureate education for some medical specialties. Health practitioners share a common duty to provide services to consumers, but diversity exists in the responsibilities of these groups.

The numbers of practitioners and their

roles have evolved over time and are expected to undergo radical change because of three factors that have transformed the health services industry. These factors are scientific and technological change, patterns of utilization, and funding for health services.

Advances in scientific understanding and technology in health services have triggered significant change in the industry and in the responsibilities of practitioners. Individual roles have become more specialized, since one person or profession cannot possess all the knowledge in a specific area of medicine. This has caused not only specialization of medical practice but also the creation of new types of health practitioners with up-to-date and unique skills to staff new technologies.

The evolution of medical knowledge, con-

TABLE 1.1. Estimated Active Supply of Selected Health Personnel and Practitioner-to-Population Ratios, 1970, 1980, and 1989

Health occupation	Estimated active supply			Percent change	
	1970	1980	1989	1970–1989	1980–1989
Physicians	290,862	427,028	562,839	93.5	31.8
Allopathic (MD)	279,212	410,955	536,755	92.2	30.6
Osteopathic (OD)	11,650	16,073	26,084	123.8	62.2
Podiatrists	7110	8880	11,950	68.0	34.5
Dentists	95,700	121,240	144,000	50.4	18.7
Optometrists	18,400	22,330	25,500	38.5	14.1
Pharmacists	112,570	142,780	160,000	42.1	12.0
Veterinarians	25,900	36,000	49,300	90.3	36.9
Registered nurses	750,000	1,272,900	1,666,200	122.1	30.8
	Practitioners per 100,000 population				
Physicians	142.7	189.8	230.6	61.5	21.4
Allopathic (MD)	137.0	182.7	219.9	60.5	20.3
Osteopathic (OD)	5.7	7.1	10.7	87.7	50.7
Podiatrists	3.5	4.0	5.0	30.0	25.0
Dentists	47.0	53.5	58.1	2.6	8.5
Optometrists	9.0	9.8	10.2	13.3	4.0
Pharmacists	55.4	62.5	64.1	15.7	2.5
Veterinarians	12.7	16.3	19.8	55.9	21.4
Registered nurses	368.9	560.0	671.0	81.8	19.8

Source: U.S. Department of Health and Human Services (1991). *United States Health & Prevention Profile 1991*, DHHS Pub. No. (PHS) 92-1232. Hyattsville, MD: Author.

centration of technological capability in the hospital, and improved reimbursement have led to increases in the absolute number of employees in nonfederal short-term general hospitals from 662,000 in 1950 to 3,110,000 in 1982 and the relative number of hospital employees per patient day from 1.78 in 1950 to 4.08 in 1982 (American Hospital Association, 1986). Recent changes in utilization of services have occurred because of a number of factors described elsewhere (Aday & Shortell, 1988). Hospital admissions and patient days per 1000 population appear to have peaked in the 1970s after years of increase. The absolute number of hospital admissions and the average daily census for nonfederal short-term general hospitals have declined every year from 1981 to 1989 with a slight increase in 1990 (American Hospital Association, 1991).

The number of physician visits for all sources and places was 5.2 in 1985 and 5.5 in 1990 (U.S. Department of Health and Human Services, 1991, p. 219). From 1982 to 1983, the net income of surgeons increased 10% while net income of general/family practitioners declined. The expected physician increase to nearly 720,000 by the year 2000 is expected to foster increased competition in medical practice (U.S. Department of Health and Human Services, 1991, p. 245).

Increasing emphasis has been placed on cost reductions and control of expenditures by major purchasers of health services. Since October 1, 1983, 5200 hospitals have been operating under the prospective payment system (PPS) for Medicare-eligible patients. This system, numerous other organized arrangements that encourage efficient use of health services, increased competition, and industry maturity have led to changes in job opportunities and entry of different types of individuals into training for the health professions. Employment in nonfederal short-term general hospitals has increased 10.1% from 1985 to 1989 (U.S. Department of Health and Human Services, 1991, p. 272). Within most health disciplines, enrollment in educational programs has either leveled off or declined in recent years (U.S. Department of Health and Human Services, 1986). Enrollment in educational programs has decreased in medicine, dentistry, and optometry, and increased in nursing and pharmacy (U.S. Department of Health and Human Services, 1991, p. 251).

Certainly, more extensive discussions are available on the health services industry (Andersen, 1985; Starr, 1982; Williams & Torrens, 1993); the health professions labor force (Sorkin, 1977; U.S. Department of Health and Human Services, 1986), and personnel planning (Edwards et al., 1983). This brief review suggests that the labor force expanded and became specialized during the past 40 years in response to increased utilization of services. Recent emphasis on cost control and efficient operations appears to be having a negative effect on demand for services, employment opportunities, and number of persons seeking career preparation in the health professions.

Environmental shifts that influence demand for services and trends in the health labor force must be considered during human resources planning. It cannot be assumed that skilled personnel will be freely available in the labor market when services are started or expanded; thus, adequate time for recruitment and training must be allowed. When services are downsized or terminated, use of tactics such as attrition or employee retraining may reduce the probability that layoffs and terminations will be required. Attention to external trends and proper planning provides for the maintenance of the organizational staff at near optimum levels of size, skills, and experience. It also reduces problems from personnel shortages or surpluses such as reductions in quality, inefficiencies, inability to deliver services, and practitioner dissatisfaction.

STRATEGIC MANAGEMENT OF HUMAN RESOURCES

Among the major environmental trends affecting health institutions are the changing financing arrangements, the emergence of new competitors, low or declining inpatient hospital occupancy rates, changes in physician/health care organizational relationships, changes in work force demographics, and capital shortages. The result has been increased competition, the need for higher levels of performance, and concern for institutional survival. Many health care organizations are closing facilities, undergoing corporate reorganization, instituting staffing freezes and/or reductions in work forces, providing services with fewer resources, changing their organizational structures and/or job designs, and developing leaner management structures with fewer levels and wider spans of control.

A variety of major competitive strategies are being pursued to respond to the current turbulent environment, including low-cost provision of traditional health services, provision of superior patient service through extra high technical quality or customer service, specialization into a few key clinical areas (i.e., centers of excellence), or diversification within health care or outside of it

(Coddington & Moore, 1987). Regardless of which particular strategies are being pursued, all health care organizations are experiencing a decrease in staffing levels in many traditional service areas and a growing staff in new ventures, specialized clinical areas, and related support services (Wilson, 1986).

Hence, staffing profiles are increasingly characterized by a limited number of highly skilled and well-compensated professionals. Health care organizations are no longer "employers of last resort" for the unskilled. At the same time, most are experiencing shortages of nursing and various allied health personnel.

The development of appropriate responses to this changing health care environment has received much attention during the past decade so that strategic planning is now well-accepted in health care organizations (Zollow, Joseph, & Furey, 1984). However, *implementation* of strategic plans has often been problematic. The process often ends with the development of goals and objectives, but without strategies or methods of implementation or monitoring of results. Implementation appears to be the major difficulty in the overall strategic management process (Porter, 1980).

A major reason for this failure of implementation has been the failure of health care executives to assess and manage the various external, interface, and internal stakeholders whose cooperation and support are necessary to implement any business strategy (i.e., corporate, business, or functional) successfully (Blair & Fottler, 1990). A stakeholder is any individual or group with a "stake" in the organization. External stakeholders include patients and their families, public and private regulatory agencies, and third-party payers. Interface stakeholders are those who operate on the "interface" of the organization and who operate in both the internal and external environments. Examples include members of the medical staff who have admitting privileges at several institutions and who are members of the board of trustees. Internal stakeholders are those who operate within the organizations, such as managers, professionals, and nonprofessional employees.

Blair and Fottler (1990) advocate determining which stakeholders are "key" for the implementation of a certain strategy at a particular level in the organization, assessing each in terms of their degree of supportiveness for the organization, and then determining an appropriate generic strategy and specific tactics for managing each stakeholder. For example, government regulatory bodies might be "nonsupportive" stakeholders; physicians might be "mixed-blessing" stakeholders; and employees might be "supportive" stakeholders. Blair and Fottler (1990) recommend "defending against" nonsupportive stakeholders, "collaborating with" mixed-blessing stakeholders, and "involving" supportive stakeholders. Implementing each of these three generic strategies could utilize a wide range of specific tactics.

Involving supportive stakeholders such as employees and human resources management is crucial to the success of any strategic plan. For example, if the human resources executives are not actively involved, then the employee planning, recruitment, selection, development, appraisal, and compensation necessary for successful implementation are not likely to occur. McManis (1987) has noted: "While many hospitals have elegant and elaborate strategic plans, they often do not have supporting human resource strategies to ensure that the overall corporate plan can be implemented. But strategies don't fail, people do" (p. 19). Yet the health care industry spends less than one-half the amount that other industries are spending in human resources administration (*Hospitals,* 1989).

Fottler, Phillips, and Duran (1990) recommend that health care executives should consciously formulate human resources strategies and practices that are linked to and reinforce the broader strategic posture of the organization. For example, a hospital that wished to differentiate itself on the basis of "functional quality leadership" should provide above average staffing; implement a sophisticated career counseling/promotion system; monitor employee attitudes; train all staff in guest relations; and appraise and reward based upon interpersonal skills and responsiveness to patients.

Such a strategic approach to human resources management includes assessing the organization's environment and mission; formulating the organization's business strategy; assessing the human resources requirements based upon the intended strategy; comparing the current inventory of human resources in terms of numbers, characteristics, or practices relative to the future strategic requirements; formulating a human resources strategy based on the differences between the assessed requirements and the current inventory; and implementing the appropriate human resources practices to reinforce the strategy and attain competitive advantage (Fottler et al., 1990). Figure 1.1 provides some examples of possible linkages between strategic decisions and human resources management practices.

The strategic human resources management approach is not currently well-recognized and well-utilized in the health care industry. This neglect of strategic human

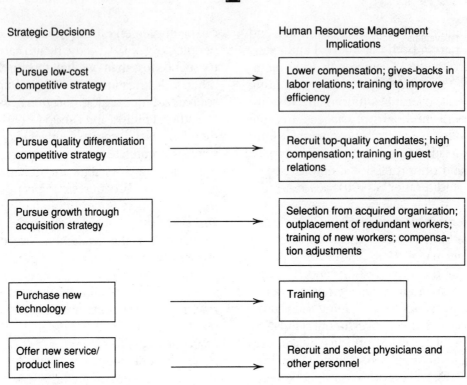

FIGURE 1.1. Examples of strategic decisions and corresponding human resources management implications.

resources consideration is particularly surprising in a labor-intensive service industry requiring the right people in the right jobs at the right times, which is currently undergoing shortages in some occupations (Cerne, 1988). In addition, there is fairly strong evidence that organizations utilizing more progressive (i.e., strategically linked) human resources approaches achieve significantly better financial results than comparable (but less progressive) organizations (Gomez-Mejia, 1988; Kravetz, 1988).

An organization that is managed strategically ensures that the functional and operational administrative systems are linked to the strategic and tactical decision-making activities of the organization. The planning, control, and management systems must be joined for the organization to be able to ensure that the plans developed by senior management are executed as intended.

As illustrated in Figure 1.2, organizations are complex entities that require constant interaction with the environment. If they are to remain viable, health services organizations must adapt their strategies to external changes. The internal components of the organization are then affected by these changes

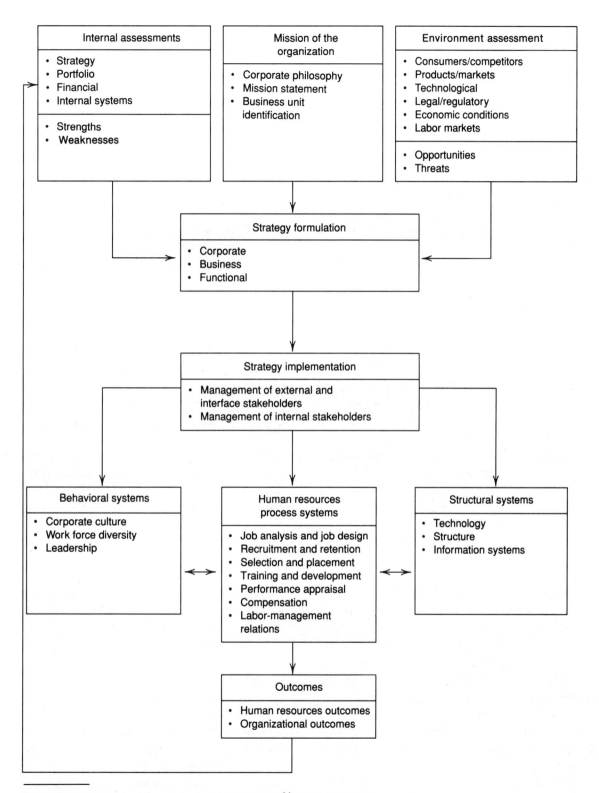

FIGURE 1.2. Model of the strategic management of human resources.

in that shifts in the organization's strategy potentially necessitate modifications in the internal structural systems, behavioral systems, and human resources process systems. There must be harmony, in turn, among these systems. The characteristics, performance levels, and the amount of coherence in operating practices among these systems influence the outcomes achieved in terms of organizational- and employee-level measures of performance.

The strategic management of human resources involves attention to the effect of environmental and internal components on the human resources process system. Because of the critical role of health professionals in delivering services in this labor-intensive industry, a major concern of health services managers should be the development of personnel policies and practices that are closely related to, influenced by, and supportive of the strategic thrust of their organizations. In addition, managers must ensure that the human resources functions are linked to the other internal design features of the organization.

Organizations, either explicitly or implicitly, pursue a strategy in their operations. Deciding on a strategy means to determine the products or services that will be produced and the markets to which the chosen services will be offered. Once these selections have been made, the methods to be used to compete in the chosen market must be identified. The methods adopted are based on internal resources available, or potentially available, for use by managers.

As illustrated in Figure 1.2, strategies should be based on consideration of environmental conditions and organizational capabilities. To be in position to take advantage of opportunities that are anticipated to occur, as well as to parry potential threats from changed conditions or competitor initiatives, managers must have detailed knowledge of the current and future operating environment. Cognizance of internal strengths and weaknesses allows management to develop plans based on an accurate assessment of the firm's ability to perform in the marketplace at the desired level.

A more detailed discussion of the significance of the legal and economic environment is presented in Chapter 2. Chapter 3 focuses on a more detailed discussion of approaches for determining organization strategy. In Chapter 4, we show the linkages among the organization's point in its own life cycle, strategy, and human resources.

STRUCTURAL SYSTEMS

The structure of an organization has a profound effect on the activities of employees. Structural concerns include deciding how task responsibilities will be allocated among employees and determining how coordination among the tasks will be achieved (Mintzberg, 1979), and these involve two features. One is the formal allocation of work roles to individuals; the second is use of administrative mechanisms to control and integrate work activity.

Implementation of strategies occurs through specific programs or services by the assignment of work to individuals, the control of worker activities so that standards of performance are achieved, and the coordination of tasks among workers for efficient operation. Thus, organizational structure should be determined by the strategy being pursued by the organization, since different strategies require work routines, control methods, and coordination patterns of distinctive types.

The several components of an organization's structure have a strong influence on human resources systems. One of these closely associated with task responsibilities of personnel is the technology applied by the institution. Another element of the structure used to control and coordinate work within or across units is the information systems that are required to assemble and organize data on human resources. A third component consists of the more traditional structural attributes of an institution, such as formalization of roles and behavior, centralization of decision making, and complexity of the institution.

Technology Within Health Services Organizations

The numerous methods of conceptualizing technology are discussed later in the text. In general, technology is conceived to include not only the equipment, supplies, and other physical materials required to provide a given service, but also the *knowledge* that must be used in the provision of the service or in the operation of the equipment.

Organizational strategy has significant implications for the technology that will be available to a health services organization. As discussed in Chapter 3, managers exercise strategic choice in determining the product lines their organizations will offer. The decision to provide selected medical services or products and to exclude others prescribes the medical technology that an institution must use. In addition, the strategic alternatives available to management in the short run are governed by the organization's current technology, including the knowledge level of its personnel.

Once a strategy, and therefore a technological thrust, has been chosen by an organization, it has an immediate effect on personnel practices of the institution. Since technology also includes the knowledge base that is required to deliver a service, an entire array of activities such as job design, human resources training and development activities, performance appraisal and compensation systems, and related activities must be orchestrated to ensure that service delivery occurs as planned. The relationships between organizational technology and human resource functions are presented in more detail in Chapter 5.

Structure for Human Resources Management

As previously stated, the methods used to allocate tasks within an organization and to achieve coordination among the tasks are structural concerns. Different strategies (e.g., markets served, methods for serving those markets) lead to different structures. Numerous authors (Chandler, 1962; Galbraith & Nathanson, 1978) have noted the changes that occur in structural features of organizations as firms attempt to serve different markets or to use new methods and practices in the strategies that they implement to gain a competitive edge.

The internal design or structure of an organization has a profound influence on the human resources systems. In turn, job design is an aspect of personnel practices that is influenced directly by structural decisions. Levels of formalization, internal complexity, and the amount of central authority used by organizations determine the appropriate design of work in the organization. Other personnel functions such as recruitment strategies, approaches to management development, and related activities are also affected by internal organizational design. The exact relationships among these factors are discussed in Chapter 5.

Information Systems

Appropriately designed management information systems (MIS) provide data required to support strategic planning and management decision making. Information concerning human resources that can be used for planning as well as operational purposes is a crucial element of such a system. External planning depends on accurate data on future numbers of professionals that will be available for the jobs required by the organization. Internal planning requires significant detail on such matters as current productivity, employee skills, work demands, and related areas. Information systems also should be designed to ensure that managers have access to the data required to support the strategies the organization is pursuing.

Human resources information systems support personnel activities by providing managers with statistics on the future need for personnel as well as information on current levels of performance and skills of employees. This information can be used to identify types of personnel to be recruited in the future and to design compensation systems and related activities. The contributions of information systems to personnel activities are discussed in Chapter 6.

BEHAVIORAL SYSTEMS

The actual delivery of health services, the provision of most support functions, the development of plans, and the coordination and control of work occur through the behavior of people and the processes by which they interact. Thus, the ability to achieve an organizational strategy depends on the nexus between organizational behavioral systems and the mission and objectives of the institution.

The actions and behaviors of individuals within the organization constitute a major focus of behavioral systems. If management is sensitive to the personal and professional requisites of these individuals, their needs and expectations from participation in the organization may be translated into commitment to the organization and motivation to accomplish tasks desired by the institution.

Additional emphasis of behavioral systems is on group attributes and the quality of leadership available for guiding the institution through major change. Another significant element of behavioral systems is the corporate culture (i.e., the characteristic day-to-day internal environment that is experienced and shared by those working within the organization). The approaches to leadership and organizational change are a third component of organizational behavioral systems that must be handled properly and linked to the mission of the firm if human resources are to be directed strategically by management.

Corporate Culture

The system of informal customs and rules that transmit the behaviors expected of employees in most situations constitutes organizational culture. The quality of the relationship between the culture of an organization and its strategy has significant implications for the potential performance of that organization. Strong cultures do an excellent job of transmitting the values and beliefs of the organization to the individual. Thus, individuals are able to determine what they are to do in the vast number of situations for which no formal rules or guidelines exist.

Corporate culture should complement the human resources management process systems. The shared values and expectations that are reinforced by culture should blend with the systems that have been established for selecting organizational members, developing their skills, and rewarding desirable behavior. It is important that management assess cultural norms and plan interventions as required. Methods for managing the corporate culture are discussed in Chapter 7.

Work Force Diversity

As the demographic characteristics of the U.S. population are changing, health care organizations face the continuing challenge of managing and integrating their work force. The recruitment, selection, training, and development of ethnic minorities and other nontraditional employees also pose a challenge. Differences in language, culture, values, and educational backgrounds may necessitate special efforts and programs to minimize problems and conflict. The management of a diverse workforce is discussed in Chapter 8.

Transformational Leadership and Leadership Development

The importance of effective leadership in determining the overall mission and direction of an organization and guiding the institution through major change cannot be overstated. Whereas contingency theory posits that appropriate organizational strategy and design are determined by environmental conditions, senior management must be cognizant of those environmental conditions and determine the response the organization should initiate. In addition, the implementation of organizational transformation and change is the responsibility of senior executives.

To survive, organizations must constantly adapt. This is demonstrated by the radical changes that have been occurring in the health services industry during the past 5 to 10 years. Managers must provide leadership to enable their organizations to make the transformations necessary in a changing environment. In Chapter 9, the approaches that are available for renewing the organization and for developing future leaders are discussed.

HUMAN RESOURCES PROCESS SYSTEMS

The processes used for human resources management may be viewed as a cycle of related activities. Job analysis, recruitment, retention, selection and placement, training and development, performance appraisal, compensation, and labor relations may be envisioned as a continuum of tasks and responsibilities that flow logically from one to another. These functions must be performed to ensure that the necessary human resources are available to support the strategic thrust of the organization.

Although each of these areas is important

and must be performed competently for the organization to function, the importance of the activity to sustaining excellence varies depending on the strategies chosen. Some strategic initiatives emphasize selection and placement activities, while others require health services managers to concentrate on refining the appraisal system. The relationships of selected strategic activities to human resources functions within the organization are discussed in Chapter 3, and the variance of these relationships to the organizational life cycle is further detailed in Chapter 4. The association between other organizational activities and human resources functions as well as the contribution of these functions to organizational performance are discussed in the sections that follow.

Job Analysis

Job analysis is a systematic process of gathering information about jobs, which results in a job description. Job descriptions provide basic information necessary to implement all of the other human resources functions successfully. Chapter 10 discusses job analysis and job design in more detail.

Recruitment and Retention

Health services organizations must have a constant influx of candidates for potential employment. New employee positions are required as market areas are expanded or services are initiated. Recruitment occurs even in the face of limited growth or decline in service capacity, because individuals with specialized skills or training who leave the organization must be replaced and because services or technologies that have been revised or modified must be staffed.

The recruitment of personnel plays an important role in helping the organization to adapt and remain competitive. Employees who have recently finished professional training are the source of information on new methods and techniques in service delivery that allow the organization to remain competitive in its traditional services. In addition, it may be necessary to recruit outside the institution if personnel with the managerial or professional skills needed to implement new strategic thrusts are not available internally.

As discussed previously, the health services industry employs a wide variety of workers. Thus, the sources of applicants and types of method used to expand the applicant pool vary depending on the occupational classification being considered. A description of recruitment methods is provided in Chapter 11, together with a discussion of retention and turnover. Obviously, it is self-defeating to invest significant resources in a successful recruitment effort if such effort is offset by high turnover rates. Retention of high-performance employees is as essential as their original recruitment.

Selection and Placement

A responsibility highly correlated with recruitment is employee selection and placement. Once the applicant pool has been filled, methods must be in place to choose the persons who will be most qualified for each job. Successful implementation of organizational strategy requires that management have a thorough understanding of the jobs that must be performed and the qualifications of individuals to fill these jobs.

Selection of competent personnel for new or unique positions created by initiation of services may be problematic. For example, an institution initiating an innovative, nontraditional service may have difficulty identifying the activities that must be performed by individuals to be employed. In addition, it may have little experience in evaluating candidates for new positions.

A number of steps are critical in the selection and placement process. Job analysis must be conducted to determine the tasks to be performed and the qualifications required to perform them. Then, criteria for predicting employee effectiveness are required, with adequate attention given to validity and reliability of the selection instrument. These activities are examined in Chapter 12.

Training and Development

Investment in the existing human capital of a health services organization through a well-managed training and development activity offers potential for significantly enhancing the ability of the enterprise to achieve its objectives. Indeed, improvement in the skills and abilities of current employees will contribute to sustained levels of performance because the technological change occurring in the health services industry requires the constant updating of the knowledge base of health professionals. The increased competency of the health services organization staff will provide significant benefits to the enterprise no matter what strategy is being pursued.

The changing environment of the health services industry itself ensures that the training and development of current staff members will contribute to organizational performance. Institutions are required to develop innovative responses to the competitive ref-

ormations taking place today. The providers of health services within organizations must be informed of the factors causing these changes, as well as the roles they can potentially play in helping management cope with change. Information on competitive shifts and marketing alternatives conveyed to current employees and medical staff will help these professionals to understand the rationale for fundamental changes that are occurring. An improved understanding should make it easier to obtain their support and advice on implementation issues.

A third factor relating the strategic thrust of the enterprise to staff training and development is that the initiation of unique strategies and tactics may call for programs to be implemented by current employees who do not possess the necessary skills. For example, strategies to become a low-cost provider (Porter, 1980) may dictate the use of internal management control methods that are foreign to supervisory staff. Management must ensure that plans for strategic initiatives include an inventory of the skills required for program implementation and must design necessary developmental activities. These and other issues in training and development are discussed in Chapter 13.

Performance Appraisal

Performance appraisal is the systematic evaluation of an employee's work behavior on criteria measuring important job-related activities. To determine the extent to which work requirements and responsibilities are met, valid, reliable criteria must be developed for a job, and job behaviors must be measured.

Performance appraisal can serve multiple purposes for management. First, it can provide guidance for the selection of individuals for promotion. When advancement criteria have been determined, employees who meet or exceed those criteria can be identified as promotion opportunities arise. Second, it can be used as a method for determining increases in employee compensation. Levels of employee performance can be measured and comparisons can be made to improve the probability of equitable rewards being given for desired performance. Third, performance appraisal can serve as a tool for identifying areas in which personnel need training and development or additional counseling. Areas in which one or a number of employees exhibit consistently inadequate performance can be identified and remedial programs to improve performance developed.

If properly designed, an appraisal system complements the strategic planning of an organization because it translates the initiatives desired by the organization into specific behaviors required of individuals. Management must identify the key activities necessary for the achievement of the institutional mission and translate those activities into employee appraisal criteria. Performance appraisal methods are discussed in more detail in Chapter 14.

Compensation Management

The compensation system of an organization can influence the strategic direction of an organization and organizational effectiveness in a number of ways as identified by Lawler (1984). First, an enterprise's ability to attract and retain conscientious workers is partially determined by the kind and level of rewards provided. Second, a compensation system may foster the achievement of desired outcomes by motivating employees if an organization can link valued rewards to the performance of essential behaviors. Third, compensation systems contribute to the corporate culture that is perceived by organizational members as well as serving to reinforce the structural systems of the organization.

The linking of compensation systems to the mission and strategies of the organization occurs through several vehicles. An assessment of the current compensation systems and their influence on behaviors should be an input to strategy development. Once a strategy has been generated, the firm must focus on the type of human resources needed and the behaviors required to make the plan effective. Then, compensation systems should be designed to reward the behaviors necessary for obtaining desired outcomes. The coupling of compensation to the behaviors required to support diverse strategic thrusts is a major component of strategic human resources management.

A difficulty health services managers face in developing compensation systems is the heterogeneity of personnel employed within an institution. This heterogeneity suggests that unique methods for compensating different types of employees may need to be developed. Variability also must be faced by larger health services delivery systems across facility sites or, as the merger of larger systems occurs, across systems in compensation programs. Such diversity means that managers must be sensitive to the need for blending these potentially different approaches for employee remuneration into a logical framework that is supportive of the mission of the organization. The methods for development of compensation packages for rewarding the diverse activities of health services organizations are discussed in Chapter 15.

Labor Relations

Senior managers seek to retain flexibility in selecting among alternatives when determining organizational strategy. Preservation of administrative flexibility (Thompson, 1967) is critical for long-term adaptability and survival for health services organizations, especially in today's volatile environment. Thus, development of a positive relationship between management and employees by practicing "preventive health" in labor-management relations is important for strategic management of human resources. This is because if groups of employees feel that management is not interested in their welfare, they may elect to have a union represent and bargain for them.

Nonunion status allows management greater flexibility in exercising its prerogatives. Loss of flexibility accompanies union status when provisions of the labor-management contract serve as a barrier to the implementation of programs or options that are being considered by management.

For example, a hospital may have agreed with a union that workers whose jobs are terminated will be shifted to other comparable positions or that present workers will be hired first if new jobs are created within their job classification. If such a facility desires to cease offering obstetric services while initiating new inpatient services for psychiatric patients, there may be an impasse. It will be almost impossible to shift personnel from obstetrics to psychiatry without significant retraining, and the obvious alternative (i.e.,

for the hospital to hire new personnel for psychiatric services) may be blocked, at least temporarily, by the terms of the union agreement. Thus, the change in services desired by the hospital cannot be implemented without major costs and delays. Discussion of methods to create a positive human relations climate in order to reduce the probability of unionization is provided in Chapter 16.

Health services organizations that already have unions should consider the future strategic thrusts they wish to follow when they negotiate new collective bargaining agreements. Otherwise, an agreement may serve as an internal constraint that inhibits the performance of the organization. If the institution decides to follow a low-cost strategy in the marketplace, the management team must be tough negotiators, granting few wage demands, holding the line on numbers of workers, and stressing productivity standards in an attempt to restrain costs.

Conversely, the negotiations of an organization wishing to compete on the basis of service quality should reflect that desire. Management should bargain to gain concessions that focus on quality of care such as use of employee assessment criteria that stress job performance and quality of care. Bonuses may be paid to employees for quality enhancement activities. The organization may emphasize funding for training and development for job improvement rather than providing larger pay increases. Less stress may be placed on reducing staffing ratios or controlling overtime pay.

These factors suggest the importance of integrating strategic considerations into the handling of labor relations and negotiating collective bargaining agreements. Approaches to labor relations and negotiations are discussed in more detail in Chapters 16 and 17.

OUTCOMES

The outcomes achieved by a health services organization depend on the environment of the organization, the mission and strategies being pursued, the internal structural systems, the behavioral systems, the human resources process systems, and the consistency of operating practices across these internal systems. The appropriate methods for organizing and relating these elements are determined by the specific outcomes desired by the managers of the health services organization and the other major stakeholders of the entity. Although numerous methods exist for conceptualizing organizational performance and outcomes (Cameron & Whetten, 1983; Goodman & Pennings, 1977), the outcomes that might be useful for this discussion can be thought of as organizational outcomes and employee outcomes.

Organizational Outcomes

For long-term survival, a health services organization must have a balanced exchange relationship with the environment. An equitable relationship must exist because the exchange is mutually beneficial to the organization and to the elements of the environment with which it interacts. A number of outcome measures can be used to determine how well the organization is performing in the marketplace and how well the organization is producing a service that will be valued by consumers.

One subset of organizational outcomes that may be used to measure the effectiveness of the exchange relationship and the performance of the organization involves the economic viability of the entity. Growth, profitability, return on investment, and related measures are methods for determining the financial performance of the organization. An organization needs to perform well financially so that funds are available for maintenance of current operations, for investment in new service development, and for return to investors if the organization is investor-owned.

Another subset of outcomes involves the nature and level of service performance achieved. Quality of services is especially critical for the health industry, and it contains several dimensions. Technical quality is the appropriate management of a medical problem through medical and other health science technology. A second component of quality, called *interpersonal,* pertains to the psychological and social interaction between provider and patient. Amenities (e.g., appetizing food, quiet room) are a third element, which Donabedian (1980) perceives to be subsumed under the interpersonal element. He also asserts that an inseparable relationship exists between technical and interpersonal quality.

A third subset of organizational measures involves the efficiency with which services are provided (i.e., the level of organizational resources required to produce units of service). Staffing ratios per occupied bed day or numbers of laboratory tests performed by discharge diagnosis are common standards used in hospitals. The ratio of the costs to units of service provided, such as the cost for types of physical therapy procedure or the cost per X-ray procedure, is another type of efficiency measure.

A fourth subset of outcomes involves the satisfaction of key stakeholders in the organization (Blair & Fottler, 1990). Satisfaction of key stakeholders is often associated with one or more of the other three subsets of organizational outcomes. For example, high technical duality tends to be associated with physician satisfaction.

Employee Outcomes

There are other purposes and criteria for the existence of organizations and for determining their level of performance. An organization should provide its work force with job security, meaningful work, safe conditions of employment, equitable financial compensation, and a satisfactory quality of work life. Health services organizations will not be able to attract and retain the numbers, types, and quality of professionals required to deliver health services if the internal work environments are not suitable. In addition, employees are a valuable stakeholder group whose concerns are important because of the complexity of the service industry.

A number of measures of the attitudes and psychological conditions of employees are available for use within the health services industry. Employee job satisfaction (Hackman & Oldham, 1975), commitment to the organization (Porter, Steers, Mowday, & Boulian, 1974), motivation (D'Aunno & Fottler, 1994), levels of job stress (Maslach, 1976), and other constructs can be used. These measures provide management with an assessment of the quality of work life in the organization. Besides being important outcomes themselves, these factors appear to be associated with economic performance in that employees tend to remain in the organization and are likely to put forth more effort and to work more effectively if the

quality of work life is improved (Macy & Mirvis, 1976).

Turnover and absenteeism are two measures of employee withdrawal from the organization. Price and Mueller (1981) have found that a number of organizational characteristics and practices cause professional employees to withdraw psychologically from hospitals and eventually to separate voluntarily from such institutions. The financial costs of recruiting replacement personnel can be quite high. In addition, the organization loses operating efficiency when new employees must be trained in organizational policies and procedures. A detailed discussion of these and other human resources outcomes is provided in Chapter 18.

Strategic Management and Outcomes

As previously mentioned, the mission and objectives of the organization will be reflected in the outcomes that are stressed by management and in the strategies, general tactics, and human resources practices that are chosen. Management makes strategic decisions that, combined with the level of fit achieved among the internal organizational systems, determine the outcomes the institution can achieve. For example, almost all health services organizations need to earn some profit for continued viability. However, some organizations refrain from initiating new ventures that might be highly profitable if the ventures would not fit the overall mission of the organization for providing quality services needed by a defined population group.

Conversely, an organization may start some services that are acknowledged to be break-even propositions at best, because the services are viewed as critical to the mission of the institution and the needs of the target market. The concerns of such an organization would be reflected not only in the choice of services offered but also in the human resources approaches used and the outcome measures viewed as important. This organization would likely place more emphasis on assessment criteria for employee performance and nursing unit operations that stress the provision of quality care and less emphasis on criteria concerned with efficient use of supplies and the maintenance of staffing ratios. This selection of priorities does not mean that efficiency of operations is ignored, but that greater weight is placed on the former criteria. The outcome measures used to judge the institution should reflect those priorities.

Another institution may place greater emphasis on economic return, profitability, and efficiency of operations. While quality of care also is important, the driving force for becoming a low-cost provider causes management to make decisions that reflect that resolve. Maintenance or reduction of staffing levels is stressed. Prohibition of overtime is strictly enforced. Recruitment and selection criteria stress identification and selection of employees who will meet minimum criteria and expectations and, possibly, will accept lower pay levels.

In an organization striving to be efficient, less energy may be spent on "social maintenance" activities designed for employee needs and to keep them from leaving or unionizing. It can be anticipated that the outcomes in this situation will reflect, at least in the short run, higher economic return and lower measures of quality of work life. Chapter 19 examines present and future human resource challenges that must be met in order to achieve positive outcomes.

SUMMARY

The intensive reliance on professionals for service delivery requires health services executives to focus attention on the strategic management of human resources in the delivery of services and to understand the factors that influence the performance of persons employed in their organizations. To assist managers in understanding these relationships, this chapter presented a model of the association that exists among strategy, selected organizational design features, and human resources management activities.

Since different strategies require work routines, control methods, and coordination patterns of distinctive types, the structure of a health services organization is determined by the strategy being pursued. Components of an organization's structure have a strong influence on human resources systems. The behavioral systems of the organization (i.e., commitment and motivation, culture, leadership) also influence the personnel functions performed by the organization.

The outcomes achieved by the organization are influenced by numerous factors. The mission determines the direction that is being taken by the organization and what it desires to achieve. The amount of integration of mission, structural systems, behavioral systems, and human resources systems defines the level of achievement that is possible. The remainder of the text addresses these issues in detail.

Discussion Questions

1. Describe the effects that reductions in both the number of applicants and the number of total enrollments in health profession schools may have on

hospitals and other provider institutions.

2. List factors under the control of health service managers that contribute to the reduction in number of applicants for training in health profession schools. Describe the steps that hospitals and other providers can take to improve this situation.

3. Describe the changes that have taken place in the distribution of health personnel among various occupational categories. What changes do you anticipate in this distribution during the next decade? Why?

4. What are the organizational advantages of integrating strategic management and human resources management? What are the steps involved in such an integration?

CASE

Affiliated HealthSystems, a regional, non-profit hospital system, was founded in 1976 by the merger of three large, urban hospitals. These institutions were tertiary care facilities that had a combined capacity of 2000 inpatient acute care beds. During the next 7 years, Affiliated HealthSystems purchased 12 hospitals located in rural communities or small towns that were within 150 miles of the three original institutions. In addition, five management contracts were initiated between Affiliated and smaller facilities. These 17 institutions were added by Affiliated in hope of increasing, or at least retaining, referrals for the three urban hospitals.

From 1984 to 1988, Affiliated began to diversify and offer a broader array of programs and services to its urban marketplace. A health maintenance organization and a pre-ferred provider organization were initiated successfully. Special services for target markets, such as the elderly and women, were offered with positive results.

In contrast, the rural hospitals are not doing so well; for example, occupancy levels are down, the cash flow at some institutions is poor, and it is difficult to recruit competent physicians and other professional staff. The system is not certain that its urban centers are receiving the volume and type of referrals that it desires. As a result, Affiliated is considering the development of outcome measures that would allow it to monitor the performance of its rural hospitals as well as its new urban community initiatives.

Case Discussion Questions

1. Describe the steps you would take to identify the measures that should be included in the performance measurement system.

2. List suggested measures you believe are important items to include in this analysis. Discuss your rationale for including each item.

REFERENCES

Aday, L.A., & Shortell, S. (1988). Indicators and predictors of health services utilization. In S.J. Williams & P.R. Torrens (Eds.), *Introduction to health services* (3rd ed.) (pp. 46–70). New York: Wiley.

American Hospital Association. (1986). *Hospital statistics*. Chicago: Author.

American Hospital Association. (1991). *Hospital statistics*. Chicago: Author.

Andersen, A. (1985). *Health care in the 1990s: Trends and strategies*. Chicago: Arthur Andersen and American College of Hospital Administrators.

Blair, J.D., & Fottler, M.D. (1990). *Challenges in health care management: Strategic perspectives for managing key stakeholders.* San Francisco: Jossey-Bass.

Cameron, K.S., & Whetten, D.A. (1983). *Organizational effectiveness: A comparison of multiple models.* New York: Academic Press.

Cerne, F. (1988). CEO builds employee morale to improve finances. *Hospitals, 62*(11), 110.

Chandler, A. (1962). *A strategy and structure.* Cambridge: MIT Press.

Coddington, D.C., & Moore, K.D. (1987). *Market-driven strategies in health care.* San Francisco: Jossey-Bass.

D'Aunno, T. & Fottler, M.D. (1994). Motivating people. In S.M. Shertell and M.D. Kaluzny (Eds.), *Health Care Management* (3rd ed.). Albany, NY: Delmar.

Donabedian, A. (1980). *Explorations in quality assessment and monitoring, Vol. 1: The definition of quality and approaches to its assessment.* Ann Arbor, MI: Health Administration Press.

Edwards, J.E., Leek, C., Loveridge, R., Lumley, R., Mangan, J., & Silver, M. (1983). *Manpower planning: Strategy and techniques in an organizational context.* New York: Wiley.

Fottler, M.D., Phillips, J.D., & Duran, C.A. (1990). Achieving competitive advantage through strategic human resources management. *Hospital and Health Services Administration, 35*(3), 341–363.

Freudenheim, M. (1990, March 5). Job growth in health care areas. *New York Times,* p. 1.

Galbraith, J., & Nathanson, D. (1978). *Strategy implementation: The role of structure and process.* St. Paul: West Publishing.

Ginzberg, E. (1990). Health personnel: The challenge ahead. *Frontiers of Health Services Management, 7*(1), 3–22.

Gomez-Mejia, L.R. (1988). The role of human resources strategy in export performance. *Strategic Management Journal, 9,* 493–505.

Goodman, P.S., & Pennings, J.M. and Associates (1977). *New perspectives on organizational effectiveness.* San Francisco: Jossey-Bass.

Hackman, J.R., & Oldham, G.R. (1975). Development of the job diagnostic survey. *Journal of Applied Psychology, 60,* 159–170.

Human resources. (1989). *Hospitals, 63,* 46–47.

Kissick, W.L. (1968). Health manpower in transition. *Milbank Memorial Fund Quarterly, 46*(1), 51–60.

Kravetz, D.J. (1988). *The human resources revolution: Implementing progressive management practices for bottom line success.* San Francisco: Jossey-Bass.

Lawler, E.E. (1973). *Motivation in work organizations.* Pacific Grove, CA: Brooks/Cole.

Lawler, E.E. (1984). The strategic design of reward systems. In C. Fombrun, N.M. Tichy, & M.A. Devanna (Eds.), *Strategic human resource management* (pp. 127–148). New York: Wiley.

Macy, B.A., & Mirvis, P.H. (1976). A methodology for assessment of quality of work life and organizational effectiveness in behavioral-economic terms. *Administrative Science Quarterly, 21,* 212–226.

Maslach, C. (1976). Burned out. *Human Behavior, 5,* 16–22.

McManis, G.L. (1987). Managing competitively: The human factor. *Health Care Executive, 2*(6), 18–23.

Mick, S.S., & Moscovice, I. (1993). Health care professionals. In S.J. Williams & P.R. Torrens (Eds.), *Introduction to health services* (4th ed.) (pp. 3269–3296). Albany, NY: Delmar.

Mintzberg, H. (1979). *The structuring of organizations.* Englewood Cliffs, NJ: Prentice-Hall.

Porter, L.W., Steers, R.M., Mowday, R.T., & Boulian, P.V. (1974). Organizational commitment, job satisfaction, and turnover among psychiatric technicians. *Journal of Applied Psychology, 59,* 603–609.

Porter, M.E. (1980). *Competitive strategy.* New York: Free Press.

Price, J., & Mueller, C.W. (1981). *Professional turnover: The cases of the nurses.* New York: SP Medical and Scientific Books.

Sorkin, A.L. (1977). *Health manpower*. Lexington, MA: Lexington Books.

Starr, P. (1982). *The social transformation of American medicine*. New York: Basic Books.

Thompson, J.D. (1967). *Organizations in action*. New York: Basic Books.

U.S. Bureau of the Census. (1991). *Statistical abstract of the United States*. Washington, DC: Government Printing Office.

U.S. Department of Health and Human Services. (1986). *Fifth Report to the President and Congress on the Status of Health Personnel in the United States*. (DHHS Publication No. HRS-P-OD-86-1.) Hyattsville, MD: Author.

U.S. Department of Health and Human Services. (1991). *United States Health and Prevention Profile 1991,* (DHHS Publication No. PHS 92-1232). Hyattsville, MD: Author.

U.S. Department of Health, Education, and Welfare. (1970). *Health manpower sourcebook*. Washington, DC: Government Printing Office.

U.S. Department of Labor, Bureaus of Labor Statistics. (1990). *Employment and earnings*. Washington, DC: Government Printing Office.

Williams, S.J., & Torrens, P.R. (Eds.). (1993). *Introduction to Health Services* (4th ed.). Albany, NY: Delmar.

Wilson, T.B. (1986). *A Guide to Strategic Human Resources Planning for the Health Care Industry*. Chicago: American Society for Healthcare Human Resources Administration, American Hospital Association.

Zallaro, R.B., Joseph, B., & Furey, N. (1984). Do hospitals practice strategic planning? *Health Care Strategic Management, 2*(2), 16–20.

CHAPTER

THE LEGAL AND ECONOMIC ENVIRONMENT

Richard I. Lehr

Robert A. McLean

Gregg L. Smith

LEARNING OBJECTIVES

Upon completing this chapter, the reader should be able to . . .

- List the major items of legislation affecting human resources management in health care organizations.
- Describe employees' basic rights and employers' basic obligations under equal employment law.
- Explain the purposes and list the major requirements of the amended National Labor Relations Act.
- Describe the ways in which the level of overall economic activity affects a health care organization's ability to attract qualified employees.
- Explain how the external labor market affects the internal wage, salary, and benefit decisions of health care organizations.
- Explain the effects of the special features of the labor markets for health care professionals, including occupational licensure, high hiring-on costs, and long training times.

INTRODUCTION

Health care managers function in a complex environment. Their actions are constrained by the regulatory, professional, ethical, economic, and technological conditions of the societies in which they work. This chapter deals with two aspects of the external environment of human resources management: law and economics. In his classic work, *Industrial Relations Systems,* Dunlop (1958) identified the legal (or "power") and economic (or "market") contexts as major aspects of the environment in which human resources management occurs.

In the United States, the management of human resources is constrained by two broad classes of laws: those designed to protect employees in the workplace and those that regulate the conduct of employers and employees in collective bargaining situations. Protective labor legislation includes regulations for wages and hours, industrial safety, and equitable treatment of individuals. Labor relations law governs both the conduct of collective bargaining and the internal affairs of labor unions. Managers who ignore either type of legislation will experience professional peril.

Similarly, the economic environment constrains the management of human resources in health care in two ways. First, every organization is affected by the overall level of economic activity; and second, the conditions of local, industrial, and professional labor markets constrain the management of human resources. For example, failure to adopt compensation policies that are consistent with prevailing labor market conditions can result in an organization's being unable to recruit adequate hours of labor.

THE LEGAL ENVIRONMENT

Concurrently, rapid changes are occurring in the health care delivery system and in the availability of legal rights to individuals in the workplace. The impact of these changes has been dramatic to health care providers who, in efforts to control costs, have become involved in downsizing, flexible scheduling, and otherwise controlling staffing needs. Cost containment may be the impetus for the staffing changes; legal issues concerning employment may be a consequence of those changes. This chapter provides an overview of the legal considerations in the health care employment context. The chapter also includes particular issues affecting health care providers, such as reduction in force decisions, flexible scheduling, and the use of temporary or contract employees.

Statutory Rights

Federal and State Statutes Prohibiting Discrimination in Employment

Federal law and most states prohibit employers from considering certain characteristics about an applicant or an employee when making employment-related decisions. These characteristics include race, color, religion, age, sex, disability, national origin, citizenship status, or veteran status. Many states also prohibit discrimination based on marital status, and a few state and city jurisdictions prohibit discrimination based on sexual preference.

The laws prohibiting discrimination in employment do not require employers to treat everyone in the same manner. Rather, an employer may treat applicants or employees differently based on factors or business reasons unrelated to an individual's protected status. Examples of business reasons include experience, objective qualifications, subjective behavior, length of service, quality or quantity of work, attendance, or any other factor that relates to job performance. No local, state, or federal law requires an employer to hire a less-qualified applicant or to retain or promote a less-qualified employee in order to comply with the antidiscrimination statutes.

The major federal statutes prohibiting discrimination in employment include Title VII of the *Civil Rights Act of 1964* (42 U.S.C.

§2000e), *the Civil Rights Act of 1991* (42 U.S.C. §1981 (A)), *the Age Discrimination in Employment Act* (29 U.S.C. §621), *the Americans with Disabilities Act of 1990* (29 U.S.C. §706), *the Rehabilitation Act of 1973* (29 U.S.C. §701), and *the Equal Pay Act of 1963* (29 U.S.C. §201). Under Title VII of the Age Act, the Rehabilitation Act, and the Americans with Disabilities Act, if an individual has reason to believe that an employer has violated the law, the individual first must file a charge or a complaint of discrimination with an administrative agency, such as the Equal Employment Opportunity Commission (EEOC). There are also state and local agencies that may investigate complaints of discrimination under state or local law. Usually, the time table for filing a complaint or charge with those agencies is longer than under the federal statutes. Thus, to be fully informed of its obligations under the antidiscrimination laws, an employer must review the laws of its community and state, in addition to the federal statutes.

Title VII of the *Civil Rights Act of 1964* became effective in July 1965 (Kleiner, McLean, & Dreher, 1988). It forbids employment discrimination based on race, color, religion, sex, or national origin. The term "sex" was amended by the Pregnancy Discrimination Act of 1978 to include pregnancy or pregnancy-related conditions. The statute does not identify a particular gender, race, color, or religion for protection. Thus, individuals who historically may not have been discriminated against in employment, such as white males, also are protected from employment discrimination based on their gender and race. The term "reverse discrimination" simply means that the members of some classifications who historically have not experienced discrimination are in fact discriminated against.

According to reports issued from the EEOC, approximately 56% of discrimination claims filed under Title VII involve discharge-from-employment decisions. However, charges of failure to hire or to promote to management positions because of sex or race receive closer scrutiny by the EEOC than most discharge claims. This scrutiny is largely due to a study by the U.S. Department of Labor of major corporations in the United States, which identified an invisible barrier, referred to as a "glass ceiling," that impedes the progression of women and minorities into managerial and executive positions throughout the country. Thus, although discharge decisions trigger most discrimination charges, hiring and promotion decisions are receiving a higher level of scrutiny from federal enforcement authorities than ever before. This is particularly the case for organizations in which women and minorities progress to staff functions rather than operational positions.

The *Age Discrimination in Employment Act* forbids employment discrimination against individuals who are 40 years of age or older. Some states forbid discrimination based on any age; however, the overwhelming majority of states that prohibit age discrimination follow the federal standard of age 40 or older. No employee, except certain highly compensated ones, may be required to retire. (There are exceptions for public safety officers and college faculty.) One of the most difficult employment decisions for an employer to make involves a long-term employee well into the protected age group whose performance has declined, but where there has not been a dramatic incident or a

particular behavior the employer can point to as justifying an aggressive action, such as discharge. As a general guideline to employers, the older the employee, the greater length of service, and the better the overall work record, the more thorough and deliberate an employer must be in deciding that such an individual is no longer effective in his or her position. The employer should focus on performance factors, not age, and should not assume that declining performance is because of age.

Title I of the *Americans with Disabilities Act* (ADA) prohibits discrimination in employment based on an individual's disability. Applying the same definition of disability as the Rehabilitation Act, the ADA protects approximately one in five American adults. For example, someone who had cancer but shows no signs of recurrence is considered protected from discrimination under the ADA. The Act also protects individuals who have long-term, if not permanent, physical or psychological conditions that impair major life functions, and persons who are regarded as having disabilities. In the latter situation, for example, an individual with high blood pressure may be on a restricted diet, which would not impair a major life function. Such an individual is protected from disability discrimination based on perceived disability because an employer may adopt stereotypes regarding the person with high blood pressure. Contagious diseases, substance abuse, and alcoholism are regarded as disabilities under this Act.

The ADA requires an employer to follow a specific time table through the interviewing and selection process. The Act does not prohibit an employer from asking an applicant questions about medical history or health condition, but it changes the timing of when such questions may be asked during the pre-employment selection process. A "conditional" offer of employment must be made before health-related questions are asked. The offer of employment is contingent on the employee's responses to medical inquiries. An employer may not withdraw the offer if a disability becomes known to him or her unless the disability interferes with the job and the employer cannot accommodate the disability.

The ADA also restricts when and what an employer may inquire about a current employee's health condition. As a general rule, unless the employer offers employees a voluntary wellness program, the employer may not ask an employee questions about his or her health condition or require physical verification of a health condition unless there is a job-related reason to do so. This does not prohibit an employer's adherence to standards issued by the Occupational Safety and Health Administration for blood-borne pathogens or other such situations.

Under the ADA, if an applicant or an employee has a disability that may interfere with job performance, the employer must assess whether it is possible to "reasonably accommodate" the individual in the job. Reasonable accommodation in essence means "barriers removal." If the disability is a barrier such that the individual cannot perform the job function, what steps can the employer take to remove that barrier? The ADA presumes that it is possible to remove barriers, so it will be an employer's burden to show that barriers removal cannot be accomplished.

The *Pregnancy Discrimination Act of 1978* prohibits employers from treating pregnancy differently from other medical conditions. Thus, if an employer offered employees sick leave benefits, pregnancy would have to be treated as any other medical condition covered by those benefits. Furthermore, although pregnancy typically is not considered a disability under the ADA, an employer may not unilaterally decide that a pregnant employee is no longer capable of performing her job functions. Note that some state laws require employers to treat pregnancy more favorably than other medical conditions.

If the local, state, or federal administrative agency is unable to resolve the discrimination charge between the employer and the individual (referred to as the "claimant" or "charging party"), the administrative agency or the individual may initiate litigation against the employer. Under the federal anti-discrimination statutes, an individual will receive a "Right to Sue" notice, requiring the individual to file suit in state or federal court within 90 days after receiving the notice or else the right to sue is lost. The time table for similar action differs under state or local ordinances. Under the Civil Rights Act of 1991, persons who claim discrimination under Title VII and the ADA have the right to try their case to a jury, and to receive compensatory and punitive damages if they prevail. Compensatory damage covers matters such as pain and suffering and emotional distress, and punitive damages, although they may be viewed as a windfall to the individual, are intended to punish the employer for its wrongful actions. Under the Age Discrimination in Employment Act, double damages may be awarded if the employer was willful in its violation of the Act. The availability of compensatory and punitive damages under local and state laws varies by location. Employment discrimination laws often are "fee shifting" statutes, which means that if it loses the case, the employer is responsible for paying the plaintiff's attorney fees.

There are other federal antidiscrimination in employment statutes with which employers must comply, although they do not require the same degree of scrutiny as the ones just reviewed. For example, the *Viet Nam Veterans' Readjustment Assistance Act of 1974* (38 U.S.C. §2021) guarantees individuals in the military or National Guard time off without a loss in seniority for purposes of military obligations and the right to reinstatement on completion of the military duty, unless the individual otherwise would have been transferred, laid off, or terminated. Changes to this law also protect an individual's pension eligibility and contributions made on behalf of the individual while on military leave. The *Fair Credit Reporting and Disclosure Act* covers circumstances in which employers may request a credit check about an applicant or employee. The purpose of this Act is so that individuals will be aware if a reporting organization indicates that their credit ratings are unfavorable. Furthermore, the individual is protected from discrimination in employment due to bankruptcy or garnishments, although there are circumstances in which there are multiple garnishments that may result in an employee's termination. The *Immigration Reform and Control Act of 1986* (29 U.S.C. §802) prohibits discrimination based on citizenship status.

Individual Employment Rights

"Individual employment rights" is a term that applies to specific behavior, employer practices, or incidents occurring at the work place. At the state level, for example, many states have enacted laws prohibiting or restricting smoking in the work place. Some states also have laws providing an employee access to his or her personnel records in certain circumstances. Other examples of state laws regarding individual employment rights include protection from loss of pay and employment if an employee is called out for jury duty, protection for a leave of absence for voting purposes, protection for an employee who blows the whistle on potential illegal employer behavior, and a requirement that employers submit letters of reference or recommendation within a specific time period after being requested by the employee.

Harassment is an area of the law that crosses between federal statutory guidelines and state judge-made or "common law." Under federal law, an individual may not be harassed by a fellow employee, superior, subordinate, patient, or visitor to the premises because of his or her status in a protected group. Such harassment, if done by a supervisor and under circumstances in which the employer does not have policies and preventive approaches in place may make the employer liable for the supervisor's behavior. For a nonsupervisory employee, it is usually required that the employer had noticed or should have known that the behavior occurred and that the employer failed to act.

Harassment based on gender and sexual harassment are two different concepts. Gender harassment involves illegal harassment toward someone because of his or her gender. For example, belittling or derogatory comments to women or about women made to others at work may constitute gender harassment and is evidence of sexual discrimination in employment. Sexual harassment involves two forms of behavior. The first involves the behavior of a supervisor to a subordinate in which the subordinate is placed in the position of submitting to sexual advances or else suffering some form of job harm. This type of harassment is known as *quid pro quo*. In this situation, there is a risk of individual liability for the supervisor and strict liability for the employer. Strict liability means that if the behavior occurred, the employer will be held responsible for the behavior of its supervisor, regardless of whether the employer knew of the behavior.

Hostile environment is a form of sexual harassment in which there may not be sexual favors sought or, if so, it is not a *quid pro quo* environment. For harassment to be of a hostile environment nature, the behavior must be unwelcomed by the individual, must be based on the prohibited factor (e.g., the individual's sex), must have been offensive and pervasive from the viewpoint of a reasonable person, and must have occurred in a situation in which the employer either knew or should have known that the behavior occurred and failed to take corrective action. This last factor is a significant difference between hostile environment and *quid pro quo* sexual harassment. There also may be individual liability for those whose behavior constitutes the hostile environment.

A delicate problem involves sexual harassment from a patient or a physician (e.g., if a patient were to make unwelcomed sexual comments to a nurse, if a physician were to make unwelcomed sexual overtures to a hospital employee). In those situations, the employer should have a policy describing behaviors that may be viewed by the health care provider as inappropriate toward an employee, how the employee should respond to the individual behaving in that fashion, and whom in the organization should be contacted by the employee regarding the behavior. Generally, for risk-management purposes in employment and health care issues, if such behavior occurred between a patient and a nurse, efforts should be made to shift a different nurse to care for that patient and also to counsel the patient and/or the patient's family about that behavior. Similarly, if the unwelcomed behavior is from a physician, the hospital administrator in charge of physician matters, for example, should be the one to discuss that behavior with the physician.

The *Family and Medical Leave Act of 1993* (29 U.S.C. §2601), provides employees with the opportunity to take as many as 12 weeks per year of unpaid leave for the birth; adoption or foster care child placement; an employee's serious health condition; or the serious health condition of an employee's spouse, child, or parent. Employees must meet certain eligibility standards in order to take a leave covered under this Act. In some circumstances, the leave may be on an intermittent or reduced schedule basis, for increments as little as 1 hour at a time. Some states have more demanding family, parental, or medical leave statutes. When there is a conflict between a more rigorous state statute and the Family and Medical Leave Act, the more rigorous provisions should be followed.

Worker's compensation is a state law procedure for an individual who is injured on the job. The purpose of the procedure is to establish a certain system for compensation of an individual who incurs medical expenses and loses earnings due to a job-related injury. Also, a purpose is to have finality, so that the employer does not have open-ended continuing litigation over work-related injuries. Most states have established what is referred to as the "exclusivity principle," which is that worker's compensation provides the sole and exclusive remedy for an individual who is injured on the job.

If an individual is injured on the job, the employer should investigate the injury promptly. This includes speaking to witnesses and even taking pictures of the work site, if appropriate. The employer should try to ascertain what occurred and whether the injury was due to carelessness on the part of the employee or someone else, or due to circumstances that were simply unavoidable. Such an approach may reduce an employer's risk of similar injuries occurring in the future. Furthermore, because of the high correlation statistically between alcohol and drug use and work-related injuries, a number of states permit employers to test employees for the presence of alcohol or drugs in their systems after job-related accidents. In some states, an individual who tests positive for alcohol or drugs when tested after a work-related injury may be precluded from receiving worker's compensation benefits.

Virtually all states with worker's compensation statutes prohibit employers from retaliating against an individual who has exercised rights under the worker's compensation law. Thus, an employer may not refuse to reinstate an employee who has missed work due to a worker's compensation injury. However, some courts have upheld an employer practice that if an employee is not at work for any reason for longer than a specific period of time (e.g., 12 months), the individual loses reemployment rights. Those types of policies must be evaluated for compliance with the ADA as well as state worker's compensation law. A claim of retaliation under worker's compensation is separate from the issue of worker's compen-

sation as the exclusive remedy for lost wages and health benefits due to the injury.

Employment contracts are perhaps the single greatest source of judicial development in the individual employment rights area. They involve claims of employment contract, promises, or misrepresentation. In every state except Montana, employees are "terminable at will," which means that unless the termination decision violates state or federal law or breaches a contract of employment with the employer, an employee may be terminated with or without cause or notice, and an employee may terminate under the same circumstances (Kleiner, McLean, & Dreher, 1988). Thus, in addition to the antidiscrimination statutes, contracts of employment may restrict an employer's right to terminate an employee with or without cause or notice. An employment contract, of course, may be written and, in some states, it may be verbal. Furthermore, promises to applicants or employees that are not kept, such as representations of job security when staff cutbacks occur throughout the organization, may result in a claim of breach of contract or misrepresentation.

Written communications to applicants or employees, such as the employment application, personnel handbook, and internal memoranda, should be analyzed from the standpoint of whether these documents create potential contract claims. If employers want employees to remain "terminable at will," employers must include the appropriate language in the organization's documents for protection. Furthermore, when an applicant is offered employment, it is often useful to offer it in writing, stating that the employment relationship is terminable at will and that the written offer of employment supersedes all previous discussions regarding the potential employment relationship. Such communication reduces the risk of an employee subsequently claiming that certain promises were made during the time he or she was recruited by the health care provider and that those promises were not kept.

Constitutional Issues

Health care providers that are part of a governmental entity should consider whether their employees are afforded protection by the United States Constitution and the constitution of the state in which the facility is located. Private-sector employees are not protected by the Constitution regarding their employers' actions. However, public-sector or governmental employees are entitled to constitutional protection in addition to the protections under most state and federal employment statutes. For example, free speech in the work place entitles an individual to be free of retaliation if the individual expresses a belief or opinion about a matter at work that would touch and concern the public (e.g., problems with quality of care), and if the manner in which the expression is conveyed is not unduly disruptive to the employer. There is no such protection for a private-sector employee, although private and public sector employees are protected from retaliation under the antidiscrimination statutes for raising a matter covered by those laws.

Employees of public-sector employers also are entitled to due process before a disciplinary or discharge decision may be implemented. For example, before termination is effective, an individual typically is entitled to a hearing, with an opportunity to hear the charges against him or her and the opportunity to present evidence in response to those charges. In some states, a pretermination hearing is required, such that the individual first hears the charges before a termination decision is made.

An additional area of constitutional protection involves unreasonable searches and seizures. For private sector health care employers, employees generally do not enjoy a constitutional expectation of privacy such that they would be immune from searches of their desks or work stations. A drug test is a "search" under the Constitution. More than 30 states have passed laws regulating how drug testing among private-sector employers should be conducted. Thus, although public employers may not as a general rule test employees randomly for drugs because that could be considered unreasonable search and seizure, private-sector employers may be limited under state law regarding drug testing.

Compensation and Employee Benefits

The *Fair Labor Standards Act* (FLSA) (29 U.S.C. §201), passed in 1938 and amended several times since then, contains provisions that are unique to health care employers. A general requirement under the FLSA is that unless an employee is exempt from minimum wage and overtime, he or she must be paid at least the minimum wage for each hour worked up to 40 hours in a work week, and time and one-half of that amount for any hours worked over 40 in that work week. There are different ways to arrive at this calculation, such as a flat hourly rate approach or an approach in which a salary is averaged over hours worked. The latter is called fixed salary for fluctuating work week. In some states, the minimum wage is actually higher than the federal minimum wage. Where there is a conflict between state and federal wage and hour law, the more stringent of the two laws prevails.

Recognizing that health care facilities have unique staffing needs and obligations, Section 7(j) of the Fair Labor Standards Act provides greater flexibility for health care employers. This section permits a health care employer to pay its employees under a system called "8/80." This means that during a 14-day period, if an employee works no more than 8 hours in a day or 80 hours for the entire 14 days, the employee is not eligible for overtime. Thus, assume that a nurse works a 7 days on, 7 days off schedule. Also assume that the nurse works 8 hours each day. If the employer did not use the 8/80 approach, and the nurse worked 7 consecutive 8-hours days, or 56 hours, the nurse would be entitled to 16 hours of overtime pay. Under the 8/80 pay system, no overtime is owed. The 8/80 pay system is widely available to employees who are not involved in direct patient care responsibilities. Employers should make employees aware of this pay system, how it works, and how they will be paid under it.

There is also a pay plan known as the "Baylor plan," which involves paying nurses, who are referred to as "Baylor nurses," over a weekend for 40 hours, although they may work only 24 hours. This plan originally developed as a recruiting approach for employers to attract nurses who wanted to work on a part-time basis. As hospitals have cut back staffing because of changes of health care cost reimbursement systems, Baylor plan employees often are the first eliminated.

The *Employee Retirement Income Security Act of 1974* (ERISA) (29 U.S.C. §1001) covers retirement, pension plans, and "welfare plans," such as health insurance or segregated funds intended for employee benefits, covering sick days, vacation pay, and severance benefits. ERISA addresses issues such as eligibility for vesting in a retirement program, circumstances of forfeiture of retirement funds, and the duty that is owed by retirement plan administrators to plan beneficiaries. Issues concerning nondiscrimination regarding the eligibility for retirement and certain welfare benefits are governed by ERISA. An employer generally may not terminate or retaliate against an employee because that employee is about to become eligible for retirement or welfare benefits.

Under ERISA, employers have greater latitude to differentiate among employees and make changes to welfare plans without prior governmental approval. A primary area in which this occurs involves changes regarding eligibility to participate in an insurance program and the nature of coverage under the insurance program. Much attention has been focused on changes that have been made to the health care benefits available to retirees. Those changes are analyzed from a standpoint of whether they violate ERISA or breach a contract of employment that was entered into with those individuals prior to their retirement.

The *Consolidated Omnibus Budget Reconciliation Act* (COBRA) covers situations in which an employee or an employee's dependents may be eligible for health insurance continuation coverage on the employee's layoff, termination from employment, or death. The Act has specific requirements for notifying individuals of their COBRA rights. COBRA may not be available if an employee is terminated due to gross willful misconduct. Some courts have followed the state law definition of "gross misconduct" under unemployment compensation statutes to determine whether an individual is ineligible for COBRA benefits. If the employer mistakenly concludes that a former employee and/ or his or her dependents are not eligible for COBRA coverage and an insurance event arises, the employer, if wrong, may be responsible for paying that cost plus fines that may accrue on a daily basis and attorney's fees.

Unemployment compensation is a short-term benefit to individuals who are separated from employment for reasons other than gross misconduct, dishonesty, or extended absenteeism. A layoff or termination due to unsatisfactory performance usually entitles the individual to unemployment compensation. The employee's claim for compensation and the employer's response and testimony at the unemployment hearing are under oath and may play a significant role if the employee pursues some of the claim against the employer (e.g., discrimination). In essence, what either party says or communicates during the unemployment process may be used as evidence in an employment discrimination or breach of contract claim filed by the employee.

The *Equal Pay Act of 1963* (29 U.S.C. §201) addresses the issue of men and women who receive different pay based on performing similar work under similar working conditions, requiring similar skill, effort, and responsibility. The expression "equal pay for equal work" evolved from the Equal Pay Act. If there is a difference in pay between a man and a woman who are performing similar work with similar requirements and working conditions, the difference in pay must be based on some other factor than difference in sex. Factors that are permissible distinctions include length of service, quality or

quantity of work, or any other factor other than sex. In the event an employer is found to violate this Act, the remedy includes raising the pay of lower-paid employees; lowering the pay of the more highly paid individuals is not permitted. It is unnecessary for a person complaining of an Equal Pay Act violation to file a complaint with an administrative agency; the individual may proceed directly to state or federal court.

Other Federal Laws

The *National Labor Relations Act of 1935* (29 U.S.C. §151) did not apply to hospitals for many years. The reason for this exclusion was that Congress was concerned that there would be disruption to the flow of health care services to patients, which could present potential safety risks. However, in 1974, the National Labor Relations Act was amended to cover hospitals, but also included provisions unique to hospitals. For example, if employees strike at a hospital, the hospital must receive greater advance notice of that strike than a nonhospital employer so that efforts can be made to mediate the dispute and the employer can have ample time to prepare for coverage in the event of strike. Furthermore, for acute care hospitals only, there are specific rules the National Labor Relations Board promulgated concerning which groups of employees may be combined for unionization purposes.

When employees seek to unionize, an issue to address is whether those employees are an appropriate "bargaining unit." This questions whether the employees share commonality of interests regarding jobs, working relationships, work conditions, and the like. The analysis of common interests is to establish a bargaining unit that facilitates bargaining between the union and employer about matters of common concern to the employees. In a rule that applies only to acute care facilities, the National Labor Relations Board has determined that unless unusual, special circumstances apply, employees will be classified into one of eight bargaining units appropriate for collective bargaining. Prior to this rule, acute care facility employees were often grouped as all professional or all nonprofessional employees. The current rule provides that employees will be in units based of registered nurses, physicians, all other professionals, technical employees, skilled maintenance employees, business office clericals, guards, and all other nonprofessional employees.

Employees protected under the National Labor Relations Act generally have the right to "solicit" about union matters, provided the individuals initiating and receiving the solicitation are not working and are not supposed to be working and provided that the solicitation occurs in nonwork areas, such as breakrooms. Employees also have the right to wear union insignias and buttons. These rules are different as they apply to health care employers. Such rules, referred to as "no solicitation, no distribution," permit hospitals to consider whether the solicitation, distribution, or wearing of union pins occurs in a patient care or patient access area. The greatest restrictions apply to the facility's patient care areas. Furthermore, a factor to consider is whether the employer permits employees to engage in other similar activity in the same patient care or access areas.

The *Worker Adjustment and Retraining Notification Act of 1988* (WARN) (23 U.S.C. §2101) covers employment decisions that are identified as mass layoffs and plant clos-

ings. A *mass layoff* is a work force reduction that results in a loss at a single location of employment during a 30-day period affecting at least one-third of the employees *and* at least 50 employees, *or* at least 500 employees. To be covered, the layoff must be expected to last 6 months or longer. A *plant closing* refers to a permanent or temporary shutdown at a single location of employment that results in a loss of employment for 50 or more employees—for example, if a hospital discontinued providing certain services that resulted in the termination of at least 50 employees during a 30-day period. The Act, as a general rule, requires employees and local governments to receive at least 60 days notice in advance of the date of the layoff or termination. There are exceptions to the 60-days notices, such as when the circumstances were unforeseeable. That is an exception that the employer is required to prove, and the employer also must comply with giving notice provisions immediately and explaining why the 60-day notice provision was not met. In addition to notifying the employee or the employee's collective bargaining representative, the employer also must notify the local or county government, to whichever the employer pays more taxes, and the state dislocated worker unit, which functions to assist employees in their attempts to secure other employment.

The *Occupational Safety and Health Act of 1970* (P.L. 91-596, 91st Congress, 5.2193) is a federal law administered by the Occupational Safety and Health Administration (OSHA), a division of the United States Department of Labor. Employers have a general duty under the Act to maintain a safe work place and to adhere to standards that OSHA promulgates for specific industries. For example, health care employers are required to adhere to OSHA standards regarding blood-borne pathogens and standards regarding establishing a hazard communication program. In addition to OSHA, states may establish safety and health requirements in conjunction with OSHA or that extend beyond the minimum thresholds required of OSHA.

The turmoil in the health care community due to cost-containment and insurance issues has forced health care employers to become more flexible in analyzing staffing needs. A two-step process to follow from a legal perspective involves asking the following questions: 1) what decision makes the most business sense for the health care employers? and 2) how does that decision fit with the employer's local, state, and federal law obligations?

Approaches for Handling Specific Employee Situations

Termination from Employment

The United States has become more productive over time; yet for many employers, this has been a result of work force reductions due to enhanced efficiency and technology. Health care employers are faced with a similar productivity challenge. For individuals, particularly those in managerial capacities, the opportunities to obtain other jobs on termination from employment may be quite limited. It is not unusual for terminated employees, therefore, to turn to the legal system to question whether they have been terminated in violation of local, state, or federal law. There are approaches health care employers may consider to try to minimize, from a risk-management standpoint, the possibility of a termination decision resulting in employment litigation.

One approach is to provide for an internal appeals process or appeals board by which the employee would have the termination decision reviewed by others within the organization. For example, if an employee believes that a termination decision has been improper, a peer review panel composed of three employees would review the decision, hear testimony from the employee and others, and review documents in the employee's personnel file and other documents related to the situation. The review panel, preferably not a permanent one, would have the authority either to order that the employee should be reinstated or to make a recommendation to management of reinstatement. For true peer review to exist, the members of the review panel should be an individual's peers. An approach for selecting the panel could be for the employee to name a member, the employee's manager to name a representative, and the Human Resources Director to name a third representative. Employers have found that this type of structure may serve as an effective approach for an employee to have his or her "day in court" without actually incurring the costs of litigation.

Another approach is mandatory arbitration of employment disputes arising on termination. This, in essence, is a contractual agreement between the employer and the employee, whereby the employee agrees to submit to arbitration regarding the question of whether the termination was illegal or in violation of some contract the employee claims that he or she had with the employer. Courts have shown an increased willingness to enforce private arbitration agreements, resulting in an expedited process for the employer and employee with less cost, and, for the employer, often less risk. Employers should be sure that the employee or applicant understands that arbitration means that the individual may not pursue another type of employment-related cause of action against the employer.

Arbitration is a form of an alternative dispute resolution process, referred to colloquially as "ADR." This procedure has become more widespread as an alternative to the delay, disruption, and cost associated with litigation in state or federal court. Mediation or conciliation is another form of ADR, in which a third party is brought in to facilitate the employer and former employee resolving their differences, instead of the matter proceeding to the administrative and judicial system.

Reduction in force (RIF) decisions are different from an individual termination decision in that an RIF typically is motivated by a change in business circumstances, rather than by an individual's job performance. Thus, if the health care employer has determined the need to cut staffing, the employer should be sure that this is done in a manner that does not violate the antidiscrimination statutes, particularly the Age Discrimination in Employment Act, and does not breach a contract that an individual arguably had with the employer. When considering a reduction in force analysis, the employer should consider the advantages and disadvantages of the following methods:

- Seniority: The advantage to making reduction in force decisions based on seniority is that it is an objective, easily understood factor. The downside of using seniority as the factor is that good performers with less seniority may be terminated, compared to less-than-top performers with greater seniority.
- Assessing who remains, based on an analysis of performance appraisals and forming a priority from those employees who are the top performers to those who are the worst performers. (A problem often arises when employee performance appraisals do not reflect the employer's assessment of the individual's job performance accurately.)
- Identify tasks that must be done by those who will remain, and then determine which employees are the most qualified to perform those tasks. Assess qualifications based on job performance and other factors, and then rank employees in order of strongest and weakest performers. Where employees are close in ranking, provide additional credit for the employee with the greater length of service.

In addition to a reduction in force, other approaches include a reduction in pay and a cutback in hours or job sharing, such that two employees work fewer hours, but neither one is laid off.

Contract Employees, Temporary Employees, and Independent Contractors

Contract employees are those who, by agreement, work generally on a part-time basis or for a fixed project and then are terminated, and to whom health care, vacation, sickness, and personal leave benefits are not extended. The trend of federal legislation is to provide insurance benefits to the approximately 35 million Americans who work but who do not receive insurance benefits from their employers. Therefore, employers who use individuals on a contract or per-project basis must assess whether these benefits apply. Furthermore, employers should consider whether benefits similarly apply in the retirement area, for which eligibility is often based on total hours worked in a given year, rather than on whether an individual is classified as a contract employee.

Employees utilized through a temporary service actually are often referred to as jointly employed by the temporary service and the entity utilizing the temporary employee. Although the health care provider may pay a fee to the temporary service, the actual day-to-day supervision of the temporary employee is conducted by the health care employer. Therefore, the most secure course of action for the employer is to assume that state and federal antidiscrimination and individual employment rights laws cover those employees who are utilized through temporary services.

Some health care providers and other employers also utilize independent contractors. The advantage of an independent contractor is that the employer saves payroll and benefits costs. However, the U.S. Department of Labor and Internal Revenue Service closely scrutinize the independent contractor classification because some employers have utilized this approach to classify individuals who truly are employees as independent contractors. An individual is a valid independent contractor if, first and foremost, the employer does not direct the individual or have the right of control regarding how the individual is to perform his or her tasks. The individual also should exist as a separate business enterprise, be recognized as such, and be responsible for his or her own equipment, licenses, taxes, and the like. As a general rule, employers should consider entering a written contract with an independent contractor. However, the longer the relationship continues and if the independent contractor does not have similar relationships with other entities, the greater the likelihood that the individual will be viewed as an employee.

The changing regulatory and competitive environment requires health care providers to be flexible and creative in deciding which individuals should be employed, promoted, or terminated from employment. When that environment is overlapped with the expansion of employment rights that has occurred from 1963 through today, one quickly sees the importance of being informed about and knowledgeable of placing the employment laws in the context of the health care provider's mission.

THE ECONOMIC ENVIRONMENT

Health care organizations manage human resources in an economic environment as well as legal one. Several features of the economic environment affect strategic human resources management. The overall level of economic activity affects both the demand for health services and the availability of potential employees. Conditions prevailing in the labor markets for health care professionals affect the compensation and employment conditions an organization must offer to attract employees. The prevailing market compensation required to attract employee characteristics, in turn, affects management's decisions about types of employees to recruit. The remainder of this chapter draws on the field of labor economics (Ehrenberg & Smith, 1991; Kleiner, McLean, & Dreher, 1988) to evaluate human resources in the health care sector.

The Economic System: Pricing and Resource Allocation

The economic system sets prices for scarce resources, allocates resources through markets and other mechanisms, determines the level of overall productive activity, and distributes the rewards for that activity among society's members. In the United States, market forces set most prices with relatively little interference from government or other authorities. Resources, including human effort, are allowed to move to their highest and most valued uses in response to price incentives. Those who would purchase goods and services, including labor, are allowed to bid for those resources and, generally, to use resources in the most cost-effective manner possible. Since colonial times, however, there have been government regulations for American economic activity (Hughes, 1977) to moderate the effects of market forces on resource allocation.

Labor markets are the arrangements by which the sellers of labor (i.e., workers) and the purchasers of labor (i.e., firms) come together to determine the number of hours of work employed and the price at which those hours will be purchased. *It is important to note that the purchase of an hour of work from an individual is not the same as the purchase of that individual for an hour.* In American labor markets, as in the economy at large, however, several deviations from unfettered market activity are the rule.

The Level of Economic Activity

Just as a rising tide lifts all ships, firms and employees in every industry are affected by the level of economic activity. The level of economic activity is usually measured by gross domestic product (GDP), the market value of all goods and services produced in the country in a year. (GDP has all but replaced gross national product [GNP] as the principal measure of economic activity in the American National Income and Product Accounts) (Carson, 1992). As GDP rises, employment increases because additional labor is required to produce more goods and services. As GDP falls, workers are "laid off." As those persons are laid off, they reduce their spending, causing GDP to fall further.

Over time, GDP grows due to three factors. First, as prices rise (as they have, to one degree or another in almost every year since World War II), GDP measured in current market prices rises. Second, as technological change progresses and as the stock of productive equipment grows, GDP measured in real (i.e., constant price level) terms grows. The latter effect is known as "economic growth" and is responsible for the rising standard of living that the people of the United States have enjoyed for virtually all of this century. Third, over long periods of time, the size of the labor force grows, allowing total output, and therefore GDP, to rise.

Since GDP has a growth trend, one can develop a better measure of prosperity and depression than the GDP level alone. (Even after long recessions, GDP is higher than in earlier periods of prosperity.) A better measure of the level of prosperity is the difference between current real GDP (i.e., GDP adjusted for changing prices) and its long-run trend value. When GDP is above its long-run trend value, the nation is in a period of general prosperity (although there will be pockets of poverty and individuals who do not share equally in that prosperity), and there may be strong upward pressure on wages and salaries. When real GDP is below its long-run trend value, the nation is in a period of recession (although there may be regions, industries, and individuals who are less affected than average). In such a time, unemployment will rise and upward pressure on wages and salaries will moderate.

Historical experience shows that the volume of economic activity need not always be adequate to employ all persons who wish to work. Table 2.1 shows GNP, GNP adjusted for changing prices, and total private employment for the United States for a series of recent years. (GNP is shown here, rather than GDP, as GNP had been the regular measure produced by American National Income and Product Accounts until very recently.) Table 2.1 demonstrates that nominal GNP (i.e., GNP in current prices) rose in every year in the

series. Real GNP, however, fell in 1980 and 1982. The latter decline in real GNP was accompanied by a decline in total private employment as well.

What causes changes in the level of GDP? Economists have debated that question for generations, beginning with Keynes's *The General Theory of Employment, Interest, and Money* (1936). Mankiw (1990) provides a review of the recent literature. In general, fluctuations in GDP have their origins in autonomous changes in GDP components and in changes in the availability of money and credit. An autonomous change in a component is one that is caused by the decisions of economic factors, rather than as a response to an earlier change in GDP.

Consumers can make an autonomous increase in spending when, in response to im-

TABLE 2.1. Gross National Product and Employment from 1975 to 1989

Year	Nominal GNP ($ millions)	Real GNP ($ millions 1982)	Total private employment (thousands)	Total private health services employment (thousands)
1975	1598.40	2695.00	62,259.00	4133.80
1976	1718.00	2827.00	64,511.00	4350.40
1977	1918.30	2959.00	67,344.00	4583.90
1978	2163.90	3115.00	71,026.00	4791.60
1979	2417.80	3192.00	73,876.00	4992.80
1980	2732.00	3187.10	74,166.00	5278.00
1981	3052.60	3248.80	75,126.00	5562.20
1982	3166.00	3166.00	73,729.00	5811.80
1983	3405.70	3279.10	74,330.00	6122.30
1984	3772.20	3501.40	78,472.00	6298.70
1985	4014.90	3618.70	81,125.00	6298.70
1986	4231.60	3717.90	82,832.00	6535.70
1987	4515.60	3945.30	85,190.00	6805.40
1988	4873.70	4016.90	88,150.00	7121.00
1989	5200.80	4117.70	90,644.00	7550.70

Sources: U.S. Department of Commerce, Bureau of the Census (1987). *Statistical abstract of the United States,* Washington, DC: Government Printing Office; U.S. Department of Commerce, Bureau of the Census (1991). *Statistical abstract of the United States.* Washington, DC: Government Printing Office; U.S. Department of Labor, Bureau of Labor Statistics (1991). *Employment, hours, and earnings, United States, 1909–1990* (Vols. 1 & 2). Washington, DC: Government Printing Office.

provements in their expectations about future income, prices, and interest rates, they decide to purchase more newly produced goods and services than they did in the past. Likewise, business firms, both investor-owned and not-for-profit, make autonomous increases in capital investment when, in response to improved expectations, they increase their spending on newly produced capital goods.

The most frequently cited source for autonomous spending changes is government. Especially at the federal level, government's ability to set its budget at will makes it a major determinant of changes in GDP. That the federal government can increase spending without increasing taxes (or can cut spending without cutting taxes) means that it can make net increases or decreases in the level of economic activity as matters of policy. An increase in the level of taxation, however, takes purchasing power away from consumers and business, causing a decrease in their purchases. It is government's net contribution (i.e., spending minus tax receipts), then, that represents the role of government in determining the level of economic activity. In addition, government's actions are major determinants of changes in consumers' and business' expectations. The commitment of government to undertake new programs can promote optimism on the part of other actors. A perceived willingness of government to fight inflation can improve the expectations of all other participants in the economy.

Business' purchases of capital goods and consumers' purchases of durable goods (e.g., automobiles, major appliances) are determined, in part, by the cost of obtaining financing (i.e., by the level of interest rates). The availability and the cost of credit are also determinants of the level of economic activity. When the Federal Reserve System acts to increase the amount of money in circulation, its purpose is to stimulate the level of GDP and employment. When it acts to reduce the stock of money in the banking system, its intent is to restrict economic activity and to reduce the level of employment.

Not all industries are affected to the same extent by changing levels of GDP. Some industries (e.g., the production of consumer durable goods), are highly sensitive to changes in GDP. Their employment and output levels respond quickly and strongly to changing macroeconomic conditions. Table 2.1 shows real GDP (RGNP, adjusted for changing prices), overall employment, and employment in the nongovernmental health services sector for 1975–1989. One can estimate relationships between GNP and employment for the economy and for the health care sector. The relationship estimated is of the following form:

(2.1) $Employment_t = a + b(RGNP_t)$.

The model tests the hypothesis that employment in each year (time is denoted by "t") depends on a constant term (a) plus a sensitivity term (b) multiplied by that year's real GNP. The model was estimated by the method of ordinary least squares.

Table 2.2 summarizes the results of estimating Equation (2.1) for total private employment and for private health care employment. For each dependent variable (employment overall or in health care), the coefficient shows the estimated sensitivity of employment to changes in that variable. The numbers in parentheses are the standard errors of the estimated coefficients. (Readers may wish to consult a standard textbook on multivariate statistics for assistance in inter-

TABLE 2.2. Results of Regression (numbers in parentheses are standard errors)

Independent variable	Total employment	Total employment	Private health care employment	Private health care employment
		Dependent variable		
Constant	12,097.45	21,352.28	−2087.51	4713.88
Real GNP	19.00	15.41	2.32	−0.32
	(0.66)	(2.82)	(0.18)	(0.26)
Time trend		357.03		262.38
		(273.36)		(24.82)
Standard error of estimate	1074.39	1046.36	293.12	94.99
R^2	0.98	0.99	0.93	0.99
Observations	15	15	15	15
Degrees of freedom	13	12	13	12

preting these results.) The R^2 for each equation shows the percentages of the total variation in employment that is explained by that equation.

In the simplest model, both total private employment and private health care employment appear to be significantly affected by the level of real GNP. That result is unsurprising and is strong, supported by highly significant estimated coefficients and by R^2s in excess of 0.90. A second set of regressions, however, tells another story. One can add a second term to account for changes in employment over time. That time trend variable is not (as the third column of Table 2.2 shows) a significant determinant of total private employment. The time trend variable is, however, a significant determinant of private health care employment. *After including the trend variable, real GNP ceases to have a statistically significant effect on employment in the health care sector.* These results show that private health care employment, in the aggregate, has grown over time without consideration of the overall level of economic activity. The essential nature of many health care services makes them nonpostponable,

even in times of economic hardship. Furthermore, Medicare coverage for the elderly is constant; as an age-related entitlement, it is not tied to current employment. Health care employers, as a whole, however, have continued, in the post-Medicare era, to expand employment despite fluctuations in the proportion of the population with health insurance.

What, then, is the overall effect of the level of economic activity on human resources management in the health care sector? When GDP is high (i.e., above its long-run trend value), the demand for labor by all firms will be strong. Not only will health care institutions compete for employees' loyalties, but other sectors of the economy will also compete for workers who might be employed in health care. That external competition will be most intense for workers with the smallest degree of specific health care training. A booming external economy will not place pressure on health care institutions for unskilled workers alone. Information systems professionals, industrial engineers, accountants, and administrators also experience improved nonhealth care opportunities in a booming economy. The pressures associated with the GDP being above its long-term trend value may force increased levels of wages and salaries for affected individuals and job categories in order to retain those employees in the face of external competition.

For some professional employees, the effect of competition from other sectors of the economy will hardly be felt. For example, most registered nurses are unlikely to defect to the banking and financial services industry, even when wages in that sector rise substantially. Wage, salary, and employment pressures for those persons trained specifically for and professionally committed to the health care sector are determined, largely, by what happens inside the health care sector (i.e., the labor markets for licensed health care professionals are little affected by the overall level of economic activity, but are affected by supply and demand forces within their own labor markets).

Labor Markets Defined

In common usage "the labor market" is considered to be a single homogeneous entity. One might hear, "the labor market is poor this month." In fact, labor markets are highly differentiated, and one can classify them along three dimensions: geographic, industrial, and occupational (Figure 2.1). Geographic labor markets are defined by the location of employment (e.g., Salina, Kansas or Syracuse, New York); industrial labor markets are defined by the nature of the good or service being produced (e.g., automobiles or hospital services); and occupational labor markets are defined by the activities in which the individual is engaged or by the professional certification required to perform those activities (e.g., registered nurse, physi-

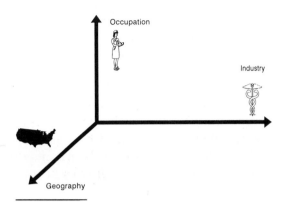

FIGURE 2.1. The three dimensions of labor markets.

cian, podiatrist, or accountant). Although every individual and every employer displays some degree of concern with each of the three labor market dimensions, most positions and most individuals identify most strongly with one of the three.

Some individuals perceive their relevant labor market geographically. These persons view their opportunities as being constrained to one locality and are concerned little, if at all, with the specific activity or industry in which they are employed. In general, the lower the degree of occupation-specific education and training, the more narrowly geographically defined is the labor market in which the individual participates. Maintenance workers, for example, may work as carpenter's helpers, janitors, or landscape workers in construction, retailing, or health care services. They tend to remain, however, in one local labor market.

Some individuals define their labor market experiences by industry. Those who move from position to position within the health care sector (e.g., moving from nurse to nursing administrator to director of human resources) define their relevant labor markets as that related to health care, with little reference to profession or location. Those who select careers in government service are among the largest group for whom industry, rather than occupation or location, defines the relevant labor market.

Individuals with a great deal of occupation-specific education and training usually remain within the profession for which they are prepared. Those individuals may move across industries and from state to state, but they seek out and consider employment opportunities within well-defined occupations. For example, a registered nurse may move from a factory's health office to a hospital and then to a long-term care facility, all the while working as a nurse. He or she may move from Wisconsin to Texas while making those industrial changes without ever changing occupation.

For professional employees, the higher the degree of training required, the greater the geographic scope of the relevant market. Thus, those who serve food in the cafeteria may be recruited from the pool of local high school graduates. Registered nurses may be recruited from RNs living within a 100-mile radius. Chief executive officers may be recruited from among all experienced hospital chief executives nationwide.

Equilibrium in Labor Markets: The Simple Case

The demand for any type of labor is a *derived demand*. This means that the demand for labor is derived from consumers' demand for the products and services that labor produces. Hospitals do not hire respiratory therapists because they like having them around. Rather, respiratory therapists find work because patients (and admitting physicians) demand respiratory therapy. In any labor market, then, the number of hours of service employed and the compensation paid for those services depends on consumers' demand for the products and services that are produced. One determinant of hiring decisions, then, is the willingness of consumers to pay for the product or service produced.

The derived demand for labor by a firm also depends on the role that labor plays in the production of the product or service that the organization sells. Firms wish to hire more of the most productive types of labor (and of other inputs) and less of the least productive types of labor. "Most productive" means that which produces the most physical product per hour. One type of labor is usually more productive than another because of the nature of the production process and because of the type of physical capital it uses, rather than because some people work more diligently than others.

Combining the two determinants of the derived demand for labor provides a complete picture of employers' hiring preferences. What matters is consumers' willingness to pay and the role of labor in production. Consumers' willingness to pay is best measured by the increase in the firms' revenue from selling one more unit of output. That measure is known as "marginal revenue" and, surprisingly, is usually not the same as the price of a unit of output.

The role of labor in the production of the organization's output is measured by the additional output contributed by employing one more hour of labor. That measure is known as the "marginal physical product of labor." One of the most basic "laws" of production is that as more hours of labor are added, the marginal physical product of labor falls (i.e., the *additional* output added by the last hour of labor is not as great for the hundredth hour as for the twenty-fifth hour in a given week, all other things held equal). Multiplying marginal revenue by the marginal physical product of labor, one calculates the marginal revenue product of labor. The marginal revenue product of labor is the firm's demand for labor (Kleiner, McLean, & Dreher, 1988).

The demand for labor (e.g., labor's marginal revenue product) is shown in Figure 2.2 as a downward sloping line. The downward slope of the demand for labor is the result of both the declining marginal physical product as more labor is hired and, in most cases, of a decline in marginal revenue as more output is sold. The axes on which the demand for labor is placed form the traditional economist's grid of price and quantity. Changes in price are assumed to be an independent variable, causing quantity responses. The price of a unit of labor is the wage. Wage appears within quotation marks in Figure 2.2 because it does not represent hourly take-home pay. Rather, the "wage" is the total compensation for an hour of labor and may include the cost of a substantial amount of nonmonetary benefits (e.g., vacation rights, life insurance, health insurance) as well as some delayed monetary compensation (e.g., pension contributions).

The supply of labor to a firm is shown in

Figure 2.2 as a horizontal line (it need not, however, be horizontal in every case). The relevant function is the cost to the firm of hiring 1 additional hour of labor, the "marginal cost of labor." *The firm should hire labor up to the point at which the cost of hiring 1 additional hour of labor (the marginal cost of labor) is equal to the additional revenue generated from hiring that hour (the marginal revenue product of labor).* Were the additional revenue from hiring 1 more hour of labor greater than the additional cost of hiring that hour, the firm would have a bargain and would want to continue to hire. Were the additional revenue from hiring 1 more hour of labor less than the cost of hiring that hour, the firm would want to lay off that hour. Equilibrium, then, is reached when the marginal cost of labor is equal to the marginal revenue product of labor, at point L* in Figure 2.2.

The model shown in Figure 2.2, like all economic models, is only a caricature of reality. The model omits any roles for interpersonal differences, regulatory constraints (e.g., minimum staffing to meet the standards of the Joint Commission on the Accreditation of Health Care Organizations), or managerial ability. The model is, however, a useful place to begin analysis of wage and employment decisions in health care organizations. Managers need not be able to measure the marginal revenue product of labor precisely in order to be able to sense whether additional hours of work would add value to the organization. Furthermore, the model illustrates several important points about labor market decisions; these include the following:

- The demand for labor by any organization is derived from the demand for its product or service and from the way different types of labor

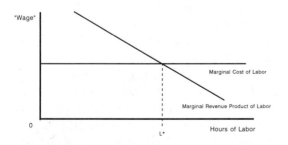

FIGURE 2.2. Neoclassical equilibrium in a homogeneous labor market.

and capital work together in producing goods and services.

- The demand for labor represents all of the labor that an organization will employ at any given marginal cost of labor.
- Higher money wages and higher nonwage costs of labor contribute to the marginal cost of labor (the "wage") and both tend to reduce the numbers of hours of labor hired when all other things are equal.

Recognizing Differences Among People and Jobs: Compensating Wage Differentials

Neither labor force participants nor the jobs they fill are homogeneous. Some individuals are more suited by temperament than others for specific positions. Some are smarter, quicker, stronger, and more diligent than others. Some positions offer "inside work with no heavy lifting," and others do not. In health care, some positions require heavy lifting (e.g., of patients), and some positions require workers to expose themselves to danger of infection or to work with dying patients. Some positions require years of education and training, while others can be filled by intelligent high school graduates.

In 1776, in *The Wealth of Nations,* Adam Smith (1937) argued that labor markets equilibrate on the basis, not of the "wage" alone, but of all of the attributes of the jobs in question. This means that dirty and dangerous jobs will, in equilibrium, pay higher "wages" (understood to include all monetary and nonmonetary compensation) than jobs that are clean and safe. If the dirty, dangerous positions were not to offer higher "wages," workers would flood to the clean, safe posi-

tions in which pay is just as good. The excess supply of labor to the clean, safe positions would depress the "wages" that employers needed to pay to attract adequate amounts of labor. The declining "wages" in the clean, safe jobs would create the necessary *compensating wage differentials* to attract adequate supplies of labor to the dirty, dangerous jobs.

Analysis of the role of education in the labor market extended the definition of compensating wage differentials to interpersonal differences among labor market participants. Workers invest in education and training. The result of that investment is enhanced productive capacity embodied in the workers. Becker (1975) called that enhanced capacity *human capital.* That there are positive returns to human capital is now well-established (Rosen, 1977). Human capital can be acquired, not only through investment in education and training but also through investment in health status (Cropper, 1977; McLean & Moon, 1980; Mushkin, 1962).

A useful way of understanding compensating wage differentials is to think of them as prices determined in *implicit markets* (Lancaster, 1966). There is an unobservable market for cleanliness in the work place. As employees cannot escape the conditions under which they work, they demand that they be compensated for accepting employment in a dirty work place. The price of a unit of dirtiness (a standardized, dirty work day, perhaps) depends on workers' collective aversion to dirty conditions (the more averse, the higher the price) and the abundance of clean work alternatives (the more openings there are in clean environments, the higher the price required to induce accepting dirty work). The supply of clean work interacts with the demand for clean work in the unobservable, but very real, market for clean work settings. The result is an equilibrium compensating wage differential for dirty working conditions.

Similar unobservable markets can be thought to exist for stressful conditions, danger of accident, educational requirements, and other employee characteristics (including, unfortunately and inefficiently, such characteristics as race and sex that are unrelated to job performance). The "wage" that any particular worker earns in any particular job is the sum of each job (or worker) characteristic's price multiplied by the amount of that characteristic that the job (or worker) offers. In equation form, the compensation of the "i^{th}" worker employed in the "j^{th}" job is equal to the following:

$$(2.2) \quad Comp_{ij} = (\text{Worker Characteristic}_{1i} \times \text{Worker Characteristic Price}_1) + \ldots + (\text{Worker Characteristic}_{ni} \times \text{Worker Characteristic Price}_N) + (\text{Job Characteristic}_{1j} \times \text{Job Characteristic Price}_j) + \ldots + (\text{Job Characteristic}_{Nj} \times \text{Job Characteristic Price}_N).$$

In this equation, Job Characteristic$_{1j}$ is the jth job's endowment of the Characteristic 1. The price of the jth characteristic is determined in its implicit market and does not depend directly on the firm in question.

Although one cannot observe the implicit market for dangerous work, one can separate the wage effects of exposure to danger in the work place statistically. Smith (1979) summarized the empirical literature on compensating wage differentials for hazardous work, noting that the overwhelming body

of evidence found such differentials to be positive, as theory suggests, and statistically significant. There is no consensus on the size of the differentials. Those who have estimated compensating wage differentials to account for variations in compensation generally have been able to explain only small parts of the variation in earnings across individuals (McLean, Wendling, & Neergaard, 1978).

One may be skeptical that wages and salaries are determined through the interaction of supply and demand in unobservable markets for worker and job characteristics. If labor economists must decompose wage effects statistically, how can employers and their employees possibly be able to take into account these effects? The implicit market analysis described here has a counterpart in practice in typical compensation systems (Kleiner, McLean, & Dreher, 1988). In many compensation systems, every job is assigned a number of points for each of several "compensable factors." If "formal education" is identified as a compensable factor (as it almost universally is), a position requiring a university degree (e.g., medical records administrator) would be assigned more points for that factor than a position requiring only a high school diploma (e.g., file clerk). The medical records technician would be assigned fewer points than a position requiring a bachelor's degree (e.g., medical records administrator), but more points than the file clerk. Each compensable factor's points are multiplied by a monetary base to determine the amount of compensation attributable to that factor. The various factor effects are added together to arrive at the total compensation for workers in the job in question. The result is an administrative system that brings to internal human resources management decisions the same result that the system of implicit markets generates in external labor markets.

External Labor Markets and Internal Labor Markets: The Need for Consistency

One may well ask, "If administrative systems determine the pay differentials associated with each compensable factor, has not the role of the labor market been eliminated? Is it not the judgments of experts that count, rather than the invisible hand of the market?" Not at all. Doeringer and Piore (1971) were the first to use the term "external labor market" to describe the influences of supply and demand *outside* the organization. Every large organization needs an internal pay structure to rationalize its personnel system and to ensure that equity among employees will be maintained. The rules that govern the determination of pay and employees' progressions through the organizational hierarchy are what Doeringer and Piore called the firm's "internal labor market."

The outcomes mandated by the internal labor market (i.e., compensation levels and allocations of labor) cannot be inconsistent with the outcomes of the external labor markets that form the organization's economic environment. Suppose, for example, the supply of and the demand for safe working conditions dictate that, to compensate laboratory technicians for exposure to biological hazards, a $2.50 per hour premium is required. For a short period of time, a hospital's internal compensation system, based on expert judgment, could mandate a premium of $1.75 per hour. Over the long run, however, technicians would desert the $1.75 premium

in favor of those organizations that pay the market-determined $2.50 premium. The "low-premium" employer would find it difficult to attract technicians and, eventually, the laboratory director would be forced to offer a higher wage for those exposed to biological hazards, even though he or she may never be aware of an implicit market for safe working conditions. The external market's equilibrium cannot be ignored in the long run. Some observers have suggested that health care professionals are relatively immune to the influence of the external labor market, displaying great loyalty to their employing institutions regardless of wage differentials. Sloan and Steinwald (1980) cite several studies that show that nurses are quite sensitive to internal/external wage differentials and are willing to change employers to obtain the benefits of higher external labor market wages. The belief that health care professionals are immune to external market influences may be only wishful thinking on the part of human resources managers.

Must a hospital's internal labor market offer hourly compensation that is *exactly* equal to that offered by the external labor market to, for example, nurses (as reflected, perhaps, by the wages offered by temporary nurse staffing agencies)? It does not. Job security is a desirable job characteristic (with its own implicit market), and nurses will be willing to take a negative compensating wage differential to obtain it. Other job characteristics and nonmonetary benefits can also serve to drive a wedge between the external labor market's equilibrium wage and the hourly pay determined in the internal labor market. What is important is that the internal compensation structure is constrained by the interactions of supply and demand (and by the outcomes of the relevant implicit markets) in the external labor market.

Special Considerations in the Labor Markets for Health Care Professionals

Human resources managers in the health care sector face some special issues that are less important in other settings. Occupational licensing restrictions are greater in number and more closely regulated in health care organizations than in most other settings (McLean, 1980). The long training time for many health professionals and the occupational attachments those individuals feel sometimes produce markets that move from disequilibrium shortage to disequilibrium excess supply, rather than movement from equilibrium to equilibrium. The difficulties of recruiting some professionals make the fixed costs of employing those individuals substantial, with interesting implications for their recruitment, compensation, and retention.

Labor economists have studied the effects of occupational licensing in a variety of settings. Licensing is a form of restriction on entry into a profession. Requiring that individuals hold a license (or degree or certificate, for that matter) is a way of holding others out of the profession (Posner, 1974). One school of thought holds that the public benefits from occupational licensing. Adherants to the "public interest theory" of licensing believe that the principal effect of licensing is to ensure that only well-qualified individuals are allowed into the regulated professions. The public benefits because a floor is set for the quality of professional services. The evidence in support of quality enhancement as a result of occupational li-

censing is mixed, at best. No licenses are either granted or denied on the basis of quality of outcomes in professional practice.

Licensing does restrict entry into the licensed occupation. Licensing, then, restricts the supply of labor to the affected occupation and raises the income of those already practicing. It is no surprise that the strongest calls for tighter licensing regulations often come from incumbents in the affected professions, as they have the most to gain from keeping others out. Interstate differences in licensing restrictions can also be used to limit the mobility of professionals from low-entry-barrier states (where professional incomes are usually low) to high-entry-barrier states (where professional incomes are usually higher).

Licensing restrictions have significant effects on every health care organization's human resources management function. First, licensing restrictions make it difficult to recruit employees for positions requiring occupational licenses. Even in the face of a serious shortage of nurses, one cannot reduce the minimum qualification for a staff nurse. The licensing restriction must be met.

Second, licensing restrictions make it difficult to substitute one type of labor for another. Efficiency and cost control would be enhanced by substituting LPNs for RNs in many activities. Licensing restrictions make those substitutions difficult, as only RNs can perform certain tasks. Licensure regulations, then, raise the cost of providing care.

A third effect of occupational licensure may reduce the hiring costs of health care organizations. In the absence of licensure, it would be difficult to observe, before hiring, which potential employees were capable of performing nursing duties, acting as medical transcriptionists, or performing laboratory tests. Licensure provides the employer with information as to which potential employees have the minimal competency to act in those capacities. For licensed occupations, then, information about minimal competencies is available at zero cost to employers. The cost of selecting those employees is, thus, reduced. The disadvantage of the availability of that cheap information is that it may discourage employers from seeking other better indicators of employee quality.

Economists' models almost always assume that the forces of demand and supply will work to achieve equilibrium in every market. In equilibrium, the price of the good or service in question is set so that the amount that purchasers wish to purchase *at that price* is just equal to the amount that sellers offer for sale *at that price.* There is, in equilibrium, neither any excess demand, which would force the price to rise, nor any excess supply, which would force the price to fall.

Economists have known for a long time that there are markets that never reach equilibrium. If the adjustment of prices and quantities is sufficiently slow, the market may move from one disequilibrium position to another, only very slowly (or never) reaching equilibrium. Freeman (1976a, 1976b) was the first to demonstrate statistically that the markets for the services of many professionals follow cobweb paths of moving from excess demand (i.e., shortage) to excess supply (i.e., surplus), never achieving equilibrium.

The market for nurses is often characterized by shortages. This means that, at the wages prevailing, employers wish to hire more hours of labor than licensed registered nurses wish to offer. That situation would, in most markets, cause wages to rise, more nurses to enter the market, and the market to reach equilibrium. In the market for RN services, however, adjustments take time. A shortage leads to higher wages, but more nurses cannot be created overnight (again, licensure requirements play a restrictive role). As higher wages become known, the number of applications for the *entering* classes in nursing schools rises. Several years elapse before the number of licensed RNs rises. During that training time, the nursing shortage persists. Higher wages may entice some nurses back into the labor force, but that effect is usually small.

The length of the training time for nurses guarantees that there is little or no feedback to nursing school applicants as to the size of nursing school classes relative to the size of the nursing shortage. The persistence of the nursing shortage during the training period is often mistaken as a need for ever larger nursing classes. Thus, several classes of nursing students may be "too large." When these students graduate, they flood the market, producing a surplus. The surplus causes nursing wages to fall, sending a signal to young career choosers that nursing is not a desirable occupation and causing a decline in the number of applicants for nursing schools. As incumbent nurses are attached to their profession, the excess supply may persist, sending too strong a signal to potential nursing school applicants. Thus, the process begins again (Figure 2.3).

In Figure 2.3, equilibrium would be achieved at a wage level (total hourly compensation, including nonwage benefits) of W* and H* hours of work employed. At that point, the numbers of hours of work that nurses wish to offer to the market is exactly equal to the number of hours of nursing services that employers wish to hire. The market, however, is temporarily out of equilibrium, with the wage of W1. At that wage level, employers wish to hire H1 hours of

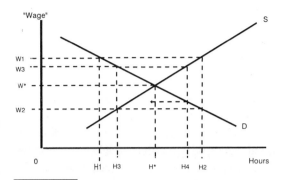

FIGURE 2.3. A cobweb model of the market for registered nurses.

labor while nurses offer H2 hours. The excess supply of labor puts downward pressure on the wage level. For example, nurses applying for positions at some hypothetical hospital are told that they are not needed unless they are willing to work in a pool of temporary staff who are not entitled to some of the benefits that comprise W1. Where does the downward pressure on wages end? Initially, wages may be depressed to the level of W2, at which all of the nursing hours offered at W1 can be hired. Why does the market "over-adjust?" The over-adjustment can arise from the fact that nurses, highly trained and specialized professionals, are reluctant to leave the labor market. Even with falling compensation, there may be little exit from the nursing profession in the short run. All of the labor offered at W1 must be employed, because few, if any, of the H2 hours will be withdrawn.

At W2, after adjustment and some occupational exit, employers demand more hours of nursing services (H2) than nurses offer (H3). Employers find that they cannot attract and retain enough nurses to meet their needs *at that level of compensation.* Upward pressure on the level of compensation may

occur in the form of increased fringe benefits. It is difficult, however, to attract nurses to the labor market. The training time is too long to prepare new entrants for the profession quickly, and the attachment of nurses to their local labor markets is often too strong for hospitals to be able to attract nurses from outside the local area. Instead, hourly compensation must rise enough to allow employers to attract all of the hours of nursing services they need at W2; that wage is W3.

The process continues and eventually reaches equilibrium if the slopes of the demand and supply curves allow a converging cobweb. The disequilibrium may persist for long periods of time if the slopes of demand and supply mandate a diverging cobweb. Diverging cobwebs (i.e., those that never reach equilibrium) are just as likely as converging cobwebs. Alternating periods of shortage and surplus in the labor markets for health care professionals (e.g., nursing, physical therapists) are predictable consequences of the long training periods in those professions, coupled with the high degree of attachment to the profession that its members display.

Hourly compensation is a variable cost to the firm (i.e., when the daily census falls, nurses and aides can be sent home). If the downturn in census is permanent, employees can be terminated. When the census rises, nurses and aides can be recalled, temporary help obtained, and new staff hired. Total hourly compensation varies with the hours that labor is actually employed, which can vary with the volume of activity. When the prospective payment system was enacted in 1983 and with repeated needs to control cost, many, if not most, hospitals have made changing nursing compensation from a fixed monthly expense to a variable hourly expense a high-priority policy.

Not all labor costs are so variable. There are fixed costs of labor, even for employees paid by the hour. Resources are required to seek out and to hire new employees, especially for the types of specialized labor employed in health care organizations. A search for a respiratory therapist may require advertisements in several newspapers, announcements in professional newsletters, payments to a "headhunter," and days of time for the human resources staff. Hiring-on expenses are fixed, in that they do not vary with the hours per week that the therapist is employed. Once hired, the new respiratory therapist will be entitled to health insurance, life insurance, disability insurance, pension benefits, and annual vacation. Those are all benefits that accrue (in virtually all settings) by virtue of employment, without reference to the number of hours worked in any given week.

Oi (1962) showed that the presence of those fixed costs of labor affects both the allocation of labor resources and the stability of employment. In the presence of fixed costs, labor costs are "quasi-fixed" (part variable and part fixed). In the neoclassical model, the firm hires labor up to the point at which the marginal revenue product of labor is equal to the marginal cost of labor (see Figure 2.2). That intersection determines both the wage and the number of hours of labor hired. Oi assumed, for simplicity, that the firm took the marginal cost of labor as fixed. In addition to that cost, the firm also bears *over the full length of employment of the employees in question,* a fixed cost component, which associated with hiring the employees and with the fixed components of compensation. Now the firm's

hours of labor decision is changed. It now hires labor up to the point at which the marginal revenue product of labor is just equal to the marginal cost of labor *plus* 1 hour's share of the fixed cost component.

What is the effect of quasi-fixity of labor cost on the hiring decision? This decision is illustrated in Figure 2.4. Because the marginal revenue product of labor must now equal the variable plus the fixed components of labor cost, fewer hours of labor are employed than when labor costs were only variable. Fixed labor costs make employers less willing to hire new employees. In the presence of fixed labor costs, the hours of work hired fall from H1 to H2. Ehrenberg (1971) demonstrated that one of the effects of labor's having quasi-fixed costs is to discourage hiring new employees and to encourage the overtime employment of incumbent workers.

There is another effect of quasi-fixity. When the marginal revenue product of labor (i.e., the demand for labor) falls, as in a recession, the fixed cost component provides a cushion of stability for the affected employees. The hiring costs that are one part of the fixed cost component are "sunk." They have

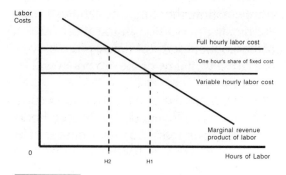

FIGURE 2.4. Labor market equilibrium with fixed costs of hourly labor.

been incurred and must be borne regardless of whether the employee hired is actually retained. Therefore, the demand for labor can fall and the employer will have no incentive to lay off the affected employees *so long as the marginal revenue product of labor is at least as great as the variable component of hourly compensation.* Laying off an employee does not save the sunk costs of hiring. Quasi-fixity makes firms slower to lay off their employees than would be the case were all labor costs purely variable.

Feldstein (1971) argued that not-for-profit hospitals set wages above market levels because they are not constrained to maximize profits and because they take a charitable posture toward their employees as well as toward their patients. Feldstein's assertion is generally consistent with recent developments in the compensation of health care professionals, especially within the hospital sector. Bishop (1977) noted the rising levels of compensation and benefits of hospital workers, as well as the growing degree of professionalism in their ranks. More recently, Fisher (1992) found rising compensaton to be the principal source of input price increases for hospitals from 1978 to 1989. Nemes (1992), citing a salary survey by Hay Management Consultants, in cooperation with *Modern Healthcare* magazine, suggested that hospitals' senior management officers have attracted public attention because of their high salary and benefit levels.

Sloan and Steinwald (1980) offer a different interpretation of the facts from that of Feldstein (1971). They argue that higher-than-market wages in hospitals may be due to the hospitals' needs to attract employees of higher-than-average quality. If that is the case, above-market wages are only compensating wage differentials necessary to attract

the qualities the hospital legitimately demands of its workers. Their empirical analysis decomposed the wage premiums of hospital workers into an employee quality component and a philanthropic wage differential component. They found almost all of the measured wage premium to be due to differences in worker quality, not to hospitals offering higher compensation than that required to attract qualified employees.

SUMMARY

Strategic human resources activities do not exist in a vacuum. Among the most important external environmental influences are the legal and economic environments that impact health services organizations. These environments must be continually scanned to manage human resources effectively. Doing so links the needs of the health care organization to the demands of the external environment (see Chapter 1).

Federal and state legislation, regulation, and court discussions have shaped the way in which most human resources functions are designed and implemented. Changes in any of these legal environment aspects are likely to have a significant impact on how human resources are managed. Thus, constant scanning of the legal environment and familiarity with these changes will aid health care executives in taking advantage of opportunities to enhance productivity while avoiding legal problems.

Health care organizations need to devote special attention to three large and growing segments of their work forces—minorities, women, and older workers. Managers need to be very clear about job requirements and performance standards, treat people as individuals, and evaluate each individual fairly relative to job requirements and performance standards. More broadly, they also need to develop procedures for ensuring procedural justice, due process, and ethical decision making. Finally, employers need to provide a place of employment free from recognized hazards to comply with all standards of health and safety established under OSHA.

The abilities of health care organizations to attract and retain adequate numbers of qualified employees depend on conditions prevailing in the economy at large. The allocation of labor to health care and the compensation that labor must be paid is strongly influenced by the economic environment. In the broadest sense, the very nature of the employment relationship is determined by the nature of the economy (e.g., free market, regulated market, command-and-control). The level and the rate of growth of economic activity influence the demand for health care services and the types and abundance of alternative employment available to health care workers. External labor market conditions strongly constrain the wage and employment decisions of health care organizations.

Some aspects of the economic environment influence decision making in health care organizations more strongly than in other firms. Health care organizations are more heavily regulated than most other types of firms, in their human resources decisions as well as in their clinical decisions. The shortage/surplus cycle seen in the labor markets for the services of several health care professions is a predictable consequence of long training times, imperfect market information, and strong occupational attachments. The fixed costs of employment may be heavier for organizations employing

health care professionals than for other types of firms. If that is the case, hourly compensation will be below marginal revenue product in health care organizations, but employment in those organizations will be especially stable. Finally, as health care organizations have emerged as modern business entities, compensation and benefits in that sector have come to resemble those in other sectors of the economy, with special compensation premiums offered for the high quality of work demanded for health care delivery.

Discussion Questions

1. What are the two most commonly used theories of discrimination for claims under Title VII of the Civil Rights Act of 1964?
2. Distinguish "quid pro quo" sexual harassment from "hostile environment" sexual harassment. For which of the two can an employer be held "strictly liable." Explain, including an explanation of the meaning of "strict liability."
3. Distinguish the requirements of the Equal Pay Act of 1963 from the concept of "equal pay for comparable work."
4. Under the FLSA, is an employee entitled to overtime pay for hours spent on a long commute? Are there exceptions? Explain.
5. For what acts or occurrences are fines imposed under the OSHA?
6. What are the major provisions of the Americans with Disabilities Act of 1990?
7. Consider all the laws, court rulings, and interpretive guidelines discussed

in this chapter and elsewhere. Describe to a health-care employer the downside risk of noncompliance as well as the benefits to be gained from full compliance.

8. Define GDP. What causes GDP to fluctuate over time?

9. What is the principal effect of fluctuations in GDP for wage-setting in health care organizations?

10. Describe and explain the three dimensions along which labor markets are defined.

11. What condition must be met for an employer to reach equilibrium in its hiring decision?

12. What is a compensating wage differential? What are some individual characteristics and some job characteristics for which one would expect to observe compensating wage differentials?

13. What are the effects of occupational licensure on the earnings and employment of health care professionals? What are the effects on the availability of the services of those professionals to consumers?

REFERENCES

Becker, G.S. (1975). *Human capital* (2nd ed.). New York: Columbia University Press.

Bishop, C. (1977). Hospitals: From secondary to primary labor market. *Industrial Relations, 16*(1), 26–34.

Carson, C.S. (1992). Replacing GNP: The updated system of national economic accounts. *Business Economics, 27*(3), 44–48.

Cropper, M.L. (1977). Health, investment in health, and occupational choice. *Journal of Political Economy, 85*(6), 1273–1294.

Doeringer, P.B., & Piore, M.J. (1971). *Internal labor markets and manpower analysis.* Lexington, MA: D.C. Heath.

Dunlop, John T. (1958). *Industrial relations systems.* Carbondale, IL: Southern Illinois University Press, reprint, 1970.

Ehrenberg, R.G. (1971). Heterogeneous labor, the internal labor market, and the dynamics of the employment-hours decision. *Journal of Economic Theory, 3*(1), 85–104.

Ehrenberg, R.G., & Smith, R.S. (1991). *Modern labor economics* (4th ed.). New York: Harper Collins.

Feldstein, M.S. (1971). *The rising cost of hospital care.* Washington, DC: Information Resources Press.

Fisher, C.R. (1992). Trends in total hospital financial performance under the prospective payment system. *Health Care Financing Review, 13*(3), 1–16.

Freeman, R.B. (1976a). A cobweb model of the supply and starting salary of new engineers. *Industrial and Labor Relations Review, 29*(2), 236–248.

Freeman, R.B. (1976b). *The overeducated american.* New York: Basic Books.

Hughs, J.R.T. (1977). *The governmental habit: Economic regulation from colonial times to the present.* New York: Basic Books.

Keynes, J.M. (1936). *The general theory of employment, interest, and money.* London: Macmillan.

Kleiner, M.M., McLean, R.A., & Dreher, G.F. (1988). *Labor markets and human resource management.* Glenview, IL: Scott, Foresman/Little, Brown.

Lancaster, K.J. (1966). A new approach to consumer theory. *Journal of Political Economy, 74*(2), 132–137.

Mankiw, N.G. (1990). A quick refresher course in macroeconomics. *Journal of Economic Literature, 28*(4), 1645–1660.

McLean, R.A. (1980). Regulation of the healthcare marketplace: A review of the issues. In D.E. Hough & G.I. Misek (Eds.), *Socioeconomic issues of health, 1980* (pp. 3–20). Chicago: American Medical Association.

McLean, R.A., & Moon, M. (1980). Health, obesity, and earnings. *American Journal of Public Health, 70*(9), 1006–1009.

McLean, R.A., Wendling, W.W., & Neergaard, P.R. (1978). Compensating wage differentials for hazardous work: An empirical analysis. *Quarterly Review of Economics and Business, 18*(3), 97–107.

Mushkin, S. (1962). Health as investment. *Journal of Political Economy, 70*(2), 129–157.

Nemes, J. (1992). Hospital executives' pay beginning to raise eyebrows. *Modern Healthcare, 22*(23), 41–52.

Oi, W.Y. (1962). Labor as a quasi-fixed factor. *Journal of Political Economy, 70*(6), 538–555.

Posner, R.A. (1974). Theories of economic regulation. *Bell Journal of Economics and Management Science, 5*(2), 335–358.

Rosen, S. (1977). Human capital: A survey of empirical research. In R.G. Ehrenberg (Ed.), *Research in labor economics* (Vol. 1, pp. 3–39). Greenwich, CT: JAI International.

Sloan, F., & Steinwald, B. (1980). *Hospital labor markets.* Lexington, MA: D.C. Heath.

Smith, A. (1937). *The wealth of nations.* New York: Modern Library Edition.

Smith, R.S. (1979). Compensating wage differentials and public policy: A review. *Industrial and Labor Relations Review, 32*(3), 339–353.

U.S. Department of Commerce, Bureau of the Census. (1987). *Statistical abstract of the United States.* Washington, DC: Government Printing Office.

U.S. Department of Commerce, Bureau of the Census. (1991). *Statistical abstract of the United States.* Washington, DC: Government Printing Office.

U.S. Department of Labor, Bureau of Labor Statistics. (1991). Employment, hours, and earnings, 1909–1990 (Vols. 1 & 2). Washington, DC: Government Printing Office.

CHAPTER

FORMULATING ORGANIZATIONAL STRATEGY

S. Robert Hernandez

LEARNING OBJECTIVES

Upon completing this chapter, the reader should be able to . . .

- Describe the evolution of planning systems used by American industry.
- List and discuss the four corporate-level strategies available to health services managers.
- List and discuss the business-level strategies available for health services organizations to gain strategic advantage over competitors.
- Participate in formulation of an organization's strategy using the process illustrated in the text.
- Describe the critical human resources issues facing strategists in each stage of the product/market life cycle.

INTRODUCTION

A critical function of health care management is development of a plan for the future actions to be taken by the organization. Senior managers must identify the major tasks to be accomplished by their firm, assign responsibility for performance of those tasks, and monitor organizational actions to ensure that the tasks are executed satisfactorily. An adequate planning system allows a health care organization to achieve organizational objectives by identifying and being responsive to environmental change through deployment of internal resources in an efficient and effective manner.

The planning system or systems that are used by an organization vary based on the sophistication of management, rates of environmental change, and level of competition experienced within a geographic region or

service sector. A planning system also must match the corporate culture of the firm as well as the complexity of the business in which the organization is competing. Major planning approaches available to health care managers are reviewed in the following section. Next, selected organizational strategies that might be used by health care institutions are presented. A guide for formulating the organization's strategy is then suggested. Selected relationships that should exist between possible business strategies and human resources functions are described at the conclusion of this chapter.

PLANNING METHODS

The methods used for the formulation of strategies and plans by organizations in the health services industry have evolved rather dramatically during the past several years. The major types of planning approaches that have been used are budgeting, long-range planning, strategic planning, and strategic management[1]. Budgeting involves planning for anticipated revenues and costs for a given time period, usually annually. Long-range planning is concerned with the projection of organizational goals, objectives, programs, and budgets during an extended period. This approach requires forecasting of environmental trends based on historical data. Strategic planning involves an organization's choices of mission, objectives, strategy, policies, programs, goals, and major resources allocations. This method is intended to de-

---

[1] Management by objectives is not a method for developing strategy but a system to plan, monitor, and control. Facility planning is seen as following strategy formulation. These are not reviewed.

fine the strategy for the firm so that internal resources and skills are matched to the opportunities and risks created within the environment. Finally, strategic management is concerned with integration among administrative systems, organizational structure, and organizational culture for both strategic and operational decision making. This approach views strategic planning as one element of administrative functioning that must be blended with other management processes for an organization to function efficiently.

Each of these methods represents a fundamentally different approach for planning and organizing the activities of a health services organization. The evolution of each of these planning approaches in the health services industry is reviewed and implications for use of these techniques in strategy development are discussed.

Budgeting

Budgeting was one of the first planning methods that was applied on a systematic basis in American industry. It emerged more than 50 years ago to assist management in the difficult task of planning, coordinating, and controlling the numerous, often disparate activities undertaken by a firm (Hax & Majluf, 1984). Although the budget is not an operational plan and some have suggested it is not planning (Marrus, 1984), it is the *expression* of the operational plan in dollars (Berman & Weeks, 1979). Budgeting converts management intentions for the organization's future actions into a financial format.

Although the budget has been available as a management tool at least since the 1930s, the adoption of budgeting as a management technique by health services organizations did not occur rapidly. One survey of hospitals in a midwest state in the early 1960s found that only 23% of hospitals prepared income and expense budgets (McNerney et al., 1962). Even worse, only 3% used budgets appropriately by involving supervisory personnel in estimating expenses and in receiving reports of financial performance. Certainly, the use of the budget has expanded dramatically in the last quarter century since the McNerney study, possibly due to increased management awareness of the value of budgeting, or the mandatory requirement for budget development as a condition for participation in the Medicare program.

Budgeting has value for institutional planning because the process requires that the hospital direct its attention toward the future and plan for it. Thus, it *raises the priority of planning* within an organization. Without annual attention to budget development, many institutions would not devote much time to a systematic consideration of future operations.

Additionally, budgeting *provides a structure* for the planning activity. It requires identification of projected revenues, expenses, capital needs, and cash flows for organizational units. Thus, the hospital is forced to consider the unique units (i.e., responsibility centers) for the organization and the varying operating requirement that might be anticipated during the coming year. Performance can be meaningfully planned, evaluated, and controlled by the responsibility centers identified through the budgeting activity.

A typical process used in the decision-making process for budget development is illustrated in Figure 3.1. This simplified version of the process suggests that the facility board establishes financial goals for the organization and gives final approval to the bud-

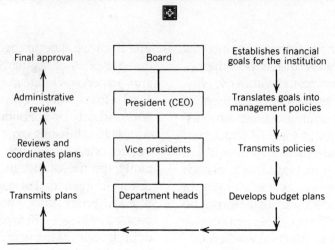

FIGURE 3.1. Budget preparation.

get. Senior management develops operational objectives and policies, establishes priorities for program development, plans for budget development including financial assumptions, and conducts the final administrative review after budgets have been developed. Line management must convert policy and operating objectives into programs by specifying resources required to accomplish approved projects.

If maximum benefit is to be obtained from this approach to planning, management must be sensitive to the importance of planning rather than financial issues, driving the budget process. The budget will have little value if it becomes a paper-shuffling exercise driven by finance as contrasted with a comprehensive institutional plan driving projected revenues and expenses.

Budgeting will be inappropriately developed as a planning tool if the process does little more than use historical data for budget projections with only incremental change anticipated over past operations. One method to overcome this myopic concern for previous operating history and incremental approach to budgeting is the use of zero-based budgeting (Dillon, 1979; Pyhrr, 1973). This

approach requires that each unit examine critically and justify each of the activities it proposes to operate during the projected budget period. While traditional budgeting processes require only that a manager justify the increases planned over previous years, zero-based budgeting requires each department to defend its entire budget request each year.

Another concern that arises if management uses budgeting as the only planning process for a hospital is that the focus is only on one aspect of hospital activities—financial performance. It is important that management prevent preoccupation with short-term return on investment at the expense of the organization's long-term growth.

Long-Range Planning

Substantial improvement in planning future operations for a firm was made with the introduction of long-range planning. The use of this method followed the rapid growth of the U.S. economy in the post-World War II era. Corporations found that 1-year budget projections were inadequate means for identifying future operating plans for organizations in the rapidly expanding economy.

Long-range planning requires that management focus the energies of the organization on an integrated approach to attainment of corporate goals and objectives. Because the future is expected to be predictable through extrapolation of previous growth, study of historical operating trends is an important component to the development of the plan (Ansoff & McDonnell, 1990; Moore, 1970). Thus, the underlying assumption of the method is that establishment of challenging objectives based on projection of environmental trends will provide direction for future growth and development by the firm.

Descriptions of long-range planning techniques were relatively widespread in the hospital and health services literature by the mid 1970s. Perlin (1976) presented a model outline for a hospital long-range plan that included several steps. The characteristics of the population residing in the facility's service area with projections of future demographic changes would be identified in one step. A planner then would forecast future community needs based on anticipated population changes and health delivery techniques, inventory current health resources and services, and conclude with future gaps or excesses in services based on a comparison of the preceding two factors. Historical utilization of an institution's programs and services would be chronicled. Then, based on the organization's mission and the gaps previously identified, the facility's plan to carry out future service programs would be developed. A long-range plan would conclude with an implementation plan that placed programs and services in short-range and long-range priorities and described physical plant requirements for plan accomplishment, manpower required, and financial resources needed. A typical flow of steps in long-range planning is illustrated in Figure 3.2.

This method represents a major improvement over the use of budgeting as a planning tool because it increases managerial awareness of and responsibility for planning. However, several limitations potentially detract from its use for charting future directions for an organization. One weakness is the assumption that the future is predictable from historical growth and utilization patterns. Complex environments that feature rapid change in operating rules, conditions of demand, and levels of competition do not allow the future to be extrapolated accurately from past operations.

A related, implicit assumption is that future performance can and should be an improvement on past operations. This assumption can lead managers to think they can control the future and achieve sustained growth when, in fact, external forces beyond management's control may influence the or-

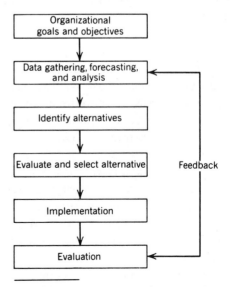

FIGURE 3.2. Long-range planning.

ganization's operations. Overly optimistic objectives can be identified because of this belief.

Another problem with long-range planning is that it frequently is developed by support staff or external consulting firms using exhaustive arrays of operating and environmental data, but without adequate involvement of either senior or line management. Meager participation by senior managers results in a plan that does not provide strategic direction for a firm because the plan may not address major issues critical for the organization's survival. This document becomes a dust gatherer that sits on a shelf and is reviewed annually, at best.

Strategic Planning

Strategic planning emerged in American industry as a reaction to changes in the nature of competition and increasing uncertainty in a firm's operating environment. Organizations were confronting environmental fluctuations that had not been projected by their long-range planning systems, and discontinuities caused significant problems for the firms (Ansoff, 1977). Long-range planning is appropriate when the firm is operating as a single dominant business or product line in an industry experiencing high market growth, when the future is relatively predictable based on previous experience, and when there is low rivalry and/or a regulated environment in the industry. However, the changes in the U.S. economy required development of planning systems that considered systematically the analysis of alternative possible futures and allowed firms in multiple markets to evaluate their options.

Given the rapid changes occurring in the health services industry described in Chapter

1 it is small wonder that many health services organizations are using strategic planning approaches in determining future directions for their organizations. These techniques allow a complex organization to evaluate multiple market and service/product opportunities while considering the strengths of the organization and its competitors.

Strategic planning focuses on the market environment facing a firm, including future actions by competitors and consumers. A major contribution of strategic planning is the use of market segmentation and portfolio analysis that allows management to assess the relative attractiveness and competitive strength of the business units of the organization.

Typically this approach to planning contains four steps (Ansoff & McDonnell, 1990). First, management conducts an *analysis of the anticipated results* of the firm's operations through projection of operating trends as well as identification of environmental threats and opportunities. These data provide levels of performance likely to be attained if management initiates no change in strategy. Then, *competitive analysis* identifies performance improvement that is possible from changes in the competitive strategies employed in current business units of the firm. Next, *portfolio analysis* allows management to establish priorities for the business units by comparing the anticipated future performance of all business areas. Because all subunits will not be anticipated to enjoy equal success, priorities for allocation of resources to business units can occur based on this analysis. Finally, *diversification analysis* provides management with an opportunity to identify new business opportunities if deficiencies exist in the current portfolio of services. The improvement in health services organization performance is possible following each of these analyses with related management actions that are suggested as appropriate. Incremental performance increases are possible from improving competitive strategies in current businesses, more efficiently allocating resources among current portfolio of businesses, and diversifying into new areas.

Strategic Management

The previously described planning systems are concerned with identifying future actions to be taken by an organization. As was initially noted, senior management's responsibilities extend beyond planning future actions and identifying major tasks to be accomplished. They also must assign responsibility for performance of those actions and monitor organizational activity to ensure that the tasks are achieved satisfactorily. Outcomes of the planning process must be integrated into the organization for implementation and evaluation.

Strategic management is concerned with linking strategic planning activities with other internal management systems, the structure of the organization, and culture of the firm. This means that management must work to see that the outcomes of strategic planning become an administrative reality. Additionally, management systems must be considered during the planning process for an organization to develop a viable strategic plan.

The issue of ensuring that the strategic planning activities are at the nexus of the organization's actions systems is a prime responsibility of senior management. The next section of this chapter identifies the relationships and techniques for achieving the organizational strategies that are desired through strategic management of human resources

within a health care organization. The remainder of this chapter is devoted to strategic planning and management processes that provide direction for the organization.

ORGANIZATIONAL STRATEGY

Many individuals do not distinguish between organizational strategy, operating tactics, and functional operating policy. The focus of strategic planning activities should be on *strategic* issues and *strategy* development, rather than operating tactics. Thus, a clear delineation of what constitutes strategy is critical. Because a complex health services organization contains many operational units and can offer a vast array of products and services to a community, a second area that requires clarification is how to identify the major subunits of an organization. These subunits, called *strategic business units,* are the starting points for development of organizational strategy. A discussion of what constitutes strategy and how strategic business units are to be identified is provided here.

Types of Strategies

Although numerous management theorists and authors have definitions of what constitutes strategy[2], Drucker (1974) captured the topic best when he stated that thinking about the mission and strategy of an organization is concerned with answering the following question: *What is our business and what should it be?* These questions trans-

---

[2] For examples of strategy definitions, see Aaker (1984); Andrews (1971); Duncan, Ginter and Swayne (1992); Hofer and Schendel (1978); and Steiner (1979).

late into *identification of the business areas in which the organization will compete.*

Health services organizations must determine what services they will provide to which market areas. Their current portfolio of services and/or business areas must be reviewed and a decision reached on what will be done with each of the services/businesses. This analysis is a corporate-level strategic decision that focuses on which areas will be *built, held, harvested, or divested.* Unique operating decisions concerning levels of investment, allocation of resources, functional policies, and related concerns are associated with each of these four strategic options that may be applied to a business unit operated by a firm.

Build

The decision by a health services organization to build a service/business area means that the institution plans to invest heavily in the service in an attempt to increase its market share of consumers receiving the service. This approach may be taken even though it means that the institution forgoes some short-term profits to build share. A system of emergicare centers may decide to implement a build strategy by retaining operating profits for development of new service delivery sites. Alternatively, the system may decide to implement the strategy by raising capital for growth by offering convertible debentures to a limited number of investors.

Hold

A decision to hold suggests that the institution has an objective to maintain its current market share. This strategy usually is associated with services or businesses that are expected to generate large cash flows that are

to be diverted to other investment opportunities. Increased levels of investment are made only to the extent that there are increases in patient demand. Many hospitals providing inpatient acute care have implicitly adopted this strategy.

Harvest

Organizations that attempt a harvesting strategy desire to increase short-term cash flows emanating from a service regardless of the consequences for that service. This strategy may be implemented by reducing staffing levels, cutting maintenance, or allowing technical obsolescence or related tactics that decrease operating costs while maintaining prices. The long-term outcome will be that the service/business will be terminated or sold. A multi-institutional system may employ this strategy with a group of hospitals it owns in an attempt to reap short-term profits before disposing of the holdings to another system.

Divest

The decision to divest means that the organization will abandon the market. Resources that would have been consumed in service delivery will be diverted to other parts of the organization. Divesting is illustrated by a multi-institutional system selling a hospital in a geographic area that it no longer wants to serve, or it could entail termination of a major service (e.g., obstetrics) by a community general hospital.

A second, related question that must be answered for strategy formulation is to determine *how the organization will compete in the delivery of the services to the markets that have been identified.* Managers must decide what general approach they will use to provide services to the areas they have identified. The answer to this question concerns what *competitive advantage* the organization will attempt to achieve. Three basic strategies that have been found to lead to sustained competitive advantage are overall cost leadership, differentiation, and focus (Hall, 1980; Porter, 1980, 1985).

Cost Leadership

Achieving overall cost leadership is an attempt by a health care provider to become the low-cost producer for an area. If a firm is able to provide services at a lower *cost* than its competitors and yet obtain reimbursement at *prices* that are comparable, it will receive above-average returns.

Although use of economies of scale through being the market share leader for a product is a common means of becoming the cost leader for industrial sector firms, numerous approaches may be used in the health services industry. Some investor-owned hospitals attempt to achieve cost leadership through management systems geared to control resources consumption (e.g., close monitoring of full-time equivalent per occupied bed). Health maintenance organizations attempt cost leadership through controlling utilization, especially hospital admissions. The methods for achieving cost leadership in health services depend on the type of organization providing the service, the consumers of the service, payer mix served by the institution, forms of reimbursement, and related factors.

Differentiation

An organization seeking to achieve differentiation desires to be perceived by consumers as offering a service that is unique on important dimensions. This uniqueness is usually associated with a premium price that can be charged for the service.

Achieving differentiation may be associated with *technical quality* of the medical care that is being delivered. The medical staff, the level of technical sophistication of equipment provided, and related matters may viewed by the community as being superior to competitors. Differentiation also may be associated with offering *patient amenities* that are valued (e.g., valet parking in crowded inner-city hospital locations; immediate access to medical personnel in emergency rooms; a reputation for having a responsive, caring nursing staff for inpatient acute care).

Focus

Organizations choosing to focus are those that target a narrow scope of competition within their community. The institution decides on a market segment or group to which it will provide a service or range of services. After choosing the target market, the institution may then have a *cost focus* or a *differentiation focus*.

One example of a focus strategy is initiation of pediatric emergency services by a community general hospital. Although there is increasing competition in many communities for the emergent patient, identifying pediatric patients as the market to be served may give a hospital a competitive advantage in a saturated urgent-care market. Targeted marketing strategies, special billing practices, separate entrances, unique employee uniforms, and related operating tactics support this strategy of focusing on the pediatric patient in need of urgent care and then differentiating the service from other emergency services available within the community.

Identifying Strategic Business Units

A fundamental concern for health care organizations is to identify their current business units by grouping related services into strategic business units (SBUs). After the services provided by the organization are logically grouped, it is then possible to define the businesses in which the organization is competing. Businesses are usually defined by the services that are provided and/or the markets that are served (Abell & Hammond, 1979). One of the primary values of identifying SBUs is that the institution can discern among the divergent markets that it serves, develop logical strategies that will be successful in these unique markets, and assign responsibility for implementing the plan.

An SBU usually contains several related services or programs. The composition of an SBU depends on the level of organization that is being examined. At the corporate level for HealthTrust or AMI, SBUs may be identified by groupings such as psychiatric hospital division, inpatient acute care hospital division, health insurance division, and preferred provider arrangements. Conversely, a multispecialty medical group may define its SBUs based on clinical services such as pediatrics, obstetrics, and general surgery.

For acute care hospitals, data may be collected and operational management decisions reached on the basis of diagnosis-related groups (DRGs). However, it is *not* practical to plan strategically using DRGs as the units for which strategies are developed because it would be almost impossible for a community hospital to develop unique market approaches for more than 400 business units. An SBU for these organizations more realistically might contain a number of DRGs in "product groupings that have economic and marketplace significance" (Alfirevic, Nackel, & Shade, 1983, p. 13). It is possible that clinical service groupings are appropriate units for SBU analysis by these hospitals.

Although there are a number of ways that one might identify SBUs, an ideal SBU might have the following characteristics (Kotler, 1990):

- It is a single business or collection of related businesses.
- It has a distinct mission.
- It has its own competitors.
- It has a responsible manager.
- It consists of one or more program units and financial units.
- It can benefit from strategic planning.
- It can be planned independently of the other businesses.

As previously stated, it is important that units designated as SBUs develop plans for the markets that they serve. In addition, these SBUs should receive resources to implement the plan and be held accountable for the plan's success or failure. Some health organizations do not delegate these latter functions to the managers at the operating unit level and require senior management oversight of these responsibilities. The separation of these activities currently appears to be working well. In any case, SBU plan development, resource allocation, and accountability for performance must be done in conjunction with an overall strategy for approaching the marketplace that is developed by corporate planning.

FORMULATING ORGANIZATIONAL STRATEGY

A model process used to generate strategy for a health care organization is illustrated in Figure 3.3. Planning begins with a mission statement that has been articulated with sufficient detail to guide organizational decision making; external and internal analyses are conducted; the portfolio is reviewed; strategies are identified and selected; implementation is accomplished; and evaluation begins. The material provided in this section, while not presented at the level of detail required to guide the production of a strategic plan, allows the reader to understand the flow of data and the rationale that supports corporate strategy development. This understanding is beneficial for comprehending the relationship between strategy and human resources functions. Detailed discussions of strategic planning approaches are offered by Aaker (1984), Duncan et al. (1990), Hofer and Schendel (1978), Nutt (1984), Peters (1985), and Steiner (1979).

Mission of the Organization

The first step in development of strategies is to identify the general direction in which the organization is headed. It is the responsibility of senior management to provide the institution with the goals and operating philosophy that will be a guide to direct the future of the firm. The communication of corporate purpose, scope of operations, self-concept, and image to important stakeholders occurs through a mission statement.

> The principal value of a mission statement as a tool of strategic management is derived from its specification of the ultimate aims of the firm. It thus provides managers with a unity of direction that transcends individual, parochial, and transitory needs. It promotes a sense of shared expectations among all levels and generations of employees. It consolidates values over time and across individuals and interest groups. It projects a sense of worth and intent that can be identified and assimilated by company outsiders, i.e., customers, suppliers, competitors, local committees, and the general public (Pearce, 1982, p. 24)

Some authors suggest that an organization requires two distinct types of mission statements (Hax & Majluf, 1984). One is concerned with articulating the mission of the entire firm and is developed at the *corporate* level simultaneously with the grouping of products/services into SBUs and the enunciation of a corporate philosophy. These elements (corporate mission statement, philosophy, and selection of SBUs) are known as

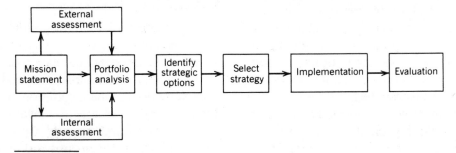

FIGURE 3.3. The strategy development process in health services organizations.

the *vision* of the firm. A second type of more detailed mission statement is required at the *business* level for each SBU. Whether developed at the corporate or business unit level, the mission statement usually specifies the products or services that will be provided, the markets that will be served, and the manner in which competitive leadership will be attained.

Product Definition

The identification of the product line of services means that management defines the *scope* of services that the organization will offer by determining the breadth of the line that will be provided. Will a complete range of patient needs be met or will the organization target a specific service? A multispecialty group may decide to change its product definition by broadening its services with the addition of a new specialty (e.g., neurology) that had not been offered previously. This decision allows the group to capture revenues that may have been lost to the group when patient referrals were made to other neurologists who were not members of the group.

Defining how an organization wishes its services to be perceived by consumers in relation to competitors providing the service is known as *positioning*. One example is positioning on the basis of a price–quality spectrum. An organization may attempt to be perceived as providing comparable services at a lower cost than its competitors. Emergicenters attempt to convince consumers that the centers can provide minor emergency service comparable to a hospital emergency room more rapidly and at a lower cost.

Products and services benefit from a positioning strategy that is clearly articulated to the target market for that service. Six potential approaches for a positioning strategy are listed below (Wind, 1982, pp. 79–81):

- Positioning on specific product features
- Positioning on benefits, problem solutions, or needs
- Positioning for specific usage occasions
- Positioning for user category
- Positioning against another product
- Product class dissociation

Market Definition

Defining the market for a business requires identifying the consumer groups to be served by the organization. The most logical delimiter for a health services organization is the *geographic boundary* of its service area. A hospital may identify its primary service area as a region that has a high relevance index (Griffith, 1972), or a generalist hospital consulting firm may decide not to offer its services beyond midwestern states.

A market also may be defined by the *consumers that desire the product*. The consulting firm that is restricting its services to the midwest also may identify its clients as senior managers of hospitals that are operating between 100 and 300 beds. This group may value the general management consulting package that is being provided more than other executives in more complex facilities.

The process of defining markets allows management to decide the *market segments* that will be served. Segmentation of a market is the process of breaking the total market into elements that share common properties. Organizations are able to develop appropriate services and provide those services more efficiently for groups that have common needs that have been identified through segmentation.

Distinct Competence

The distinct competence of an organization refers to an advantage that the institution holds over its competitors. The advantage may emanate from the competitive advantages of cost leadership, differentiation, or focus that were previously discussed. Alternatively, an organization may possess an asset that provides it with an advantage over competitors. A hospital may have a reputation for an outstanding nursing staff that is well-respected within the community. A nursing home may have evolved into an organization offering a complete array of vertically integrated services for the elderly. A hospital system may have facility sites that are conveniently located near transportation arteries. Articulating the distinct competence for the organization helps management to design strategies that reinforce strengths.

External Assessment

An external analysis focuses on elements that are relevant for organizational performance but are outside the institution's boundaries. The purpose of this assessment is to determine the major opportunities that might be available to the firm and potential threats that might prevent the organization from achieving desired outcomes. This analysis often consists of identifying and analyzing patient groups or consumers, competitors, industry conditions, and general environmental factors.

Consumer Groups

The first issue in external analysis is to identify the markets currently being served by the institution, to select markets that potentially could be served, and to determine how to segment these markets. As noted, the process of segmentation groups consumers into clusters that share common characteristics. The demand for services by consumers should be relatively homogeneous within the group and heterogeneous to demand by other groups. Analyzing consumer groups assists management in identifying increases or decreases in demand that might be associated with changing needs or requirements by the groups that are studied. This knowledge assists in making investment decisions across alternative product/market opportunities.

Competitor Analysis

The result of competitor analysis is identification of the threats or opportunities that will occur from the probable moves and reactions of competitors (Sammon, 1984). This information is obtained by building a competitor's response profile (Porter, 1980), which includes their future goals, current strategy, assumptions about market conditions, and current strengths and weaknesses.

This profile should include an estimation of the competitor's financial goals as well as a determination of its interest in long-term versus short-term performance. The extent to which the competitor will stress quality versus cost in the provision of services is important to note. Recording the values and beliefs of the competitor's senior managers will provide insight into the reason that specific services and programs are initiated. Knowledge of the structure of the competitor's organization provides information about who key decision makers are, the methods they use to handle the medical staff, and their ability to respond rapidly to its competition's initiatives.

The competitor's assumptions about its

own operation and the health services industry also should be a component of the profile. How has it assessed its organization? What does it believe are its strengths and weaknesses? How will its perceptions influence likely thrusts? What does it view as future utilization patterns for the health services industry? What are the *actual* strengths and weaknesses of the competition?

The above information can be used to determine how the competitor will respond to new services that you may decide to offer or to your decision to terminate some of your current services. It also can be used to anticipate strategic thrusts it may be planning.

Analyzing competitors also improves understanding of consumer responses to product offerings. Cognition of the strategies, operating practices, and successes and failures of competing organizations helps management to know the attributes that appeal to various market segments. For example, close monitoring of an innovative service provided by a major competitor will allow management to decide which benefits and features will be included in their own version of the service.

Additionally, this analysis validates consumer analysis and provides clues as to potential market opportunities that may become available (Abell & Hammond, 1979). It is possible that identification of the product/markets served by competitors will result in recognition of an area unserved by other institutions.

Industry and Environmental Analysis

A third major component of external assessment is concerned with analyzing trends in the industry as well as overall environmental conditions. *Industry analysis* is intended to identify the competitive factors that lead

to success in a given product/market and to determine the relative attractiveness of an industry/market for the firm. The forces that drive competition (Porter, 1980) and the manner in which firms are organized for delivery of services are areas to examine. An additional need is for projections of demand and number of competitors currently providing services or anticipated to begin service delivery for the market. This information allows identification of the stage of the life cycle for the industry.

The environment provides the context in which industry operating rules and practices exist. *Environmental analysis* is concerned with identifying trends and major events that potentially have an effect on an industry and, ultimately, the strategy of an organization. Just as the environment is one step removed from and above an industry, so is environmental analysis related to, but broader than, industry analysis. Components of environmental analysis may be divided into five dimensions (Aaker, 1984). The areas to be monitored include the following:

1. Technology: new technologies and the life cycle of current technology
2. Government: legislative and regulatory actions, tax policies, and values held toward the health industry
3. Economics: interest rates, economic health of local firms, and general economic conditions
4. Culture: lifestyle trends that affect consumption of health and related services
5. Demographics: trends in age, income, education, and geographic location

A major component of industry and environmental analysis for health services organizations must include projections of the future availability of selected types of health professionals. For many types of professionals, state licensure boards provide counts of individuals practicing in an area. Of course, individuals may retain their licenses without intending to practice, so these figures are misleading. Historical labor force participation rates are helpful in determining the size of the current manpower pool.

Identifying the numbers of individuals in professional training is necessary to determine the potential size of the pool from which new employees may be recruited. Historical data on the success rate of the organization in attracting new recruits to work in the institution will provide at least a crude measure of the inflow of future workers that might be anticipated.

Internal Assessment

An internal assessment is intended to provide a detailed understanding of attributes of the organization that are of strategic importance. The outcome of this assessment should be a listing of the firm's strengths that might be used for competitive advantage. In addition, problems or weaknesses that might hinder performance must be recognized.

An inventory of current internal capabilities, resources, operating characteristics, and actions provides the basis for this assessment. Webber and Peters (1983) suggest that the following areas be examined:

- Management and governance
- Functional programs and services
- Human resources
- Medical staff
- Financial resources and results
- Physical facilities

- Basic values and culture of the organization
- Interrelationships of the above

Although a description of each of these areas is beyond the scope of this chapter, some discussion of the human resources and medical staff inventory is required. Management must maintain separate databases on personnel and medical staff that can be used both for the day-to-day operation of the institution as well as for strategic planning.

For strategic purposes, these databases include demographic information, career information, a skills profile, productivity measures, and utilization statistics. These data provide management with the basis for understanding the characteristics of its personnel and medical staff. This information can be used for determining how well the organization is currently functioning as well as for identifying the organization's future internal capabilities for implementation of programs and services that might be planned.

After current capabilities, resources, operating characteristics, and actions of the health care organization are inventoried, these attributes can be compared to performance levels that are standards in the industry or that are desired by management. The result of this assessment is a list of attributes viewed as institutional strengths and a list of organizational weaknesses. These attributes, when combined with the previously developed external opportunities and threats, provide data to be used in assessing the institution's portfolio of goods and services.

Portfolio Assessment

The analysis of the portfolio of SBUs operated by the firm examines the service mix of an organization to determine if the overall array of business units is appropriately balanced. This analysis typically requires that the SBUs of the organization be placed on a matrix that contains two parameters. One parameter describes characteristics (e.g., desirability) of the market or industry in which the SBU is competing, and the other illustrates the strength of the business unit in that unique market. Several techniques are used to conduct portfolio analysis including the market growth rate-relative market share analysis known as the Boston Consulting Group (BCG) Business Grid, the industry attractiveness-competitive strength analysis based on a GE-type Business Screen, and the industry maturity-competitive approach analysis known as the Product Life-Cycle Portfolio Matrix.

BCG Business Grid

This method of examining the holdings of an organization is based on pioneering work that was conducted by the Boston Consulting Group in the early 1960s. This easily understood analysis focuses on the growth rate for the market of a business and the relative market share that the business commands. As illustrated in Figure 3.4, the annual market growth rate for a business is shown on the vertical axis, and the relative market share of the SBU to its largest competitor is shown on the horizontal axis.

The market growth rate illustrated in Figure 3.4 ranges from 0 to 20%, although values above or below those numbers are possible. Because a growth rate above 10% is considered high, the vertical axis is divided into

[3] The cut off for high versus low growth rates is normally selected as the average growth for that industry, assuming that all SBUs are competing in the same industry (Hax & Majluf, 1984).

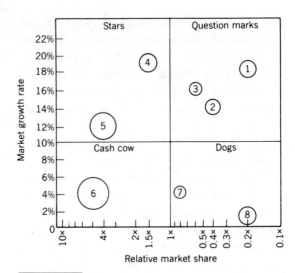

FIGURE 3.4. The Boston Consulting Group's growth-share matrix. (Reprinted from *Long Range Planning,* February 1977, Heldey, B., Strategy and the business portfolio, vol. 10, p. 12, Copyright 1977, with kind permission from Pergamon Press, Ltd., Headington Hill Hall, Oxford OX3 0BW, UK.)

high and low growth markets at 10%[3]. The relative market share, shown in log scale with equal distances representing the same percentage increase, has the midpoint of the horizontal axis as 1. This occurs when the organization's share exactly equals its largest competitor. A value of 2 on the scale occurs when the firm's SBU has twice the sales as the next strongest firm and a market share that is half that of the strongest competitor is represented by the .5 value. The matrix is divided into four quadrants by these midpoints. The relative share and growth rate of these markets suggests management decisions for the SBUs operating in these four markets.

The lower left quadrant contains the *cash cows.* These SBUs operate in low-growth markets with relatively large market share. The strong market position suggests that they should be able to generate positive cash flow because they have potential for economies of scale and higher profit margins. Investment needs should not be great because they are situated in a mature market with a low-growth rate. Funds from these businesses are used to support SBUs in other, high-growth markets.

The upper left quadrant contains the *stars* that are high-growth, high-share SBUs. They require funds to support growth in demand for services, but they also are in a position to perform well financially because of their strong competitive position as market leaders. Stars usually do not generate surplus cash because this high-growth market attracts new firms, and the organization must reinvest to maintain share. These SBUs may be cash users if competitors begin major efforts to gain relative market share that must be countered.

The upper right quadrant contains *question marks,* also known as wildcats, that have relatively low market share in fast-growth markets. These SBUs need to fund growth, but are not able to obtain funding internally because they are not far enough down the experience curve. These businesses are in the worst position because of their growth needs and low market shares. They should be grown to become stars or should be divested.

The lower right quadrant contains the *dogs,* which are not profitable because of their weak competitive position in a low-growth market. Because growth in this market is low, increases in market share are costly. These businesses should be phased out when possible.

After the SBUs have been plotted on the matrix, the organization must determine how balanced the portfolio appears. Too many question marks or dogs or an inappropriate mixture of exclusively stars or cash

cows cause management to attempt to change its investment mix.

Although this approach has merits, several factors detract from use of this analytical tool in the health care industry without modification. One issue is that growth rate is not an adequate criterion for determining the desirability of a market for investment decisions. Health providers have multiple stakeholders with numerous, often conflicting, goals and objectives for the organization. The allocation of capital based on market growth alone is not a responsible approach to this complex situation.

Additionally, the success of market share leadership associated with cost reductions is meaningful only in volume businesses. Health providers that concentrate on small segments of the market can focus on a defensible niche that is not easily penetrated by market leaders. Thus, market share leadership is not always an adequate criterion for determining the strength of a business.

GE-Type Business Screen

Recognizing that market growth rate is only a proxy for market attractiveness and that relative market share is one measure of the competitive strength of a firm, an approach was used by GE in the early 1970s to provide composite measures of market attractiveness and competitive strength. Industry attractiveness is represented on the vertical axis by as many factors as is considered relevant. This is accomplished by an organization first identifying the criteria that are considered important by the firm. These may be based on institutional objectives as well as a determination of the organizational stakeholders' desires. Second, the criteria are weighted because each is not anticipated to be equally important. These weights

TABLE 3.1. Health Service Market Attractiveness

	Weight	Score	Total
Profitability	0.20	5	1.00
Payer mix	0.10	4	0.40
Market size	0.20	5	1.00
Growth potential	0.15	3	0.45
Referral network	0.20	4	0.80
Ease of entry	0.05	2	0.10
Level of investment required	0.10	4	0.40
	1.00		4.15

should add to 1. Third, individual services or business units are rated. Rating may be on a 5-point scale, with 1 being very unattractive and 5 being very attractive. Finally, each weight is multiplied by each rank, and the results are summed to determine the overall score for a service. An example of this rating process is shown in Table 3.1.

In a similar manner, the competitive strength of the organization in each market should be assessed. The key success factors for each service to be competitive are identified. The relative importance of these is then determined. Third, the strength of the organization on each success factor is noted. Finally, the overall strength is identified by multiplying each weight times each rank, and the results are summed to obtain the overall score for a service. An example is shown in Table 3.2.

TABLE 3.2. Hospital Strengths

	Weight	Score	Total
Competitive advantage	0.05	5	0.25
Market share	0.10	4	0.40
Public perception	0.15	4	0.60
Medical staff support	0.35	2	0.70
Location	0.15	5	0.75
Plant and equipment	0.15	4	0.60
Support staff	0.05	4	0.20
	1.00		3.50

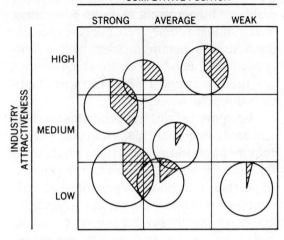

FIGURE 3.5. Market attractiveness/business position matrix. (Reprinted by permission from page 32 of *Strategy Formulation: Analytical Concepts* by Charles W. Hofer and Dan Schendel. Copyright © 1978 by West Publishing Company. All rights reserved.)

After the value for each service has been identified, the services can be plotted on a matrix (Figure 3.5). Examining the matrix provides a determination as to how well the services of the firm fit the overall values of the firm and have adequate strength to succeed in the market.

Product Life-Cycle Matrix

The life-cycle approach is based on an analogy to the biological cycle that living matter experiences through stages of embryonic development, growth, maturity, and decline. Products and services (Kotler, 1990), organizations (Kimberly et al., 1980), and industries (Porter, 1980) are believed to follow a similar pattern from their inception to their decline. Each stage in the life of a service, business unit, or industry is characterized by changes in demand for the service, number of competitors, profitability, cash flow, and other features of market conditions. A life-cycle model is illustrated in Figure 3.6.

Although Figure 3.6 represents an expected, or "normal," life cycle, the curve does not always have the same shape as that illustrated. Some services may have an introductory phase followed by rapid growth and then experience sharp, immediate decline. Other services may have long periods of maturity and never enter decline; still others may enter decline and then observe a revival in demand.

The general market conditions associated with each phase of the life cycle have been identified by Porter (1980) for industry evolution and by Kotler (1990) for product evolution. The first phase, or *introductory* stage, occurs when the service has just been introduced and there is limited consumer knowledge of the service, with resulting low utilization and revenue levels. Managerial time must be devoted to developing markets for the services because organization capacity is underused. Uncertainty exists among providers as to the technology that will be most

effective, as no common standards have evolved. Because product quality may be erratic, control should be exerted over service delivery, possibly through narrowing the scope of service so that operations are better managed. Image and credibility with the financial community may be critical because of the funding required to support growth and the uncertainty associated with new services.

During the second phase, the *growth* stage, consumer knowledge of the service increases and demand rises. Technical quality improves considerably. Reliability and differentiation become more critical because consumer expectations increase. Organizations experience increased use of existing capacity, and profits grow as costs are spread over larger volume. More providers enter the market and offer a broader scope of services that further expand the market. The potential exists for segmented services because of diverse consumer demand. Because the opportunities for shifts in relative market share are greatest during this stage, major efforts may be directed toward market penetration.

At *maturity,* Kotler (1990) identifies three

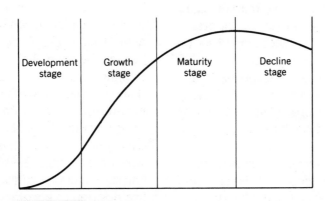

FIGURE 3.6. A life-cycle model.

substages that exist. He describes the three as follows:

> In the first phase, growth maturity, the sales-growth rate starts to decline because of distribution saturation. There are no new distribution channels to fill, although some laggard buyers still enter the market. In the second phase, stable maturity, sales become level on a per capita basis because of market saturation. Most potential consumers have tried the product, and future sales are governed by population growth and replacement demand. In the third phase, decaying maturity, the absolute level of sales now starts to decline, and customers start moving toward other products and substitutes. (p. 367)

The slow rate of demand growth and overcapacity leads to intense competition for market share. Consumers are more cost conscious and technically knowledgeable. Sophisticated cost analysis is needed to provide data required to identify and prune unprofitable services from the broad service line initiated during the growth stage. Also, correct pricing is essential because cross-subsidization, through average cost pricing, may not be possible. Service delivery innovation is directed toward identifying lower-cost delivery methods.

Defending the remaining market share that an organization possesses is important. Existing consumers are encouraged to increase their use of the scope of services offered by the institution, an approach that is less costly than winning new consumers. Providers become more selective in terms of the groups to whom they will provide services.

The final phase, *decline,* is evidenced by a significant drop in demand. This reduction may occur rapidly or gradually. There is uncertainty as to whether this downturn is permanent or a short-term condition that will self-correct. If the downturn represents a sharp movement toward market extinction, management must withdraw as soon as possible to prevent significant losses. Gradual decline suggests that management might be able to harvest some profits from the market by controlling service delivery costs and efficiently providing services. Alternatively, pockets of demand may remain that allow highly selective marketing to be initiated toward those niches. Finally, decline may be temporary, and aggressive marketing tactics could renew demand.

Strategy Identification and Selection

The above methods for analyzing portfolios contribute to management understanding of the organization-environment interface. These conceptual tools, combined with important data on market conditions and internal capabilities, are valuable aids in determining future directions for health care organizations. Decision algorithms have been developed to augment the previously described portfolios.

Strategic decisions for business areas of organizations are facilitated by the BCG Business Grid. Because market growth rate is beyond the control of management (Abell & Hammond, 1979), focus shifts to market share and allocation of funds. One successful long-term strategy is financing efforts to increase market share of question marks from cash generated by cash cows. This produces stars that eventually become cash cows. Question marks not in an adequate competitive position to become stars should not receive infusions of cash and should be allowed to descend to become dogs with the decline in market growth rate.

The GE-type Business Screen also provides insights into appropriate portfolio investment decisions. Harvesting or divesting should occur when business strength and industry attractiveness are low, and investment and growth should occur when they are high.

The Product Life-Cycle Matrix provides direction for managers interested in strategy formulation. Hillestad and Berkowitz (1984) suggest a *strategy action match* to match the organization's life cycle with the marketplace

life cycle to determine appropriate managerial action. This match is illustrated in Figure 3.7. During the service introduction, an organization should "go for it" and strive for overall market leadership, limit service variations, concentrate on quality, establish high prices, and make related moves.

"Differentiation" is attempted during the growth stage. At maturity, a "necessity" approach is used if the organization must initiate a service for competitive reasons, does not currently provide it, and will not obtain market leadership. "Maintenance" is an attempt to retain market share without undue

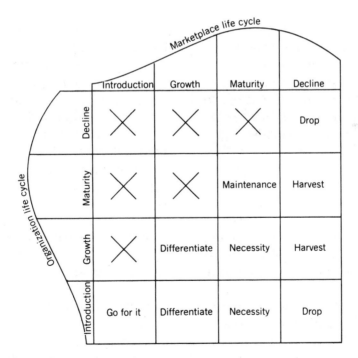

Legend
X = Position cannot occur

FIGURE 3.7. Strategy action match matrix. (Reprinted from *Health Care Marketing Plans: From Strategy to Action, 2nd Ed.,* by S. Hillestad and E. Berkowitz, p. 123, with permission of Aspen Publishers, Inc., © 1991.)

investment of funds. Finally, the decline stage suggests that an organization either harvest or divest the service. Interestingly, Porter (1980) suggests that a firm may not only harvest or divest during decline, but also may attempt to find a defensible niche or maintain a market share leadership position if conditions warrant.

Organizational Strategy and Human Resources Management

Human resources functions should have a direct supportive relationship to the formulation and implementation of organizational strategy. *The strategic management of human resources is concerned with ensuring that qualified personnel are available to staff the portfolio of business units that will be operated by the organization.* This assurance means that qualifications for operation of the units must be determined; appropriate personnel must be recruited and selected; development of manpower to meet future needs must occur; and adequate rewards must be provided to attract and retain valuable employees.

Unfortunately, only a few progressive organizations seek to include human resources management activities in the strategy planning process even though data are available to support decision making (Tichy, Fombrun, & Devanna, 1984). The general role that human resources functions should play in the strategy of health care organizations is discussed in the following section. Then, the relationship of these functions to the portfolio of services managed by the organization is described.

Recruitment and Selection

Recruitment and selection are concerned with methods for hiring individuals and the internal movement of personnel to positions. Matching qualified individuals to appropriate jobs is crucial for organizational performance. Health care organizations must design selection systems that support the organization's strategy. For example, if an organization plans to diversify, management must have careful analysis of types of persons needed to staff and manage the new enterprise. Diversification by large health systems may be hindered if new products or services that are developed are not well-managed. Early development of selection criteria and hiring of individuals for the diversification will ensure that staff is in place when the new venture is initiated.

The organization also must monitor the internal flow of individuals and identify persons who have attributes that match those required for the emerging business strategies. Skills that mark persons as upwardly mobile may change if shifts occur in the strategic thrust. Inpatient acute care managers need the ability to work well with the medical staff, numerous community groups, and others. Determining who is eligible for career advancement in this situation requires assessment of interpersonal abilities (along with other skills). However, new ventures in health insurance, real estate, or other entrepreneurial activities may require that greater emphasis be placed on bargaining skills. Thus, the types of data used to identify persons for advancement and the priority weights attached to the measures may change with different market thrusts.

Comparably, health care organizations must match their key executives to business units that may be pursuing strategies that require unique skills. The advent of portfolio management in health services means that organizations offer an array of services that are situated at different stages of the life cycle. As discussed later, services at different stages of development require distinct managerial capabilities. Individuals should be placed with services at development stages that match their competence.

Development

Identification of needed skills and active management of employee learning for the future in relation to explicit corporate and business strategies will contribute to organizational stability. The process of enhancing an individual's present and future skills most frequently occurs through training on the job. Health care organizations must develop job rotation sequences and other early career developmental tracks aimed at producing people capable of handling key positions.

One approach for identifying personnel with high managerial potential and for developing these persons is succession planning (Hernandez, Haddock, Behrendt, & Klein, 1991). This type of program frequently begins with a review process that evaluates the current management skills of persons in supervisory positions. Individual development plans allow managers to improve deficiencies and strengthen skills. Organizations involved in succession planning are thus able to evaluate and develop managers and have available "promotability ratings" that allow comparison of candidates for management vacancies.

Health systems that have competed exclusively in one market segment (e.g., inpatient acute care) have specific types of experiences planned for developing executives. With the emergence of alternative service delivery systems and diversification into services only tangentially related to health care, human resources managers must devote considerable attention to planning early career experiences for management personnel who will operate these new ventures.

Appraisal

Appraisal is concerned with systematic examination and evaluation of positions and employees. Obviously, the entire human resources planning system depends on valid, reliable appraisals. Recruitment, selection, and placement require that skills needed in positions be accurately described. Then, the capabilities of candidates for those positions must be assessed to ascertain that an appropriate match is achieved.

Compensation systems require support from valid appraisal methods. The reason for this requirement is that rewards can be allocated on the basis of performance only if performance standards for a job have been established and if the performance of the incumbent can be measured.

Finally, management development depends on accurate data from the performance appraisal system. Summary information on the strengths and weaknesses of managerial personnel can be analyzed to surface training and development needs.

Compensation

To be effective is securing behaviors that are desired from managers, compensation must be tied to the performance needed by the organization. Compensation systems appear to influence factors that subsequently influence organizational outcomes. Persons who are attracted to work for an organization and who remain are swayed by the types of compensation systems used; high performers frequently are attracted to organizations offering merit-based compensation systems (Mobley, 1982).

A major consideration for individuals responsible for designing compensation systems is that the systems drive managers toward long-term goals. If rewards are tied to short-term results, it will be difficult to get managers to focus on long-term goals when results may not be known for years. The difficulty of designing compensation systems to accomplish this task is discussed in the next section of this chapter.

Portfolio Analysis and Human Resources Management

The portfolio analysis methods that were described previously have positive and negative attributes in terms of their ability to guide the human resources management process of health care organizations. The GE-type Business Screen is a thoughtful method for surfacing often implicit views of outcomes desired by organizations and converting these to explicit measures. However, this method gives few clues regarding the relationship of the portfolio of services being provided to the human resources management issues that must be addressed.

In a comparable manner, the BCG Business Grid does an excellent job of guiding the suggested flow of funds among business unit choices. However, it too does not lend itself to clarification of human resources planning requirements.

The Product Life-Cycle Matrix has more intuitive appeal. The stages of the cycle of development for services suggest market conditions that lead to critical issues that must be faced by senior management. These issues, in turn, require that selected elements of the human resources system be used to address the issues that are raised. In addition, the skills required of managers vary based on the stages of the life cycle of the services being managed. Identification of the competencies needed assists in development of criteria for selection, appraisal, compensation, and development of managerial personnel across the business units of the organization.

Each of the four stages of the life cycle is examined to identify the management issue that must be faced. The human resources function or tactic that is critical during the stage is noted. Finally, the managerial skills most important for handling business units during that stage of the life cycle are listed.

Introduction

As previously noted, during the introductory stage of the life cycle, the service is not widely known and considerable time must be devoted to identification and development of markets. Because the best methods for producing the service are relatively unknown, the scope of services offered must be limited and concentration must be placed on maintaining the quality of services offered. The dominant competitive issue that must be faced by the organization is associated with identifying methods to be employed to *develop the market*.

Because this is a new venture for the institution, the major concerns for the human resources management system are *recruiting and selecting* competent managerial personnel to staff the enterprise. Additionally, other individuals must be recruited to staff all of the positions required for the new unit to be able to deliver services. Internal or external sources of personnel must be considered. Criteria for selection of appointments must be developed.

Because of the uncertainty associated with the technology required to deliver the service, the managers responsible for these new ventures must be able to handle ambiguity well. Rapid changes in the methods used to provide the service or in the expectations placed on employees means that these managers also must have good interpersonal skills to handle the disturbances that are likely to occur.

Managers and other employees of the health services organization must be entrepreneurial and exploit new markets or variations in service delivery techniques that improve operations. Knowledge of new services marketing tactics is critical. Skills in financing the new services or in budgeting and projecting the economic results of business unit operations are required.

Growth

The growth stage is characterized by increase in consumer knowledge of the service and rise in consumer demand. The largest shifts in relative market share occur during the growth stage. Improvements in quality and in the availability of differentiated services provide a competitive edge for health care organizations that are able to institute these enhancements. Thus, the significant managerial issue that must be handled during the growth stage relates to the ability of the organization to *meet market demand* for the service.

The ability to respond to rapid changes and to maintain or increase market share is improved by the organization having managers and other health professionals within the institution who are exceptionally knowledgeable about opportunities occurring in the market and who have technical knowledge of the production capabilities of their units. The human resources function that takes on increased importance during this stage is concern for *management development* activities.

Improving the current and future effectiveness of managers during the growth stage is critical for several reasons. First, managers who were selected to operate these business units may have general management training but little knowledge of health services, or they may be health professionals without formal training in business and marketing principles. During this stage managers must have both technical product knowledge and marketing-management competence. Marketing skills that are required include methods to increase market share or begin market penetration tactics. Thus, a concern for human resources management is ensuring that either experiential or technical training activities are planned to develop expertise necessary in this type of market.

As demand for the service increases, more organizations will enter the market and current providers will expand operations. Thus, a second reason that management development is critical for this stage is that demand will grow for managers knowledgeable about operation of these units. For example, it is expected that managed care and health maintenance organizations (HMOs) will increase in importance, and new sites may begin operations in the near future. However, large HMO systems have devoted inadequate attention to identifying and developing individuals to manage these new sites. Thus, a seller's market exists for managers with HMO experience. Corporations interested in expanding their managed care activities need to develop individuals for projected growth or they will be unable to implement their plans successfully.

Maturity

During maturity, the rate of increase in growth of demand drops sharply. Consumers are more cost conscious and knowledgeable about service features. The scope of services that was broadened during the growth stage may be a liability now and pruning of services occurs. *Competition* is the dominant competitive issue facing the organization. Cost analysis and cost-cutting methods are required to keep the services of the organization competitively priced. Defending market share in a mature to declining market is essential for continued survival.

Appraisal and *compensation* are crucial functions performed by human resources managers during this stage. The character of compensation systems changes from loose, informal methods appropriate for a rapidly changing environment to a more structured, formal approach as industry maturity takes place. Human resources personnel must spend greater time and effort developing and fine-tuning this formal system to ensure that equity is engineered into the process. Compensation also may take on increased significance to managers of mature service units because less intrinsic satisfaction may be derived from managing these units during periods of increased competition.

Valid appraisal of managerial performance is important because the reduction in demand for an organization's services may result from overall market conditions, or it might arise from judgmental errors by management. Additionally, managers of business

units may be eligible for promotion into senior, general management positions. The appraisal system and succession planning system must be able to identify successful managers at the business unit level so that compensation will be equitable and simultaneously identify individuals who have talents needed for higher levels of management or for corporate positions.

Decline

The final stage of market conditions is associated with significant drops in consumer demand. An organization may decide to divest itself of the business, remain in the market for an extended period and harvest profits from the service, identify a suitable market niche for the organization, or attempt to maintain a market share leadership role if it is believed that demand for the service will be relatively enduring. The dominant issue or concern facing management will depend on the strategic decision that is made. Divestment simply means that a suitable buyer for the service is found or that the business unit is terminated. Attempting a harvesting position suggests that *cost control* must occupy managerial attention. Conversely, finding a market niche or attempting to maintain leadership suggests that *redevelopment* is to occur.

Given the decline in demand for services, fewer business units may be operated and cost reduction strategies are in order. Thus, the major activities for the human resources manager concerns performing *outplacement* services for individuals who will not be retained, or in engineering *selective retention* of personnel and their replacement in other operating units of the organization. This matter will be of increasing concern as

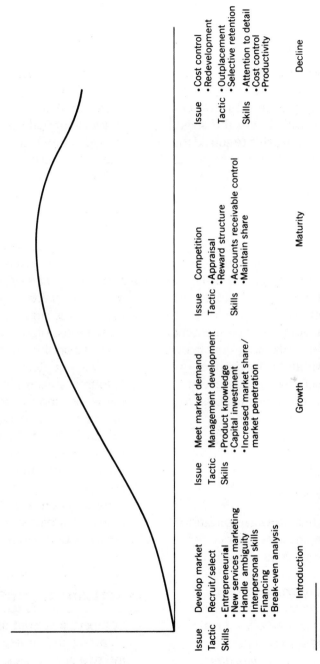

FIGURE 3.8. Integration of the human resources management process into a life-cycle model.

health services organizations face downsizing issues with health care reform.

Human Resources Management

The above discussion described the management issue during each stage of the life cycle of a product and the human resources function or tactic critical during the stage, and suggested managerial skills required for handling business units at various stages of growth. This information is illustrated in Figure 3.8. The association of a human resources function or tactic with each stage of the life cycle does not mean that other functions are not necessary during that stage. This illustration is used to identify the activity that is *most critical* during the listed stage.

This material serves as a guide to suggested interrelations that should exist between human resources management functions and strategic planning and management activities within health services organizations. Other sections of the text provide greater detail on the methods for accomplishing these activities.

MANAGERIAL IMPLICATIONS

The following are managerial implications of formulating an organizational strategy for health services organizations:

1. *Several planning approaches have been used by health services organizations, but an emphasis must be placed on strategic planning and strategic management in today's competitive marketplace.* Organizational strategies that might be used by health services

institutions require determining the "business" of the organization and the methods that will be used to compete in those businesses.

2. *The formulation of the organization's strategy begins with a well-articulated mission statement.* Analysis of external opportunities and threats, as well as internal strengths and weaknesses, provides input in determining the alternative services that a health services organization should include in its portfolio. Portfolio analysis also suggests strategies that should be followed for the services that the organization decides to provide.

3. *Relationships exist among business strategies, stages of product life cycle, and human resources functions.* Life-cycle stages suggest critical issues that must be handled under different market conditions. These issues require that varying elements of the human resources system be used to address the issues and that the skills required of managers vary based on the stages of the life cycle of the service. Identification of the competencies needed assists in development of criteria for selection, appraisal, compensation, and development of managerial personnel across the business units of the organization.

Discussion Questions

1. Compare and contrast strategic planning and strategic management. Of the two approaches, which one do you think is more difficult for management to realize? Why?

2. Three approaches to achieving competitive advantage for a business are cost leadership, differentiation, and focus. Is it possible for a community general hospital to use both a cost leadership and differentiation method with separate services in the hospital? Explain your response.

3. A variety of tools are available for analyzing a portfolio of strategic business units. Which of these tools would you suggest health services managers use when attempting to gain insight into the aptitudes and skills required for the manager of a soon-to-be-developed business unit? Explain your selection.

4. Describe the approach you would take to determine the stage of Product Life Cycle for the following services: 1) coronary artery bypass graph, 2) in-vitro fertilization, and 3) home health care.

CASE

Lakeview Medical Center was founded in 1895 when civic leaders in a midwestern town united to establish a home for the sick-poor. Over time, the scope of services was expanded to include maternity care, sick infants and children, and a full array of health services needed by the community. The Medical Center increased in size to become a 577-bed, acute care hospital with numerous affiliated activities. The foundation that controls the hospital also controls a family practice center, a fitness and sports medicine program, a health promotion center, three urgent care centers, a hospice, two skilled nursing facilities, and a patient transport service with several helicopters and ground ambulance capabilities.

There is a feeling among some of the administrative staff that the organization has become "overstretched" in its attempt to provide the number of services that it does. Additionally, numerous opportunities arise to develop new service ventures at the Medical Center. The management team is in the process of considering methods that can be used to prioritize the services currently provided as well as to help in the process of considering new ventures. The team's concern is that each of the services currently offered makes a somewhat different contribution both to the Medical Center and to the community. Additionally, numerous stakeholders have desired outcomes that are achieved by the operation of some services and not others.

Case Discussion Questions

1. Describe the method or methods you would use to determine priorities for both existing and potential services that the Lakeview Medical Center might offer.
2. What criteria would you choose for selecting among the various services and how would you choose the criteria?
3. The business units of the Medical Center provide services at different stages of the product life cycle. What implications does this situation have for the human resources functions of the Medical Center?

REFERENCES

Aaker, D.A. (1984). *Developing business strategies*. New York: Wiley.

Abell, D.F., & Hammond, J.S. (1979). *Strategic market planning*. Englewood Cliffs, NJ: Prentice-Hall.

Alfirevic, J., Nackel, J., & Shade, D.M. (1983). Prospective payment and case mix management. *Osteopathic Hospitals*, August, 11–15.

Andrews, K. (1971). *The concept of corporate strategy*. Homewood, IL: Dow-Jones-Irwin.

Ansoff, H.I. (1977). The state of practice in planning systems. *Sloan Management Review, 18*(2), 1–24.

Ansoff, H.I., & McDonnell, E.J. (1990). *Implanting strategic management* (2nd ed.). Englewood Cliffs, NJ: Prentice-Hall.

Berman, H.J., & Weeks, L.E. (1979). *The financial management of hospitals* (4th ed.). Ann Arbor, MI: Health Administration Press.

Dillon, R. (1979). *Zero-base budgeting for health care institutions*. Germantown, MD: Aspen Systems.

Drucker, P.F. (1974). *Management: Tasks, responsibilities, practices*. New York: Harper and Row.

Duncan, W.J., Ginter, P.M., & Swayne, L.E. (1992). *Strategic management of health care organizations*. Boston, MA: PWS-Kent.

Griffith, J.R. (1972). *Quantitative techniques for hospital planning and control*. Lexington, MA: Lexington Books.

Hall, W.K. (1980). Survival strategies in a hostile environment. *Harvard Business Review, 58*(5), 75–85.

Hax, A.C., & Majluf, N.S. (1984). *Strategic management: An integrative perspective*. Englewood Cliffs, NJ: Prentice-Hall.

Heldey, B. (1977). Strategy and the business portfolio. *Long Range Planning, 10*(1), 9–15.

Hernandez, S.R., Haddock, C., Behrendt, W.M., & Klein, W.F. (1991). Management development and succession planning: Lessons for health service organizations. *Health Care Management Development, 10*(4), 19–30.

Hillestad, S.G., & Berkowitz, E.N. (1984). *Health care marketing plans: From strategy to action*. Homewood, IL: Dow Jones-Irwin.

Hofer, C.W., & Schendel, D. (1978). *Strategy formulation: Analytical concepts*. St. Paul: West Publishing.

Kimberly, J.R., Miles, R.H., and Associates (1980). *The organizational life cycle*. San Francisco: Jossey-Bass.

Kotler, P. (1990). *Marketing management: Analysis, planning, and control* (7th ed.). Englewood Cliffs, NJ: Prentice-Hall.

Marrus, S.K. (1984). *Building the strategic plan*. New York: Wiley.

McNerney, W.J., et al. (1962). *Hospital and medical economics: A study of population, services, costs, methods of payment, and controls* Vol. 2. Chicago: Hospital Research and Educational Trust.

Mobley, W.H. (1982). *Employee turnover: Causes, consequences, and control*. Reading, MA: Addison-Wesley.

Moore, R.F. (Ed.). (1970). *AMA management handbook*. New York: American Management Association.

Nutt, P.C. (1984). *Planning methods for health and related organizations*. New York: Wiley.

Pearce, J.A. (1982). The company mission as a strategic tool. *Sloan Management Review, 23*(1), 15–24.

Perlin, M.S. (1976). *Managing institutional planning*. Germantown, MD: Aspen Systems.

Peters, J.P. (1985). *A strategic planning process for hospitals*. Chicago: American Hospital Publishing.

Porter, M.E. (1980). *Competitive strategy*. New York: The Free Press.

Porter, M.E. (1985). *Competitive advantage*. New York: The Free Press.

Pyhrr, P.A. (1973). *Zero base budgeting*. New York: Wiley.

Sammon, W.L. (1984). Competitor intelligence: An analytical approach. In W.L. Sammon, M.A. Kurland, & R. Spitalnic (Eds.), *Business competitor intelligence: Methods for collecting, organizing, and using information* (pp. 91–143). New York: Wiley.

Steiner, G.A. (1979). *Strategic planning*. New York: The Free Press.

Tichy, N.M., Fombrun, C.J., & Devanna, M.A. (1984). Organizational context of strategic human resource management. In C. Frombrun, N.M. Tichy, & M.A. Devanna (Eds.), *Strategic human resource management* (pp. 19–31). New York: Wiley.

Webber, J.B., & Peters, J.P. (1983). *Strategic thinking: New frontier for hospital management*. Chicago: American Hospital Publishing.

Wind, Y.J. (1982). *Product policy: Concepts, methods, and strategy*. Reading, MA: Addison-Wesley.

CHAPTER

MANAGING HUMAN RESOURCES OVER THE ORGANIZATIONAL LIFE CYCLE

Myron D. Fottler

Howard L. Smith

INTRODUCTION

After reading this chapter the reader should be aware of the critical importance of the health care organizations stage in its organizational life cycle. This chapter also describes how strategies and human resources practices change during the organization's life cycle. Finally, the matching of strategy and human resources practices is a continual challenge at each life-cycle stage. After reading this chapter, readers should be better able to link strategy and practices at each life-cycle stage.

In recent years, particular emphasis has been placed on the need to study organizations as they evolve in their life cycles. As mentioned in Chapter 3, each stage in the organizational life cycle may be associated with particular issues and problems in addition to those associated with human resources.

This chapter discusses the nature of the organizational life cycle, strategies for managing organizational decline, and appropriate human resources management strategies and tactics at each stage of the organizational life cycle. Examples from the health care industry are also provided.

ORGANIZATIONAL LIFE CYCLES

People, products, markets, and even societies have life cycles, which include birth, growth, maturity, old age, and death. At every life-cycle stage, a typical pattern of behavior emerges that poses particular challenges to management. As the organization passes from one phase of its life cycle to the next, different roles are emphasized, and the different role combinations that result produce different individual and organizational behaviors.

However, it also should be remembered that at any point in the organizational life cycle, various organizational subunits and the organization as a whole may be in different phases of the cycle. Such a situation may necessitate some strategies and tactics different from those required elsewhere in the organization. For example, if a hospital suffering declining inpatient census and revenue decides to start an HMO, it may need to recruit a director who is capable of entrepreneurial planning and implementation of managed care concepts. The compensation package would probably involve some incentives for the director based on enrollment and revenue, even though such incentives may not exist within the hospital itself.

Several authors have discussed organizational life cycles and the nature of problems at each stage. We use a four-stage model of start-up, growth, maturity, and decline based on the work of Adizes (1979) and Quinn and Cameron (1983). By observing the development of organizations through the life-cycle stages, it may be possible to predict the major problems, decisions, and opportunities to be faced by organizations and to provide some suggestions for appropriate organizational responses.

Start-up Phase

The start-up phase for most organizations is usually typified by *creativity and entrepreneurship*. Marshalling resources, creating an ideology, and finding an ecological niche are the emphasized activities. The dominant competitive issue is to identify methods to develop a market for the particular good or service. Because the best methods of producing the service are generally not well-known, the scope of services offered must be limited, and managers must concentrate on maintaining the quality of services offered.

Managers must be entrepreneurial and develop or exploit new markets or new methods of delivering existing services. At the same time, they must be adept at raising needed capital and recruiting new personnel with appropriate skills. Building a team from the newly recruited personnel is a challenge that requires either development of an ideology (i.e., a concept of what the organization is about) or charismatic leadership.

Producing results is a key value. What counts at this stage of organizational life is not what one thinks, but what one does. Most people in such an organization, including the CEO, are out selling and doing. There are few staff meetings.

The start-up organization is highly centralized and best described as a one-man show. There are few policies, systems, or procedures, and sometimes only rudimentary budgets. The administrative system is very primitive. There is no long-range planning.

The organization is so busy doing that it is usually inundated by short-term tactical pressures. Management often misses some long-term opportunities. When it does perceive opportunities, it tends to move fast and to make decisions intuitively. Because it lacks experience, almost every opportunity becomes a priority.

The dangers to the organization are twofold. First, the organization is spread so thin that it may run out of capital. Second, the personification of its managerial process (i.e., the founder's trap) may preclude the development of appropriate administrative structures and processes.

The Growth Phase

The growth phase is characterized by an emphasis on meeting market demands from consumers as well as development of an internal management structure. Increases in consumer knowledge and consumer demand for the service occur at this stage. The organization finds and exploits one or more market niches on the basis of quality or price differentials. There is an emphasis on responding to changes in market demand and on exploitations of new markets to continue the pattern of growth.

To handle the growth in revenues and employment while complying with various external requirements, administrative structures are developed. At this stage, there is still a high level of cohesion among employees and commitment to the organization. Face-to-face communication and informal structures are common. There is a sense of mission and dedicated service to the organization. However, the administrative role is increasing in importance, and more time is spent on planning and coordinating meetings. Training programs and various standardized personnel procedures are established. A computer is installed to manage information.

These activities may take time away from the entrepreneurial role, which enhances long-run survival and growth, or from producing results in the short term. A "healthy" growth phase is one in which the production of short-term results is temporarily sacrificed for the sake of integrating the required administrative systems.

There is often a tension between those seeking more stability and predictability (i.e., the administrative orientation) and those seeking continued growth and entrepreneurship. The first group feels that policies and organizational systems are necessary if the organization is going to survive and grow in the long run, whereas the second group feels that the first group is stagnating the organization.

At the latter stages of the growth phase, the organization has a healthy balance among a short-term results orientation, a long-term entrepreneurial role, and appropriate administrative policies and procedures. Rates of growth in revenue and profits (or "surplus") have become more stable and predictable.

However, at the latter stages of the growth phase some early signs of aging begin to appear. There may no longer be a great gap between the aspiration levels of top management and expected achievements. As the group becomes more satisfied with the status quo, energy and pressure for change are reduced. The mental aging of top management, the infeasibility of increasing market share, and an ambiguous organizational structure with unclear lines of authority and responsibility also can reduce aspiration levels in the latter stages of the growth phase. When these effects are present, momentum based on past actions becomes the prime determinant of present growth. Slowdown is inevitable.

The Mature Organization

In the mature organization, the rate of increase in revenue and profit drops sharply. There are no serious declines or losses, but the organization has reached a rough equilibrium with its environment. The range of services that expanded during the growth phase may be narrowed as unprofitable or low-volume services are pruned. Competi-

tion increases in many of the service lines, and there is an emphasis on efficiency as a means of achieving or maintaining competitive prices.

The maturity phase is also characterized by *formalization* and *control.* Procedures and policies become institutionalized, goals are formalized, flexibility is reduced, and conservatism predominates. The administrative system of policies and procedures is enhanced and institutionalized. Employees spend more time with each other than working on producing results. A climate of personal friendships develops, meetings proliferate, the climate becomes more formal, and a sense of urgency is lost. New ideas are received without enthusiasm, and there is reluctance to rock the boat. An eagerness to excel and a "results orientation" declines. The climate is relatively stable.

What counts in the mature organization is not what you did or why you did it, but *how* you did it. There may be more emphasis on the style by which things are accomplished rather than the actual end results themselves. Form is more important than function.

Individual managers are rewarded for loyalty and for not making waves. Criticisms and threatening questions are not expected or allowed. The organization's climate rewards conformity. Those unable or unwilling to adapt to such a climate typically leave. The result is an organization that has become even more insular.

To maintain growth in revenues, the mature organization is inclined to raise prices rather than to generate new products or penetrate new markets. Eventually prices are raised to the inelastic portion of the products' demand curves. Total revenues decline.

Sometimes the mature organization acquires a growth organization to compensate for its own inability to grow or the lack of internal entrepreneurial activity. In other cases, the cash-rich, mature organization is acquired by a smaller, growing organization. In either case, the marriage can be very rocky. The two cultures usually are not compatible. The mature organization's policies and procedures may stifle the growth organization, or perhaps the management of the growing organization is unable to cope with the mature organization's problems.

In the case of some mature organizations, decline is averted when the organization is able to decentralize, expand its domain (or market), renew its adaptability to the environment, and develop new subsystems. Health care organizations that develop into horizontally or vertically integrated multi-institutional systems represent one example of the phenomenon.

The Decline Stage

In the decline stage, the organization can no longer pretend that the problems identified above are temporary. Significant decreases in consumer demand for services or products are occurring. The strategic decision to be faced by top management is whether to sell the organization to potential buyers, identify a suitable market niche and try to maintain market share in that submarket, or remain in the present markets and attempt to harvest profits. Which strategy is most appropriate depends on internal and external factors such as whether a suitable buyer exists or whether the organization has the potential to undercut the competition in terms of price.

Within the declining organization, a fight for personal survival begins. Managerial paranoia rises. Managerial behavior accelerates the organizational decline as managers

fight each other rather than the competition. Creative capabilities are directed into ensuring personal survival by eliminating or discrediting fellow employees rather than creating better products and services. The more productive employees are feared because of their productivity and either leave or are terminated cleverly or encouraged to find positions elsewhere.

This process eventually results in a stifling bureaucracy, which allows no innovation or change. Very little, if anything, gets done. Systems, rules, procedures, and forms predominate. Conflict is minimal or nonexistent. The organization buffers itself from the external environment by allowing few linkages and ignoring relevant information from (or about) that external environment.

In the decline portion of the life cycle, the administrative role predominates. Employees assume that unless something is explicitly assigned and permitted, it is probably not allowed or expected. Employees do not initiate or take chances. They wait to be told what to do. Finance and accounting managers have much greater power than production or marketing managers. Budgetary controls are emphasized, and new expenditures are rarely approved.

In a later section of this chapter, we examine in more detail the nature and causes of organizational decline, appropriate strategies and tactics for managing decline, and organizational constraints in managing decline. From the latter half of the 1980s into the 1990s, most health organizations are experiencing organization decline in whole or in part. The management of declining organizations requires skills, strategies, and tactics different from those used in the management of growing organizations. In addition, the management of human resources in the decline phase of the organizational life cycle requires strategies and tactics different from those used during the growth phase. These differences are discussed in the final section of the chapter.

ORGANIZATIONAL DECLINE

The term "decline" has two principal meanings in the organizational literature (Durham & Smith, 1982). First, it is used to denote a cutback in the size of an organization's work force, profits, budget, and clients. It has also been used to describe the general climate or orientation of an organization that shows evidence of stagnation, bureaucracy, and passivity. This latter condition of decline may or may not result in a loss of revenue. Decline-as-stagnation does not necessarily imply an absolute decreased revenue, whereas decline-as-cutback does. Stagnation is more often reflected as a decrease in the rate of increase than as an actual decrease. Stagnation is more likely to occur during periods of abundance, whereas cutbacks are more likely during periods of scarcity. This chapter focuses primarily on decline-as-cutback.

The most frequently cited causes of organizational decline reflect administrative inadequacies, administrative motivation, and external factors. In the for-profit sector, the first two causes are considered primary, whereas in the nonprofit and public sectors the third appears to be the most important. Problems of decline in hospitals are typically due to changes in their external environments, particularly regulatory and reimbursement changes (i.e., prospective payment systems). Lack of support in the external environment may also result from the inability of administrators to adapt to

changes in that environment. (Levine, 1978a, 1978b; Pfeffer & Salancik, 1978).

Table 4.1 indicates the major causes (both external and internal) of decline in health care organizations since the 1980s. The reasons for organizational decline are not these changes alone or mismanagement per se. Rather, decline is due to the inability of health care executives to adapt to those

TABLE 4.1. Major Causes of Organizational Decline in Health Care

I. External factors
  A. Declining support in the external environment
    1. Shift from "rapid-growth" to "slow-growth" industry
    2. Shift from "open-ended" to "close-ended" funding
  B. Increased emphasis on competition and cost containment
    1. Oversupply of hospital beds and physicians
    2. Prospective reimbursement and managed care plans
    3. State laws (e.g., Massachusetts, New Jersey) limiting reimbursement
    4. Competitive bidding for both public and private insurance contracts
    5. Unwillingness of private corporations and private insurers to allow significant "cost shifting" to private patients and employees
    6. Growth of employer coalitions to reduce costs
  C. Capital shortage
  D. Defensive medicine used to prevent litigation
  E. Rapid obsolescence of medical equipment and technology
II. Internal factors
  A. Lack of management experience in managing retrenchment
  B. Inability of management and other members of the dominant coalition to diagnose the causes of decline correctly
  C. Unwillingness or inability of management to implement necessary changes due to inertia, lack of understanding, or a weak power position
  D. Ill-configured or incorrectly implemented strategies designed by management to address external pressures
  E. Failure to integrate or network with physicians
  F. Conflicts among clinicians (e.g., physicians versus nurses) over philosophy of care and methods of case management

changes by making necessary modifications in strategy or tactics.

Levine (1978a) has defined four basic causes for loss of external environmental support. *Organizational atrophy* or inertia results when an organization habitually maintains programs based on their previous (rather than present) utility. Previous success may desensitize managers to environmental changes, and they therefore become more vulnerable to future failure. *Political vulnerability* is reflected in a public agency's inability to resist budget cuts. Factors contributing to such vulnerability (according to Levine) include small size, internal conflict, changes in leadership, lack of a base of expertise, and the absence of a positive self-image and history of excellence.

Problem depletion is a major cause of loss of legitimacy. Benson (1975) has stressed the importance of legitimacy as an organizational resource and has noted the tendency of some public agencies to overemphasize the acquisition of resources and to overlook the value of cultivating political acceptance. Public funding support for particular organizations, for example, tends to rise and fall depending on the perceived legitimacy of the values such agencies embody. *Environmental entropy* results from the reduced capacity of the environment to support a particular organization. Whereas the literature on business organizations emphasizes finding another market niche, the literature in the public sector emphasizes scaling down operations.

Changes in Ecological Niches

A major external cause of organizational decline is a significant change in the ecological niche in which the organization exists.

A niche is the environmental habitat of a population of organizations. It can be defined as a set of physical, biological, and social conditions that provide resources for, or place constraints on, the performance of an organizational population (Zammuto, 1982). Moreover, niches in a social exchange system are partially determined by the willingness of people to purchase the products or services produced by a population or organizations (Boulding, 1981).

The organizational domain refers to that part of the population's niche in which each organization operates. An organization's domain is defined by the clientele served, the technology employed, and the services or products produced (Meyer, 1975). It is identified by examining the major activities pursued by an organization (Cameron, 1981). It is that part of the niche that each member of the organizational population creates and inhabits.

Changes in ecological niches may produce conditions of decline for a population of organizations. Adaptation by individual organizations in an evolving niche occurs through domain responses. Organizations modify their domains in response to changes in the population's niche (Zammuto & Cameron, 1985). For example, a niche that remains constant in shape might be shrinking in size. A domain response would be to begin shifting activities to other niches that are not shrinking.

The two dimensions of niche change (shrinkage or shifting) can be used to construct a typology of decline. The cells in Figure 4.1 represent four different types of environmental decline that vary by type of change in niche configuration and by the continuity of change (Zammuto & Cameron, 1985). Organizations that encounter a continuous

	Continuity of Environmental Change	
	Continuous Change	Discontinuous Change
Change in Niche Size	Erosion	Contraction
Change in Niche Shape	Dissolution	Collapse

FIGURE 4.1. A topology of environmental decline. (From Zammuto, R. F., and Cameron, K. S. (1985). Environmental decline and organizational response. In B. M. Staw and L. L. Cummings (Eds.), *Research in Organizational Behavior,* Vol. 7. Greenwich, CT: JAI Press; reprinted by permission).

decrease in the size of their niche experience *erosion.* This form of environmental decline reflects a gradual reduction in the amount of organizational activities the niche will support. An example of erosion is provided by the experience of many elementary school systems during the 1970s. A decreasing birthrate during the 1960s produced a gradual and continuous reduction in enrollments during the 1970s, requiring many school systems to reduce their level of operations.

Organizations that encounter a discontinuous decrease in the size of their niche experience *contraction.* A sudden decrease in

available resources or in the demand for the goods and services produced is often the cause of contraction. The sudden contraction of the market for nonfilter cigarettes in 1954 after widespread publicity linking smoking to various health hazards (Miles & Cameron, 1982) provides an example of this type of decline.

Dissolution is the form of decline that occurs when one niche evolves into another. For example, the gradual shift in the demand for educational programs during the 1970s, from the humanities and social sciences to the professions and applied life and physical sciences, created conditions of dissolution for the college and university population (Zammuto, 1984).

Collapse refers to a rapid, dramatic condition of decline in which the existing niche of a population is more or less abolished and replaced by a new niche demanding different forms of performance. For example, fluorocarbon producers in the United States experienced collapse during the 1970s after scientists predicted that fluorocarbon propellants and coolants would deplete the ozone layer in the upper atmosphere and result in globally higher rates of skin cancer. The federal government quickly banned the use of fluorocarbons in most products (Post, 1978), and the niche for producers of other propellants, such as carbon dioxide, rapidly expanded.

The cell that best describes the health care industry in general during the late 1980s and the 1990s is dissolution. The health care niche is experiencing *continuous* change in *shape*. Of course some segments, such as inpatient care, may erode or contract. This typology is discussed later in the chapter when we examine potential managerial strategies and tactics for preventing or reversing decline.

Early Symptoms

The symptoms of organizational decline brought on by changes in ecological niche and the environment vary according to the stage of decline itself. In the initial stage decline may be viewed as just another crisis to be conquered. Whetten (1980a, 1980b) has observed that our society inculcates values of self-determination and self-confidence. We are taught that success can be willed and that no obstacle should deter us from reaching an objective. As a result, administrators may fail to admit that decline exists until it has

become apparent to all (Scott, 1976; Starbuck & Hedberg, 1977). Budget cutbacks may be viewed as *temporary* due to transient economic conditions. As a consequence, it is not unusual to observe administrators who are unwilling and/or unable to plan for necessary changes. Other common planning symptoms include a leadership vacuum, lack of a clearly defined strategy, various administrative extremes (e.g., too much innovation in the development of services, or too little), and failure to adapt to rudimentary changes in the external environment (Ford, 1980a).

Early organizing symptoms include the lack of a system for generating organizational renewal and extremes in formalization and centralization (Levine, 1979; Miller, 1977). High degrees both of formalization and centralization, as well as low degrees of each, are associated with decline (Thompson, 1967). Highly structured organizations tend to filter information, while "loose" structures tend to provide too many gaps in their communications systems.

The process of motivation usually suffers from a failure to define objectives and reward employees based on contribution, as well as an unwillingness of competent administrators to remain with the deteriorating organization (Scott, 1976). Perhaps as a result, decisions made by administrators at this point are often inappropriate and tend to exacerbate the problems associated with decline (Hedberg, Nystrom, & Starbuck, 1976). The area of control is often deficient in the early stages of decline because a negative feedback control system is lacking, as well as quantitative performance measures (Miller, 1977; Summers, 1977). It should be noted that studies discussing these early symptoms are based on casual observation and case studies.

Later Symptoms

Although the earlier symptoms tend to persist, new and potentially more damaging symptoms develop as the decline process continues. Much of our present understanding of these symptoms is a result of inferences from studies on the effects on *individuals* of crisislike events such as disasters and sudden bereavement or personal loss (Fink, Beak, & Taddeo, 1971; Janis & Mann, 1977). Responses to these events tend to follow a pattern of initial shock (numbed inaction), then "defensive retreat" (denial, refusal to change), and then a period of acceptance of the new situation and eventual adjustment to it. When this pattern is applied to organizations, it is the first two stages, which have been labeled "the crisis syndrome," that have received the most attention (Hermann, 1963). Empirical evidence based on studies of a wide variety of organizations lends support to this conceptual framework (Dunbar & Goldberg, 1978; Hall & Mansfield, 1971; Starbuck, Greve, & Hedberg, 1978).

One of the most interesting case studies of the crisis atmosphere that usually accompanies the onset of organizational deterioration examined two state hospitals forced to merge and to reduce their work force in the face of budgetary cutbacks (Jick, 1979a, 1979b). The characteristics of the crisis syndrome emerged in full view as job insecurity and general uncertainty swept the organization. Each dimension of the early crisis phases was clearly observed, as interpersonal relations, communication, and leadership deteriorated.

This research creates a picture of considerable stress experienced by the majority of employees as a result of budget cutbacks (Holsti, 1978). The morale of those who remained in the organization was severely damaged, and their productivity declined. Many other skilled employees left for what they saw as better opportunities. The net result was understaffing due to a combination of employee attrition and loss of motivation among those who remained. Studies of the crisis syndrome have empirically demonstrated these symptoms over and over again in nonprofit public sector organizations.

The crisis syndrome typically is accompanied by a series of organizational effects that are much more serious from the viewpoint of the long-term viability of the organization. First, administrators often begin to participate in an increasing number of meetings to plan short-run strategy or resolve conflicts related to the obvious organizational decline (Jick, 1979a). A system for administering change may be almost totally lacking (Summers, 1977). Also, there tends to be less long-range *planning* (sometimes none) and more orientation to the short run (Summers, 1977; Whetten, 1980b). Long-range planning is difficult due to increased interpersonal and interunit conflict (Levine, 1979), which makes it harder to get good information for problem identification and problem solution purposes (Hall, 1976; Smart & Vertinsky, 1977; Starbuck et al., 1978). The tendency to centralize decision making may be attributable to the environmental hostility, which demands quick responses and rapid coordination of organizational activities (Mintzberg, 1979). To survive in the short run, the organization chooses centralization. This tendency does not contradict the earlier discussion indicating that some declining organizations exhibit extreme decentralization and low degrees of formalization. Ford (1980b) explains this phenomenon by proposing that a structural hysteresis occurs, wherein the impact of growth and decline on administrative ratios is asymmetrical.

Third, the *motivation* of employees in the later stages of organizational deterioration tends to be extremely problematical. There is less encouragement of subordinate involvement and participation in all areas. The organization exhibits a complicated tangle of rules and regulations, extensive paperwork and forms, and the need to involve several departments to achieve even minor goals. Many individual symptoms (noted above), such as employee resistance to change and conflict, occur at the departmental and organizational levels as a result of these motivational problems.

Fourth, the crisis environment affects *decision making* by discouraging innovative solutions to problems and encouraging "group think" (Janis, 1972). This tendency toward conformity is reinforced by the high turnover rates and by the increased proportion of long-term employees that results when those who leave are not replaced. Employees who stay in a declining organization are more likely to share common norms and values, to reach consensus more easily, to have similar perceptions of the organization, and to be more committed to it (Starbuck, 1976). As a result, habitual or routine ways of perceiving the environment tend to predominate. Research has shown that high degrees of identification with the organization and long employee tenure are negatively related to certain measures of effectiveness and creativity (Rondine, 1975).

Finally, the *control* system at the later stages tends to operate by complaint (Summers, 1977). The assumption is that if a particular function is not performed up to the standards expected, someone will complain. A reduction in complaints, or their absence, is viewed as an indication that all is well. There might also be too many or too few

controls (Miller, 1977). The control system also tends to emphasize efficiency measures rather than effectiveness measures, which might have greater long-term potential for reversing the deterioration process (Miller & Friesen, 1980; Whetten, 1981).

It is emphasized that both the crisis syndrome and the tendency of administrators to respond to severe decline through increasing centralization and formalization have been well-documented through empirical work. The other later symptoms of decline discussed in this section have much less empirical support and should be viewed as hypotheses for further testing.

Constraints in Managing Decline

Health care executives are typically not prepared to cope with, or to manage effectively, conditions associated with organizational decline (Goldsmith, 1989). Even if they are prepared, there are severe constraints on their freedom of action.

First, the experience of most health care executives has largely been in responding to conditions of growth. Abundant financial resources and steadily increasing demand for services made conditions of growth almost universal during the 1950s, 1960s, and 1970s. Expansions of physical plant facilities and services were typical.

Second, the values and ideology of our culture emphasize growth and expansion as indicative of effectiveness. Whetten (1980a) has noted that large size is widely lauded as a desirable organizational characteristic because it enhances economies of scale and the organization's ability to absorb the shocks accompanying environmental change. Managers are typically evaluated positively if they produce more, obtain a larger budget, or expand their organizations. When the reverse occurs, negative evaluations normally result.

Third, factors operating in the institutionalized environments of health care organizations often severely constrain the available strategies and tactics. For example, the ability of many public sector health care organizations to modify their domains is limited by the corporate charter. Domain creation or consolidation strategies may not be legal. Moreover, the civil service systems under which some manage their human resources may constrain tactical options. Minimum staffing, personnel licensure, promotion policies, and indigent care requirements are all examples of such constraints.

Finally, administrators in both health care and non-health care organizations tend to define conditions of decline exclusively as a resources allocation problem or a problem of efficiency (Cameron, 1983). They respond conservatively rather than innovatively. Whetten (1981) has noted several examples of administrators in higher education who have emphasized internal resources allocation aimed at operating more efficiently at the expense of longer-term strategies for ensuring effectiveness.

The same phenomenon has been observed in health care organizations and is attributed to the conservative nature of the dominant coalition and its unwillingness to propose solutions not compatible with the existing organizational culture (Fottler, Smith, & Mueller, 1986). Not only are these conservative approaches contrary to prescriptions from management theory, but empirical evidence indicates that the exclusive emphasis on conservative, efficiency-oriented coping mechanisms leads to ineffective performance and even organizational death (Hedberg et al., 1976; Starbuck et al., 1978; Whetten, 1980a).

Whetten (1981) has argued that managers tend to focus on efficiency at the expense of effectiveness and to respond conservatively rather than innovatively when facing decline for at least six reasons. First, organizational effectiveness has been extremely difficult to define and measure, particularly in service industries. Because efficiency is more easily measured than effectiveness, it is given more attention by administrators. Most institutions have budget (efficiency) monitoring devices in place, but few have any mechanisms to measure effectiveness.

Second, the stress resulting from having to face conditions of decline compels individuals to engage in conservative and self-protective behaviors (Whetten, 1980a). A common side effect of decline is personal stress among managers. Research has shown that the consequences of such stress are (a) engaging in anxiety-reducing behaviors at the expense of problem-solving behaviors, (b) reducing the risk of mistakes (which are more visible under conditions of decline) by becoming conservative, (c) restricting the communication network, (d) reducing the number of participants in decision making, (e) enforcing rules more closely, (f) rejecting contrary evidence more readily, (g) perceiving the tasks and decisions to be more difficult, and (h) being prone to "group think" (Hall & Mansfield, 1971; Hermann, 1963; Janis, 1972; Staw, Sandelands, & Dutton, 1981).

Third, there is a tendency to pursue strategies that were successful in the past (e.g., during conditions of abundance and growth) even though they are inappropriate under current conditions of decline (March & Simon, 1958). In times of abundance, the major concerns were related to resources allocation rather than resources acquisition. The same pattern often carries over to the decline phase of the organizational life cycle, where it is clearly inappropriate except as a stopgap to buy time for implementation of a long-term resources acquisition strategy.

Fourth, the tendency toward passive leadership by administrators is also consistent with attribution theory, according to which individuals tend to believe that success (e.g., growth) is due to personal factors and failures (e.g., decline) to environmental factors beyond their control. Because the causes of decline are outside of the administrator's control, no proactive responses are forthcoming.

Fifth, health care institutions are frequently structured as loosely coupled systems, governed by committees and semiautonomous units. They are similar to political organizations in having multiple stakeholders to satisfy, each with vested interests, some of which are conflicting. Multiple interests groups and semiautonomous units make consensus on any decision unlikely, and resistance from some group to almost any strategy is virtually guaranteed. A consistent, innovative strategy for coping with decline is difficult to develop.

Miles and Snow (1978) refer to organizations without consistent strategies as "reactors." Research has found them to be the least effective of all organizational types (Snow & Hrebiniak, 1980). Because stakeholder conflict is heightened under conditions of decline, administrators are even more likely to "satisfice" by adopting conservative (e.g., efficiency-oriented) strategies to ameliorate this conflict.

Sixth, many creative and innovative managers are the first to leave an organization when decline occurs (Hirschman, 1970). These individuals are often the most marketable to other organizations. Declining organizations often do not attempt to retain these individuals because their entrepreneurial talents may not be perceived as valuable under decline conditions. The managers who are left as decline accelerates are often the least innovative ones, who tend to play it safe.

Finally, innovation itself may be viewed as one of the causes of decline. When rapid growth is the norm, organizations often experiment and expand to the point that services and facilities are difficult to maintain with stable or declining resources. Previous innovations are now viewed as financial burdens. One response is to eliminate innovative services and to avoid instituting alternatives.

STRATEGIC AND TACTICAL RESPONSES

Strategic responses refer not only to reactions or adaptations of the organization, but also to practice and anticipatory moves as well. Organizations are not completely at the mercy of an immutable environment, with no choice but to adapt. As noted previously, they can implement strategies that influence and even alter the population niche in which they exist (Miles & Cameron, 1982; Pfeffer & Salancik, 1978). Strategic responses, therefore, refer to actions taken by organizations to alter their domains and influence the niches in which they operate. Our model contains strategies of five types: domain defense, domain offense, domain creation, domain consolidation, and domain substitution (Zammuto & Cameron, 1985).

Domain defense strategies are oriented toward preserving the legitimacy of the existing domain of activities and buffering the organization from encroachment of the environment. These strategies are externally oriented and frequently involve attempts to manipulate or change the nature of the organization's environment (e.g., generating coalitions of support among key resources providers). Domain offense strategies are designed to do more of what the organization already does well. These strategies help to generate organizational slack by expanding current activity levels (e.g., expanding the market for current products or introducing new forms of a product). Domain creation strategies supplement current domains of activity with completely new domains. Diversification and innovation are often a part of domain creation strategies (e.g., forming a subsidiary in another domain, where current organizational expertise can still be utilized).

Domain consolidation strategies involve reducing the size of the domain occupied by the organization. Activities peripheral to the core domain of the organization are eliminated, and the organization becomes more specialized (e.g., divesting unprofitable divisions or products). Domain substitution strategies are designed to replace one domain with another. In the extreme case, the carrying capacity of the original niche completely disappears; no evidence of the earlier domain is left after domain substitution occurs. For example, when the cure for polio was found, the March of Dimes became an organization oriented toward birth defects. Table 4.2 provides some examples of specific approaches some health care organizations are currently implementing under each of the five generic strategies.

The strategic responses presented in the

TABLE 4.2. Some Examples of the Five Strategic Alternatives for Managing Decline in Health Care Organizations

Domain Defense
- Developing or enhancing political coalitions to reduce threat
- Becoming a preferred provider for employees of particular organizations
- Activating boards of trustees for political action

Domain Offense
- Providing enhanced services to a target segment of the service community (e.g., no-delay admitting procedures for certain employee groups)
- Increased advertising of services through various media
- Sponsoring and/or participating in community health care events

Domain Creation
- Opening new clinics in areas of wellness, stress management, and chemical dependency
- Offering contract management services to other hospitals
- Opening satellite facilities with ambulatory services

Domain Consolidation
- Divesting unprofitable or low-volume inpatient services
- Divesting unprofitable units (e.g., HMO)

Domain Substitution
- Substituting free-standing emergency clinic services for in-hospital emergency services
- Substituting commercially insured or self-pay patients for Medicare or Medicaid patients

model are expected to be the most effective strategies for coping with the particular type of decline identified. However, as mentioned previously, they are not expected to be the only strategies selected by organizations under these conditions because many types of strategy can be pursued concurrently or in sequence. This means that organizations may perform more than one strategy at a time, or they may pursue one strategy for a time and then change to another. The strategies identified in this model, however, are more likely to foster successful adaptation to the different conditions of decline than are domain strategies of other types (Burns & Mauet, 1989).

Figure 4.2 summarizes the four conditions of decline together with their impact on competition, the types of organization likely to be successful, and the appropriate strategic response when the conditions of decline are predicted in advance so that there is adequate lead time (e.g., continuous change) and when they are not (e.g., discontinuous change).

Erosion

Under the condition of erosion, competition within the population will gradually increase as the niche shrinks. Specialist organizations will be better able to adapt because of their greater efficiency. Generalist or strategist organizations have fewer economies of scale in resource acquisition and utilization.

When erosion is predicted, domain offense is likely to be the best strategic response. The goal of domain offense is to expand the resource base and the market share, and implementing this strategy helps the organization to ensure that it will maintain or increase its share of the existing niche, even though that niche is getting smaller. This strategy prevents the organization from being squeezed out of the shrinking niche

	Contingency of Environmental Change	
	Continuous Change	Discontinuous Change
Change in Niche Size	**Erosion** Competition: Slow increase Successes: Specialists Strategies: Domain offense predicted domain consolidation not predicted Tactics: Small, incremental change (fine-tuning)	**Contraction** Competition: Rapid increase Successes: Specialists Strategies: Domain defense if predicted; domain consolidation if not predicted Tactics: Change by deletion; substantial selective or across-the-board cutbacks
Change in Niche Shape	**Dissolution** Competition: Moderate increase Successes: Generalists Strategies: Domain defense then domain creation if predicted; domain substitution if not predicted Tactics: Search for new alternatives; change by addition	**Collapse** Competition: Overall decrease Successes: Strategists Strategies: Domain creation if predicted; domain substitution if not predicted Tactics: Change by substitution; trial-and-error use of past solutions

FIGURE 4.2. Strategic and tactical responses to four types of organizational decline. (From Zammuto, R. F., and Cameron, K. S. (1985). Environmental decline and organizational response. In B. M. Staw and L. L. Cummings (Eds.), *Research in Organizational Behavior*, Vol. 7. Greenwich, CT: JAI Press; reprinted by permission).

by competition from stronger or more specialized organizations.

When erosion is not foreseen, or when the organization is faced with a short lead time, domain consolidation is predicted to be the more appropriate initial strategy. Because implementing domain offense often requires substantial lead time, an organization is expected to focus on strategies of consolidation. This has been the response of many colleges and universities to declining revenues. At the University of Wisconsin, for example, three different incremental cuts in the budget were received throughout the 1980 to 1981 academic year. These cuts had not been unanticipated because the budget had already been appropriated by the legislature (Kauffman, 1982). The response of the institution was to eliminate all nonessential expenditures and activities. Photocopying was restricted, as was faculty travel. Contingency funds were eliminated, and the availability of noncore courses was limited. Resources were consolidated and focused solely on core areas of acknowledged high priority. In the 1990s, this same pattern has been replicated throughout the nation as higher educational institutions struggle to deliver education on a proportionally declining resources base.

Since erosion involves continuous shrinkage in the size of the niche, it is not likely to present an immediate threat to organizational survival. Management tactics will therefore emphasize small incremental adjustments, fine-tuning, and a redistribution of resources to improve efficiency. A conservative stance of "weathering out the storm" is typical (Hall & Mansfield, 1971). Examples of what health care organizations have done to fine-tune their organizations to improve efficiency include hiring freezes to reduce

labor costs, reeducation of physicians concerning costs, and general institutional cost containment programs.

Contraction

Under conditions of contraction, there is a discontinuous reduction in niche size. Competition increases dramatically within the industry as each organization tries to protect its share of services in the face of declining demand. Again specialist organizations have a competitive advantage because of their greater efficiency. Given the lack of adequate lead time, organizational failures are much greater among nonspecialist organizations compared to the erosion cell.

Strategically, when contraction (e.g., sudden shrinkage in niche size) is predicted, domain defense strategies are the most likely to be successful. The organization must preserve its legitimacy and ensure that its domain remains viable, even though the niche is smaller. Domain defense strategies are implemented to help buffer the organization from environmental encroachment. When contraction is not predicted, domain defense strategies, which require lead time to implement, are not likely to occur. Therefore, domain consolidation to preserve the organization's core domain is expected. The organization has little time and few resources with which to respond when an unexpected decline in the resources base occurs, and consolidation (i.e., marshalling resources around a core area of expertise) is the most likely strategy.

The most common tactic in response to contraction is a "threat-rigidity response" (Staw et al., 1981), which leads to cutback and retrenchment (e.g., change by deletion). Minor adjustments are unlikely to be effective because of the suddenness of the niche shrinkage. Thus, the magnitude of the tactical response is usually larger than in the erosion cell. Elimination of weaker services and significant layoffs of employees are examples of tactics used by health care organizations to respond to contraction.

Dissolution

Under conditions of continuous change in niche shape, there will be a moderate increase in competition as the carrying capacity of the original niche is reduced by movement toward a new niche. Generalist organizations will exhibit a greater adaptive potential than specialist organizations because their broader domains offer more options for responding to changes in niche shape. Increased failures will be experienced by specialist organizations with the "wrong" specializations.

The dissolution cell describes continuous environmental change: Here, a decrease in the acceptability of organizational outcomes creates a change in the shape of a niche. This type of decline is likely to produce incremental, but proactive, adjustments, and the search for new alternatives will be a central activity. Because organizations must change the nature of their activities to survive, change by addition is most likely to be effective. Organizations facing decline by dissolution, therefore, may actually choose to *expand* for the sake of adapting.

When dissolution is foreseen, effective organizations are predicted to implement domain defense strategies in an effort to build political slack and to preserve their legitimacy and the acceptability of their outputs. The orientation is toward exploiting the environment so that the impact of niche change on the organization may be inhibited. Do-

main defense is expected to be followed, however, by domain creation strategies so that the organizational domain can be located in a more viable part of the niche. Domain creation diversifies organizational domains and decreases the risk of having a continued state of dissolution, where the outputs of the organizations finally become completely unacceptable.

When dissolution is not predicted in advance, domain substitution is the strategy likely to be most effective. Caught by surprise, the organization is required to change domains to survive. Confronted by qualitative niche changes, the organization is expected to engage in different activities to facilitate its entry into the new niche. With no advance prediction of decline, there is little possibility of altering the environment itself (as in domain defense), so the strategic emphasis must point toward guaranteeing organizational survival. Substituting a supported domain in the evolving niche for the threatened domain is therefore a likely response of successful organizations.

Examples of the expected tactics to deal with dissolution in the health care field are long-range planning and market research to diagnose outlook for various market segments. Open discussion of the possibility of offering new and innovative ambulatory and long-term care services is also important.

Collapse

In the fourth cell, decline by collapse, the shape of the niche changes suddenly. Competition is likely to decrease because the rapid collapse of the original niche drives many competitors out of business. Strategists— organizations that can move quickly to take advantage of rapidly evolving portion of the niche—are most likely to be successful.

Experimentation with past successful activities is the most likely tactical response because threat produces a constriction of the new alternatives considered in search procedures, although it does not constrict search per se (Staw et al., 1981). Structural adjustment is expected to occur by substituting more acceptable activities for old activities, but the substituted activity is expected to be within the institution's area of expertise. The first satisfactory alternative is likely to be accepted because there is neither the time nor the inclination to search widely (Hall & Mansfield, 1971; Hermann, 1963).

When collapse is predicted, domain creation strategies can be implemented. These strategies allow the organization to form and nurture new domains of activity in addition to current domains. The organization becomes more generalized or diversified in an attempt to adapt to the collapsing niche. The goal of domain creation is to maintain support for the activities conducted in what remains of the original niche while expanding into the evolving portion of the niche or into other less threatened niches.

Nonpredicted collapse leaves the organization with little choice but to substitute an already existing domain that has some support for the domain that is now threatened. Lead time is not available to nurture a diversification effort (i.e., domain creation). Instead, the organization concentrates on maintaining viability. Domain substitution, therefore, is the most likely strategic choice.

REINSTITUTING GROWTH

Although the preceding sections have described the typical stages through which organizations pass if they are not actively managed, decline and death are not inevitable.

Proactive management can strategically direct an organization to seek out and exploit new markets, reduce unprofitable operations, and avoid or reduce bureaucracy. Even organizations that are in the decline phase may be reinvigorated by "new blood," new ideas, or both. In the health care industry, two major approaches to reversing stagnation or decline are transformational leadership and corporate restructuring.

Transformational Leadership

Transformational leadership typically occurs when there is a significant "performance gap" between what the key stakeholders desire and what they receive from the organization. It typically involves a new CEO or leadership team, which challenges the existing norms, values, and culture. There is an attempt to transform a stagnant or declining organization by adding new people with new ideas and goals, developing a new culture, reducing the influence of certain key individuals not attuned to the new goals, and creating a new vision of the organization and its mission. New leadership is usually required in this process because the old leadership is either unable or unwilling to make such fundamental changes.

According to Kaluzny, Jaeger, and Habib (1987), the major collective task of any organization is to negotiate an acceptable accommodation with its environment. As the environment changes, so too must the organization, or it risks decline and death. In health care, this pressure has led to interesting collaborative relations in response to a threatening environment (Foreman & Roberts, 1991; Miller & Walmsley-Ault, 1990). A stagnant or declining organization has obviously failed to respond to environmental change. Transformational leadership, one response to this failure, triggers a search for solutions by the organization.

Organizations initiate actions that have the least invasive effects on themselves and yet achieve acceptable performance (Shortell & Wickizer, 1984). Time and other resources for solving problems faced by various individuals and departments are limited. As a consequence, the search for solutions is also restricted and begins with existing routines and standard operating procedures. Thus, searches are usually executed in a hierarchical fashion, beginning with those that have the least invasive implications for the organization (Smith & Kaluzny, 1986).

Kaluzny et al. (1987) propose the following hierarchical order for transformations required when there is a "performance gap":

1. *Environmental manipulation:* Activities or programs that affect the environment, to make it more compatible with the organization and its ongoing operations
2. *Process modifications:* Activities or programs that affect internal operating processes without affecting the basic structural configuration or basic mission of the organization
3. *Strategic modifications:* Activities or programs that affect the basic goal or mission of the organization
4. *Reconfiguration:* The development of a new organizational form

Transformational leadership is usually necessary to accomplish the latter two stages and probably not necessary to accomplish the first two stages because the transformations are not as significant and fundamental. However, even with transformational leadership, the process of making strategic modifi-

cations or structural reconfigurations is problematic. Attempts to make an organization more compatible with its environment through strategic or structural transformations so that it can continue or resume growth are not always successful.

Because the culture of an organization tends to select and retain certain types of people and to reinforce certain types of behavior, change does not come easily or quickly. Individuals are very resistant to any change they perceive as adverse. Some combination of "new blood," deletion of "old blood," communication of new values and goals, reinforcement of the new values and goals, board support, and the passage of time is required for successful implementation of strategic or structural change.

Such attempted transformations require reinforcement at the operational level, including human resources management activities. Recruitment and selection of all new employees, but particularly managerial employees, must reinforce the new values. goals, and missions. Those with experience or knowledge in the newer growth areas are preferred. Likewise, those with experience or knowledge related to projected areas of decline or deletion should be avoided. Performance appraisal and compensation practices should also reinforce the new values, goals, and missions.

Numerous authorities underscore that organizational renewal begins at the operations level (Beer, Eisenstat, & Spector, 1989; Kanter, 1989). Transformational leadership implies that top managers nurture the conditions by which renewal is fostered at the customer level. Human resources development through recruitment, selection, training, and career-path management represents an important mechanism available to managers in ensuring that organizational renewal is linked with individual renewal (Bartlett & Goshal, 1990). The goal is to achieve a balance at which the organization culture and human resources capabilities mesh with the vision articulated by top leaders (Bice, 1990). The end result is a transformed organization.

Although innovation is the responsibility of each staff member, chief executives in health care organizations are still responsible for creating a climate conducive for change (Coyne, 1990). From the 1960s to the 1980s, David Jones, who founded Human Inc. with Wendell Cherry, established conditions in which the nursing home chain grew into a multihospital system, and then was transformed into a vertically integrated health care system. His challenge is to stimulate the next innovative evolution of the corporation—possibly a national network of vertically integrated markets (Johnsson, 1991a). Other examples of chief executives setting the tone for innovation in hospitals abound, whether by transforming a hospital through downsizing into a medical center, by establishing management budgets for creative ideas (i.e., specific objectives for formulating new service delivery concepts), or by investing in unconventional medical technology (e.g., proton beam accelerator to treat cancer) (Johnsson 1990). Chief executives typically function as catalysts for change.

Corporate Restructuring

A second major method by which some health care organizations have been able to avoid stagnation and decline is corporate restructuring. This means adding or deleting divisions, adding new services, and/or becoming part of a multi-unit system through merger. Clearly, it is not necessary for an organization to choose *either* transformational leadership *or* corporate restructuring. Both may be implemented simultaneously and often are.

Throughout the 1980s, health care organizations pursued diversification strategies in an effort to revitalize their operations and essentially to improve their prospects relative to the organizational life cycle. In the 1990s, this emphasis on diversification continues, albeit with growing interest in vertical integration. The scorecard on diversification as an effective response to organizational decline is mixed (Clement, 1987, 1988). As shown in Table 4.3, a survey of 524 hospitals nationwide demonstrates that service diversification carries risk as well as return (*"Diversification Success,"* 1990). Freestanding outpatient surgery centers, outpatient diagnostic centers, physical rehabilitation and home health services are rising stars because 60% of the hospitals surveyed report making money on the new service strategies. However, the precise profit margins were not reported. Meanwhile, the hospitals participating in the study had less than a 40% chance of making money on preferred pro-

TABLE 4.3. Diversification Strategy Scorecard

Rising stars (>60% Chance of making money)
- Freestanding outpatient surgery centers
- Freestanding outpatient diagnostic centers
- Physical rehabilitation
- Home health services

Question marks (>40% Chance of making money)
- Cardiac rehabilitation
- Industrial medicine
- Psychiatric services

Dogs (<40% Chance of making money)
- Preferred provider organizations
- Women's medicine
- Skilled nursing unit

Source: *Hospitals*, Vol. 65, No. 9, by permission, May 5, 1991, Copyright 1991, American Hospital Publishing Inc.

vider organizations, women's medicine, and skilled nursing units.

Diversification, therefore, is not a panacea. For example, related diversification by a university hospital into hotel accommodations for patients and families may not work equally well for other university hospitals (Zuckerman, D'Aunno, & Vaughan, 1990). Successful diversification requires understanding inherent differences in diversification strategies, commitment to differentiating services after diversification has occurred, and willingness to enter new territory as a "first mover" (Shortell, 1990). By the 1990s, the adoption of diversification strategies began to be tempered by recognition of the importance of vertical integration (Fox, 1989). The prognosis is that more hospitals, and especially hospital systems, will become vertically integrated in the future (Brown & McCool, 1990).

As a solution to their failure to grow or out of concern for simple survival, many hospitals have turned to various collaborative forms referred to as "multihospital systems," or simply as "systems" (Fottler, Schermerhorn, Wong, & Money, 1982). Such systems are defined as two or more hospitals owned, leased, or contract-managed by a central organization.

The alleged advantages of systems include increased access to capital, reduction in duplication of services, economies of scale, improved productivity and operating efficiencies, access to management expertise, enhanced employee career mobility, easier employee recruitment, improved access through geographical integration of various levels of care, improvement in quality through increased volume of services for specialized personnel, and increased political power to deal with planning, regulation, and reimbursement issues (Fottler & Vaughan, 1987). Despite these advantages, their actual achievement is difficult. There is a general consensus that hospital systems have yet to fully provide the anticipated benefits to those hospitals joining the systems (Greene, 1989).

The rapid growth in systems between 1960 and 1980 initiated speculation that the majority of all hospitals would join systems by 1990. However, the actual growth has been much more moderate than predicted by some. In 1980, systems accounted for 31% of all hospitals and 35% of all beds. By 1985, these percentages had grown to 38% and 39%, respectively (Fottler & Vaughan, 1987). During the same period, the number of systems shrunk from 267 to 250, indicating that consolidation was occurring. A smaller number of larger systems is emerging.

Horizontal integration (i.e., buying additional hospitals) accounted for the bulk of growth in systems during the 1970s. However, from 1980 to 1985, systems have emphasized vertical integration (i.e., purchase of ambulatory facilities) while deemphasizing horizontal integration. The net impact of these trends is to make it more difficult for unaffiliated, freestanding hospitals to survive in the future by joining systems (Fottler & Vaughan, 1987).

A recent study of acquisition strategies of multihospital systems found that all systems studied were expected to become vertically and horizontally integrated health care services organizations (Alexander, Lewis, & Morrisey, 1985). No system saw itself solely as a provider of hospital services. Instead the strategy called for provision of both insurance and health care delivery. Insurance services were usually linked to participation in preferred-provider or health maintenance organizations. Health care services were viewed on a continuum of ambulatory-primary care, acute inpatient care, and post-discharge recuperative or chronic care services.

Systems have become more particular about the hospitals or other organizations they are willing to acquire. They look primarily to favorable market and management fundamentals in determining which hospitals are likely candidates for merger or acquisition. Limits to the future growth of systems, in addition to their reluctance to purchase marginally profitable facilities, include limits on access to capital, antitrust constraints, and a lack of leadership vision (Alexander et al., 1985).

Multi-institutional systems themselves are subject to life cycles that influence their structure and ultimately their human resources management. For example, many hospital systems are confronting the tenuous balance between centralized and decentralized governance in the 1990s (Greene, 1991a). In many situations, system boards have overruled local or individual hospital member decisions. In other cases, hospital systems (and hospitals) are destructuring to focus greater attention on local operations and markets (Burda, 1990; Greene, 1991a; Johnsson, 1991b; O'Donoghue, 1991). These transitions ultimately disrupt the organization climate and may distract staff from their responsibilities. However, there also are other more fundamental human resource concerns from the evolution of hospital systems (Kinzer, 1990).

What are the human resources implications of acquisition of freestanding facilities by large systems? From the viewpoint of the acquired institution the worst-case alternative to not being taken over is that all employees will lose their jobs. In the less urgent event of a slow decline. employment will decline by attrition, salary increases will be small or nonexistent, and opportunities for advancement few. So the benefits to the employees of the acquired institution may include continued employment, merit salary increases, and career mobility. In addition, research indicates that systems attempt to stabilize the work force and to improve personnel recruitment and retention policies (Alexander et al., 1985).

However, the chief executive officer in the acquired hospital is seldom kept on. Department directors and other administrative staff also may lose their jobs after acquisition. If the hospital is overstaffed, nonadministrative personnel may be laid off.

Management of the system faces the challenge of modifying the culture of the newly acquired institution, integrating it into the existing system, and returning it to profitability. In addition to implementing new accounting and management information systems, the system must recruit, retain, appraise, and compensate employees in the newly acquired organization in a way that will reinforce the values, missions, and goals it wishes to pursue. Interim conflicts are to be expected. Complete integration of the newly acquired organization is usually a long-term process.

Thus, the search for continued growth is eventually problematical in all organizations. Only proactive management policies that continually examine the organization's structure, strategy, and processes can hope to perpetuate such growth (Langland-Orban & Krasik, 1991). Even in these cases, however, the challenges are significant and short-term setbacks almost inevitable. Human resources management strategies and tactics must reinforce the strategic and structural changes management is attempting to make.

HUMAN RESOURCES CHALLENGES OVER THE ORGANIZATIONAL LIFE CYCLE

Matching Human Resources to the Organizational Life Cycle

There are a number of human resources issues that are more and less important at different points in an organization's life cycle. The growth phase poses problems and challenges different from those of the decline phase and thus requires both different business strategies and different human resources strategies.

Assume that a hospital in the maturity phase of its organizational life cycle has diversified by acquiring an exercise/wellness center. Should the compensation package of the parent be extended to the new addition, which competes in an industry where benefits are not as generous? Or again, assume that a hospital whose inpatient business has been stable for many years finds that its health maintenance organization is growing very rapidly and holds a strong position in an expanding market. Are the hospital's traditional criteria for selecting, promoting, and compensating health care executives appropriate to the management of this growing sector? Do personnel policies in recruitment, selection, training, and compensation developed during a hospital's growth cycle still fit during the maturity phase and the decline phase?

These examples indicate not only that different human resources policies are called for during different phases of the life cycle, but that a given organization might have different subunits at different points in their life cycles at the same time. In the latter case, the application of uniform personnel policies to all subunits would be inappropriate.

The conditions of decline facing some segments of the health care industry (e.g., inpatient hospital care) stem from both federal policy (e.g., prospective payment systems) and increased competition. The duration of the decline promises to be long term for these segments. The conditions of decline are serious enough to threaten the survival of many health care organizations, whose choice of domain is generally limited by their stakeholders. Multiple stakeholders exist both inside and outside of these organizations, demanding different types of performance and threatening to withdraw support. The demand for traditional services is decreasing, and public support is tenuous.

For all of these reasons, the management of organizational decline in health care organizations is particularly problematic. After a strategy for preventing or reversing organizational decline has been developed, its successful implementation depends on how well human resources are managed.

Matching Human Resources to Strategic Objectives

The examples above also illustrate the problem of matching human resources to strategic management of the organization. Effective organization and management of human resources is both a precondition for successful implementation of strategy and a reflection of that strategy. Attracting and retaining the right people, motivating and rewarding them for good performance, designing appropriate training programs, and planning for the replacement of key people are fundamental to the implementation of the organization's strategy.

Although these principles are not in dispute, health care executives have been slow to adapt them to the portfolio concept of managing diverse organizational activities. Whereas the theme of personnel management has typically been to develop uniform policies and procedures, the portfolio concept of strategy formulation maintains that both human and capital requirements vary according to the strategic posture of the business unit. Human resources systems must be congruent with the strategy of the business units they are meant to support, even if this leads to considerable variation in programs across the organization.

A business unit positioned in a growth industry with a strategy calling for investment, risk taking, and aggressive pursuit of market share will need different kinds of people and will manage them differently from a business unit positioned in a mature or declining industry. The challenge, therefore, is to support a diversity of business unit strategies while maintaining equity and consistency with overall organizational objectives. All too often, however, those charged with the management of human resources are excluded from both the process of strategy formulation and implementation.

Life Cycle, Strategy, and Human Resources Management

Table 4.4 integrates both the preceding discussion and the human resources management functions covered in upcoming chapters. Five stages in the organizational

and/or service unit life cycle are delineated, including two conditions of decline: terminal and reversible. Generic strategies most appropriate at each stage are noted, along with specific human resources strategies and tactics required for successful implementation of these strategies.

Start-Up Phase

In the start-up stage, the dominant value is entrepreneurship and the major generic strategy is domain creation. The human resources area is typically underdeveloped, informal, and designed to support the dominant entrepreneurial values and strategies. There is little or no human resources planning, and career planning is informal because career opportunities develop naturally as the organization grows.

Because of the high mortality rates of new organizations, there is an understandable emphasis on the short run, "the here and now." Consequently, the recruitment and selection of risk takers (i.e., entrepreneurs) to meet present needs for domain creation are critical. The emphasis is on external recruitment because the organization does not have a large enough base of experienced personnel to rely on internal recruitment for most positions.

There is little formal training, and most of what exists occurs on the job rather than in classroom settings. The emphasis is on creating a cadre of professional, technical, and managerial personnel to meet the requirements for the emerging activities. Performance appraisals tend to be informal and geared to evaluating the individual employee's future contributions. Compensation tends to reflect a policy of incentives based on market share, successful risk taking, and

TABLE 4.4. The Relationship of Organizational/Service Unit Life-Cycle Stage, Generic Strategies, and Human Resources Management Strategies and Tactics

	Organizational or service unit life-cycle stage				
	Start-up	Growth	Maturity	Reversible decline	Terminal decline
Dominant Values	Entrepreneurship	Revenue growth / Market share	Competitiveness	Entrepreneurship	Cost control
Generic Strategies	Domain creation	Domain offense / Domain creation	Domain defense / Domain offense	Domain defense / Domain offense / Domain creation	Domain consolidation / Domain substitution
Strategies and Tactics					
1. Major challenge	1. Recruit/select for present activities	1. Recruit/select for future activities	1. Develop appraisal/reward systems	1. Recruit/select for new activities	1. Manage reduction in force/redeployment
2. Human resources planning	2. Little or none	2. Meet critical manpower needs through job information system and flexible retirement	2. Greater effort to motivate and retain best employees; cross-functional job rotation	2. Planning for selective retention; more closely integrated with strategy; broader job tasks	2. Planning for phased disengagement and outplacement
3. Career planning	3. Informal; natural career growth	3. Rewards for developing subordinates; career counseling	3. Provide opportunities for job enrichment, lateral transfers, formalized, career ladders	3. Avoid early retirement; match new needs with skills of those retained	3. Little or none
4. Recruitment/selection	4. Recruit risktakers for present activities; fill	4. Recruit for present and future activities;	4. Less external recruitment; more	4. Recruit executives skilled in reversing	4. Little or none; recruit executives skilled in

114

	existing positions mainly from external sources	long-range perspective; emphasis on selection of "best" candidates internally and externally	internal recruitment; fewer positions to be filled; marketing specialists recruited	decline; recruit entrepreneurs	service termination
5. Training/management development	5. Little formal training; on-the-job training to meet skill requirements of new activities	5. Generic formal training to meet requirements in growth areas; upgrade key personnel	5. Integrate training with career ladders; produce skills necessary to implement strategy	5. Training to meet organization needs	5. Little or none
6. Performance appraisal	6. Informal; emphasize potential for future contributions	6. Measure formal subordinate development as well as future potential; assessment centers	6. Emphasize employee productivity	6. Appraise to determine retention based on present and future contribution	6. Appraisal based on managers' ability to manage disengagement
7. Compensation	7. Based on gaining market share, willingness to take calculated risk, and service improvements; more incentives; fewer benefits	7. Based on building effective organization and subordinate development; more benefits	7. Based on contributions to government/consumer relations or bottom-line performance; fewer incentives; more benefits	7. Based on generating new resources; incentives for entrepreneurs	7. Based on risk avoidance, cost control, and annual profits; flexible separation packages
8. Labor relations	8. Preventive labor relations	8. Preventive labor relations or efforts to prevent greater union penetration	8. Preventive labor relations or productivity bargaining	8. Preventive labor relations, or minimize impact of union by "giveback" bargaining	8. Preventive labor relations or negotiations to terminate services

service improvements. Fringe benefits are limited. The key issue in labor relations is to prevent a union election victory by meeting employee needs in other ways (e.g., good communication, informality, charismatic leadership, competitive wages, unique growth opportunities).

A health care organization in the start-up stage will emphasize recruiting marketing managers to develop new markets (domain creation) and physicians to provide the necessary services after these markets have been established. When these two groups are in place, other professional and administrative staff are recruited as needed. The evolution of new services within health care organizations may also necessitate similar human resources responses. Whether a hospital adds an ambulatory care center (Bigelow & Arndt, 1991), geriatric units (Capitman et al., 1988), coordinated care programs (Warrick, Christianson, Williams, & Netting, 1990), or some other initiative, intra-organizational start-ups require commensurate attention to human resources development.

Growth Phase

The growth phase is usually accompanied by increasing formalization of policies and procedures to minimize inequities in different subunits of the organization. Part of this formalization process is increased long-range planning and recruitment/selection for staffing *future,* as well as present, needs. Job posting and job information systems become institutionalized to enhance internal recruiting. Retirement systems tend to be flexible enough to allow the organization to retain its most productive experienced employees irrespective of age.

During the growth phase, managers should be rewarded for developing subordinates and helping them plan their careers within the organization. Recruitment and selection activities are not only more formalized, but they are based on objective data generated through job analysis so that the "best" candidates are chosen: this usually means those who can provide or expand existing services (domain offense) or provide or create new services in growth areas (domain creation).

Training also becomes more formalized during the growth phase and tends to focus on developing the individual employee through generic approaches (i.e., training that is not specific to the employee's present position). This type of training facilitates upgrading of key personnel to growth areas offering greater responsibility. Performance appraisal also tends to be both more formal and more developmental than in the start-up phase. There is an emphasis on subordinate development as well as the individual's future potential. Assessment centers to predict the future potential of administrators are common in the growth phase.

Compensation for managers is usually based on their contribution to the building of an effective organization to cope with the experienced growth as well as subordinate development. Benefits for all employees increase and become institutionalized during the growth phase because resources are available to fund such benefits and the desire exists to recruit top talent to meet growing demands.

Labor relations continues to be preventive during the growth phase unless some portion of the organization's employees becomes unionized. In this event, a policy of containment is usually adopted wherein the organization attempts to constrain further union gains among the work force and to prevent significant union contract inroads into what are viewed as management prerogatives.

There are presently fewer health care organizations in the growth phase than there were in the 1950s, 1960s, and 1970s. Growth organizations either provide ambulatory services (e.g., wellness) or services to the elderly (e.g., nursing homes). In the past, the existence of a cost-plus reimbursement environment allowed growing organizations to become bureaucratized and also overspecialized in terms of work force skills. Growing health care organizations today tend to be leaner and to employ personnel with broader skills. Especially pertinent is the inclusion of clinical staff through both informal and formal networking strategies (Perry, 1991; Shortell, 1989). As in the case of non-health care organizations, the growing phase is characterized by human resources management activities aimed at employee development (through training, job posting, and career counseling) to fill future openings.

Maturity Phase

In the maturity phase of development, an organization's human resources system becomes institutionalized and standardized. The goal is to respond to both legal and employee pressures for equity, while allowing the organization to continue doing what it is already doing with perhaps some expansion of existing activities. This requires that the organization become more competitive in its existing markets in terms of price, quality, or service. Teamwork is emphasized (Horak, Guarino, Knight, & Kweder, 1991). Achieving such a competitive edge requires sophisticated appraisal and reward systems

to measure and reward employee productivity.

Human resources planning emphasizes motivating and retaining the best employees through job enrichment, cross-functional job rotation, lateral transfers, and an emphasis on internal recruitment when higher-level positions are open. Promotion opportunities, however, are more limited than during the growth phase. This situation is partly offset by the more formal nature of career planning, which allows employees to follow well-defined career paths and to be aware of the qualifications required for higher-level positions in their own career paths. The organization's emphasis is on internal recruitment; little external recruitment occurs for positions other than entry level. Because competitiveness requires consumer awareness of the organization and its services, more marketing specialists are recruited.

Training is also geared toward preparing employees for higher-level positions as well as improving their productivity in their present positions. Training needs are identified by analyzing employee deficiencies noted in the performance appraisal forms. The compensation package often rewards those who are effective in dealing with government or consumers as well as bottom-line performance. There are fewer incentive packages at this stage and more employee benefits.

Preventive labor relations continues for nonunion organizations in the maturity phase, while those that have been organized attempt to remain or become competitive by engaging in productivity bargaining. The latter approach is an attempt to control unit labor costs by making compensation increases contingent on productivity increases (Fottler & Maloney, 1979).

Health care organizations in the maturity

phase often attempt to compete by increasing their marketing efforts aimed at both patients and physicians (Lape, 1991). This means that the marketing role is enhanced, and marketing specialists, often from other industries, are recruited to coordinate the effort. At the same time, physicians are evaluated more critically in terms of their contribution to revenue (Smith & Fottler, 1985). Pressure is exerted on those who are far out of line with their colleagues with respect to resources use for particular diagnoses. Upgrading of personnel appraisal systems for other employees is also common during the maturity phase.

Reversible Decline Phase

When an organization is experiencing decline that is viewed as reversible, domain defense followed by domain offense and domain creation are the appropriate generic strategies. The organization is likely to have administrative personnel capable of implementing the first two strategies because these are implemented during the previous maturity phase. Consequently, key human resources challenges are to revitalize the organization and to recruit entrepreneurs who are skilled in domain creation.

Human resources planning becomes more closely aligned with the strategy of reversing decline. The trend toward job specialization is reversed as job task definition becomes broader. Selective retention of the employees capable of contributing to the new areas of growth is emphasized. Many organizations encourage early retirement when trying to reverse decline, but this often leads to loss of the experienced, skilled employees most needed for future growth. A better alternative is to provide flexible work alternatives for key employees (e.g., phased retirement, part-time employment).

The reversal of decline requires the recruitment of executives who have had success in reversing similar declines. Executives who have experienced only growth or stability usually will not manage the situation well, as noted previously in the chapter. The recruitment of entrepreneurs to develop new growth areas is also a critical challenge.

The training programs at this phase are geared to meet immediate organizational needs for domain defense, offense, or creation. Individual employee development for the future is not emphasized. The role of the performance appraisal system is to assess both present contribution and future potential in the areas of future growth. Compensation is often based on potential contribution to new areas of growth, and entrepreneurs are able to negotiate incentive packages. Labor relations remains preventive unless unionization has already occurred. In this event, the emphasis is on "giveback" bargaining, which calls for management aggressiveness in winning compensation and work rule concessions from the union.

Hospitals across the country have typically faced some degree of decline in their inpatient areas within the last 10 years. While they are lobbying and marketing to protect their revenue base and to expand current services (domain defense and domain offense), they are also planning and implementing domain creation strategies. Among the new activities has been development of HMOs, substance abuse clinics, exercise facilities, freestanding emergency clinics, and consulting services of various types.

These attempts to reverse decline in core areas have required hospitals to recruit personnel experienced in the new areas, together with marketing personnel. These individuals are often recruited from other industries and are offered incentive compensation packages that reward the successful development of the opportunity. Failure is penalized by loss of the position. At the same time, present employees are being appraised with greater sophistication in an attempt to determine their present productivity and future potential contributions. Obviously, scrutiny of physician practice patterns to determine contributions to both revenue and costs is a major part of this effort.

Terminal Decline Phase

After the organization has determined that a service unit or the whole organization is facing terminal decline with no possible reversal, the emphasis is on the systematic management of reduction in force and redeployment to other areas in the organization (in the case of a service unit). Control of costs (efficiency) is important because the goal is to avoid losing money during the terminal phase.

There is little or no career planning, training, or management development because future opportunities in the service unit or the organization are nonexistent. Human resources planning emphasizes phased disengagement and outplacement of current employees (Fottler & Schuler, 1984). The only recruitment that occurs involves hiring executives who are skilled at phasing out organizations or subunits of organizations.

Performance appraisal is based on the manager's ability to manage disengagement with a minimum of conflict and avoidance of further economic losses if possible. There is no future orientation. Rewards for executives are based on risk avoidance, cost con-

trol, and annual profits. Separation packages for executives are flexible and individually negotiated. If there is a labor union, negotiations may be held to agree on the process of termination and on the benefits/services terminated employees may expect to receive.

When a health care organization faces terminal decline, it often attempts to find a buyer (e.g., a large chain) to which it can sell out. However, the chains are becoming more selective, and this option may be shrinking for many declining organizations. If all other avenues for reversal of the decline have proved fruitless, the organization begins to plan for termination. This means communicating the decision to terminate and the reasons for this decision. Plans for phased reduction in force and outplacement then need to be implemented.

SUMMARY

All organizations and subunits of organizations evolve and go through predictable phases. At each stage in the organizational life cycle, different strategies for growth, revitalization, and survival are appropriate. Successful formulation and implementation of these strategies are required if the organization is to avoid premature decline and death. The implementation of such strategies requires appropriate human resources strategies and tactics as discussed above. Ignorance of the appropriate linkages between business strategies and human resources strategy/tactics may mean organizational failure even if the strategy itself is appropriate.

Health care organizations need to be aware of where they are in terms of their organizational and service subunit life cycles. This knowledge will help them to develop and implement appropriate organizational strategies supported by reinforcing human resources strategies and tactics. The increasingly competitive health care market will penalize organizations that fail to formulate and implement appropriate strategies.

The start-up and growth phases of the organizational life cycle tend to emphasize strategies Miles and Snow (1978) describe as "prospector." The prospector organization innovates early in the face of product/market opportunities. It also pursues a particular type of "differentiation" strategy (Porter, 1980). This involves creating value that is perceived as unique. It may take many forms, including unique product or service attributes, quality, or service. Costs are not a key ingredient.

At the operational level, there is an emphasis on open communications, informality, and productivity. Although the administrative structure is developing during the growth phase, the emphasis is still on entrepreneurial activity and producing results. Aspirations exceed achievements.

During the maturity and decline phases, the strategic emphasis is on either cost leadership or focus (Porter, 1980). Cost leaders are often market share leaders and pay great attention to asset use, employee productivity, and discretionary expenses. Consumers purchase the products or services primarily because they cost less than equivalent offerings by competitors. Focus involves competing in a narrow segment based on consumer type, service type, geography, or other factors. In Miles and Snow's (1978) terms, organizations involved with cost leadership or focus tend to be "defenders" or "reactors." A defender maintains a stable offering and may choose to exploit its stability in the form of low costs or other competitive weapons. A

"reactor" follows the lead of other organizations and consequently fails to achieve the benefit of early exploitation.

At the operational level, the maturity and decline phases are characterized by bureaucracy and declining internal response to the external environment. The administrative structure becomes an end in itself, and innovation is discouraged.

Management of the health organization also needs to be aware of differences in life stage and strategies in different subunits. These differences require different human resources strategies and tactics to implement the subunit strategy successfully. Bureaucratic uniformity in the human resources system across the entire organization may stifle some units and provide too much flexibility to others. Health organizations will have to determine which policies should be uniform (and therefore centralized) and which ones need to be flexible and nonuniform (and therefore decentralized).

Discussion Questions

1. Why do most organizations eventually experience stagnation and decline? Is such stagnation and decline inevitable? What managerial actions may facilitate continued growth (if so desired) while preventing or postponing decline? What actions accelerate such decline?

2. What are the early and later symptoms of organization decline?

3. Discuss the five types of generic strategies for responding to organizational decline, give specific health care examples for each, and indicate under what conditions each is appropriate.

4. What are the major causes of organizational decline in health care?
5. How can health care organizations prevent or reverse organizational stagnation or decline? Be sure to include strategic and tactical responses.
6. Discuss each of the five stages in the organizational or service unit life cycle in detail. What are the major human resources challenges at each stage?
7. Why is it important to match business strategies with human resources strategies and tactics? Give specific examples of such matching.

CASE

Mr. Smith is the administrator of Metropolitan Hospital, a nonprofit institution located in a medium-size southern city. Since the early 1980s, the inpatient occupancy rate has fallen steadily to 50.2% during the most recent year. With the approval of the board of directors, the hospital has recently established an Independent Practice Association (IPA) model HMO with linkages to a variety of other health care facilities. This program now must be properly priced and marketed to prospective enrollees through physicians and employers.

Mr. Smith and Mr. Kelley (the personnel director) have been interviewing prospective candidates for the position of administrator of the new IPA. Several issues that require decisions have been raised during these interviews. The applicants view this opportunity as a high-risk entrepreneurial activity. They are concerned with the possibility of failure and subsequent loss of position. At the same time, they feel success in promoting this program is crucial to the hospital's future and should be associated with significant re-

wards for the administrator and other members of the administrative team. In addition to the issue of incentive compensation, the applicants have also discussed autonomy in terms of both strategy and tactics (including freedom from the hospital's human resources policies and procedures).

Mr. Smith and Mr. Kelley have made no commitment to anyone, but Mr. Kelley feels the hospital's policies should apply to all employees. You are an administrative resident at the hospital and they have asked your opinion.

Case Discussion Questions

1. Should the hospital modify its personnel policies and procedures to accommodate its new venture into HMOs? Why or why not? How could the administration defend itself against charges of inequity?
2. What would be the implications of uniform personnel policies and procedures and lack of administrator autonomy on the probable success of this venture? Why?

REFERENCES

Adizes, I. (1979). Organizational passages: Diagnosing and treating life cycle problems in organizations. *Organizational Dynamics, 8,* 3–25.

Alexander, J.A., Lewis, B.L., & Morrisey, M.A. (1985). Acquisition strategies of multihospital systems. *Health Affairs, 4,* 49–66.

Bartlett, C.A., & Goshal, S. (1990). Matrix management: Not a structure, a frame of mind. *Harvard Business Review, 68*(4), 138–145.

Beer, M., Eisenstat, R.A., & Spector, B. (1989).

Why change programs don't produce change. *Harvard Business Review, 67*(6), 85–92.

Benson, J.K. (1975). The interorganizational network as a political economy. *Administrative Science Quarterly, 20,* 229–249.

Bice, M. (1990). Corporate culture must foster innovation. *Hospitals, 64*(22), 58.

Bigelow, B., & Arndt, M. (1991). Ambulatory care centers: Are they a competitive advantage? *Hospital and Health Services Administration, 36*(3), 351–363.

Boulding, K.E. (1981). *Evolutionary economics.* Beverly Hills: Sage.

Brown, M., & McCool, B.P. (1990). Health care systems: Predictions for the future. *Healthcare Management Review, 15*(3), 87–94.

Burda, D. (1990). Untangling management structures. *Modern Healthcare, 10*(17), 20–28.

Burns, M., & Mauet, A.R. (1989). Patrolling the turbulent borderland: Managerial strategies for a changing health care environment. *Healthcare Management Review, 14*(1), 7–12.

Cameron, K.S. (1981). Domains of organizational effectiveness in colleges and universities. *Academy of Management Journal, 24,* 25–47.

Cameron, K.S. (1983). Strategic responses to conditions of decline: Higher education and the private sector. *Journal of Higher Education, 54,* 359–380.

Capitman, J.A., Prottas, J., MacAdam, M., Leutz, W., Westwater, D., & Yee, D.Y. (1988). A descriptive framework for new hospital roles in geriatric care. *Healthcare Financing Review, 12*(2), 17–25.

Clement, J.P. (1987). Does hospital diversification improve financial outcomes? *Medical Care, 21,* 988–1001.

Clement, J.P. (1988). Corporate diversification: Expectations and outcomes. *Healthcare Management Review, 13,* 7–13.

Coyne, W. (1990). Innovation as a competitive advantage. *Hospitals, 64*(10), 88.

Diversification success varies, survey shows, (1990). *Hospitals, 65*(9), 16.

Dunbar, R.L.M., & Goldberg, W.H. (1978). Crisis development and strategic response in European corporations. In C.F. Smart & W.T. Stanbury (Eds.), *Studies in Crisis Management* (pp. 112–148). Toronto: Butterworth.

Durham, J.W., & Smith, H.L. (1982). Toward a general theory of organizational deterioration. *Administration and Society, 14,* 373–400.

Fink, S.L., Beak, J., & Taddeo, K. (1971). Organizational crisis and change. *Journal of Applied Behavior Science, 7,* 15–37.

Ford, J.D. (1980a). The administrative component in growing and declining organizations: A longitudinal analysis. *Academy of Management Journal, 23,* 615–630.

Ford, J.D. (1980b). The occurrence of structural hystersis in declining organizations. *Academy of Management Review, 5,* 561–575.

Foreman, S.E., & Roberts, R.D. (1991). The power of health care value-adding partnership: Meeting competition through cooperation. *Hospital and Health Services Administration, 36*(2), 175–190.

Fottler, M.D., & Maloney, W.F. (1979). Guidelines to productivity bargaining in the health care industry. *Health Care Management Review, 4,* 375–388.

Fottler, M.D., Schermerhorn, J.R., Wong, J., & Money, W.H. (1982). Multi-institutional arrangements in health care. *Academy of Management Review, 7,* 67–79.

Fottler, M.D., & Schuler, D.W. (1984). Reducing the economic and human costs of layoffs. *Business Horizons, 27*(4), 9–15.

Fottler, M.D., Smith, H.L., & Mueller, H.J. (1986). Retrenchment in health care organizations: Theory and practice. *Hospitals and Health Services Administration, 31,* 29–43.

Fottler, M.D., & Vaughan, D.G. (1987). Multihospital systems. In L.F. Wolper & J.J. Pena (Eds.), *Health care administration: Principles and practice* (pp. 246–265). Rockville, MD: Aspen Systems, 1987.

Fox, W. (1989). Vertical integration strategies: More promising than diversification.

Healthcare Management Review, 14(3), 49–56.

Goldsmith, J. (1989). A radical prescription for hospitals. *Harvard Business Review, 67*(3), 104–111.

Greene, J. (1989). Promises, promises. *Modern Healthcare, 19*(42), 24–36.

Greene, J. (1991a). Hospitals dismantle elaborate corporate restructuring. *Modern Healthcare, 21*(19), 31–33.

Hall, D.T., & Mansfield, R. (1971). Organizational and individual response to external stress. *Administrative Science Quarterly, 16,* 533–547.

Hall, R.I. (1976). A system pathology of an organization: The rise and fall of the old *Saturday Evening Post. Administrative Science Quarterly, 21,* 185–211.

Hedberg, Bo.L.T., Nystrom, P.C., & Starbuck, W.H. (1976). Camping on seesaws: Prescriptions for a self-designing organization. *Administrative Science Quarterly, 21,* 41–65.

Hermann, C.F. (1963). Some consequences of crisis which limit the viability of organizations. *Administrative Science Quarterly, 8,* 61–82.

Hirschman, A.O. (1970). *Exit, voice, and loyalty.* Cambridge: Harvard University Press.

Holsti, O.R. (1978). Limitations on cognitive abilities in the face of crisis. In C.F. Smart & W.T. Stanbury (Eds.), *Studies in Crisis Management* (pp. 86–104). Toronto: Butterworth.

Horak, B.J., Guarino, J.H., Knight, C.C., & Kweder, S.L. (1991). Building team on a medical floor. *Healthcare Management Review, 16*(2), 65–71.

Janis, I.L. (1972). *Victims of group think.* Boston: Houghton Mifflin.

Janis, I.L., & Mann, L. (1977). Emergency decision-making: A theoretical analysis of responses to disaster warnings. *Journal of Human Stress, 32*(2), 35–48.

Jick, T.D. (1979a). *Process and impacts of a merger: Individual and organizational perspective.* Unpublished doctoral dissertation, Cornell University, Ithaca, New York.

Jick, T.D. (1979b). Mixing qualitative and quantitative methods: Triangulation in action. *Administrative Science Quarterly, 24,* 602–611.

Johnsson, J. (1990). CEOs as risk takers—From visions to reality. *Hospitals, 64*(22), 24–34.

Johnsson, J. (1991a). David Jones: Reinventing humans for the 1990s. *Hospitals, 65*(10), 55–56.

Johnsson, J. (1991b). Hospitals dismantle elaborate corporate restructuring. *Hospitals, 65*(B), 41–46.

Kaluzny, A.D., Jaeger, B.J., & Habib, K.M. (1987). *Multi-institutional systems management.* Owings Mill, MD: National Health Publishing.

Kanter, R.M. (1989). The new managerial work. *Harvard Business Review, 67*(b), 85–92.

Kauffman, J.F. (1982). Some perspective on hard times. *Review of Higher Education, 6*(1), 69–78.

Kinzer, D.M. (1990). Twelve laws of hospital interaction. *Healthcare Management Review, 15*(2), 15–19.

Langland-Orban, B., & Krasik, E.R. (1991). Successful business planning for new programs in health care organizations. *Evaluation and the Health Professions, 14*(1), 76–81.

Lape, D.H. (1991). A winning proposition. *Health Progress, 72*(8), 61, 70.

Levine, C.H. (1978a). Organizational decline and cutback management. *Public Administration Review, 38,* 316–325.

Levine, C.H. (1978b). More on cutback management: Hard questions for hard times. *Public Administration Review, 38,* 316–325.

March, J.G., & Simon, H. (1958). *Organizations.* New York: Wiley.

Meyer, M.W. (1975). Organizational domains. *American Sociological Review, 40,* 599–615.

Miles, R.E., & Snow, C.C. (1978). *Organizational strategy, structure, and processes.* New York: McGraw-Hill.

Miles, R.H., & Cameron, K.S. (1982). *Coffin nails and corporate strategies.* Englewood Cliffs, NJ: Prentice-Hall.

Miller, D. (1977). Common syndromes of

business failure. *Business Horizons, 20*(3), 43–53.

Miller, D., & Friesen, P.H. (1980). Momentum and revolution in organizational adaptation. *Academy of Management Journal, 23,* 591–614.

Miller, J.W., & Walmsley-Ault, J. (1990). The hospital-health center collaborative: A model for ambulatory care. *Journal of Ambulatory Care Management, 13*(4), 22–27.

Mintzberg, H. (1979). *The structuring of organizations.* Englewood Cliffs, NJ: Harper & Row.

O'Donoghue, C., Sr. (1991). A change from the top. *Health Progress, 72*(6), 64–67.

Perry, L. (1991). Advising group to hospitals: Snap up physician practices. *Modern Healthcare, 21*(5), 40.

Pfeffer, J., & Salancik, G. R. (1978). *The external control of organizations: A resource dependence perspective.* New York: Harper & Row.

Porter, M. (1980). *Competitive strategy.* New York: Free Press.

Post, J.E. (1978). *Corporate behavior and social change.* Reston, VA: Reston.

Quinn, R., & Cameron, K.S. (1983). Life cycles and shifting criteria of effectiveness. *Management Science, 29,* 33–51.

Rondine, T. (1975). Organizational identification: Issues and implications. *Organizational Behavior and Human Performance, 13,* 95–109.

Scott, W. (1976). The management of decline. *Conference Board Record, 13*(6), June, 56–59.

Shortell, S.M. (1989). Study shows what industry will need to succeed in '90s. *Modern Healthcare, 19*(42), 38–42.

Shortell, S.M. (1990). Diversification benefits innovative leader. *Modern Healthcare, 20*(10), 38.

Shortell, S., & Wickizer, T.M. (1984). New program development: Issues in managing vertical integration. In J.R. Kimberly & R.E. Quinn (Eds.), *Managing Organizational Transitions* (pp. 164–192). Homewood, IL: Irwin.

Smart, C., & Vertinsky, I. (1977). Designs for crisis decision units. *Administrative Science Quarterly, 22,* 640–657.

Smith, D.B., & Kaluzny, A.D. (1986). *The white labyrinth: A guide to the health care system* (2nd ed.). Ann Arbor, MI: Health Administration Press.

Smith, H.L., & Fottler, M.D. (1985). *Prospective payment: Managing for operational effectiveness.* Rockville, MD: Aspen Systems.

Snow, C., & Hrebiniak, L. (1980). Strategy, distinctive competence, and organizational performance. *Administrative Science Quarterly, 25,* 317–336.

Starbuck, W.H. (1976). Organizations and their environments. In M. Dunnette (Ed.), *Handbook of industrial and organizational psychology* (pp. 1–23). Skokie, IL: Rand McNally.

Starbuck, W.H., Greve, A., & Hedberg, Bo.L.T. (1978). Responding to crisis. *Journal of Business Administration, 9,* 111–137.

Starbuck, W.H., & Hedberg, Bo.L.T. (1977). Saving an organization from a stagnating environment. In H. Thorelli (Ed.). *Strategy + structure = performance* (pp. 212–234). Bloomington: Indiana University Press.

Staw, B.M., Sandelands, L.E., & Dutton, J.E. (1981). Threat-rigidity effects in organizational behavior: A multilevel analysis. *Administrative Science Quarterly, 26,* 501–524.

Summers, J. (1977). Management by crisis. *Public Personnel Management, 4,* 194–200.

Thompson, J.D. (1967). *Organizations in action.* New York: McGraw-Hill.

Warrick, L.H., Christianson, F.G., Williams, F.G., & Netting, F.E. (1990). *Hospitals and Health Services Administration, 35*(4), 505–524.

Whetten, D.A. (1980a). Sources, responses, and effects of organizational decline. In J. Kimberly & R. Miles (Eds.), *The organizational life cycle* (pp. 342–374). San Francisco: Jossey-Bass.

Whetten, D.A. (1980b). Organizational decline: A neglected topic in organizational science. *Academy of Management Review, 5,* 577–588.

Whetten, D.A. (1981). Organizational responses to scarcity—Exploring the obstacles to innovative approaches to retrenchment in education. *Educational Administration Quarterly, 17*(3), 80–97.

Zammuto, R.F. (1982). *Assessing organizational effectiveness: Systems change, adaptation, and strategy.* Albany: SUNY Press.

Zammuto, R.F. (1984). Are liberal arts colleges an endangered species? *Journal of Higher Education, 55,* 184–211.

Zammuto, R.F., & Cameron, K.S. (1985). Environmental decline and organizational response. In B.M. Staw & L.L. Cummings (Eds.), *Research in organizational behavior: Vol. 7* (pp. 223–262). Greenwich, CT: JAI Press.

Zuckerman, H.S., D'Aunno, T.A., & Vaughan, T.E. (1990). The strategies and anatomy of university hospitals in competitive environments. *Hospital and Health Services Administrations, 35*(1), 103–120.

PART TWO

STRUCTURAL AND BEHAVIORAL SYSTEMS

CHAPTER

THE ROLE OF STRUCTURE AND TECHNOLOGY

Bruce Fried

James W. Begun

LEARNING OBJECTIVES

Upon completing this chapter, the reader should be able to . . .

- Identify three key dimensions of an organization's structure.
- Identify characteristics of the simple structure, machine bureaucracy, and professional bureaucracy.
- Understand how selected human resources functions (e.g., job design, selection and placement, performance appraisal, compensation management, training and development) differ in the simple structure, machine bureaucracy, and professional bureaucracy.
- Identify several examples of recent changes in the technology of health care organizations that affect human resources.
- Classify the technologies of different health care organizations and their subunits based on the degree of routineness of the technologies.
- Understand how selected human resources functions (e.g., job design, selection, performance appraisal, reward systems, development) differ based on the routineness of the technology of an organization or subunit.

INTRODUCTION

Two key attributes of organizations that have significant effects on human resources management functions are the structure and the technology of the organization. In this chapter, we focus on these two attributes because they are of critical importance to the design of effective human resources systems.

In this chapter, a conceptual overview of each attribute is provided, followed by dis-cussions of how each affects selected human resources management functions. The impact of organizational structure and technology on functions such as job design, selection, training and development, performance appraisal, and rewards, is considered. After reading this chapter, students and managers should be better able to identify and classify types of organizational structures and technologies and identify human resources management practices that are appropriate for those different types of structures and technologies.

CONCEPTUALIZING ORGANIZATIONAL STRUCTURE

Central to the smooth functioning of any organization is a set of rules and norms, procedures, and roles that govern the distribution of tasks in the organization. These rules, roles, and procedures determine the way in which the organization differentiates and integrates work activities, and together they are referred to as the organization's structure. Typically, an organization's structure is formally defined by an organizational chart and by organizational policies and procedures, including job descriptions. Power relationships among organizational members and unwritten norms also contribute to defining an organization's structure. These formal documents and informal relationships determine who performs organizational tasks and how the tasks are integrated in the production of a product or service. In this way, structure has a direct impact on human resources in an organization and is interrelated to the organization's technologies for producing outputs.

Levels and Dimensions of Structure

Organizational structures can be investigated at several different levels, especially in large, complex organizations. First, most organizations are linked to other organizations formally through contracts, buying-selling relationships, or interlocking boards, and less formally through communications, liaison personnel, or social contacts. *Interorganizational* structures define the ways in which tasks are differentiated and coordinated among the multiple organizations. Structure at the *organization* level refers to the division of tasks within a whole organization, while *subunits* of organizations, such as departments, have structural characteristics of their own. Structures at each level may vary substantially, requiring different human resources management policies or flexibility in the application of the same policies.

It is important to note the distinction between formal organizational structures, which are reflected in written documents, and informal structures, which may complement or conflict with the formal structures. It is critical that managers recognize that both types of structures exist and that changes in formal structures often are insufficient to produce an expected outcome unless the formal changes are accompanied by changes in informal structures. For example, many organizations have a problem with employee pilfering of office supplies. An informal norm that supports employee use of small quantities of office supplies for personal needs may be more powerful and thus more important to address than written policies restricting employee access to and use of supplies.

In order to describe organizational structures, we employ the three key dimensions of structures: *formalization, centralization,* and *complexity.* Formalization refers to the degree to which roles, rules, and procedures are specified in writing. Formalization attempts to standardize behavior across large numbers of employees. Formalization promotes equity in treatment of individuals in the same categories (e.g., workers in the same job classification are evaluated in the same time frame) and across time (e.g., new employees are offered the same fringe benefits available to existing employees). Formalized policies and procedures serve as part of an organization's "memory bank," thus eliminating the need to repeatedly debate and decide complex and controversial issues.

Centralization is the degree to which discretion over decisions is concentrated at a single point, usually at the top of the organization or at the top of subunits of the organization. An organization may be decentralized as a whole organization, with authority dispersed to subunits, but its subunits may be centralized, with significant authority invested in one position at the top of the subunit. Centralization facilitates quick and standardized decision making, often at the expense of involvement of other parties in the process.

Complexity is the degree of task differentiation within the organization—the number of different tasks being performed. Complexity can be introduced vertically by adding hierarchical layers of workers, or horizontally by adding new roles or activities to the organization. Horizontal complexity is indicated by job specialization. As more specialized jobs are added to an organization, its complexity grows. Although often necessary for efficient production of services, horizontal specialization makes it more difficult for organizations to coordinate their different functions. Most organizations group workers horizontally based on their function (e.g., nursing, dietary services) and/or the product or service to which they contribute (e.g., oncology services, health promotion programs). Horizontal differentiation of workers by geographic area also is common in large organizations, with workers assigned to different regional divisions of the organization.

Vertical complexity is indicated by the number of hierarchical levels in the organization. More levels make it more difficult for top management to control work activities. Often, vertical and horizontal complexity accompany each other, because as job specialization increases, more coordinating managers (i.e., vertical complexity) are added to the hierarchy.

Patterns in Organizational Structure

Despite the fact that each organization is structurally unique, patterns of structural variation can be observed across different organizations. Typologies of organizational structures convey the essence of these major patterns. Typologies are simplified images designed to summarize and communicate succinctly.

One useful typology of organizations was developed by Mintzberg (1983), who delineates five major organizational types. The *simple structure* is usually highly centralized but not highly formalized or complex. Many small business organizations fit this mold, with decision-making power retained at a strategic apex. This centralization enables the organization to move quickly in response to changes in the organization's external environment. Within health care, simple structures are represented by such organizations as small firms that produce or distribute medical supplies, waste management services, or temporary nursing services. Small delivery organizations, such as the solo or small group medical practice, also have many characteristics of the simple structure. In these organizations, control is likely to be centralized in a dominant physician-owner, and rules, policies, and procedures are likely to be informal rather than written.

A second type of organization is the *machine bureaucracy,* which is highly formalized, relatively complex, and centralized. Tasks are specialized, and a wide variety of rules and procedures (i.e., formalization) serves to coordinate operations throughout the organization. Often, simple structures evolve into machine bureaucracies as they grow. Within the health care arena, machine bureaucracies are approximated by large health insurers, pharmaceutical manufacturers, and dietary service distributors. The nursing home, under the centralized control of an administrator, may also have many machine bureaucracy features.

A form of organization related to the machine bureaucracy is the *divisionalized form,* which introduces decentralization into the machine bureaucracy through the creation of separate divisions. Each division functions separately like a machine bureaucracy.

The machine bureaucracy can be contrasted to the fourth type of structure, the *professional bureaucracy,* which, as the name implies, has many professional members, resulting in a lower degree of centralization and formalization, while complexity is even higher. Professional specialists have a wide range of autonomy in decision making, unlike in the machine bureaucracy. For professional employees, behavior is controlled by standardized professional education rather than the extensive formalization found in the machine bureaucracy. The general hospital, with its vast array of skilled clinical groups, is an example of the professional bureaucracy. By its nature, most health care delivery takes place in organizations that have key attributes of the professional bureaucracy.

The *adhocracy* is the last of Mintzberg's forms, and it is the least common of the five. Adhocracies are flexible organizations composed of separate project groups that shift in composition over time. Adhocracies exhibit low levels of formalization and centralization, but are considered highly complex structures. Specialists do their work in small project teams. This form of organization encourages innovation and promotes rapid response to external environmental changes.

THE INFLUENCE OF ORGANIZATIONAL STRUCTURE ON THE HUMAN RESOURCES FUNCTIONS

Human resources managers must be familiar with the structural characteristics of their organization and each of its subunits because of their implications for human resources management. To illustrate these implications, we discuss the influence of an organization's structure on six important human resources management functions: job analysis and design, recruitment and retention, performance appraisal, compensation management, and training and development.

Examples are drawn primarily from health services organizations that represent simple structures, machine bureaucracies, and professional bureaucracies.

Structure and Job Analysis and Design

In small, simple organizations, roles exhibit low specialization, and there are relatively few job titles. In a small outpatient urgicenter, for example, a single individual may handle patient telephone calls and cash receipts, schedule appointments, transcribe medical dictation, maintain medical records, and perhaps even perform some clinical services. In these settings, it is important that workers understand the need for role flexibility and role interchangeability. Otherwise, resistance to the undertaking of a wide variety of tasks can be expected.

As organizations increase in structural complexity, new issues regarding job design begin to arise. Specialists are assigned tasks that are increasingly narrow, and role interchangeability declines. As medical groups reach a size of about six physician members, for example, there are pressures to hire a professional manager (Hamity & Gauss, 1982). This development has a direct impact on the job design of the clinical workers, who are more able to focus on their clinical responsibilities. The role of a group practice manager is a difficult one, however, as he or she may answer to a number of physicians, who may not coordinate their demands; and nonmedical personnel, who report to the manager, may be pressured to respond to the conflicting demands of physicians and other clinicians. To be effective, the decentralization of authority to the manager from the physician-owners must be formalized and endorsed by the physicians. A clear chain of command helps to clarify reporting relationships, but physicians must support the formal system of authority in everyday interactions as well.

Formalized job descriptions may number in the single digits in the small group medical practice, in double digits in the nursing home, and in triple digits in the hospital. The job description manual of the American Society for Hospital Personnel Administration (ASHPA) (1985) of the American Hospital Association, for example, lists 335 different job descriptions for hospital workers. In large hospitals and other bureaucracies, job analysis is a highly formalized process. The incumbent in a particular job may complete a questionnaire, with final development of the job description and job specifications being a product of collaboration between the department head and the human resources management department. Depending on the position, the documentation can become quite elaborate. Moreover, given the high degree of change in hospital jobs over time, some hospitals attempt to audit all positions periodically.

Although the elaborate process of job analysis in hospitals would appear to clarify the design of jobs, overspecialization has been associated with such task characteristics as low autonomy, lack of variety, and lack of identity (Bechtold, Szilagzyi, & Sims, 1980). In turn, these attributes influence the level of employee satisfaction and ultimately the retention of personnel. The implication is that in machine and professional bureaucracies it may be necessary to redesign jobs at the expense of specialization (i.e., to expand task autonomy, identity, and variety in an attempt to make the work more inherently meaningful).

However, the reversal of specialization through the redesign of jobs can create problems. If employees who are affected by the redesign are unionized, unions may resist the task changes. This is particularly likely if existing work rules are threatened. The inherent limitations in certain jobs (e.g., housekeeping), lack of employee desire for redesign, and the impossibility of redesigning all jobs in a bureaucracy pose additional obstacles to restructuring roles to promote job satisfaction.

In addition to its influence on the content and scope of specific jobs, structure is important in grouping the myriad of jobs and in establishing relationships among the jobs. In most bureaucracies (e.g., nursing homes, hospitals), functional departments are the major way to group different jobs. Departmentalization in hospitals is extensive, as indicated by departments ranging from dietary and housekeeping to nursing and the various specialized clinical services. Further differentiation is visible in the various systems of reporting relationships. Neuhauser (1972) notes that physicians use a loose, organic structure; nurses and skilled technicians use a more hierarchical structure; and less skilled personnel use an even more hierarchical structure. Central management is less able to redesign tasks in the more skilled clinical areas of health care organizations.

The need for coordination across departments raises basic operational issues in the machine bureaucracy and more difficult issues in the professional bureaucracy. For example, whereas nursing homes generally can emphasize traditional hierarchy and rules as the basic means of coordination, the complexity of hospitals usually creates pressure to develop additional bases for departmental relationships. Unit managers, scheduling departments, and management committees all exemplify structural elaboration to meet the greater need for lateral coordination in hospitals, but the best known mechanism is probably the patient care team. Consisting of the physician who is responsible for the patient and the other personnel (e.g., nurses) who assist, the teams form and dissolve as patients enter and leave the hospital. However, formalization remains important, especially because the patient's record is a crucial coordinating device for the different team members. As Neuhauser (1972) notes, this is basically a matrix organizational structure. Vertical coordination, through the departments, exists simultaneously with horizontal coordination, through the clinician who heads the team. Nurses and other health personnel are located in functional departments, but they are brought together to attend particular patients under a physician's supervision. The unity of command principle notwithstanding, effective coordination makes this "two bosses" approach appear to be functional. The logical extension of this structure is a "product" structure wherein nonphysician personnel are located in the different clinical departments of the medical staff. That structure explicitly recognizes that physicians have authority over basic operational activities of other clinicians. Product structuring is more common in hospitals that are complex (i.e., offer a diversity of services) and that face competitive pressures in the product areas. When product areas are not defined around medical departments, as is often the case, new roles for nonphysician administrators and clinicians are rapidly developing. Appropriate design of these positions is critical to the ability of product managers to effectively do their work (Charns & Tewksbury, 1993).

Structure and Recruitment and Retention

The processes used to select and place employees in organizations also are affected by the employing organization's sructure. As organizations increase in size, formalization, and complexity, they are more likely to employ sophisticated selection and placement methodologies, such as job analysis and testing of new employees. Centralized control of such functions in a human resources department, typical of machine and professional bureaucracies, facilitates the wider use of sophisticated selection and placement methodologies.

Recruitment and retention of applicants selected by the organization are critical issues for any health services delivery organization, particularly for the professional bureaucracy that employs a large number of highly specialized clinicians. Organization structures can affect recruitment and retention profoundly. In the simple organizational structure, recruitment and retention are made difficult by the fact that formalization is low. Job descriptions and job specifications are basic elements in the recruitment process, and the employee's understanding of responsibilities is a key to retention. In simple structures, where recruiting and retention are apt to be tangential tasks for heads of the organization, negative consequences may accrue. New employees may misunderstand their responsibilities. Adequate socialization and training may not occur. The initial search for candidates may be too limited, and screening may be superficial.

As organizations become more formalized, recruiting and retention are more likely to be assigned to human resources management personnel. The process of recruiting is likely to be more systematic. A large group practice manager, for instance, is likely to make the time to interview candidates and to scrutinize references. Information about expectations is likely to be written and, therefore, less easily misunderstood. In the nursing home and hospital, recruiting and retention are likely to be pursued more systematically to achieve a large, complex work force. As the need for more specialized personnel increases, so does the reach of recruitment efforts, such as the use of national trade publications or contacts with academic health science centers. Moreover, hospitals may draw on nonstandardized recruitment methods (e.g., use of a nurse registry) to meet their distinctive needs.

In comparison to simpler organizations, the complexity of a hospital usually requires a more elaborate and formalized orientation for new employees. Indeed, the orientation is likely to occur at three levels: hospital-wide, departmental, and job-specific.

Most health care organizations experience periodic problems recruiting and/or retaining specific types of clinical providers (e.g., nurses or physical therapists). Structural attributes of the organization can be manipulated to address such problems. In simple structures, recruitment and retention efforts can draw on the attractiveness to many candidates of the less formalized structure—managers are freer to tailor rewards to the needs of specific individuals. Of particular relevance to recruitment and retention success in professional bureaucracies is the structural dimension of centralization. Clinical personnel desire autonomy in the governance of patient care delivery, and centralized structures often frustrate such desires. Motivation and job satisfaction can be addressed by decentralized management struc-

tures, which assign decision-making responsibility to functional departments, patient care units, or individual clinicians to the extent possible.

Structure and Performance Appraisal

In simple organizational structures, appraisal of employees is relatively informal, as managers frequently either observe directly or participate in the work activities of the employees. This informal process provides the basis for reaching judgments about attendance, interpersonal skills, quantity and quality of work, and job knowledge. Use of formal evaluation instruments often is seen as unnecessary, particularly because performance decisions are centralized in a supervisor with whom employees have constant personal contact.

The predominance of informal interaction in the simple structure can create two basic difficulties in the appraisal of employees. First, a fair evaluation process requires that an employee understand both the tasks and the standards of performance that will be the basis for evaluation. It is assumed that an employee will acquire much of this information during socialization, but this is sometimes an unreliable way to communicate the basis of performance review, particularly in an organization that emphasizes informal norms and role interchangeability. For example, even if it is assumed that all staff answer the telephone in a small medical group practice, a nurse who does not understand the informal norm and ignores the ringing telephone might object to being called "uncooperative" in an evaluation. To ensure a fair appraisal process, it is important to make both the job tasks and performance standards clear. A second difficulty in the evaluation of employees involves the process of appraisal. An informational evaluation that entails some undocumented, brief oral comments provides no benchmark data for future reference. The supervisor might forget the specifics of the discussion, and the employee, who expects a reward due to future changes in work behavior, might be disappointed. Written performance reviews help to avoid this kind of situation, and they are particularly helpful to a manager who may incur legal liability because of inability to document the basis for an employee's dismissal.

In a professional bureaucracy, the danger of a split between the appraisal process for "clinical" and "administrative" employees exists. In the eyes of the physician-owners of many medical group practices, for example, the core operational activity, the delivery of medical services, is the most important work. Because physicians work closely with medical support staff who contribute to these core activities, a subtle favoritism toward these employees can arise. The result can be a systematic bias in the evaluation process, which creates inequity in the merit rewards of the compensation program. The practice manager must work closely with physicians to avoid this problem.

In the small group practice, evaluation of physician performance reflects the modest hierarchical structure of the organization. With a small number of members, there is no real need for a formal quality assurance structure. Instead, one of the physicians in the group usually is delegated this responsibility on an informal basis. Evaluation commonly arises in response to problems. For example, events such as patient complaints, a malpractice suit, a reduction in income,

and a decrease in patient load are likely to result in a discussion between the "quality assurance" physician and the alleged offender. Because the scale of the organization is small, it is easy to communicate with other members and to convene a formal meeting of the governing board if necessary.

As horizontal complexity of structures develops, the appraisal function becomes more systematized, and employees are more likely to be evaluated by persons qualified in their area of expertise. The process of evaluation also is affected by the increase in formalization of the professional bureaucracy, compared to the simple structure. Evaluation often involves a standardized form; reviews are more likely to occur at regular intervals, and a written assessment in the employee's record can provide benchmark data for determining the relative change in an employee's performance. In the machine bureaucracy, appraisal criteria for many positions are also subject to a high degree of quantification.

In large machine and professional bureaucracies, appraisal can become quite elaborate. For example, hospital nurses may be assessed on several dimensions—clinical, patient/family and staff education, professional development, and other factors. Within each category there may be numerous items ranging from documentation of patient condition on admission to the unit to attendance at in-service continuing education programs. In addition to the checklist response (e.g., "exceeds standards") to each item, there often is a request for supplementary written comments. This material generally is then reviewed in a formal meeting of a supervisor and employee. Formal systems of evaluation may include management by objectives (MBO), which is particularly useful in large, complex bureaucracies because it provides a direct link between the organization's goals and individual performance expectations. This relationship frequently is unclear to employees in large organizations, which have numerous departments and hundreds of employees. In the professional bureaucracy, an additional problem is the desire of professional groups to be appraised by their peers, rather than by administrative personnel and organization-wide appraisal standards. Peer review is more important in the appraisal processes of professional bureaucracies than other organizations.

Because a supervisor's evaluative judgments are a common source of employee grievances, it is important to note the character of grievance procedures in different health care delivery structures. In simpler structures such as small group practices, the procedure often takes the simple form of an "open door" policy by the practice manager. The hospital or nursing home grievance process, however, is likely to be more formalized. Written documents, a specified route of appeal, and final review, often with formal employee representation, have become common in hospitals.

Greater formalization of the appraisal process also affects evaluation of the performance of physicians and other clinicians. In many group practices, evaluation of physician activities is informal, possibly being the function of a quality assurance committee if one exists. The Joint Commission on the Accreditation of Healthcare Oganizations, however, requires that accredited hospitals have a complete quality assurance program. The evaluation of physicians activities in multihospital systems is even more complex. The system's board of directors is obligated to oversee the quality assurance programs

of its member facilities, but to fulfill this responsibility, the board must deal with the vertical complexity of the chain structure. The board, management, and medical staff of each member hospital often design and agree on their own quality assurance procedures, subject to the system board's approval. Formal rules and procedures usually are established concerning the frequency of reports and the apropriate channels of communication. The relationship between structural factors and appraisal extends to managers in multiunit chains. With two boards—a system corporate board and a local hospital board—top managers face greater vertical complexity. Indeed, a hospital's chief executive officer may be evaluated on the basis of different goals, which are established by the different levels. At the local level, a chief executive officer may be held accountable for such functions as planning and organization and marketing of the hospital, while the corporate officer may evaluate the individual based on coordination of multiunit services, marketing of the system, and participation in system meetings.

Structure and Compensation Management

Generally, the formality and degree of complexity of a compensation program are related to the complexity of an organization's structure. In simple structures, elaborate pay-grading scales are unnecessary. But simple structures have particular compensation management issues. First, role interchangeability and cross-training tend to "homogenize" jobs. As a result, it is more difficult to establish salary differentials that are based on a clear and distinct valuation of each position. If everyone does many different tasks, distinctive job valuation becomes more difficult. Ultimately, the primary tasks of each position are used to justify salary differences among job titles; to legitimize their compensation programs, managers must be careful to emphasize this point. A second problem is that the upper end of a salary range implicitly sets a limit on the salary advancement of an employee in that position. With advancement in position and salary blocked, personnel difficulties (e.g., loss of initiative or high turnover) are not unusual. A final hazard is that the compensation process will not receive the attention it deserves. For instance, a common complaint of office assistants in small medical group practices is that physicians forget to review the assistants' salaries. However, informal interaction enables such employees to exert direct personal pressure concerning salaries. The result is that physicians may make unsystematic salary decisions.

As formalization and administrative specialization increase in the machine and professional bureaucracy structures, so does the formalization of compensation policies. Certain basic compensation matters—vacation, fringe benefits, and sick leave—are more likely to be stated explicitly in a personnel manual. The salary review process becomes more regularized. Managers usually have regular conferences with employees. In hospitals, centralized salary systems are highly formalized. Job analyses establish the relative salary ranges for each position. A highly formalized compensation program tends to centralize managerial control over salaries. However, the greater likelihood of unions in more complex bureaucracies represents a decentralizing force in salary administration. In bargaining with union representatives, management shares some power over the bureaucracy's compensation program.

Often, an outgrowth of vertical complexity in the bureaucracy is the emergence of separate salary programs for managerial employees (e.g., department heads and up). Incentive programs for managerial employees are becoming more common in these settings. Incentive programs can be used additionally to link the work of individuals to the goals of the organization. In the professional bureaucracy, where professionals may perceive their professional goals to be at odds with those of the organization, incentive programs can be an important tool for integrating professionals into the organization.

Structure, Training, and Development

In the simple organizational structure, training and development are affected by the complexity of tasks undertaken by employees. For less complex tasks, training and development are likely to be handled informally by face-to-face interaction as needed or as convenient. A manager or clinician who wants a task (e.g., the greeting of patients) performed in a certain way, will personally instruct the employee. Another feature of the simple structure is that employees are likely to be cross-trained on the organization's less complex tasks. With few employees, such training enables individuals to substitute for each other in the event of absences due to vacation or illness. Paradoxically, continuity in the functioning of the organization is enhanced by the decrease in specialization. Second, the lack of horizontal and vertical complexity, which limits the possibilities for internal promotion or transfer, is related to the degree of investment in external employee training, such as continuing education courses. At a certain point, additional training will cause employees to exceed the skill requirements of their job titles. With the limitation on internal promotion, the more highly trained employees may seek opportunities for advancement elsewhere.

As structures increase in complexity and jobs become more specialized, training is likely to be delegated to specialists, and cross-training is less common. In nursing homes and hospitals, the training and development function is elevated in importance due in part to the formal requirements of externally imposed regulations. The numerous internal policies and procedures of nursing homes and hospitals, which serve to standardize the behavior of many individuals, often require careful introductory training. In this vein, new nurses often are assigned to an internship program for several weeks. Hospitals and large nursing homes are likely to have training coordinated by the human resources management department or an even more specialized training and development division or department. Another manifestation of the complexity and decentralization of the large bureaucracy is the delegation of such functions to different functional or product service divisions of the organization.

Specialization is one reason for the greater commitment of professional bureaucracies to training programs. The division of the hospital medical staff into departments according to specialty, for example, provides a logical organizational basis for transmitting specialized knowledge. As a result, most large hospitals have formal medical residency training programs. Nursing departments, which historically have provided training programs in technical areas, also have performed a similar function. Hospitals are more likely to be involved in develop-

mental programs in areas such as patient education, community health education, undergraduate and graduate medical education, and continuing medical education. The diversity of educational programs reflects the hospital's more elaborate horizontal differentiation.

As in other health care organizations, individual on-the-job training is important in hospitals and nursing homes. However, given the sizable number of employees in a particular functional area, there is a greater tendency to use a formal instructor and a systematic format. In addition, a growing number of hospitals use multi-institutional cooperative structures as a way to share educational services efficiently.

It is important to note that many complex health care organizations underinvest in training. Shortell (1982) mentions two structural factors among the reasons for this. First, the intensive horizontal specialization of labor has undermined the incentive "for hospitals to 'cross-train' employees through job rotation or related programs" (p. 15). Second, although many hospital nursing diploma schools are now closing for economic reasons, historically these institutions have had a significant role in training nurses. With subservience to administrative and medical staff needs as a basic orientation, the nurses so trained were an "all-purpose resource," performing functions that ranged from housekeeping to unit management administration to diagnosis and treatment of patients. Some researchers adopt the view that an unforeseen consequence of this "all-purpose resource" approach to nursing training has been the much lamented "nursing shortage" that has been the source of much vexation for the health care delivery system during the past 10 years. Although the increase in the supply of nurses has substantially exceeded the population growth rate throughout the 1980s, the tendency for nurses to assume clerical, custodial, and other non-clinical functions has helped to create a situation in which the demand for nurses functioning in a strictly clinical role continues to surpass the supply.

In response to the increasingly competitive health care market, hospitals have begun to emphasize training that meets their operational needs. For example, hospitals have recognized that cross-trained allied health personnel can make significant contributions to productivity, a development that would mark the reversal of greater horizontal complexity in the hospital division of labor. This development is particularly useful for smaller hospitals, where structural complexity is lower (Vaughan, Fottler, Bamberg, & Blayney, 1991). Another change in training and development relates to the complex interorganizational structures

within which many health care organizations, including nursing homes and hospitals, are embedded. The development of divisional structures within health care has prompted the possibility of lifetime employment relationships. This possibility varies for managers, physicians, nurses, and others, but a decrease in the turnover of any group of personnel may prompt organizations to invest in training that meets their particular needs. Multi-institutional systems, particularly investor-owned ones, already provide a variety of training courses to managers and clinical workers. The importance of such training for increasing productivity—especially in organizations with elaborate vertical complexity—is an additional factor underlying the trend toward more investment in training and development.

Table 5.1 summarizes some of the differences in human resources management that emerge under the three different types of organizational structures. Compared to sim-

TABLE 5.1. Selected Characteristics of Human Resources Management Functions in Three Structural Settings

Human Resources Functions	Simple Structure	Machine Bureaucracy	Professional Bureaucracy
Job analyses and design	• Low specialization • Role interchangeability • Informal	• Moderate specialization • Clear roles • Hierarchical arrangement of jobs	• High specialization • Clinical-administrative conflict • Horizontal coordination problems among positions
Selection and placement	• Low formalization	• High formalization	• High formalization for positions where credentials required • Partially decentralized to professional departments
Performance appraisal	• Direct observation • Informal; high potential for favoritism	• Highly formalized • Quantitative	• Decentralized review by peers important, but can create inequities across departments
Compensation management	• Informal; potential for inequity	• Highly formalized and elaborate	• Incentives important to integrating professionals in the organization
Training and development	• Face-to-face training • Cross-training common • Limited incentive for development	• Routinized training and development	• Profession-specific training and development • Cross-training may aid productivity

ple structures, bureaucracies develop more formalized and complex procedures for job analyses and design, recruitment and retention, selection and placement, performance appraisal, compensation management, and training and development. Specialized roles or departments are delegated responsibility for the management of human resources management in the bureaucracy. In the largest and most complex bureaucracies, particularly professional bureaucracies, these functions may be decentralized to departments or divisions of the organization so that professionals may be recruited and managed according to the particular needs and demands of their own profession.

TECHNOLOGICAL CHANGE IN HEALTH SERVICES ORGANIZATIONS

Just as organizational structures vary, there are many different technologies in health services organizations, all of which have an impact on how work is conducted. As an illustration, let us explore the case of a community general hospital at which the physicians on staff are interested in acquiring a new scanner based on an emerging new technology. Physician interest in this new technology is motivated by the desire for patients to have access to state-of-the-art technology. Also, however, physicians and managers have learned that some patients are transferring to a neighboring hospital that has already installed this new equipment. How does the hospital decide whether to purchase this new technology? The decision cannot be made by the physicians alone be-

cause the new equipment will most likely require extra space, substantial funding, additional human resources, and staff training. The impact of this and many new technologies is significant. It is the responsibility of the hospital manager to assess the potential impact of this new technology on the hospital. Some of the most important questions to be discussed by the senior management team include: How does this technology fit the mission of the hospital? What other resources, including human resources, are necessary? And, how will the new equipment affect the services currently being provided in other departments?

Although medical technology tends to be the dominant one that influences the operations of health services organizations, other *paraprofessional* groups bring their own technologies or sets of techniques to the organization. Nurses and social workers, for example, may not require special equipment to carry out their work, but the social-psychological support to patients that is usually provided by nurses and social workers is an important component of their technological repertoire. Technology is therefore defined quite broadly as the knowledge, procedures, and equipment used to transform unprocessed resources into finished goods or services (Perrow, 1967; Rousseau, 1979). Technology includes machines and technical equipment as well as the technical knowledge and skills of participants. Every organization does work and possesses a technology for doing that work (Scott, 1992).

Consider a 100-bed nursing home that, for the past 50 years, has served primarily elderly persons. The average patient is older than 80 years of age, and two-thirds of the patients are women. The board of the facility has decided to close half the beds and remodel the physical space to provide support services to AIDS patients. This decision was made partly on the basis of new funding available from the federal government specifically for AIDS services. However, the type of social-psychological services nurses and social workers have been providing may not be appropriate for the new clientele. Accordingly, this change will require the retraining of nurses and social workers to impart the knowledge, skills, and attitudes required for serving this new population. It also may require new approaches to recruitment and selection.

One of the biggest changes currently taking place in health services organizations is the introduction of computers to manage both clinical and management information systems. Data processing, communications, and office automation, as branches of information technology, are becoming increasingly important components of health services, especially in hospitals. The whirlwind of activities in *information technology* is enough to catch even the most experienced health services managers off guard. Many hospitals have extensive in-house capabilities with respect to the decisions that must be made about hardware, software, networks, and so forth. These changes carry obvious human resources implications. For example, new occupational groups are emerging to handle the complexities of information technology; these include highly specialized technicians who not only understand computers and their programming but also have some insights into the information needs of managers and clinicians.

The work of clinicians may be dramatically changed as a result of the introduction of information technologies. Physicians, for example, have access to a variety of technologies allowing them to improve medical record keeping, to acquire current medical knowledge, and to help make diagnostic and protocol management decisions. The success of many of these initiatives has been limited, however, due to sociopolitical and logistical problems. For example, some physicians are slow to adopt these technologies because of a perceived loss of rapport with patients, loss of control over decision making, or the incompatibility of new technologies with traditional office practice (Shortliffe, Wulfman, Rindfleisch, & Carlson, 1990). Sociotechnical principles suggest that employers must satisfy employees' needs within the technical requirements of an organization's production system. Unless the human element is considered in the implementation of new technology, it is unlikely that we will reap the full benefits of new technologies.

Another example of the impact of computers on human resources might be found in a large teaching hospital. Suppose it has been decided to computerize the patient information system to allow all patient data, including orders for tests, drugs, and treatments, to be entered into a computer terminal at each patient's bedside by the physician. These orders will be communicated to the relevant service departments automatically. The introduction of this system, however, may make the 40 unit clerks in the hospital redundant because they will no longer be required to transcribe the orders for the physicians. The union local is particularly interested in the unit clerks' case because it wants to ensure that alternative employment is made available to them in the hospital. Some physicians may also be concerned because

CONCEPTUALIZING ORGANIZATIONAL TECHNOLOGY

this change requires a major alteration in traditional behaviors.

Although the classical approaches to management recognize the importance of work in organizations, the concept of technology and its influence on the organization is not explicitly recognized in these approaches. Dubin (1958) and Woodward (1965) pioneered research pointing to technology as a determinant of structure and performance.

In her studies of 100 British manufacturing firms, Woodward (1965) confirmed the general hypothesis that organizational performance is dependent on an appropriate "fit" between the technology employed by the organization and organizational structure. She developed a classification scheme of the three basic types of manufacturing technology—small batch production, mass production, and continuous process production. Small batch production involves the production of customized products produced as one-of-a-kind items or in small quantities. Examples of this type of technology include aerospace equipment, custom-made clothing, and research. In mass production technologies, such as automobile manufacturing and book publishing, the same product is produced repeatedly, either in large batches or in long production runs. Continuous process production is a type of technology that produces the same product for an extended period of time, such as motor oil and nuclear power. Since her work, other forms of technology production have emerged, such as flexible cell production

(Hull & Collins, 1987). This technology, used mainly to produce machine metal parts, utilizes a cell of computer-controlled production machines connected together by a flexible network of conveyors that can be rapidly reconfigured for different production tasks. As described in the discussion of organizational structure, the type of technology employed will in large measure indicate the type of structure most likely to lead to high levels of performance. Organizations using mass production technologies, for example, may benefit from relatively centralized decision making with standardization of most work procedures (i.e., a machine bureaucracy). A medical research organization, however, would likely function poorly with this type of design. The customized nature of most research requires great flexibility and decentralization, and an adhocracy, in which employees do their work in small project teams, would be most appropriate.

Thompson (1967) was concerned with the relationship between technology and structure. He described three types of technology that focused on the conversion of inputs into outputs. *Long-linked* technologies involve serial interdependence of actions: A must be completed before B, and B must be completed before C. *Mediating* technologies link clients to customers who wish to be interdependent (e.g., banks). *Intensive* technologies use a variety of techniques depending on feedback from the object being transformed. To illustrate intensive technologies, Thompson used the general hospital, where the type of service provided varies according to a patient's needs at a particular time.

Arising from his interest in the impact of computers on organizations, Whisler (1970) developed the concept of *information technology*. Information technology was defined as the sensing, coding, transmitting, translating, and transforming of information. Whisler saw information as a technology of control, believing that older technologies were an extension of man's muscle (i.e., tools), and newer technologies are an extension of man's brain with the potential of being a partner or even taking control.

Perrow (1965, 1967) had a particular interest in human services organization technology. He described technology as the process whereby basic material is taken into an organization and certain acts are performed on it in series, with the raw material ultimately altered in a desired fashion. Perrow (1970) described the work performed in organizations according to its degree of *routineness.* Routineness is assessed by the extent to which raw materials are predictable and the nature of the techniques (or technology) for transforming the raw materials.

The nature of raw materials was thus considered key in human services organizations because actual human beings, not inanimate objects, comprise raw materials. In assessing routineness, three characteristics of raw materials were described: their variability, their instability, and the extent to which they are understood. Perrow maintained that it is workers' *perceptions* of raw materials that are important. If they perceive the material as stable and uniform (regardless of whether it is objectively so), they will act on it in a standardized way. Accordingly, organizations may attempt to standardize raw materials to reduce variability and to minimize exceptional cases (Perrow, 1970).

The selection of appropriate techniques or technologies is also key to understanding how organizations cope with transforming raw materials. The search process is particularly important when exceptions occur in the nature of raw materials. The search process may be logical and analytic, for example, where techniques can be applied with predictable outcomes. Search behavior may be unanalyzable when outcomes are unpredictable and the search relies on intuition, inspiration, guesswork, or some other unstandardized procedure (Perrow, 1967). The dimensions of Perrow's technology concept are summarized in Figure 5.1.

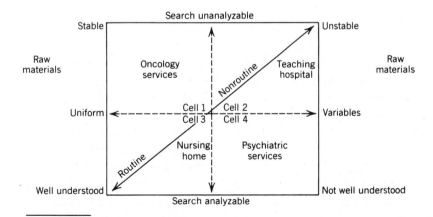

FIGURE 5.1. Perrow's technology techniques. (Adapted from Perrow, C. (1967). A framework for the comparative analysis of organizations. *American Sociological Review, 32,* 194–208.)

Four different technological situations may occur, shown as cells 1, 2, 3, and 4 in Figure 5.1, and different types of health services organizations may be illustrative of the four sets of technological circumstances. For example, in a large, complex teaching hospital (cell 2) the raw materials (patients) are typically unstable, variable, and not well understood; and often the search processes to find appropriate treatment methods are difficult to identify or analyze. In contrast, in a nursing home (cell 3) patients are relatively stable, uniform, and well understood; and the techniques for caring for the elderly are relatively well-defined. Situations 1 and 4 are less clear-cut. Certain organizations providing psychiatric services are illustrative of cell 4, insofar as patients' problems are not well understood but do tend to be treated in standardized ways (e.g., drug therapy). Illustrative of Cell 1 organizations are those providing services to oncology patients. The characteristics of certain cancers may be well understood, but the search for appropriate techniques is unanalyzable (i.e., a variety of treatments may be used with unpredictable outcomes).

With the emergence of new technologies, particularly in the manufacturing sector, we are seeing new approaches to the conceptualization of technology (Snell & Dean, 1992). There is an emerging literature, for example, on the relationship between human resources practices and just-in-time inventory control (Huang, Rees, & Taylor, 1983; Klein, 1991), total quality management (Oliver & Davies, 1990), and advanced manufacturing technology (Gunn, 1987). There is debate about whether firms should upgrade employee skills when implementing new technologies or use new technology to *minimize the need* for skills development and worker decision making.

Environment, Strategy, Structure, and Technology

The development of an organizational strategy depends partly on a systematic assessment of the organization's external environment. This assessment is aimed at determining the opportunites and threats confronting the organization. The central premise underlying these activities is that organizations have the capability of adapting to varying environmental conditions (Hickson, Hinings, Pennings, & Schneck, 1971). These adaptations help the organization to survive over the long run (Aldrich, 1979) and short run (Pfeffer & Salancik, 1978).

Figure 5.2 illustrates the relationship among an organization's environment, strategy, structure, and technology. We illustrate the complex relationships among these factors through an example of a community general hospital located in a small resort town on the southern California coast. The hospital has 200 acute care beds and offers a range of ambulatory care programs. The most important environmental factor facing the board of the hospital is the changing demography of the community the hospital serves; this includes increasing numbers of elderly persons because they find this area to be an ideal retirement center. Currently 25% of the population is older than 65 years of age, and this proportion is increasing. The elderly, who often have multiple health problems, are being admitted to the hospital for both minor and major procedures; once they are in the hospital they often stay for extended periods. The board and senior management team have clarified that services for the elderly are an important part of the hospital mission; however, they are concerned about the effect of the increasing lengths of stay on the hospital's overall per-

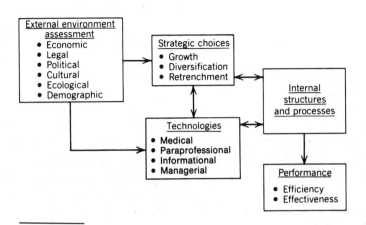

FIGURE 5.2. Environment, strategy, and technology.

formance. The range of strategic choices includes adding more acute care beds, cutting back on the services to the elderly, or providing alternative services for the elderly. Close examination of the health problems of the hospital's elderly patients revealed that a large portion of admissions were for ophthalmological procedures, especially cataract surgery. The hospital, therefore, made a strategic decision to set up a new ambulatory program in gerontological ophthalmological procedures, especially cataract surgery. This change involved the adoption of a new set of technologies (i.e., ambulatory cataract surgery), as well as a change in the structure of the organization (i.e., a new program focused on ophthalmological services for the elderly). This case provides an example of a particular strategic choice influencing the form of technology used as well as a change in the structure of the organization. The technology included the space, equipment, operating room, and day beds required for the new program. It also included the knowledge that this type of surgery could be performed safely on an outpatient basis with predictable success. In terms of human resources needs, it was necessary to employ an ophthalmologist experienced in gerontological work. Information technologies were also required to monitor the clinical and financial outcomes of the program. A variety of structural changes were possible to accommodate this new program. For example, a matrix structure could have been established, whereby staff from already existing departments could be "loaned" to the program for specified periods of time. Alternatively, the program could have been established as a stand-alone program with its own permanent staff.

Although this example serves to illustrate how certain strategic choices may lead an organization to select one or more particular technologies, it is conceivable that the relationship between strategy and technology could be reversed. In other words, there is the potential for a new technology, developed within the organization, to influence strategic choices. For instance, a rehabilitation center may have an exceptionally strong prosthetics service, with biomedical researchers who are at the cutting edge of their field. Senior management may decide that the development of prostheses should become an important product line and that other health services organizations in the community will be offered the opportunity to purchase prosthetic services from the center. In this case, the technology of the organization could influence the strategy selected by the senior management team.

THE INFLUENCE OF TECHNOLOGY ON THE HUMAN RESOURCES FUNCTIONS

Technology thus has a pervasive effect on health services organizations and on their employees. Discussion has focused on the relationships among technology, organizational structure, performance, and strategy. We move now to an analysis of the impact of technology on the major human resources management functions: job design, personnel selection, performance appraisal systems, reward system development, and occupational development.

Technology and Job Design

Job design is concerned with specifying the tasks a particular position should contain and the level of task specialization that is appropriate. It also requires decisions about the extent to which the tasks may be standardized and what knowledge and skills are necessary (Mintzberg, 1983). All of these decisions require detailed understanding of the technologies to be used by the job incumbent. Various approaches have been used to determine the design of individual positions, as described below.

The scientific management school had a pervasive influence on job design because of its emphasis on specialization and routinization of tasks to increase efficiency (Porter, Lawler, & Hackman, 1975). Among the effects of this approach were boredom and alienation because of the repetitiveness of work. One response to this problem was *job rotation* (i.e., individuals would be assigned for a period of time to several related jobs). This approach was common in nursing departments in hospitals in the 1950s and 1960s. This approach was largely unsuccessful. Nurses were unable to develop their specialized technical expertise in a particular area and, consequently, did not find the work rewarding. In this instance, technological specialization was not compatible with job rotation.

Job enlargement emerged in the 1940s and 1950s in response to overspecialization. Instead of breaking work down into smaller components, which tended to become repetitive and monotonous, job enlargement combined several tasks together to form a more complete whole. Often the enlargement of the tasks and responsibilities was accompanied by greater freedom for individuals to choose the procedures for completing the work as well as the pace of work. Suppose, for example, that medical technologists in a clinical laboratory are responsible for carrying out a variety of routinized and standardized clinical tests. With a specialization approach, each technologist is assigned to complete one single type of test on all of the patients who require it. With a job enlargement program, each technologist is assigned patients and is able to perform the full range of tests that has been prescribed for his or her patients. One of the main criticisms of job enlargement programs is that they often leave the basic nature of jobs unchanged and may simply result in more work for individual employees.

The *job enrichment* approach to job design is based on Herzberg's (1968) two-factor theory of motivation and satisfaction. Job enrichment increases the amount of control individuals have over their own work. This control in turn acts as a motivator by increasing responsibility, recognition, and opportunities for growth. An example of job enrichment in health services organizations is primary care nursing. In contrast with traditional approaches to nursing, a primary care nurse is assigned a case load of patients and assumes responsibility for the nursing services to be provided to those patients throughout their stay. Primary care nursing was introduced in psychiatry, where continuity of the patient-nurse relationship is critical to positive clinical outcomes.

Job enrichment programs, however, have not always been successful because they often fail to take into consideration the individual's needs and characteristics. Not everyone is ready for job enrichment, and not everyone wants it (Ferris & Gilmore, 1984).

The *job characteristics model* (Hackman & Oldham, 1976, 1980) attempts to identify the conditions under which jobs generate high levels of internal work motivation. The model, shown in Figure 5.3, assumes that when internal work motivation is high, good performance on the job generates positive feelings and provides self-reward. Poor performance leads to negative feelings and, therefore, limited personal rewards. Three conditions must be met to increase internal work motivation. The worker must (1) derive a sense of personal meaningfulness from the work, (2) experience responsibility for outcomes of the work, and (3) have knowledge of the actual results of the work activities. Three job characteristics—skill variety, task identity, and task significance—contribute to the person's experiences of meaningfulness of the work. Experienced responsibility for the outcomes of the work comes from the degree of autonomy in the job. Knowledge of the results of the work is achieved by way of feedback. Three moderators—individual knowledge and skills, growth need strength, and the job context—potentially influence individuals' ability to achieve internal work motivation.

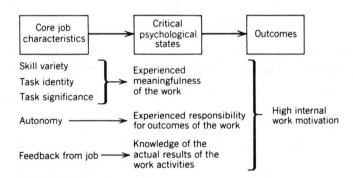

FIGURE 5.3. Job characteristics that foster three psychological states. (From J. Richard Hackman and Greg R. Oldham, *Work Redesign.* (Figs. 4.2 & 4.6), © 1980 Addison Wesley Publishing Company, Inc. Reprinted by permission.)

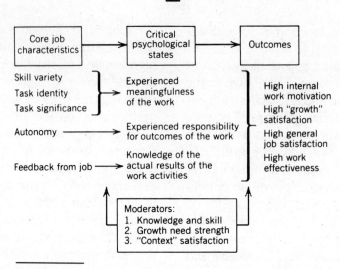

FIGURE 5.4. The complete job characteristics model. (From J. Richard Hackman and Greg R. Oldham, *Work Redesign.* (Figs. 4.2 & 4.6), © 1980 Addison Wesley Publishing Company, Inc. Reprinted by permission.)

Hackman and Oldham (1980) have developed a job diagnostic survey to assess all of the components in the job characteristics model. After the diagnosis has been made, changes can be considered according to certain principles as summarized in Figure 5.4.

The relationships between technology in health services organizations and the main approaches to job design are illustrated in Figure 5.5. Relatively routine tasks can be broken down into highly specialized activities, and detailed standards can be developed

for their performance. For example, consider a hospital employee whose job involves the routine and repetitive task of wrapping instruments for sterilization in a central supply room. Two design approaches might be used in this situation. Job rotation might be used (i.e., having different people rotate into the position). The cost to the organization would be low in this case because there are few specialized procedures to learn. Job enlargement might also be used to broaden the scope of the job to include such activities

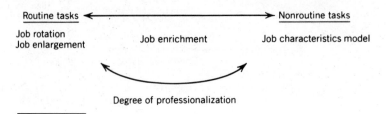

FIGURE 5.5. Technology and job design methods in health services organizations.

as packaging other supplies and delivering instruments to the users.

At the other end of the continuum are nonroutine tasks. For these types of jobs, we suggest the application of the job characteristics model as an approach to job design. Physicians, nurses, social workers, and pharmacists represent highly specialized occupational groups, and these professionals are expected to work relatively autonomously and to make decisions under uncertain conditions. Professionals are also more likely to be responsive to internal motivating factors. The service ideal underlying professional commitment is entirely compatible with the job characteristics model.

Technology and Personnel Selection

The development of valid selection criteria is a persistent problem in health services organizations. We suggest that there exists an important relationship between the nature of the job-related technology and the development of selection criteria. Because of the rapidity of technological change in health services organizations, selection criteria for certain jobs are in a state of flux. Technological changes are ongoing and essentially irreversible, whether referring to the use of automation and computers, new inventions, or innovative techniques and procedures. Technological change, therefore, requires the selection of individuals capable of adapting to technological change.

New developments in technology also may change the relative importance of a position to a health services organization and thereby alter the criteria for successful performance and the processes of selection. For example, prospective payment systems have dramatically changed the role of the medical records department; the position of medical records administrator has expanded in importance to the point that this person's performance may be critical to the viability of the organization. New skills are required of individuals assuming this role. Because this expanded role is relatively new, earlier job specifications may be obsolete, and the characteristics and performance of former job incumbents are likely to be irrelevant in predicting success. The selection process itself may be affected by the expanded role. Because of the increased importance placed on medical records administration, the selection process for this position may have to be upgraded. For example, additional personnel, representing groups with which the medical records department must now interact (e.g., physician and nurses) may need to be involved in the selection process.

Although technological change often requires retraining or acquiring individuals with new sets of skills, other skill areas may become obsolete. For example, the accounting clerk, trained and skilled in the management of debits and credits, may become less essential in hospitals that have developed automated data processing systems. Technological change may also require individuals to adopt new social skills. For example, star performers who previously operated in privileged or isolated circumstances may find themselves working in teams or project groups requiring a level of interpersonal skills not heretofore needed. Constructing valid criteria to predict success is increasingly difficult in an environment of rapidly changing technology.

Selection decisions represent the next major step in the selection process. Optimally selection decisions are made by matching individual qualifications to job requirements. Objective and subjective data may be used in assessing job applicants. Objective data include information on education and experience, references, and results of performance tests. Subjective data, which enter into almost every selection decision, are generally of a judgmental and intuitive nature. Subjective data are usually obtained from interviews, references, and other indirect information sources.

After job criteria have been established and information about applicants collected, decisions must be made about the manner in which criteria will be combined and weighed. Two methods have been suggested as valuable ways to combine information: intuitive judgment and systematic combination (Feldman & Arnold, 1983; Meehl, 1954). The intuitive judgment method requires an individual in the organization to review all information on applicants and to base a decision on an overall impression. Systematic combination, however, involves quantification of all information on applicants, with weights assigned to different criteria. Here, selection is not an intuitive process, although judgment may be involved in assessing applicants on each criterion. Comparisons among applicants are straightforward; the applicant receiving the highest score is selected for the position. It has been found that the best selection decisions are made when objective *and* subjective information about applicants is used, and that information should be combined systematically to arrive at a selection decision.

What is the relationship between the technology required of a particular position and the selection process, especially in terms of the choice of selection critiera? Figure 5.6 shows that jobs may be classified along two dimensions. The first dimension, which is related to the degree of job routineness, is the level of understanding of job-related technologies, or means-ends relationships. For some jobs, such as a laboratory technician or housekeeper, the technology is relatively routine. For others, such as a home care coordinator and clinical nurse specialist, the work is more nonroutine (i.e., it is less clear how tasks are to be accomplished). The second dimension reflects the degree to which there are clear job specifications and valid and reliable selection criteria. Although a well-planned and well-executed job analysis for certain jobs will yield job specifications and selection criteria, the reliability and validity of these criteria are not always clear. For example, there may be relatively strong confidence in criteria for hiring a person for a hospital pharmacist position. The applicant's education, experience, and references probably will provide most of the information required for a selection decision. The job of intensive care unit (ICU) nurse, however, may be quite different. Appropriate training and experience are important, but the job of an ICU nurse requires considerable teamwork and the ability to handle stress. The criteria for assessing these qualities are generally less valid and reliable than criteria for other areas.

Figure 5.6 indicates that the choice of an appropriate selection strategy depends on the level of understanding of job-related technologies, the confidence one has in the job specifications, and the reliability and validity of selection criteria. Cell 1 includes the jobs for which there is a high level of understanding of job-related technologies, as well as high confidence in job specifications and selection criteria. Such jobs as food tray assembler, X-ray developing machine

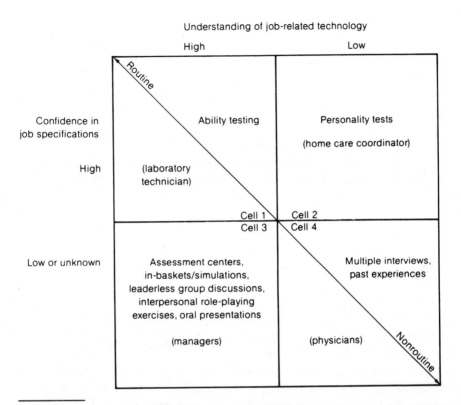

FIGURE 5.6. Type of selection process as determined by job-related, technological certainty and confidence in job specifications.

operator, laboratory technician, and cashier fall into this category. For each of these jobs, the required tasks are clear and unambiguous and there is high confidence in the validity of job specifications and selection criteria. Objective criteria may be established for these positions, including credentialing and ability testing.

Cell 2 includes jobs for which there is low understanding of the job-related technologies but high confidence in the job specifications and the reliability and validity of selection criteria. The positions of home care coordinator and psychiatric aide are examples. The home care coordinator, for example, must possess a community orienta-

tion, have knowledge about community resources, and understand the medical and social dimensions of disease. The job specifications are, therefore, clear. However, the job of home care coordinator has considerable uncertainties. Despite similarities among cases (e.g., formal admitting and discharge criteria to be followed), each case represents a unique situation. Each case requires intuitive judgment and unstandardized analytic approaches. Thus, in the case of home care coordinator, there is high confidence in the job specifications (i.e., we know the kind of person we are looking for), but little understanding of how this person will actually accomplish the work. The implications for selection procedures are clear; similar to jobs in cell 1, it is necessary to ensure that successful applicants meet the job specifications. Understanding that successful performance would require some relatively "unspecifiable" skills, it is essential to place additional emphasis on interviews and tests to assess assertiveness, intellectual ability, interpersonal skills, and decision-making abilities. Of particular importance in designing selection procedures for this type of job is ensuring their construct validity. In other words, if it is determined that leadership skills are critical for successful performance as a home care coordinator, then procedures used to assess leadership must in fact measure this trait.

Cell 3 represents jobs for which there is high understanding of job-related technologies but low confidence in the specifications for effective performance of the job. An example of this type of job is the manager of an ambulatory pediatric clinic. The technology of this job is clear and includes budgeting, supervising clerical personnel, and coordinating work schedules. Because the work of the clinic is fairly routine and predictable, these management tasks are correspondingly routine. However, in addition to the mechanical aspects of the job, there are intangible aspects as well. These features of the managerial role thus reduce the level of confidence in objective job specifications. For some management roles, applicants may need to be evaluated through simulations, leaderless group discussions, and oral presentations. Note the distinction between jobs falling in Cell 2 and those in Cell 3. In Cell 2, we know the *kind* of person we are looking for (i.e., clear job specifications) and we test to determine whether applicants can do the job. In Cell 3, we know the *skills* the job incumbent must have (i.e., job-related

technology), but we test to determine which applicants we feel would be most successful.

For the final group of jobs, located in Cell 4, there is minimal understanding of the job-related technologies and low confidence in job specifications. Relatively new or unique jobs (e.g., researchers, chiefs of medical staff, chief executive offers) may fall into this category. Because of the absence of knowledge about the job-related technologies and lack of confidence in job specifications, considerable emphasis is placed on techniques that analyze biographical data, as well as reports on past experiences and use of multiple interviewers.

Technology and Performance Appraisal Systems

Performance appraisals are used for a variety of purposes, including decisions about salary increases and promotions, individual development and motivation, employee selection and placement, discipline, and personnel and organizational planning. Four recurrent problems exist in the area of performance appraisal: (1) arriving at a single overall performance evaluation based on a series of different ratings, (2) convincing managers to grant rewards on the basis of merit (3) obtaining greater employee involvement in the performance appraisal process, and (4) reconciling the developmental and administrative requirements of appraisal systems (Teel, 1980). There are other issues as well, such as overcoming rater bias, time pressures, and negative attitudes toward the performance appraisal process.

This section focuses on the first of these problems, which involves deciding precisely what should be measured and developing performance measures. As we shall see, rapidly changing technologies have exacerbated the criteria-specification problem.

The specification of performance appraisal criteria is a recurrent problem in performance appraisal. One of the central issues is whether to evaluate traits, behaviors, or outcomes of work. Trait approaches, now largely outdated, evaluated such items as appearance, self-confidence, alertness, ambition, and initiative. Resembling grammar school report cards more than adult performance appraisal instruments (Klatt, Murdick, & Shuster, 1985), trait approaches tend to be paternalistic and subjective. More important, they do not measure desirable job-related behaviors, productivity, or quality of work.

There is an ongoing debate over the merits of behavioral versus outcome-oriented performance criteria. Behavioral approaches identify critical job-related activities and behaviors and appraise employees on their performance of these activities. The use of behaviorally anchored rating scales (BARS) is a popular application of this approach. Outcome approaches focus on the results of employee performance rather than behaviors. Management by objectives (MBO) is one example of such an approach.

Many factors affect the choice of the approach in measuring performance, including organizational norms and practices and how the performance appraisal information will be used. It is also necessary to consider the nature of the job itself and the technology that will be used to get the job done. Specifically, the type of appraisal method used depends on the extent to which knowledge about the transformation process or means-ends relationships is available and whether there exist valid and reliable performance measures (Lee, 1985). Figure 5.7 clarifies the impact of the presence or absence of these two factors on the type of performance appraisal procedures appropriate to different types of technology.

Where there is high knowledge of the transformation process (i.e., routine technology), and reliable and valid performance measures are available (cell 1), performance may be assessed through monitoring behavior or outputs. For example, the work of a dietary aide or an admissions clerk would fall into this category. The technology required for each of these jobs is clearly defined and requisite job-related behaviors are unambiguous. Performance appraisal criteria may, therefore, be based on behavior or output.

Cell 2 refers to jobs in which there is a relatively low level of knowledge about the technology, but reliable and valid indicators of performance exist. Here, performance appraisal should focus mainly on outputs rather than behaviors. Examples of jobs of this type are health educator and community health worker. Although behavioral guidelines could and should be specified for these jobs, one could limit the creativity and performance of a job incumbent by linking appraisal criteria too stringently to behavioral guidelines. The "technologies" used to educate patients or to relate to various cultural groups are not clearly understood and require subtleties and sensitivities that are not easily measured. Outputs for these jobs, however, are relatively easy to measure. For example, to appraise the performance of a patient educator, one could measure the number of patients counseled, patient satisfaction with the educator, or patient behavior or attitude change. For the community health worker, it is possible to evaluate whether target groups of patients are receiving the appropriate array of services, and the level

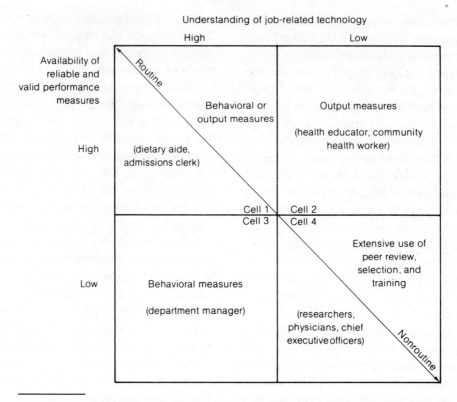

FIGURE 5.7. Choice of appraisal methods by understanding of job-related technology and availability of reliable and valid performance indicators.

of patient and family satisfaction with the services.

Other jobs employ technologies that are well understood, although reliable and valid measures of performance are few (cell 3). Department managers generally fall into this category. Generally, we know what managers should do, but it is difficult to develop output-based performance measures. For example, we can count the number of performance appraisals conducted by a department manager, but assessing whether the appraisal process has enhanced individual and departmental performance is not straightforward. Even where department performance may be measured, it may be difficult to attribute

performance levels to the manager. Thus, the basis for evaluating the performance of a manager may at times be limited to behaviors rather than outputs.

A final job category is found in Cell 4. Here, the nature of the technology is limited, and there are few valid or reliable performance measures. The work of researchers, physicians, and chief executive officers exemplifies this type of job. Development of performance appraisal criteria is difficult, and great reliance is placed on extensive and costly selection procedures. Those involved in assessing performance for such jobs frequently rely on multiple observers and raters as well. For jobs in Cell 4, consensus among raters or observers is generally superior to behaviorally or output-oriented performance appraisal formats.

Technology and Reward System Development

The primary purpose of reward systems is to motivate effective individual or group performance. Reward systems may have other uses including attracting high-quality members to join the organization and minimizing absenteeism and tardiness.

Organizations can encourage effective performance by the use of two types of rewards. *Intrinsic* rewards are rewards that are valued in and of themselves by the worker, and *extrinsic* rewards are those that are provided by external agents. Intrinsic rewards are frequently referred to as self-administered because they are concerned with an individual's feeling about the job in terms of personal competence and accomplishment, responsibility and autonomy, and growth and development. Extrinsic rewards usually include the rewards directly controlled by the organization (e.g., pay, fringe benefits, recognition, promotion). Four basic requirements have been identified as essential to any reward system (Lawler, 1971, 1977); these include the following:

1. It must provide individuals with sufficient reward to satisfy basic needs for food, shelter, safety, and security.
2. It must compare favorably with reward systems in other organizations.
3. It must be perceived by organizational members as fair and equitable.
4. It must be flexible, so that it can be adapted to individual needs.

With respect to individual rewards, Lawler (1977) suggests the following characteristics that are essential to ensure effectiveness:

1. Rewards must be perceived to be of sufficient importance to organizational members.
2. Rewards must be visible, and there must be a clear relationship between performance and rewards.
3. Rewards should be structured such that they can be administered frequently without losing their potency.

In addition, the reward system must not cost so much that the price of using it outweighs any benefits in performance that might be derived. Some of the most common methods of reward include pay, promotion, fringe benefits, status symbols, and special symbolic rewards.

What relationship exists between the nature of technology in health services organizations and the characteristics of rewards that may be effective in motivating performance? Building on the previous discussion in this chapter, it would appear that similar relations may exist between the nature of the technology and reward systems. For example, for a housekeeping aide, the tasks are routine and easily specified, the job-related technology can be clearly specified, and there exist reliable and valid indicators of performance; thus extrinsic rewards will have the greatest effect for such jobs. In these circumstances, the reward (e.g., pay) can be directly linked to measurable performance of relatively routine tasks.

In contrast, a physician must make decisions with a great deal of uncertainty (i.e., perform nonroutine tasks), the job-related technology may not be easily specified, and the reliability and validity of performance measures is somewhat suspect; thus he or she is more likely to be responsive to intrinsic rewards. These rewards will come from the individual's sense of "doing a worthwhile job" and particularly, in health services organizations, from feelings of providing a quality service. Clearly, the nature of the technology and the requirement for highly professional staff in health services organizations influence the types of rewards that will be effective in motivating performance (Chusmir, 1986).

Technology and Occupational Development

Most of the literature on careers in organizations focuses on the life cycle of individual careers, beginning with the development of career choice and identity, evolution of personal values and career choice, early career issues, mid- and later career issues, and retirement. The manner in which one moves through a career also varies according to occupation. For example, occupational groups that are highly professionalized (e.g., physicians, nurses, social workers) are influenced in their career development by professional associations, which provide extensive socialization to professional values throughout the career development cycle. Standards and expectations of performance by professionals within health services organizations are often more likely to be determined outside the organization by professional associations than by the organization itself (Mills & Posner, 1982). Similarly, ongoing technological change, especially in medicine, is likely to affect career choices and development. The higher the initial investment of an individual in education for a par-

ticular occupation, the less likely the person is to leave that occupation. Accordingly, the profession plays a very important role in ensuring that its members keep abreast of new technological developments.

In contrast, occupational groups that are relatively unskilled or nonprofessional (e.g., unit clerks) may approach career choices from a different perspective. The investment in the preparation for a particular position of this type is relatively low, and the major source of socialization is likely to be the organization itself. Accordingly, in situations of routine technology, a health services organization will play an important role in influencing the value system of new employees. Organizational socialization may include an in-house training program to teach routine tasks; in addition, standards of performance and expectations are likely to be well-defined. Individuals who are employed to complete relatively routine tasks requiring few specialized skills are more likely to change jobs frequently during their work careers because any retraining costs are at the expense of the organization rather than the employee.

In summary, the characteristics of technology in health services organizations determine the numbers, types, and levels of professional and other occupational groups necessary for the organization to meet its goals. Different occupational groups vary in their degree of professional identity and socialization, and these will set the framework for career development. Where the position is responsible for routine, nonspecialized tasks, the organization itself must assume greater responsibility for socializing individuals for these positions.

The sample decision tree shown in Figure 5.8 reveals a clear relationship between the

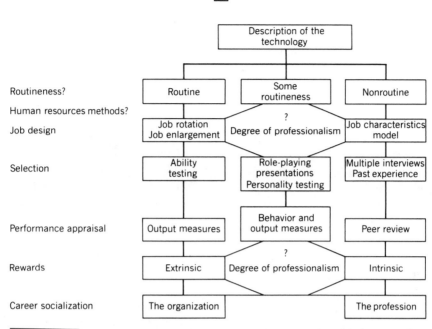

FIGURE 5.8. Decision tree for matching human resources management to technology.

nature of the technology and the principal methods for achieving the human resources function in the organization. Where the technology is more routine, it is likely that job design will be achieved through the specification of highly specialized tasks. Techniques of job rotation and job enlargement may be useful to alleviate the boredom workers experience in completing these tasks. Selection process for jobs when the tasks are routine will rely on ability testing, as well as on the assessment of skills in preparation for the job through demonstration of ability. Performance appraisal will be achieved through output measures because these can be directly linked to job performance. Reward systems for employees whose jobs entail routine tasks will come from extrinsic sources (i.e., from others) and will include such tangibles as pay, improved working conditions, and fringe benefits. The organi-

zation itself will assume the greatest responsibility for socializing individuals to fulfill these roles.

In contrast, where jobs entail the completion of nonroutine tasks and the continuous handling of exceptional cases, the job characteristics model will be most appropriate. Selection processes will be more difficult and will incorporate several methods, including personality testing, multiple interviews, and careful examination of applicants' prior performance. Performance appraisal methods will be difficult because the expected behavior in response to nonroutine tasks cannot easily be specified or standardized. The most likely approach will include techniques for peer review. Persons occupying these positions will experience rewards that are intrinsic (i.e., stemming from personal feelings about their jobs and the knowledge that they are doing well). The main influence on career socialization can be expected to come from the professional association of the particular group, especially in relation to the standards of practice. The profession itself will be the most important reference group for persons occupying positions with non-routine tasks.

SUMMARY

Throughout this chapter, we have developed ideas about how organizational structures and technologies influence the ways in which human resources are managed in health services organizations. Due to the increasing rate of change in health care organizational structures and technologies, health services managers of the future will need to assume a more proactive stance in identifying and assessing the potential impact of these developments on human resources functions.

In conclusion, we present three general guidelines to assist health services managers in assessing and preparing for technological and structural changes.

1. *Identify changes in structures and technologies.* It is important that human resources managers be alert to any form or variety of technological or structural change occurring within their own organizations. In addition, managers should scan the environment for new trends that potentially could be integrated into their own organizations. Managers can learn from the experiences of other organizations that have already adopted the structure or technology.
2. *Identify the level(s) of the organization affected by the new structure or technology.* Many changes have effects at all levels—individual positions, work groups, the whole organization, or groups of organizations—with the consequences of the change differing at each level.
3. *Match human resources management practices with the characteristics of technologies and structures.* Table 5.1 and Figure 5.8 give general guidelines for thinking about this matching process. The guidelines in the tables are suggestive, not definitive. It is the challenge of management to use those guidelines as a stimulus for identifying and implementing changes that are most appropriate to the manager's specific setting and situation.

Discussion Questions

1. Consider the situation of a human resources manager who changes jobs, moving from a 500-bed not-for-profit, general hospital to a large medical specialty group practice. What differences in organizational structure and technology is the manager likely to encounter? What are the implications for how the manager should function differently in the medical group practice setting?
2. Today, many health care organizations are implementing quality management programs. Are quality management programs a form of new technology for organizations? What are the likely implications of quality management programs for organizational formalization and centralization? What new issues do they present for human resources managers?

3. Contrast the structure and technology of a hospital emergency department with the structure and technology of a hospital dietary department. Should human resources management practices vary between the two departments?

REFERENCES

Aldrich, H.E. (1979). *Organizations and environments.* Englewood Cliffs, NJ: Prentice Hall.

American Society for Hospital Personnel Administration (ASHPA). (1985). *Health care occupations: A comprehensive job description manual.* Hastings, MN: Regina Publications.

Bechtold, S.E., Szilagzyi, A.D., & Sims, H.P. (1980). Antecedents of employee satisfaction in a hospital environment. *Health Care Management Review, 5*(1):77–88.

Charns, M.P., & Tewksbury, L.J.S. (1993). *Collaborative management in health care: Implementing the integrative organization.* San Francisco: Jossey-Bass.

Chusmir, L.H. (1986). How fulfilling are health care jobs? *Health Care Management Review, 11*(1), 27–32.

Dubin, R. (1958). *The world of work.* Englewood Cliffs, NJ: Prentice Hall.

Feldman, D.C., & Arnold, H.J. (1983). *Managing individual and group behavior in organizations.* New York: McGraw-Hill.

Ferris, G.R., & Gilmore, D.C. (1984). The moderating role of work context in job design research: A test of completing models. *Academy of Management Journal, 27*(4), 885–892.

Gunn, T.G. (1987). *Manufacturing for competitive advantage.* New York: Free Press.

Hackman, J.R., & Oldham, G.R. (1976). Motivation through the design of work: Test of a theory. *Organization Behavior and Human Performance, 16,* 250–279.

Hackman, J.R., & Oldham, G.R. (1980). *Work redesign.* Reading, MA: Addison-Wesley.

Hamity, G.I., & Gauss, J.W. (1982). A profile of the group practice administrator. *Medical Group Management, 29*(4):30–34.

Herzberg, F. (1968). One more time: How do you motivate employees? *Harvard Business Review,* 53–62.

Hickson, D.J., Hinings, C.R., Pennings, J.M., & Schneck, R.E. (1971). Structural conditions of interorganizational power. *Administrative Science Quarterly, 16*(2):216–229.

Huang, P.Y., Rees, L.P., & Taylor, B.W., III. (1983). A simulation analysis of the Japanese just-in-time technique (with kanbans) for a multiline, multistage, production system. *Decision Sciences, 14,* 326–344.

Hull, F.M., & Collins, P.D. (1987). High technology batch production system: Woodward's missing type. *Academy of Management Journal, 30,* 786–797.

Klatt, L.A., Murdick, R.G., & Schuster, F.E. (1985). *Human resource management.* Columbus, OH: Merrill.

Klein, J.P. (1991). A reexamination of autonomy in light of new manufacturing practices. *Human Relations 44,* 21–38.

Lawler, E.E., III. (1971). *Pay and organizational effectiveness.* New York: McGraw-Hill.

Lawler, E.E., III. (1977). Reward systems. In J.R. Hackman & J.L. Suttle (Eds.), *Improving life at work* (pp. 57–82). Glenview, IL: Scott, Foresman.

Lee, C. (1985). Increasing performance appraisal effectiveness: Matching task types, appraisal process, and rater training. *Academy of Management Review, 10*(2), 322–331.

Meehl, P.E. (1954). *Clinical versus statistical prediction: A theoretical analysis and a review of the evidence.* Minneapolis: University of Minnesota Press.

Mills, P.K., & Posner, B.Z. (1982). The relationship among self-supervision, structure and technology in professional service organizations. *Academy of Management Journal, 25*(2), 437–443.

Mintzberg, H. (1983). *Structure in fives: Designing effective organizations.* Englewood Cliffs, NJ: Prentice Hall.

Neuhauser, D. (1972). The hospital as a matrix organization. *Hospital Administration, 17*(4), 8–25.

Odiorne, G.S. (1984). *Strategic management of human resources.* San Francisco: Jossey-Bass.

Oliver, N., & Davies, A. (1990). Adopting Japanese-style manufacturing methods: A tale of two (UK) factories. *Journal of Management Studies 27,* 555–570.

Perrow, C. (1965). Hospitals: Technology, structure, and goals. In J.G. March (Ed.), *Handbook of organizations* (pp. 133–164). Skokie, IL: Rand McNally.

Perrow, C. (1967). A framework for the comparative analysis of organizations. *American Sociological Review, 32,* 194–208.

Perrow, C. (1970). *Organizational analysis: A sociological view.* Belmont, CA: Wadsworth.

Pfeffer, J., & Salancik, G.R. (1978). *The external control of organizations.* New York: Harper & Row.

Porter, L.M., Lawler, E.E., III, & Hackman, J.R. (1975). *Behavior in organizations.* New York: McGraw-Hill.

Rousseau, D. (1979). Assessment of technology in organizations: Closed versus open system approaches. *Academy of Management Review, 4,* 531–542.

Scott, W.R. (1992). *Organizations: Rational, natural, and open systems.* Englewood Cliffs, NJ: Prentice Hall.

Shortell, S.M. (1982). Theory Z: Implications and relevance for health care management. *Health Care Management Review, 7(4),* 7–21.

Shortliffe, E.H., Wulfman, C.E., Rindfleisch, T.C., & Carlson, R.W. (1990). *An integrated oncology workstation.* Bethesda, MD: National Cancer Institute.

Snell, S.A., & Dean, J.W. (1992). Integrated manufacturing and human resources management: A human capital perspective. *Academy of Management Journal, 35*(3), 467–504.

Teel, K.S. (1980). Performance appraisal: Current trends, persistent progress. *Personnel Journal, 59,* 297.

Thompson, J.D. (1967). *Organizations in action.* New York: McGraw-Hill.

Vaughan, D.G., Fottler, M.D., Bamberg, R., & Blayney, K.D. (1991). Utilization and management of multiskilled health practitioners in U.S. hospitals. *Hospital and Health Services Administration, 36*(3), 397–419.

Whisler, T.L. (1970). *Information technology and organizational change.* Belmont, CA: Wadsworth.

Woodward, J. (1965). *Industrial organization.* London: Oxford University Press.

CHAPTER

6

INFORMATION SYSTEMS FOR HUMAN RESOURCES MANAGEMENT

Charles J. Austin

James A. Johnson

Gary Drucker Palestrant

LEARNING OBJECTIVES

Upon completing this chapter, the reader should be able to. . .

- Differentiate between strategic and operational objectives for an HRIS in a health services organization.
- Participate in the planning, selection, and implementation of an HRIS.
- Understand the responsibilities of executive managers in overseeing the development of an HRIS.
- Avoid the common problems and pitfalls encountered by many organizations in the design and development of an HRIS.

INTRODUCTION

Information is an essential tool for managers in the recruitment, retention, utilization, and evaluation of human resources in health services organizations. Because they support the strategic goals and objectives of the organization, information systems play an important role in planning and management of human resources. These systems also serve important personnel administration operational programs, including employee record keeping, budget control, compensation, benefits management, and government reporting.

This chapter discusses human resources information systems (HRISs) and their *strategic* and *operational* use in health care organizations. Specific topics include the following:

1. The role and functions of an HRIS for human resources management

2. The relationship of an HRIS to other information systems
3. The process of planning, developing, and implementing an HRIS
4. The implications of effective HRIS utilization for health services managers

THE BACKGROUND OF INFORMATION SYSTEMS UTILIZATION IN HEALTH SERVICES ORGANIZATIONS

Three general categories of information systems are used in health care organizations. These are clinical information systems, systems that support administrative operations, and executive decision support systems (Austin, 1992).

Clinical information systems support direct patient care activities. These include automated systems for medical records storage and retrieval, computer-assisted clinical decision making, computer-assisted medical instrumentation, support of clinical departments (e.g., laboratory, radiology, pharmacy, emergency room), support of nursing activities, and clinical research and education.

Operational administrative systems assist managers in nonpatient care activities. Examples include general ledger and cost accounting systems, patient accounting systems, payroll, human resources management, materials and facility management, and office automation.

Executive decision support systems relate to strategic policy matters that transcend day-to-day operations. They can assist in long-range planning, evaluation of organizational performance, continuous quality improvement, and analysis of program impact on the community.

The information systems in all three categories are interrelated. Furthermore, successful utilization of information depends on the extent to which information systems are integrated (i.e., the ability to communicate and share information for many applications).

Increasingly, health services organizations have electronic linkages of their information systems to external organizations, including insurance companies for claims processing, government agencies for required reporting and transmission of withholding tax and Social Security data, and national databases for retrieval of clinical information. To promote electronic communication and sharing of clinical and financial information, many hospitals also provide linkages of their information systems to personal computers in physicians' offices.

The 1990s have seen continued improvement in computer hardware, software, and telecommunications systems for use in health care organizations. Many of the early hospital information systems installed in the 1960s and 1970s were developed by in-house staffs of systems analysts and computer programmers. More recently, however, most health care organizations have purchased generalized computer software from commercial vendors who specialize in this field. Many organizations, particularly larger hospitals, have installed computer networks in which systems purchased from several different software vendors are linked together in an "open architecture" format.

THE ROLE AND FUNCTION OF INFORMATION SYSTEMS FOR HUMAN RESOURCES MANAGEMENT

The Human Resources Information System (HRIS)

Managing human resources effectively requires information from several sources. Computer technology enables hospitals and other health care organizations to combine human resources information into a single database that can be used to support multiple personnel and managerial functions. A human resources information system (HRIS) is the integration of software, hardware, support functions, and system policies and procedures into an automated process designed to support the strategic and operational activities of the human resources department and managers throughout the organization (Ceriello, 1991).

An HRIS database maintains an inventory of people, job skills, and positions, and its system draws on these inventories for transaction processing, reporting, and tracking. The HRIS provides a foundation for a set of analytical tools that assist managers in establishing objectives and in evaluating the performance of the organization's human resources programs. The level of system complexity progresses from low to high as it affects and supports increasingly sophisticated decisions and activities.

A health care organization usually aspires to several key goals in automating its human resources management function. The HRIS should provide timely, efficient, thorough, and accurate personnel information and analysis. A second goal for an HRIS generally is to provide an effective match of the needs, skills, and interests of the human resources department staff with other users and departments (Ceriello, 1991). An HRIS also provides uniform processing and utilization of human resources information throughout the organization for a diverse group of the system's users.

Strategic Objectives for an HRIS

In a recent survey of more than 800 human resources executives in the health care industry, human resources strategic planning was identified as the most critical issue they will face in coming years (Melton, 1990). Human resources professionals must be involved in these strategic planning activities. Unfortunately, human resources professionals are sometimes overlooked or are asked to participate in the planning process late, making it difficult to use the information and expertise they can bring to the planning activities fully.

Increasing numbers of executives are recognizing that an effective HRIS can help fashion and support a health care organization's strategic mission. Broderick and Boudreau (1992) stress the role human resources information technology can play in improving human resources management as well as contributing to competitive advantage. As a key component of an organizationwide integrated information system, a strategic HRIS provides important information about human resources needs and capabilities; this information can assist the management team in establishing the organizational mission and setting goals and objectives to set it in motion. An HRIS can become an action tool to help lead an organization toward trans-

---

STRATEGIC USE OF HRIS

A physician recruitment system can be a key strategic component, as well as a competitive tool, as a hospital strives to fulfill its health service mission. In the wake of changes in reimbursement, growing competition for physicians, and changing community needs, administrators on the strategic planning committee at St. John's Regional Medical Center in Joplin, Missouri, developed plans to address both short-term and long-term needs by developing a physician recruitment system.

The medical center purchased and implemented a recruitment database software system that could operate in a real-time environment and could be updated frequently. By controlling the work flow of the recruiting function, administrators and managers can plan searches and coordinate physician site visits. This recruitment database of approximately 35,000 physicians has allowed the hospital to offer the optimum mix of medical services to the community and to react quickly in the highly competitive marketplace of physician recruitment

Fanning, R.J. (1992). Physician database eases staffing headaches. *Healthcare Informatics,* June, 9(6), 46–48.

forming and redesigning health care in the community.

Manpower planning and allocation are critical links between the human resources strategy plan and the organizational business plan. Assessment of future needs requires information about current employee levels and skills, along with projections of patient needs. Also required are analytical tools for asking "what if" questions when exploring alternative service strategies (Martin, 1988).

A health care organization that utilizes computerization in its human resources function will experience a number of strategic advantages. First, an HRIS enables a hospital's human resources department to take a more active role in organizational planning. Computerization can make forecasting more timely, cost effective, and efficient. Second, an HRIS integrates and stores in a single database all of the organization's human resources information that may have been filed in separate physical locations previously. Thus, a human resources department could take a more global view of its human resources assets and could interpret its strategic contributions in more meaningful ways. Third, an HRIS can accelerate the process of comparing costs and benefits of human resources activities.

Employees are the lifeblood of a health services organization; they are its most important resource. In order to retain a competitive market share, many health care organizations are developing new methodologies to address recruiting issues. For example, nursing administrators at the Dana-Farber Cancer Institute have developed and implemented a computerized nursing recruitment program to meet the increased competition among health care facilities for

skilled nursing personnel (Garre, Lutey, & McElroy, 1990).

The need for collection, analysis, and management of human resources information has outpaced the development of human resources information systems in many health care organizations. This is further complicated by an increasing trend toward the development of integrated hospital information systems (Martin, 1988).

Austin (1992) estimates that hospitals spend 60% to 70% of their operating budgets on employee salaries and benefits. Management must be able to measure and understand the tremendous investment that it has in such a labor-intensive organization. Omachonu (1991) points out that the challenge facing management information systems in health care is one of supporting productivity and quality efforts by generating reliable and adequate information. Thus, a good human resources information system is very important in assisting management in work force planning and productivity analysis.

Cybernetic models have been used to describe systems for strategic decision support and managerial control in health services organizations (Austin, 1992) (Figure 6.1). Wright and McMahan (1992) use such a model to describe a human resources management system. *Inputs* to the system include knowledge, skills, and abilities that must be developed through programs of recruiting and employee development. Human resources system *outputs* are evaluated through measures of job performance and employee satisfaction.

Effective mechanisms for feedback concerning outputs must be incorporated so that progress is monitored and strategies are ad-

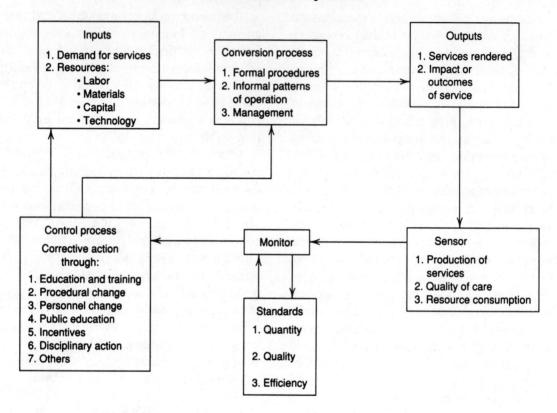

Generalized Management Control System (Cybernetic)
for a Health Services Organization

ENVIRONMENT

FIGURE 6.1. A cybernetic, generalized management control system for a health services organization. (From Austin, C. J. (1992). *Information systems for health services administration.* Ann Arbor, MI: AUPHA Press/Health Administration Press; reprinted by permission.)

justed accordingly. Human resources outputs that can be monitored through an HRIS include the following:

- Voluntary and involuntary turnover
- Unfilled job vacancies
- Employee attitudes
- Physician and patient attitudes

- Financial outcomes
- Growth of service volume
- Deficiencies identified in performance appraisals
- Proportion of new positions filled internally
- Work force demographics
- Benefit utilization

In this example, managerial control and feedback provided by the cybernetic system could include the following:

- Automatic position control linked to the hospital's budget
- Labor analysis reports for each cost center
- Inventory of special skills of employees
- Labor cost allocations with linkage to the hospital's payroll system
- Management reports on employee productivity and quality of services provided to patients

Operational Objectives for an HRIS

When human resources activities are not automated, it takes a tremendous amount of time, manpower, and money simply to ensure that proper records are being maintained to comply with government guidelines and regulations. Compared to a manual system, an HRIS offers benefits such as increased data accuracy, increased processing speed, more useful and sophisticated reporting, and enhanced productivity.

An effective HRIS can facilitate the easy storage and retrieval of human resources records that are vital for hospital operations. In addition, to comply with various federal employment laws, hospitals must follow several human resources record-keeping requirements. An HRIS streamlines such compliance by automating relevant data collection and reporting.

Basic Components of an HRIS

An HRIS generally includes the following set of related components: human resources planning, personnel administration, recruit-

HRIS AS A TRAINING TOOL

Computer-assisted instruction (or CAI) enabled the 468-bed El Camino Hospital in Mountain View, California, to cut training costs, comply with OSHA and JCAHO requirements, improve training quality and flexibility, and increase turnaround time for training personnel. The hospital purchased and implemented a computer-assisted instruction program which is fast, easy to use, and cost efficient.

This portable, Macintosh-based system can be wheeled-around to various sites throughout the hospital and has benefitted El Camino in important ways. In the first year, the CAI system has resulted in a 50 minute training timesaving per employee. Times for self-paced training are determined by individual staff. Since implementation, costs to administer OSHA- or JCAHO-mandated training has decreased 46 to 55 percent. In one training module, the hospital has realized an annual savings of $41,213.

Leonard, K. (1992). OSHA, dollars & fun: Counting CAI's benefits. *Healthcare Informatics,* September, 9(9), 66–68.

ment and employment, pension administration, benefits management, payroll, compensation, training and staff development, employee and industrial relations, and government reporting including the Occupational Safety and Health Act (OSHA), worker's compensation, Equal Employment

Opportunity/Affirmative Action (EEO/AA), and Consolidated Omnibus Budget Reconciliation Act of 1975 (COBRA) (Figure 6.2). In a typical hospital human resources department that uses a computerized system, all of these components and functions would be linked by integrated screens, modules, or subsystems and all information would be retrieved from a single human resources database. This database would include the following components:

1. Personnel information, including employee name, address, Social Security number, birthdate, and marital status

2. Job-related information, including job title, department, employment date, last promotion date, supervisor, and salary history

3. Benefits information, including medical and dental contributions, life and disability insurance coverage, and pension data

4. Miscellaneous information, such as special skills, physical limitations, bonuses, and disciplinary actions

The HRIS should be updated periodically to comply with the federal government's current laws and regulations concerning the work force. The system could assist human

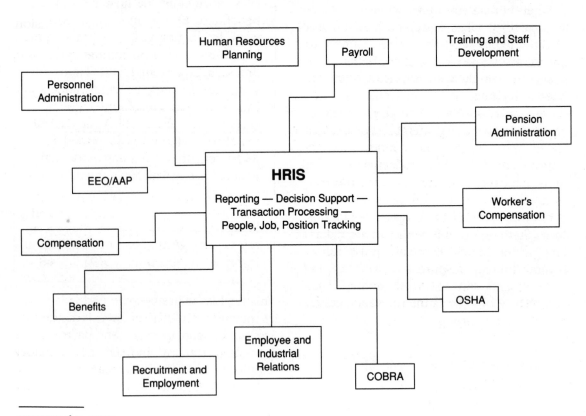

FIGURE 6.2. HRIS components.

resources department staff members in tracking terminated employees still receiving benefits under the government's COBRA plan. Affirmative action and EEO reporting can assist managers in avoiding discrimination and maintaining diversity in employment.

A recruitment and employment subsystem also could enable the human resources department to match applicants to available positions in a cost-effective manner. When an applicant is hired, relevant information would be transferred automatically to other subsystems (e.g., compensation, benefits management, training and staff development), thus eliminating costly multiple data entry.

An attendance tracking function, closely integrated with the payroll system, could enhance labor productivity analysis. Such a subsystem enables the human resources department to track different types of absences (e.g., sick leave, vacation, unexcused absences), and to report attendance and absence statistics by organizational unit. Combined with payroll system data, an HRIS could utilize such information to produce analytical reports (e.g., ratios of net revenue to employee cost).

In addition, with information stored in a centralized human resources management database, a flexible reporting system could provide listing, summary, or analytical reports on demand. Lists of employees could be produced by department, salary grade, position classification, and/or other categories, and summary reports could be generated to focus on numbers rather than individuals (e.g., statistics regarding minority and female employment). Analytical reports support management decisions by providing quantitative and qualitative analysis of current staffing and other human resources issues.

Milkovich and Boudreau (1991) point out that there are both technical questions and organizational development issues that must be addressed in specifying the requirement for an HRIS. Technical design issues include the following:

1. The amount and types of data to be included in the HRIS database
2. The availability of these data from internal and external sources
3. The degree of decision support capability to be included
4. The extent of integration among system components to be included

The organizational development dimension includes issues such as the following:

1. The amount of effort devoted to understanding users' expectations from the system and enhancing user knowledge of system capabilities
2. Development of safeguards to protect system security and privacy of employee information
3. Cooperation among staff members from the human resources department and technical staff from the information systems department of the organization (Milkovich & Boudreau, 1991)

This final issue has become particularly important recently. In an era when data regarding potentially sensitive personnel issues must be maintained for legal and regulatory purposes, security of information and individual privacy have become paramount concerns for the human resources manager. Information such as medical status, drug abuse, sexual harassment, marital status, AIDS testing, and action by licensure boards often must be maintained in the personnel record. Milkovich and Boudreau (1991) emphasize that technology creates new obligations and responsibilities. Controlling access via multilevel password security and other sophisticated means is important to protect confidential human resources information in an automated system.

RELATIONSHIPS OF HRIS TO OTHER INFORMATION SYSTEMS

Human resources information systems cannot exist in isolation. They must be able to exchange data with other information systems, both internal systems and those external to the health services organization. Figure 6.3 depicts the major system interfaces that must be established for the HRIS to be able to meet strategic and operational objectives.

Internal System Linkages

An interface between the HRIS and the organization's payroll system provides a bidirectional flow of information between the two systems. The payroll system can provide information about employee compensation, benefits, salary history, time and attendance history, and related items for management analysis and reporting by the HRIS. The HRIS also can maintain basic employee demographic information (e.g., age, sex, position classification) for use in payroll calculations.

A similar bidirectional linkage to the budgeting system facilitates the analysis of labor costs and productivity by organizational unit. At the operational level, this linkage can be used to maintain position control within established budgetary limits.

A much less obvious interface requirement is linkage of the HRIS to clinical data systems in the organization. Sophisticated staff scheduling and workload assignments systems require the linkage of staffing information with data on patients classified by diagnosis and acuity level. A description of computer software available for this purpose, particularly in the nursing service area, is included later in this chapter. At the strategic level, productivity analysis requires the ability to link employee workload to units of service required in providing patient care.

External System Linkages

The HRIS must be able to communicate also with external organizations and data sources if all system objectives are to be met. Many hospitals and health services organizations have established electronic communication with systems operated by government agencies for transmission of withholding tax and Social Security data and for submission of required regulatory reports (e.g., EEO, affirmative action, COBRA). Similar linkages with insurance company systems can be used for providing information on employee benefit premium payments and for electronic processing of claims.

At the strategic level, health care organizations need comparative information on workload and staffing levels at other institutions of comparable size and mission. Many hospitals participate in cooperative systems of this kind, such as the MONITREND program operated by the American Hospital Association or systems operated by state

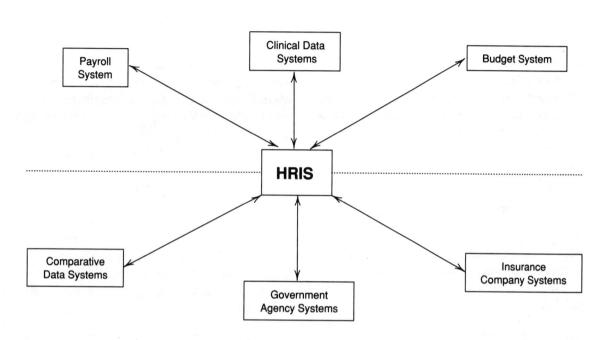

FIGURE 6.3. System interfaces.

hospital associations. Information can be exchanged electronically with these systems if appropriate interfaces are established.

DEVELOPING AND IMPLEMENTING AN HRIS

Planning for the development and implementation of an HRIS should be guided by the institution's strategic information sys-

tems plan. The institutional plan will outline the health services organization's overall approach to computer systems architecture, integration of systems, priorities for individual applications, data definition and data coding standards used to ensure system compatibility, and the general approach to software development. Following these institutional guidelines is essential to ensure that appropriate interfaces to related systems can be established.

Project Organization

The HRIS development project should be carried out by a team of key user department employees, management representatives, and information analysts (Figure 6.4). The project team should be chaired either by a knowledgeable manager from the human resources department (i.e., vice president for human resources or key assistant) or by a senior analyst from the information systems department. If a senior systems analyst is chosen to chair the project team, the individual selected must have broad knowledge of and experience with the organization and its human resources programs. The project should employ a user–driven, rather than technology–driven, focus regardless of who chairs the project team.

One representative from each major de-partment using information from or generating information for the HRIS should serve on the project team. A representative of senior management should be included to ensure that strategic objectives are considered and included in the system specifications. Because physicians come in frequent contact with employees of the hospital or health services organization, it is advisable to invite the medical staff to appoint a representative to the project team.

Technical personnel can be assigned to the team as needed. These requirements will be greater for systems to be developed in-house; they will be lower when vendor-supplied software is to be acquired. Consultants can be used as necessary, but the consultant's role should be restricted to facilitating the process and serving as a source of technical information regarding hardware and soft-

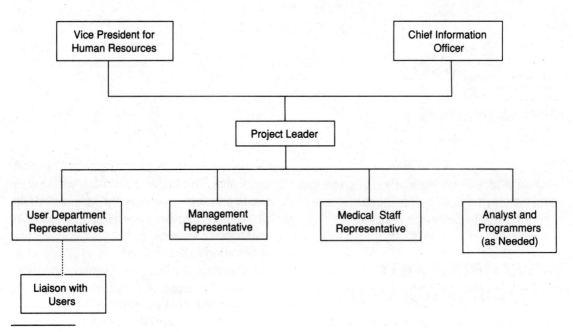

FIGURE 6.4. HRIS project organization.

ware availability. The system planning must be done by those who know the organization and its human resources requirements.

Once organized, the project team should agree on a work schedule of regular meetings and individual assignments. Estimates of time requirements for each team member should be drawn up and submitted to the appropriate department manager and central administration for review and approval. "The best insurance against a poorly developed information system is the active and enthusiastic involvement of user personnel at all stages of the project" (Austin, 1992, p. 71).

Analysis of Functional Requirements and Statement of System Specifications

Systems analysis is an important first step in the development of an HRIS. It is the process of analyzing current information practices and developing functional requirements for applications to be included in the new information system. "Systems analysis is the process of collecting, organizing, and evaluating facts about information system requirements and the environment in which the system will operate" (Austin, 1992, p. 72).

Broderick and Boudreau (1992) offer a conceptual framework for matching human resources management objectives with specific computer applications available to the manager. They group computer applications into three categories: 1) transaction processing/reporting/tracking systems, 2) expert systems, and 3) decision support systems.

Transaction processing systems provide a necessary detailed database for use by the

HRIS. They can support operational objectives related to cost leadership by reducing paper handling, standardizing reporting, increasing the accuracy of personnel processing, improving report turnaround time, and providing early warning of deviations from personnel management goals in areas such as recruiting, staffing, and retention.

Expert systems support decisions based on complex rules and knowledge determined through analysis of the previous experience of experts in a field. "Expert systems can be applied to many HR [human resources] decisions. For example, using historical data on the number and quality of recruits from various sources, where should we recommend our new division recruit to meet its hiring goals?" (Broderick & Boudreau, 1992, p. 13).

Decision support applications can support strategic decisions in which rules are not always well-defined. "Which combinations of people and skills will produce the most productive teams in our major business divisions? Which assignments and career development experiences produce executives best able to manage diversity and change?" (Broderick & Boudreau, 1992, p. 14).

Most human resources information systems in hospitals and other health care organizations focus on operational transaction processing. Inclusion of senior management representatives on the project team will help to provide a focus on strategic, as well as operational, objectives in the definition of system requirements.

After the analysis of requirements for the HRIS has been completed, the project team should prepare a written set of system specifications detailing which functional applications are to be included in the new system.

These applications might include (but not be limited to) the following:

- Manpower planning
- Skills assessment
- Recruiting
- Employment records
- Wage and salary management
- Labor relations
- Benefits management
- Education and training
- Safety and security
- Staff scheduling and assignment
- Management reporting for assessment of productivity and quality of human resources utilization in the organization

These written functional specifications for the HRIS system should be reviewed by all departments to use or be affected by the system and by the executive management team of the health services organization. After agreement on functional requirements has been obtained, the project team can proceed with system selection and implementation.

Selecting the HRIS System

Using the statement of functional requirements as a guide, the project team must choose between an in–house design and programming effort or the purchase of commercial software for implementing the HRIS. Most health services organizations today choose the packaged software approach in order to avoid the cost of in–house design and programming. If this option is followed, the project team must be satisfied that available software products will meet the majority of the requirements as outlined in the functional specifications for the system. The team must also be assured that the necessary interfaces among the HRIS software and other information systems, both internal and external, can be constructed.

Information on the availability of HRIS software can be obtained from a number of sources including the following:

1. Professional and trade association journals
2. Software directories
3. Attendance at professional meetings and trade shows
4. Discussions with colleagues at other institutions
5. Consultants who specialize in human resources management and/or health care information systems
6. Computer manufacturers and software vendors

The section at the end of the chapter entitled "Sources of Information About HRIS Software" provides a listing of selected information sources. Directories such as the *Hospital Software Sourcebook* (McKenzie, 1993) and the annual market directory published by *Computers in Healthcare* can be particularly helpful in obtaining information about vendors and the products they offer. However, these directories will not provide information about the quality of these products, and the project team must turn to other sources (e.g., users of specific software packages, consultants) to determine general levels of satisfaction with products available in the marketplace.

The following are the most important factors to be used in evaluating packaged software for use in health services organizations:

1. Congruence with organizational requirements
2. Level of satisfaction of other users of the software
3. Degree of compatibility with existing computer hardware
4. Requirements for building interfaces among the software package under consideration and other existing information systems in the organization
5. Frequency of updates to the software provided by the vendor
6. System maintenance requirements
7. Costs, including those for purchase or lease of the software; implementation (including computer hardware additions or modifications, building system interfaces, system testing, and personnel training); and new releases and maintenance after the system is implemented

The project team may choose to employ a Request for Proposals (RFP) for major HRIS software acquisitions. After information on available software has been obtained, the team should determine which software products appear to match organizational requirements most closely. After initial vendor screening has been conducted, the RFP is then submitted to those remaining on the list of qualified bidders.

Ceriello (1991) discusses the following reasons for using an RFP in selecting HRIS software:

1. The RFP defines user goals and requirements.

2. The RFP simplifies decision making.
3. The RFP saves time and facilitates comparisons of vendor responses.
4. The RFP reduces the potential for errors. (Ceriello, 1991)

Development and utilization of an RFP is a complex and time-consuming process that is not necessary in all situations. For smaller system acquisitions, a less formal process requiring limited documentation may be more appropriate. A request for information (RFI), rather than an RFP, could be used to obtain general information about software products and to help in prescreening of vendors.

After the HRIS system has been selected, the project team turns to the important tasks of system implementation.

Implementing the HRIS

Implementation of the human resources information system involves more than just installing new software. Other steps in the process include equipment acquisition and installation (if necessary), construction of interfaces with other information systems, personnel training, file conversion, system testing, and final documentation of the new system.

Implementation of the HRIS may require that computer terminals, printers, and/or personal computers be ordered and installed in several departments of the hospital or health services organization. Additional telecommunication linkages may be required to connect the new system to the organization's central computer or to decentralized computing equipment in other departments. The project team must take responsibility for necessary space planning, ordering, and installation of equipment.

As discussed previously, interfaces to other software (e.g., payroll, budgeting system) must be developed when installing the HRIS. In some cases, the HRIS vendor may take responsibility for providing the necessary connections. Alternatively, the in–house programming staff may carry out this important task, which must be completed before system testing begins.

Training of personnel who will operate and use the HRIS is a very important component of the implementation phase of the project. Project team members should be trained first, and they can then take responsibility for developing the necessary training programs in their respective departments. The software vendor will be required to provide some or all of the necessary training, but this must be carefully monitored and supervised by in–house staff. "A well–designed and well–managed training program can help overcome employee anxiety and potential resistance to change and make the difference between a successful and unsuccessful system implementation" (Austin, 1992, p. 184).

Implementation of the HRIS may require an initial file conversion step in which paper records are converted to electronic storage for use in the new system. For facilities with a large number of employees, this can be a time-consuming task that must be carefully planned and supervised. Careful editing and checking of information entered into the electronic database are essential.

After all of the other implementation steps have been completed and the software has been installed, a comprehensive test of the HRIS should be carried out prior to acceptance and operational use of the system. The test should be conducted under actual operational conditions to the extent possible and should involve all users' departments. The system test should be designed to ensure that system objectives as specified in the functional requirements are met and that operational procedures and software are functioning properly. The health services organization should not take responsibility for the HRIS software from the vendor until this test has been satisfactorily completed.

The last task in system implementation is completion of all system documentation, both operating procedures for user departments and technical documentation of computer software and hardware components. Good documentation will facilitate effective utilization of the system and training of new personnel as they join the organization.

After the HRIS system has been in use for some reasonable period of time (at least 6 months), a postimplementation evaluation should be conducted. The evaluation should cover the degree to which the system meets original objectives and functional requirements, the degree of user satisfaction, costs and benefits, and analysis of system error rates.

PITFALLS TO AVOID

Human resource managers and information professionals should be cognizant of some of the pitfalls to avoid in developing and implementing an HRIS. Several of these are as follows:

- Lack of clearly defined goals and expectations
- Failure to relate the system to strategic priorities
- Inadequate cost-benefit analysis at the beginning of the project

- Lack of integration of HRIS components
- Failure to integrate the HRIS with other hospital systems
- Inadequate user participation on the project team responsible for system design and development
- Insufficient management support for the design and development effort
- Inadequate personnel training prior to system operation
- Inadequate system testing during the implementation process

SUMMARY

Information can and should play an important role in the strategic management of human resources in health services organizations. As a key component of an organization's management information system, the HRIS assists managers in planning and evaluating human resources programs, which contribute to the accomplishment of strategic goals and objectives. Careful planning and allocation of staff is a critical component of business planning in the organization. An HRIS that is well-designed and implemented can serve both strategic and operational functions in the management of human resources.

The development of an HRIS is a major project that should be carried out by an interdisciplinary team of system users, management representatives, and information analysts. Thorough analysis of functional requirements should precede any decisions about hardware and software acquisition. Necessary interfaces to other information systems, both internal and external to the organization, must be constructed as part of system implementation. Protection of the confidentiality of sensitive employee information is an important consideration in system design and selection. Comprehensive employee training and system testing should be conducted prior to placing the system into operation.

Executive management must support all aspects of system development and implementation. The chief executive officer and senior human resources manager must ensure the following:

1. The organization has an information systems plan that is linked to the goals, objectives, and priorities in the institution's strategic plan.
2. The HRIS is planned and developed in accordance with the guidelines and priorities in the information systems plan.
3. Users are involved in all phases of the project, and the system is developed with a user-driven focus rather than an information-technology focus.
4. Adequate attention is paid to integrating the HRIS with other components of the health care organization's management information system.
5. The HRIS is periodically evaluated with changes incorporated to improve the quality of the system continually.

Discussion Questions

1. Can a single HRIS meet both strategic and operational objectives in a health services organization? Why or why not?
2. What role should human resources department personnel and other users play in the planning, selection, and implementation of an HRIS? Describe the composition of an HRIS project

development team for a 400-bed community hospital.

3. Discuss the responsibilities of executive management in providing oversight to the development of an HRIS for a health services organization.

4. Why is integration of information systems in a hospital important? Discuss the major interfaces that need to be created between an HRIS and other internal and external information systems.

5. What are some of the potential pitfalls in implementing an HRIS? Briefly describe an implementation strategy designed to avoid these pitfalls.

6. Identify three software packages that might be used as components of an HRIS for a hospital. Prepare brief descriptions of each software package and discuss the major factors you would use in evaluating each of them.

REFERENCES

Austin, C.J. (1992). *Information systems for health services administration* (4th ed.). Ann Arbor, MI: AUPHA Press/Health Administration Press.

Broderick, R., & Boudreau, J.W. (1992). Human resource management, information technology, and the competitive edge. *Academy of Management Executive, 6*(2), 2–17.

Ceriello, V.R. (1991). *Human resource management systems.* New York: Lexington Books.

Fanning, R.J. (1992). *Physician database eases staffing headaches. Healthcare Informatics, 9*(6), 46–48.

Garre, P.P., Lutey, L.M., & McElroy, L.S. (1990). Apply technology today—A computerized nursing recruitment database. *Computers in Nursing, 8*(1), 10–15.

Leonard, K. (1992). OSHA, dollars & fun: Counting CAI's benefits. *Healthcare Informatics, 9*(9), 66–68.

Martin, A.L. (1988). Information systems for human resources management. In M.D. Fottler, S.R. Hernandez, & C.L. Joiner (Eds.), *Strategic management of human resources in health services organizations* (pp. 141–177). New York: Wiley.

Melton, V.B. (1990). Human resources strategic planning: The human resources professional as architect In N. Metzger (Ed.), *Handbook of health care human resources management* (2nd ed.) (pp. 17–19). Rockville, MD: Aspen Publishers.

Milkovich, G.T., & Boudreau, J.W. (1991). *Human resource management* (6th ed.). Homewood, IL: Irwin.

Omachonu, V.K. (1991). *Total quality and productivity management in health care organizations.* Norcross, GA: Industrial Engineering and Management Press.

Wright, P.M., & McMahan, G.C. (1992). Theoretical perspectives for strategic human resource management. *Journal of Management, 18*(2), 295–320.

SOURCES OF INFORMATION ABOUT HRIS SOFTWARE

McKenzie, J.R. (Ed.). (1993). *Hospital software sourcebook.* Rockville, MD: Aspen Publishers, Inc.

This comprehensive directory contains an extensive listing of personnel and human resources management systems. Brief descriptions of the individual software packages are included.

Computers in Healthcare: Annual market directory issue. Published by Cardiff Publishing Co., 6300 S. Syracuse Way, Suite 650, Englewood, Colorado 80111.

This directory is published annually as a special issue of *Computers in Healthcare.*

Names and addresses of software vendors are included. Vendors are listed by subject categories, including personnel/human resource management. Descriptions of individual software packages are *not* included.

Ceriello, V.R. (with Christine Freeman). (1991). *Human resource management systems.* New York: Lexington Books.

Appendix C contains sources of HRMS vendors, a listing of information sources for generic human resources software that is not specific to the health care field.

HRIS software buyer's guide. Published annually by the *Personnel Journal,* 245 Fischer Ave., Costa Mesa, California 92626.

Directory of human resources services, products, and suppliers. Published annually by the American Management Association, 135 W. 50th Street, New York, New York 10020.

CHAPTER 7

MANAGEMENT OF CORPORATE CULTURE

Stephen J. O'Connor

E. Jose Proenca

LEARNING OBJECTIVES

Upon completing this chapter, the reader should be able to . . .

- Define and discuss the role of organizational culture in both the strategic management of human resources and the attainment of organizational goals/objectives.
- Give examples of health care and non-health care organizations where culture and cultural values have played a major role in facilitating or impeding organizational success.
- Understand how health care executives might develop strong cultures that support organizational goals, match the organizational strategy to the culture, and relate cultural values to such human resource functions as selection, orientation, training, performance appraisal, and compensation.

INTRODUCTION

Although a great deal of managerial attention is typically given to such activities as planning and marketing, strategy formulation, budgeting, design issues, information systems, operations, and finance, the fact remains that the attainment of organizational objectives can be accomplished only through the activities of its members. Thus, the quality of an organization's employees plays an instrumental role in the proper execution of strategy and in the achievement of stated organizational objectives. How a health care organization goes about recruiting, selecting, socializing, rewarding, promoting, training, and in general, treating these employees through its human resources practices can be traced, in large part, to its corporate or organizational culture (Sathe, 1985a). Illustration 1 presented as follows describes an organization that went to the great and unusual lengths of finding suitable re-employment opportunities for all of its 1200 displaced employees following a hospital closure. The incident provides an excellent example of how organizational culture can affect health care human resources management practices and vice versa.

The 1980s saw a growing interest in the management of organizational culture. Books such as *In Search of Excellence* (Peters & Waterman, 1982). *The Art of Japanese Management* (Pascale & Athos, 1981), and *Corporate Cultures* (Deal & Kennedy, 1982) popularized the concept of culture among management practitioners. Academic journals such as *Administrative Science Quarterly* dedicated entire issues to the subject. Since Pettigrew introduced it to the field of organizational science in 1979, numerous articles on organizational culture have appeared in the literature.

The concept of organizational culture is an important one for health care managers to consider because of its ability to influence organizational and individual performance. As with all other organizational phenomena, the principal goal of managing culture is to improve performance. The literature suggests that the incorporation of cultural insights into decision making is helpful in planning mergers and acquisitions (Mirvis & Sales, 1990); in strategic management (Wilkins, 1983); in recruitment and selection (Deal & Kennedy, 1982); in socialization and career planning (Sathe, 1985a); in improving leadership, creativity, and innovativeness (Ott, 1989); in fulfilling consumer expectations and sustaining total quality management efforts (Rakich, Longest, & Darr, 1992);

in improving profitability and market share (Atchison, 1990); and in improving productivity (Kopelman, Brief, & Guzzo, 1990). In addition, it can influence individual-level performance by its impact on employee satisfaction, morale, pride (Atchison, 1990), and commitment (Nystrom, 1993).

This chapter discusses health care organizational culture. It discusses what it is, what it is capable of achieving strategically, how it can be shaped and controlled through human resources management practices, and how it can be harnessed to realize desired organizational goals.

IN THE REAL WORLD

ILLUSTRATION 1: FINDING JOBS FOR 1200 LAID-OFF EMPLOYEES: HEALTH ONE'S GOAL[1]

I n the summer of 1991, Metropolitan-Mount Sinai Medical Center, one of the Twin Cities' prominent downtown hospitals, permanently closed its doors—to patients and to more than 2000 full- and part-time employees.

The strategy used to cope with the predicament—finding new jobs for 1200 displaced employees who sought re-employment—has strengthened the corporate culture and saved from $8 million to $16 million in potential layoff-related costs. The success of the strategy also brought Health One Corporation, the parent company of Metropolitan-Mount Sinai, an award for Excellence in Managing Corporate Change.

Paula Eubanks, of *Hospitals* magazine, interviewed Tom McLaughlin, the former vice president of human resources at Metropolitan-Mount Sinai, about how commitment to aggressive job placement, job development, and training enabled Health One to stick to its principles.

Hospitals: In approaching the impending layoff, Health One executives said they decided to "do the right thing" and find jobs for displaced employees. How did

you decide to what extent the hospital system would be willing to go to do that?
McLaughlin: Well, it's not hard when Don Wegmiller is the [Health One] president. He said, "Find jobs for all of them."

Hospitals: What part did top managers play in establishing the tone of the layoff process?
McLaughlin: The senior managers of the hospital and Health One were critical to the effort. We had a placement task force that was made up of the chief administrative officer of Health One, the chief financial officer, the senior vice president of our diversified company, the vice president of our medical affairs division, the chief operating officers of Mercy and Unity, and the chief operating officer of Health One United Hospital. Those people were absolutely critical because they set the policy. They challenged our policy proposals and sent us back to the drawing board and really owned it; they owned the policy. Then they went back to their own facilities and said, "Guys, let's do it. This is what we're going to do; this is why we're going to do it; and we all have to

pull together." We couldn't have done that without such support.

Hospitals: Had these executives gone through previous experiences that enabled them to do something like "own" it instead of "rubber-stamp" it?

McLaughlin: The Health One-Health Central merger occurred in January of 1987, so that was a process of identifying who the leadership of that new company was. And again I have to refer back to Wegmiller and the senior vice president of human resources making a commitment to building a single company with a unified company culture and consolidating human resources systems across the company. Don had a vision of Health One as what he calls a "seamless system." He was thinking of patients at the time, but I think we've tried to make it a seamless system for our employees as well so that it's one company and one culture.

Hospitals: How does Health One define what it wants that culture to be?

McLaughlin: The closest thing to a definition is reflected in our employee relations principles. They say, "Health One recognizes employees as its most important asset and, therefore, is committed to creating an environment that supports the personal and professional growth of employees."

Hospitals: Do you remember a time when the management team turned to those principles for guidance?

McLaughlin: One of the elements in the principles says, "Promote employment security for all employees." So we asked, "Does this mean when times are good, or does this mean when times are tough?" One of the criticisms of this statement by employees was, "That's just a bunch of guys up in the ivory tower putting this

plan together." There was not that much ownership for it throughout the organization. So it was met with a whole lot of skepticism [by employees] who said, "Well, we'll see whether we live it or not."

But I would say that there was a pretty strong commitment to the principles on the part of the managers. Interestingly enough, as we began to share this with the union leadership, the union leaders took strong ownership of it; they said, "We really like this. And we want you to become this. Maybe you're not this now, but we want to help you become what you say you believe in."

Still, I think the average rank-and-file employees were rather skeptical about it all.

Hospitals: How did employees learn they were going to get pink slips?

McLaughlin: One of the things I found some other Twin Cities companies doing was hauling people into a big auditorium and giving them the word. Or they would have "hit teams" that would go through the building, saying, "You're laid off; you're leaving." I thought that was horrible.

So we made a commitment that anybody who was going to lose their job—which was damn near everybody—was going to get the word from someone with whom they already had a relationship. We made sure that the supervisors were the ones who gave messages out and gave the slips to their employees. And I'm really proud that we did it this way.

Hospitals: During all of this, were you able to sleep at night?

McLaughlin: Yes. I didn't have that problem at all. But I had a delayed reaction. It was after I moved to my new job, once the whole thing was over, that I started

to have sleepless nights. But when you're going through it, you are so engaged in the policy, union contract, and interpretation issues. There is so much intensity around all of this; and I hate to say this, but it's extremely stimulating. So you don't have time to feel the grief. Most of us didn't start going through a real grieving process until after it was all done.
Hospitals: Where is the Health One organization in terms of "healing"?
McLaughlin: I think the best test of that is

how we will handle future layoffs—when people see that other Health One employees who lose their jobs are treated as well as the people from Metropolitan-Mount Sinai.

The fact is, we've had to do more layoffs. There are 28 people whose positions we're eliminating here. We have 28 jobs already lined up for them, even before we announce the layoffs. They will all get job offers, and we'll give them 6 weeks' notice. ◈

[1] Excerpted from *Hospitals,* Vol. 66, No. 1, by permission, January 5, 1992, Copyright 1992, American Hospital Publishing, Inc.

DEFINING ORGANIZATIONAL CULTURE

The Algonquinian-speaking Indians of North America believed in a concept called *manitou* (Salisbury, 1982). *Manitou* refers to a manifestation of spiritual power (Baraga, 1850), a supernatural strength or metaphysical energy that gave rise to spirits and natural forces (Gove, 1971). To the Algonquin, everything that could not be comprehended was attributed to *manitou.* Similarly, the very modern concept of organizational culture has been described as a mystical, magical (Atchison, 1990; Deal & Kennedy, 1982; Morgan, 1986), and invisible (Kilmann, 1984) power that can appear to influence organizations in supernatural ways. Many of the apparently inexplicable and irrational acts that occur in organizations can be attributed in large part to the concept of organizational culture (Schein, 1985). Much like the concept of *manitou,* culture feels illusory; nevertheless, it is a very real phenomenon

governing the beliefs and behaviors in organizations. For this reason, an understanding of culture is *essential* for health care managers. If ignored, not adequately considered, or poorly understood, it can work quite like a supernatural force controlling health care organizational behavior.

Because many different meanings and connotations have been attributed to culture (Schein, 1985), the term tends to be especially confusing. For example, microbiologists grow bacterial cultures. Anthropologists analyze ethnic cultures. Others refer to highly civilized societies as being cultured and more primitive ones as being uncultured. In this latter regard, European societies are often thought of as being more highly refined than American culture, especially in areas such as the arts, literature, music, architecture, and fashion. This view of culture, as measured disparities in level of social refinement, although still commonly used, is old-fashioned and should not be confused with contemporary notions of organizational culture in any way.

What then is corporate or organizational culture? Innumerable definitions have been advanced in the literature, but an exclusive definition of the concept does not exist (Ott, 1989). Cryptic explanations such as "the glue that holds organizations together," "the lubrication that makes the gears mesh," or "the way we do things around here," while conveying the fundamental essence of what is meant by the term, are not nearly complete enough to be useful on their own (Duncan, 1989b). However, the reader will see that these abbreviated descriptions become more meaningful as the concept becomes better understood.

Perhaps the best place to begin gaining a true understanding of organizational culture is to examine Schein's (1985) definition and three-level model. Schein (1985) defines culture as the:

> pattern of basic assumptions—invented, discovered, or developed by a group as it learns to cope with its problems of external adaptation and internal integration—that has worked well enough to be considered valid and, therefore, to be taught to new members as the correct way to perceive, think, and feel in relation to these problems. (p. 9)

In addition, culture exists in three interacting, hierarchical levels called 1) artifacts, 2) beliefs and values, and 3) basic underlying assumptions (Schein, 1985).

Artifacts

Artifacts represent the most visible and objective aspect of organizational culture (Duncan, 1989b). Anything in an organization's physical, social, and emotional environment potentially can be a cultural artifact. Examples of artifacts include group member dress and deportment, facility layout and de-cor, furnishings and equipment, written documents, spoken words, and work outputs.

Artifacts serve as the highly visible manifestation or outgrowth of culture, and are thus relatively easy to examine and describe. For this reason, many writers have tended to view artifacts *as the culture* (Nystrom, 1993). Anthropologists who examine fragments of pottery, jewelry, and tools excavated from an archeological site are examining artifacts of a culture. The difficult task is to infer the content of the culture based on those artifacts. Likewise, when one views the immense Pacific Island Culture collection, made famous by the late Dr. Margaret Mead, in New York's Museum of Natural History, one is not observing a complete culture—only artifacts of that culture. Thus, although cultural artifacts are easily observed, they tend to be difficult to decode without the benefit of the information contained in the two levels beneath them (Sathe, 1985b). Specific categories of artifacts include symbols; language; ceremonies and rituals; stories, myths, and legends; and heroes and heroines.

Symbols

Symbols are physical representations of shared values that can be used to fortify a culture by evoking in workers a profound sense of self-esteem and pride. Symbols can be almost anything—a sculpture, building, picture, expression, logo, or award.

Language

Language is such an important element that a culture cannot remain in tact without it. The significance of language derives from its ability to influence how people think, behave, and perceive. In Navajo language, for example, corresponding words for *boss, sub-*

ordinate, or *hierarchy* do not exist (Ott, 1989). As such, members of this culture cannot be expected to assimilate easily into formal bureaucratic structures without changing the language and attenuating their culture.

Language contains expressions, phrases, jargon, and acronyms that cultural outsiders may not be able to interpret. The vernacular of the health administration subculture is replete with representative jargon (e.g., matrix structure, strategic business units, corporate culture) and an alphabet soup of acronyms (e.g., HMO, TQM, PPS, DRG, MIS). Likewise, the language of interns and residents is central to the physician socialization process. Konner's (1987) "Glossary of House Officer Slang" (pp. 379–390) provides more than 200 expressions and acronyms used by American interns and residents. These types of expressions are indispensable to members of the culture, but are virtually incomprehensible to people from the outside. To genuinely comprehend and influence a culture, one must learn to speak its language.

Ceremonies and Rituals

While ceremonies refer to the occasional events when a culture's values and assumptions are deliberately showcased (Deal, 1985), rituals refer to the habitual and customary approaches to work that convey and sustain culture. Organizational activities such as meetings, strategic planning, and the process of budgeting can become ritualized approaches to work from which "people learn, celebrate, and reshape core values" (Deal, 1985, p. 310). A classic example is the scrubbing and gowning process of surgical culture (Deal, 1985). Konner (1987) describes this mechanical and protracted hand washing as being:

> so exceedingly thorough, that it [is] like a ritual confirmation of the germ theory, a self-reteaching of that theory, every day. The gowning and gloving [are] equally ritualistic but more dramatic, since they [involve] nurses attending the surgeon . . . like priestesses who . . . [are] responsible for the purity of the ritual and who [will] pounce mercilessly on a technical blemish. (p. 37)

Stories, Myths, and Legends

Accounts of previous incidents in an organization's history are known as stories. Stories impart the ideal standard suggestive of a culture's favored values, behaviors, and outlooks by delivering "their core messages implicitly, metaphorically, and usually symbolically. They tend to have a greater impact on attitudes than most other forms of verbal communication" (Ott, 1989, p. 32). As such, members of the culture better retain the central ideas communicated in stories than through other types of communiques that may be more to the point, but much less intense. As time progresses, some stories may become less factually accurate by being embellished and accentuated. These types of stories are known as *myths* and *legends*. Organizational members are aware that the truth may be slightly misrepresented, but a myth or legend still serves the same function as the more factually correct story.

Heroes and Heroines

All organizational stories contain characters known a *heroes* and *heroines*. These key individuals epitomize the core cultural elements that the organization wishes to preserve or bolster. Heroes and heroines are role models (Deal, 1985) who render testimony to the significance and vitality of the values underlying the culture.

The illustration below is a powerful example of a genuine cultural story in use at a large, religiously affiliated university hospital.

IN THE REAL WORLD

ILLUSTRATION 2: NORMA JEAN FRANK: THE COURAGEOUS PHILOSOPHY OF AN OPTIMISTIC LEADER[2]

According to Thelma Frank, there are two ways of looking at life. "You can be defeated by life, or you can take what life has to offer and run with it—up until the last minute." Thelma's daughter Norma Jean Frank, was a student of the later philosophy.

A highly respected administrator at St. Louis University Hospital, Norma Jean Frank struggled against the adversities of diabetes, blindness, and kidney failure during the last years of her life. On her death in October, 1984, Frank's co-workers demonstrated their admiration by establishing the Norma Jean Frank Memorial Fund, in which money donated in Norma's memory would be used to establish a dialysis unit at the hospital.

On June 29, 1989, a dedication was held to celebrate the opening of the Norma Jean Frank Dialysis Unit. The funds, more than $225,000, came from the gifts and pledges of more than 500 Medical Center employees who gave graciously in Norma's memory.

Thelma Frank, a dedicated hospital volunteer, was one of her daughter's greatest admirers and supporters. In 1983, she donated one of her own kidneys for what turned out to be an unsuccessful trans-

plant for her daughter. When Norma's illness left her legally blind and in need of daily dialysis, Thelma was there, offering whatever help she could give, both on the job and at home. But helplessness was not a word familiar to the younger Frank's vocabulary.

In 1983, nearly a year after her eyesight began to fail, Norma received a master's degree in allied health sciences from Webster University. "She used tapes to study," explained her mother. "At work she used a talking computer and special glasses. She was prepared to learn braille, if it would have helped her continue her work."

What kind of person affects the lives of co-workers in such a way that they would give so much?

"Norma was a hard-working, ingenious, well-organized administrator," said Leonard Laskowski, Ph.D., director of the clinical microbiology laboratory at the hospital. "Her achievements in microbiology are noted in *Who's Who in America,* as well as the *Dictionary of International Biographies.*"

Others who knew Norma recall her contributions toward improving patient care, including food service and medication distribution for hospital patients. For these and other contributions, Frank was named the first recipient of the hospital's Caring Award, now known as the Norma Jean Frank Caring Award. She is also remembered as a creative thinker and a solid decision maker. However, her professional achievements are only part of what made Norma a heroine in the eyes of those who knew her.

"When she was lab supervisor, she always tried to remember her employees' birthdays and anniversaries," recalled Dr. Laskowski.

"She was a great teacher and her lessons will be with me always!" said another admirer.

"This was her world," explained her mother. "She had other interests. She was a figure skater and an artist. But she really never thought about herself. She always thought of others." Norma Jean Frank was the kind of person who planned Christmas throughout the year. She kept lists of her employees' clothing sizes, the names and ages of their children, likes, dislikes, and even favorite colors. She lived to serve others.

A letter written by a hospital staff member serves as eloquent testimony to the memory of Norma Jean Frank: "All too often our true feelings go unspoken," he wrote. "We say 'Good morning,' 'How are you today,' 'Can we meet later and talk about this or that?' But what we wanted to say was "You are one terrific lady, Norma Jean Frank. You are an inspiration to all of us and you have shown us daily the meaning of courage."

[2] This illustration is from McDonald, B. (1989). Norma Jean Frank: The courageous philosophy of an optimistic leader. *Chart,* Fall, p. 10; reprinted by permission of St. Louis University Medical Center.

Beliefs and Values

Knowledge of the second level of culture—beliefs and values—can offer insights into how individuals explicitly interpret, account for, and uphold their actions as organizational members (Sathe, 1985b).

Values, perhaps better referred to at this level as *espoused values,* refer to the *conscious* outcomes that are considered desirable or meaningful to organizations (Beyer, 1981). An organization's espoused values are relatively easy for the membership to voice and on which to agree. Typically, they are expressed in documents such as mission or philosophy statements (Gibson, Newton, & Cochran, 1990).

Beliefs, although similar to espoused values, are less of an aspiration and more of a conscious understanding of what is believed to be *real* and *true* in an organization. Whereas "beliefs provide cognitive justification for organizational action patterns, . . . values provide the emotional energy or motivation to act on them" (Ott, 1989, p. 40). The incident described in Illustration 1 provides an example of this values/beliefs distinction in a health care culture. Health One Corporation maintained an explicit, conscious desire (i.e., value) to promote employment security for all employees. Although this principle was expressly valued by the organization's top management, it did not serve as a belief initially because employees viewed it with a great deal of skepticism. To the extent that the expressed value of employment security is upheld consistently and lived throughout the organization, it will become a belief. Employees will come to see this value as something that is real and true, and not just empty rhetoric.

Basic Underlying Assumptions

The level that comes closest to characterizing a culture is that of basic underlying assumptions (Ott, 1989; Sathe, 1985b; Schein, 1985). The assumptions operating at this level, although unstated and unrecognized, strongly regulate behavior (Kilmann, 1984) by showing members which actions are regarded indisputably as appropriate or inappropriate to the group.

Espoused values can often be detected by asking people about them directly or by reading about them in organizational literature. Underlying assumptions, however, are "the out-of-conscious system of beliefs, perceptions, and values" (Ott, 1989, p. 42). They are much more difficult to uncover because they have dropped from awareness and exist only in the subliminal backwaters of the mind.

Espoused values are normative statements of desired outcomes or conditions that an organization believes ought to exist. However, espoused values do not become basic underlying assumptions automatically unless they work effectively and repetitively over time. To the degree that espoused values, or any other ways of behaving or perceiving, *work* over time, they will inevitably fall from the organization's consciousness and become collectively and implicitly acceptable. When this occurs, they will not be questioned, challenged, or even talked about, thus making it extremely difficult for even organizational members to articulate them.

However, because they represent the intrinsic "way we do things around here," they will be earnestly adhered to. It is this level of basic underlying assumptions that comes closest to giving meaning to the idea of culture.

An example of a basic underlying assumption operating in modern American culture is that we respect and honor our elderly parents and grandparents. The idea that they should be left to die unattended when they become too old, frail, and burdensome is repulsive to us. Rarely is this assumption talked about explicitly. However, if someone were to challenge it seriously, such as when former Colorado Governor Richard Lamm publicly stated, "the old should die and get out of the way"; the tacit assumption—that it is very wrong to hurry the deaths of the elderly because they may be a burden to others—became explicit (i.e., surfaced) in the public reaction that followed.

We can contrast this implicit value with pre-twentieth century arctic Inuit culture, in which it was believed proper to abandon the elderly by leaving them to freeze to death or to be eaten by wild animals when they became unable to contribute to tribal survival adequately (Salloway, 1982). In that particular culture, the notion that the elderly "should die and get out of the way" was not challenged nor debated vigorously. In fact, the elderly themselves often indicated when their time had come. Jack London's (1981) short story *The Law of Life* recounts how an old man left to die did not complain about his treatment, rather he affirmed that it "was the way of life, and it was just" (p. 280). Because this practice effectively and consistently allowed Inuit families and tribes to survive in an inordinately harsh physical environment, as time progressed, the practice fell from conscious consideration and became a basic underlying assumption (i.e., "the way we do things around here").

It is also important to recognize that consciously espoused values do not always correspond with deeper underlying assumptions. For example, a new hospital administrator who has not had the opportunity to explore the organization's culture fully, may be at a loss to explain the very strong resistance to the hospital's publicly stated values of: 1) patients are the reason we exist; 2) all employees will be treated fairly, equitably, and with dignity; and 3) employees are encouraged to participate in the management process. By taking the time to examine the culture carefully, it would become apparent that it is not a supernatural force bringing about this resistance, but espoused values that are at odds with the basic underlying assumptions that maintain that: 1) patients are the problem; 2) women and minorities are second-class citizens; and 3) employees cannot be trusted to be empowered with managerial responsibilities.

In sum, all health care organizations possess specific and identifiable cultures (Deal, 1990) that are characterized by a pattern of beliefs, behaviors, and unspoken underlying assumptions that are conveyed to, and shared by, all members (Conner, 1990). An organization's culture can be analyzed in terms of artifacts and/or espoused values and beliefs, but the surest (and most difficult) way to grasp it is to understand its basic underlying assumptions.

CULTURAL STRENGTH

Organizational cultures can be characterized as being strong or weak. In strong cultures, a dominant and unified set of shared assumptions is adhered to consistently by members throughout the organization (Rakich, Longest, & Darr, 1992). Sathe (1985b) specifies three attributes that contribute to a culture's strength: 1) thickness, which represents the number of underlying assumptions in use by members; 2) extent of sharing, which denotes the degree assumptions are shared throughout the organization; and 3) clarity of ordering, which refers to how evident it is that some assumptions are more prominent than others. Strong cultures tend to be thick, widely shared, and ordered more clearly than weak cultures.

A health care organization can benefit from a strong and widely shared culture in a variety of ways. First, it can provide employees with a clear sense of direction, meaning, and guidance (Atchison, 1990), which can obviate the need for extensive or restrictive systems of bureaucratic control (Ott, 1989). Second, strong cultures can allow health care organizations and their employees to achieve valued outcomes. In a strong culture, employees are able to identify better with the organization and consequently tend to demonstrate greater commitment, cooperation, loyalty (Martin, Feldman, Hatch, & Sitkin, 1983), satisfaction, morale, and pride (Atchison, 1990). Third, a strong culture is imperative for the establishment and perpetuation of high technical and consumer-perceived service quality (Albert, 1989; O'Connor & Bowers, 1990). Last, strong and widely shared cultures are also likely to improve decision making and communication (Sathe, 1985a), as well as to facilitate succession planning (Schein, 1985). For these reasons, health care organizations that feature strong cultures are frequently viewed as superior performers (Nystrom, 1993).

Alternatively, weak cultures are splintered

and lack consensus on, and commitment to, the overarching values, beliefs, and assumptions that characterize the dominant culture. In other words they are cultures in disarray (Rakich, Longest, & Darr, 1992). They emerge from the existence of splinter groups, conflicting subcultures, and a general lack of *shared,* organization wide values and assumptions.

The lack of connectedness and *esprit de corps* brought about by weak cultures can result in situations in which animosity, conflict, and divisiveness run rampant and even the most minor problems become overblown. Absent a collective focus, employees find themselves "compelled to use their own values as a basis for making decisions, they are inclined to say, 'You haven't given me anything to believe in, so I'm going to make decisions in my own best interest'" (Atchison, 1990, p. 130).

Weak cultures usually are viewed unfavorably because they frequently create a less gratifying work experience, and consequently employees who are reluctant to work very hard on behalf of the organization. Additionally, weak cultures can have a negative impact on an organization's bottom line by insidiously contributing to erosion in profitability, productivity, and market share (Atchison, 1990).

Subcultures

Unfortunately, the cultures of many health care organizations tend to be weak and in disarray (Bice, 1984). This is due largely to the fact that they harbor numerous and diverse subcultures that must be fused together to achieve organizational objectives (Lombardi, 1992). Although some of these subcultures are supportive and advance the values of the principal culture, others conflict by maintaining distinct and rival value systems.

Subcultures can be categorized into three groups called: 1) enhancing, 2) orthogonal, and 3) counterculture (Siehl & Martin, 1984). As the name suggests, the *enhancing* subculture is supportive and very much in harmony with the principal culture. An example might be a hospital's sponsoring religious congregation. The *orthogonal* subculture partially overlaps the principal culture by sharing some of the same values, but also simultaneously adheres to others that are different. An example of an orthogonal subculture might be a radiology group organized as an independent professional corporation that contracts exclusively with a specific hospital. *Countercultures* are confederate subcultures that are inimical to the value structure of the overall organizational culture. Because trade unions can be conceived as counterorganizations that often are at ideological odds with the main organization, they exemplify the archetypal counterculture (Morgan, 1986).

In health care organizations, subcultures can emerge almost *anywhere a group can be identified,* such as on nursing units, in service-line programs and ancillary departments, as well as among governing bodies. However, the presence of numerous and assorted professional subcultures such as nursing, administration, medicine, and other health-related occupations is probably most responsible for the observation that health care organizations are culturally weak. Different professions arise from distinctive theoretical paradigms and professional socialization processes that leave their imprint in the form of unique frames of reference that serve to shape priorities and guide organizational activity differentially. Thus, for example, although physicians are considered essential to the functioning of most health care organizations, their distinctive and strong professional subculture frequently clashes with the dominant culture (Myer & Tucker, 1992; Raelin, 1986), as well as the administrative subculture (O'Connor & Shewchuk, 1993; Shortell, 1991).

Most complex health care work places possess weak cultures due to their highly differentiated and professionalized nature, which contributes to the formation of orthogonal and countercultural subcultures. Indeed, the need to bring order to this chaos can be quite daunting. Nevertheless, the obligation for doing so rests squarely with the chief executive officer (CEO) (Stevens, 1991; Zuckerman, 1989), who must clarify purposes and values as well as convey them continuously through as many vehicles as possible (Filerman, 1989). Accordingly, the CEO must act as: 1) a role model, and 2) as a skilled storyteller (Atchison, 1990).

As the leading behavioral role model, the CEO can do much to facilitate a desired culture. Because "actions speak louder than words," a leader's behavioral conduct conveys more convincing messages than oral and written exhortations. The aphorism, "Walk your talk" (Nystrom, 1993, p. 47) is especially valuable in this regard. The introductory illustration demonstrates how instrumental the CEO and senior management staff of Health One Corporation were in creating a strong and unified culture by acting as appropriate role models.

In addition to playing the proper roles, the CEO must develop skills in orchestrating artifactual expressions—symbols; language; ceremonies and rituals; stories, myths, and legends; and heroes and heroines—that furnish insights into the main culture (Deal, 1985; Sathe, 1985b).

A Cautionary Caveat

Although strong cultures are considered generally desirable, it is important to note that they do not *always* enhance performance. Inappropriate values and beliefs, particularly when widely shared and strongly adhered to, may cause organizations to march in the wrong direction and to resist change efforts.

The content of culture, as described by specific types of values and beliefs is, therefore, equally critical in influencing organizational performance (Sathe, 1985a). Environmental conditions may make some types of cultures more appropriate than others. In high-tech, research-driven environments, hospitals whose cultures stress values such as innovation and risk-taking may be more successful than hospitals that share risk-aversion and traditionalism as values. In stable environments, however, the opposite may be true. Cultures emphasizing efficiency and tradition may outperform those that place a high priority on constant and unnecessary change.

Accordingly, in rapidly changing environments such as health care, even strong and appropriate cultures may not always improve performance. As environmental opportunities and threats change, values and norms that have worked well in the past may no longer suffice. Organizations would have to discard old values and beliefs and adopt new ones. In such cases, adaptive cultures are called for (Kotter & Heskett, 1992). Organizations whose cultures promote flexibility and adaptability in values and norms are more likely to survive and to succeed in turbulent environments.

Health care administrators seeking to manage culture for superior performance need to understand the relationship between the two concepts. How does organizational culture influence performance? It is believed that culture affects performance through other organizational practices (Sathe, 1985a). The following sections address the interaction of culture with two such practices—strategic management and human resources management.

ORGANIZATIONAL CULTURE AND CORPORATE STRATEGY

Organizational culture affects and is affected by the strategic context of the firm. It influences the various steps of the strategic management process, from environmental analysis and goal setting, to strategy formulation, implementation, and control. It influences the kinds of strategies selected by an organization, and it determines the effectiveness with which the selected strategies are implemented. The strategies adopted by an organization also affect its culture. Every strategy has an unique configuration of structure, management systems, and organizational processes that it imposes on an organization. This unique configuration is likely to affect the existing culture of the organization (Joyce & Slocum, 1990).

Managers' perceptions of cultural values in the organization affect the manner in which they monitor, interpret, and evaluate environmental issues. An issue such as managed competition may be interpreted as a threat by administrators of hospitals with tra-

ditional, risk-averse cultures. The same issues may be perceived as an opportunity in hospitals with innovative, risk-taking cultures. An organization's culture may also determine the aspects of the environment to which it gives higher priority. Hospitals with innovative, research-oriented cultures may pay more attention to the technological aspects of the environment. Religious hospitals with charity-oriented cultures may be more concerned about the social aspects of the environment.

An organization's culture is also reflected in its mission and objectives. Hospitals with a mission to provide "high-tech" care are often characterized by innovative cultures, whereas those with missions to provide "high-touch" care have patient-focused cultures. The former will have objectives in the areas of medical research and technology acquisition, and the latter will have objectives in the area of patient satisfaction.

Strategy formulation is ideally an analytical decision-making process based on economic realities. In practice, however, this process is often biased by political and cultural realities within the organization (Bower & Doz, 1979). Incomplete financial information often forces managers to use value-based judgments in evaluating strategic alternatives and making strategic choices. Often, strategies that make the best economic sense are discarded because they run afoul of the values of powerful subcultures within the hospital. Cost containment strategies may have to be pared down in the face of quality-related values. Cultural values also provide a framework that facilitates the interpretation of large amounts of information that would otherwise overwhelm the decision maker.

Strategy implementation is facilitated when organization members' values are incorporated in business strategies. Strong cultures ensure that values and beliefs are shared by both managers and employees and improve the chances that employees' values are represented in the strategies selected by management. As a consequence, employees are committed to strategy adopted by the organization and motivated to implement this strategy more effectively. If physicians and managers share the belief that costs can be cut without sacrificing quality, then it will much easier to implement a cost containment strategy. Managers could promote effective implementation by incorporating physician values (in the form of quality safeguards) in the cost containment practices.

It has been widely recommended that organizations find a fit between their strategies and their cultures (Deshpande & Parasuraman, 1986; Schwartz & Davis, 1981; Shrivastava, 1984). Organizations whose strategies match their cultures are likely to perform better than organizations whose cultures clash with their strategies (Bourgeois & Jemison, 1982). Strategy-culture congruence results in the formulation of better strategies and superior implementation. Lack of congruity, however, results in conflicts of interest, confusion, and resistance to implementation.

CULTURAL FORMATION, MAINTENANCE, AND CHANGE

The association between human resources management practices and organizational culture is best understood in the context of the formation, maintenance, and change of culture. Selection, socialization, compensation, reward systems, and removal are some commonly suggested means for the propagation of culture (Sathe, 1985a). In order to understand the relationship between human resources strategies and the culture of an organization, we have to look at culture formation from a behavioral point of view.

The Behavioral Aspect of Culture

Thompson and Luthans (1990) describe culture as socially learned values and norms that help organization members cope with their experiences. What are the implications of this statement? First, it implies that culture formation involves learning through social interaction. Culture is a system of values that have been learned during a period of time as a result of past experiences, both successful and unsuccessful. Second, it implies that behavior is connected to the development of culture. Organization members modify their behaviors by observing others and learning which behaviors are rewarded and which ones are disciplined (O'Reilly, 1989; Thompson & Luthans, 1990). The learning and behavioral aspects of culture are fundamental to its formation and transmission.

According to social learning theory (Bandura, 1977), learning occurs either through direct experience or through vicarious processes. Direct learning follows the notion that behavior is a function of its consequences (Skinner, 1938). Individuals learn which behaviors are expected and which ones are not by recognizing the connection between their various behaviors and the consequences of such behaviors. Accordingly, they modify their behaviors, repeating those that result in favorable consequences and reducing the frequency of those that produce unpleasant reactions.

Management can aid this learning process by providing feedback to the employee. Positive feedback reinforces the behavior and negative feedback deters its occurrence. This interaction between management and employees facilitates the learning process and leads to the formation of culture. The same holds true for interactions between employees and their peers, mentors, or subordinates. By learning to associate behaviors with consequences, employees learn to cope with experiences in the organization. The feedback they receive enables them to articulate the behavioral norms in the organization, and as they accumulate this knowledge, they develop an understanding of the organization's culture. Management propagates the culture by providing the feedback and reinforcement.

The behavior-consequence association can also be learned vicariously. Employees learn by observing what happens to other employees or by hearing about the experiences of others through formal (e.g., memos, meetings) or informal (e.g., newsletters, grapevine) channels of communication. The direct and indirect learning of the connection between behaviors and consequences leads to a modification of behaviors to maximize favorable outcomes. As these behaviors are internalized into norms and values, culture is formed. The formal and informal communications can be used by management as transmitters of culture.

Thompson and Luthans (1990) also suggest that employees learn by recognizing the appropriate antecedents for a particular behavior. A behavior that is appropriate in some situations may not be tolerated in others. Organizations that place a higher value on autonomy in certain administrative tasks may demand absolute adherence to rules in certain clinical procedures. Once again, the learning process here occurs through direct experiences as well as through vicarious

means. As employees develop a knowledge of the antecedents-behaviors links in the organization, they improve their perception of the organizational culture.

The preceding discussion can be summarized by stating that direct and vicarious social interactions allow members to interpret the relationships among antecedents, behaviors and consequences in an organization. This facilitates individual assimilation of behavioral norms and values within the organization. As more employees are exposed to a common set of experiences, there is a shared perception of the values and beliefs in the organization, and a strong culture develops.

The extent to which management can influence the formation, transmission, and change of culture depends on its ability to dictate the antecedents and consequences of behavior in the organization. Human resources management practices and policies constitute an important avenue available to management for this purpose.

The Role of Human Resources Practices in Culture Transmission

Human resources management strategies such as selection, socialization and development, and rewards systems and performance evaluation can be used to set the antecedents and consequences in the organization. They can also reinforce those behaviors that management wants internalized in the form of organizational culture.

Selection

In addition to the interactions within the organization, employee perceptions of organizational culture are influenced by predispositions formed outside of the organization. The society from which an organization draws its human resources inculcates certain norms and values in its members. In the course of a lifetime of social interaction with family, friends, and institutions (e.g., schools, churches, work organizations), individuals go through a continuous process of matching antecedents-behaviors-consequences to form a host of behavioral norms and values.

These extra-organizational norms and values influence an individual's perception of the organizational culture when he or she joins the organization. They also may influence an individual's image of the organization before joining it. Organizations may be variously perceived as having task-oriented or people-oriented cultures (Sheridan, 1992). Some hospitals may be viewed as having highly stressful but high-paying work environments. Others may be seen as low-paying organizations but with pleasant, low-stress environments. Perceptions of an organization will determine the kind of individuals who seek employment in it. Applicants who thrive on competition, and who place a relatively high value on compensation may be attracted to high-pay, high-stress organizations. Those who value cooperation and pleasant working conditions are likely to be willing to sacrifice pay for low-stress work environments.

Societal predispositions require management to review the values and expectations of potential employees carefully. Selection and recruitment practices should ensure that applicants whose values are compatible with those of the organization will be hired and that applicants whose values are incompatible will be screened out (Chatman, 1991). In addition to job-related criteria such as skills, knowledge, intelligence, and ability, selection processes should also include cri-

teria measuring the fit of values between the applicant and the organization.

Organizations are recognizing that the formation, maintenance, and change of culture is facilitated by hiring individuals whose values and expectations match the profile desired by the organizational culture. Conversely, the selection of individuals with values that are inconsistent with or contrary to the culture make the management of organizational culture even more difficult (Trice & Beyer, 1993). Organizations are finding it useful to provide applicants with information about the organization. If candidates perceive a mismatch between their values and those of the organization, they can withdraw from the recruitment process.

Organizations are trying to learn as much as they can about applicants by spending time with them prior to hiring. The pre-hiring stage has become an important part of the recruitment process. Potential employees are invited to spend time with different members of the organization. Applicants whose values match those of successful members of an organization have a better chance of being selected (Rothstein & Jackson, 1981). Traditional recruitment practices have given way to psychological testing and structured interviews. Illustration 3 describes the practices used by hospitals to develop a profile of candidates' values that are then compared with predetermined profiles of an ideal candidate for the job.

Socialization and Development

Human resources managers can use selection practices to match the external experiences of applicants to the organization's culture. In a similar fashion, they can use socialization to direct the internal experi-

IN THE REAL WORLD

ILLUSTRATION 3: HOSPITALS PROBE APPLICANTS' VALUES FOR ORGANIZATIONAL 'FIT'[3]

Hospital human resources managers are increasingly seeking ways to identify job candidates who share their organizational values. Irvine Medical Center in California uses testing and interviews to evaluate employee-hospital congruence on values such as service orientation, proactiveness, and teamwork. It has found that selection of employees who share its core values has greatly reinforced its corporate culture. Lutheran General Hospital in Park Ridge, Illinois, conducts a structured interview for internal and external candidates seeking positions at the supervisory level and above. The interview seeks to ascertain the applicants' feelings about five values held dear by the Lutheran Health Care System: respect, servanthood, stewardship, creativity, and collaboration.

According to Carson Dye, vice president at St. Vincent Medical Center in Toledo, Ohio, these hiring practices achieve better results than the "chit-chat" interviews and reference checks that are currently the norm in the industry.

[3] Excerpted from *Hospitals,* Vol. 65, No. 20, by permission, October 20, 1991, Copyright 1991, American Hospital Publishing, Inc.

---

ences of employees toward the formation and assimilation of organizational culture. Organizational socialization is a process by which individuals learn the values and behavioral norms that contribute to the culture. Learning occurs through a variety of activities that facilitate social interaction.

Mentor programs are a commonly used form of socializing new employees. New recruits are encouraged to form relationships with senior organizational personnel. The senior member serves as a source of cultural information for new recruits who want to learn the antecedent-behavior-consequence links in the organization. New employees can use the values and norms of their mentors to guide their own behaviors (Terborg, Castore, & DeNinno, 1976).

For employees who have been in the organization for some time, socialization serves to foster maintenance or even change of culture. Training and development is a form of socialization often used for this purpose (Van Maanen, 1977). Employees go through intensive training programs aimed at reinforcing existing values and norms, or in case of change, replacing existing values and norms with new ones. Existing perceptions of culture are very difficult to change. Change will come only in incremental form unless concerted efforts are made through comprehensive organizational development programs.

Effective socialization techniques also may include the use of clear career paths and management role models to exemplify

IN THE REAL WORLD
ILLUSTRATION 4: RETREATS ADVANCE THE CORPORATE CULTURE[4]

A retreat for hospital managers can be a useful tool in developing or changing an institution's corporate culture, according to Diane Iorfida, senior vice president for human resources for the 768-bed University Hospitals of Cleveland in Ohio. To achieve the best results, Iorfida recommends that the retreat should have culture as a clearly stated objective and that collectively participants should address questions such as: Who are our customers? What do they want? What values does the institution need to deliver what they want? What human resources management practices (e.g., hiring and pay programs) will nurture those values? Neutral outside facilitators are needed to help participants differentiate between their individual and institutional values. Karen Poole, administrator of 93-bed Women's and Children's Hospital in Lafayette, Louisiana, suggests that even retreats that were not originally planned for culture development can provide the dynamic atmosphere in which management can propagate culture.

[4] Excerpted from *Hospitals,* Vol. 65, No. 18, by permission, September 20, 1991, Copyright 1991, American Hospital Publishing, Inc.

strong, visible values. Employees who perceive their organizations as having intensive socialization and support programs are more committed to the organization. This indicates that socialization promotes the direct, as well as vicarious, learning of norms and values, thus helping in the creation, maintenance, and change of organizational culture. Illustration 4 demonstrates the use of retreats as a socialization tool for the development of culture.

Reward Systems and Performance Evaluation

Reward systems represent a powerful tool for influencing an organization's culture (Kerr & Slocum, 1987). One of the lessons from the behavioral perspective of culture is that organizations can facilitate the learning of behavioral norms by providing a range of reinforcements through a variety of reinforcing agents. Motivation theory stipulates that individuals will gravitate toward behaviors associated with positive reinforcement and away from behaviors that produce negative reinforcement. Hence, rewards and penalties play an important role in the learning process and its outcomes.

Individuals qualify for rewards according to their ability to meet a variety of needs and wants. Extrinsic rewards such as salary increases, bonuses, promotions, stock awards, and other prerequisites may be preferable to some employees. Intrinsic rewards, such as the provision of a sense of achievement, responsibility, and competence, may provide a more positive reinforcement for others.

In addition to rewards, performance evaluation processes also influence organizational culture. Evaluation protocols specify what is expected from employees. They communicate the values and norms that the organization expects its employees to conform to and they set out the consequences that individuals can expect to face as a result of their behaviors and performance. They represent another way by which organizational members learn the antecedents-behavior-consequence linkage. Kerr and Slocum (1987) described how two combinations of rewards and evaluation systems, which they termed as the *hierarchy-based system* and the *performance-based system,* produced two different types of cultures in organizations.

In the hierarchy-based system, superiors evaluated performance of employees largely through subjective criteria based on interdepartmental cooperation, interactions with consumers, interpersonal relationships, and teamwork. Rewards were largely in the form of salary, with increases according to formal salary plans or perks based on rank and tenure. Bonuses constituted a very small percentage of the total compensation and were based on team, rather than individual, performance. Promotion was largely from within. These rewards and evaluation criteria emphasized the importance of long-term commitment, cooperation, teamwork, and the dependence of subordinates on superiors. The cultures of organizations that adopted a hierarchy-based reward system were characterized by values and norms that emphasized fraternal relationships, loyalty to the organization, sense of tradition, pride in organizational membership, and conformity to the common good rather than to individual wants.

The performance-based system evaluated employees solely on objective and measurable performance criteria. Quantitative outcomes such as return on assets, pre-tax profits, and sales and production figures were used as evaluation criteria. Rewards were directly based on performance and results, not on the methods by which results were achieved. Rewards were largely in the form of bonuses and stock awards and were based on individual, rather than on team, performance. Hiring from outside was more common than promotion from inside, and perks based on tenure were rare. These rewards and evaluation protocols emphasized individual initiative and performance, short-term commitment, and independence from peers. The culture of organizations with performance-based reward systems were found to include values and norms that emphasize contractual relationships, loyalty to self, limited interaction with other organizational members, and priority of individual needs over organizational needs.

Organizations do not only differ in types of reinforcements; they also have different types of reinforcing agents. Management, professional associations, peers, subordinates, and superiors are some of the sources that individuals rely on for reinforcement of behavior. In new organizations that are preoccupied with stabilizing work norms, work groups develop that become additional sources of reinforcement. These groups may often encourage norms and values different from or opposite to the ones supported by management, which leads to the development of subcultures and countercultures (Siehl & Martin, 1983). The transmission or change of culture through rewards is thus not entirely under the control of management. The influence of professional and peer groups may have to be taken into account when designing incentive systems.

Assessing Culture

Any attempt to create, change, or reinforce a given health care organizational culture requires that some method be available for its assessment. However, because culture is multitiered and ill-defined, it is not surprising that issues surrounding its measurement have been hotly debated. The heart of this controversy centers on the relative merits of quantitative versus qualitative methods of cultural assessment.

Quantitative methods, which utilize techniques such as standardized questionnaires and interview formats, quasi-experimental designs, and multivariate statistical analyses, have been criticized for their unsuitability (Deal & Kennedy, 1983) and apparent lack of success in providing penetrating insights into organizational cultures (Van Maanen, Dabbs, & Faulkner, 1982). As a result, the state of organizational culture research and assessment is increasingly turning to qualitative methods such as participant observation, interactive probing, and ethnography.

It is important to remain flexible on this issue (Duncan, 1989a) because the most appropriate method may depend on the level of culture we wish to assess (Rousseau, 1990). Although qualitative techniques, such as interactive probing, may be the only ones compatible with surfacing basic underlying assumptions, quantitative survey methods may be better suited for eliciting organizational values, norms, and beliefs.

Rousseau (1990) provides an excellent overview of the qualitative-versus-quantitative debate and makes the strong case for using a variety of methods when assessing organizational culture. In addition, she provides a comparison of several widely known culture assessment tools that are likely to be of value to health care management prac-titioners and researchers. Several of these and others are included in the following list of instruments for assessing organizational culture:

1. Kilmann-Saxton Culture-Gap Survey (Kilmann & Saxton, 1983)
2. Organizational Value Congruence Scale (Enz, 1986)
3. Organizational Culture Profile (O'Reilly, Chatman, & Caldwell, 1991)
4. Corporate Culture Survey (Glaser, 1983)
5. Organizational Norms Opinionnaire (Alexander, 1978)
6. The Culture Audit (Wilkins, 1983)

SUMMARY

Culture is an ethereal concept that is one of the more mysterious and magical elements operating in health care organizations. Given its supernatural aura and assessment difficulties, some health administrators readily attribute all facets of organizational life to it, and others just ignore it. The point remains, however, that all health care organizations maintain specific and distinct cultures that can serve to influence performance positively or negatively. Thus, it behooves the health care manager to attempt to understand the organization's culture and to set in motion appropriate interventions when necessary.

In conclusion, we offer several guidelines.

1. *Know your culture.* Because organizational- and individual-level performance is related to culture, understanding the culture can provide baseline information for future performance improvements. Knowing your culture means more than being

familiar with norms, beliefs, and the espoused values articulated in documents such as the mission statement; it means being cognizant of basic underlying assumptions as well.

2. *Create a strong, appropriate, and flexible culture.* Strong cultures are generally preferred to weak ones because of the clear sense of meaning and guidance they offer employees. However, given the high rate of change and turbulence associated with the health care environment, strong and appropriate cultures can become strong and *inappropriate* ones quickly. For this reason, cultural flexibility is paramount. Senior-level managers play a key role in correcting inappropriate cultures and reinforcing appropriate ones. In addition, careful attention to human resources management practices (e.g., selection, socialization and development, reward systems and performance evaluations, dismissal) is necessary.

3. *Match organizational strategy to organizational culture.* Strategies that incorporate the values of managers as well as other organizational members generally tend to be implemented more effectively. Managers in charge of strategy formulation should perform a cultural audit of their organization before they generate and evaluate strategic alternatives. One of the evaluation criteria should be the fit between the behaviors demanded by the strategy and the behaviors stemming from the organizational culture values.

4. *Employ value congruence as one of the selection criteria in the hiring process.* Candidates whose values are congruent with the values of the organization will be more committed to the organization. They will also be more satisfied and will remain longer in the organization. Hiring practices should include structured interviews aimed at identifying the value fit between applicants and the organization. Key organizational personnel should spend time with candidates to convey the value systems of the organization.

5. *Tailor evaluation and compensation systems to reward culturally correct values and behaviors.* Employees will engage in behaviors that produce positive evaluations and rewards. Organizational monitoring and reward systems should be designed so as to provide reinforcement of those behaviors considered desirable by the organizational culture. Continuous reinforcement of such behaviors will internalize them as norms and values.

6. *Use socialization to propagate, maintain, or change culture.* Use mentor programs, pre-hiring seminars, and orientation programs as socialization techniques to inculcate organizational culture into new recruits. Management development seminars, employee training programs, retreats, social gatherings, and ceremonies can be used to maintain or change cultural values and beliefs among existing employees.

Discussion Questions

1. Is it possible for a strong health care organizational culture to be an ineffective one? Explain.
2. What kinds of cultural changes will hospitals have to make in order to

adapt to the changing health care environment? How can these changes be achieved most efficiently?

3. Referring to the cultural story in Illustration 2, can you identify the heroine(s) and examples of symbols and ceremonies in use? Although not explicitly revealed, can you discern the major cultural values the story seeks to communicate?

4. What are the cultural implications of the total quality management movement in the health care industry? Can culture provide a solution to the cost-versus-quality debate?

5. "Any culture becomes dysfunctional over time." Explain.

6. What steps are required to change a dysfunctional culture?

CASE: THE RECALCITRANT MEDICAL STAFF

St. Vincents Hospital is a 200-bed hospital in a Northeastern city. The institution was established in 1908 by the Sisters of Charity, a Roman Catholic religious order. The hospital has been known for providing humane patient care in a Christian environment.

In 1985, the hospital joined a nonprofit, Catholic, multi-unit system based in the Northeast called Health Care Services, Inc. The reasons for the merger were to achieve economies of scale and lower purchasing costs and to obtain greater managerial expertise in certain areas.

Recently, however, St. Vincents has been receiving pressure from the home office to reduce patient lengths of stay and total costs per case, both of which are above the average for the city. Sister Elizabeth, the administrator of the hospital, has spoken with Dr. Thurston, president of the medical staff, about the problem. His response was that he would discuss the issue, but was "reluctant to push too hard" because it might be viewed as "infringing on the physician's right to practice good medicine."

After meeting with the medical staff, Dr. Thurston reported strong resistance to "any type of controls on the practice of medicine." The staff also asked him to express disappointment that Sister Elizabeth would even raise the issue. In their view, each case is unique, and only the attending physician can determine what length of stay or total expenditure is reasonable. The staff also stated that bureaucratic standards on averages for large numbers of dissimilar cases are irrelevant and that Christian institutions, above all others, should support the principle that patient care comes first.

Several months went by, and the performance level of the facility did not improve. As occupancy rates declined, the hospital began to develop deficits. Pressure on Sister Elizabeth increased, and she knew she had to do something. Although she sympathizes with the medical staff in terms of their concern with patient care, she is also disturbed by their unwillingness to curb their use of resources and their support of one another.

Case Discussion Questions

1. What is the major problem? How did it develop?

2. What alternatives does Sister Elizabeth have? What are the advantages and disadvantages of each?

3. What solution would you propose?

Why? Provide a step-by-step plan for implementation of your proposal.

4. How can such a problem be avoided in the future?

REFERENCES

Albert, M. (1989). Developing a service-oriented culture. *Hospital & Health Services Administration, 34*(2), 167–183.

Alexander, M. (1978). Organizational Norms Opinionnaire. In J.W. Pfeiffer & J.E. Jones (Eds.), *The 1978 Annual Handbook of Group Facilitators* (pp. 81–88). La Jolla, CA: University Associates.

Atchison, T.A. (1990). *Turning health care leadership around: Cultivating inspired, empowered, and loyal followers.* San Francisco, CA: Jossey-Bass.

Bandura, A. (1977). *Social learning theory.* Englewood Cliffs, NJ: Prentice Hall.

Baraga, F. (1850). *A theoretical and practical grammar of the Otchipwe language, the language spoken by the Chippewa Indians; which is also spoken by the Algonquin, Otawa and Potawatami Indians, with little difference. For the use of missionaries and other persons living among the Indians of the above mentioned tribes.* Detroit, MI: Jabez Fox.

Bice, M.O. (1984). Corporate culture and business strategy: A health management company perspective. *Hospital & Health Service Administration, 29*(4), 64–78.

Bourgeois, L., & Jemison, D. (1982). Analyzing corporate culture in its strategic context. *Exchange: The Organizational Behavior Teaching Journal, 7*(3), 37–41.

Bower, J.L., & Doz, Y. (1979). Strategy formulation: A social and political process. In D.E. Schendel & C.W. Hofer (Eds.), *Strategic management: A new view of business policy and planning* (pp. 52–166). Boston: Little, Brown.

Chatman, J.A. (1991). Matching people and organizations: Selection and socialization in public accounting firms. *Administrative Science Quarterly, 36,* 459–484.

Conner, D. (1990). Corporate culture: Healthcare's change master. *Healthcare Executive, 5*(2), 28–29.

Deal, T.E. (1985). Cultural change: Opportunity, silent killer, or metamorphosis. In R.H. Kilmann, M.J. Saxton, R. Serpta, & Associates (Eds.), *Gaining control of the corporate culture.* San Francisco, CA: Jossey-Bass.

Deal, T.E. (1990). Healthcare executives as symbolic leaders. *Healthcare Executive, 5*(2), 24–27.

Deal, T.E., & Kennedy, A.A. (1982). *Corporate cultures.* Reading, MA: Addison-Wesley.

Deal, T.E., & Kennedy, A.A. (1983). Culture: A new look through old lenses. *Journal of Applied Behavioral Sciences, 19,* 498–505.

Deshpande, R., & Parasuraman, A. (1986). Linking corporate culture to strategic planning. *Business Horizons, 29,* 28–37.

Duncan, W.J. (1989a). *Great ideas in management: Lessons from the founders and foundations of management practice.* San Francisco, CA: Jossey-Bass.

Duncan, W.J. (1989b). Organizational culture: "Getting a fix" on an elusive concept. *The Academy of Management Executive, 3*(3), 229–236.

Enz, C. (1986). *Power and shared values in the corporate culture.* Ann Arbor, MI: UMI.

Eubanks, P. (1991a). Hospitals probe job candidates' values for organizational 'fit'. *Hospitals, 65*(20), 36, 38.

Eubanks, P. (1991b). Retreats advance the corporate culture. *Hospitals, 65*(18), 58.

Eubanks, P. (1992). Finding jobs for 1,200 laid-off employees: Health One's goal. *Hospitals, 66*(1), 43–44.

Filerman, G.L. (1989). Toward a future of consequence: The education of a health service administrator. In G.L. Filerman (Ed.), *A future of consequence: The manager's role in health services* (pp. 3–28). Arlington, VA: Princeton University Press.

Gibson, C.K., Newton, D.J., & Cochran, D.S. (1990). An empirical investigation of the nature of hospital mission statements. *Health Care Management Review, 15*(3), 35–45.

Glaser, R. (1983). *The corporate culture survey.* Bryn Mawr, PA: Organizational Design and Development.

Gove, P.B. (1971). *Webster's third new international dictionary, unabridged.* Springfield, MA: G. & C. Merriam Co.

Joyce, W.F., & Slocum, J.W. (1990). Strategic context and organizational climate. In B. Schneider (Ed.), *Organizational climate and culture* (pp. 130–150). San Francisco: Jossey-Bass.

Kerr, J., & Slocum, J.W. (1987). Managing corporate culture through reward systems. *Academy of Management Executive, 1*(2), 99–108.

Kilmann, R.H. (1984). *Beyond the quick fix: Managing five tracks to organizational success.* San Francisco: Jossey-Bass.

Kilmann, R.H., & Saxton, M.J. (1983). *The Kilmann-Saxton culture-gap survey.* Pittsburgh: Organizational Design Consultants.

Konner, M. (1987). *Becoming a doctor: A journey of initiation in medical school.* New York: Penguin Books.

Kopelman, R.E., Brief, A.P., & Guzzo, R.A. (1990). The role of climate and culture in productivity. In B. Schneider (Ed.), *Organizational climate and culture* (pp. 282–319). San Francisco: Jossey-Bass.

Kotter, J.P., & Heskett, J.L. (1992). *Corporate culture and performance.* New York: Free Press.

Lombardi, D.N. (1992). *Progressive health care management strategies.* Chicago: American Hospital Publishing.

London, J. (1981). The law of life. In L. Teacher & R.E. Nicholls (Eds.), *The unabridged Jack London* (pp. 279–284). Philadelphia: Running Press.

Martin, J., Feldman, M., Hatch, M., & Sitkin, S. (1983). The uniqueness paradox in organizational stories. *Administrative Science Quarterly, 28,* 438–453.

McDonald, B. (1989). Norma Jean Frank: The courageous philosophy of an optimistic leader. *CHART, 12,* 10.

Mirvis, P., & Sales, A. (1990). Feeling the elephant: Culture consequences of a corporate acquisition and buy-back. In B. Schneider (Ed.), *Organizational climate and culture* (pp. 345–382). San Francisco: Jossey-Bass.

Morgan, G. (1986). *Images of organizations.* Newbury Park, CA: Sage Publications.

Myer, P.G., & Tucker, S.L. (1992). Incorporating an understanding of independent practice physician culture into hospital structure and operations. *Hospital & Health Services Administration, 37*(4), 465–476.

Nystrom, P.C. (1993). Organizational cultures, strategies, and commitments in health care organizations. *Health Care Management Review, 18*(1), 43–49.

O'Connor, S.J., & Bowers, M.R. (1990). An integrative overview of the quality dimension: Marketing implications for the consumer-oriented health care organization. *Medical Care Review, 47*(2), 193–219.

O'Connor, S.J., & Shewchuk, R.M. (1993). Enhancing administrator-clinician relationships: The role of psychological type. *Health Care Management Review, 18*(2), 57–65.

O'Reilly, C.A. (1989). Corporations, culture, and commitment: Motivation and social control in organizations. *California Management Review, 31*(4), 9–24.

O'Reilly, C.A., Chatman, J., & Caldwell, D.F. (1991). People and organizational culture: A profile comparison approach to assessing person-organization fit. *Academy of Management Journal, 34*(3), 487–516.

Ott, J.S. (1989). *The organizational culture perspective.* Chicago: Dorsey Press.

Pascale, R., & Athos, A. (1981). *The art of Japanese management.* New York: Simon & Schuster.

Peters, T., & Waterman, R. (1982). *In search of excellence.* New York: Harper & Row.

Pettigrew, A. (1979). On studying organizational cultures. *Administrative Science Quarterly, 24*(4), 570–581.

Raelin, J. A. (1986). *The clash of cultures: Managers and professionals.* Boston: Harvard Business School Press.

Rakich, J.S., Longest, B.B., & Darr, K. (1992).

Managing health services organizations (3rd ed). Baltimore: Health Professions Press.

Rothstein, M., & Jackson, D. (1981). Decision-making in the employment interview: An experimental approach. *Journal of Applied Psychology, 65,* 271–283.

Rousseau, D.M. (1990). Assessing organizational culture: The case for multiple methods. In B. Schneider (Ed.), *Organizational climate and culture* (pp. 153–192). San Francisco: Jossey-Bass.

Salisbury, N. (1982). *Manitou and providence: Indians, Europeans, and the making of New England, 1500–1643.* New York: Oxford University Press.

Salloway, J.C. (1982). *Health care delivery systems.* New York: Westview Press.

Sathe, V. (1985a). *Culture and related corporate realities.* Homewood, IL: Irwin.

Sathe, V. (1985b). How to decipher and change corporate culture. In R. H. Kilmann, M.J. Saxton, R. Serpta, & Associates (Eds.), *Gaining control of the corporate culture* (pp. 230–261). San Francisco: Jossey-Bass.

Schein, E.H. (1985). *Organizational culture and leadership: A dynamic view.* San Francisco: Jossey-Bass.

Schwartz, H., & Davis, S. (1981). Matching corporate culture and business strategy. *Organizational Dynamics, 10,* 30–48.

Sheridan, J.E. (1992). The relationship between organizational culture and employee retention. *The Academy of Management Journal, 35*(5), 1035–1056.

Shortell, S.M. (1991). *Effective hospital-physician relationships.* Ann Arbor, MI: Health Administration Press.

Shrivastava, P. (1984). Integrating strategy formulation with organization culture. *The Journal of Business Strategy,* Winter, 103–111.

Siehl, C., & Martin, J. (1984). The role of symbolic management: How can managers effectively transmit organizational culture? In J.G. Hunt, D.M. Hoskig, C.A.

Schriesheim, & R. Stewart (Eds.), *Leaders and managers: International perspectives on managerial behavior* (pp. 227–269). New York: Pergamon Press.

Siehl, C., & Martin, J. (1990). Organizational culture: A key to financial performance. In B. Schneider (Ed.), *Organizational Climate and Culture.* San Francisco: Jossey-Bass.

Skinner, B.F. (1938). *The behavior of organisms.* East Norwalk, CT: Appleton & Lange.

Stevens, R.A. (1991). The hospital as a social institution, new fashioned for the 1990s. *Hospital & Health Services Administration, 36*(2), 163–173.

Terborg, J., Castore, C., & DeNinno, J. (1976). A longitudinal field investigation of the impact of group composition on group performance and cohesion. *Journal of Personality and Social Psychology, 34,* 782–790.

Thompson, K., & Luthans, F. (1990). Organizational culture: A behavioral perspective. In B. Schneider (Ed.), *Organizational Climate and Culture* (pp. 314–344). San Francisco: Jossey-Bass.

Trice, H.M., & Beyer, J.M. (1993). *The cultures of work organizations.* Englewood Cliffs, NJ: Prentice Hall.

Van Maanen, J. (1977). Toward a theory of the career. In J. Van Maanen (Ed.), *Organizational careers: Some new perspectives* (pp. 67–130). New York: Wiley.

Van Maanen, J., Dabbs, J.M., & Faulkner, R.R. (Eds.). (1982). *Varieties of qualitative research.* Beverly Hills: Sage Publications.

Wilkins, A. (1983). The culture audit: A tool for understanding organizations. *Organizational Dynamics, 12*(2), 24–38.

Zuckerman, H.S. (1989). Redefining the role of the CEO: Challenges and conflicts. *Hospital & Health Services Administration, 34*(1), 25–28.

CHAPTER

MANAGING A DIVERSE WORK FORCE

Gail W. McGee

Richard M. Shewchuk

LEARNING OBJECTIVES

Upon completing this chapter, the reader should be able to . . .

- Describe the demographic trends that are changing the nature of the work force.
- Offer a useful definition of "cultural diversity."
- Identify different organizational typologies for managing cultural diversity and delineate the characteristic values or assumptions underlying each approach.
- Describe specific management strategies associated with each of the different approaches.
- Identify and describe characteristics and assumptions of multicultural (Stage 5) organizations.

INTRODUCTION

The environment in which health care organizations operate is characterized by constant change and upheaval. In recent years, hospitals and other health care organizations have had to keep pace with significant technological developments and confront a challenging array of new regulatory and reimbursement mechanisms. At stake is the organization's survival. Its viability, quite simply, is likely to depend on how well and how quickly it can perceive and adapt to changing environmental conditions.

One of the most critical elements of the changing health care environment concerns the demographic and cultural profile of the work force that is emerging in the United States. Surprisingly, this element has received relatively little research attention. Until recently, the work force employed in most

organizations could be described as being "monolithic" with respect to its demographic and cultural characteristics. In general, the typical employee conformed to a "homogeneous ideal" that was found in most corporate settings. Loden and Rosener (1991) noted that the ideal or successful employee embodied several specific attributes; "he" was between the ages of 35 and 49 and was married with children, college educated, heterosexual, in good physical condition, tall, Protestant or Jewish, and competitive. However, it also must be recognized that, to some degree, the concept of the typical employee traditionally has been influenced by the specific occupational roles found in a particular organizational setting. In health care organizations, for example, nurses and allied health personnel have tended to be fairly homogeneous with respect to gender. Similarly, the demographic profile of hospital administration employees, especially those who have attained upper management positions, also has tended to conform to fairly well-defined characteristics. The concept of the "homogeneous ideal" and the historically close correspondence between occupational roles and the demographic profiles of the employees who have occupied those roles have helped to define a management dynamic in which assimilation and conformity were dominant strategies for developing a productive work force. In organizations in which the majority of employees conformed to an "ideal type," a management approach based on relatively narrowly defined norms, values, and expectations of a homogeneous work force, although perhaps somewhat constrictive, was nonetheless, probably functional.

However, as the growth rate of the work force slows in general and as the traditional pool of potential employees shrinks, the concept of the "homogeneous ideal" will become obsolete. Concomitantly, as organizations face fierce competition for entry-level and skilled workers and need to turn to nontraditional entrants who are currently entering the work force at a more rapid rate, the emerging work force of the 1990s will be characterized by its diversity. Consequently, management practices that seemed to be appropriate when most employees were thought to be similar (and when those who were different were encouraged to adapt to the norm) will become less effective, and even dysfunctional, in work places where there are many different individuals, each of whom requires understanding and respect (Jamieson & O'Mara, 1991). To survive in this new environment, health services organizations must develop a new management paradigm.

In this chapter, we argue that conventional management approaches should be supplanted by approaches that utilize fully the benefits of diversity and minimize potential costs (Cox, 1991). First, we define the concept of diversity as it relates to individual differences. We then explore several environmental realities that have generated interest and concern for diversity management issues. Next, we describe several different approaches that organizations have adopted in dealing with diversity. Finally, we conclude by outlining specific strategies that have been used by various organizations to manage the impact of a diverse work force effectively.

DEFINING DIVERSITY

Morrison (1992) stated that the term diversity, which is relatively new in human resource circles, "is confusing and controver-sial" (p. 4). She pointed out that diversity has been discussed under many labels, including affirmative action, civil rights, quotas, and reverse discrimination. She noted that the concept of work force diversity is continuing to evolve, which contributes to the ambiguity in its definition. For example, Jamieson and O'Mara (1991) view diversity as a product of the characteristics of individuals, defining it as "a workforce (sic) of individuals who bring different resources and perspectives to the workplace (sic) and who have distinctive needs, preferences, expectations, and lifestyles" (p. 14). Thomas (1991), however, defines diversity from a management perspective, calling it "a holistic approach to creating a corporate environment that allows all kinds of people to reach their full potential in pursuit of corporate objectives" (p. 167).

One of the most straightforward definitions of diversity was provided by Loden and Rosener (1991), who referred to diversity simply as "*otherness* or those human qualities that are different from our own and outside the groups to which we belong, yet present in other individuals and groups" (p. 18). Although many managers tend to think of work force diversity somewhat narrowly, in terms of race and gender, Loden and Rosener noted that diversity must be viewed along a number of different dimensions. They identified two dimensions of diversity, which they labeled as *primary* and *secondary*. Primary dimensions are defined as "those immutable human differences that are inborn and/ or that exert an important impact on our early socialization and an ongoing impact throughout our lives" (p. 18). Primary dimensions include age, ethnicity, gender, physical abilities and qualities, race, and sexual or affectional orientation. They defined secondary dimensions of diversity as "mutable differences that we acquire, discard, and/

or modify throughout our lives" (p. 19), including such factors as education, income, geographic location, marital status, and religious beliefs.

Jamieson and O'Mara (1991) defined work force diversity as "a workforce (sic) of individuals who bring different resources and perspectives to the workplace (sic) and who have distinctive needs, preferences, expectations, and lifestyles" (p. 14). According to Jamieson and O'Mara, the most notable dimensions along which the American work force is changing are age, gender, culture, education, physical abilities and disabilities, and personal values.

WHY MANAGE DIVERSITY? EXPLORING ENVIRONMENTAL REALITIES

Currently, several demographic forces are altering the work force that is available to health services organizations. Much of what we know about work force that will evolve during the next 10 years derives from the Hudson Institute's *Workforce 2000* comprehensive analysis of emerging trends in employment patterns (Johnston & Packer, 1987). In essence, the *Workforce 2000* analysis and a subsequent study by Towers Perrin and the Hudson Institute (1990) indicate that as we approach the year 2000, employers are likely to encounter increasing competition for a shrinking pool of skilled workers. It appears that the recruitment and retention of "knowledge workers" will present an especially difficult challenge for health services organizations in particular (Towers Perrin & Hudson Institute, 1990). Much evidence indicates that the work force of the near future will not "look like, think like, act like,

or have the same desires as the workers of the past" (Jamieson & O'Mara, 1991, p. 13). In the section that follows, we examine some of the primary forces that are changing the work force. We also briefly discuss some of the implications that a changing work force has for health services organizations.

The Aging of the Work Force

The "graying of America" is potentially the single most significant demographic force that will influence management strategies of health services organizations in the foreseeable future. Aside from the obvious implications that a growing elderly population has for the organization and delivery of health services, older persons are likely to be an important source of labor for hospitals, nursing homes, and other health services organizations that will be confronted with a slowly growing pool of well-educated and skilled employees.

The large baby boom cohort (i.e., approximately one-third of the U.S. population that was born between 1946 and 1961) in concert with a much smaller baby bust cohort (i.e., individuals born in the 10 years following the baby boom) is influencing the U.S. work force in a dramatic fashion. As the baby boom cohort ages, the average age of the population will also increase, reaching age 36 by the year 2000 (Johnston & Packer, 1987). Paralleling the aging of the population is an aging work force. By the year 2000, the average American worker will be 39 years of age, 10 years older, on average, than the average American worker in 1976. In addition, it is projected that within the next 25 years, approximately one-fourth of the work force will be at least 55 years of age (Fyock, 1990).

The so-called "birth dearth" and the resulting smaller baby bust cohort also are having a considerable influence on the work force. This smaller birth cohort is the primary reason that it is anticipated that the annual growth rate of the work force, which is currently increasing by less than 1% per year, will be slower than at any time since the great depression (Johnston & Packer, 1987).

There are at least two realities that accompany an aging and slowly growing work force. The first, which is likely to be a boon to health services organizations, is that there will be an extremely large pool of workers 55 years and older who are well-educated, highly skilled, and eager to work. Less fortuitous will be the increased competition for promotion to top management positions, potentially higher payrolls, and workers who are less flexible with respect to retraining or relocations (Offermann & Gowing, 1990) . In contrast to the expanding ranks of middle-age and older workers, an acute decline in the number of young workers entering the labor force is expected to occur during the coming decade. As a consequence, health services organizations are likely to experience intense competition in their attempts to recruit and retain adequately trained, entry-level employees (Jamieson & O'Mara, 1991). Furthermore, the limited ability to hire a supply of younger and lower-paid workers will make it more difficult for organizations to diversify rapidly or to expand operations in response to changing environmental conditions.

The graying of America is adding a new dimension of diversity to the work place. Those health services organizations that wish to manage the impact of this environmental reality effectively "will use more older workers; accommodate these workers' range of needs and lifestyle preferences; accept the challenge of managing a potentially less adaptable workforce (sic); and rethink careers, progression, and strategies for recruiting and retaining entry-level workers" (Jamieson & O'Mara, 1991, p. 18).

Women in the Work Force

The continuing influx of women into the work force is another dominant demographic trend that holds far-reaching implications for health services organizations. During the last three decades, employment patterns have been altered dramatically as increasing numbers of women entered the work force. In 1950, 34% of women worked in paying jobs outside of the home and made up about 30% of the work force. At present, 57.5% of women working in jobs outside of the home comprise approximately 46% of the U.S. work force. It is anticipated that by 2000, 61% of women will occupy approximately 47.5% of all paying jobs in this country (Fernandez, 1991; Johnston & Packer, 1987). Despite representing a growing share of the work force, it appears that the rate at which women continue to enter the work force is slowing somewhat. Johnston and Packer (1987) report that in contrast with the 14 million women who entered the work force between 1970 and 1980, approximately 5 million fewer women are projected to enter the work force between now and 2000. However, even considering the trend toward slower growth, women will still represent about three-fifths of all new entrants into the work force between 1985 and 2000.

Many of the women who enter the work force are married mothers of young children. In fact, Hoffman (1989) has observed that 71% of mothers in two-parent families have full-time employment outside of the home and, as a group, represent one of the most rapidly growing segments of the work force. There is considerable evidence that supports the notion that most women, including mothers of young children, work primarily because of economic need. In fact, reporting on the results of a Gallop poll, Johnston and Packer (1987) note that only a small percentage of working women with children prefer full-time employment with regular hours; most would like part-time jobs with flexible hours or jobs that would permit them to work at home.

As the feminization of health services organizations further evolves, new management approaches will be required to capture the potential of this large pool of workers fully. In particular, attention must be focused on developing family-friendly benefits, human resources policies and practices that allow women to balance their career and home responsibilities effectively. It is possible that in addition to appearing more attractive to potential employees, health services organizations that provide assistance with child care arrangements and institute policies that allow flexible work options (e.g., job sharing, voluntary reduced time, flextime, compressed work week, work-at-home options) could prevent or help resolve much of the family-work conflict that can undermine women's productivity (Jamieson & O'Mara, 1991).

If health services organizations are to benefit optimally from a feminized work force they must resolve several lingering management practices that discriminate against women. It is especially important to remove the many barriers that deny women access to upper management levels (Morrison, 1992). The issue of differential salaries is another gender bias issue that should be addressed by organizations hoping to attract and retain qualified women. Undergirding these and other changes that must occur are educa-

tional and training initiatives and "a thoroughgoing reform of the institutions and policies that govern the workplace (sic), to insure that women can participate fully" (Johnston & Packer, 1987, p. xxv) .

Minority and Immigrant Workers

The increasing rate at which people of color born in the United States and new immigrants to this country enter the work force is a third dominant demographic trend that will have a profound influence on health services organizations. It is estimated that native-born people of color, primarily African Americans, Latinos, and Asians, will comprise only slightly less than one-third (29%) of the new work force entrants during the 15-year period that began in 1985. During the same period, it is also expected that the approximately 600,000 people who immigrate to this country each year (most from Latin America and Asia) will make up another 14% of the new entrants to the work force. As a result of their rapid entry into the work force, minority and immigrant workers will occupy an average of 26% of all jobs nationwide by 2000 (Fernandez, 1991; Johnston & Packer, 1987; Jamieson & O'Mara, 1991).

The overall impact of this changing demographic profile will be significant. According to some sources, the concept of "minority" will assume a different meaning in some regions of the country, where much of the population will consist of people of color. Of particular significance to health services organizations is the fact that many of these new workers are being raised in poverty with many of its attendant disadvantages, especially being "ill-served by the nation's school system" (Offermann & Gowing, 1990, p. 97). Johnston and Packer (1987) suggest that the lack of adequate education and training could place minority workers at a distinct disadvantage as jobs are created in which more education and higher skill levels are required (p. xxi).

In light of the impending shortage of qualified workers, it seems clear that health services organizations would be well-served if they were to commit educational and training resources to those segments of minority and immigrant populations that are in need of such assistance. However, effective management of a culturally diverse work force will entail more than helping nontraditional employees gain entry into the work force. If health services organizations are to integrate people of various cultural, ethnic, and racial backgrounds into the workplace successfully, they also must implement programs that foster a recognition and appreciation of the meaningful differences that employees manifest.

Other Dimensions of Diversity

Another population segment that traditionally has been underrepresented in the work force, but that is expected to participate more extensively in the future, is a large population of people with disabilities and a growing population of people with HIV disease. Although a majority of persons with disabilities express a desire to work, for several reasons, only approximately one-third of the working-age members of this population have found their way permanently into the work force (Jamieson & O'Mara, 1991, p. 25). In the past, many disabled persons confronted significant social and physical barriers that made it difficult to obtain employment. However, it seems certain that many of these barriers should be dismantled

as organizations begin to comply with the recently legislated Americans with Disabilities Act. This law includes provisions that "prohibit discrimination in employment against individuals who, with reasonable accommodation, can perform the essential functions of a job."

It can be reasonably expected that health services organizations may wish to help offset the developing work force shortage by integrating qualified workers from the large population of disabled persons and a growing number of persons with HIV disease into the work place. Effective strategies for enhancing the productivity of the many elements of this population demand innovative and flexible work approaches that accommodate workers' limitations. Also called for are concomitant educational efforts that are directed at enhancing all employees' levels of tolerance and understanding of this dimension of otherness, thereby helping to remove the attitudinal barriers that interfere with cooperative work place efforts.

Concurrent with the very observable work force changes that are already occurring, health services organizations are likely to encounter workers who possess diverse attitudes, motivations, and values that may seem to be at odds with those that were held by the traditional work force. Although perhaps less obvious, these psychologically oriented dimensions of diversity are very salient for workers and can have an important influence on productivity levels. Characteristic of the value orientation of the emerging workforce is an "increased desire for autonomy, self-development. . . more meaningful work experiences, as well as more involvement in decisions pertaining to themselves" (Offermann & Gowing, 1990, p. 98). One would expect that health services organizations would gain some advantage over competitors in terms of being able to attract and retain qualified workers in productive roles, by acknowledging the validity of each employee's values and attitudes. Although this is an area that requires additional research, Jamieson and O'Mara (1991) suggest that value-sensitive management policies are those that link reward and recognition mechanisms with employee values, allow a large measure of worker autonomy and self-management, and seek and consider employee input concerning decisions that affect the quality of life in the work place.

The evolving work force of today's health services organizations reflects, to a large degree, the major demographic transitions that are occurring within society at large. Accumulating evidence suggests that the rate of work force growth is slowing and that, unlike the traditional, predominantly white male work force of the past, this new work force will be older and have more women, minority, immigrant, and disabled workers. Furthermore, it is likely that employees will express values and attitudes that are unfamiliar

to most managers. Taken together, these transitions pose a significant challenge for health services organizations. In the section that follows, we examine several approaches organizations have adopted in dealing with issues of diversity.

DIFFERENT APPROACHES TO DIVERSITY: ORGANIZATIONAL TYPOLOGIES

Just as definitions of diversity have varied somewhat, so have typologies that describe organizational approaches to handling diversity. Morrison (1992) described five organizational approaches to diversity, including: 1) the golden rule approach, 2) assimilation, 3) righting the wrongs, 4) the culture-specific approach, and 5) the multicultural approach (Table 8.1).

The golden rule approach relies on the biblical notion of, "Do unto others as you would have them do unto you." Organizations adopting this approach rely on individ-

TABLE 8.1. Organizational Approaches to Diversity

Stage	Morrison (1992)	Thomas (1991)	Cox (1991)	Adler (1991)
Do nothing/denial of differences or impacts of diversity	Golden rule			Parochial
Acknowledge differences; avoid problems by avoiding diversity	Assimilation		Monolithic	Ethnocentric
Acknowledge differences; take action only if legally mandated	Rights the wrongs	Affirmative action	Plural	
Acknowledge differences; minimize inevitable dysfunctional impacts by fostering understanding and acceptance	Culture-specific	Valuing cultural differences		
Full recognition of differences, problems, and benefits; productively encourage and manage diversity	Multicultural	Managing cultural diversity	Multicultural	Synergistic

ual integrity and morality to make diversity work (i.e., all individuals should be treated equally). Differences among employees based on age, gender, race, ethnicity, and so forth are not recognized explicitly by organizations that ascribe to the golden rule approach.

Assimilation, however, "calls for shaping people to the style already dominant in an organization" (Morrison, 1992, p. 6). Organizations that adopt this approach expect individuals to suppress their differences and to accommodate the notion of the "homogeneous ideal."

The third approach, righting the wrongs, targets groups who have suffered past discrimination, and attempts to compensate for past injustices. Organizations that favor this approach rely primarily on legal mandates for guidance in handling diverse employees.

The culture-specific approach, according to Morrison (1992), is used to prepare employees for particular international assignments. Thus, the focus of this approach is quite narrow and likely to bring about short-term, superficial understanding of diversity.

The multicultural approach "involves increasing the consciousness and appreciation of differences associated with the heritage, characteristics, and values of many different groups, as well as respecting the uniqueness of each individual" (Morrison, 1992, p. 7). Organizations that embrace this approach consciously acknowledge differences among employees along a number of dimensions and promote understanding and respect of such differences.

A similar typology, reflecting an organization's strategy for dealing with cultural diversity, was offered by Thomas (1991). He notes that organizations can use a strategy of: 1) complying through affirmative action,

2) simply valuing cultural differences, or 3) proactively managing cultural diversity. The goals of the first approach are to provide opportunities for upward mobility for minorities and women and to comply with legal and social responsibilities. However, the affirmative action approach, as a singular strategy for dealing with diversity, has significant disadvantages. Although such an approach may succeed in increasing numbers of women and minorities in key positions, little is done to change negative attitudes toward these individuals. Indeed, in many cases, a "backlash" of negative attitudes may occur, resulting in charges of reverse discrimination and feelings that all minorities and women achieve key positions through quotas rather than qualifications.

The goals of the second approach, valuing diversity, are to establish quality interpersonal relationships, to reduce conflict, and to minimize overt expressions of racism, ethnocentrism, and sexism. Essentially, such an approach is aimed toward eliminating or minimizing the negative impact of a culturally diverse work force. The focus of this strategy is on avoiding trouble rather than on maximizing benefits.

According to Thomas (1991), "acceptance, tolerance, and understanding of diversity are not by themselves enough to create an empowered work force. To empower a diverse group of employees to reach their (sic) full potential, managing diversity is needed" (p. 25). Thus, organizations adopting the third strategy of proactively managing diversity view cultural differences as offering specific advantages. Organizations adopting this strategy recognize and confront the realities of the 1990s (e.g., changing demographics of the U.S. work force, increased competition, external pressure for quality products and services) and believe that they will achieve a competitive advantage only by fully integrating and utilizing a culturally diverse work force.

Cox (1991) presented a typology describing three organizational prototypes that differ according to six factors: 1) mode of acculturating diverse employees, 2) methods and degree of structural integration of diverse employees, 3) methods and degree of informal integration of diverse employees, 4) degree of cultural bias within the organization, 5) identification (e.g., loyalty, commitment) of employees, and 6) degree of intergroup conflict among diverse employees. He viewed these prototypes as representing different stages of development in an organization's ability to deal effectively with diversity.

The first type of organization, which Cox labeled as *monolithic,* is characterized by assimilation of diverse employees (i.e., conforming to a homogeneous norm), minimal structural and informal integration of diverse others, presence of prejudice and discrimination against diverse employees, large gaps in the degree of organizational commitment of diverse versus dominant employees, and low intergroup conflict due to high homogeneity. Thus, the monolithic organization reflects the first, or least effective, stage of development in managing cultural diversity.

The *plural* organization reflects "middle ground" on the six factors identified by Cox (1991) and is the second stage of development. This organization also is characterized by assimilation of diverse others, but has greater structural and informal integration of diverse employees, less prejudice and discrimination, and smaller gaps in employee identification than the monolithic organization. However, intergroup conflict may be higher in a plural organization because heterogeneity is greater although prejudice and discrimination still exist.

The organization that handles diversity most effectively, according to Cox (1991), is the *multicultural* organization. This organization incorporates diverse employees into its work force by recognizing differences and valuing heterogeneity. Diverse employees are fully integrated into the organization, both structurally and informally, resulting in little intergroup conflict. Prejudice and discrimination are minimal, as are gaps in the level of employee commitment among groups.

Adler (1991) offered yet another typology of organizations, based on their recognition of the potential impact, both positive and negative, of cultural diversity. She stated that "the extent to which managers recognize cultural diversity and its potential advantages and disadvantages defines the organization's approach to managing that diversity" (p. 104). According to Adler, the most common organizational approach is to ignore the impact of diversity (i.e., to assume that differences among people are irrelevant). Adler (1991) maintains that managers in such organizations confuse judgment with recognition; she stated:

> Recognition occurs when a manager realizes that people from different cultural groups behave differently and that that difference affects their relationship to the organization. People from one ethnic group are not inherently any better or worse (judgment) than those from another group; they are simply different. To ignore cultural differences is unproductive. . . . Judging cultural differences as good or bad can lead to inappropriate, offensive, racist, sexist, ethnocentric attitudes and behaviors. Recognizing differences does not. Choosing not to see cultural diversity limits our ability to manage it. (p. 97)

Organizations in which managers ignore the potential impact of cultural diversity are labeled "parochial" by Adler (1991). Parochial organizations neither benefit from employee diversity nor resolve problems associated with such differences.

A second type of organization, labeled "ethnocentric" by Adler (1991), assumes that cultural diversity among employees has clear disadvantages, but no advantages. Such organizations seek to minimize the source and impact of cultural diversity by selecting a monocultural work force and by forcing diverse others to assimilate to the values, attitudes, and behaviors of the predominant group. Obviously, ethnocentric organizations fail to benefit from the diversity that exists among the work force.

In contrast, the "synergistic" organization, according to Adler (1991), recognizes the potential advantages and problems associated with a culturally diverse work force. Such organizations, which Adler believes are uncommon, directly address potential problems (e.g., miscommunication, lack of consensus regarding appropriate behaviors) while simultaneously embracing the benefits offered by diversity among its employees (e.g., greater creativity and flexibility).

Summary of Typologies

The various typologies discussed above are summarized and compared in Table 8.1. Basically, organizations might be viewed along a diversity continuum, ranging from passive denial to proactive management of the impact of a diverse work force. Stage 1 organizations deny the importance of cultural differences, assuming that *equal* treatment for all will naturally prevail and will result in perceived equity and productivity. Morrison's (1992) golden rule organizations and Adler's (1991) parochial organizations adopt this approach.

At Stage 2, organizations acknowledge that differences exist, assume that they are counterproductive, and seek to minimize problems by consciously avoiding diversity in their work force. Such organizations may avoid diversity through the selection process or through assimilation of the limited number of "others" who do enter the work force. Morrison's (1992) assimilation, Cox's (1991) monolithic, and Adler's (1991) ethnocentric organizations are at Stage 2 of the diversity continuum.

Stage 3 organizations, like those at Stage 2, acknowledge that differences among people exist and view them as generally dysfunctional. Organizations at this stage, however, actively seek to expand the diversity of the work force, but only within the boundaries mandated by law. Diversity is seen by such organizations as a necessary evil. Organizations labeled by Morrison (1991) as "righting the wrongs" and by Thomas (1991) as "affirmative action" are representative of this stage.

At Stage 4, organizations recognize that diversity is a way of life and realize that benefits may accrue to the organization if greater understanding and acceptance can be fostered among employees. Thus, educational efforts may be undertaken by such organizations to enhance understanding of cultural differences and to minimize problems related to communication or conflict. Stage 4 organizations, however, still fail to achieve maximum benefit from the diversity of employees because their efforts are directed only toward minimizing problems, not toward developing strengths. Organizations fitting this description are labeled by Morrison (1991) as "culture-specific" and by Thomas (1991) as "valuing cultural differences." Cox's (1991) plural organization combines elements of Stages 3 and 4 (i.e., complying with legal mandates and making some efforts to minimally integrate diverse employees and to lessen dysfunctional effects of diversity).

Stage 5 organizations clearly understand both the problems and the benefits associated with employee diversity. They view the management of a diverse work force as an ongoing activity that necessitates fundamental changes in the values and assumptions that define the organization's culture. Cultural differences are recognized fully, and efforts are made to develop an organizational culture that supports differences, develops individual strengths, and benefits from the range of experiences, values, and skills offered by its diverse others. Multicultural organizations (Cox, 1991; Morrison, 1992), organizations that manage cultural diversity (Thomas, 1991), and synergistic organizations (Adler, 1991) are organizational types described as operating at Stage 5.

Although these five stages seem to reflect the range of philosophies and actions that might be found in different organizations, it should be noted that the categories are not mutually exclusive. Morrison (1992), for example, concludes that "perhaps the most promising approach to diversity is one that combines the premises and practices of several of the approaches . . . particularly the goals of the multicultural approach and the affirmative action types of practices in the approach of righting the wrongs" (p. 8). Likewise, Thomas (1991) stated that effective

managers cannot rely exclusively on any of the three strategies that he described, but "will want to use all three" (p. 26) to achieve maximum productivity.

As organizations move through the continuum to the latter stages, it is likely that they retain characteristics of earlier stage organizations. Thus, the process might be viewed as cumulative or additive; organizations retain some practices (e.g., affirmative action) while adding new ones (e.g., training and education). As organizations advance toward Stage 5, they do not reject worthwhile policies or practices of the past; rather, they refine beneficial policies, discontinue policies or practices that are detrimental, and extend efforts to include new and innovative approaches to managing employee diversity.

CHARACTERISTICS AND ASSUMPTIONS OF MULTICULTURAL COMPANIES

Loden and Rosener (1991) surveyed 50 organizations, both public and private, that are innovators in managing diverse employees. Their goal was to identify the underlying values or assumptions that are shared by such organizations. Labeled "leading-edge organizations," they were described as "those with a declared commitment to the value of diversity that are actively engaged in a variety of efforts aimed at institutionalizing this philosophy" (p. 160). Loden and Rosener (1991) found three common characteristics among the 50 organizations: 1) support and involvement of top management; 2) operating philosophy of different but equal and 3) expanded, more flexible definitions of effective performance. Loden and Rosener (1991) stated that within leading-edge institutions, senior-level managers have "become visibly and philosophically identified with efforts to promote a culture of diversity" (p. 161). Senior-level managers serve as critical role models for other employees and act as protagonists in efforts to change underlying cultural values. They also emphasized that managers in leading-edge organizations recognize the distinction between equality and sameness. Because they understand true differences among diverse employees (e.g., communication styles), these managers adapt their styles to accommodate varying needs. Finally, leading-edge organizations tend to be more flexible in their definitions of effective performance. Loden and Rosener (1991) stressed that organizations need not sacrifice performance standards; rather, they recognize that high levels of performance can be attained in different ways. For example, traditional approaches to identifying employees with management potential have tended to be gender-biased (e.g., emphasizing the value of competitive, combative behavior, rather than supportive behavior). Loden and Rosener (1991) stated that performance assessment tools "need to be modified to reflect the diverse communication styles of the multicultural workforce (sic)" (p. 164).

Furthermore, Loden and Rosener (1991) delineated three common assumptions among leading-edge organizations. First, such companies assume that employee diversity is a competitive advantage, rather than a disadvantage. They recognize that a culturally diverse work force can serve as a "means of enhancing their recruitment, marketing, and customer service effectiveness" (Loden & Rosener, 1991, p. 164). Second, leading-edge companies assume that the organization is in transition; they recognize the need for continuous monitoring and alteration of the organization's culture, policies, and practices. Finally, leading-edge companies assume that they must change the organizational culture, rather than the people. They have abandoned the practice of assimilation (i.e., forcing diverse others to "fit" their organization) and have embraced the idea that the organization's culture must change to support a variety of diverse others.

STRATEGIES FOR MANAGING A DIVERSE WORK FORCE

Morrison (1992) reported the results of in-depth interviews of managers in 16 organizations that were considered to be "role models in developing diversity in management" (p. 271). She reported that organizations used many different strategies for dealing with work force diversity; however, she also observed much overlap in strategies. The seven practices that ranked highest were: 1) top management intervention and influence; 2) targeted recruitment of women and persons of color for entry-level, nonmanagerial jobs; 3) internal advocacy groups; 4) reliance on equal employment opportunity statistics and employee profiles; 5) incorporation of diversity into the performance review process; 6) targeting of women and people of color in the management succession process; and 7) revision of promotion criteria to include diversity goals.

Morrison noted that the 16 organizations in her study engaged in 52 different practices related to diversity, and "that more than half of the organizations . . . used at least 20 different practices as part of their diversity efforts" (p. 78). Further examination of these 52 practices suggested that they comprised three broad categories: 1) accountability practices, 2) development practices, and 3) recruitment practices.

Twenty-three different practices appeared to fit the accountability category. Accountability practices included such things as the use of internal advocacy groups; inclusion of diversity in performance evaluation, promotion decisions, management compensation, and management succession planning; policies against racism or sexism; inclusion of diversity in the mission statement; and internal audits or surveys regarding cultural diversity.

Eighteen practices were considered to be development-related, including such things as diversity training programs, formal mentoring programs, support groups, job rotation, career planning, and targeted job assignments for diverse employees. Eleven recruitment practices were cited, including targeted recruitment of diverse employees for nonmanagerial and/or managerial positions, recruitment incentives for diverse persons, partnerships with nontraditional organizations or groups, and creation of a corporate image of supportiveness for diverse individuals.

Morrison (1992) also provided guidance for organizations considering the implementation of diversity-related strategies. Specifically, she recommended that organizations: 1) match practices to the organization's problems and culture, 2) select practices that provide for sustained leadership development within the organization, 3) choose practices

that will reach as many employees as possible, 4) provide the necessary education and training to support each practice and to ensure its successful implementation, and 5) be reasonable—narrow the list of problems and strategies to a few immediate priorities.

In addition, Morrison (1992) offered several steps for organizations to follow if they are interested in developing effective programs for managing cultural diversity. The first step is discovery of problems and issues. She stated that "finding and understanding the most significant problems in your organization . . . is a basic first step in making headway on diversity issues" (p. 164). Organizations hold rich information related to existing problems; such information may be captured by asking employees about their knowledge, perceptions, or attitudes (e.g., through focus groups or survey instruments) or by utilizing existing personnel data. Both objective and perceptual data are important during the discovery phase.

Second, organizations must strengthen top management's commitment to the process. She stated that "the commitment of an organization's leaders to diversity is so important that it warrants emphasis as a separate step in the diversity process" (p. 184). Top management must recognize that the process represents a long-term effort and must endorse it through words and actions.

Third, organizations must choose a balanced strategy. Specific practices should reflect all three overarching strategies (i.e., accountability, development, and recruitment), and they should support both short-term and long-term goals.

Fourth, organizations should identify ways to evaluate the results of their diversity-related efforts to determine whether they are achieving desired goals. If not, they should reexamine both goals and practices. Morrison (1992) stated that "the degree of emphasis that organizations place on results may separate those that succeed in their diversity efforts from the field of hopefuls" (p. 226).

Finally, Morrison (1992) recommended that organizations "plan beyond the short-term impact of diversity practices" (p. 251). Initial plans should include both short-term and long-term goals; continuous evaluation and revision must take place to ensure that momentum is maintained.

SUMMARY

In summary, effective human resources managers must recognize the increasing demographic and cultural diversity in the United States and its work force, and they must understand the significant challenges that such changes will present to organizations. Human resources managers must assume the responsibility for developing plans and strategies that are designed specifically to help them compete for an increasingly limited pool of knowledgeable and skilled employees. A key element of their success will be the degree to which they understand and appreciate meaningful differences among employees; such understanding must provide the underpinning for human resources policies and practices that will optimize the organization's ability to attract, retain, and utilize fully qualified employees. Finally, effective human resources managers must become familiar with the wide array of strategies available to them in their efforts to manage and benefit from an increasingly diverse work force. They should evaluate strategies in light of their own organization's goals and culture. They must select strategies with great care and consideration in order to preserve what is valuable within their organization, while simultaneously changing goals or cultural values that are unlikely to be effective in the context of the rapidly emerging, nontraditional work force.

Discussion Questions

1. Discuss the management implications of the demographic changes that are occurring in today's work force.
2. Using specific examples, identify the primary and secondary dimensions of diversity and suggest how these dimensions might influence management philosophy and practices.
3. Compare and contrast different organizational typologies for managing a diverse work force. Address underlying values, assumptions, strategies, policies, and practices.

REFERENCES

Adler, N.J. (1991). *International dimensions of organizational behavior* (2nd ed.). Boston: PWS-Kent.

Cox, T., Jr. (1991). The multicultural organization. *Academy of Management Executive, 5*(2), 34–47.

Fernandez, J.P. (1991). *Managing a diverse work force: Regaining the competitive edge.* Lexington, MA: D.C. Heath.

Fyock, C.D. (1990). *America's work force is coming of age.* Lexington, MA: D.C. Heath.

Hoffman, L.W. (1989). Effects of maternal employment in the two-parent family. *American Psychologist, 44,* 283–292.

Jamieson, D., & O'Mara, J. (1991). *Managing workforce 2000: Gaining the competitive advantage.* San Francisco: Jossey-Bass.

Johnston, W.B., & Packer, A.H. (1987).

Workforce 2000: Work and workers for the twenty-first century. Indianapolis: Hudson Institute.

Loden, M., & Rosener, J.B. (1991). *Workforce America! Managing employee diversity as a vital resource.* Homewood, IL: Business One Irwin.

Morrison, A.M. (1992). *The new leaders: Guidelines on leadership diversity in America.* San Francisco: Jossey-Bass.

Offermann, L.R., & Gowing, M.K. (1990). Organizations of the future: Changes and challenges. *American Psychologist,* 45(2), 95–108.

Thomas, R.R. (1991). *Beyond race and gender: Unleashing the power of your total work force by managing diversity.* New York: AMACOM.

Towers Perrin & Hudson Institute. (1990). *Workforce 2000: Competing in a seller's market.* Valhalla, NY: Towers Perrin.

CHAPTER

9

LEADERSHIP DEVELOPMENT

Barbara Arrington

Richard S. Kurz

Cynthia Carter Haddock

LEARNING OBJECTIVES

Upon completing this chapter, the reader should be able to . . .

- Outline the reasons that leadership and the development of health care leaders are critical strategic concerns as the U.S. health care system moves into the twenty-first century.
- Distinguish between transactional and transformational leadership and describe the underlying premises and characteristics of each.
- Explore the question, "Can leaders be developed?".
- Describe generic approaches to leadership development.
- See the application of these approaches in specific leadership development programs and the application of leadership development concepts to specific issues facing the field of health care administration.

INTRODUCTION

The competitive challenges of the 1980s forced many U.S. health care organizations to rethink how they were organized and managed for high-quality, cost-effective performance. Years of resource abundance under cost-based reimbursement during the late 1960s and throughout the 1970s had created growth in the health care industry, but had also produced large and unwieldy bureaucracies. The tedious decision making these organizations engendered made flexibility in increasingly demanding environments and responsiveness to shifting markets extremely difficult. "This disastrous hardening of corporate arteries prompted the press, . . . schools, and corporations to

reexamine management effectiveness. Attention turned to leadership as one of the key factors" (Conger, 1992, p. 9).

As the health care sector moves through the 1990s, dramatic changes in system financing and organization, as well as in roles and relationships, are predicted. Alterations in the demographic and lifestyle profiles of our communities, upheavals in domestic and international markets, and increasing governmental involvement in and responsibility for health care financing are stimulating interest in health care system reform. As these stimulants have interacted with the rapidly escalating expectations of system customers, health care administrators have searched for ways to improve continually the performances of their organizations and the system.

Although limited consensus exists concerning exactly what changes are needed, more attention is being focused on leadership as the essential ingredient in creating and sustaining the high levels of organizational quality and cost performance that these changes will require. The Healthcare Forum (1992) recently conducted a national investigation that studied the disparities between the leadership values and competencies currently practiced and those that will be needed to lead the U.S. health care system into the twenty-first century.

Six specific transformational competencies were deemed most critical to outstanding organizational performance by the study participants. These are mastering change, systems thinking, shared vision, continuous improvement, redefining health care, and serving the public or community (Table 9.1). The Healthcare Forum study found that a nationwide cross-section of health care leaders agrees with critics of the health care sys-

TABLE 9.1.   Transformational Competencies Critical to Organizational Performance

Competency	Definition
Mastering change	The ability to view change as an opportunity for new experiences, alternative operations, and calculated risk taking
Systems thinking	The ability to understand relationships and patterns in defining and solving complex problems
Shared vision	The ability to craft a collective organizational vision of the future and to energize current reality toward its attainment
Continuous improvement	The ability to create and sustain a "never satisfied" attitude that supports the ongoing and continuous improvement of service quality and clinical outcomes
Redefining health care	The ability to focus on healing and changing lifestyles and the interplay of spirit, mind and body in nurturing health
Serving public/community	The ability to pursue organizational goals, objectives, and actions in the context of a larger social consciousness and commitment

Source: Data from Healthcare Forum. (1992). *The leadership gap study.* San Francisco: Author.

tem. They agree that the current systems of financing and organization are irretrievably broken and that tinkering through piecemeal reform will not produce the necessary solutions.

> What is needed is a new type of leadership . . . to move health care into the 21st (sic) century. Today's health care practices—even the most successful and effective—will not be adequate for the future . . . The Study findings . . . suggest that health care is between paradigms . . . To move from the old paradigm to a new paradigm requires leaders willing to retire outmoded skills and assumptions. Leaders—different from their predecessors—transformational leaders. (Healthcare Forum, 1992, p. 2)

In this chapter, we explore the definitions of leadership and why it is needed in health care organizations. In so doing, we address the distinction between transactional and transformational leadership and outline the debate regarding the possibility of leadership development. This discussion is followed by descriptions of various leadership development programs and their application in specific situations.

DEFINITIONS OF LEADERSHIP

Leadership, as one of the world's oldest preoccupations, has been a subject creating substantial curiosity since time began (Bass, 1990). Prophets, priests, and kings—the leaders of ancient cultures—were the heroes of myths, the sources of authority in biblical stories, and the focal points around which the Greek and Latin classics were conceived.

Since the advent of research on the workings of complex organizations, leadership has continued to be of considerable interest. Beginning with early studies of the personal traits of leaders (Bass, 1990) and continuing through contingency models of leadership (e.g., Fiedler, 1967), it became clearer that leadership is an incredibly complex subject. Perhaps as a result of this inherent complexity, there have been almost as many definitions of leadership as there are persons who have attempted to define it. In addition to the sheer number of definitions, Pfeffer (1977) noted that many of these definitions are ambiguous.

An important breakthrough in our understanding of the concept of leadership and an important step in addressing the concept's complexity occurred in 1978 with the publication of James MacGregor Burns' book *Leadership*. In this political and organizational consideration of leadership, Burns characterized leaders as either transactional or transformational. *Transactional* leadership occurs when one person takes the initiative, making contact with others for the purpose of an exchange of valued things (Burns, 1978, (pp. 19–20). *Transformational* leadership "occurs when one or more persons engage with others in such a way that leader and follower raise one another to higher levels of motivation and morality" (Burns, 1978, pp. 19–20). Burns' concepts of transactional and transformational leaders were similar to the portraits of managers and leaders, respectively, which Zaleznik (1977) had drawn from clinical evidence independently.

Transactional approaches rely on leaders' promises of rewards and benefits to subordinates for the subordinates' fulfillment of agreements with the leader. An example of this view is perhaps best seen in the adage, "A fair day's work for a fair day's pay." In contrast, transformational approaches feature the leader asking followers to transcend their own interests for the good of the group, organization, or society; to consider their longer-term needs for development, rather than their needs for the moment; and to become more aware of what is truly important and of true value (Bass, 1990). It should be noted that Burns (1978) considered leaders to be either transformational or transactional, but not both. Likewise, Zaleznik (1977) believed that managers and leaders are very different people, with different backgrounds, personalities, and adult characteristics. Therefore, both Burns (1978) and Zaleznik (1977) did not conceive that the same person could exhibit both transactional and transformational leadership approaches.

Since the publication of *Leadership* (Burns, 1978), a number of authors have built on the ideas presented in this seminal work. Many of these authors have modified its leadership paradigm. Bass (1985) proposed that transformational leadership augments the effects of transactional leadership on the efforts, satisfaction, and effectiveness of subordinates and that leaders could be both transactional and transformational. Tichy and Devanna (1986) identified a number of characteristics of transformational leaders through a series of case studies. They described the hybrid nature of transformational leadership, whereby transformational leaders also could use transactional approaches.

Kotter's (1990) distinction between leadership and management is similar in many ways to what Burns (1978) called transformational and transactional leadership, respectively. According to Kotter, leadership produces change by establishing direction, aligning people, and motivating and inspiring. Management brings a measure of order and consistency to organizations by planning and budgeting, organizing and staffing, and controlling and problem solving. Although management and leadership, as defined by Kotter (1990), are distinct concepts, it is possible that one individual may exhibit both. Also, Burns' (1978) transformational leadership has many elements similar to those outlined by Senge (1990) as those needed by leaders of learning organizations. These are developing vision, values, and purpose; providing meaning to subordinates' work; and fostering subordinates' learning.

The practical relevance of transformational and transactional concepts of leadership is illustrated by the identification of patterns of behaviors associated with each type of leadership based on subordinate perceptions. Through a factor analysis of items evaluated by a group of military officers, two factors have been associated with transactional leadership and three others with transformational leadership (Bass, 1985). These factors are discussed below.

Transactional Leadership

The transactional form of leadership was found to consist of two leadership behavior patterns termed *contingent reward* and *management by exception*. In the contingent reward approach, the leader identifies tasks to be done to accomplish a goal, explains them to subordinates, and indicates the outcomes that will accrue to them if tasks are performed and the goal accomplished. Typically, the rewards are praise for work well done and recommendations for pay increases. Path-goal theory (Evans, 1974; Georgopolous, Mahoney, & Jones, 1957; House, 1971; House & Mitchell, 1974) is used to explain why the contingent reward approach works. This approach also identifies contingencies, such as worker experience and task complexity, that influence the relationship between leader and follower. An example of transactional leadership through the contingent reward approach is found in *The One Minute Manager* (Blanchard & Johnson, 1982).

A second transactional leadership process is management by exception, or contingent punishment. In this case, the leader intervenes with subordinates only when something goes wrong. This type of leadership is often advocated for use with skilled professionals, such as physicians or nurses, especially by the professionals themselves. The use of management by exception without coincident use of reward does not appear to be effective (Bass, 1985). Without opportunities for positive reinforcement, relationships become negative and soon deteriorate.

The function of transactional leadership is to maintain the organization's operation rather than to change it. The development of efficient methods to carry out tasks is the role of the transactional leader (Burns & Becker, 1988). This concept of leadership is well-suited to theories that concentrate on the formal structure of organizations and their function of goal attainment (Fayol, 1949; March & Simon, 1958; Taylor, 1911; Weber, 1947). In sum, transactional leadership is the process through which those in formal positions achieve existing organizational goals by clarifying subordinates' expectations about the outcomes of their effort and by reducing role ambiguities and conflict. Kotter's (1990) conception of management follows this idea. Management brings order and consistency to an organization through planning and budgeting, organizing and staffing, and controlling and problem solving. In contemporary health care organizations, this order and consistency, whether termed transactional leadership or management, is needed at all organizational levels.

Transformational Leadership

As noted previously, three patterns of transformational behavior were identified through factor analysis of subordinate perceptions (Bass, 1985). The first factor is charisma, "an endowment of an extremely high degree of esteem value, popularity, and/or celebrity-status attributed by others" (Bass, 1985, p. 39). Eighteen items loaded on this factor, three of which are listed below as illustrations:

- He or she makes everyone around enthusiastic about assignments.
- I have complete faith in him or her.
- He or she is a model for me to follow.

Intellectual stimulation is the second transformational factor (Bass, 1985). This dimension indicates the transformational leader's ability to create in others increased awareness of problems and their solutions. In other words, such leaders focus on and promote strategic thinking among their associates. Subordinates are not aroused to action, but rather to conceptualization of their environment. The following three items loaded on this factor:

- His or her ideas have forced me to rethink some of my own ideas that I had never questioned previously.
- He or she enables me to think about old problems in new ways.
- He or she has provided me with new ways of looking at things that used to be a puzzle for me.

Individualized consideration is the third and final transformational factor identified by Bass (1985). This factor consistently appears in factor analyses of leadership behavior (Bowers & Seashore, 1966; House & Baetz, 1979). This dimension has two aspects. One is the leader's concern for subordinates as individuals with unique problems, which is often expressed through one-to-one interaction focused, perhaps, on job-related or personal issues. The second aspect is the leader's attempt to develop subordinates. This element may take many forms, such as delegation, team building, or mentoring. The following are examples of the items in this factor:

- You can count on him or her to express appreciation when you do a good job.
- He or she makes me feel we can reach our goals without him or her if necessary.
- He or she treats each subordinate individually.

The function of transformational leadership is to produce constructive, sometimes dramatic, change. This is done not through organizing followers and designing organizational structures and processes but rather through calling followers to commitment to a transcendent goal. Transformational leadership takes a long-term view and appeals to followers' values. Kotter's (1990) leadership concept follows this idea. As the need for leadership to take health care organizations into the twenty-first century is recognized, transactional leadership will remain necessary but transformational leadership will be the critical requirement. If health care organizations are to meet the challenges of cost control, access, and quality in the 1990s and beyond, leaders who can produce constructive, perhaps even dramatic, change are needed.

DEVELOPMENT OF LEADERS

Can Leaders Be Developed?

If transformational leaders are needed in contemporary health care organizations, one might ask, "How can transformational leaders be developed?" However, some writers begin not by asking this question but by asking, "*Can* transformational leaders be developed?" The answer given to this latter question is not universally yes; rather, the extent to which nurture is viewed as more significant than nature varies. After carefully analyzing the potential for development, Zaleznik (1977) concluded that leaders, as opposed to managers, can be assisted in reaching positions of authority but that a distinct personality structure is essential. In Zaleznik's view, leaders have "twice-born" personalities, resulting from weak parental attachments that produced "inner directedness" and a sense of separateness. Unlike managers, who are more socially oriented, leaders seek risk rather than security, focus on the meaning of action rather than policy and procedures, and are able to empathize with others rather than merely understanding their roles in a structure.

Similar to Zaleznik, Kuhnert and Lewis (1987) used differences in individual development as the basis of a theory of transformational leadership. They suggested that transformational leadership reflects the mature adult development of personal standards and transcendental values in the leader. In contrast, those who use only transactional approaches are arrested at lower developmental levels and are focused on their own immediate needs, feelings, and interpersonal connections. Transformational leaders have the capacity to take a perspective on interpersonal relationships and to achieve a self-determined sense of identity. They can choose the leadership option most appropriate to a given situation and may at times employ transactional methods to lead. However, transactional leaders have not reached a level of personal development that allows them to use transformational leadership approaches.

Although some would argue that the role of heredity and early childhood experience is primary in determining transformational leaders, advocates of the ability to develop both transactional and transformational leadership can be found. While Kotter (1990), Conger (1992), and others highlight the influence of heredity (e.g., intelligence, physical stamina) and childhood experiences on leadership development, they recognize that individuals do have the capacity to learn and change after adolescence, and that educational and career experiences can enhance both transactional and transformational leadership (i.e., management and leadership, in Kotter's terms) in individuals. This view has been articulated further by proponents of professional graduate education in health administration (Kurz, 1986) and in business (Tarr, 1986).

How Are Leaders Developed?

Having defined leadership and concluded that, indeed, leadership can be learned, one must then ask, how? Assuming an individual has the potential to lead (i.e., the presence of some genetic predisposition to leadership, childhood and adult life experiences that encourage the growth of leadership capacity, and/or motivation and desire to lead), there are several approaches to turning potential into reality.

Hall (1984) noted that organizations involved in leadership development tend to focus on talent identification rather than on learning and development. If one takes Zaleznik's (1977) view that leaders are born and not made, this approach may be a correct one. However if one takes Kotter's (1990) perspective that transformational leadership can be developed, this approach has serious deficits.

Even in organizations in which emphasis is not only on talent identification, there are deficiencies in the training and career development targets and strategies that organizations employ. Hall (1984) outlined four outcomes that measure career effectiveness and therefore can serve as targets for development. These are performance (i.e., attainment of present work goals); attitudes (i.e., present feelings about one's career, such as involvement, commitment, and conflict); adaptability (i.e., preparation to meet future career demands); and identity (i.e., a measure of the congruence and integration of the person's self-perceptions over time). According to Hall (1984), performance improvement through the acquisition of short-term, task-related skills is generally the focus of training and development. Typically, longer-term activities concerned with personal development are not addressed by organizational training and development efforts but may be more appropriate targets for the development of transformational leaders.

Hall (1984) described three strategies for attaining the four targets outlined above. The first strategy is cognitive and is concerned with altering thoughts and ideas. Examples of activities that employ the cognitive strategy are university seminars and orientation programs. The second strategy is behavioral, entailing the attempt to change behavior directly. Examples of this second strategy include role-playing and apprenticeships. An environmental strategy represents the third category. This strategy consists of interventions aimed at altering the individual's immediate work area and can be seen in activities such as job rotation and working on project teams. Most organizational training and development efforts have used cognitive strategies. However, these may not be appropriate for the development of transformational leaders. Behavioral and environmental strategies may be more effective for this purpose.

Conger (1992) identified four essential elements of transformational leadership development. These are personal growth, improvement of conceptual abilities, feedback, and improvement of "teachable skills" (Table 9.2). The following sections describe the assumptions, content, and processes typical of each of these approaches and explore the construction of an ideal framework for leadership development.

TABLE 9.2.   Approaches to Leadership Development

Approach	Description
Personal growth	Clarifying an individual's identity, attitudes, personal needs and interests; building the self-esteem essential to leadership
Conceptual capacity	Building awareness of different models of leadership and the roles and responsibilities ascribed to leadership; expanding the conceptual thinking skills required for leadership
Feedback	Systematic feedback on interpersonal and managerial behaviors from co-workers; helping individuals to see and to move beyond their interpersonal blocks to increased effectiveness
Refinement of "teachable skills"	Deliberate skill-building education; developing and refining skills identified as essential to good leadership

Source: Data from Conger, J.A. (1992). *Learning to Lead.* San Francisco: Jossey-Bass.

The Personal Growth Approach

The primary assumption of personal growth is that leaders are passionate individuals, viscerally aligned with their dreams, their genius, and their competence, and energized to fulfill their promise (Conger, 1992). Through personal growth experiences, individuals engage with their inner selves, it is argued, and, in so doing, become individually motivated to high performance and better able to formulate a vision and to motivate others. Risk taking, teamwork, self-acceptance, personal mastery, emotional competence, reaching for one's potential, balanced living, and being open to possibilities and opportunities constitute the thematic underpinnings of this approach.

Through confidence-building exercises and feedback, this approach builds and fortifies self-esteem. In addition, personal growth may occur as a person recognizes needs that may get in the way of him or her being a leader. Many of the programs of the Center for Creative Leadership, the Outward Bound wilderness training programs, and Kouzes' Leadership Challenge program derive from this understanding of leadership development.

The Conceptual Approach

"I know, therefore I am"—awareness—is the driving assumption of the conceptual approach to leadership development. Comprehension of how leaders act and the domains in which they function is created through demonstration, explanation, and simulated experience using theory, theories in use, models, and cases. This comprehension encourages the motivated individual to develop and sustain a lifelong commitment to learn-ing to lead. The focus on conceptual ability is twofold. First, leaders must be able to think conceptually (i.e., in a broad-based strategic way). Second, leaders must be able to conceptualize the leadership role itself (i.e., to understand the distinction between the leadership and managerial roles and to know how to be and act like a leader). The earliest organizationally developed training programs as well as graduate programs in management, generally, and in health administration, specifically, are examples of this approach.

The Feedback Approach

Proponents of the feedback approach assume that effective feedback creates an understanding of individual strengths and weaknesses and motivates individuals to improve their practices. Feedback, which targets behaviors that are known or believed to be related to leadership effectiveness, is expected to support the development of positive skills and the diminishment of ineffective behaviors.

> Feedback is the process of giving a person information about the impact of his or her behavior. This impact may be on other people or on the completion of a task. Feedback can have multiple purposes; it can be intended to change behavior, to improve performance, to deal with stress, or to enrich a relationship. To be effective, feedback should encourage the maintenance of desired behavior, assist in solving a problem, or enable greater productivity. (Center for Creative Leadership, 1988)

Many tools have been developed to provide individuals with feedback and to help them construct individual plans for remediation and growth. The Leadership Development Program of the Center for Creative Leadership is an example of a program designed primarily from a feedback perspective; many leadership development programs using other approaches include feedback as a component.

The Skill-Building Approach

Skill-building approaches emphasize the teaching of key leadership skills. Through demonstration and experiential exercises, participants in this type of development are taught and practice skills that characterize a particular leadership model or constellation of models. Skill building is one of the older forms of leadership development. Skill programs emphasize both the simpler transactional skills and the more complex transformational skills. Many of the programs developed by the Healthcare Forum and by such groups as Innovation Associates fall primarily into this category.

The Ideal Approach

Taken alone, none of the approaches detailed above is adequate to develop and enhance leadership competence. Rather, a balanced, integrated, and iterative system of development is needed.

Although limited empirical work has been done evaluating the effectiveness of these approaches over time, a recent study of leadership development programs by Conger (1992) reached several significant conclusions. Conger concluded that, to be effective, a program must combine all four approaches: personal growth, enhancement of conceptual abilities, feedback, and skill building. In most cases, the best programs are likely to achieve awareness only, rather than mastery, as current programs provide too little time and too few opportunities for practice, feedback and reinforcement to accomplish real behavioral change. Even if time, practice, feedback, and reinforcement were adequate to nurture and sustain individual motivation, the receptiveness of most organizations to the intended behavioral change is limited at best. As noted earlier, Hall (1984) asserted that most organizations utilize cognitive strategies for development rather than behavioral or environmental strategies.

> Realistically . . . a well-designed leadership program could result in something roughly like the following: (1) no behavioral change and little enhanced awareness for perhaps 10 to 20 percent of the participants, (2) an expanded conceptual understanding of leadership for another 30 to 40 percent, (3) some positive incremental behavioral change (in addition to conceptual understanding) for an additional 25 to 30 percent, and (4) significant positive behavioral change for 10 percent. (Conger, 1992, p. 181)

Conger (1992) contended that both the content and processes of leadership development will need to undergo radical change for real, sustainable growth in leadership capacity to occur. Why is it, he asks, that after more than two decades of leadership development activity we are inundated with the byproducts of poor leadership in our organizations? The culprits of consequence for the limited effectiveness of current leadership development endeavors are not the individual program participants, but the organizations to which they return.

Most organizations, by and large, are comfortable with and welcome managers of stability, rather than leaders of change. Preferring stability, Hall (1984) contended, organizations have relied excessively on short-term performance improving cognitive approaches to leadership development, doing little to develop adaptability, attitudes, and identity, which are longer-term and/or nonspecific task focused. Senge (1990) argued that organizations are designed, jobs are defined, and organizational members are taught to think in ways that are antithetical to accepting, following, and thriving under what we are coming to understand as "good leadership" (i.e., transformational leadership).

In its 1992 study, the Healthcare Forum found that the most conventional practices of our health care organizations include such things as hierarchical management structures, risk minimization, short-term profit maximization, incentive-based performance, and linear thinking. If the leadership necessary to enter the twenty-first century successfully is to become prevalent in health care organizations, organizational structures and processes must be redirected in ways congruent with transformational leadership. These would include cross-functional, integrating structures emphasizing continuous improvement, mastery of and comfort with change, team learning, shared vision, and systems thinking.

Hall's (1984) third developmental strategy relates to the construction of organizational environments conducive to learning and employing transformational leadership. Conger (1992) argued that any organization entering into leadership development must understand that long-term commitment of both the individual and the organization is essential for any development program to be effective. All transformational leadership programs should emphasize critical competencies, multiple sessions, pre- and post-participation

interaction, innovative adult education methods, and the positioning of leadership development program participation at key developmental transition points in developing leaders' careers.

SPECIAL CASES OF LEADERSHIP DEVELOPMENT IN HEALTH CARE

Having considered the fields of leadership and leadership development generically, we now consider leadership development in the health care sector. Three special cases are of particular interest. The first is the effectiveness of academic programs in health care administration in the development of transformational leaders. If one believes that the answer to the question "Can transformational leaders be developed?" is yes, then management education can and should play an important role in developing such leaders. The second involves the increasing feminization of health care administration and our understanding of women's development as transformational leaders. Although much research has been devoted to management and leadership development, possible gender differences associated with this development have received limited attention. Finally, we consider leadership for continuous improvement, a core competence for health care leadership (Healthcare Forum, 1992).

Academic Programs

Although education for leadership is seen as being of major importance in higher education (Bass, 1990), some writers argue that the effect of academic programs on managers and their later success is minimal (McCall, Lombardo, & Morrison, 1988). Critics say that little of what is taught in colleges or even in graduate management education really prepares graduates for what they will face in the "real world."

Health care administration and business programs at both the graduate and undergraduate levels have emphasized mastery of transactional skills in the areas of organizational behavior and development, operations management, marketing, finance, accounting, and information systems. Program emphasis on student acquisition of these skills is a response to the demands of the functional, hierarchical structures of most contemporary health services organizations. This approach to management education has received substantial criticism in the past 10 to 15 years. Although impressed with the technical knowledge of program graduates, critics are dissatisfied with their limited interpersonal skills and their inability to understand the interdependence of the political, structural, human resources, and cultural aspects of organizations. Critics believe that the result of this problem "is that graduates of management programs lack the capacity to deal with the uncertainty and constant change of organizational life" (Kurz, 1991).

This criticism of academic management programs and their outcomes leads us to the question of whether management education can facilitate the development of transformational leaders. Transformational leaders must have a broad knowledge of industry and organization, social relationships in the industry and organization, an excellent reputation and track record, strong interpersonal skills, and personal values. Can health care administration education furnish these? To answer this question, each of these character-

istics of transformational leadership is considered below in relation to areas in traditional health care administration curricula.

Health care administration programs can support the progressive evolution of a broad knowledge base by including content on epidemiology and health care systems. Epidemiology contributes to an individual's understanding of health and disease in human populations, the phenomena that health systems are intended to address, as well as methods of inquiry and techniques for further investigation. Content on health care systems introduces students to the issues of quality, access, and costs that are inherent to systems and the financial, political, and social structures through which communities address these issues.

Accomplishment of the second and third aspects of transformational leadership, a broad set of solid relationships and an excellent track record and reputation, can occur best through experience in work settings, either real or simulated. In academic programs, learning has traditionally been individual; one reads, studies, writes, and is tested alone. Success in the work place, however, is largely accomplished in groups.

> The complexity of most modern organizational tasks, the necessity for broad participation to achieve commitment to programs, and the isolation resulting from task specialization in organizations require group forms of organizing (committees, task forces, project teams, boards, etc.) to achieve coordination on projects. No single person, working alone, can float a bond issue, produce a jet fighter, or market a new laundry detergent. (Bowen & Jackson, 1986, p. 22)

Group projects have been used for instruction, but these projects are typically of such short duration that students cannot see the benefits of forming solid work groups. Moreover, the success and failure of these groups are not analyzed so that the causes of group results (good or bad) can be understood. Programs can and should be more creative in developing working relationships among students that demonstrate the long-term utility of these relationships and begin to refine students' abilities in forming and maintaining them.

Health care administration programs also can demonstrate the significance of reputation and track record to students through a number of activities. Students can be allowed to select teams based on their prior knowledge of each other, as well as information that each student has an opportunity to present prior to group formation. After groups are created, each person can be given the opportunity to assess how he or she was viewed by others and how it affected their selection. Such an approach is perhaps a minimal start, but it begins to illustrate how past activities influence one's ability to function in a specific situation. An essential aspect of management education is to learn that choices regarding one's actions will have significant impact on the perceptions of others, one's ability to work in a group, and one's ability to lead.

Academic programs can also accelerate the development of the interpersonal skills needed for transformational leadership. These skills are necessary for an individual to exhibit transformational leadership qualities such as inspiration, caring for others, and empowerment. In each instance, the ability to communicate is essential for the development of the relationship between leader and follower. The development of interpersonal skills as part of a course of study in health

services administration is an achievable goal. The techniques for training in this area are known and provided in many college and university departments. Courses in interpersonal skills are offered by communication, psychology, and social work departments. This training typically begins in courses such as organizational behavior, but frequently stops short of meaningful progress in improving the capabilities of most students. For example, role-playing may be attempted in exercises addressing negotiation, conflict resolution, and performance appraisal. These exercises typically are restricted to one class period and have limited impact on changing behavior. The role of health services management programs may be to assess student skills in this area and link those in need of further training with appropriate, specialized work offered through their program or by other departments on campus. In addition, some classroom exercises (e.g., Boozer & Maddox, 1992) are now available for teaching about interpersonal aspects of transformational leadership.

Finally, academic programs can support students in developing a strongly held set of values and can enhance their ability to use them in making decisions. A program's ability and desire to alter a student's values may be limited, but programs can assist students in identifying their own values and in addressing the implications of these values for their actions. This can be done through inclusion of ethical content in technical courses (e.g., planning, human resources management), as well as in courses that specifically address ethical principles and issues. Such coursework does not espouse a particular set of values but rather provides a systematic means for considering the relationship of personal values to action in situations where conflicting individual and organizational needs occur.

The capacity of academic–degree-granting programs to develop technical skills and analytical abilities is widely accepted by both health services executives and university faculty. The capacity of these programs to develop transformational leadership qualities is present but largely untapped. In the past, some instructors have been unwilling to take on the formal role of influencing student outcomes in the affective or attitudinal domain, focusing rather on students' intellectual development (Stark, 1990). This focus clearly must change if the development of transformational leaders is to be achieved. In addition, the measurement of educational outcomes, including longitudinal measures of graduates' performance, will be important in this effort. Individual health administration programs and the field through the accreditation process, for example, are beginning to allocate greater attention to these developmental outcomes, and in so doing, respond to their critics.

Women's Leadership Development

The "feminization" of the American work force is a subject about which much has been written. By the year 2000, almost 50% of the U.S. work force will consist of women, and more than 60% of all women will work outside of the home. Women will comprise about three-fifths of the new entrants into the labor force between the late 1980s and the year 2000 (Hudson Institute, 1987).

"Feminization" is also a word that could be applied to the field of health care administration. Although traditionally a field largely made up of white male practitioners (with the exception of Catholic nuns), many women have entered the field since the late 1970s. In the 1981 to 1982 academic years, the proportion of women enrolled in accredited master's programs in health services administration reached 50%, with this proportion growing to almost 60% by the 1990 to 1991 academic year (Association of University Programs in Health Administration, 1992). The percentage of affiliates of the American College of Healthcare Executives (ACHE) who are women grew from 13.9% in 1985 to 23.3% in 1991 (ACHE, 1992).

Although several studies have documented women's career progression and attitudes about their careers in health care administration (e.g., Barkowski & Walsh, 1992; Cyphert, Levey, Weil, & Levey, 1990; Haddock & Aries, 1989), little is known about the differential impact of gender on the development of women's approaches to management and leadership. This is also true, not only for women in health care administration, but also for women in management, in general. Although it is generally recognized that women are developmentally different from men (Gallos, 1989), there has been little exploration of how these differences may affect management and leadership development specifically.

A recent study of male and female mangers, sponsored by the International Women's Forum, found significant differences in how men and women describe their approaches to leadership (Rosener, 1990). The men in the study were more likely than women to describe themselves in ways that were characteristic of transactional leadership. These men tended to view job performance as a series of transactions with subordinates, exchanging rewards for services rendered or punishment for inadequate performance. They were also more likely than women respondents to use power that comes from their organizational position (i.e., formal authority). Women respondents described themselves in ways that were more characteristic of transformational leadership, getting subordinates to transform their own interests into the interests of the group through concern for a broader goal. They were also more likely to ascribe their power to personal characteristics such as charisma, interpersonal skills, hard work, or personal contacts rather than to organizational position. Rosener (1990) labeled this style of leadership described by female respondents "interactive leadership" (p. 120).

Similar to Rosener, Helgesen (1990) found several differences between male and female managers. Helgesen performed a number of case studies of highly successful female managers and compared her results to those of Mintzberg (1973), who had studied a group of male managers. Helgesen found that women tended to take a longer-term view that did men; she called this the "ecology of leadership" (p. 25). Women also saw their own identities as complex and multifaceted, seeing their positions as only one element of who they were; male managers tended to define themselves by their position. Like the women in Rosener's (1990) study, the women in Helgesen's (1990) case studies placed great emphasis on sharing information with those with whom they worked.

Both Rosener's (1990) and Helgesen's (1990) studies clearly exhibit differences in the way that males and females approach leadership. Although it may be imprudent to generalize these findings to every single male or female manager, it is apparent that there are real differences. This should perhaps not be surprising given what we know

about differences between men's and women's psychological and cognitive development (e.g., Belenky, Clinchy, Goldberger, & Tarule, 1986; Gilligan, 1982). As we consider the development of leadership, especially transformational leadership, we must recognize that women may employ a different set of learning strategies or make sense of their experiences in ways that are qualitatively different from men (e.g., Gallos, 1993). This appears to be the case in a recent study sponsored by the Center for Creative Leadership (Van Velsor & Hughes, 1990). In studying the differential effect of gender, the ability of women to learn from other people was remarkably different from that expressed by men. There were differences in the frequency of learning types reported as well. Reflective learning about self and about self in relation to the organization was high in the top third of experiential lessons reported by women. In contrast, "how-to" learning focused on skill mastery was high in the top third reported by men.

When reviewing what we know about leadership development, we should be careful to remember that most of what we know is based on a male leadership model. There may be differences in how women lead and in how women develop leadership skills. This is especially important given the current emphasis on training and development as a way for women to break the "glass ceiling" (Loden & Rosener, 1991; Morrison, 1992; Morrison, White, & Van Velsor, 1987; U.S. Department of Labor, 1991, 1992) and reports that women currently have more restricted access to management development opportunities than do men (Barkowski & Walsh, 1992; U.S. Department of Labor, 1991, 1992). Clearly, management attention and further research in this area are needed.

Continuous Improvement

Continuous improvement, identified as a critical competency by the Healthcare Forum (1992) leadership study, by Nolan (1992), and by Batalden and Nolan (in press), is being embraced as a guiding principle and management philosophy by many health care administrators and as a strategic focus by a growing number of health care organizations. Leaders determined to pursue continuous improvement in their organizations must answer the following three fundamental questions (Nolan, 1992):

- What are we trying to accomplish?
- How will we know that a change is an improvement?
- What changes can we make that will result in improvement?

Five leadership commitments are central to answering these questions and, thus, to developing and sustaining continuous improvement (Nolan, 1992). These are the following:

- To establish and maintain a sense of purpose
- To help people feel comfortable with change
- To maintain a balance between vision and coaching
- To provide an environment of cooperation and concern for people
- To build the system of improvement

To establish and maintain a sense of purpose in a health care organization, leaders must ask and find an answer to the question, "Why do we make what we make?" (Batalden, 1992). The answer should identify a vision for the organization and an under-standing of community need for the services that are provided as well as customer knowledge of them. The vision provides an idealized goal for the health care organization (Kotter, 1988), and community need and customer knowledge illuminate its current reality. As Senge (1990) suggests, when the vision of an organization is compared to its current reality, a tension is created that can drive its transformation.

Leaders must also answer the question, "How do we make what we make?" (Batalden, 1992). In this case, their answer must include developing a customer focus for the organization, providing an environment of cooperation and concern for people, and maintaining a long-term view toward relationships. The criteria for quality established by customers must become the basis for all decisions and actions in the organization. Batalden and Nolan (in press) argued that the indicators of customer focus are not difficult to identify. "The extent of customer focus in an organization is easy to measure. One only has to review the important decisions, actions, and investments of the last six months and determine the primary factors that were considered" (Batalden & Nolan, 1993, p. 9).

If the organization is to function as a system, leaders must create cooperation, not competition, among its parts. A customer focus must extend to internal as well as external customers against whose needs the organization judges its efforts to improve quality. For cooperative relationships to develop and exist among individuals, communication must be clear and commitment must be long-term. Such relationships among individuals in an organization will produce mutual trust as genuine concern for the needs of others becomes the basis of decision making.

Finally, leaders must build a system of improvement by asking, "How can we improve what we make?" (Batalden, 1992). The leadership of the organization retains the responsibility to set strategic direction and to identify the processes in the organization that must be redesigned to improve quality. Improvement depends on adequate levels of individual and organizational investment and knowledge for improvement.

Continuous improvement is not a free good. Leadership and organizational capacity for improvement can be acquired only through the investment of personal and organizational resources—intellect, emotion, finances, and time. First, individuals must be willing to adopt a philosophy of continuous personal and professional improvement through learning. For many, this represents a fundamental change in thinking concerning their own lives and their work in organizations.

Second, organizations must be willing to expand their definitions of and investments in professional development to include the knowledge, skills, and competencies associated with continuous improvement. As decision making flows down in the organization, managers and workers must learn new roles as process investigators, process designers, and process managers, as well as those of facilitator, coach, and teacher. Everyone must learn to create and use knowledge through cross-functional teams.

It has become clear that to advance the rate and nature of improvement in health care systems, leaders must acquire new knowledge that goes beyond the professional knowledge (i.e., knowledge of subject and discipline as well as the values that support their use) on which previous improvements have been based. However, professional knowledge cannot be ignored. Health care organizations must maintain current levels of investment in the technical development of both clinical and managerial employees.

In medicine and other clinical professions, specialists have identified topics of concern or subject matter that can be addressed by several disciplines. Acquired immunodeficiency syndrome (AIDS), for example, can be addressed through both internal and preventive medicine. These disciplines provide accepted concepts, principles, and methods for understanding and studying this phenomenon. In addition, each of these disciplines is both advanced and constrained by a set of values that sets expectations for those practicing them. When a new subject appears, such as AIDS, leadership must improve health care by acquiring and disseminating new knowledge on the subject from each appropriate discipline. To obtain better quality, based on professional knowledge, one simply must learn more and add sophistication to the provision of care.

Improvement through the application of professional knowledge also has been exercised in health care administration. Advances in health care administration have been made through new knowledge of organizational structuring (e.g., multi-institutional system arrangements and strategic alignments); health care financing mechanisms and reimbursement [e.g., prospective financing based on diagnosis-related groups (DRGs) and managed care organizations]; and health care marketing (e.g., demographic and lifestyle market segmentation and sophisticated computer technologies).

Advocates of continuous improvement argue that the professional knowledge approach has advanced quality but is insufficient to support optimum quality in a health care organization. In addition to professional knowledge, health care administrators must accumulate a different kind of knowledge—the essential knowledge needed for improvement. The "core of this knowledge is Deming's system of 'profound knowledge' " (Batalden & Nolan, 1993, p. 11). This system of "profound knowledge" consists of four elements that sustain continuous improvement. They include the following:

- Appreciation of the system
- Knowledge of variation
- Knowledge of psychology
- Theory of knowledge

These elements may be viewed as the content of a curriculum for leadership of continuous improvement. Each component is unique, yet interrelated in its application.

Any health care organization is a system of highly interdependent parts—people, technology, and processes—with a shared purpose that requires cooperation among individuals and departments and flexibility in the performance of processes. Optimization of parts of the system, as often occurs through professional improvement, does not necessarily result in optimization of the system as a whole. System knowledge implies an understanding of the parts and the relationships among the parts that ensure performance.

Leaders must also acquire and spread knowledge of variation. By their very nature, systems experience variation. Variation in systems can result from the effects of what Shewhart (1980) labels special or idiosyncratic causes and/or common or consistent causes of action. Variation in a system that emanates from special causes (an unstable

system) can be decreased by understanding the special causes and eliminating them. Donald B. Berwick (personal communication, January 6, 1993) refers to this as variation requiring first-order change. Systems experiencing only common cause variation (i.e., stable systems) usually need to pursue fundamental, second-order (D. B. Berwick, personal communication, January 6, 1993) change to effect improvements in their functioning. Leaders must develop knowledge of the statistical tools and methods that allow one to distinguish special and common causes, ensure statistical competence organizationwide, and exercise this competence in the identification of and amelioration of causes of variation.

The third area of knowledge is psychology. Specifically, leaders must understand and balance intrinsic and extrinsic motivation. Intrinsic motivation for improvement comes from believing that one is participating in worthwhile activity, from enjoying one's work and taking pride in one's achievements, from being in an environment that supports participation in improving the system, and from being recognized and appreciated for the work one does (Nolan, 1992). Intrinsic motivation results from participation in meaningful decisions about one's work or the functioning of the organization. Feelings of competence and esteem result from workers attributing to themselves the cause for tasks in which they participated and at which they succeeded. Extrinsic motivation (e.g., the use of job-based, merit compensation systems) often creates competition, rather than cooperation, among individuals and groups. Extrinsic motivators can be short-lived and often costly to continue, and can create conflict.

Finally, leaders must employ a theory of

knowledge through which continuous improvement in the system can occur. Such a theory fundamentally applies the scientific method to identifying the common and special causes of organizational phenomenon and uses this new knowledge to predict future events. Once created, this theory of knowledge and the techniques for acquiring it [e.g., the plan-do-check-act (PDCA) cycle] must be spread throughout the organization to be used by all.

SUMMARY

This chapter began with a consideration of the reasons leadership and the development of health care leaders are critical strategic concerns as the U.S. health care system moves into the twenty-first century. Most essentially, demands for a revitalized delivery system and the likelihood of altered financing, competition, and regulation call for a new type of leadership. This new type of leadership—transformational leadership—requires a philosophy and skill set that are currently uncommon in the industry.

What is transformational leadership? The chapter provided the answer to this question by first exploring the concept of leadership and its differential definition across time. The descriptive phrase, transformational leader, was introduced by Burns (1978), juxtaposed to the concept of transactional leadership. Transactional leadership occurs when one person takes the initiative, making contact with others for purposes of exchange. Transformational leadership occurs when individuals perform in such a way that follower and leader interactively increase the levels of personal and organizational morality and motivation.

In exploring the concepts of transactional and transformational leadership, very quickly the question of whether leaders can be developed arose. The chapter reviewed the multiple opinions found in the literature concerning this question and asserted that, indeed, leaders can be made. We learned, however, that the making of a leader is an involved enterprise for which there are several approaches: personal growth, enhancement of conceptual capacity, feedback, refinement of "teachable skills," and the ideal approach. Many of the available leadership development programs can be categorized into one or two of the first four approaches; the ideal approach, which incorporates all four approaches, is not currently in place and available.

Finally, the chapter examined the application of leadership development concepts in three cases specific to health care: the effectiveness of academic programs in developing leaders, the development of women as leaders, and leadership for continuous improvement. Each of these creates a special challenge to the health care sector. On the basis of the material presented in this chapter, the following provide helpful guidelines for health care executives:

1. Leadership and the development of health care leaders are of critical strategic concern as the U.S. health care system moves into the twenty-first century.
2. It is essential for health care administrators to understand the distinction between the concepts of transactional and transformational leadership.
3. The outcomes of transactional leadership are clear mutual expectations of the leader and followers

and organizational consistency and coherency. The outcome of transformational leadership is to produce constructive, sometimes dramatic, change. Although transactional leadership remains necessary in organizations, transformational leadership is the critical requirement for health care organizations as they face the changes and challenges of the twenty-first century.

4. Although heredity and childhood experiences do exert some influence on individuals' capacities for leadership, individuals have the capacity to learn and change after adolescence. Educational and career experiences can enhance both transactional and transformational leadership.

5. To be effective, a leadership development program should combine the personal growth, enhancement of conceptual abilities, feedback, and skill-building approaches in a balanced, integrated, and iterative system of development.

Discussion Questions

1. Briefly outline the forces that make leadership and the development of health care leaders critical strategic concerns for health care organizations as they move into the twenty-first century.

2. Distinguish between the concepts of transactional and transformational leadership. Identify the premises underlying each concept, the resulting relationship between leader and followers for each, and the outcome of each. Explain why each type of

leadership is needed in health care organizations.

3. Briefly describe the personal growth, enhancement of conceptual abilities, feedback, and skill-building approaches to leadership development. Give examples of each approach.

4. As the vice president for human resources of a large vertically and horizontally integrated health care delivery system, you have been asked to design a leadership development program for senior-level executives in the system. Briefly outline the objectives of the program you will develop, the general premises on which you will base your design, examples of the specific strategies for development that your program will employ, and the method by which you will evaluate the effectiveness of the program.

REFERENCES

American College of Healthcare Executives. (1992). *Biographical dictionary of membership.* Chicago: Author.

Association of University Programs in Health Administration. (1992). *Annual survey of health administration programs, 1991: Enrollment, graduates, and program characteristics.* Arlington, VA: Author.

Barkowski, S.C., & Walsh, A. (1992). Executives in health care administration: Where do women stand? *Health Care Financial Management, 46*(7), 47–55.

Bass, B.M. (1985). *Leadership and performance beyond expectations.* New York: Free Press.

Bass, B.M. (1990). *Handbook of leadership.* New York: Free Press.

Batalden, P.B. (1992). *Organizing health administration as a system.* Paper presented at the Quality Improvement Research Symposium, sponsored by the

Association of University Programs in Health Administration, Nashville, Tennessee.

Batalden, P.B., & Nolan, T.W. (in press). Knowledge for the leadership of continual improvement in healthcare. In R.J. Taylor (Ed.), *Manual of health services management.* Rockville, MD: Aspen.

Belenky, M.F., Clinchy, B.M., Goldberger, N.B., & Tarule, J.M. (1986). *Women's ways of knowing: The development of self, voice, and mind.* New York: Basic Books.

Blanchard, K., & Johnson, S. (1992). *The one minute manager.* New York: Morrow.

Boozer, R.W., & Maddox, E.N. (1982). An exercise for exploring organizational spirituality: The case of teaching transformational leadership. *Journal of Management Education, 16*(4), 503–510.

Bowen, D.D., & Jackson, C.N. (1986). Curing those ol' "omigod-not-another-group-class" blues. *The Organization Behavior Teaching Review, 10*(4), 21–31.

Bowers, D.G., & Seashore, S.E. (1966). Predicting organizational effectiveness with a four-factor theory of leadership. *Administrative Science Quarterly, 11,* 238–263.

Burns, L.R., & Becker, S.W. (1988). Leadership and decision making. In S.M. Shortell & A.D. Kaluzny (Eds.), *Health care management: A text in organization theory and behavior* (2nd ed.) (pp. 142–186). New York: Wiley.

Burns, J.M. (1978). *Leadership.* New York: Harper & Row.

Center for Creative Leadership. (1988). *Essentials of constructive feedback.* Greensboro, NC: Author.

Conger, J.A. (1992). *Learning to lead.* San Francisco: Jossey-Bass.

Cyphert, S.T., Levey, L., Weil, P.A., & Levey, S. (1990). Attitudes and career experiences of male and female health care executives. *Healthcare Executive, 5*(6), 17–19.

Evans, M.G. (1974). Extensions of a path-goal theory of motivation. *Journal of Applied Psychology, 59,* 172–178.

Fayol, H. (1949). *General and industrial management.* London: Pitman.

Fiedler, F.E. (1967). *A theory of leadership effectiveness.* New York: McGraw-Hill.

Gallos, J.V. (1989). Exploring women's development: Implications for career theory, practice, and research. In M.B. Arthur, D.T. Hall, & B.S. Lawrence (Eds.), *Handbook of career theory* (pp. 110–123). Cambridge: Cambridge University Press.

Gallos, J.V. (1993). Women's experiences and ways of knowing: Implications for teaching and learning in the organizational behavior classroom. *Journal of Management Education, 17*(1), 7–26.

Georgopolous, B.S., Mahoney, G.M., & Jones, N.W. (1957). A path-goal approach to productivity. *Journal of Applied Psychology, 41,* 345–353.

Gilligan, C. (1982). *In a different voice: Psychological theory and women's development.* Cambridge: Harvard University Press.

Haddock, C.C., & Aries, N. (1989). Career development of women in health administration: A preliminary consideration. *Health Care Management Review, 14*(3), 33–40.

Hall, D.T. (1984). Human resource development and organizational effectiveness. In C.J. Fombrun, N.M. Tichy, & M.A. Devanna (Eds.), *Strategic human resource management* (pp. 159–182). New York: Wiley.

Healthcare Forum. (1992). *The leadership gap study.* San Francisco: Author.

Helgesen, S. (1990). *The female advantage: Women's ways of leadership.* New York: Doubleday.

House, R.J. (1971). A path-goal theory of leadership effectiveness. *Administrative Science Quarterly, 16,* 321–338.

House, R.J., & Baetz, M.L. (1979). Leadership: Some empirical generalizations and new research directions. In B.M. Staw (Ed.), *Research in organizational behavior* (Vol. 1, pp. 341–423). Greenwich, CT: JAI Press.

House, R.J., & Mitchell, T.R. (1974). Path-goal theory of leadership. *Journal of Contemporary Business, 5,* 81–97.

Hudson Institute. (1987). *Workforce 2000:*

Work and workers for the twenty-first century. Indianapolis, IN: Author.

Kotter, J.P. (1988). *The leadership factor.* New York: Free Press.

Kotter, J.P. (1990). *A force for change.* New York: Free Press.

Kuhnert, K.W., & Lewis, P. (1987). Transactional and transformational leadership: A constructive/developmental analysis. *The Academy of Management Review, 12*(4), 648–657.

Kurz, R.S. (1986). Health administration education: Assumptions, guidelines, and future directions. *Journal of Health Administration Education, 3*(3): 382–392.

Kurz, R.S. (1991). Health administration education for the learning organization: Shifting the educational paradigm. *Journal of Health Administration Education, 9*(4): 503–517.

Loden, M., & Rosener, J.B. (1991). *Workforce America: Managing employee diversity as a vital resource.* Homewood, IL: Business One Irwin.

March, J., & Simon, H. (1958). *Organizations.* New York: Wiley.

McCall, M.W., Lombardo, M.M., & Morrison, A.M. (1988). *The lessons of experience: How successful executives develop on the job.* Lexington, MA: D.C. Health.

Mintzberg, H. (1973). *The nature of managerial work.* New York: Harper & Row.

Morrison, A.M. (1992). *The new leaders: Guidelines on leadership diversity in America.* San Francisco: Jossey-Bass.

Morrison, A.M., White, R.P., & Van Velsor, E. (1987). *Breaking the glass ceiling: Can women reach the top of America's largest corporations?* Reading, MA: Addison-Wesley.

Nolan, T.W. (1992, December). *Ten things that I have learned helping organizations focus on quality.* Paper presented to the National Forum on Quality Improvement in Health Care, Orlando, Florida.

Pfeffer, J. (1977). The ambiguity of leadership. *Academy of Management Review, 2,* 104–112.

Rosener, J.B. (1990). Ways women lead. *Harvard Business Review, 68*(6), 119–133.

Senge, P. (1990). *The fifth discipline.* New York: Doubleday.

Shewhart, W.A. (1980). *Economic control of quality of manufactured products.* American Society for Quality Control (Reprint of a 1931 version published by D. VanNostrand).

Stark, J.S. (1990). Approaches to assessing educational outcomes. *Journal of Health Administration Education, 8*(2), 210–226.

Tarr, C. (1986). Can leadership be taught? *Cornell Enterprise, 2*(2), 23–25.

Taylor, F. (1911). *The principles of scientific management.* New York: Harper & Row.

Tichy, N.M., & Devanna, M.A. (1986). *The transformational leader.* New York: Wiley.

U.S. Department of Labor. (1991). *A report on the glass ceiling initiative.* Washington, DC: Government Printing Office.

U.S. Department of Labor. (1992). *Pipeline of progress: A status report on the glass ceiling.* Washington, DC: Government Printing Office.

Van Velsor, E., & Hughes, M.W. (1990). *Gender differences in the development of managers: How women managers learn from experience.* Greensboro, NC: Center for Creative Leadership.

Weber, M. (1947). *The theory of social and economic organization.* (Translated and edited by A.M. Henderson & Talcott Parsons) New York: Oxford University Press.

Zaleznik, A. (1977). Managers and leaders: Are they different? *Harvard Business Review, 55,* 67–80.

PART THREE

HUMAN RESOURCES PROCESS SYSTEMS

CHAPTER

JOB ANALYSIS

Myron D. Fottler

LEARNING OBJECTIVES

Upon completing this chapter, the reader should be able to . . .

- Distinguish job analyses, job descriptions, and job specifications.
- Describe the methods by which job analyses are typically accomplished.
- Discuss the relationship of job requirements (as developed through job analyses, job descriptions, and job specifications) to other human resources management functions.
- Describe the steps involved in a typical job analyses.
- Describe the relationship between job analyses and strategic human resources management.

INTRODUCTION

In previous chapters, we have discussed the effects of the internal and external environments on the process of strategic human resources management. In particular, we have emphasized the importance of the economic and legal environment. The interaction between an organization and its environment has important implications for the organization's internal organization and structure. For example, the environment affects how the organization organizes human resources to achieve specific objectives and perform different functions necessary in carrying out the organization's mission and goals. The organization will formally group the activities to be performed by its human resources into basic units referred to as *jobs*.

In this chapter, we discuss the value of job analysis, which clearly and precisely spells out the requirements of each job. We will emphasize that the results of job analyses

(i.e., job descriptions and job specifications) provide the foundation for making objective and legally defensible decisions in managing human resources.

DEFINITIONS

Job analyses are sometimes called the cornerstone of strategic human resources management because the information they collect serve so many human resources functions. *Job analysis is the process of obtaining information about jobs by determining the job's duties, tasks, and/or activities.* The procedure involves undertaking a systematic investigation of jobs by following a number of predetermined steps specified in advance of the study (Ash, 1988). When completed, job analysis results in a written report summarizing the information obtained from the analyses of 20 or 30 individual job tasks or activities. Human resources managers use these data to develop job descriptions and job specifications.

A job description is a written report about a job and the types of duties it includes. Because there is no standard format for job descriptions, they tend to vary in appearance and content from one organization to another. However, most job descriptions contain the job title, a job identification section, and a job duties section. They *may* also include a job specifications section because job specifications may be prepared as separate documents or included as part of the job descriptions. *A job specification describes the personal qualifications an individual must possess in order to perform the duties and responsibilities contained in a job description.*

Typically, the job specification describes the skills required to perform the job and the physical demands the job places on the employee performing it. Skills relevant to a job include education and experience, specialized knowledge or training, licenses, personal abilities and traits, and manual dexterities. The physical demands of a job refer to the condition of the physical work environment, work place hazards, and the amount of walking, standing, reaching, and lifting required to perform the job. Figure 10.1 provides an example of a combined job description/job specification for the position of staff nurse in a hospital labor and delivery department.

ST. VINCENT'S HOSPITAL
Birmingham, Alabama

CRITERIA BASED JOB DESCRIPTION AND PERFORMANCE STANDARDS

JOB TITLE   Staff Nurse
DEPARTMENT   Nursing—Labor and Delivery

DATE 8/17/92   JOB CODE 2339   FLSA STATUS Nonexempt

DEPARTMENT APPROVAL: _____

PERSONNEL APPROVAL: _____

ADMINISTRATIVE APPROVAL: _____

JOB SUMMARY

Assesses, prescribes, delegates, coordinates, and evaluates the nursing care provided. Ensures provision of quality care for selected groups of patients through utilization of nursing process, established standards of care, and policies and procedures.

SUPERVISION

A. SUPERVISED BY: Unit Manager, indirectly by Charge Nurse
B. SUPERVISES: No one
C. LEADS/GUIDES: Unit Associates/Ancillary Associates in the delivery of direct patient care

JOB SPECIFICATIONS

A. EDUCATION
    —Required: Graduate of an accredited school of professional nursing
    —Desired:
B. EXPERIENCE
    —Required: None
    —Desired: Previous clinical experience
C. LICENSES, CERTIFICATIONS, AND/OR REGISTRATIONS: Current R.N. license in the State of Alabama; BCLS and certifications specific to areas of clinical specialty preferred.
D. EQUIPMENT/TOOLS/WORK AIDS: PCA infusors, infusion pumps and other medical equipment, computer terminal and printer, facsimile machine, photocopier, and patient charts
E. SPECIALIZED KNOWLEDGE AND SKILLS: Ability to work with female patients of child-bearing age and newborn patients in all specialty and subspecialty categories, both urgent and nonurgent in nature.

FIGURE 10.1. An example of a combined job description/job specification. (Reprinted with permission of St. Vincent's Hospital.)

F. PERSONAL TRAITS, QUALITIES, AND APTITUDES: Must be able to: 1) perform a variety of duties often changing from one task to another of a different nature without loss of efficiency or composure; 2) accept responsibility for the direction, control, and planning of an activity; 3) make evaluations and decisions based on measurable or verifiable criteria; 4) work independently; 5) recognize the rights and responsibilities of patient confidentiality; 6) convey empathy and compassion to those experiencing pain or grief; 7) relate to others in a manner that creates a sense of teamwork and cooperation; and 8) communicate effectively with people from every socioeconomic background.

G. WORKING CONDITIONS: Inside environment, protected from the weather but not necessarily temperature changes. Subject to frequent exposure to infection, contagious disease, combative patients, and potentially hazardous materials and equipment. Variable noise levels. Also subject to rapid pace, multiple stimuli, unpredictable environment, and critical situations.

H. PHYSICAL DEMANDS/TRAITS: Must be able to: 1) perceive the nature of sounds by the ear; 2) express or exchange ideas by means of the spoken word; 3) perceive characteristics of objects through the eyes; 4) extend arms and hands in any direction; 5) seize, hold, grasp, turn, or otherwise work with hands; 6) pick, pinch, or otherwise work with the fingers; 7) perceive such attributes of objects or materials as size, shape, temperature, or texture; and 8) stoop, kneel, crouch, and crawl. Must be able to lift 50 pounds maximum with frequent lifting, carrying, pushing, and pulling of objects weighing up to 25 pounds. Continuous walking and standing. Must be able to identify, match, and distinguish colors. Rare lifting of greater than 100 pounds.

JOB RESPONSIBILITIES AND PERFORMANCE STANDARDS

**Assigned
Weight**

10%   1. UTILIZES THE NURSING PROCESS (i.e., ASSESSMENT, PLANNING, IMPLEMENTATION, AND EVALUATION) IN THE PROVISION OF PATIENT CARE IN ACCORDANCE WITH THE STANDARDS OF CARE AND POLICIES AS WRITTEN
Assessment
— Admission assessment includes at least the following:
  * Patient identification
  * Current medical history
  * Current obstetrical history
  * Reason for admission
  * Relevant physical, psychological, and sociological status
    Allergies
    Drug use
    Disabilities
    Impairment
    Surgical Consent Form
    Medical Consent Form
    Pediatrician's Consent Form
— Assessments performed in accordance with the patient care standard, S–2–7010–VI:
  * Admission physical assessment
  * Affected system each shift
  * Labor patients:
    Maternal temperature q 4 hours
    Maternal pulse q 4 hours
    Maternal blood pressure q 1 hour
    Pitocin order
    Vaginal exam prior to Pitocin
    Epidural level of anesthesia hourly
    FHR q 30 minutes during 1st stage
    FHR q 15 minutes during 2nd stage

10%   — Plan of care
* Conceptualized plan of care is developed for each patient:
Identify one nursing diagnosis pertinent to this patient's care.
Identify one nursing intervention related to this diagnosis.
Identify to whom this plan of care should be communicated.
* Nursing intervention(s) relative to the identified nursing diagnosis is documented.
* Written plan of care is initiated on patients whose stay in Labor and Delivery exceeds 24 hours (Exception: patients in labor).
* Plan of care mutually developed with patient and/or SO.
* Written plan of care updated in response to changes in patient care needs.
* Plan of care consistent with medical plan of care.
* All components of the written plan of care are included:
Date
Problem number
Nursing diagnosis
Nursing orders
Patient goal(s)
Projected resolution date
* Patient goals stated are:
Realistic
Measurable
* Patient's response to care given is documented.
* Changes in patient's condition are documented.

10%   2. DETERMINES CONDITION OF PATIENTS AND CLASSIFIES APPROPRIATELY
— Appropriate acuity level is determined based on care provided to the patient/SO.
— All asterisk (*) items have narrative documentation.

5%   3. DEMONSTRATES KNOWLEDGE OF DISCHARGE PLANNING REHABILITATIVE MEASURES AND COMMUNITY RESOURCES BY MAKING APPROPRIATE AND TIMELY REFERRALS
— Initial assessment of discharge needs is accomplished through a complete patient/family history on admission.

5%   4. DEMONSTRATES KNOWLEDGE AND UNDERSTANDING OF TEACHING/LEARNING PROCESS AND IMPLEMENTS PATIENT TEACHING TO MEET LEARNING NEEDS OF PATIENT AND/OR SIGNIFICANT OTHER
— Patient and/or significant other are involved in the identification of learning needs for short-term teaching/counseling during labor.
— Patient teaching during labor is evidenced by anticipatory guidance relative to all procedures and events.

5%   5. ASSUMES RESPONSIBILITY FOR ASSIGNING, DIRECTING, AND PROVIDING CARE FOR GROUPS OF PATIENTS
— Demonstrates necessary skills and knowledge to make appropriate assignments and considers the following factors when making patient care assignments:
* The patient's status
* The environment in which nursing care is provided
* The competence of the nursing staff members who are to provide the care
* The degree of supervision required by and available to the associates
* The complexity of the assessment required by the patient
* The type of technology employed in providing nursing care
* Relevant infection control and safety issues
— Demonstrates the necessary skills and knowledge to provide care for patients in accordance with the Nursing Department and unit specific required skills and competencies
— Compassionately gives personal patient care to provide comfort and well-being to the patient, acknowledging psychological needs

— Delegates aspects of care to other nursing staff members as appropriate
— Appropriately documents and communicates pertinent observations and care provided

10%   6. ADMINISTERS MEDICATIONS, INTRAVASCULAR FLUIDS, AND TREATMENTS IN ACCOR-
DANCE WITH HOSPITAL STANDARDS AND FEDERAL REGULATIONS
— Demonstrates or obtains knowledge of drugs and fluids to be administered
— Accurately administers medications and intravascular fluids as ordered and scheduled
— Accurately and completely documents administration and patient's response to drugs and intravascular fluids
— Demonstrates ability and appropriate technical skills and procedures in accordance with physician's orders and nursing policies and procedures:
  * Procedures and treatments performed in a timely manner
  * Makes adequate preparation for performance of procedures and/or treatments
— Completes appropriate documentation

10%   7. MAINTAINS EFFECTIVE COMMUNICATION WITH SUPERVISORS, HOSPITAL ASSOCIATES, MEDICAL STAFF, PATIENTS, FAMILIES, AND VISITORS
— Enhances cohesiveness of unit staff group through effective interpersonal communication
— Communicates with all persons involved in a patient's care in a manner that facilitates timely meeting of stated goals
— Utilizes approved lines of authority and channels of communication in sharing concerns
— Actively participates in a minimum of four (4) interdepartmental meetings annually
— Interacts effectively with patients, families, and/or significant others
— Supports problem-solving approach to both unit and patient needs
— Follows through on problems that may compromise patient care by using the appropriate chain-of-command
— Gives a thorough concise change of shift report

5%   8. RESPONDS APPROPRIATELY TO ENVIRONMENTAL AND SAFETY HAZARDS AND FUNCTIONS EFFECTIVELY IN EMERGENCY SITUATIONS
— Recognizes, takes action, and reports unsafe acts or situations involving patients, visitors, or staff
— Responds promptly and appropriately to environmental and safety hazards
— Promptly removes unsafe equipment from patient care areas and notifies the appropriate department
— Functions promptly and effectively in codes, emergencies, or other stressful patient situations
— Identifies high-risk patients and monitors accordingly
— Complies with hospital and departmental policies and procedures concerning infection control
— Demonstrates correct and safe technique in the use of equipment according to specific product information and policy and procedure manuals
— Maintains a clean, neat, and safe environment for patients, visitors, and staff according to hospital and unit policies

5%   9. UTILIZES HOSPITAL SYSTEMS EFFECTIVELY TO ENSURE ECONOMICAL USE OF EQUIP-
MENT AND SUPPLIES
— Effectively utilizes unit dose, classification, pneumatic tube, beepers, emergency checks, and services of other hospital departments
— Demonstrates appropriate economical use of supplies and equipment
— Ensures appropriate handling of charges
— Accurately utilizes the computer system
— Correctly initiates and discontinues daily charges when indicated
— Ensures that supplies and equipment necessary for patient care are stored in an organized and efficient manner
— Follows appropriate procedure for obtaining and returning or cleaning and/or disposing of equipment and supplies

5%   10. DEMONSTRATES THROUGH ACTIONS THE ACCEPTANCE OF LEGAL AND ETHICAL RESPON-
SIBILITIES OF THE PROFESSIONAL NURSE
— Documents effectively, accurately, and in a timely manner, on the patient's medical record according to hospital and department standards and policies
— Adheres to drug handling regulations
— Exhibits knowledge of reportable incidents, appropriate documentation, and follow-up
— Maintains current State R.N. license
— Protects patients' rights to privacy and confidentiality
— Demonstrates professional responsibility for nonprofessional group members
— Accurately transcribes or verifies accuracy of physician orders

5%   11. ASSUMES RESPONSIBILITY FOR KEEPING SKILLS CURRENT AND KNOWLEDGE UPDATED THROUGH STAFF DEVELOPMENT AND CONTINUING EDUCATION PROGRAMS
— Actively seeks learning experiences
— Appropriately verbalizes learning needs
— Attends a minimum of eight (8) hours or eight classes of relevant continuing education/ staff development programs annually
— Maintains current Educational Profile.

10%   12. COMPLETES A VOLUME OF WORK THAT ENSURES OPTIMUM PRODUCTIVITY WHILE MAIN-TAINING QUALITY PATIENT CARE
— Completes care of assigned patients in a timely manner
— Assists other associates in completing their assignments in a timely manner
— Supports cost-effective methods for improving patient care
— Willingly accepts adjustment of posted schedule to meet unit emergencies and patient care needs as requested
— Demonstrates an ongoing awareness of, and participation in, the Quality Review (QR) program
— Is alert to potential QR problems and actively participates in solving such problems
— Responds with improved performance to results obtained from QR monitors
— Does not incur excessive unscheduled overtime

5%   13. PARTICIPATES IN ASSIGNED COMMITTEES, CONFERENCES, PROJECTS, STAFF DEVELOP-MENT PROGRAMS, AND STAFF MEETINGS
— Attends and actively contributes to assigned committees, projects, and so forth
— Assists immediate supervisor in the orientation and performance evaluation of associates
— Actively supports departmental projects
— Effectively implements approved departmental changes
— Adapts to changes in a positive, professional manner
— Attends staff meeting or reads and signs all minutes of staff meetings not attended

The associate is expected to perform this job in a manner consistent with the values, mission, and philosophy of St. Vincent's Hospital and the Daughters of Charity National Health System.

Reviewed/Revised By:

_____ Date _____

_____ Date _____

_____

This job description is meant to be only a representative summary of the major duties and responsibilities per-formed by incumbents of this job. The incumbents may be requested to perform job-related tasks other than those stated in this description.

LIMITATIONS AND GUIDELINES

Although human resources managers consider job descriptions a valuable tool for performing human resources functions, several problems are frequently associated with these documents (Grant, 1988). First, they are often poorly written and provide little guidance for the job holder. Second, they are generally not updated as job duties or specifications change. Third, they may violate the law by containing specifications not related to job performance. Fourth, the job duties they include are often written in vague, rather than specific, terms. Fifth, they can limit the scope of activities of the job holder in a rapidly changing environment.

Today's legal environment has created a need for higher levels of specificity in job analysis and job descriptions. Federal guidelines now require that the specific performance requirements of a job be based on *valid* job-related criteria (Equal Employment Opportunity Commission, Civil Service Commission, Department of Labor, & Department of Justice, 1978). Employment decisions that involve either job applicants or employees and are based on criteria that are vague or not job related are increasingly being challenged successfully. Managers of small health care organizations, where employees may perform many different job tasks, must be particularly concerned about writing specific job descriptions.

When writing job descriptions, it is essential that employers use statements that are terse, direct, and simply worded. Unnecessary phrases and words should be eliminated. Typically, the sentences that describe job duties begin with verbs (see Figure 10.1). The term *occasionally* is used to describe those duties that are performed once in a while. The term *may* is used for those duties performed only by some workers on the job.

Excellent job descriptions are of value to both employee and employer. They can be used to help employees learn their job duties and to remind them of the results they are expected to achieve. For the employer, they can serve as a base for minimizing the misunderstandings that occur between supervisors and their subordinates relative to job requirements. They also establish management's right to take corrective action when the duties specified in the job description are not performed at all or are performed at an inappropriate standard.

THE JOB ANALYSIS PROCESS

Figure 10.2 illustrates the elements of the job analysis process and the functions for which it is used. Conducting job analyses is usually the primary responsibility of the human resources department or the individuals charged with these functions. Although job analysts are typically responsible for the job analyses program, they usually enlist the cooperation of the employees and supervisors in the departments in which jobs are being analyzed. It is these supervisors and employees who are the sources of much of the job information generated through the process.

Steps in Job Analysis

The process of conducting a job analysis involves a number of steps. Although health care organizations may differ in the exact job analysis procedures, the following steps

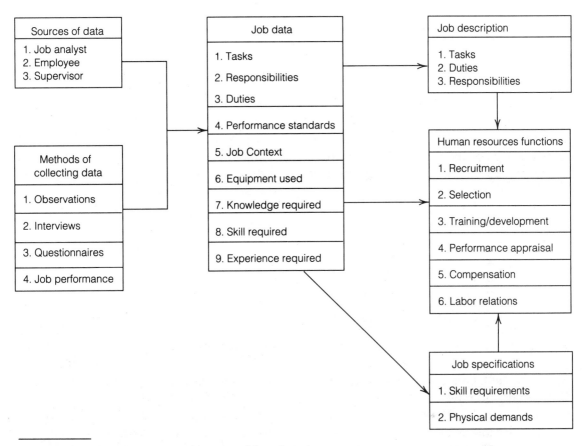

FIGURE 10.2. The elements and functions of the job analysis system.

provide a general guide (Anthony, Perrewe, & Kacmar, 1993).

The first step is to determine the purpose of the job analysis. As a result of rapid growth or downsizing, jobs may have changed in their content. Such changes may cause employee salaries to be inequitable. The purpose of conducting the job analysis should be explicit and tied to the organization's overall business strategy in order to increase the probability of a successful job analysis program.

The second step is to identify the jobs to be analyzed. All jobs are analyzed if no previous formal job analysis has been performed. If the organization has undergone changes that have affected only certain jobs or if new jobs have been added, then only those jobs are analyzed.

The third step is to explain the process to employees and determine their levels of involvement. Employees should be informed of whom will be conducting the analysis, why it is needed, whom to contact to answer questions and concerns, the schedule of events, and their roles in the process. In addition to good communication, a committee elected by employees may serve as a verification check and may reduce employee anxiety. Such committees can also help answer questions and concerns employees may have.

The fourth step consists of actually collecting the job analysis information. Managers must decide which method or combination of methods will be used and how the information will be collected. Various alternatives are discussed in the next section of this chapter.

The fifth step is to organize the job analysis information into a form that will be useful to managers and employees. This form consists of job descriptions and job specifications as described previously. The job descriptions can vary from very broad to very specific and precise. The level of detail depends on the needs of the organization as noted in the first step of the process. As noted later in this chapter, the job specifications must be linked directly to the job description (i.e., it must be relevant to the job).

The sixth and final step is to review and update the job analysis information frequently. Particularly in a dynamic environment such as health care, jobs seldom go unchanged for long periods of time. Even if no major changes have occurred within the organization, a complete review of all jobs should be performed every 3 years (Mathis & Jackson, 1985). More frequent reviews are necessary when major organizational changes occur.

Data Collection Methods

Job information is collected in several ways depending on the purpose to be served by the organization. Typically, the organizational chart is reviewed to identify the jobs to be included in the analysis. Often restructuring, downsizing, merger, or rapid growth will initiate the job analyses review. A job may be selected because it has undergone undocumented changes in job content. As new job demands arise and the nature of the work changes, compensation for the job also may have to change. The employee or the manager may request a job analysis to determine the appropriate compensation. The manager may also be interested in documenting change for recruitment, selection, training, and performance appraisal purposes.

Managers should consider a number of different methods to collect job analysis information because it is unlikely that any one method will provide all of the necessary information needed for a job analysis. Among the most popular methods of data collection are observation of tasks and behaviors of the job holders, interviews, structured questionnaires and checklists, job performance, and critical incidents.

Observations require job analysts to observe the job holders performing their jobs. The observations may be continuous or intermittent based on work sampling (i.e., observing only a sampling of tasks performed). For many jobs, observation may be of limited usefulness because the job does not consist of physically active tasks. For example, observing an accountant reviewing an income statement may not provide valuable information. Even with more active jobs, observation does not always reveal vital information such as the importance or difficulty of the task. Given the limitations of observation, it is helpful to incorporate additional methods for obtaining job analysis information.

Employees knowledgeable about a particular job (i.e., the employee holding the job, supervisors, or former job holders) may be interviewed concerning the specific work activities that comprise the job. Usually a structured interview form is used to record information. The questions asked correspond to the data needed to prepare a job description and job specification. Employees may be suspicious of the interviewer and his or her motives, especially if the interviewer asks ambiguous questions. Because interviewing can be a time-consuming and costly method of data collection, managers and job analysts might prefer to use the interview as a means to answer specific questions generated from observations and questionnaires.

The use of structured questionnaires and checklists is most efficient because it is a quick and inexpensive way to collect information about a job. If possible, it is desirable to have several knowledgeable employees complete the questionnaire for verification. Such survey data often can be quantified and processed by computer. Follow-up observations and interviews are not uncommon if a questionnaire or checklist is chosen as the primary means of collecting job analysis information.

Although questionnaires and checklists provide the employer with a simplified method for obtaining job analysis information, the questionnaire must be extremely detailed and comprehensive so that valuable information is not missed. Compared to other methods, questionnaires are cheaper and easier to administer but more time-consuming and expensive to develop. Management must decide whether the benefits of a simplified method of data collection outweigh the costs of its construction.

Strategically, managers would favor methods of data collection that do not require a lot of work and up-front costs if the content of the job changes frequently. Another option might be to adopt an existing structured questionnaire. Among the more widely used structured questionnaires are the Position Analysis Questionnaire (PAQ), the Management Position Description Questionnaire (MPDQ), and the Functional Job Analysis (FJA). Irrespective of whether the questionnaire is developed in-house or purchased from a commercial source, rapport between analyst and respondent is not possible unless the analyst is available to explain items and clarify misunderstandings. Without such rapport, such an impersonal approach may have adverse effects on the respondents' cooperation and motivation.

Finally, the analyst can actually perform the job in question. This approach allows exposure to the actual job tasks as well as the job's physical, environmental, and social demands. It is appropriate for jobs that can be learned in a relatively short period of time. However, it is inappropriate for jobs that require extensive training and/or are hazardous to perform.

Relation to Other Human Resources Functions

Not surprisingly, job requirements as documented in job descriptions and job specifications influence many of the human resources functions that are performed as a part of managing employees. When job requirements are modified, corresponding changes must be made in other human resources activities. Job analysis is the foundation for forecasting future needs for human resources as well as plans for such activities as training, transfer, or promotion. Frequently, job analysis information is incorporated into the human resources information systems.

Prior to attempting to recruit capable employees, recruiters need to know the job specifications for the positions they are to fill. This includes all of the knowledge, skills, and abilities required for successful job performance. The information in the job specifications is used in notices of job openings and provides a basis for attracting qualified applicants while discouraging unqualified applicants. A failure to update job specifications could result in a pool of applicants who are unqualified to perform one or more job functions.

Until 1971, job specifications used as a basis for employee selection decisions often bore little relation to the duties to be performed under the job description. Then in *Griggs v. Duke Power Company* (401 U.S. 424) (1971), the Supreme Court ruled that employment practices must be job-related. When discrimination charges arise, employers have the burden of proving that job requirements are job-related or constitute a business necessity. Employers must now be able to show that the job specifications used in selecting employees for a particular job relate specifically to that job's duties.

Job analysis is faced with several legal constraints largely because it serves as a basis for selection decisions, compensation, performance appraisals, and training. These constraints have been articulated in the 1978 *Uniform Guidelines for Employee Selection Procedures* (Equal Employment Opportunity Commission, Civil Service Commission, Department of Labor, & Department of Justice, 1978) and several court decisions. Section 14.c.2 of the *Uniform Guidelines* states that "there shall be a job analysis of the important work behaviors required for successful performance." To determine this, organizations should conduct job analyses to help them determine the skills, knowledge, and abilities individuals need to perform the jobs. After this is known, selection procedures can be developed (Thompson & Thompson, 1982).

Where job analyses have not been performed, the validity of selection decisions has been challenged successfully (*Albermarle Paper Company v. Moody* (422 U.S. 405) (1975). Numerous court decisions regarding promotion and job analysis also exist. In *Rowe v. General Motors* (325 U.S. 305) (1972), the court ruled that a company should have written objective standards for promotion in order to prevent discriminatory practices. In *U.S. v. City of Chicago* [573 F. 2nd 416 (7th Cir.)] (1978), the court ruled that the standards should describe the job for which the person is being considered for promotion. In both cases, these objective standards can be determined through job analysis (Nobile, 1991).

Any discrepancies among the knowledge, skills, and abilities demonstrated by a job holder and the job requirements contained in the job description and job specification for that position provide clues to training needs. The formal qualification requirements set forth for higher-level positions serve to indicate how much more training and career development are needed for employees to advance to these positions. Because training and career development can be quite costly, up-to-date job descriptions and specifications help to ensure that training programs and other assignments reflect actual job requirements of the higher-level positions. Good job analysis data also allow for more effective career planning because the relationships among jobs and job families are more clearly understood.

The requirements contained in the job description should provide the criteria for evaluating the performance of the individual holding a particular job. Results of the performance appraisal may reveal that certain specified job requirements are not specific or job-related. This situation may subject the employer to charges of unfair discrimination unless the job description and/or specifications are rewritten to be more specific and job-related. Then the performance appraisal instrument can be redone to reflect the updated and more valued information. More critical and less critical job requirements could then be specified with confidence.

In determining the rate to be paid for performing a particular job, the relative worth of the job as determined by job evaluation is one of the most important factors. Before jobs can be ranked in terms of their overall worth to an organization or compared to jobs in other similar organizations through pay surveys, their requirements must be understood thoroughly. A job's worth is based on its requirements in terms of the necessary skills, knowledge, effort, responsibility, and ability, as well as the conditions and hazards under which the work is performed. Job descriptions and specifications provide such understanding to those who must make job evaluation and compensation decisions.

Prior to the *Uniform Guidelines* (Equal Employment Opportunity Commission, Civil Service Commission, Department of Labor, & Department of Justice, 1978) and the associated court cases discussed previously, labor contracts required consistent and equitable treatment of unionized employees. The information provided by job analysis is helpful to both management and unions for contract negotiations and for avoiding or resolv-ing grievances, jurisdictional disputes, and other conflicts. For these reasons, unionized employers have found it advantageous to prepare written job descriptions and job specifications.

STRATEGIC ASPECTS OF JOB ANALYSIS

This section explores the linkages among the health care organization's external environment, human resources practices, and job analyses. As the external environment and business strategies change in the dynamic health care environment of the 1990s, so too must human resources practices and job analysis information. Failure of the job analysis information to keep pace with the other changes will result in poorer individual and organizational performance. This section examines job analysis in the changing health care environment.

The dynamic nature of today's health care organization brings into question the logic of job analysis. More specifically, it must be assumed that the job analyzed today will consist of the same set of duties and functions tomorrow. This may not be the case in many health care organizations by design or otherwise as the environment forces various types of corporate restructuring and job restructuring. Thus, one could be recruiting, selecting, and training based on job requirements that are obsolete. For example, computerization and downsizing may alter substantially the nature of jobs and personal employee characteristics needed to meet new job requirements successfully.

If health care executives have a clear view of how jobs are going to be restructured in the future, then a *future-oriented* job analysis may be undertaken. This approach requires health care executives to identify future duties and tasks for those jobs that are expected to change. The extent to which skills required of the present duties and tasks overlapped or contributed to the future duties and tasks is a key judgment area for executives. Those judgments might determine the weights placed on various aspects of present performance and could form the basis for retention decisions in a downsizing situation.

In these times of intense competitive pressure, total quality management, continuous quality improvement, and flexibility, a future-oriented job analysis can offer a solution when organized and anticipated change is going to occur. However, what approach should be taken by an organization that desires to be more flexible but cannot plan for or anticipate the exact nature of future changes?

A second approach to the dynamic health care environment under the above conditions is *generic job analysis.* The traditional job analysis approach serves to constrain desired change and flexibility by compartmentalizing and specifically defining presumably static job characteristics. It impedes shifting decision making downward in the organization, cross-training employees, and getting employees involved in quality improvement efforts (Blayney, 1992). Reducing the number of job titles and developing fewer but more generic job descriptions can provide needed flexibility to manage unanticipated change.

For example, Nissan Motor Company has only one job description for hourly wage production employees. This description is generic and gives the organization the opportunity to use employees as needed. Cross-training and multiple job assignments can occur. The company rejects explicit and specific job descriptions because they are static and prevent innovation and continuous improvement.

Another approach to generic job analysis is to focus on understanding the personal characteristics important for performance in an innovative and continuous improvement environment. The focus here is not on specific duties and tasks, but on the personal qualities necessary to function in a continuous improvement culture (e.g., flexibility, innovativeness, the ability to work as part of a team). These personal characteristics should be an important part of the job specification because they are consistently important even though duties and tasks may be in flux.

Both future-oriented job analysis and generic job analysis offer promise in terms of managing health care organizations in a dynamic environment. However, they also pose certain challenges. First, health care executives may not be able to make accurate judgments about the requirements of future jobs (even when the likely changes are known). Second, how will employees react to generic job descriptions? They may experience role conflict and role ambiguity. Third, future-oriented and generic job analysis may not meet the legal requirements for job descriptions and job specifications described previously in this chapter.

SUMMARY

Job analysis is the collection of information relevant to the preparation of job descriptions and job specifications. An overall written summary of the task requirements for a particular job is called a job description and an overall written summary of the personal requirements an individual must possess in order to successfully perform the job is called a job specification. Job analysis information developed in the form of job descriptions and job specifications provides the basic foundation for all of the human resources management functions.

Some combinations of available job analysis methods (i.e., observation, interviews, questionnaires, job performance, critical incidents) should be used because all have advantages and disadvantages. Key considerations regarding the choice of methods should be the fit between the method and the purpose, cost, practicality, and an overall judgment concerning the appropriateness of the methods for the situation in question. The primary purpose of conducting the job analysis should be described clearly to ensure that all relevant information is collected. In addition, time and cost constraints should be specified before choosing one or more of the available data collection methods.

Health care executives in the human resources area should follow the following steps when conducting a job analysis: 1) determine purpose, 2) identify jobs to be analyzed, 3) explain the process to employees, 4) collect job analysis information, 5) organize the information into job descriptions and job specifications, and 6) review and update frequently.

Job descriptions and job specifications, as derived from job analysis, must not only be done, but the process must be valid, accurate and job-related. Otherwise, the health care organization may face legal repercussions, particularly in the areas of employee selection, promotions, and compensation. The *Uniform Guidelines* of 1978 and associated court cases provide guidelines for avoiding charges of discrimination in the development of job analysis data.

Finally, in today's rapidly changing health care environment, health care executives should consider the potential advantages of future-oriented job analysis when change is more predictable and generic job analysis when change is less predictable. Both are relatively new concepts that may have legal or practical limitations that must be considered before they are fully adopted.

Discussion Questions

1. Why should health care executives conduct a job analysis? What purpose does it serve?
2. What are job descriptions and job specifications? What is their relationship to job analysis?
3. Consider the position of the registered nurse in a large hospital. Which of the five methods of job analysis would you use to collect data on the position and why?
4. Describe the steps involved in the job analysis process.
5. How can the existence of a high-quality job analysis make a particular human resources function, such as employee selection, less legally vulnerable?
6. Are jobs static or do they change over time? What might cause a job to change over time? What implications does this have for job analysis?
7. Describe and discuss future-oriented job analysis and generic job analysis. How might each be used to help health care executives cope with a rapidly changing and competitive environment? What are some potential pitfalls of each approach?

REFERENCES

Albermarle Paper Company v. Moody. (1975), 442 U.S. 407.

Anthony, W.P., Perrewe, P.L., & Kacmar, K.M. (1993). *Strategic human resources management.* Fort Worth, TX: Dryden Press.

Ash, R.A. (1988). Job analysis in the world of work. In S. Grael (Ed.), *The job analysis handbook for business* (pp. 3–23). New York: Wiley.

Blayney, K.D. (Ed.). (1992). *Healing hands: Customizing your health team for institutional survival.* Battle Creek, MI: W.K. Kellogg Foundation.

Equal Employment Opportunity Commission, Civil Service Commission, Department of Labor, & Department of Justice. (1978). *Uniform guidelines for employee selection procedures* as reproduced in the *Federal Register, 43*(166) (August 25, 1978), 38290–38315.

Grant P.C. (1988). Why job descriptions don't work. *Personnel Journal, 67*(1), 53–59.

Griggs v. Duke Power Company. (1971). 401 U.S. 424.

Mathis, R.L., & Jackson, J.H. (1985). *Personnel/human resources management.* St. Paul, MN: West Publishing.

Nobile, R.J. (1991). The law of performance appraisals. *Personnel, 35*(1), 1.

Rowe v. General Motors. (1972), 325 U.S. 305.

Thompson, D.E., & Thompson, T.A. (1982). Court standards for job analysis in test validation. *Personnel Psychology, 35,* 865–874.

U.S. v. City of Chicago (1978). 573 F. 2nd. 416 (7th Cir.).

CHAPTER

RECRUITMENT AND RETENTION

Jacqueline Landau

Michael Abelson

The authors would like to acknowledge the contribution of Geoffrey Hoare, Ph.D., University of Washington. He co-authored an earlier version of this chapter, which was published in 1988.

The authors also acknowledge the assistance provided by a number of human resources executives who provided information about their organizations' practices. These persons included the following: Michael Howe, Senior Vice-President, Human Resources, Health One; Frank St. Denis, Vice-President of Human Resources, Health West; Larry Smally, Vice-President of Human Resources, Hospital Group, National Medical Enterprises; and Robin Walker, Vice-President, Tyler and Company.

LEARNING OBJECTIVES

Upon completing this chapter the reader should be able to . . . .

- Discuss the strategic importance of the recruitment process.
- Describe the turnover process.
- Explain the differences between functional/dysfunctional turnover and controllable/uncontrollable turnover.
- Conduct a turnover audit.
- Describe the recruitment process.
- Identify and evaluate internal and external recruitment services.
- Implement recruitment plans.
- Evaluate the recruitment process.
- Describe the relationship between recruitment and retention.

INTRODUCTION

Staffing, the process of moving employees into, through, and out of positions to facilitate the accomplishment of the organization's strategic objectives, is one of the most important human resources management functions (Milkovich & Boudreau, 1988). Recruiting, the process of seeking, attracting, and screening qualified applicants, and forming a pool from which job candidates are selected, is an integral part of the staffing function. Health care organizations cannot operate effectively if they cannot attract quality applicants to fill their work force requirements. This is particularly important in times of low unemployment when fewer people are available to work or when there is a shortage of skilled personnel. Service organizations, such as hospitals and clinics, are labor intensive and therefore vulnerable to shortages. Selection strategies, training programs, appraisal and compensation systems, and career development programs can have only limited success if organizations cannot attract the employees they need.

Training programs, appraisal and compensation systems, and career development programs can also have only limited success if organizations cannot retain the employees they have acquired. Although all human resources functions can have an impact on retention, recruitment sets the stage for initial work experiences. The more carefully an organization plans and implements its recruitment policies and practices, the less likely turnover will be a problem.

There are few industries that employ personnel with such a range of expertise as health care. Physicians, nurses, technicians, and semiskilled employees work interdependently in caring for patients. All of these caregivers and support staff are becoming increasingly dependent on administrators, who know the characteristics of the service area, ways to generate demand for service through marketing, and the intricacies of reimbursement (Kaluzney & Shortell, 1983). Several trends are making this already complex situation more complicated and are changing the recruiting and retention needs of health care organizations.

The health care industry is dramatically changing the mix of types of services offered as the burden of disease shifts. Health care in the United States is moving from an era of treating cases of acute, infectious diseases to managing patients with chronic diseases who experience acute episodes periodically (Miller & Miller, 1981). At the same time, as third-party payers have demanded reductions in the cost of care, user-friendly technologies have developed that allow a number of treatments to be given outside of the hospital. The proliferation of clinical settings, including ambulatory surgery, skilled nursing and long-term care facilities, and home care, has created demands for types of personnel different from those found in a traditional community hospital. Furthermore, the linking of hospitals and alternative care facilities into multi-unit diversified health care corporations has created a number of new management tasks, and hence manpower requirements (Hoare, 1987). These positions in the corporate infrastructure, in headquarters and regional offices, for example, may entail planning, productivity analysis, or performance auditing. However, tertiary care facilities continue to need highly trained staff to work with increasingly complex technology and very sick patients.

In the 1980s, hospital managers focused on cost containments and profitability more than they ever had previously (Anderson & Wootton, 1991). The number of hospitals decreased due to closings, mergers, and acquisitions, and from 1983 to 1986 employment in hospitals declined by 2.3% (Anderson & Wootton, 1991). There were staff cuts, hiring freezing, and increased use of contract services. It appeared that recruitment and retention were no longer going to be critical issues. By 1989, however, hospital employment increased 6.9%, as hospitals developed services in expanding alternative care markets (e.g., outpatient surgery, home health care) (Anderson & Wootton, 1991). Between 1983 and 1989, the number of marketing, advertising, and public relations managers employed by hospitals increased more than 70%; the number of medical and health services managers increased 40%; the number of registered nurses increased 13%; and the number of physical, occupational, and recreational therapists increased 20% (Anderson & Wootton, 1991). In general, the need for people in occupations that involve the use of new complex technology or are directed at managing costs has increased; the need for people in occupations that involve direct patient care has decreased (Anderson & Wootton, 1991).

Clearly, the range and mix of skills required by health care personnel are expanding. This will complicate the work of a health care corporation's personnel department. For example, a large community hospital built a 12-bed hyperbaric chamber to treat burn and trauma patients but found few individuals qualified to work there. The hospital had to choose either to train nurses to work in those conditions or to recruit deep-sea divers familiar with hyperbaric technology and train them in nursing. Either alternative would be costly and time-consuming, particularly if those individuals whom they decided to hire and train soon left for other jobs. Therefore, retention issues must be considered in the design and implementation of any recruitment strategy.

This chapter begins with a discussion of turnover, the turnover process, the distinction between functional and dysfunctional turnover, and the degree to which dysfunctional turnover can be controlled. Then, the chapter explains how to conduct a turnover audit to determine the extent to which there is a need to manage turnover more effectively. Next, factors that affect the individual turnover decision are discussed. Finally, the three basic steps of the recruitment process (i.e., planning, implementation, and evaluation) are reviewed, and the implications of the process for retention and turnover are discussed.

EMPLOYEE TURNOVER

Turnover is the process of employee intraorganizational and interorganizational movement. Intraorganizational movement occurs when an employee moves from one position to another within the same organization, either within the same department or across organizational departments. Interorganizational movement occurs when an individual moves from one organization to another. This latter type of movement is what is more traditionally associated with turnover. In order to support the strategic goals of the organization, both intraorganizational and interorganizational movement must be managed effectively.

The Turnover Process

Turnover is a multistage process (Mobley, 1977). The decision to stay at or leave an organization begins with a person's perception regarding how satisfied he or she is with the current position (Figure 11.1). The more satisfied people are, the less likely they are to leave the organization. Another factor that is most directly related to this stage of the

turnover process is the level of commitment people feel toward the organization (Mowday, Porter, & Steers, 1982). The more their personal goals and values match those of the organization, the more committed they are to the organization and the greater the likelihood is that they will stay. If people are highly committed to the organization's goals and values but are not satisfied with their present position, they are more likely to seek opportunities within, as opposed to outside, the organization. A decision to consider leaving the current position may be the result of thinking greater satisfaction can occur from another job. For example, a hospital technician may like his or her current job but may become aware of opportunities in other parts of the organization or in other organizations that more satisfactorily meet his or her personal needs.

In the second stage of the turnover process, the person thinks about leaving his or her current job. Employees may begin thinking about leaving because of dissatisfaction with various aspects of the job itself (Porter & Steers, 1973), opportunities elsewhere (March & Simon, 1958), or because of friends who are either in the process of leaving or

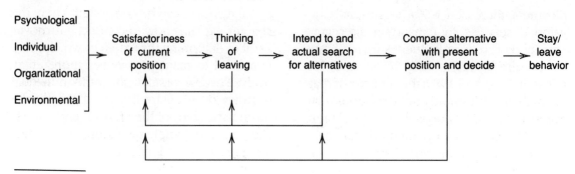

FIGURE 11.1. The turnover process.

who have left already (Krackhardt & Porter, 1985). A nurse may be somewhat satisfied with his or her current position but may think about leaving after speaking with a fellow nurse who has identified a job at another hospital that more closely meets his or her personal needs.

In the third stage of the turnover process, the person searches for alternative employment. The more frustration or dissatisfaction an employee experiences with the current job, the greater the likelihood the person will actually search for another position (Kahn, Wolfe, Quinn, Snock, & Rosenthal, 1964). This position may be within or outside of the organization. Some people discuss leaving but never actually search for work elsewhere. These people are at the thinking-of-leaving stage and have not truly evolved to the next stage in the process. A pharmacist, for example, may frequently state a personal desire to quit but may never examine other work alternatives.

In the fourth stage of the turnover process, the employee compares alternatives with the present job and makes a decision. The more the employee searches for employment elsewhere, the more probable his or her leaving. The pharmacist or nurse who has obtained information proactively concerning numerous job opportunities has a greater likelihood of leaving than does the person who only browses the Sunday want advertisements.

The fifth and final stage of the turnover process is the actual staying or leaving behavior. Although intent to leave is often related to actual staying or leaving, intentions do not always predict behavior. An employee may acquire additional information concerning the current job or potential new opportunities that may affect the decision.

Several other issues regarding the turnover process must be considered. First, because turnover is a process, management can attempt to influence the employee's decision to stay or leave at any time during the process. The ability of management to influence the turnover decision positively depends on management skill and how advanced the employee is in the turnover process. The further the employee proceeds in the process, the more difficult it is to change the direction of his or her decision.

A second issue that complicates management's ability to manage turnover proactively is that not all employees progress through the process in the same way. Some employees may move from one stage to the next very methodically. Others may progress rather quickly, even appearing to skip stages. Still others may seem to make abrupt decisions and announce that they are leaving even though they never appeared to be dissatisfied (Sheridan & Abelson, 1983). Management can influence employee turnover decisions best by focusing on symptoms that might be signs of employee dissatisfaction and by attempting to address the turnover issue as it is evolving instead of waiting until the employee has decided to leave and gives formal notice.

Functional and Dysfunctional Turnover

In some instances, turnover actually may increase organizational effectiveness (Dalton & Tudor, 1979). The departure of poorly performing staff will be functional for the organization if they can be replaced by employees who are more competent. The departure of people who create conflict and/or turmoil in the work place is also functional.

Furthermore, many organizations, especially health care organizations in rural settings, find themselves decreasing the number of staff in order to deal with organizational costs effectively. This downsizing can be functional if it has long-term benefits for the organization. Replacement of some employees may bring new ideas and increased energy into the organization, resulting in a significant long-term gain. In fact, an effective strategy for faster and more dramatic change is to hire administrators from outside of the organization.

Dysfunctional turnover occurs when valued employees leave (Dalton & Tudor, 1979). The departure of competent workers can have a severe impact on the organization. This is especially true when a number of high performers leave at approximately the same time (Krackhardt & Porter, 1985). Furthermore, although certain levels of turnover are functional, too much turnover can reduce stability in the organization and contribute to problems. The simultaneous departure of several nurses from an intensive

care unit may contribute to lower levels of patient care until new nursing staff can be hired and trained. The departure of employees in crucial and/or specialized areas (e.g., emergency rooms, operating rooms, burn units) can be dysfunctional for the health care organization. Personnel shortages could force these typically profitable units to close. Figure 11.2 includes a partial list of examples of both functional and dysfunctional turnover.

Turnover Avoidability

Not all turnover is avoidable and controllable by management or the individual (Abelson, 1987). Figure 11.3 includes an avoidability matrix. Understanding and using this matrix can be beneficial in planning for future staffing needs. Quadrant 4 of the matrix gives examples in which neither the organization nor the individual has any control over turnover, such as instances of severe medical problems and death.

Quadrant 2 gives examples in which people voluntarily leave, but the organization has no control. For example, an individual may decide to enhance his or her career and leave the organization to pursue additional education. Numerous family-related reasons are also beyond the control of an organization. A spouse may choose to move to another location or an employee may choose to remain at home to care for a child, spouse, and/or another family member. Under these conditions, it may be difficult for organizations to persuade people to stay.

There are also a number of situations in which the organization has control over the turnover decision, and the employee has none (see quadrant 3 in Figure 11.3). For example, the organization may fire poor per-

---

Functional turnover occurs when:
- Low performers leave
- People who create conflict and/or turmoil leave
- Effective downsizing occurs
- People leaving allows for hiring people from the outside, resulting in faster and more dramatic change

Dysfunctional turnover occurs when:
- High performers leave
- A number of people leave at the same time causing scheduling problems and additional stress
- Difficult-to-replace staff leave
- Competent staff in crucial positions leave

FIGURE 11.2. Functional and dysfunctional turnover.

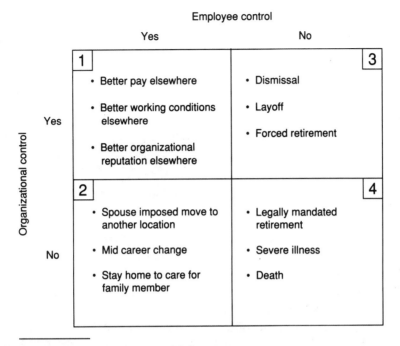

FIGURE 11.3. Turnover Avoidability Matrix.

formers. In most situations, these turnovers will be functional for the organization, at least in the short term.

Quadrant 1 lists a number of situations in which turnover may be controlled by both the individual and/or the organization. Employees may leave for companies with better pay, working conditions, management, or reputations. Both the employee and the organization have some control in dealing with any of these issues.

When evaluating turnover, organizations should recognize that not all turnover is controllable or problematic. Effective organizations attempt to focus on areas that they can control. One way to control turnover is to recruit and hire people that match the organization's needs and culture.

Organizational Turnover Audit

A turnover audit helps the organization identify the proportion of turnover that it needs to control. The first step in conducting an audit is to determine the turnover rate for a particular unit during a specific period of time. For example, a large, center-city hospital has determined that nursing staff turnover in intensive and intermediate care units during a 12-month period of time is 40% (Figure 11.4). The percentage was calculated by dividing the total number of people leaving the unit by the number of positions in the unit during the specified time period.

The second step of the turnover audit is to determine what percentage of this turnover is dysfunctional. In the example given

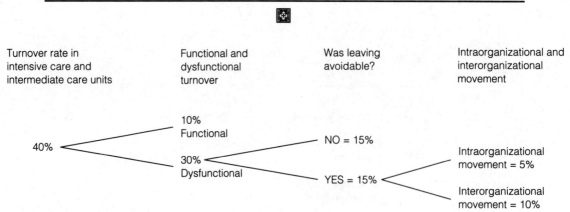

FIGURE 11.4. Turnover audit.

above, the organization determined that three-quarters of turnover was dysfunctional.

In the third step of the audit, the proportion of dysfunctional turnovers that occurred for controllable reasons is determined. In the example above, the organization determined that about 50% of the dysfunctional turnover was controllable. Therefore, only 15% of the total turnover was both detrimental to the organization and within the organization's control.

In the fourth step of the turnover audit, intraorganizational and interorganizational movement are examined. In the example, two-thirds of the employees left for other organizations, and one-third stayed within the organization. Therefore, only 10% left the organization for reasons that were dysfunctional and avoidable.

Each step of the turnover audit provides potentially valuable information. The first step can be used to determine the total percentage of individuals to be recruited and hired for the units being audited. The second step identifies that one-quarter of those leaving are not performing effectively so their leaving is actually healthy for the organization. These turnovers may be the result of faulty recruitment, placement, and/or training. The respective human resources func-

tions can use this information to evaluate and modify their practices. The third step in the analysis identifies the number of competent people leaving the organization for reasons the organization can control. These turnovers are detrimental to the units under study and should be managed more effectively. The fourth step identifies the true number of quality employees who are leaving for other organizations for reasons that are within the organization's control. These are the turnovers that are most detrimental to the organization and are those that should be scrutinized most closely to determine organizational practices that need to be changed.

Factors that Affect Turnover Decisions

Four sets of factors influence turnover decisions; these are psychological, individual, organizational, and environmental. Examining these factors leads to a better understanding of how to use the information obtained in the turnover audit to intervene in the turnover process more effectively (see Figure 11.1) and to enhance recruitment and other human resources management policies.

Psychological Factors

Satisfaction and commitment, the two primary psychological factors that affect employee turnover decisions, have already been discussed. Both general satisfaction and satisfaction with the work itself have been found to be better predictors of turnover than satisfaction with pay and satisfaction with supervision (Mobley, 1982). However, research has demonstrated that commitment to the organization may have a greater influence on turnover than employee satisfaction (Abelson, 1983; Porter, Steers, Mowday, & Boulian, 1974). When individuals see their goals and values appropriately matched with those of the organization, they are much more likely to remain loyal to that organization.

Individual Factors

Biographical factors such as age, formal education, tenure, and family responsibility are also related to employee turnover decisions (Mobley, 1982). Younger employees with greater formal education and less organizational tenure have more opportunities outside of the organization and thus are more likely to leave. Also, people in urban locations may be more likely to leave for other jobs than those in rural locations, and dual-career families or those with strong attachments to the local community are more likely to search for alternatives intraorganizationally.

Other individual factors, such as the level of ability, current skill level, performance level, and personal aspirations, affect intraorganizational and interorganizational movement strategies (Abelson, Ferris, & Urban, 1988). Organizations generally wish to retain competent individuals with high aspirations.

Providing these people with organizationally specific skills training will increase the likelihood that they will stay in their current position or transfer internally.

Organizational Factors

Characteristics of the organization that affect turnover decisions include size and type of facility (Abelson, 1987). Organizations with more employees and/or beds may have a more impersonal culture, resulting in higher turnover. Organizations that are growing may have low turnover, because they can provide their employees with greater career opportunities. Geriatric and other long-term care facilities tend to have the highest turnover levels. Although, they may have a core of staff that is highly motivated to remain, it is not unusual for them to have a greater than 75% turnover rate among certain staffing specialties (e.g., nursing). Hospitals and clinics, however, typically have a 25% to 35% turnover level.

Professional school affiliation also can affect organizational turnover decisions. Students from these affiliate programs frequently obtain their clinical experience in the affiliated hospital. This enables the student to obtain a lot of information about the hospital and the hospital to obtain a lot of information about the student, facilitating the job choice and selection process.

Environmental Factors

The environment also has tremendous impact on employee turnover decisions. Physical characteristics of the metropolitan area (e.g., site, geographic location) can influence an employee's decision to stay with or leave an organization (Abelson, 1986), as may general economic conditions. Typically, as employment rates increase, so do turnover rates. When fewer opportunities exist in other organizations, most people are less motivated to begin looking elsewhere for employment.

A number of other environmental factors specifically affect turnover decisions in health care organizations, such as the number of facilities in the marketplace competing for the same personnel. Also, the cost-effective movement toward outpatient care in the 1980s and 1990s allows numerous types of organizations to offer similar services. Furthermore, the advent of AIDS, as well as a shift in philosophy toward preventive care, suggest that an even larger number of organizations will be offering similar health care services in the future. The greater the competitiveness, the greater the likelihood of additional employment opportunities in the environment and the greater the likelihood of employee turnover.

Human Resources Factors

Human resources factors can affect the turnover rate as well. An organization that staffs its departments effectively and develops and rewards its employees will have low turnover. The second half of this chapter explains the recruitment process and how it is related to retention. The following chapters discuss how the organization can select, train, develop, evaluate, and reward its employees effectively.

THE RECRUITMENT PROCESS

The recruitment process, as the first step in employee staffing, can have a tremendous impact on retention. As mentioned previously, the recruitment process consists of three basic steps—planning, implementation, and evaluation.

To develop an effective recruiting program, six familiar questions must be answered: why, what, who, where, when, and how? The organization's plan explains *why* types of positions must be filled and *what* types of people are needed to fill those positions, *who* will do the recruiting for each job category, from *where* candidates will be recruited, and *when* the recruiting process must begin to ensure that the positions are filled by a specified time. After these decisions have been made, the plan can be *implemented* and a pool of candidates selected. To do this one needs to ask *how* the organization will attract qualified candidates and disqualify those who are clearly unsuitable. Then the program is *evaluated,* and the planning process begins again. The steps in the recruitment process are listed in Figure 11.5.

RECRUITMENT PLANNING

Why? Demands for New Strategies in Human Resources

Cultures are systematic patterns of thoughts shared by organizational and subunit members that influence perceptions and behavior. Cultures may be particularly strong in professionally dominated organizations because practitioners may have deeply ingrained work attitudes and patterns of behavior as a result of professional training and socialization (see Chapter 7). Recruiting individuals who use different treatment protocols or have different work norms may be one of the only ways to change these organizations (Mintzberg, 1979).

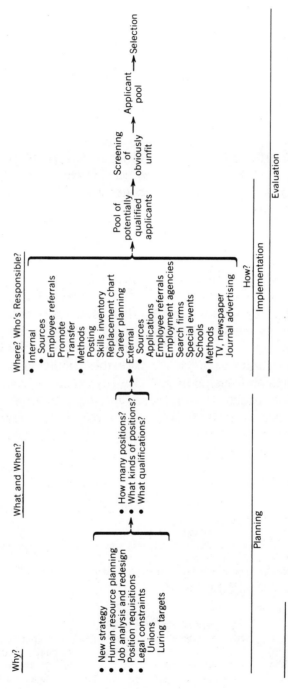

FIGURE 11.5. Steps in the recruitment process. (Adapted by permission from p. 149 of *Personnel and Human Resource Management*, Second Edition, by Randall S. Schuler; Copyright © 1984 by West Publishing Company. All rights reserved.)

Because of dramatic changes in the type of work in health care organizations, human resources planning and its recruitment component must be closely tied to the overall planning process. Planning can be divided into the following three timeframes (Ackoff, 1970):

- Strategic planning (3- to 10-year horizon)
- Tactical planning (1- to 3-year horizon)
- Operational planning (1-year horizon)

Plans focusing on each of these timeframes should be updated periodically. Information generated by this ongoing planning process could change the focus or the scope of the recruitment effort. Table 11.1 outlines the linkages between organization-wide planning and recruitment.

Changes in an organization's strategic plans, such as diversification and vertical integration of services (Goldsmith, 1981), could require dramatic changes in human resources, which in turn would call for new recruitment plans. For example, if a hospital starts an HMO, some physicians may need to be recruited. Their availability will need to be determined before the feasibility of this strategy can be assessed. During a longer time period, the case mix of an institution may change as a result of demographic changes in the service area from migration or from aging of the population. This could create incremental annual changes in staffing patterns, which over time would lead to significantly different manpower requirements and recruitment needs.

At the tactical level, as hospitals "downsize" and shift more services into satellite offices, internal recruiting strategies may need to change. There may be a number of employees who would rather transfer to a satellite clinic than be laid off. Testing and training may be necessary, however, to prepare these individuals for new jobs. Such changes would affect annual recruiting quotas and the size of the recruiting budget.

The reasons an organization recruits different kinds of employees, including phy-

TABLE 11.1.   Linkages between Organization-Wide and Recruitment Planning

Strategic Planning	Tactical Planning	Operational Planning
Organization-wide tasks	*Organization-wide tasks*	*Organization-wide tasks*
Define mission	Identify new programs and ventures	Develop budgets
Compare strengths and weaknesses with environment's opportunities and threats	Specify objectives	Quantify performance goals
Articulate strategy	Specify manpower needs including amount and type	
Set long-range goals		
Recruiting tasks	*Related recruiting tasks*	*Related recruiting tasks*
Assess feasibility of attracting different categories of needed staff	Project recruiting needs based on new positions, attrition, layoffs, and productivity changes	Set recruiting goals by job category based on projected surplus or deficits, staffing authorizations, succession planning, and promotions and transfers
Analyze labor force composition, labor force supply, demographic changes, and internal labor force	Develop recruiting strategies for each staff category	

Source: From David J. Cherrington, THE MANAGEMENT OF HUMAN RESOURCES, Third Edition. Copyright © 1991 by Allyn and Bacon. Reprinted by permission.

sicians, will continue to change. As these evolutionary changes occur, an effective recruiting strategy will help to prevent the following:

- A shortage of labor
- Excessive use of overtime or excessive use of contract labor (e.g., pool nurses)
- Excesses of full-time equivalent (FTE) employees compared to some standard such as occupied beds or patient visits
- High training costs of new hires
- A mismatch between applicants' skills and actual job demands
- Physician or patient dissatisfaction with staff's performance
- A poor image in the eyes of potential employees, suggesting that the organization has not been favorably represented in recruiting activities

A shortage of labor, excessive use of overtime, or a mismatch could lead to increased stress and/or dissatisfaction of employees. As discussed previously, these factors, in turn, could lead to increased turnover, which would increase recruitment and training costs, perpetuating a vicious cycle.

What and When? Number and Type of Positions and Timing of the Search

Before any recruiting takes place, management must determine how many positions must be filled and what kinds of positions they include. For physicians, this is a strategic decision under the purview of the board, medical staff, and top administrator that affects the service mix and, in the long run, the viability of the organization. Decisions

about nurses, department managers, and hourly workers have been the responsibility of the personnel function in the organization. In small organizations, these decisions are usually made on an ad hoc basis when line management informs personnel through employee requisition forms that a position has been vacated or a new one created. However, large organizations, particularly those that need highly skilled employees, must forecast their needs far in advance to ensure adequate staffing. Their need for employees in the future is determined by the strategic plans and the goals of the organization and by the turnover audit. Equal Employment Opportunity Commission (EEOC) regulations and Affirmative Action goals also must be considered. Organizations may be required to recruit specific minorities to redress past inequities. These needs must be compared to projected availability of human resources, and demands must be reconciled with supply. The results of this process will indicate to personnel staff the number and kinds of positions that need to be filled within a specific timeframe.

The personnel staff must then determine how long it will take to fill positions successfully. Factors to be considered include the state of the economy, the technical and educational requirements of the positions to be filled, and lead time for posting and advertising positions, and receiving and screening responses. Unskilled labor may be recruited in a week, but it may take 18 months to recruit a physician specialist. For positions for which there are dire shortages (e.g., nurses), special recruiting efforts such as trips to professional conventions and job fairs will have to be planned far in advance.

The economy affects recruitment in several ways. First, a better economy suggests there will be greater turnover of current employees. Second, the amount of unemployment will determine the size of the available labor pool. This will affect various employee categories differently, but the amount of unemployment should be considered when timing and determining the scope of a recruitment effort. Regional migration patterns that are economically motivated can also change the labor pool, and thus change recruitment plans. The technical and educational requirements of positions can tax the local labor pool. In these instances, a wider search is needed, lengthening the amount of time required.

Decisions also have to be made about how many individuals to recruit for each job opening, because not all candidates will be acceptable, and some acceptable candidates will decline job offers. Historical data can be used to calculate yield ratios, comparing the number of candidates at each stage of the selection process to the number of candidates who make it to the next stage. Figure 11.6 shows an example of what yield ratios might look like when recruiting a nurse anesthetist.

In the past, physician recruitment either has not been done at all or has been done

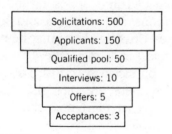

Solicitations: 500
Applicants: 150
Qualified pool: 50
Interviews: 10
Offers: 5
Acceptances: 3

FIGURE 11.6. Yield ratios for various recruiting steps (Adapted from Calhoun, 1966; Cherrington, 1987).

by the medical staff; now, because of the strategic importance of recruiting the right kinds of subspecialists, hospital administration has become involved. An institution cannot implement a plan to diversify into certain services unless it has medical staff members willing to admit patients of those kinds. Also, as the number of staff model HMOs grows, the number of salaried physicians is increasing. Recruiting and selecting these physicians will become an increasingly important responsibility of management (Berger & Schoen, 1981).

Deciding what types of physician are needed on the hospital's medical staff and, hence, what types need to be recruited, is one area in which recruitment planning is tied inextricably to strategic and operational planning. This is always an executive function, but it is a support service that could be centralized in larger multiunit corporations. Analyzing medical staff for replacement purposes entails the following steps:

• Categorize staff by specialty and prioritize based on importance to current plans.
• Note which physicians contribute more to the facility's profits. For cost-plus patients, indicators include number of admissions, total patient days, and number of ancillary procedures. As prospective payment becomes the norm, however, more sophisticated measures will need to be developed. Someone who admits many patients for long stays that are not totally reimbursed could jeopardize the hospital's financial position.
• Note whether these physicians are located in parts of the service area where the facility captures a strong

market share. Also note whether they are in areas where the hospital hopes to improve its position.

- The physicians' ages also should be listed. In this way, one can predict when they will be reducing the size of their practices or retiring. Knowing when medical staff members in key subspecialities are retiring will indicate which type of staff to recruit and when.
- Conduct a turnover audit for physicians and use this information to gain insight into recruitment needs.

Table 11.2 shows how this information can be displayed for easier analysis. Such an array quickly reveals any gaps in the current complement of physicians on the staff (Kropf & Greenberg, 1984) that may be due to the unavailability of certain key support staff (and facilities). This would indicate further recruitment needs. Also, future gaps can be identified as key physicians retire or reduce their practice. Any plans should also compare medical staff needs to the projected array of specialists at competing institutions. A similar analysis can be done of the age structure of senior management personnel, who are often costly to replace (Ray, 1977).

As shown in Table 11.2, efforts should soon be under way to replace some of the chief admitters at this hypothetical facility. National standards indicate shortages of chief admitters (Goldsmith, 1981; Jacobsen & Rimm, 1986, Steinwachs et al., 1986), and several key admitters will be retiring soon. Recruiting a physician and allowing adequate time for him or her to build up a practice

TABLE 11.2. Physician Analysis for Recruitment

Specialties	Percentage of Profits	Ages	Years to Retirement	Additional Physicians Needed Based on Rational Norms (GEMENAC)	Office Location Important?
I. Subspecialty (prioritized by strategic importance)				13	
Chief admitters					
1. (Prioritized	5	59	6		×
2. by	3	35	30		
3. productivity	3	42	23		
4. or	5	58	7		×
5. contribution					
· to					×
·					
·					
n. profits)					
II. Subspecialty				4	
Chief admitters					
1.	4	56	9		
2.	1	51	14		×
·					
·					
·					
n.					

Source: Adapted from Kropf, R., & Greenberg, J. A. (1983). *Strategic analysis for hospitals.* Germantown, MD: Aspen.

takes several years, so efforts should be started immediately. Possibly each of the senior key admitters could be encouraged to take on a partner who will eventually take over the practice.

After a position has been targeted, it can take 18 months and cost as much as $15,000 to recruit a physician (Cejka & Taylor, 1986; Garofolo, 1984). The board or medical staff may be reluctant to accelerate this process by incurring the cost of identifying the need and using a search firm. They should consider, however, revenue that could be generated if the needed physician was admitting patients 6 months sooner (Garofolo, 1984).

Who Is Responsible for Recruiting?

In most large organizations, recruiting is a function of the personnel department. Depending on the size of the department, recruiting may be the responsibility of the director, a staffing unit, or a recruiting unit. The personnel staff recommends policy and strategy to top-level management; seeks applicants from various sources, including the organization itself; screens applicants; and forms an applicant pool (Cherrington, 1987). When recruiting managers, physicians or some technical staff, or line managers (e.g., department heads, clinical chiefs) will take a more active role in the recruitment process. The complexity of federal regulations often requires that a personnel department member, such as an Affirmative Action officer, be in a position of functional authority (Koontz & O'Donnell, 1984) over line staff, perhaps with authority to veto certain applicants or to reopen the process if correct procedures were not followed. This protects the organization from litigation from applicants who felt they were not treated fairly. A recruit-

ment plan, then, should state who should be involved and how each person will participate in the relevant phases of the process.

As caregiving facilities coalesce or merge into multiunit alliances and systems, many of the technical aspects of recruitment and other personnel functions are being centralized. Indeed, recruiting on a wider geographic scope is espoused as one of the benefits of system affiliation (Zuckerman, 1979). The recruitment functions that lend themselves to centralization include the following:

- Evaluating a facility's needs
- Developing a computerized skills bank that can be adapted for use by facilities
- Advertising and screening for needed technicians, nurses, managers, or physicians
- Tracking of laws and regulations, such as Affirmative Action guidelines
- Training facility staff to comply with regulations (e.g., when screening applicants)
- Evaluating the cost-effectiveness of facilities' recruitment systems

Where? Recruiting Sources and Methods

Internal Recruiting

One of the best *sources* of job applicants consists of the organization's present employees. They are familiar with the culture and operations of the organization, and therefore, may be promoted or transferred into open positions with confidence that they will learn quickly. Also, promotions are one of the best motivators organizations have at their disposal. Career opportunity at all hierarchical levels can account for the way people involve themselves in their work. Studies have shown that dramatic increases in opportunity can lead to increased career aspirations, higher work commitment, a sense of organizational responsibility, and decreased intention to quit (Kanter, 1977; Landau & Hammer, 1986; Vardi & Hammer, 1977). Sometimes union contracts require management to consider internal candidates before looking outside of the organization. The contract also may specify criteria to be used in developing an internal applicant pool (e.g., those with the greatest seniority must be considered first).

There are several *methods* an organization can use to facilitate internal recruiting. First,

job vacancies can be posted in public access areas and in company newsletters or bulletins. This gives the employees the opportunity to apply for positions that fit their needs. Second, the organization can maintain a computerized skills inventory. This inventory may contain information on technical skills, supervisory experience, degrees obtained, language skills, and even career aspirations. When a position becomes vacant or a new position is created, the organization will be able to locate any potential candidates quickly.

A third method of identifying candidates for management slots is succession planning and the use of a replacement chart (Figure 11.7), which is a convenient way to show who

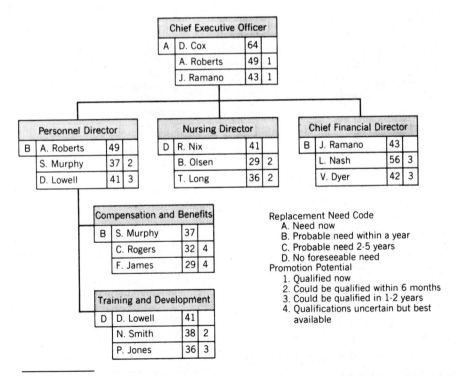

FIGURE 11.7. Replacement chart. (From David J. Cherrington, THE MANAGEMENT OF HUMAN RESOURCES, Third Edition. Copyright © 1991 by Allyn and Bacon. Reprinted by permission.)

is qualified to fill the different managerial positions in the facility. This approach is applicable internally only in large facilities, but it is a useful way to keep track of managers working in various units in the system. By identifying transfers that best match the needs of the positions with the career aspirations of the employees, there should be a reduction in turnover as a result of increasing employees' satisfaction. At Holy Cross Health System Corporation in South Bend, Indiana, "a senior-management committee gathers information, conducts inventories of management, uses a data base to outline current management's strengths and weaknesses, and identifies future top-management qualities" (Powills, 1989).

External Recruiting

Although there are several advantages to recruiting internally, there are also some disadvantages. When organizations need to shift direction quickly, bringing new people with new ideas and new ways of doing things may be easier than trying to change all of the current employees. Also, the manpower an organization needs for the future may not always be available internally. This is particularly true in health care organizations, where rapid expansion and technological developments constantly create a demand for new skills. Then, the organization must depend on the external labor market to fulfill its manpower requirements.

External recruitment becomes necessary as rapid diversification creates the need for new knowledge and skills not found in a traditional health care setting. For example, insurance salespersons are needed to market prepaid health service packages to employees. There has been some movement to recruit managers from outside industries just to infuse more "business sense" into hospitals or systems. It is not clear that this will be cost-effective because of the unique characteristics of service industries, in general (Sasser et al., 1978), and hospitals, in particular (Shortell & Kaluzny, 1983). The advantages and disadvantages of internal and external recruitment are summarized in Table 11.3.

The scope of the external search will depend on the types of positions to be filled. The organization can generally rely on the local labor market to fill lower-level un-

TABLE 11.3. Advantages and Disadvantages of Internal and External Recruiting

Promotion from Within	
Advantages	*Disadvantages*
Greater motivation for good performance	Creates a narrowing of thinking and stale ideas
Greater promotion opportunities for present employees	Creates political infighting and pressures to compete
Better opportunity to assess abilities	Requires a strong management development program
Improves morale and organizational loyalty	
Able to perform the job with little lost time	

External Hiring	
Advantages	*Disadvantages*
New ideas and new insight	Loss of time due to adjustment
Able to make changes without needing to please constituent groups	Destroys incentive of present employees to strive for promotions
Does not change the present organizational hierarchy as much	No information is available about the individual's ability to fit with the rest of the organization

Source: David J. Cherrington, THE MANAGEMENT OF HUMAN RESOURCES, Third Edition. Copyright © 1991 by Allyn and Bacon. Reprinted by permission.

skilled and semiskilled positions. Nurses or highly trained technicians may need to be recruited from a regionwide labor market. This may require strong affiliations with allied health schools in the area. Managers may need to be recruited nationally from health care and related industries. Physicians may need to be recruited nationally for certain subspecialities. Residency programs traditionally have been used to attract new physicians to an area in the hope that they will remain after completing their residencies.

Whether the scope of the search is narrow or wide, an organization can utilize many different *sources* to attract and identify applicants. These include direct applications; employee, medical staff, and other referrals; private and public employment agencies; executive search firms; special events; and high schools, colleges, and universities. Television, radio journal, and newspaper advertisements are the chief *methods* used to attract recruits.

Direct Applications

If the organization has a good reputation and convenient location, direct applications (e.g., walk-ins, unsolicited write-in applications) may provide a large enough pool to fill all semiskilled and some technical positions at very little cost.

Employee, Medical Staff, and Other Referrals

Many organizations rely on current employees to refer qualified applicants. Some organizations give cash bonuses to employees who encourage friends or relatives to apply for positions, if the applicant is hired. Additional cash bonuses may be paid if the referrals remain employed by the organization for a specified time period.

The medical staff is probably not an adequate recruitment source for physicians because of its geographic limits and the hospital's changing needs. However, the hospital exists in a complex network of relationships with suppliers, salespeople, licensing agents, and so forth. These contacts are used to generate potential applicants. For example, sales representatives of suppliers to physicians' offices often can identify experienced, but unhappy, physicians.

Private and Public Employment Agencies

Private employment agencies charge fees to perform many of the prescreening functions an organization would usually perform, such as finding qualified applicants, doing preliminary interviewing, and obtaining application blank information. Many of them specialize in, for example, nursing or technical personnel. The quality of private employment agencies varies tremendously, so the organization may have to do some searching before finding one that meets its needs adequately.

Public employment agencies are operated by the states under the auspices of the U.S. Training and Employment Service. All men and women who collect unemployment insurance are required to use this service, which is free to both seekers and organizations. Public employment agencies now utilize computer systems to match applicants with jobs. Few, however, take advantage of this service because employers complain that the referrals often are poorly qualified and not always interested in accepting employment (Heneman, Schwab, Fossuem, & Dyer, 1986).

Executive Search Firms

These highly private employment agencies usually seek candidates currently earning $40,000 or more. They are more expensive and more aggressive than other private agencies, generally charging half an executive's annual salary as a fee. Whereas most private employment agencies rely on candidates who are actively looking for positions, executive search firms, often called "headhunters," will approach highly qualified professionals who are currently employed and had not been looking. Industry norms forbid hospitals to recruit employees directly from one another. Thus, headhunters may serve a useful purpose by broadening the pool of applicants for organizations that need upper-level executives. A list of characteristics of reputable search forms is provided in Table 11.4.

As more health care organizations use executive search firms, organizations must be doubly careful to provide their managers with enough intrinsic and extrinsic incentives to ensure that they will not be lured away by competitors. This also increases the importance of ensuring that subunits do not develop turnover cultures in which quitting is the coping mechanism for any problem on the job.

Special Events

Job fairs and meetings of professional societies provide a convenient setting for an organization's recruiter to meet with potential employees or search firms. Job fairs are often regional events in which employers in certain industries can meet with interested applicants and promote their organizations' job openings.

High Schools, Colleges, and Universities

Educational institutions are good sources of applicants for positions that require very little experience. High schools and vocational schools are good applicant sources for low-skilled and trade positions. In some communities, businesses develop and partially fund training programs in conjunction with educational institutions. This arrangement provides the businesses with a readily available pool of qualified applicants.

Colleges and universities are good applicant sources for nursing and managerial positions, as well as physicians. Many universities now have specialized programs in health care administration. The Association of University Programs in Health Administration (AUPHA) publishes a directory of all member graduate and undergraduate health administration programs in the United States and Canada. A number of these require students to participate in either summer internships or longer residencies before graduating. Also, there is a growing number of competitive fellowships being offered. These usually require a 2-year commitment and often are based in the corporate offices of multiunit systems.

Advertisement

Other than working with the sources mentioned previously, the major method of recruiting is through advertising. Organizations can advertise position openings in newspapers and journals, on television and radio, and even on billboards. Organizations often consult with advertising agencies to determine the most effective media and content of a recruitment campaign.

TABLE 11.4. Characteristics of Reputable Search Firms

Service	Reputable Agencies	Questionable Agencies
Recruiting	Engage in selective recruiting occasionally, and then only to fill the urgent needs of client companies at their specific requests. Most applicants obtained through newspaper advertising.	Do all of their recruiting through a large, heavily indoctrinated staff of "counselors." Prospects are called at home between 6 P.M. and 8 P.M. and on Saturdays. This builds reservoir of applicants. No selective recruiting for specific jobs.
Applicant motivation	Encourage applicants to seek positions commensurate with their highest skills and to set salary requirements at high but realistic levels.	Promise salary advantage to raise recruitment volume. Later, urge applicants to reduce salary demands to ensure faster placements.
Resumès	Always provide personnel managers with résumés whether requested or not. Encourage applicants to prepare detailed résumés in a professional manner. Help them to revise their résumés when necessary.	Do not provide personnel managers with résumés if it can be avoided. Insist on blind interviews. Standard pretext: "We are selling you the man, not an employment record."
Screening applicants	Interview in depth to be certain that applicant is qualified in every particular for job he or she is seeking. Give approved tests when need is indicated. Question applicant to determine whether he or she is emotionally qualified for job and is likely to have a rapport with prospective employer.	Spend minimum of time to get basic information. No testing by "counselors." Start here to maintain control of applicant and condition him to accept first job offer.
Screening companies	Study employers' record for fair employment practice. Do not send applicants to companies known to have poor reputations for job security, salaries, or benefits.	None.
Placement follow-up	After a reasonable interval, contact both applicant and new employer to determine whether both are satisfied.	None.
Advertising	Advertise only the existing job, not an imaginary opening so dramatized as to attract applicants.	None, or very little.
Counselors	Employ only experienced, professional counselors with proven records for placing the right people in the right jobs.	No previous experience in personnel work is required. Persons with background in selling goods or services are preferred. Persuasive telephone voice is an asset.
Job orders	Never send an applicant out for an interview unless a specific job order requesting his or her qualifications has been received.	Rarely match applicants with job orders, except for general job category. Theory is that companies will be satisfied with applicants who approximate job descriptions. Frequently try to "pump in" applicants.
Personnel managers	Try to understand their problems. Don't demean them by attempts to reach department or division managers.	Regard company personnel managers as inefficient clerks. Try to bypass them whenever possible.
Fees	Either make firm agreements with client companies so that the latter pay fees or inform applicants that fees will be chargeable to them.	Tell applicants virtually all fees are company-paid, but have no firm, contractual agreements with companies. Applicants must sign contracts requiring them to pay the fees if they accept jobs and the companies refuse to pay.

Source: From Metzger, N. (1981). *Handbook of Health Care Human Resources Management.* Rockville, MD.

Advertisements should convey the qualifications and major responsibilities of the position, as well as the working conditions. If the organization is a government contractor, the advertisement must indicate that the organization is an Equal Opportunity Employer. An advertisement implying that a candidate of a particular race, sex, religion, age, and/or nationality is preferred over others is illegal, unless the organization can prove that these characteristics are bona fide occupational requirements. According to Section 703(e) of Title VII of the Civil Rights Act of 1964, an organization may discriminate on the basis of race, sex, religion, age, or national origin only if the attribute is a bona fide occupational qualification (BFOQ), reasonably necessary to the normal operation of that particular business or enterprise.

In developing an advertising campaign, an organization must also take into consideration the message it wants to convey to the public and the audience it wants to target. Lower-level, unskilled, and semiskilled workers can be reached best through want advertisements in local newspapers or radio advertisements. Professional and technical workers are more likely to respond to advertisements in trade publications. Placing advertisements in publications of these types is particularly worthwhile if the level of expertise required for the position is not available through the local labor market. Trade and professional journals are distributed nationally and sometimes internationally, so they reach a wider and more specialized audience. A good list of journals and mailing lists for advertising job openings to the nursing labor market is given by Filoromo and Ziff (1980).

Evaluating Recruitment Sources

Organizations must evaluate the effectiveness of various recruiting sources periodically. Questions that should be asked about each source include the following:

1. What is the ratio of costs to benefits in terms of number of applicants referred, interviewed, selected, and hired?
2. How effective are applicants hired from various sources in terms of job performance and absenteeism?
3. How long do hires who were obtained from a particular source remain employed by the organization?

Only a few studies have investigated the effectiveness of different recruitment sources. This research has found that employee referrals are the best source in terms of employee tenure, and newspaper advertisements and employment agencies are the worst (Decker & Cornelius, 1979; Gannon, 1971; Heneman, Schwab, Fossuem, & Dyer, 1986). A study of research scientists showed that employees recruited through college placement offices and newspapers did not perform as well as those who responded to a professional journal or convention advertisements or those who made contact based on their own initiative (Breaugh, 1981). Those who were recruited through newspaper advertisements were also absent twice as frequently as others (Breaugh, 1981). Clearly, however, the effectiveness of a recruitment source depends on the type of position that must be filled. Table 11.5 shows the best recruiting methods for different job categories.

TABLE 11.5. Relevant Recruiting Sources by Personnel Category

Source	Unskilled	Technical/Professional	Managers	Physicians
Employee referrals	×	×		
Promotion	×	×	×	
Transfers	×	×	×	
Job posting	×	×		
Direct applications	×	×		
Employment agencies	×	×	×	
Search firms			×	×
Special events		×		
Schools		×	×	×
Temporary help	×	×		
Interns and residents			×	×
Newspaper advertisements	×	×	×	
Journal advertisements		×	×	×

How? Implementing Recruiting Plans

Attracting Recruits

A well-developed plan is essential for attracting job applicants. This is particularly important when the unemployment rate is low or when the organization must fill highly specialized positions for which few candidates are available. Organizations can convey information about themselves through the sources described above, including television, trade journals, community events, and brochures; however, the recruiter is most important in conveying a positive image of the organization to the applicant during screening interviews.

A study by Dean and Wanous (1984) showed that turnover in organizations could be decreased by as much as a 28% if candidates were given more realistic job previews. A more recent review of several studies showed that realistic job previews could decrease turnover by at least 9% (McEvoy & Cascio, 1985). Job candidates should be told both the negative and positive aspects of a job and career path within an organization so that they might make informed choices. Otherwise, there will be a mismatch between the employee's and employer's expectations, the employee may become dissatisfied and quit. If a turnover audit reveals that employees are leaving soon after they are hired, unrealistic job previews may be causing the problems. Realistic job previews are most effective in reducing turnover and increasing satisfaction when candidates can be selective about accepting job offers, when realistic information is not readily available about the job from other sources, and when the candidates might have difficulty in coping with certain job demands (Breaugh, 1983). Even if turnover is not a problem, realistic job previews should be developed (Wanous, 1989). If the recruiter presents a balanced picture of the job and the organization, applicants are more likely to view the organization as caring and trustworthy (Meglino, DeNisi, Youngblood, & Williams, 1988). This should improve yield ratios.

The effectiveness of any recruiting message depends not only on its contents, but also on the credibility of its sources. Organizations should select their recruiters carefully and make sure they are trained for the position. Studies have shown that candidates prefer recruiters who are middle-aged, have an important position within the organization, have a comfortable rapport, take the time to talk and listen, and are knowledgeable about the candidate and job vacancy (Rynes & Miller, 1983). Unfortunately, many organizations give the job of recruiting to new employees, who have little credibility with applicants and may not know very much about the organization. They may be effective in screening applicants, but they cannot provide candidates with the information needed.

Recruitment and Retention of Nurses and Physicians

Extraordinary efforts may be needed to attract nurses and/or physicians to a facility and to retain them. The financial viability of many hospitals is already being threatened by a shortage of these employees (Powills, 1989). Suburban and rural hospitals have been particularly hard hit (O'Leary, 1992).

The centrality of nurses and physicians to hospitals justifies the sometimes extraordinary efforts made to attract them. The factors mentioned above—realistic job previews and credible interviews—are important when enticing nurses to accept positions, but they are only a beginning. Unfortunately, many organizations are turning to short-run, quick-fix solutions to solve their nursing shortage problems. Hospitals are offering higher salaries, free vacations, increased benefits such as flexible hours and child care facilities, and sign-on bonuses of up to $4,000 (Male & Clarke, 1991). Organizations have also tried emphasizing the quality of work life at the hospital and the interesting variety of patients and treatment modalities.

Margrif (1991) argues that hospitals must develop a long-range approach to the nursing shortage by recognizing that individual performance is a function of organizational support, individual attributes, and work effort. Organizations must provide intrinsic as well as extrinsic rewards. Margrif (1991) suggests that physicians and nurses should be encouraged to work together as a team to speed patient recovery. He also suggests implementing a hospital suggestion plan at the nursing floor level to ensure efficient delivery of hospital services. If a hospital develops a reputation as being a place where nurses' contributions are valued, recruiting will become a much easier job.

Developing a supply of new nursing resources is another long-term strategy for ending the nursing shortage. Nursing schools have been developed by some larger hospitals, and many others have professional school affiliations. Students from these programs frequently obtain their clinical experience in the affiliated hospitals. This allows the student to obtain valuable information about the organization and the organization to obtain valuable information about the individual, facilitating the recruitment and selection process and improving retention.

Senior management at Guthrie Healthcare System ended its nursing shortage by identifying and recruiting an untapped pool of students who had a true interest in nursing, but who did not have the funds available to pursue a nursing education (Meyer, Mannix, & Costello, 1991). In July 1988,

Guthrie Healthcare System began a new program—the Guthrie Nursing Care Opportunity Program—that made financial support available for baccalaureate nursing education offered through Mansfield University (Meyer et al., 1991). "Virtually all education-related expenses could be covered, including tuition, books, housing, transportation, and other expenses such as child care" (Meyer et al., 1991, p. 449). In addition, at the completion of the program, all students would be offered positions at a competitive salary in the Guthrie Healthcare System, and, in return for financial support, they would be obligated to remain within the Guthrie System for 1 year. "After 1 year, students had the option to continue employment as a method of repayment or to repay the funds directly. The loaned funds (principal and interest) would be forgiven at the rate of 25%, or up to $4,000, per year of full-time employment in the Guthrie Healthcare System" (Meyer et al., 1991, p. 449). The program was heavily marketed in newspapers and over radio and TV. Guthrie received more than 900 inquiries and succeeded in solving its nursing shortage.

Physicians generally have been recruited by word of mouth, but now health care organizations must use sophisticated marketing strategies to attract physicians in key groups such as family practice, pediatrics, obstetrics and gynecology, and internal medicine (O'Leary, 1992). Physician recruiters at MacNeal Hospital in Berwyn, Illinois, give the following recruitment tips:

- Gather leads through advertising in clinical journals, networking, and direct mail.
- Bring in identified candidates and show them around, including gowning up

surgeons and bringing them into the operating room.
- Include after-hours socializing in which family life-style issues can be discussed.
- Establish the new recruit in a practice by finding a site, getting it going, and providing financial support.
- Provide office signage, business cards, and extensive marketing support (O'Leary, 1992).

A well-planned hospital information system can support physician recruiting activities by helping to identify the type of physician the institution needs, describe the type of medical practice a physician can expect, support the institution's strategic plan for the future, and demonstrate the institution's ability to assist a physician with his or her office billing and other administrative functions (Poggio, 1992). The key information needed by physician recruits includes the following: inpatient volume, outpatient volume, ambulatory surgery procedures, inpatient surgery by type, deliveries (normal and c-section), patient profiles by age and sex, payment policy and profiles, account management information (e.g., volume in dollars and collection rates), number of new patients, and availability of computer systems for clerical work, billing and other support (Poggio, 1992). Various incentives for physician and nursing recruiting are shown in Table 11.6.

Many rural hospitals, for example Monroe Clinic, S.C. in Monroe, Wisconsin, have preceptor relationships with universities (O'Leary, 1992). Students from the University of Wisconsin use the Monroe Clinic as part of their training rotations. This is very important to the recruitment effort because it enables candidates to gather firsthand infor-

TABLE 11.6. Incentives for Physicians and Nurses

Practice Opportunity Factors	Incentives
Financial	
Income	Income guarantees during the transition
Insurance	Complete coverage or at group rates; professional help at designing and
Malpractice	managing a coverage plan
Health	
Disability	
Life	
Pension program	Complete coverage or at group rates; help at designing and managing
	a coverage plan
Productivity	Performance incentives, bonuses
Vacation	Costs paid
Continuing education	Leaves and allowances
Practice environment	
Hospital	A case mix that fits the physician's interests; special staff, equipment, and
	facilities; facility's future plans
Office	Assistance in locating, setting up, staffing, managing an office; low-cost
	rent or low-interest loans
Professional relationships	
Peers	Professional membership; well-orchestrated interviews; group practice
	membership; or help in recruiting partners
Referrals	Clear information on utilization patterns; introductions to primary care
	physicians or prepaid plans; a physician referral service
Coverage	Help in joining or forming a group
Medical school or teaching	A plus for some physicians
opportunities	
Community	
Housing	Help in locating and financing a home; moving costs
Quality of school systems	Clear information on both public and private schools through college
Job opportunities for spouse	Information and professional contacts and help in job search
Social and cultural opportunities	Club memberships; personal contacts; a well-planned visit
Recreational opportunities	Club membership; visit
Location; climate, geography	Visit
population	

mation about the institution. Monroe also involves retired physicians in the recruitment process as goodwill ambassadors (O'Leary, 1992).

Screening Recruits

In addition to attracting good candidates, the recruitment process serves to disqualify unsuitable candidates. Reviewing applica-tions or resumés and interviewing are the main ways to perform initial screening. It is important that this process be done consistently. Consistent screening is possible only if clear criteria are applied to each applicant by trained screeners. Choosing appropriate screening and selection criteria is discussed in Chapter 12. For screening purposes, it is only necessary that the criteria be legal and define the prerequisite knowledge and skills for the job.

The recruitment interview, besides providing an opportunity to impart information about the organization, is a time to screen out unsuitable job applicants. Whereas the organization wants to use the interview to attract good candidates and eliminate unsuitable candidates, from the candidates' perspective the purposes are to receive an invitation to be considered seriously for a position and to find out as much as possible about the job and the organization. In both cases, the first item usually takes top priority, so both the candidate and the organization spend their time trying to look good. As a result, neither the candidate nor the organization obtains the information necessary to make an informed decision. The organization may select an employee based on inaccurate information, and the employee may accept a position without really knowing what the job or organization is like. Careful use of screening criteria in a well-delineated interviewing procedure can maximize the amount of information gleaned from an interview.

During the screening process it is very important to keep accurate records of applicants and to respond promptly to all contacts. If good records are not kept, the selection process cannot proceed smoothly and qualified candidates may be lost because of slow organizational response. Recruiting entails significant contact with the community; therefore, all applicants should be treated politely. A person who is not suitable for the current position may be an ideal candidate for a future position.

Recruitment and the Law

Recruitment is the first step in the selection process. There can be no selection process if an organization does not have a pool of candidates. Because choice of recruitment policies and procedures influences the number and kinds of individuals who will make up the applicant pool, the entire recruitment process must meet EEOC guidelines. Title VII of the Civil Rights Act of 1964 and the Civil Rights Act of 1991 prohibit discrimination on the basis of sex, race, religion, or national origin. Organizations must evaluate whether their choice of recruiting source is disproportionately eliminating minority groups from the applicant pool. They must also make sure to screen candidates on the basis of bona fide occupational qualifications only.

According to the provisions of the EEOC uniform guidelines, the following questions may not be asked of candidates either in screening interviews or on application forms, unless the organization can prove that the qualification is a business necessity (Lowell & DeLoach, 1982):

1. *Names used previously* (Names could indicate a candidate's marital status, sex, or national origin.)
2. *Height and weight,* unless these are Bona Fide Occupational Qualifications (BFOQs).
3. *Age* (The Age Discrimination in Employment Act of 1967 and its amendments protect employees older than 40 years of age.)
4. *Religion*
5. *Race/color*
6. *Citizenship* (Asking whether candidates are citizens of the United States is legal, but asking whether they are naturalized or native-born citizens or asking for the date of citizenship is illegal.)
7. *National origin*

8. *Education requirements,* unless these are a BFOQ (Asking for dates of attendance and graduation may be construed as illegal because these dates may indicate an applicant's age.)

9. *Military status* (An organization may ask if the candidate is a veteran but may not ask questions regarding type of discharge or branch of military in which he or she served.)

10. *Arrest records* (Applicants cannot be disqualified because of arrest records because an arrest does not mean the individual was guilty, and minorities are arrested more frequently than nonminorities.)

11. *Name and/or address of a relative,* unless the applicant is a minor

12. *List of physical handicaps, defects, or past illnesses* (An organization may ask whether applicants have any physical handicaps or illnesses that, even with reasonable accommodation, would interfere with their job performance.)

13. *Marital status and/or names and ages of children* (These questions adversely affect women.)

14. *Sex* (This question cannot be included on an application blank unless it is a BFOQ.)

15. *Housing* (Questions cannot be asked regarding whether an applicant owns his or her own home, rents, or lives in a house or apartment.)

Several of these questions can be asked after an applicant has been hired; for example, number and ages of children is information needed for insurance purposes. Also, questions such as race and/or national origin can be asked if they are to be utilized for research purposes only (e.g., filling out EEOC reports), and this is clearly stated on the application blank.

Recruiting physicians creates a number of different legal problems relating to not-for-profit tax status (Mulhausen & Tracy, 1986) and Medicare fraud and abuse laws. Some of the incentives needed to attract physicians, such as subsidized office space or income guarantees, may constitute "private inurement." This is forbidden if a not-for-profit status is to be maintained with the IRS. If those or similar inducements can be construed as a quid pro quo for referrals of Medicare patients, the hospital is at risk of violating fraud and abuse laws (Bonds, 1992). Therefore, thought must be given to what incentives will be offered when recruiting physicians.

EVALUATING THE RECRUITMENT PROCESS

Evaluating the recruitment process is extremely important both to ensure the success of the institution's strategy and to allow the efficient functioning of other personnel functions such as selection or training. Strategically important indicators, although not solely measures of poor recruiting, would focus on physicians or professional support staff. These include the following:

- Loss of market share to competitors from lack of subspecialists in high demand areas
- Low quality of care, hence an unacceptable incidence of errors or even malpractice claims because of insufficient or unqualified staff
- Physician dissatisfaction with the quality of the nursing and support staff
- High turnover of recent hires

Other personnel activities can depend on the effectiveness of recruiting. For example, any selection activity will have limited utility if quality applicants cannot be located within a specified timeframe. For this reason, all aspects of the recruitment process, including sources (internal or external), methods, and administration, should be evaluated in terms of the costs and benefits to the organization. A variety of measures can be used at different steps in the recruiting process to evaluate the effectiveness of attracting qualified applicants. For each recruiting source and method, data can be collected on the number of applicants, costs per applicant, and time required to locate applicants (Milkovich & Glueck, 1985). After candidates have been screened and selected, data also can be collected on the costs and time elapsed per hire. Also, yield ratios can be calculated comparing visits offered to the total number of applicants, offers extended to either the number of visits accepted or the number of qualified applicants, and offers accepted compared to the number of offers extended (Milkovich & Glueck, 1985). Data should be kept on the number of minority and female applicants and hires compared to the total number of applicants and hires to ensure that the organization is meeting its Equal Employment Opportunity and Affirmative Action goals.

The determination that a recruiting system is attracting applicants in a timely manner is not sufficient to judge its effectiveness. The quality of applicants also should be assessed by tracking the progress of new hires in terms of job performance and turnover. These behavioral outcomes, however, may be indicators of poor work environment, an inefficient selection system, a poor training program, or other problems not related to the recruitment process. These other possibilities should be investigated before any changes are made in the recruitment process.

Evaluation of the costs of recruitment should include both direct and indirect costs. Direct costs include fees paid to agencies, telephone and travel expenses, entertainment, salaries of recruiting staff, and advertising fees. Indirect costs include the time involvement of operating managers, physicians, and board members (Milkovich & Glueck, 1985). Because these costs are usually underestimated (Cejka & Taylor, 1986) if initial plans are made, the search often seems to be not cost-effective.

Finally, the administrative components of the recruitment process should be evaluated. Are data on candidates stored so that information is easily accessible? Is the organization responding to applicants in a timely manner? If the response time is too long, good candidates may be lost to other organizations. Also, a lack of response to unqualified candidates may promote a poor public image.

SUMMARY

Recruiting is and will continue to be an important function of human resources in health care. As illustrated in Table 11.7, the relevance of recruitment varies by job category. The difficulty of answering the questions of what, where, why, and when also varies by job category. All levels of the organization are involved in an effective recruiting campaign.

The continuation of current trends in health care means that recruiting will remain a strategically important function. Diversification into alternative service delivery set-

TABLE 11.7. Summary of Key Issues by Personnel Category

| Recruiting Issues | Staff Categories | | | |
	Unskilled Workers	Technical/Professionals	Managers	Physicians
New needs?		Yes	Yes	Yes, primary care gatekeepers
Planning				
Why?		New strategy	New strategy	More control
Who's responsible?	Personnel	Department heads; personnel	Top management	Management and medical staff
What positions?	Same	New settings—alternative delivery system (ADS)	New setting—ADS	Salaried, gatekeepers
When?	Short lead time	Moderate lead time	Moderate lead time	Moderate to long lead time
Where available?	Local	Local, regional; lateral placement	Regional, national; other industries	National; residency programs
Implementation				
How?				
Attracting	Ads, walk-in, agencies, etc.	Ads, agencies, etc.	Search firms, national trade journals	Search firms; joint ventures; service incentives
Screening		Professional registry	Important	Important
The law[a]	EEOC/AA; unions	EEOC/AA, unions		Tax, Medicare, antitrust questions
Evaluation	Short-range; operational measures	Short to mid-range impact	Strategic impact and measures	Strategic impact and measures
Future needs		Changing	Increased importance	

[a] EEOC = Equal Employment Opportunity Commission; AA = Affirmative Action.

tings will continue to require staff with new sets of skills. Because of vertical integration into larger, multiunit, comprehensive health care organizations, skilled managers will continue to be in demand. Complicated clinical management decisions revolving around the issues of quality and quantity of care will continue to create a need for physician administrators.

These new staffing needs will mean that health care organizations will be competing for personnel with other industries as never before. This will require sophisticated recruiting to ensure an adequate supply of applicants. At the same time, cost-containment pressures may decrease the attractiveness of health care facilities as places to work. An effective recruiting system can increase the retention rate of employees, and provide a real competitive advantage to an organization.

Discussion Questions

1. Explain the five-stage turnover process.
2. Describe functional and dysfunctional turnover and give examples of each.
3. What are the four steps of a turnover audit? How can the information obtained from an audit be used to improve organization effectiveness?

4. What are the best recruitment sources for physicians? Why?
5. How would you evaluate the relative effectiveness of various recruitment sources for registered nurses?
6. What factors impact the turnover and retention of registered nurses? Why?
7. Discuss the advantages and disadvantages of internal and external recruitment.
8. According to the EEOC Uniform Guidelines certain questions may *not* be asked of job applicants, either in screening interviews or on application forms unless the organization can prove business necessity. List 10 of these questions and indicate *why* they may be illegal.

REFERENCES

Abelson, M.A. (1983). The impact of goal change on prominent perceptions and behaviors of employees. *Journal of Management, 9*(1), 65–79.

Abelson, M.A. (1986). Strategic management of turnover: A model for the health service administrator. *Health Care Management Review, 11*(2), 61–71.

Abelson, M.A. (1987). Examination of avoidable and unavoidable turnover. *Journal of Applied Psychology, 3,* 382–386.

Abelson, M.A., Ferris, G.R., & Urban, T.F. (1988). Human resource development & employee mobility. In R.S. Schuler, S.A. Youngblood, & V.I. Huber (Eds.), *Readings in personnel and human resource management* (pp. 320–329). St. Paul, MN: West Publishing.

Ackof, R.L. (1970). *A concept of corporate planning.* New York: Wiley.

Alfred, T.M. (1967). Checkers or choice in manpower management. *Harvard Business Review, 45*(1), 157–169.

Amante, L. (1989). Help wanted: Creative recruitment tactics. *Personnel, 66*(10), 32–36.

Anderson, K., & Wootton, B. (1991, March). Changes in hospital staffing patterns. *Monthly Labor Review,* 3–9.

Berger, J.E., & Schoen, S. (1981). Future of physician recruiting. *Group Practice Journal, 30*(4), 7–10.

Bonds, R.G. (1992). Hospitals should have strategies for safer physician incentives. *Modern Healthcare, 22*(13), 25.

Breaugh, J.A. (1981). Relationship between recruiting sources and employee performance, absenteeism, and work attitudes. *Academy of Management Journal, 24,* 142–147.

Breaugh, J.A. (1983). Realistic job previews: A critical appraisal and future research directions. *Academy of Management Review, 8,* 612–619.

Bureau of Health Professions. (1980). *The recruitment shortage of registered nurses: A new look at the issue.* Washington, DC: U.S. Department of Health and Human Services.

Calhoun, R.P. (1966). *Managing personnel.* New York: Harper & Row.

Cascio, W.F. (1991). *Applied psychology in personnel management* (4th ed.). Englewood Cliffs, NJ: Prentice Hall.

Cejka, S.A., & Taylor, M.W. (1986). When is the right time to add a physician? *Medical Group Management, 33*(5), 18.

Cherrington, D.J. (1987). *Personnel management: The management of human resources* (2nd ed.). Dubuque: W.C. Brown.

Cohen, P.D. (1979). Medical school and hospital affiliation relationships: An interorganizational perspective. *Health Care Management Review, 6*(1), 43–50.

Dalton, D.R. & Tudor, W.D. (1979). Turnover turned over: An expanded and positive perspective. *Academy of Management Review, 4,* 225–235.

Dean, R.A., & Wanous, J.P. (1984). Effects of realistic job previews on hiring bank tellers. *Journal of Applied Psychology, 69,* 61–68.

Decker, P.J., & Cornelius, G.T. (1979). A note

on recruiting sources and job survival rates. *Journal of Applied Psychology, 64,* 463–664.

Elnicki, R. (1977). Turnovers. In F.A. Sloan (Ed.), *The geographic distribution of nurses and public policy* (pp. 117–139). Washington, DC: Government Printing Office.

Filoromo, T., & Ziff, D. (1980). *Nurse recruitment: Strategies for success.* Rockville, MD: Aspen.

Flory, J. (1990). Hospitals increase efforts to attract physicians. *Hospitals, 64*(13), 54–55.

Gannon, M.J. (1971). Source of referral and employee turnover. *Journal of Applied Psychology, 56*(3), 226–228.

Garofolo, F. (1984). What medical staffs need to know about recruiting physicians. *Hospital Medical Staff, 12*(6), 18–24.

Goldsmith, J. (1981). *Can hospitals survive?* Homewood, IL: Dow Jones-Irwin.

Hauser, M.C. (1991). Attracting top candidates in troubled times. *Hospitals, 65*(12), 60.

Heneman, H.G., Schwab, D.P., Fossuem, J.A., & Dyer L.D. (1986). *Personnel and human resource management.* Homewood, IL: Dow Jones-Irwin.

Hoare, G.A. (1987). New managerial roles in multi-organizational systems: Implications for health administration. *Journal of Health Administration Education, 5*(3), 423–439.

Jacobsen, S.J., & Rimm, A.A. (1986). Primary care physicians: HMOs versus the GMENAC. *New England Journal of Medicine, 315*(5), 324.

Kahn, R.L., Wolfe, D.M., Guinn, R.P., Snock, J.D., & Rosenthal, R.A. (1964). *Organizational stress: Studies in role conflict and ambiguity.* New York: Wiley.

Kaluzny, A.D., & Shortell, S.M. (1983). Challenges for the future. In S.M. Shortell & A.D. Kaluzny (Eds.), *Health care management* (pp. 492–522). New York: Wiley.

Kanter, R.M. (1977). *Men and women of the corporation.* New York: Basic Books.

Kirnan, J.P., Farley, J.A., & Geisinger, K.F. (1989). The relationship between recruiting source, applicant quality, and hire performance: An analysis by sex, ethinicity, and age. *Personnel Psychology, 42,* 293–308.

Koontz, H., O'Donnell, C., & Weihrich, H. (1984). *Management* (8th ed.). New York: McGraw-Hill.

Krackhardt, D., & Porter, L.W. (1985). When friends leave: A structural analysis of the relationship between turnover and stayers' attitudes. *Administrative Science Quarterly, 30,* 242–261.

Kropf, R., & Greenberg, J. (1984). *Strategic analysis for hospitals.* Rockville, MD: Aspen.

Landau, J., & Hammer, T.H. (1986). Clerical employees' perceptions of intraorganizational career opportunities. *Academy of Management Journal, 29,* 385–404.

Larkin, H. (1990). Hospitals struggle to overcome intensive care shortage. *Hospitals, 64*(17), 67.

Lowell, R.S., & DeLoach, J.A. (1982). Equal employment opportunity: Are you overlooking the application form? *Personnel, 59*(4), 49–55.

Male, R., & Clarke, K. (1991). Recruitment, retention, and return: The NHS and the 3 R's. *Personnel Management, 12*(2), 46–49.

March, J.G., & Simon, H.A. (1958). *Organizations.* New York: Wiley.

Margrif, F.D. (1991). The human resource role in addressing the nursing shortage. *Health Care Supervisor, 9,* 53–58.

McEvoy, G.M., & Cascio, W.F. (1985). Strategies for reducing employee turnover: A meta-analysis. *Journal of Applied Psychology, 70,* 342–353.

Meglino, B.M., DeNisi, A.S., Youngblood, S.A., & Williams, K.J. (1988). Effects of realistic job previews: A comparison using an enhancement and reduction preview. *Journal of Applied Psychology, 73,* 259–266.

Metzger, N. (1981). *Handbook of health care human resources management.* Rockville, MD: Aspen.

Meyer, R.H., Mannix, M.N., & Costello, T.F.

(1991). Nursing recruitment: Do health care managers gear strategies to the appropriate audience? *Hospital and Health Services Administration, 36,* 447–453.

Milkovich, G.T., & Boudreau, J.W. (1988). *Personnel/human resource management: A diagnostic approach* (5th ed.). Plano, TX: Business Publications.

Milkovich, G.T., & Glueck, W.F. (1985). *Personnel/human resources management: A diagnostic approach* (4th ed.). Plano, TX: Business Publications.

Miller, A.E., & Miller, M.G. (1981). *Options for health and health care: The coming of postclinical medicine.* New York: Wiley.

Mintzberg, H. (1979). *The structuring of organizations.* Englewood Cliffs, NJ: Prentice Hall.

Mobley, W.H. (1977). Intermediate linkages in the relationship between job satisfaction and employee turnover. *Journal of Applied Psychology, 62,* 237–240.

Mobley, W.H. (1982). *Employee turnover: Causes, consequences, and control.* Boston: Addison-Wesley.

Moscovice, I. (1984). Health care professionals. In S.J. Williams & P.R. Torrens (Eds.), *Introduction to health services* (2nd ed, pp. 308–331). New York: Wiley.

Mowday, R.T., Porter, L.W., & Steers, R.M. (1982). *Employee-organizational linkages: The psychology of commitment, absenteeism, and turnover.* New York: Academic Press.

Mulhausen, M.R., & Tracy, K.L. (1986). What are the risks of physician recruitment programs? *Health Financial Management, 6*(8), 42–56.

O'Leary, J. (1992). "Physician recruitment: A three-step strategy. *Hospitals, 66*(4), 84.

Poggio, F.L. (1992). Physician recruitment: The role of the hospital information system. *Healthcare Financial Management, 12*(4), 56–62.

Porter, L.W., & Steers, R.M. (1973). Organizational work and personal factors in employee turnover and absenteeism. *Psychological Bulletin, 80*(2), 151–176.

Porter, L.W., Steers, R.M., Mowday, R.T., &

Boulian, P. (1974). Organizational commitment, job satisfaction, and turnover among psychiatric technicians. *Journal of Applied Psychology, 59,* 603–609.

Powills, S. (1989). Employee hotline: CEOs act to solve labor strategies. *Hospitals, 63*(8), 48–53.

Price, J. (1977). *The study of turnover.* Ames: Iowa State University Press.

Price, J.L. (1981). *Professional turnover: The case of nurses.* New York: SP Medical and Scientific Books.

Ray, K. (1977). Managerial manpower planning—A systematic approach. *Long Range Planning, 10*(2), 21–30.

Robbins, S.A., & Rakich, J.S. (1989). Hospital personnel management in the early 1990s: A follow-up analysis. *Hospital and Health Services Administration, 34,* 385–396.

Rosenblatt, R.A., & Moscovice, I.S. (1982). *Rural Health Care.* New York: Wiley.

Rynes, S.L., & Miller, H.G. (1983). Recruiter and job influences on candidates for employment. *Journal of Applied Psychology, 68,* 147–154.

Salipante, P., & Goodman, P. (1976). A social information processing approach to job attitudes and task design. *Administrative Science Quarterly, 23,* 224–250.

Sasser, W.E., Olsen, R.P., & Wyckoff, D.D. (1978). *Management of service operations.* Boston: Allyn & Bacon.

Schein, E. (1985). *Organizational culture and leadership.* San Francisco: Jossey Bass.

Schuler, R.S. (1984). *Personnel and human resources management* (2nd ed.). St. Paul, MN: West Publishing.

Sheridan, J.E., & Abelson, M.A. (1983). Cusp catastrophe model of employee turnover. *Academy of Management Journal, 26,* 418–436.

Shortell, S.M., & Kaluzny, A.D. (1983). Organization theory and health care management. In S.M. Shortell & A.D. Kaluzny (Eds.), *Health care management* (pp. 5–37). New York: Wiley.

Steinwachs, D.M., Weiner, J.P., Shapiro, S., Batalden, P., Coltin, K., & Wasserman, F. (1986). A comparison of the requirements for primary care physicians in HMOs with projections made by the GMENAC. *New England Journal of Medicine, 314,* 217–222.

Tichy, N.C., Fombrun, J., & Devanna, M.A. (1982). Strategic human resource management. *Sloan Management Review, 23*(1), 47–61.

Vardi, Y., & Hammer, T.H. (1977). Intraorganizational career mobility and career perceptions among rank and file employees in different technologies. *Academy of Management Journal, 20,* 622–634.

Wanous, J.P. (1989). Installing a realistic job preview: Ten tough choices. *Personnel Psychology, 42,* 117–134.

Zuckerman, H.S. (1979). Multihospital systems: Promise or performance. *Inquiry, 17*(3), 291–314.

CHAPTER

SELECTION AND PLACEMENT

Jacqueline Landau

Daniel S. Fogel

LEARNING OBJECTIVES

Upon completing this chapter, the reader should be able to . . .

*   Describe the steps in a selection process.
*   Explain how job descriptions are developed and used within organizations.
*   Describe the differences between conventional and quantitative job analyses.
*   Decide which job analysis methods are most appropriate for your organization.
*   Describe how to establish a reliable and valid selection process.
*   Evaluate the extent to which a selection system meets federal regulations.
*   Identify different types of selection instruments and assess the pros and cons of each.
*   Evaluate the utility of the selection process.
*   Suggest at least two methods for the placement of employees.

INTRODUCTION

Health care is a service industry with care levels ranging from clinic, outpatient, emergency, and ambulatory surgery, to inpatient, long-term, skilled nursing. Hospitals are in the process of diversifying. In the past few years, hundreds of nonprofit hospitals have been restructured into holding companies so that they could move into some of the other health care areas dominated previously by for-profit hospitals. Diversification is forcing hospitals to strengthen their marketing and long-range planning departments and to find staffs to handle such issues as cost accounting, labor productivity, and financial modeling (Coddington, Palmquist, & Trol-

linger, 1985). Also, the advent of Medicare's Prospective Payment System (PPS) requires hospitals to become increasingly competitive by building a market niche, creating product differentiation, and using resources more efficiently.

According to the American Hospital Association, most hospitals today have no financial reserves (Earle & Pfannkuche, 1991). At the same time, purchases of health care services have become more aggressive and demanding (Earle & Pfannkuche, 1991). These changes, as mentioned in Chapter 11, create needs for individuals with qualifications different from those required in the past. In addition to having the appropriate credentials and fitting with the organization's culture, employees must be aware of the economic ramifications of their use of resources and delivery of patient care. For example, previously most health care administrators received formal training in clinical, public health, or health care/public administration. Now, increasing numbers of administrators have Master's of Business Administration degrees and private sector business experience (Eubanks, 1992). These administrators provide health care organizations with the entrepreneurial spirit, managerial skills, and understanding of business issues needed for survival today.

As the need for employees with flexibility and diverse skills and abilities has increased, the number of hospital employees has decreased (Coddington et al., 1985). Health care organizations must learn to do more with less, which means that matching the right person to the right job has become increasingly important. Organizations can ill afford a nonproductive, dissatisfied employee. The skills, abilities, motivations, and career goals of individuals must match the job requirements. Therefore, the selection and placement of employees must be planned and implemented with care.

Health care organizations also may find themselves becoming more vulnerable to charges of negligent hiring and retention. Negligent hiring is a legal doctrine under which an employer may be charged with hiring or retaining an individual who causes harm to a third party (Fenton, Kinard, & David, 1991). In these cases, courts pay very close attention to the adequacy of the employer's pre-employment investigation into the employee's background. An organization that has a well-planned and executed selection and placement system is less susceptible to law suits.

OPENING DILEMMA: HIRING A NEW VICE PRESIDENT

Methodist Medical in Southern Heights is a holding company that owns a 500-bed hospital in the northeast. Methodist just acquired several ambulatory care facilities, participates in several HMOs, and is considering acquisition of two other hospitals and a physician's practice. The Board of Trustees has just given approval to the hospital's CEO, Sarah Brandy, to hire a Vice President of Strategic Planning, a new position for the organization. The Board's goals for hiring a person are to have the person be responsible for obtaining more information about the competitive environment in which the hospital operates, to learn more about Methodist's competitive advantages, and to develop and use a more systematic approach to planning.

Brandy was puzzled about how to go about designing this position and hiring a person to fill it. Should she hire someone from another industry, even if the person has no health care experience? Should she train someone from within the hospital? What requirements are important for this position?

Brandy asked her Human Resources Vice President, Dr. Landis, to design a process that would lead to hiring a person who could fill the strategic planning position. Brandy gave the HR manager two guidelines. First, she asked Landis to include as many key people as possible in the process of defining the position. Because this was a new position, Brandy believed that several of the key constituents throughout Methodist should be consulted. Second, Brandy wanted to hire a person who could be part of the top management team. Brandy's management style was to include her key staff in all major decisions. Thus, she believed the Vice President of Strategic Planning position should include a requirement that the person have the skills to work in teams.

Brandy asked Landis to try and complete the selection design within 1 month so they could begin recruiting a person to fill the position. Landis returned to his office and began to think about the design of the selection process and the steps needed to fulfill both Brandy's requirements and to ensure a reliable and valid selection process.

DESIGNING THE SELECTION PROGRAM

Selection is the process of collecting and evaluating information about an individual, deciding whether to extend an offer of employment, and placing the individual in the appropriate job. Such employment could be either a first position for a new employee or a different position for an existing employee. The selection process is constrained by legal and environmental factors that protect the future interests of the organization and the individual (Gatewood & Field, 1990).

Designing the selection program involves seven primary steps, which are outlined in Figure 12.1: conducting a thorough *job analysis;* defining employee effectiveness and deciding how it will be measured (i.e., *choosing criteria*); *choosing predictors* of employee effectiveness and deciding what the *selection instruments* should be; collecting scores on both the criteria and predictors; and examining the relationship between the two (i.e., *testing the validity* of the selection instru-

ments) (Heneman, Schwab, Fossum, & Dyer, 1986). After the relationship between criteria and predictors has been established, the organization must determine, based on cost-benefit analysis, minimal acceptable scores on selection instruments. Finally, the organization must establish how the selection process will be implemented and what records should be kept regarding each candidate. The objectives of these steps is to produce a reliable and valid selection process that is in compliance with federal regulations and will aid the organization in accomplishing its strategic human resources goals.

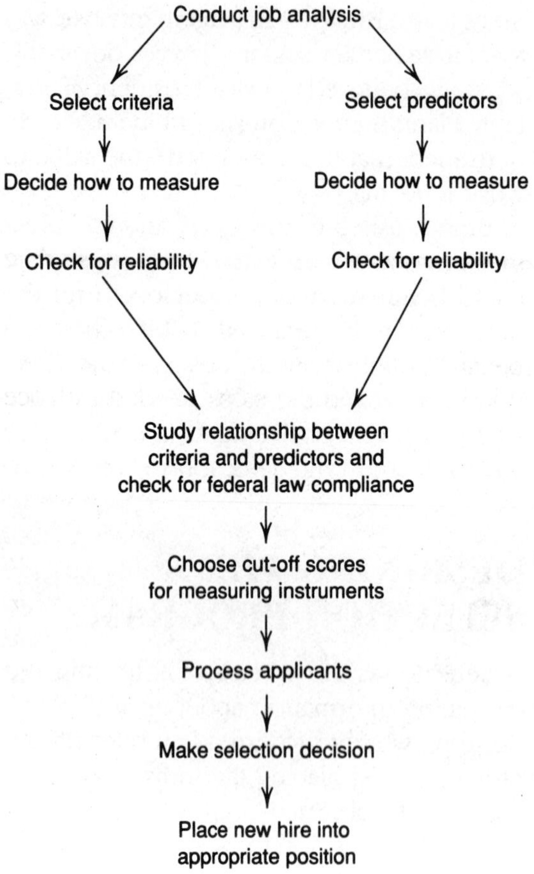

Job Analysis

Job analysis consists of two components: describing the tasks, responsibilities, activities, and working conditions of a job (i.e., preparing a job description); and identifying the qualifications needed for adequate job performance, including skills, abilities, and experience (i.e., preparing the job specifications). It is a purposeful, systematic process for collecting information about the important and work-related aspects of a job. Without this information, the organization will not know what types of people it needs to hire, what kinds of instruments must be developed to predict job performance, or how to evaluate the effectiveness of the selection process. The *Uniform Guidelines on Employee Selection Procedures,* which provides a framework for determining whether tests and other selections devices are in compliance with federal law prohibiting discrimination, specifically state that a thorough job analysis must be the basis for the design of a selection procedure (Equal Employment Opportunity Commission, 1978).

Job analysis also becomes very important as the needs of the organization change and

FIGURE 12.1. The selection process.

new positions are created. For example, many medium-sized hospitals are now hiring executives with nursing backgrounds and making them vice presidents of patient services (Souhrada, 1990). More hospitals now also have physician marketing departments (Flory, 1990). Although the majority of physician marketers have health care backgrounds, recruiters are looking to fill these positions with people who have MBAs (Flory, 1990). These jobs must be analyzed carefully to determine exactly what skills are needed for effective performance.

The first step in the job analysis process is deciding what kinds of data to collect. Relevant information may include tasks performed and percentage of time spent on each task, working conditions, supervisory responsibilities, reporting relationships, job hazards, physical requirements, machines and equipment used to perform the job, and materials or services produced. The type of data collected depends on the following: 1) how the data are going to be used, 2) the accessibility and accuracy of the data, and 3) the relevance of the data to the job.

This information may be gathered using several different methods, such as observation, interviews, diaries, recording instruments, and questionnaires. Factors to consider when choosing a method include geography, physical environment, technology, complexity and routinization of the job, background of the job holders, and social factors (Henderson, 1979). For example, if the environment is hazardous or the job complex, direct observation may be difficult. For hazardous jobs, unobtrusive observational techniques, such as recording devices, could provide information safely. For complex jobs, interviews or questionnaires might be the best choice for gathering data. Diaries could be useful if job incumbents are committed and motivated to record their daily activities.

Choice of method also depends on the job analysis procedure selected by the organization—*conventional* or *quantitative*. The conventional procedure begins with a job analyst interviewing supervisors and job incumbents and administering a questionnaire. The data then are summarized into a standard format on the basis of the subjective interpretation of the analyst. Supervisors and incumbents are given an opportunity to change and approve the description. The final description usually contains three sections. In the first section, the job is identified by title, location, and number of incumbents. In the second section, the job is defined in terms of its purpose, its relationship to other jobs and overall organizational objectives, and the end results. In the third section the job is described in terms of its major duties, degree of discretion, supervisory responsibility, and perhaps training and experience required (Milkovich & Boudreau, 1988). Figure 12.2 shows an example of a conventional job description for a registered nurse.

Another example of a conventional approach to job analysis is the functional procedure used by the U.S. Training and Employment Service. Information regarding this procedure is contained in the *Handbook for Analyzing Jobs* (U.S. Department of Labor, Manpower Administration, 1972) and descriptions of approximately 20,000 jobs are listed in *Dictionary of Occupational Titles* (U.S. Department of Labor, 1977).[1] The descriptions include five categories of information: worker functions; work fields; machines, tools, and equipment; materials,

---

[1] A supplement to the U.S. Department of Labor (1977) *Dictionary of Occupational Titles* was published in 1986.

Title: Registered nurse

STAFF NURSE:

Less than 24-hour care units: Labor/Delivery, Dialysis, Emergency Room, Operating Room, Recovery Room, Clinic

SUMMARY:

To function as a member of the total nursing team on their assigned unit. The staff nurse is expected to utilize the nursing process in planning care with the patient, significant others, and the health care team. Through assessment and planning, he or she should formulate, document, and evaluate continuously the nursing care plans, nurses' notes, and accurate patient care conferences.

RELATIONSHIPS:

Responsible to head nurse and/or charge nurse.

Workers supervised: Ancillary nursing personnel of unit interrelationships: Works closely with all members of the health care team, patients, and their families. The staff nurse is responsible and accountable for quality nursing care of assigned patients. The staff nurse is also responsible for duties assigned by the charge nurse.

ASSESSMENT:

1. Initial assessment of patient is complete according to unit time guide.
2. Basic head-to-toe assessment at beginning and conclusion of procedure or stay.

PLANNING:

1. Documentation will reflect standard of care specific to the given care.
2. Documentation of nursing care will reflect compliance with the medical plan of care.
3. Documentation of patient care planning will be reflected in the nursing documentation.
4. Patient teaching/D/C planning will be reflected in nursing documentation as appropriate to the needs of the patient.
5. Psychosocial needs of patients will be identified.

INTERVENTION:

1. Transcribes routine physician's orders (includes proper utilization of forms, requisitions) according to policy
2. Administers medications according to policy; assesses outcomes for effectiveness, toxicity, side effects; is aware of usual dosage
3. Initiates and monitors IV therapy including fluids, blood, blood products, and TPN according to policy
4. Performs IV assessments and care (assessment of rate, site; dressings and tubing changes)
5. Handles controlled substances according to policy
6. Monitors and records vital parameters (TPRs, BPs, weights, I & Os, head circumferences, abdominal girths)
7. Provides comfort, hygiene of patients (A.M. care, P.M. care, baths, mouth care, skin care, shampoos, positioning, T & D hose, etc.)
8. Collects specimens: ensures correct disposition, tests as appropriate (urine, blood, sputum, stools; tests specimens for S & A, hematest, reducing substances, pHs, etc.)
9. Uses equipment correctly and appropriately to patient's needs (Med. pumps, Gomso suction, beds, scales, Emerson suction, Pluravacs, oxygen equipment)
10. Complies with all infection control policy and procedures (isolation, hand washing, etc.)
11. Utilizes appropriate resources/supplies when assisting with or performing procedures (dressings, wound care, drains and drain care, urethral catheterizations; assisting with LPs, paracentesis, thoren-centesis, bone marrows, kidney biopsies, insertions of central lines cutdowns)
12. Recognizes and handles emergency situations in a prudent manner
13. Notifies charge nurse or physician of change in patient status or condition
14. Completes documentation of all patient care activities
15. Provides nutritional support (PO feedings, calorie counts, gastrostomy feedings, N.G. feedings)

FIGURE 12.2. Conventional job description.

16. Provides for safety of patient within environment (side rails, call lights; correct use: restraints, wheelchairs, stretchers, etc.)
17. Provides post-mortem care, including completion of death certificate according to policy

EVALUATION:

1. Reassesses patient as situation warrants and documents accordingly
2. Completes transfer stamp or discharge assessment, as appropriate
3. Contributes information to the discharge planning form as indicated

MISCELLANEOUS:

1. Correctly utilizes incident reports/first report of injury
2. Knows visiting policies and enforces as appropriate
3. Participates in change of shift report, transfer report, and so forth
4. Correctly uses telephone system, paging system, on-call schedules, and Executone system
5. Conforms with dress code
6. Is aware of and able to use correctly inter- and intradepartmental resources (consultations, social service, diabetic teaching program, biomedical engineering, etc.)
7. Maintains a professional and therapeutic relationship with patient, family, and health care team
8. Checks crash carts as assigned
9. Handles patient classification (demonstrates ability to classify patients by TMC H/C acuity system)
10. Utilizes manual, knows location, content
11. Certified to initiate IVs and/or venipunctures

products, subject matter, and services; and worker traits. Jobs are described according to their relationships to data, people, and things, and are identified by the function the worker performs. Within each of these three categories, workers may perform several functions ranging from simple to complex. (For a modified version of this approach, see Fine & Wiley, 1971.)

Some critics believe that conventional job analysis procedures are too subjective because they depend heavily on the opinion of the job analyst. *Quantitative methods* rely on computer analyses of tasks and worker traits. The quantitative method includes asking job incumbents to complete a structured questionnaire that includes items on all aspects of their job. Incumbents are usually asked to rate the listed tasks in terms of their importance and the time it takes to perform and learn them. Knowledge, skills, and abilities are measured in terms of importance and prior experience required (Milkovich & Boudreau, 1988). Because questionnaires take considerable time, expense, and effort to develop, they are usually purchased from consultants who have spent years validating and refining the instruments. Widely known examples of these questionnaires include the Position Analysis Questionnaire (PAQ) and Control Data Corporations's Position Description Questionnaire (PDQ).[2] After the questionnaires have been completed, the data are entered into a computer, analyzed statistically, and summarized. The costs of analyzing the data can be considerable and

[2] Information regarding the PAQ and the PDQ, respectively, is available from PAQ Services, Post Office Box 337, Logan, Utah 84321, and Control Data Corporation, 8200 34th Avenue South, Minneapolis, Minnesota.

should be considered before choosing a quantitative procedure. In general, when choosing a job analysis method, the following questions should be considered:

1. Is the instrument available "off-the shelf"?
2. Can the method be applied to a variety of jobs?
3. Can data from different sources be compared easily while using this method?
4. How much job analyst training is required?
5. How many respondents or sources of information are needed to obtain dependable job analysis data?
6. To what extent will the method be acceptable to the job incumbent?
7. Is the method valid and reliable?
8. How useful is the measure for developing selection measures for a particular job?
9. What is the estimated cost of the method?

Choosing Criteria

The second step in the selection process is choosing which criteria to use and how to measure the criteria. Questions to be considered include the following:

- Does the organization want to select people who will be successful in filling current job vacancies, or does it want to focus on future positions?
- Does the organization want to hire people who are likely to leave after a couple of years, or is it looking for stable, long-tenured employees?
- Does the organization want employees who already have specific skills and abilities, or does it want employees who are able to learn on the job?

The central criterion for almost every organization is job performance, but the aspects of job performance that are important will vary according to the organization and job. After the central criterion has been chosen, more specific criteria are selected. If the central criterion is job performance, job descriptions can be used for determining more specific criteria. If the central criterion is the ability to move up the hierarchical ladder rapidly, job descriptions of future positions, rather than current vacancies, must be referenced.

Next, methods for measuring the specific criteria must be chosen. A frequently used measure of job performance is the score on a performance appraisal instrument; however, for low-skilled and highly mechanized jobs, a count of how many items are produced within a certain time frame without wastage may be more indicative.

Choosing Predictors

The next step in the selection process is choosing the predictors and selection instruments. The analyst, based on his or her knowledge of job specifications, hypothesizes that certain individual characteristics are related to job performance. For example, a relationship might be hypothesized between the ability to analyze financial statements and successful job performance as a hospital administrator. Next, the analyst must decide how to measure these characteristics. Perhaps the ability to analyze financial statements could be demonstrated by previous management experience in making investment decisions. This information could be obtained through a resume, interview, or reference check. Modern organizations have a wide choice of selection instruments, including ability and personality tests, job simulations, interviews, reference checks, application blanks, and assessment centers. The choice of method will depend on the characteristic being measured, the type of position being filled, and the costs to the organization. Each method has advantages and disadvantages, which are discussed later in the chapter. In a 1991 study, Fenton et al. surveyed both private and public hospitals ranging in size from 130 to 15,000 employees to see what pre-employment screening methods were used most frequently. Table 12.1 summarizes the results of their study. The pre-screening tools used varied depending on the position, but in general, reference checks and interviews were the most popular methods.

The Relationship Between Predictors and Criteria

The relationship between criteria and predictors can be determined through statistical or nonstatistical methods. To determine accurately whether the use of the predictors improves the organization's chances of selecting the best people for the job, analysts must ascertain the *reliability* and the *validity* of the chosen predictors.

Reliability

Reliability refers to the consistency of the measuring instrument. If two interviewers interview the same candidate using the same questions and format, will their conclusions about the candidate be similar? If one candidate takes the same intelligence test twice in one week, will he or she receive approximately the same score on the test each time? Both of these questions address the issue of reliability.

The reliability of a selection instrument can be estimated using several different methods, including test-retest reliability, alternate forms reliability, split-halves reliability, and inter-rater reliability. Test-retest reliability is determined by measuring candidates more than once on the same instrument. If the test scores are approximately the same each time, the instrument is reliable. To determine alternate forms reliability, candidates are measured on two different versions of an instrument that are intended to measure the same characteristics. Again, if the scores are approximately the same, the instrument is reliable. To estimate reliability using the split-halves method, a candidate is measured on one instrument. Then the items on the first half of the test are correlated with the items on the second half of the test. If the correlation is high, the instrument is considered to be reliable. Yet, this method only can be used if the instrument purports to measure only one characteristic. Inter-rater reliability measures the consistency of use of the instrument rather than the consistency of the instrument. For example, if two interviewers who use identical instruments to evaluate a candidate reach different conclusions, the inter-rater reliability is very low.

Validity

The issue of validity has to do with whether you are measuring what you think you are measuring. In other words, are the selection instruments really measuring job performance? Validity can be determined

TABLE 12.1. Hospital Pre-Employment Screening Tools by Position

Hospital Employees Directly Involved with Patient Care*	Letters of Reference	Telephone Calls to Previous Employees	Review of Employment Application Form	Information Gathered in Employment Interview	Evaluation of Diplomas, Licenses, Certificates	Discussions with College Professors and Others	Check of Criminal Record, if Accessible	Mandatory Drug Testing	Physical Examination or Health Record	Polygraph (Public Institutions)
1. Anesthetists (63)	45	49	55	59	55	12	13	4	9	0
2. Nurses (93)	84	89	89	89	89	23	18	12	9	0
3. Nurses aides and orderlies (92)	84	86	82	82	82	7	18	12	9	0
4. Pharmacists (90)	84	83	88	88	88	3	19	8	9	0
5. Phlebotomists (88)	67	78	74	76	74	5	13	6	9	0
6. Technicians (x-ray, laboratory, etc) (91)	86	86	77	76	77	5	18	10	9	0
7. Therapists (91)	73	75	71	70	71	21	19	10	9	0
Hospital Employees Not Directly Involved with Patient Care*										
1. Administrative personnel (92)	88	90	88	88	88	22	17	10	9	0
2. Custodians (90)	71	76	90	81	90	0	20	10	9	0
3. Food service personnel (88)	72	72	86	86	86	3	18	11	9	0
4. Maintenance personnel (91)	79	80	90	88	90	3	20	11	9	0
5. Medical records personnel (92)	80	84	90	90	90	6	17	11	9	0
6. Clerical personnel (93)	72	79	88	88	88	3	14	6	9	0
7. Security personnel (73)	60	65	60	68	60	4	35	20	9	0

* Numbers in parentheses equal number of responses.

Source: Reprinted from Fenton J. W., Kinard J. L., and David F. R., Negligent Hiring and Retention: Some Evidence of Hospital Vulnerability, *Health Care Management Review*, Vol. 16:1, pp. 73–81, with permission of Aspen Publishers, Inc., © 1991.

through either data-based methods or non-empirical, logical methods.

There are two data-based or empirical methods: the predictive validity model and the concurrent validity model. Predictive validity is determined by collecting predictor data (e.g., scores on a test) from job applicants. Applicants then are selected for hire on the basis of some other predictor that has already been tested for validity (e.g., how well they performed in interviews). Several months later, performance data are collected on these new hires and correlated with the original assessments. If the correlation is high, the test can be said to predict job performance (i.e., it is valid).

Although this strategy of determining validity is methodologically sound, it has some serious drawbacks. First, the test scores cannot be validated until several months have elapsed, and most organizations cannot wait that long for selection data. Second, to conclude anything from statistical analyses, an organization needs a relatively large sample of new hires at a particular point in time.

The concurrent validity model is a less time-consuming, more practical method. Information on the performance of current employees is collected, and scores are obtained from the current employees on the predictor in question. These scores are then correlated with the performance data. Although this method is much quicker to use, it does have a few disadvantages. First, current employees already have been screened by the organization, so they are likely to receive higher scores on the predictor than a random sample of applicants would receive. Analysts will find less variance among scores of current employees, which will limit the maximum possible correlation coefficient between the predictor and the criterion, a problem referred to as restriction of range. Second, employees who were not able to perform the job probably will have left the organization either voluntarily or involuntarily, decreasing the variance of the criterion. Third, current employees will have had the opportunity to learn on the job, which could increase their scores on the predictors. Despite these problems, the *Uniform Guidelines on Employee Selection Procedures* (Equal Employment Opportunity Commission, 1978) recommends the use of this procedure when predictive validity is not feasible.

Under certain conditions, empirical, data-based validity testing is neither practical nor necessary. For example, a small nursing home is not going to have enough employees in any one job category to be able to conduct an empirical study. When statistical data-based validity is not practical, validity may be determined through nonempirical, logical methods. The organization may have to rely on results from studies in other organizations, or, as recommended by the *Uniform Guidelines on Employee Selection Procedures* (Equal Employment Opportunity Commission, 1978), may use a content validity strategy. These nonempirical methods are used to make rational judgments about whether there is a similarity between the predictors and job performance and whether the predictors tap the entire domain of job performance. These nonempirical methods can be defended easily when the selection instrument is a job simulation, in which the applicant is asked to perform the actual tasks required by the position.

A controversy has developed in recent years over whether it is necessary to validate each component of the selection process or just the overall results. The *Uniform Guide-*

lines on *Employee Selection Procedures* state that as long as the total selection process does not have an adverse impact, the organization does not have to validate each component of the process. This is called the "bottom line" concept. However, in 1982 the U.S. Supreme Court, in *Connecticut v. Teal* [29 FEB 1 (1982)], ruled five to four that the results of one step of the selection process were enough to establish a case of disparate impact. Although the Teal decision has been criticized severely (Blumrosen, 1984; Thompson & Christiansen, 1984), organizations must be ready to prove that no portion of their selection processes cause adverse impact.

THE SELECTION PROCESS AND FEDERAL REGULATIONS

The five legislative acts that have the greatest impact on the selection process are the Civil Rights Act of 1964 (Title VII, amended in 1972), the Civil Rights Act of 1991, the Age Discrimination in Employment Act of 1967 (amended in 1978), the Vocational Rehabilitation Act of 1973, and the Americans with Disabilities Act of 1990. As briefly mentioned in Chapter 11, Title VII declares it illegal for an organization to do the following:

1. Fail, refuse to hire, discharge any individual, or otherwise to discriminate against any individual with respect to his or her compensation, terms, conditions, or privileges of employment because of the individual's race, color, religion, sex, or national origin
2. Limit, segregate, or classify employees or applicants for employment in any

way that would deprive, or tend to deprive, any individual of employment opportunities or otherwise adversely affect his or her stature as an employee because of such individual's race, religion, sex, or national origin (Arvey, 1979).

The Age Discrimination in Employment Act extended protection to employees who are older than 40 years of age. To discriminate on the basis of age, an employer must be able to demonstrate that doing so is a legitimate business necessity. It is also illegal to impose requirements or conditions on workers of one age group not imposed on other age classes (Player, 1992). "An employer may not, for example, require employees over the age of 50 to take physical or mental tests not given to workers under 50" (Player, 1992, p. 137).

The Vocational Rehabilitation Act of 1973 extended protection to those who were physically or mentally handicapped. The act requires employers with federal contracts of more than $2500 to take Affirmative Action to hire and promote these individuals. The Americans with Disabilities Act is more encompassing, defining "disability" as a medically recognized physical or mental impairment. An employer may be found guilty of discrimination by doing the following:

1. using qualification standards, employment tests or other selection criteria that screen out or tend to screen out an individual with a disability or a class of individuals with disabilities unless the standard, test, or other selection criteria is shown to be job related for the position in question or is consistent with business necessity; or
2. by failing to select and administer employment tests in the most effective

manner to ensure that, when such test is administered to a job applicant or employee who has a disability that impairs sensory, manual, or speaking skills, such test results accurately reflect the skills, aptitude, or whatever other factors of such applicant or employee that such test purports to measure. (Player, 1992, pp. 162–163)

The 1978 *Uniform Guidelines on Employee Selection Procedures* (Equal Employment Opportunity Commission, 1978) and the *Principles for the Validation and Use of Personnel Selection Procedures* (Society for Industrial and Organizational Psychology, Inc., 1987) provide a framework for determining the proper use of selection procedures. Both publications encourage organizations to use selection procedures that are valid (i.e., predictive of job performance). An organization does not have to conduct validity studies unless the selection process has an adverse impact on a particular group of individuals. However, the courts have not agreed on the exact definition of *adverse impact.*

The two methods that have been used most frequently to determine adverse impact are disparate rejection rates and population comparisons. The disparate rejection rate method involves comparing the ratio of minority hires to minority application and the ratio of nonminority hires to nonminority applicants. The *Uniform Guidelines on Employee Selection Procedures* (Equal Employment Opportunity Commission, 1978) state that a selection rate for any racial, ethnic, or sex subgroup that is less that four-fifths (i.e., 80%) of the rate for the group with the highest rate will generally be regarded as evidence of adverse impact.

For certain types of positions (e.g., heart surgeon), there may be fewer minority than nonminority individuals with the requisite job qualifications. In such cases, a large discrepancy between the ratio of the number of minorities in the relevant labor market with the appropriate qualifications to the number of minorities in the relevant labor market, and the ratio of the number of nonminorities in the relevant labor market with the appropriate qualifications to the total number of nonminorities in the relevant market, can be used to establish proof that a particular minority group is less likely to have the requisite qualifications.

The population comparison method described by the Equal Employment Opportunity Commission (1978) compares the ratio of the number of minorities employed to the total number of employees with the ratio of the number of nonminorities in the relevant geographic area to the total number of people in the relevant geographic area. The meaning of the term *relevant geographic area,* however, is open to interpretation.

According to the landmark 1971 Supreme Court Case, *Griggs v. Duke Power* [3FEP, Cases 175 (1971)], as soon as adverse impact is demonstrated, the employer bears the burden of proving that its selection requirements are related to job performance, a business necessity, or a bona fide occupational qualification (BFOQ). An example of the use of a selection requirement based on business necessity would be hiring applicants of a certain race to demonstrate cosmetics formulated for members of that race. An example of a BFOQ would be hiring only females to be attendants in a ladies room.

In *Wards Cove Packing v. Antonio* (1989, 49FEP Cases 1519), the U.S. Supreme Court reversed itself on the burden of proof issue. The court ruled that the plaintiff had the responsibility for showing that the employer had no legitimate business reason for its selection practices. Partially in response to this ruling, the Civil Rights of Act of 1991 was passed. This act shifts the burden of proof back to the employer. The Civil Rights Act of 1991 also provides that individuals alleging intentional discrimination under Title VII, the Vocational Rehabilitation Act of 1973, or the Americans with Disabilities Act of 1990 can demand a jury trial. These individuals can recover punitive and compensatory damages for emotional pain, suffering, and inconvenience. This act increases the employers' risks of employment discrimination litigation (*Pennsylvania Employment Law Letter,* 1992).

To further comply with regulations, organizations must make certain that only job-related questions are asked on application blanks and during interviews. Chapter 11 outlines the questions that are forbidden by federal law; however, certain states have additional regulations. For example, in Massachusetts, applicants cannot be asked if they have been convicted of a first-degree misdemeanor, but only if they have ever been convicted of a felony, because studies have shown that blacks are disproportionately convicted for misdemeanors (*Massachusetts General Laws Annotated,* 1982).

In sum, the five legislative acts are designed to protect applicants and workers. The protection is against employers who use other than job-related criteria to select employees. To avoid lack of compliance with these Acts, an employer should do all it can to develop reliable and valid selection procedures.

Selection Instruments

In this section, we discuss nine selection instruments frequently used by health care organizations. Table 12.2 presents a brief overview of these methods, including their benefits and drawbacks.

Application Blanks

Almost all organizations require applicants to complete application blanks as the first step in the selection process. The types of questions typically asked are illustrated in Figure 12.3. The application blank serves

TABLE 12.2. Selection Instruments in Health Care Institutions

Instrument	Benefits	Problem Areas
Tests	Availability	Aptitude tests are controversial and difficult to validate
Interviews	Easy to use; can help obtain information on "intangibles"; have credibility in court cases	Unreliable and probably not valid in most cases; time-consuming
Reference checks	Verify application	Reference givers not willing to state true feelings
Job simulation	Verify application	Costly
Credentialing	Rigorous	Costly; leads to in-breeding
Licensing	External validation of skills	May eliminate effective employees
Application blanks, resumes	Focuses information in one location; good for initial screening	Tendency to analyze data subjectively
Assessment centers	Job-related, reliable and valid	Very costly
Controversial methods	Unique data	Reliability/validity uncertain; invasion of privacy

An Equal Opportunity-
Affirmative Action Employer
The Hospital does not discriminate on the basis of race, color,
religion, national origin, sex, age, veterans status or disability.

MASSACHUSETTS GENERAL HOSPITAL
APPLICATION FOR EMPLOYMENT

PERSONAL

NAME (Last, First, Middle)	DATE	SOCIAL SECURITY NO.

MAILING ADDRESS	CITY, TOWN	STATE	ZIP CODE	TELEPHONE - HOME ( )

LOCAL ADDRESS (If different)	CITY, TOWN	STATE	ZIP CODE	TELEPHONE - WORK ( )

Are you a U.S. Citizen? ☐ No ☐ Yes   Do you have authorization to work in the U.S.? ☐ No ☐ Yes

If No, type of work visa

Have you ever been employed at Mass. General Hospital? ☐ No ☐ Yes, Department   Dates

Have you ever applied for a position at Mass. General Hospital? ☐ No ☐ Yes, Dates

How did you hear about openings at Mass. General Hospital? Please be specific ☐ School _____

☐ Job Fair _____   ☐ Ad _____   ☐ Agency _____   ☐ Other _____

JOB INTEREST — POSITION DESIRED

1.   2.

AVAILABILITY — HOURS and DAYS · SCHEDULE

Indicate number of hours per week you can work
☐ Less than 12 Hrs.   ☐ 12-24 Hrs.   ☐ 24-30 Hrs.   ☐ 40 Hrs.

Indicate below the hours (a.m. or p.m.) and days you can work

☐ Full Time   ☐ Days
☐ Part Time   ☐ Evenings
☐ Temporary Summer   ☐ Nights
☐ On Call   ☐ Weekends

	SUN	MON	TUES	WED	THURS	FRI	SAT
START							
FINISH							DATE AVAILABLE

EDUCATION · NAME AND ADDRESS OF SCHOOL

		DATES ATTENDED	DIPLOMA OR DEGREE	MAJOR OR SPECIALTY
HIGH SCHOOL	School	From	☐ No ☐ Yes Type	
	City, State, Zip Code	To		
COLLEGE	School	From	☐ No ☐ Yes Type	
	City, State, Zip Code	To		
OTHER (Specify)	School	From	☐ No ☐ Yes Type	
	City, State, Zip Code	To		
OTHER (Specify)	School	From	☐ No ☐ Yes Type	
	City, State, Zip Code	To		

PROFESSIONAL LICENSES REGISTRATIONS and CERTIFICATES

TYPE	REG. NO.	EXPIRATION DATE	STATE
TYPE	REG. NO.	EXPIRATION DATE	STATE

Have you applied for other professional licenses or registration in Massachusetts? ☐ No ☐ Yes, Type   EXPECTED DATE OF RECEIPT

RELATED EXPERIENCE — Please Indicate

☐ Healthcare   ☐ Medical Terminology   ☐ Supervisory   ☐ Laboratory / Research

☐ Dictaphone   ☐ Computer Mainframe   ☐ PC Specify Software / Computer Language
☐ Cash Register

☐ Fiscal Patient Accounting   ☐ ICD-9   ☐ CPT-4   ☐ 3rd Party Billing   Speed (WPM)

Language(s) Spoken Fluently?

SPECIAL SKILLS — List special skills that amplify your qualifications for employment.

MGH FORM 0010564 (1/92)   #913   100/Pkg

FIGURE 12.3. Sample application blank.

FIGURE 12.3. *Continued*

THE FOLLOWING INFORMATION IS VOLUNTARY AND WILL BE MAINTAINED IN CONFIDENCE BY THE MASSACHUSETTS GENERAL HOSPITAL HUMAN RESOURCE DEPARTMENT.

Any information collected will be used for Federal government reporting requirements, emergency medical communication, and the implementation of various hospital policies. It is MGH's committment to our policy of non-discrimination and affirmative action in employment.

SEX	RACE	DISABILITY	VETERAN
1 ☐ Male	1 ☐ Black	1 ☐ No	1 ☐ No
2 ☐ Female	2 ☐ White	2 ☐ Yes	2 ☐ Vietnam Era
	3 ☐ Hispanic	3 ☐ Yes - Accommodations?	3 ☐ Vietnam Era, Disabled
	4 ☐ Asian	Explain _____	4 ☐ Disabled Other
	5 ☐ American Indian	_____	5 ☐ Yes, Other _____
	6 ☐ Other _____	_____	

Name (last, first, middle) _____ Date _____

PRIOR WORK AND VOLUNTEER EXPERIENCE — List most recent experience first. You may include unpaid experience.
PLEASE COMPLETE ALL PRIOR WORK EXPERIENCE INFORMATION EVEN IF SUBMITTING A RESUME.

In order that we may verify prior experience, have you used another name in your previous jobs?
☐ No ☐ Yes, give name and organization (check previous name box)

1

ORGANIZATION	PREVIOUS NAME	DATES FROM / TO /	HOURS WORKED PER WEEK _____
ADDRESS (No. and Street)		TITLE OR POSITION	SALARY
CITY STATE ZIP CODE		MAJOR DUTIES	
SUPERVISOR'S NAME TEL. # DEPT.			
REASON FOR LEAVING		I give the Massachusetts General Hospital authorization to contact this employer	☐ No ☐ Yes

2

ORGANIZATION	PREVIOUS NAME	DATES FROM / TO /	HOURS WORKED PER WEEK _____
ADDRESS (No. and Street)		TITLE OR POSITION	SALARY
CITY STATE ZIP CODE		MAJOR DUTIES	
SUPERVISOR'S NAME TEL. # DEPT.			
REASON FOR LEAVING		I give the Massachusetts General Hospital authorization to contact this employer	☐ No ☐ Yes

3

ORGANIZATION	PREVIOUS NAME	DATES FROM / TO /	HOURS WORKED PER WEEK _____
ADDRESS (No. and Street)		TITLE OR POSITION	SALARY
CITY STATE ZIP CODE		MAJOR DUTIES	
SUPERVISOR'S NAME TEL. # DEPT.			
REASON FOR LEAVING		I give the Massachusetts General Hospital authorization to contact this employer	☐ No ☐ Yes

4

ORGANIZATION	PREVIOUS NAME	DATES FROM / TO /	HOURS WORKED PER WEEK _____
ADDRESS (No. and Street)		TITLE OR POSITION	SALARY
CITY STATE ZIP CODE		MAJOR DUTIES	
SUPERVISOR'S NAME TEL. # DEPT.			
REASON FOR LEAVING		I give the Massachusetts General Hospital authorization to contact this employer	☐ No ☐ Yes

5

ORGANIZATION	PREVIOUS NAME	DATES FROM / TO /	HOURS WORKED PER WEEK _____
ADDRESS (No. and Street)		TITLE OR POSITION	SALARY
CITY STATE ZIP CODE		MAJOR DUTIES	
SUPERVISOR'S NAME TEL. # DEPT.			
REASON FOR LEAVING		I give the Massachusetts General Hospital authorization to contact this employer	☐ No ☐ Yes

REFERENCES: I give Mass. General Hospital permission to contact all my former employers ☐ No ☐ Yes	If no, indicate clearly which ones and reason why in comments area.

Have you attached an additional Prior Work and Volunteer Experience Form? ☐ No ☐ Yes Resume? ☐ No ☐ Yes

CRIMINAL CONVICTIONS: Past Criminal Convictions are not a bar to employment, but will be considered in relation to specific positions.

Have you ever been convicted of a felony? ☐ No ☐ Yes

If yes, please provide the details including the crime for which you were convicted, the date of conviction and the court where you were convicted.

COMMENTS:

LIE DETECTOR TEST: It is unlawful in Massachusetts to require or administer a lie detector test as condition of employment or continued employment. An employer who violates this law shall be subject to criminal penalties and civil liability.

I certify that my answers to the above questions are true and complete. I understand falsification of any of the above facts or other information supplied by me is grounds for immediate dismissal. I understand that final offer of employment will be based on the Hospital receiving, with my approval, any required business or personal references.

Your Signature   Date

several purposes. First, the instrument can be used to disqualify applicants who are obviously unsuitable for the position. Second, the application information can serve as a reliability check, easily verified through reference checks and compared to information obtained through interviewing. Third, data needed for personnel files, such as address and Social Security number, can be collected. Fourth, application blanks may contain information needed for reports to the Equal Employment Opportunity Commission about sex, race, and national origin, but only if these items are blocked off in a special section stating that these items will be used for research and reporting purposes only. To be on the safe side, many organizations have eliminated these potentially problematic questions. Instead, they have each applicant fill out an additional card, which is kept in a separate file.

Critics of application blanks claim that the information they contain is analyzed much too subjectively, often by employees who have little idea how to interpret the information. Researchers believe that application blanks could be much more effective as selection tools if items were weighted on the basis of statistical analysis in terms of their importance. Then, the screening staff could score the information simply according to a predetermined format. These instruments, called *weighted application blanks,* have been found to be valid predictors of job performance (Reilly & Chao, 1982).

Tests

Tests have been developed to tap numerous individual characteristics, including intelligence, dexterity, aptitudes, interests, and personality; many organizations use tests as part of the selection process. The most frequent types of tests are ability, personality, and performance. Ability tests measure aptitudes or achievements from previous jobs or formal learning. The nursing or physicians' tests are ability tests. Personality tests measure thoughts, attitudes, and behaviors that define an individual. An example of a personality test is the widely known Rorschach Inkblot Technique. Performance tests are more directly related to specific jobs. An example is an assessment center, a technique that is discussed later in this chapter. Health care organizations typically include testing as part of the selection procedure for lower-level positions, and for some professional positions. Medical transcriptionist, pharmalogical, frequency computation, and computer skills tests are some of the more frequently used instruments.

Considerable controversy exists over the use of tests as selection devices. Much of the discrimination litigation has focused on the adverse impact of tests on minority groups. In the landmark case *Griggs v. Duke Power* [3FEP Cases 175 (1971)], the U.S. Supreme Court declared that scores on an intelligence test could not be used as a basis for choosing employees for transfers because the test had an adverse impact on minority candidates. Duke Power lost the case because it was unable to prove that intelligence was related to job performance. If a test is used for selection purposes, the organization must be ready to prove that the test is both reliable and valid. Because this process can be very expensive and time-consuming, some organizations have abandoned using tests. Yet, some tests have been proven to be both reliable and valid predictors of job performance in certain types of occupations. *The Standards for Educational and Psychological Testing* (American Psychological Association, American Educational Research Association, & National Council on Measurement in Education, 1985) provide guidelines for evaluating psychological tests. Information on reliability, validity, and group norms for various tests is provided in *The Tenth Mental Measurements Yearbook* (Conoley & Dramer, 1989).

A widespread controversy also has developed over the use of aptitude tests in personnel selection. Schmidt and Hunter claim that professionally developed aptitude tests "are valid predictors of performance on the job and in training for all jobs in all settings, and are equally valid for minority and majority applicants" (1984, p. 200). They also claim that the use of cognitive ability tests to select employees can produce considerable labor cost savings for organizations. Their view contradicts the findings of many studies conducted before 1980 and the theories incorporated into the *Uniform Guidelines on Employee Selection Procedures* (Equal Employment Opportunity Commission, 1978). According to Schmidt and Hunter (1984), most of the conflicting results among studies regarding the adverse impact and validity of aptitude tests have been caused by statistical error. Therefore, they argue that organizations should not be required to validate tests for particular subgroups of employees and occupations if information on the reliability and validity of these tests for other organizations and groups is already available.

Interviews

The interview is one of the most frequently used selection devices. There are several interview formats, including nondirective, semistructured, and structured. In the nondirective interview, the interviewee determines the course of the interview; few, if any, questions are planned in advance. In the semistructured interview, basic questions are planned in advance to guide the flow of the interview. Yet, the interviewer is not restricted to the use of these questions and may use additional questions when appropriate during the interview. The structured interview resembles a questionnaire to which the interviewee responds orally. Both the question and the response formats are planned in advance of the interview. This method of interviewing is usually the most reliable, but is not very practical for selecting employees because it tends to inhibit the flow of discussion and does not allow the interviewer to probe relevant areas that arise during the interview. Generally, the semi-structured interview is preferred because it provides structure and freedom. The nondirective interview is too unreliable for selection purposes, although this method is used often by untrained interviewers.

Interviews can be conducted on an individual or group basis. The individual interview is the typical one-on-one situation. The inter-rater reliability of interviews given on an individual basis is impossible to determine, unless each interviewer asks each candidate the same questions. Yet, collecting this redundant information is usually a waste of time. In group interviews, either one or more interviewers may collect information from a group of candidates simultaneously, or multiple interviewers may question one candidate at the same time. The former type of interview is stressful for the candidates, who are placed in a highly competitive situation. The latter type of interview can save time when the decision about whom to hire is to be made by more than one person.

Little evidence exists to indicate that the interview is either reliable or valid (Arvey & Campion, 1982). Interviews are subject to a variety of biases and prejudices. In a review of studies on interviews, Schmitt (1976) concluded that interviewers tended to rate more favorably candidates who were similar to themselves in attitudes and race. Also, in one study, interviewers tended to rate male candidates more favorably than female applicants, but the outcome depended partially on the types of positions for which the candidates were applying. Females were rated lower when applying for typically "masculine" jobs, whereas males were rated lower when applying for typically "feminine" jobs (Arvey, 1979). More recent research on the interview has not found a bias in favor of either gender (McDonald & Hakel, 1985). Some evidence indicates that white applicants are sometimes rated more favorably than black applicants (McIntyre, Moberg, & Posner, 1980), but in one study of large organizations, the reverse was found to be true, probably due to awareness of the importance of complying with Equal Employment Opportunity legislation (Newman & Kryzstofiak, 1979).

Studies also have indicated other biases in the employment interview. Negative information tends to be weighted more heavily than positive information (Schmitt, 1976). Therefore, candidates are taught to respond to the often-asked question "What are your weaknesses?" by suggesting a strength (e.g., "I work too hard."). Some studies have shown that the outcome of the interview may depend on the strength of the preceding interviewees (Wesley, Yukl, Kovacs, & Sanders, 1972). College recruitment offices suggest that average students not schedule interviews to follow the session of someone who is at the top of the class.

First impressions have also been found to have a significant impact on the outcome of the interview (Farr, 1973). The interview is not the first piece of information an interviewer has about a candidate. An interviewer almost always sees a resume and sometimes a grade point average, references, or an application blank for each candidate. On the basis of this information, the interviewer forms a hypothesis about the candidate and seeks to confirm it throughout the interview (Dipboye, 1982). One study showed that 88% of the time the post-interview decision is made on the basis of preinterview information (Springbett, 1958).

Because the interview is a time-consuming method fraught with biases, why is it used so frequently to select candidates? First, some recent studies have shown that when interviewer competence is controlled, and interviewer questions are closely linked to job analysis results, the validity of the interview increases (Arvey, Miller, Gould, & Burch, 1987; Campion, Pursell, & Brown, 1988; Harris, 1989). Second, the interview serves purposes other than selection. The interview is an opportunity for the organization to sell itself and to provide information to the candidate. Also, the interview provides a vehicle for the candidate and employer to get to know each other and to decide whether they will be able to work well together. Unfortunately, this decision is often based on faulty information because both the interviewer and applicant, in attempting to make favorable impressions, often suppress important and realistic information. Finally, very few cases dealing with interviews have been litigated. Therefore, interviews are safer selection instruments to use than tests, which must be validated and checked for reliability. Discrimination in the interview is extremely difficult to prove because witnesses are seldom present, and the candidate often has no way of knowing how the interview information is combined with other data to reach a decision.

Organizations can increase the reliability and validity of their selection interview by adhering to the following basic guidelines suggested by Gatewood and Field (1990):

1. Restrict the use of the interview to the most job-relevant characteristics.
2. Limit the use of preinterview data about applicants.
3. Adopt a semistructured format by predetermining the major questions.
4. Use job-related questions.
5. Use multiple questions for each characteristic.
6. Develop a formal scoring format to evaluate separately each applicant characteristic.
7. Use multiple interviewers simultaneously whenever possible.
8. Train interviewers in the processes and pitfalls of selection interviews.

Reference Checks

Reference checks have become increasingly important in recent years as more people have been caught providing fraudulent information on application blanks and in resumes (LoPresto, Mitcham, & Ripley, 1986). Through the use of reference or background checks, an organization can verify an applicant's educational background and work experience. Backgrounds are usually checked through telephone interviews and by asking applicants for letters of recommendation. For lower-level employees, the former approach is used most frequently, whereas written references are frequently requested when the applicant is a professional.

Many organizations now prefer telephone checks, even though they are very time-consuming, because few people are willing to write an unfavorable reference. Since the passage of the 1974 Freedom of Information Act and various state regulations regarding privacy, people have been even more reluctant to write unfavorable references, because applicants may have access to the records, and authors of such letters could be subject to litigation. For fear of litigation, some organizations will not even allow their employees to give references over the telephone. They are permitted only to verify that an applicant was employed by the organization and to give the dates of employment and job title. A "catch 22" situation exists for employers. Case law indicates the importance of obtaining background information prior to hiring, yet concern about defamation of character leads past employers to be reluctant to provide such information (Gatewood & Field, 1990). Also, individuals making selection decisions based on written recommendations have difficulty discriminating between honesty and politely positive statements. This is a highly subjective judgment that is open to many biases.

Job Simulation

Job simulation, methods of duplicating actual job tasks before full-time employment, are used in a unique way in the health care industry. Employees who have been hired may be given provisional status until they can demonstrate specific job-related skills. Nurses, for example, are asked to pass a series of tests to demonstrate their clinical skills and ability to use particular equipment and procedures (e.g., starting IVs). Nurses who fail these tests during the probationary period are dismissed or trained. Probationary periods range from 2 weeks to 6 months,

although 3 months is the average length of time.

Credentialing

A unique selection process in hospitals is the credentialing of physicians for appointment to the medical staff. The objectives of this process are: 1) to ensure that care is rendered by appropriately qualified individuals, 2) to ensure that each eligible applicant is afforded equal opportunity to be appointed to the medical staff, and 3) to ensure that adequate information pertaining to selection criteria is reviewed by appropriate individuals and committees before a final recommendation is made to the governing boards. A typical procedure for credentialing is presented in Figure 12.4. This complex example involves a hospital's board of directors and its medical staff. The medical staff does not usually get involved in selection, however, unless the applicant is a chief administrator or a physician.

Licensing

The need for selection testing in the health care environment is minimized by strict licensing and certification requirements. Any health care facility approved by the Joint Commission for the Accreditation of Hospitals (JCAH) is required to use licensing as a selection criteria for most clinical, professional, and technical positions. Registered nurses can have a variety of educational backgrounds ranging from diploma programs to either 2 or 4 years of college. However, anyone who is certified as a registered nurse must take and pass the state board examination. Specialty certification on either the state

Qualifications for appointment

1. Appointment to the medical staff is a privilege that shall be extended only to professionally competent individuals who continuously meet the qualifications, standards, and requirements set forth in these bylaws and in such policies as are adopted from time to time by the board.
2. Only physicians, dentists, oral surgeons, and podiatrists who: 1) are currently licensed to practice in this state; 2) possess current, valid professional liability coverage in amounts satisfactory to the hospital; and 3) can document their background, experience, training, and demonstrated competence, their adherence to the ethics of their profession, their good reputation and character, and their ability to work harmoniously with others sufficiently to convince the hospital that all patients treated by them in the hospital will receive quality care and that the hospital and its medical staff will be able to operate in an orderly manner shall be qualified for appointment to the medical staff. The word "character" is intended to include the applicant's mental and emotional stability.
3. No individual shall be entitled to appointment to the medical staff or to the exercise of clinical privileges in the hospital merely by virtue of the fact that: 1) he or she is licensed to practice any profession in this or any other state, 2) he or she is a member of any particular professional organization, or 3) he or she had in the past, or currently has, medical staff appointment or privileges in other hospitals.
4. No individual shall be denied appointment on the basis of sex, race, creed, color, or national origin.

Conditions of appointment

Duration of initial provisional appointment. All initial appointments to the medical staff, regardless of the category of the staff to which the appointment is made, and all initial clinical privileges shall be provisional for a period of 12 months from the date of the appointment or longer if recommended by the executive committee. During the term of this provisional appointment he or she shall be evaluated by the chairman of the department or departments in which he or she has clinical privileges, and by the relevant committees of the medical staff and the hospital as to his or her clinical competence and as to his or her general behavior and conduct in the hospital. Provisional clinical privileges shall be adjusted to reflect clinical competence at the end of the provisional period, or sooner if warranted. Continued appointment after the provisional period shall be conditioned on an evaluation of the factors to be considered for reappointment set forth in these bylaws.

Rights and duties of appointees. Appointment to the medical staff shall confer on the appointee only such clinical privileges as have been granted by the board and shall require that each appointee assume such reasonable duties and responsibilities as the board or the medical staff shall require.

Time requirements for promotion. The period of time and qualification requirements stated in these bylaws for promotion from provisional status may be altered as to specific applicants by the board on its own motion or as recommended to the board by the executive committee.

Application for initial appointment and clinical privileges information. Applications shall be in writing and shall be submitted on forms prescribed by the board. Application information should include the following:

1. The names and addresses of at least three physicians, oral surgeons, podiatrists, or other practitioners, as appropriate, who have had recent extensive experience in observing and working with the applicant and who can provide adequate information pertaining to the applicant and who can provide adequate information pertaining to the applicant's present professional competence and character, and the name and com plete address of at least one appointee to the active staff not professionally associated in practice with the applicant who attests to this
2. The names and addresses of the chairmen of each department of any and all hospitals or institutions at which the applicant has worked or trained (i.e., the individuals who served as chairmen at the time the applicant worked in the particular department) (If the number of hospitals in which the applicant has worked is great or if a number of years have passed since the applicant worked at a particular hospital, the credentials committee and the board may take into consideration the applicant's good faith effort to produce this information.)

FIGURE 12.4. Sample credentialing policy and procedure.

3. An agreement to accept committee assignments and such other reasonable duties and responsibilities as shall be assigned to him or her by the board and entire medical staff

4. Whether the applicant has ever withdrawn his or her application for appointment, reappointment, and clinical privileges, or his or her medical staff appointment before final decision by a hospital's or health care facility's governing board

5. Whether the applicant's membership in local, state, or national professional societies or his or her license to practice any profession in any state, or his or her narcotic license has ever been suspended, modified, or terminated (The submitted application shall include a copy of all the applicant's current licenses to practice, as well as a copy of his or her narcotics licenses, medical, dental, or podiatry school diploma, and certificates from all postgraduate training program completed.)

6. Whether the applicant has currently in force professional liability coverage or qualifies under the state's Malpractice Act, the name of the insurance company, and the amount and classification of such coverage

7. Applicant's malpractice claims

8. A consent to the release of information from the applicant's present and past malpractice insurance carriers

9. Applicant's physical and mental health

10. Convictions of a felony and details about any such instance

11. Citizenship and visa status of the applicant

12. Such other information as the board may require

Undertakings: Every application for staff appointment or reappointment shall be signed by the applicant and shall contain the following:

1. The applicant's specific acknowledgment of his or her obligation on appointment to the medical staff to provide continuous care and supervision to all patients within the hospital for whom he or she has responsibility

2. An agreement to abide by all bylaws, rules, and regulations of the medical staff as shall be in force from time to time during the time he or she is appointed to the medical staff

3. An agreement to accept committee assignments and such other reasonable duties and responsibilities as shall be assigned to him or her by the board and entire medical staff

4. An agreement to provide the hospital current information regarding all of the questions on the application form at any time

5. A statement that the applicant has received and had an opportunity to read a copy of the bylaws of the hospital and bylaws, rules, and regulations of the medical staff as are in force at the time of his application and that he or she has agreed to be bound by the terms thereof in all matters relating to consideration of his or her application without regard to whether he or she is granted appointment to the medical staff or clinical privileges

6. A statement of willingness to appear for personal interviews

7. A statement that any misrepresentation or misstatement in, or omission from the application whether intentional or not, shall constitute cause for automatic and immediate rejection of the application resulting in denial of appointment and clinical privileges (In the event that an appointment had been granted prior to the discovery of such misrepresentation, misstatement, or omission, such discovery may result in summary dismissal from the medical staff.)

8. A statement that the applicant will: 1) refrain from fee splitting or other inducements relating to patient referral; 2) refrain from delegating responsibility for diagnoses or care of hospitalized patients to any individual who is not qualified to undertake this responsibility or who is not adequately supervised; 3) refrain from deceiving patients as to the identity of an operating surgeon or any other individual providing treatment or services; 4) seek consultation whenever necessary; and 5) abide by generally recognized ethical principles applicable to his or her profession. Burden of providing information: The applicant shall have the burden of producing adequate information for a proper evaluation of his or her competence, character, ethics, and other qualifications, and of resolving any doubts about such qualifications.

Source: Adapted from the bylaws of a 500-bed, denominational hospital in the southcentral part of the United States.

or national level furthers the role of certification in the selection process.

Assessment Centers

The assessment center is used primarily to identify candidates who would be successful in managerial positions. Candidates are evaluated by a group of assessors as they perform a series of individual and group tests, usually over 2 or 3 days. Although assessment centers were developed during World War II to evaluate candidates for the Office of Strategic Services, the first industrial use of this method is attributed to AT&T (Howard, 1984). The purpose of AT&T's first programs was to decide which of their current employees were promotable to higher levels of management.

Assessment center participants are usually evaluated on the following dimensions: leadership, organizing and planning, decision making, oral and written communication skills, initiative, energy, analytical ability, resistance to stress, use of delegation, behavior flexibility, human relations competence, originality, controlling, self-direction, and overall potential (Howard, 1984). These dimensions are assessed by evaluating behavior in a host of situational tests, including in-baskets, leaderless group discussions, and fact-finding exercises. In addition to these situational tests, participants are interviewed and asked to take projective and paper-and-pencil aptitude tests.

In the in-basket exercise, the candidate plays the role of a manager who has just returned to the office after a week-long trip and finds a huge stack of items including letters, memos, reports, and messages (i.e., the contents of the in-basket). The applicant, playing the role of the manager, is told that the manager will be leaving town again the next day and he or she must respond in some way to each item. After the exercise, the candidate is frequently asked to explain his or her actions and decision processes.

In the leaderless group discussion, a group of candidates is given a problem to solve, such as deciding who to promote or what disciplinary action to take against an employee. The group is required to come to a group decision about the problem. As the name implies, no leader is designated.

In the fact-finding exercise, individual candidates are given information about an organization, its problem, and possible alternative solutions. Group members then select, present, and justify the best alternative from the limited information available, both orally and in writing.

After the assessment center exercises have been completed, the assessors review candidate performance and complete a written evaluation. Each candidate is usually evaluated by more than one assessor who must be trained extensively in evaluation. The assessors may be members of management who themselves have gone through the assessment center, or they may be psychologists.

Studies have shown that inter-rater reliabilities are high for the final assessment evaluations and for several components of the assessment process. The validity of the overall evaluation also has been shown to be high compared to the validity of alternative selection procedures. Yet, some of the components of the assessment center are not valid across all organizations (Howard, 1984). The main drawback to the assessment center is that it is extremely costly and time-consuming. It is a feasible selection alternative only for large organizations or when selection may be critical to the survival of the firm. To date, assessment centers have not been used extensively as selection tools in the health care industry. However, in a sampling of 10 local hospitals, one reported using an assessment center to determine the promotability potential of department heads to higher-level administrative positions. Applicants were evaluated on 15 criteria as they performed a role-playing exercise, an in-basket test, and an interview.

Assessment centers could also be useful in identifying candidates for the position of head nurse. To date, most health care organizations rely heavily on past performance and intuition when selecting a head nurse manager (Turner, 1991). However, a good nurse may not necessarily be a good manager. Placing candidates in a simulated work environment in which managerial performance can be evaluated by trained observers may provide more relevant information than past clinical performance (Turner, 1991).

Physical Examinations

Many organizations require job applicants to undergo physical examinations before a hiring decision is made. The results may be used to screen out candidates with physical or mental handicaps that would prevent them from performing the job, or to protect the organization from workers compensation claims based on preemployment conditions (Cherrington, 1991). Additionally, health care organizations use physical examinations to screen out applicants with contagious diseases. Whether all applicants for health care positions should be tested for HTLV-III antibodies is currently one of the most controversial issues facing the health

care industry today. The HTLV-III blood-test indicates whether a person has been infected by the AIDS virus, but not whether that person has or will develop the acquired immunodeficiency syndrome (Kadzielski, 1986). Under current federal law, employers are neither authorized nor prohibited from testing job applicants for HIV (Fulton, 1991). Although state regulations require most health care providers to screen employees for contagious diseases, AIDS cannot be transmitted through casual contact and therefore these regulations may not apply (Harris, 1987). A number of states have enacted statutes prohibiting HIV-testing without prior formed consent and counseling of the person to be tested (Fulton, 1991). Health care organizations that receive federal funding can test for HIV only after a conditional offer of employment has been extended (Fulton, 1991). According to the Americans with Disabilities Act, an organization can refuse to hire an individual who is HIV-positive only if that person presents a direct threat to the health and safety of others. Even in that case, the organization must determine whether the risk of transmission could be eliminated by "reasonable accommodations" (Fulton, 1991). Unfortunately, if a health care organization hires an employees who is HIV-positive and the employee transmits the virus to a patient or co-worker, the organization may be faced with a very large personal injury lawsuit.

Controversial Selection Methods

Organizations are continually searching for new methods of selecting employees; several selection methods that have become increasingly popular in recent years have generated considerable controversy. These include honesty testing, graphology, and drug screening.

In 1988, Congress passed the Employee Polygraph Protection Act (Public Law 100-347) to prevent the denial of employment opportunities by prohibiting the use of lie detectors by employers involved in or affecting interstate commerce. The act includes all types of tests, whether mechanical or electrical, or those in which the results are used for the purposes of rendering a diagnostic opinion regarding the honesty or dishonesty of an employee. Yet, several organizations use these devices to identify possible security risks, particularly when employees are being hired to handle large sums of money. Critics of polygraphs (including the American Medical Association) claim that the technology has not been proven to be reliable, and the dangers of a false-positive outcome (i.e., data indicating that the applicant is lying when in fact he or she is telling the truth) are too great (Patrick & Iacono, 1989). Furthermore, critics argue that polygraph testing is an invasion of privacy because questions are often asked regarding such topics as arrest records and marital history (Kaler, 1985). Supporters argue, however, that polygraphs do not have to be 100% accurate to be useful because other selection devices, such as tests, which explain as little as 25% of the variance of performance, are often accepted by the courts (Horvath, 1985). Proponents also argue that selection decisions are never based solely on polygraph test results, and the information these tests provide is not currently obtainable by any other means (Horvath, 1985). The courts, however, have usually sided with the critics ("Can you pass," 1986).

Some health care organizations use paper-and-pencil tests, rather than polygraphs, to assess honesty. A couple of recent reviews found that paper-and-pencil honesty tests have adequate validities (Sackett, Burris, & Callahan, 1989; Sackett & Harris, 1984). Townsend (1992) argues, however, that utility rather than validity should be the real issue. Because theft is an infrequent behavior, the cost of replacing honest applicants who fail the test would not be offset by catching the small number of thieves (Townsend, 1992). Townsend (1992) recommends honesty testing only for those jobs in which an opportunity for serious theft exists. Cascio (1991) suggests that an applicant's score on an honesty test should only be considered as one piece of information. A candidate who passes all other selection requirements should not be rejected on this basis alone.

Graphologists believe that a person's suitability for a job can be determined by handwriting analysis. They claim that graphology is a very accurate assessment device because it is next to impossible for applicants to disguise their handwriting. One company, the pioneer in computerized handwriting analysis, reports that its clients have ranged from construction companies and security firms to entertainment companies ("Can you pass," 1986). The validity of graphology, however, has not been determined, and an organization would have a difficult time defending a graphology-based decision in court.

The most controversial screening device at the current time is drug-testing. Nearly 25% of Fortune 500 corporations now do routine urinalysis on employees and job applicants to try to detect disease or illegal drug use ("Medical testing," 1985). Just 3 years ago, 10% of the same corporations were participating in these screening tests ("Medical testing," 1985). This testing is sometimes combined with blood tests to detect drug abuse, genetic predisposition to disease, and the presence of the AIDS virus. Detecting drug abuse is particularly relevant for health care organizations because employees have easy access to drugs.

The Centers for Disease Control (CDC) estimates that it costs less than $5 to do an initial screening and $20 to $50 for confirmation of the results ("Medical testing," 1985). The CDC found that some laboratories testing for drugs had a false-positive error rate as high as 66%. Some facilities gave false-negative results (indicating that a person is not taking a drug when he or she really is) 100% of the time when testing for certain drugs ("Medical testing," 1985). In other words, tossing a coin would have predicted the sample results with about the same reliability. Human resources professionals can expect, however, to see an increase in this type of testing because of the magnitude of the problem. The Alcohol, Drug Abuse and Mental Health Administration estimated that reduced productivity due to alcohol and drug abuse in the United States cost more than $99 billion in 1983 (Dogoloff, Angarola, & Price, 1985). However, until drug- and blood-screening procedures are perfected, organizations that use these procedures to disqualify applicants may find themselves in court fighting a downhill battle. One large laboratory that does drug-screening claims that the most important step is to determine whether the use of drugs being screened for impairs performance. The technology of effective drug-testing will quickly surpass the ability of organizations to set and use effective policies and procedures related to drug-screening (personal communication, Dr. Thomas F. Puckett Laboratory, P.O. Box 1549 Hattiesburg, Mississippi 39402). Some health care organizations use paper-and-pencil tests to assess tendencies toward violence and

drug abuse, rather than urinalysis tests. These tests, however, are usually required only for security personnel. The following six key elements should be included in a drug-testing policy statement:

1. The employer should clearly state which drugs are under examination and the relationship of taking these drugs to job performance.
2. The applicant should be given a chance to list any drugs taken in the last month and under what conditions.
3. The applicant and employer should discuss why the test is being given.
4. If the first test is positive, the applicant should get further testing by a licensed laboratory.
5. Test results should be disclosed only to those who have a job-related reason to know the results.
6. The applicant should be given a chance to explain his or her results before any final action is taken.

DETERMINING THE UTILITY OF THE SELECTION PROCESS

The selection process does not end after the selection instruments have been demonstrated to be reliable and valid. The organization must decide how the individual components of the process are to be combined and what the instruments' cutoff scores should be. Three procedures can be used to make the final selection of employees: the multiple-hurdles approach, the compensatory approach, and the hybrid approach (Milkovich & Boudreau, 1988). If the organization chooses the multiple-hurdles approach, the applicant must pass one component of the process before proceeding to the next. A cutoff point is chosen for each predictor. If the organization uses a compensatory approach, each candidate completes all of the components and a hiring decision is based on a weighted composite of all of the predictors. The premise of this approach is that strengths in certain areas can compensate for weaknesses in others. The most common approach is the hybrid approach, for which candidates must demonstrate some minimum requirement (e.g., college degree or certain number of years of experience) before continuing, so that those who are clearly unqualified can be quickly eliminated. Yet, as soon as the candidates have passed the minimum qualifications, they proceed through the rest of the process.

Regardless of the type of approach used by the organization, the usefulness of the predictors needs to be determined. The square of the regression coefficient (i.e., coefficient of determination) indicates the job performance variance explained by the predictors (i.e., the validity of the predictors), but it does not account for situational factors that might influence the utility of the procedure. Taylor and Russell (1939) suggested considering three factors when determining the utility of a selection device: the validity coefficient, the base rate, and the selection ratio. As noted in Chapter 11, the selection ratio is the number of applicants hired compared to the total number of applicants. If the selection ratio is high, spending time and money developing selection instruments is a futile endeavor because almost everyone who applies for the job needs to be hired. This, of course, indicates that the organization has an ineffective recruitment strategy.

If the selection ratio is low, the organization can afford to be very selective, and thus predictors are needed that can discriminate between qualified and unqualified candidates.

The base rate of success is the percentage of the current work force considered to be effective job performers. If the base rate is already high, a new predictor would need to have an extremely high validity coefficient to be of any use. If the base rate is low, even a predictor with marginal validity could save the organization money.

Using the base rate, selection ratio, and validity coefficients, Taylor and Russell (1939) developed tables that indicate the improvement in successful job performance that could be expected using a new predictor. Table 12.3 shows that with a base rate of 50% and a selection ratio of .20, if a new predictor has a validity coefficient of .40, the base rate of successful performance could increase from 50% to 73%.

No selection procedure, however, is 100% valid. Errors always occur, and an organization must decide before a cutoff point is chosen for a particular predictor which type of error is least costly: false-negative or false-positive. Figure 12.5 shows two sets of the

TABLE 12.3. Example of Taylor-Russell Tables

Correlation Coefficient	Selection Ratio[a]			
	.20	.40	.60	.80
.20	.61	.58	.55	.53
.30	.67	.62	.58	.54
.40	.73	.66	.61	.56

[a] Proportion of employees rated satisfactory (base rate = .50)
Source: Adapted from Taylor, H. C., & Russell, I. T. (1939). The relationship of validity coefficients to the practical effectiveness of tests in selection: Discussion and tables. *Journal of Applied Psychology, 23,* 565–578. Copyright 1939 by the American Psychological Association.

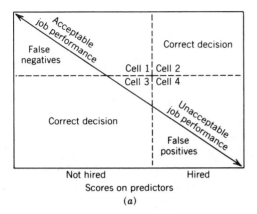

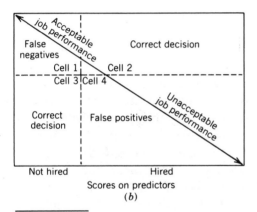

FIGURE 12.5. Types of selection errors.

four possible situations resulting from selection. In each case, Cell 2 includes applicants who received high scores on the predictors, were hired, and performed well on the job. Cell 3 includes applicants who were not selected because they received low scores on the predictors and would not have been successful. In both cases, no errors have been made. Cell 1, however, includes applicants who were rejected because they received low scores on the predictors but would have been satisfactory employees if they had been hired. This is called a false-negative error. Cell 4 contains applicants who were hired because they scored high on the predictors, but performed unsatisfactorily. This is called a false-positive error. The costs of both false-positive errors and false-negative errors have to be weighed before cutoff points for predictors are established. A high cutoff point will increase the possibility of false-negative errors as indicated by the proportionately larger size of Cell 1 in Figure 12.5, and a low cutoff point will increase the possibility of false-positive errors, as seen in Cell 4 of Figure 12.5. The cost of making a false-positive error could be extremely high when filling a physician's position or chief administrator position. However, when a file clerk position needs to be filled, the organization may be more willing to risk a false-positive than a false-negative decision. The costs of training or replacing an unsuccessful candidate would not be high, and recruiting costs could be reduced by lowering the cutoff point.

Recently, methods have been developed that enable the organization to assess the value of its selection procedures in dollar terms. The method of Schmidt, Hunter, McKensie, and Mildrow (1979) is based on asking supervisors to estimate the dollar value of a job at different performance levels. They then estimate the value added by a selection device, based on its ability to improve performance. Cascio (1990), instead of asking supervisors to estimate the dollar value, estimates that the average salary paid for a job reflects its value. Jobs are broken down into major activities, and supervisors assign a portion of the total salary to each activity. Then the supervisors rate their subordinates' performance on each activity and calculate how much the job is worth currently, and how much it would be worth if the selection instrument improved performance. These methods are currently being refined and hold promise for the future.

PLACEMENT OF EMPLOYEES

Most health care managers believe that as soon as they hire a person little else needs to be done as part of the selection process. Yet, in some cases the most important task remains (i.e., placing the person into his or her job). Placement is a process of introducing a new employee to his or her job and work environment.

Placement involves many activities. For example, after the employee has accepted a job, the organization then needs to take responsibility for the new employee's introduction into the health care unit in which he or she will be working. The less specific the job placement (e.g., a new nurse hired into a nursing pool), the more a manager needs to make sure the new employee is placed appropriately and learns about the organization.

Yet, the most important aspect of placement is the process of socialization. Socialization is the process by which employees learn the values, norms, and required behaviors that permit them to participate as a member of the organization. The most important finding from research is that a formalized program from the beginning of a person's employment is better than an informal program for socializing employees (Jones, 1986). Several techniques can be used to achieve socialization. One technique, *realistic job previews,* involves giving recruits a realistic idea of what lies ahead by presenting both positive and negative aspects of the job. This activity lowers unrealistically high expectations and can help the organization to achieve a more satisfying work outcome in terms of lower turnover, higher commitment to the job, and increased productivity.

Another technique that speeds the socialization process is *mentoring.* Mentoring is the process of forming and maintaining an intensive and lasting relationship between a senior employee and a junior employee. The mentor may be called a teacher, coach, or sponsor. Many organizations are becoming aware of mentoring as a way to facilitate a new employee's career. This process has been used in the medical field, particularly with new physicians during their internships.

Some health care organizations have formal mentoring programs (Matthes, 1991). Successful programs tend to have several of the same characteristics, four of which are important for health care organizations. First, proteges should select a mentor at two or more grades above the protege's level. Second, mentoring works best when it is one-on-one and includes both career development and personal, psychosocial discussions. Third, a mentor and protege should establish a nonfault way to end the relationship if it is no longer productive for either party. Finally, a productive relationship is both flexible in length and intensity. Research results have demonstrated the importance of mentors for career development (Kram, 1985; Scandura, 1992). A mentoring program could be particularly beneficial for nurses and other professionals who are newly appointed to managerial positions.

Career management is yet another technique for socialization. Career management or career planning is a problem-solving and decision-making process aimed at optimizing the match between individual's needs and values and work-related experiences. This process of managing one's career is a complicated set of interactions between the employee and employer. The major reasons for mentioning this process here is that the management of an employee's career is part of the responsibility of the employer and begins as the employee is placed in a new job (Feldman, 1988). This management process is particularly important for employees who are placed in technical jobs (e.g., nurses) yet will progress toward management jobs. Physicians' roles are changing rapidly as they are placed in roles different from those they expected when they went to school. Specific career management planning can be used to facilitate the change. For example, new physicians are now receiving more information about the health care industry, management skills, and management career options available to them. Cleveland Clinic implemented the Office of Practice Management and Executive Program in Practice Management for these purposes (Dunbar, 1991). Chapter 13 has more information about health care training and development.

SOLVING THE DILEMMA

Landis now had to design a selection process. Landis decided to refer to the *Dictionary of Occupational Titles* (U.S. Department of Labor, 1977) for information on Vice Presidents of Strategic Planning. He also acquired information and sample job descriptions from other hospitals who have already hired such people. He decided not to use a quantitative method for job analysis because it

would be expensive and Methodist was hiring only one person for a unique position.

Landis also consulted with the other key managers as to the job requirements for the new position and the specific skills needed for the new position. He spent most of the discussion time on defining the dimensions of job performance for this new position.

A final decision he made was to select a person with experience. He talked with Brandy about this decision and they thought this approach was best for Methodist. They wanted the person to be with the organization for a long period of time. Landis and Brandy decided on these requirements after calculating the cost of training and lost time that would be incurred by hiring an inexperienced person.

Landis reviewed all possible selection instruments and decided that the most important ones for hiring a Vice President of Strategic Planning were interviews, reference checks, application blanks, and resumes. He wanted to use a semistructured interview, including questions that would help him and the other interviewers assess the applicants' knowledge of strategic planning and the application of this knowledge to health care. Landis decided that the interviewers must include the Chief of Staff, a Board member who is on the Human Resource Committee of the Board, and several key managers. Landis included in the list of interviewers a consultant who had expertise in both health care and senior management selection.

To establish the reliability and validity of these questions, Landis asked the same consultant to help phrase and test the questions. The key questions Landis and Brandy wanted to ask were those about actual problems that the Vice President of Strategic Planning would be asked to solve when on the job.

SUMMARY

Selection of employees for health care organizations is more important than ever before. Organizations are growing and changing more quickly because of unstable environments. Moreover, although the need for employees with flexibility and diverse skills and abilities has increased, the number of employees in health care has decreased. The manager's challenge is to select the employee who can offer the widest variety of skills to the organization.

This chapter outlines the critical steps in selecting employees for a health care environment. The process begins with a job analysis to establish the parameters for selecting employees in a particular job category. After job analysis, the human resources professional proceeds through a series of technical steps to ensure the reliability and validity of the selection process. Finally, determining the utility of the selection process helps to personalize and further validate an organization's approach to selecting employees.

The future of health care will include a renewed interest in human resources selection. Human resources professionals must become involved in strategic planning by helping an organization both to define its needs for employees and to obtain and maintain an effective work force. Selection could very well be one of the critical dimensions that defines the competitive edge of a particular health care institution.

Discussion Questions

1. How is the selection process related to the strategic goals of the organization?
2. What are the seven primary steps in designing a selection system?
3. What issues should be considered when choosing a job analysis method?
4. You are the associate personnel director of a hospital. Your boss wants you to develop a process for screening dishonest job candidates. What methods might you use, and what would be the pros and cons of each?
5. What are the key elements that should be included in a drug testing policy statement?
6. What factors would you consider in evaluating the effectiveness of your selection process?

REFERENCES

American Psychological Association, American Educational Research Association, & National Council on Measurement in Education (Joint Committee). (1985). *Standards for educational and psychological testing.* Washington, DC: American Psychological Association, Inc.

Arvey, R.D. (1979). *Fairness in selecting employees.* Reading, MA: Addison-Wesley.

Arvey, R.D., & Campion, J.E. (1982). The employment interview: A summary and review of recent research. *Personnel Psychology 35,* 281–322.

Avery, R.D., Miller, H.E., Gould, R., Burch, P. (1987). Interview validity for selecting sales clerks. (1984). *Personnel Psychology, 40,* 1–12.

Blumrosen, A.W. (1984). The bottom line after Connecticut v. Teal. In R.S. Schuler & S.A. Youngblood (Eds.), *Readings in personnel and human resource management* (2nd ed.). St. Paul, MN: West Publishing.

Campion, M.A., Pursell, E.D., & Brown, B.K. (1988). Structured interviewing: Raising the psychometric properties of the employment interview. *Personnel Psychology, 41,* 25–41.

"Can you pass the job test?" (May 5, 1986). *Newsweek,* 46–53.

Cascio, W.F. (1991). *Applied psychology in personnel management* (4th ed.). Englewood Cliffs, NJ: Prentice Hall.

Cherrington, D.J. (1991). *The management of human resources* (3rd ed.). Boston: Allyn & Bacon.

Coddington, D.C., Palmquist, L.E., & Trollinger, W.B. (1985). Strategies for survival in the hospital industry. *Harvard Business Review, 63,* 129–138.

Connecticut v. Teal. (1982). 457 U.S. 440.

Conoley, J.C., & Dramer, J.L. (Eds.). (1989). *The tenth mental measurements yearbook.* Lincoln: University of Nebraska Press.

Dipboye, R.L. (1982). Self-fulfilling prophecies in the selection-recruitment interview. *Academy of Management Review, 7,* 579–586.

Dogoloff, L., Angarola, R., & Price, S. (1985). *Urine testing in the workplace.* Washington, DC: American Council for Drug Education.

Dunbar, C. (1991). Back to school at Cleveland clinic. *Computers in Healthcare, 12*(3), 25–28.

Earle, P.W., & Pfannkuche, A. (1991). Looking for Mr. Goodexec. *Health Systems Review, 24,* 44–46.

Equal Employment Opportunity Commission. (1978). Uniform guidelines on employee selection procedures. *Federal Register. 43*(166).

Eubanks, P. (1992). The new nurse manager: A linchpin in quality care and cost control. *Hospitals, 66*(8), 22–30.

Farr, I.L. (1973). Response requirements and primacy effects in a simulated selection interview. *Journal of Applied Psychology, 57,* 228–233.

Feldman, D.C. (1988). *Managing careers in organizations.* Glenview, IL: Scott Forseman.

Fenton, J.W., Jr., Kinard, I.L., David, F.R. (1991). Negligent hiring and retention: Some evidence of hospital vulnerability. *Health Care Management Review, 16,* 83–81.

Fine, S.A., & Wiley, W.W. (1971). *An introduction to functional job analysis. A scaling of selected tasks from the social welfare field. Methods for manpower analysis* (Vol. 4). Kalamazoo, MI: W.E. Upjohn Institute for Employment Research.

Flory, I. (1990). Hospitals increase efforts to attract physicians. *Hospitals, 64,* 87–88.

Fulton, S.P. (1991). Aids and employees: Exploring uncharted territory. *Nursing Homes,* May/June, 37–4I.

Gatewood, R.D., & Field, H.S. (1990). *Human resource selection* (2nd ed.). Chicago: Dryden.

Griggs v. Duke Power. [3FEP Cases 175(1971)].

Harris, M.A. (1989). Reconsidering the employment interview: A review of recent literature and suggestions for future research. *Personnel Psychology, 42,*691–723.

Harris, S. (1987). AIDS poses employer dilemma. *American Health Care Association Journal, 12,* 43–44.

Henderson, R.I. (1979). *Compensation management: Rewarding performance.* Reston, VA: Reston Publishing.

Heneman, H.G., Schwab, D.P., Fossum, I.A., & Dyer L.D. (1986). *Personnel/human resource management.* Homewood, IL: Irvin.

Horvath, F. (1985). Job screening. *Society, 22*(6), 43–46.

Howard, A. (1984). An assessment of assessment centers. In R.S. Schuler & S.A. Youngblood (Eds.), *Readings in personnel and human resource management.* (2nd ed.) (pp. 183–199). St. Paul, MN: West Publishing.

Jones, G. (1986). Socialization, tactics, self-efficacy, and newcomers' adjustments to organizations. *Academy of Management Journal, 29,* 262–279.

Kadzielski, M.A. (1986). Legal implications for health care providers. *Health Progress,* May, 48–52.

Kaler, I.K. (March 11, 1985). A mole among the gerbils? *Newsweek,* pp. 14–15.

Kram, K.E. (1985). *Mentoring at work: Developmental relationships in organizational life.* Glenview, IL: Scott Foresman.

LoPresto, R.L., Mitcham, D.E., & Ripley, D.E. (1988). *Reference checking handbook.* Alexandria, VA: American Society for Personnel Administration.

Massachusetts General Laws Annotated Vol. 22A. (1982). St. Paul, MN: West Publishing.

Matthes, K. (1991). *Beyond the myths and magic of mentoring.* New York: Josey-Bass.

McDonald, T., & Hackel, M.D. (1985). Effects of applicant race, sex, suitability, and answers on interviewer's questioning strategy and ratings. *Personnel Psychology, 38,* 321–334.

McIntyre, S.D., Moberg, I., & Posner, B.Z. (1980). Preferential treatment in preselection decisions according to sex and race. *Academy of Management Journal, 23,* 738–749.

Medical testing. (August 19, 1985), *Fortune, 112*(4), 58.

Milkovich, G.T., & Boudreau, I. (1988). *Personnel/human resource management: A diagnostic approach.* Plano, TX: Business Publications.

Newman, J.M., & Kryzstofiak, F. (1979). Self reports versus unobtrusive measures: Balancing method variables and ethical concerns in employment discrimination research. *Journal of Applied Psychology, 64,* 82–85.

Patrick, C.I., & Iacono, W.G. (1989). Psychopathy, threat, and polygraph test accuracy. *Journal of Applied Psychology, 74,* 347–355.

Pennsylvania Employment Law Letter. (1992). *2*(4).

Player, M.A. (1992). *Federal law of employment discrimination in a nut shell.* St. Paul, MN: West Publishing.

Public Law 100-347. (102.Stat. 646 et. seq. 29 U.S.C 2001 et. seq.).

Reilly, R.P., & Chao., G.T. (1982). Validity and fairness of some alternative employee selections procedures. *Personnel Psychology, 35,* 1–62.

Sackett, P.R., Burris, L.R., & Callahan, C. (1989). Integrity testing for personnel selection: An update. *Personnel Psychology, 34,* 791–804.

Sackett, P.R., & Harris, M.M. (1984). Honesty testing for personnel selection: A review and critique. *Personnel Psychology, 37,* 221–245.

Scandura, T.A. (1992). Mentorship and career mobility. *Journal of Organizational Behavior, 13*(2), 169–174.

Schmidt, F.L., & Hunter, J.E. (1984). Employment testing: Old theories and new research findings. In R.S. Schuler & S.A. Youngblood (Eds.), *Readings in personnel and human resource management* (2nd ed.) (pp. 200–212). St. Paul, MN: West Publishing.

Schmidt, F.L., Hunter J.E., McKensie, R.C. & Mildrow, T.W. (1979). Impact of valid selection procedures on workforce productivity. *Journal of Applied Psychology, 64,* 609–626.

Schmitt, N. (1976). Social and situational determinants of interview decisions: Implications for the employment interview. *Personnel Psychology, 29,* 79–102.

Society for Industrial and Organizational Psychology, Inc. (1987). *Principles for the validation and use of personnel selection procedures* (3rd ed.). College Park, MD: Author.

Souhrada, L. (1990). New job titles link business with patient care. *Hospitals, 64,* 88.

Springbett, B.M. (1958). Factors affecting the final decision in the employment interview. *Canadian Journal of Psychology, 12,* 13–22.

Taylor, H.C., & Russell, J.T. (1939). The relationship of validity coefficients to the practical effectiveness of tests in selection: Discussion and tables. *Journal of Applied Psychology, 23,* 565–578.

Thompson, D.E., & Christiansen, P.S. (1984). Court acceptance of Uniform Guidelines provisions. The bottom line and the search for alternatives. In R.S. Schuler & S.A. Youngblood (Eds.), *Readings in personnel and human resource management* (2nd ed.). St. Paul, MN: West Publishing.

Townsend, J.W. (1992). Is integrity testing useful? *HR Magazine, 96,* 32–38.

Turner, B.A. (1991). The psychological impact of the head nurse manager in transition: Organizational roles for minimizing stress. *Health Care Supervisor, 9*(3), 23–28.

U.S. Department of Labor, Manpower Administration. (1972). *Handbook for analyzing jobs.* Washington, DC: Government Printing Office.

U.S. Department of Labor (1977). *Dictionary of occupational titles.* Washington, DC: Government Printing Office.

Wards Cove Packing v. Antonio. (1989). (U.S. Supreme Court, No. 87-1387).

Wesley, K.N., Yukl, G.A., Kovacs, G.A., & Sanders, R.E. (1972). Importance of contrast effects in employment interviews. *Journal of Applied Psychology, 56,* 45–48.

CHAPTER

TRAINING AND DEVELOPMENT

Howard L. Smith

Myron D. Fottler

LEARNING OBJECTIVES

Upon completing this chapter, the reader should be able to . . .

- Describe and discuss the nature and significance of training and staff development in attaining strategic objectives.
- Describe, discuss, and implement the various components of an effective staff development program.
- Understand and anticipate future issues and trends in staff development.
- Understand what distinguishes more successful efforts to link staff development to attainment of the organization's strategic objectives.

INTRODUCTION

Training consists of planned programs designed to improve performance at the individual, group, and/or organizational levels. Improved performance in turn implies that there have been measurable changes in knowledge, skills, attitudes, and/or social behavior. Traditionally, lower-level employees were "trained" while higher-level employees were "developed." This distinction between the learning of hands-on skills versus interpersonal and decision-making skills, has become too imprecise to be useful. Thus, the terms *training* and *staff development* are used interchangeably in this chapter.

In most organizations, including those in the health services sector, employee training and staff development programs are an apparent enigma (Levine, 1981). On the one hand, such programs are prevalent in organizations. Few executives would admit that they lack a formal orientation, training, or staff development program. This is especially true in the health care field, in which continuing education is a requirement for many professional licenses. On the other hand, most executives would also admit that they do not believe their program is a primary strategic factor that is instrumental in achieving exceptional organizational performance. Health care executives need to fully contemplate this apparent paradox. If employee training and staff development programs are so prevalent in organizations, why are they not more highly valued for their contribution to organizational performance?

The answers to this question are varied, but they inevitably distill to one main idea. Employee training and staff development programs are undervalued because traditionally executives have not expected them to improve dramatically or otherwise affect organizational performance. As a result, most staff development programs have lived up (or down) to the expectations that have been set for them. Without an active incentive to perform otherwise, staff development programs have sought and attained mediocre performance. Naturally, there are exceptions to this generalization, but they are difficult to identify. As a rule, there has been little motivation for staff development programs either in health care or in business corporations to produce measurable improvements in employee or organizational performance. Without a proper incentive, many staff development programs have become complacent and content with less than extraordinary standards.

Any health care executive who is interested in the strategic management of people must at some point address the paradox presented by employee training and staff development programs. In short, such programs can be a liability, a minimal expectation, or an asset. Staff development programs are a liability when they excessively consume resources and do not offer an adequate return on investment. They represent a minimal expectation when they help health care professionals retain credentials or provide an adequate orientation to the new employee. However, these outcomes provide less than a health care executive should tolerate. At the very least, employee training and staff development programs should contribute extensively to an organization's strategic management. They should establish a foundation for excellence in personal, work unit, program, departmental, and organizational performance.

This chapter explores the nature and scope of employee training and staff development programs in health care organizations. An overview of staff development programs provides a complete understanding of the different dimensions such programs can assume within health care organizations. A rationale is presented for linking employee development to improved performance. This orientation underscores the discussion above in the sense that health care executives have expected too little in the way of meaningful results for too long from staff development programs. Yet, there are new forces in the health care organization environment that are instrumental in rectifying these past deficiencies.

This chapter also defines the primary components of a staff development program through a visual model. This model is primarily a tool to understand better the basic ingredients underlying a staff development program. The staff development needs of specific personnel in health care organizations—physicians, nurses, and administrators—are addressed in the context of fine-tuning development programs to meet the special needs of key professionals. Additionally, programmatic planning for staff development is elucidated in terms of setting objectives and assessing alternatives. Finally, the importance of assessing the performance of employee development programs is discussed, along with an exploration of feasible methodologies, anticipated outcomes, and managerial implications.

DEFINITIONS, GOALS, AND SIGNIFICANCE OF STAFF DEVELOPMENT

Employee development should be an integral aspect of the strategic management of organizations. By deriving the highest quality output attainable from each and every staff member, an organization is prepared to meet competition, respond to regulatory constraints, overcome reimbursement limitations, or address the key factors that eventually separate successful organizations from unsuccessful organizations. This conclusion is true for virtually every organization, but there is added significance for health care organizations in view of their labor intensity.

Before staff development can begin to attain its proper prominence in health care organizations, however, it is essential that executives understand the many different definitions and concepts of staff development (McGehee & Thayer, 1961; Snow & Grant, 1980; Swansburg, 1968). Without question, the term "staff development" means different things to different people. To some it may merely represent the introduction an employee receives on entering an organization. To another it may be training and skill development acquired throughout the job experience. To still another, employee development may imply a methodical effort to facilitate employee growth over the entire career span. Staff development consists of all of these efforts and more.

The challenge before health care executives is to understand the broader meaning of staff development not only as a concept, but also as a method for formulating and implementing the strategic direction of an organization. This can be accomplished only when executives are well-grounded in the continuum of concepts representing staff development. The goal is to envision the organization as a unique ensemble of human resources. As these resources develop and grow in depth, the beneficiary is ultimately the organization. Its capacities are much more robust, its set of skills more diverse and better prepared for utilization. In short, the organization becomes a logical extension of its human components. By developing the individuals who comprise the organization, staff development programs concomitantly nurture the growth of the parent organization.

The implications of this philosophical view for staff development are far-reaching. By viewing staff development as a strategic prerequisite for organizational development, a more realistic management approach can be conceived. Staff development is then recognized as one of the best means available to executives to actually shape the capability and identity of their organizations. This is consistent with the research on organization culture (e.g., Japanese management, searches for excellence), which suggests that exceptional organizational performance is not an artifact of human effort but is a distinct end result from human activity (Pascale & Athos, 1981; Peters & Waterman, 1982). Thus,

the organization can achieve excellence in low-cost, high-quality health care delivery (or other service and production efforts) only when the staff members comprising the organization are supported and encouraged in the pursuit of the limits of their abilities. By constantly raising these limits, staff development becomes a primary strategy for long-run excellence in organizational performance.

The Continuum of Staff Development

Just what constitutes staff or employee development? The terms need to be clarified before we progress further in the analysis of this strategic concept. The map for negotiating the terminology presented in Table 13.1 is not presumed to exhaust all possibilities, but it indicates a variety of employee training and staff development programs. In fact, there are so many programs that we offer some general categories that are most representative of the options normally available in organizations. It is our belief that Table 13.1 is a convenient beginning from which to create a staff development program: One or all of its options ultimately may provide the foundation for programmatic activity by an organization.

The implications from Table 13.1 for the strategic management of employee development programs are numerous, but one point should be underscored. There is no single best way to organize a staff development program. A contingency approach is preferred (Hofer, 1975). In other words, executives must examine the specific setting of an organization to determine what type of staff development program is appropriate. Relevant variables in that setting, such as task technol-

TABLE 13.1. Differentiating Employee Development Concepts

Concept	Objectives	Scope of Skill Diversity	Emphasis on Personal/Career Growth	Training Site	Frequency
Orientation training	To introduce staff to the mores, behaviors, and expectations of an organization	Narrow	Narrow	Internal	Single instance
Training	To teach staff specific skills, concepts, or attitudes			Internal	Sporadic
Inservice education	To teach staff members about skills, facts, attitudes, and behaviors largely through internal programs			Internal	Continuous
Continuing education	To facilitate the efforts of staff members to remain current in the knowledge base of their trade or profession through external programs designed to achieve external standards			External	Continuous
Career development	To expand the capabilities of staff beyond a narrow range of skills toward a more holistically prepared person	Broad	Broad	Internal and external	Continuous

ogy, type of service or product, number of employees, prior staff development program efforts, budgeted resources, extent of external constraints, organizational goals, and experience of the work force ultimately determine the nature of a staff development program for any specific organization. In some cases only an employee orientation program is needed. In other cases, a comprehensive program is appropriate. The program content, objectives, and scope of effort are contingent on the situation.

For example, a private group practice consisting of three pediatricians with two secretarial and two nursing staff members has decidedly unique staff development needs compared to a 30-physician, multispecialty group practice with 90 supporting staff members. Among the factors characterizing the pediatric group practice are the following: there are fewer resources available to fund staff development; no organizational administrative infrastructure is present to plan for

or acquire staff development resources; there is much closer supervision between the physicians and the support staff (thereby allowing more opportunities for on-the-job training); the physicians are positioned better to interpret performance variances or motivational difficulties and to react accordingly; and the set of skills needed to run the clinic is less diverse. Precisely the opposite can be said for the multispecialty group practice. It is a larger scale organization, and its staff development needs, correspondingly, are much more varied and complex. Hence, it must adopt an entirely different model if it expects to manage the strategic aspects of staff development.

Table 13.1 also implies that a number of terms are used interchangeably when referring to staff development. Employee development, staff development training, orientation, management development, inservice education, continuing education, and other terms are often used synonymously. In many cases, a person will use different terms to describe similar staff development efforts. The value of Table 13.1 is that it clarifies the diversity of terms and concepts. Because staff development programs are quite variable, it is vital to use the correct term with the appropriate concept. However, it is also possible to refer to the generic activity of orienting, training, teaching, or otherwise developing employees as staff development or employee development. We will use these terms interchangeably throughout this chapter to imply effort directed toward developing human resources.

As indicated in Table 13.1, at least five major staff development efforts should be identified on the continuum of an employee training and development program. These efforts are defined according to their respective objectives, scope of skill diversity, emphasis on personal and career growth, training site, and frequency. It is useful to repeat that a staff development program should be viewed as a continuum of programmatic effort. There is no single best way. In other words, training should not be evaluated as somehow less important for organizational performance than continuing education. In the right organizational context, a training program may indeed be even more valuable in contributing to organizational performance than a continuing education program.

Objectives

There is a range of objectives underlying staff development programs. Orientation training attempts to introduce staff to the values, mores, beliefs, behaviors, standard operating procedures, policies, and expectations of an organization. When a small nursing home expands its capacity by 30 beds,

for example, it must hire additional employees. All new employees may meet as a group to learn about the mission and goals of the nursing home, emphasis on patient satisfaction, as well as standard operating procedures for reporting to and leaving work and other prevalent policies needed to complete work each day. The new employees may be divided into smaller groups according to department to receive specific information needed for successful integration in their respective departments.

In contrast, career development is designed to continually expand the capabilities of staff beyond a narrow range of skills and toward a more comprehensive set of capabilities. Each employee is viewed as requiring continual nurturing in terms of education, training, mentoring, and experience in order to develop into a valuable asset to the organization. For example, the nursing home administrators in a large chain of nursing homes may receive periodic training and in-service education on specific managerial skills from the corporate office. They are also encouraged through a system of promotional incentives and reimbursement to continue their education at local universities. Additionally, a plan is developed for them to progress beyond the facility level to the corporate level. As should be apparent in Table 13.1, orientation training and career development are at opposite ends of a continuum because of the end results each strives to accomplish.

Increased competition for promotion, constant innovation in technology, pressure for equal employment opportunities, corporate mergers and restructuring, and employees' desires to get the most out of their careers are all major forces pushing all organizations to offer career development programs. Pressures of competition have also increased the desire of health care organizations to make better use of their employees' knowledge and skills and to retain those who are valuable to the organization. Career development programs can benefit managers, supervisors, subordinates, and the entire organization (Leibowitz, Farren, & Kaye, 1986).

It is, therefore, important that a career development program should be *viewed* as a dynamic process that attempts to meet the needs of managers, their subordinates, and the organization. Individual employees are responsible for initiating their own career planning. They need to identify their knowledge, skills, abilities, interests, and values in order to set goals and develop career plans. Managers should offer continuing assistance in the form of feedback on individual performance, information about the organization, job information, and information about career opportunities. The organization is responsible for supplying support for employee self-assessment, training, and development. Significant career growth can occur when individual initiative combines with organizational opportunity.

To succeed, a career development program requires management support, well-defined goals, effective communication, and compatible human resources policies. Such a program should include a comprehensive inventory of job opportunities with carefully organized progressions from one job to the next. Career development is a greater challenge in health care than it is in most other industries because of the extreme fragmentation of the occupational structure (Fottler, 1992). Consequently, in health care more effort must be expended to break down barriers among job families and to develop multiskilled job descriptions.

Training is generally focused on teaching staff members specific skills, concepts, or attitudes. For example, if the head nurse in the urology ward observes that some patients' catheters are becoming clogged after surgery, nurses may receive a 20-minute refresher course on the proper irrigation of catheters. Or, the admission clerks may receive 4 days of training about guest relations and insurance counseling. In these cases, the training serves to provide the employee with a specific skill or to reinforce previously learned behavior.

Inservice education is concerned with teaching staff members skills, facts, attitudes, behaviors, or concepts through largely internally designed programs. Inservice education is often confused with continuing education. Continuing education attempts to achieve broader professional or vocational requirements—usually according to externally established standards—than inservice education. In contrast, an inservice program addresses more specific skills, facts, attitudes, or behaviors through internally generated efforts. Continuing education usually relies on external training or education resources (e.g., college or university courses) to accomplish its objectives. In this sense, inservice education is more nearly aligned with training (i.e., emphasis is on learning specific facts or skills). Continuing education more closely approximates career development (i.e., in the course of continuous learning of relevant skills, facts, attitudes, concepts, or other knowledge, the staff member evolves as a person or a professional).

Skill Diversity and Personal Growth

Table 13.1 provides an overview of the variability among staff development concepts on the extent of skill diversity and emphasis on personal and career growth. Although not every staff development program can be neatly characterized in this manner, and there is much variance in how programs compare to the interpretations offered in Table 13.1, it is generally true that orientation training programs are narrow with respect to skill diversity and personal and career growth. By contrast, career development programs address a very broad scope of skill diversity. They also are directed toward a spectrum of personal or career growth subjects. The orientation program emphasizes one specific event in an employee's career—acquaintance with the employing organization. Career development emphasizes the evolution of employees and their careers. Granted, the initial orientation program is invaluable for getting off to a proper start, but it cannot replace the successive acquisition of a variety of skills that provide a foundation for personal growth.

Training Site and Frequency

Staff development programs generally can be offered through two basic methodologies. The training site may be either internal or external. Internally generated programs rely extensively on inhouse resources for education or training, and external programs mainly incorporate external resources, but the two forms are not necessarily mutually exclusive. Table 13.1, however, suggests the main emphasis for single programs of different types. Orientation training almost always incorporates onsite training, with internal personnel or staff presenting the content of the program. The same is typically true for training and inservice education programs. Continuing education programs, however, rely mainly on an external experience from professional societies or from teaching in-

stitutions to accomplish their goals. Career development combines both an extensive internal focus (i.e., heavy reliance on mentoring and job rotation) and an external focus (i.e., participation in professional societies and academic training).

The frequency of staff development programs also varies as indicated by Table 13.1. Orientation training usually happens once or is limited to a short series of courses during a relatively brief period. Career development, by way of comparison, begins when an employee joins an organization and continues until retirement. The frequency of application of the other staff development concepts varies from sporadic to continuous. The point is that the staff development program objective is the criterion that determines the frequency; there should be no preconceptions on this score.

Significance of Staff Development

There are five major reasons that health services organizations provide employee training and development. First, such training may improve employee performance. Employees who perform unsatisfactorily because of a deficiency in skills are prime candidates for training. Sometimes a new or newly promoted employee will not possess the skills and abilities required to be competent on the job. Although training cannot solve all problems of ineffective performance, a sound training and development is often instrumental in minimizing these problems.

Second, all employees need to continually update their skills in response to technological, organizational, and managerial changes. Such changes often change the design of jobs as new functions are added and old functions deleted. For example, the restructuring of health care organizations has created new positions, deleted others, and modified still others. Individuals employed in new and restructured positions are candidates for training or retraining.

Third, training may facilitate the solution of many organizational problems. Health care executives are expected to attain high goals in spite of personal conflicts, vague policies and standards, scheduling delays, inventory shortages, high levels of absenteeism and turnover, and a restrictive legal environment. Training is one important way to solve many of these problems.

Fourth, training can prepare employees for promotion. One important way to attract, retain, and motivate personnel is through a systematic program of career development. Promotion from within supported by an extensive training effort is an important component of a career development system. Organizations that fail to provide such a system often lose their most promising employees.

Fifth, training can be used to orient new employees. Most health care organizations make an effort to orient new employees to the organization and the job although the orientation may not necessarily be well done. The orientation process can reduce the difficulties encountered by new employees (Geromsi, 1989; Jones, 1986). Research shows that orientation programs can reduce employees' anxiety, save supervisor and coworker time, develop positive attitudes about the organization, and create realistic job expectations (Berger & Huchendorf, 1989; Gomersall & Myers, 1966; Marion & Frieb, 1969; Solomon, 1989).

Although the importance of staff development programs has already been alluded to, it is vital to underscore their strategic relevance. Such programs should provide a dis-

tinctive ability of organizations to perform better. In this sense, staff development is valuable because it helps organizations in the following areas:

- Accomplishment of work unit, departmental, and organizational goals
- Accomplishment of individual goals
- Integration of individual and organizational goals
- Implementation of a philosophy of human development within the organization culture

These factors make staff development invaluable to the health care organization facing a competitive market in which third-party reimbursement is increasingly constrained and large-scale corporations are actively involved.

Figure 13.1 captures the essence of the rising importance of staff development to organizational performance, namely that staff development programs should lead to better performance. It is this causal link, which heretofore has been neglected by staff development programs, their directors, and health care executives, that provides the strategic relevance of employee training and staff development programs. Quite simply, staff development programs have been permitted to languish in a state of mediocrity. As a result they have not promoted the type of organizational culture that is essential for attaining the highest levels of performance.

The strategic relevance of staff development programs must be founded on their ability to attain goals. This is the acid test of most organizational investments. However, staff development efforts can achieve the highest level of success when they also address the individuals comprising organiza-

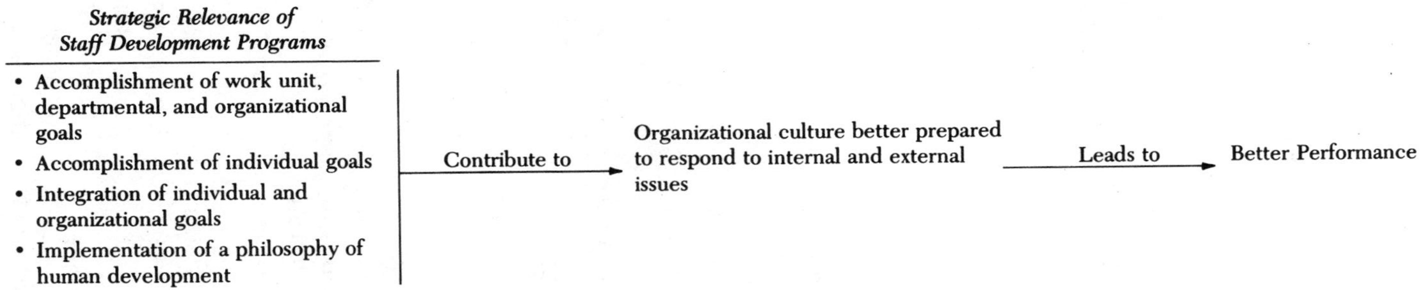

Strategic Relevance of
Staff Development Programs

- Accomplishment of work unit, departmental, and organizational goals
- Accomplishment of individual goals
- Integration of individual and organizational goals
- Implementation of a philosophy of human development

Contribute to →

Organizational culture better prepared to respond to internal and external issues

Leads to →

Better Performance

FIGURE 13.1. The causal link of staff development's strategic relevance to better performance.

tions. Consequently, these programs must primarily accomplish organizational goals while attending to the aspirations of individuals. Really effective employee training will help to integrate the individual and the organization. This is a very powerful combination. When employee and organizational interests coincide, there are phenomenal opportunities for instilling a corporate culture committed to excellence in performance, however those goals are defined.

With the proper combination of individual and organizational emphasis, it is apparent that the organization is interested in implementing a philosophy of human development. Health care executives need to take such a possibility into serious consideration. The creation of an organizational culture that supports the growth of its employees is more likely to be one that accomplishes goals while remaining flexible enough to address the challenges of the future. By investing in the development of its human resources, an organization automatically invests in its own future.

Figure 13.1 conveys these points graphically. The strategic relevance of staff development programs contributes to an organizational culture that is better prepared to respond to internal and external issues. In turn, this leads to better performance. This is the causal link. A focus on goal attainment nurtures an organizational culture that can meet the challenges of the organizational environment. In the final analysis, it is this culture that comes to represent the high standards of performance.

Organizational Goal Accomplishment

As far as organizations and their managers are concerned, the primary strategic value of staff development is that it facilitates goal accomplishment (Morrow-Winn, 1983). Specifically, *any* staff development program should produce such tangible end results as the following:

- Higher employee productivity
- Understanding and achievement of cost control
- Activation of employee responsibility for improving organizational services and performance
- Understanding and achievement of quality control
- Adaptability to change, resulting in constructive responses that build capacities for goal attainment
- Integration of personnel within a corporate culture that promotes organizational identity while underscoring service
- Knowledge of the need and mechanisms of attaining a mutually supportive work context that facilitates the completion of others' tasks as well as the accomplishment of individual tasks
- Ability to deliver optimal services and products given the constraints of budgeted resources
- Maximization of work unit goals without sacrificing departmental or organizational goals

Numerous other organizationally oriented end results are possible from staff development programs. However, the preceding list captures the essence of the *potential* organizational contribution from staff development. The strategic management problem for health care executives is to orchestrate their staff development efforts to achieve these outcomes (MacStravic, 1984).

The bottom line for staff development as

a strategic management issue is its capacity to facilitate attainment of work unit, departmental, or organizational goals. If a staff development program does not demonstrate this ability in today's health care environment, management must seriously assess whether the organization should be making any investment in the program. Most health care organizations no longer have the luxury of slack resources to waste on programs that do not provide an adequate return on investment. The ultimate validation of this capacity is attainment of prespecified goals.

Although organizational goal attainment is the focal point of staff development, health care executives should realize that conflicts may arise among work unit, departmental, and organizational goals. To a certain extent, staff development programs may help alleviate the contention among work unit, departmental, and organizational efforts. Normally, staff development is designed to help employees perform more effectively in their work units. Yet, the work unit exists only in program, departmental, and organizational contexts. Hence, the thrust of staff development should be to improve employee performance in a specific work unit, yet not at the expense of the department or the organization.

For example, the hospital pharmacy that instructs its staff in inventory control establishes a basis for exceptional cost control as a work unit. However, if the training encourages the pharmacy staff to institute an excessively elaborate system of control, it will be difficult for other personnel—nurses—to obtain patient medications, and the hospital will not want to accept the tradeoff of lower nurse productivity for the sake of a marginal decrease in pharmaceutical losses. In this illustration, the work unit (i.e., the pharmacy) is maximizing its goal attainment (i.e.,

inventory control) at the expense of other departments and the organization as a whole. Thus, staff development must secure organizational goal attainment within the context of supportive work units and departments.

Individual Goal Accomplishment

If staff development had the sole purpose of helping organizations to achieve their goals, it would be excessively unidimensional. For staff development to be meaningful to both organizations and individuals, it must provide for individual and organizational goal accomplishment (McConnell, 1984). To the extent that staff development can be designed to achieve this mutual goal orientation, employees will be more interested in deriving the most from the experience. This is only natural. When staff development is in tune with what employees want to attain during the course of their careers and employment, workers will be more likely to seriously invest the commitment necessary to improve their skills, behavior, attitude, or knowledge.

Does staff development always accomplish both employee and organizational goals in the best programs? Unfortunately, the answer to this question is no. There will always be cases of organizations that need employees to develop in some manner, yet employees are reluctant to make a conscientious effort in growth. For example, nursing staff may resist in-service training on how to handle troublesome or abusive patients because they are inundated by work and believe that the special demands of prima donnas are the responsibility of the psychological or psychiatric service.

Alternatively, the staff may desire training in how to handle the troublesome or abusive supervisor, but the employee training program does not have such a curriculum available, nor can it spare the expense necessary to generate it. In this case, the organization's staff development program conflicts with the individual goals of employees. Realistically, these conflicts between individual and organizational goals are bound to occur. However, it is incumbent on staff development directors to be sensitive to the individual goals of staff members. Organizational intentions should dominate staff development efforts, but they must be properly tempered by attention to individual goals. A harmonious balance will help promote greater commitment to the staff development program in the final analysis.

Integration of Individual and Organizational Goals

A staff development program can be invaluable in integrating individuals and organizations. The most prosperous organizations are those that are able to alleviate the contention between individual self-interest and organizational self-interest (Culbert & McDonough, 1980). Employees who are able to integrate their own goals within the context of an organization and its goals are more likely to perform better on the job. Staff development programs are merely one mechanism for achieving a satisfactory resolution of individual and organizational goals, but there is little question that they are strategic in this respect, given the extent to which staff development can clarify intentions and reinforce the rationale for efforts.

Implementation of Organizational Culture

Finally, staff development is conducive to implementing organizational culture. Such programs transmit the expectations and mores of an organization to new employees, reinforcing these norms throughout specific programmatic efforts. Through these and other mechanisms, staff development represents a philosophy of management on the part of an organization toward its employees. Such philosophies are beneficial in generating trust and confidence from employees toward the organization and its intended efforts.

To implement organizational culture effectively, staff development programs must be comprised of a full continuum of orientation, training, inservice and continuing education, and career development components. In other words, staff development programs must retain a consistent exposure to employees if they intend to contribute to defining and reinforcing an organization's culture. Incremental efforts will not accomplish results as effective or as durable as a planned and coordinated staff development program.

For example, consider the mental health clinic that has a staff development program consisting of orientation training and continuing education. What opportunities are there to instill or reinforce organizational culture? They are limited because the continuing education is obtained invariably from external sources that are unable to address the specific characteristics or context of the clinic. The orientation training is the only point of departure for explaining the existing culture. In contrast, a mental health clinic whose staff development program incorporates orientation training, training, inservice education, continuing education, and career development is better prepared to underscore its cultural expectations continuously and to thereby facilitate the shaping of a homogeneous culture.

INCENTIVES FOR UPGRADING STAFF DEVELOPMENT PROGRAMS

The incentives for upgrading the effort and resources organizations expend on their staff development programs are numerous, but there is one critical idea: namely, that the emphasis on staff development must undergo a metamorphosis. Staff development particularly should be seen from a strategic perspective. For years, health care organizations have approached staff development as a nonessential—an effort that is prevalent but not something to be nurtured, expanded, or otherwise cultivated. These low expectations and investments have yielded mediocre results. However, health care executives are beginning to realize that their organizations are comprised of human resources who make the difference between success and failure. Business organizations have always realized this because the role of the incentive system has always been paramount. Health care organizations are now confronting the matter of incentive systems, and the experience has altered many traditional expectations and perspectives.

The primary result for employee training from a new set of incentives in the health field is the metamorphosis of staff development, as portrayed in Figure 13.2. Most health care executives and their organizations have been unable to rise above a traditional view of staff development according to which there is no strategic emphasis to these programmatic efforts. Staff development has consistently been seen as a support or auxiliary function, subordinate to other critical operations of health care organizations. Essentially, staff development has been designed to address internal goals (i.e., training of employees in specific skills to help them perform their work tasks better or to maintain licensure or accreditation. In short, traditionally staff development programs have maintained a limited scope of effort. They have not been directly oriented to performance other than in very superficial ways.

Figure 13.2 indicates that several new incentives are prevalent in the health care field. The rise of competition, tighter operating margins, emphasis on performance, and a new vocabulary (describing new concepts) are forces reshaping the perception of many health care executives of staff development programs. In essence, a metamorphosis has been stimulated by the traditional view of staff development combined with the new incentives. The outcome is contemporary view of staff development.

The new age of staff development is decidedly a more exciting and more active period. Under the contemporary version, staff development maintains a strategic emphasis because of its performance orientation. In brief, contemporary staff development programs facilitate better performance by personnel and by the organization as a whole. In the contemporary version, staff development is designed to address internal and external goals. It has a much more comprehensive scope. It is directly linked to performance. These unique and meaningful changes in staff development have resulted from the pressures in the health care environment.

What are the new incentives in the health care system that demand upgrading staff development programs? Why has staff development gone from insignificance to strategic importance? The answers to these questions are related to several fundamental changes in the health system that threaten every provider.

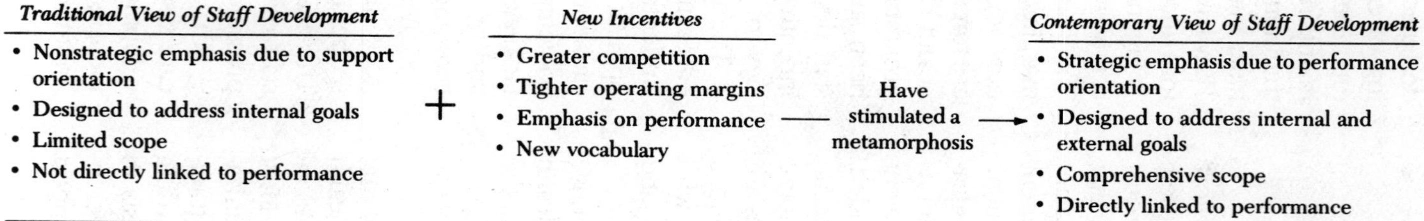

Traditional View of Staff Development

- Nonstrategic emphasis due to support orientation
- Designed to address internal goals
- Limited scope
- Not directly linked to performance

\+

New Incentives

- Greater competition
- Tighter operating margins
- Emphasis on performance
- New vocabulary

Have stimulated a metamorphosis ⟶

Contemporary View of Staff Development

- Strategic emphasis due to performance orientation
- Designed to address internal and external goals
- Comprehensive scope
- Directly linked to performance

FIGURE 13.2. The metamorphosis of staff development.

1. *Greater competition is now apparent in the health system because of deregulation, acceptance of marketing, corporate involvement and many other factors* (Smith & Reid, 1986). Health care organizations must form new strategic responses to competition. First, however, staff must be informed of the shift, and the plans to become competitive must be formed. In short, a new set of skills (i.e., in marketing) must be communicated to the staff, which must henceforth exercise them.

2. *Health care organizations are now facing tighter operating margins that emphasize efficiency, productivity, and profitability.* The fact is that consumers, employers, third parties, and the government are unable to continue funding rising health care costs. This has stimulated a number of policy changes by third-party insurers and the government. Most notable is the use of prospective pricing, which has reduced the possible margin on services (Smith & Fottler, 1985). There is less slack and more control over expenditures. To remain financially solvent, health care organizations must produce goods and services more efficiently. This is possible when staff are better trained because higher productivity and more efficient performance eventually add to profitability. However, fundamental to these achievements is more efficacious staff development, which recognizes the strategic ramifications of employee performance and is programmatically orchestrated to promote such ends.

3. *Health care organizations are demanding better performance from staff members because they recognize that investments in staff that are not accompanied by specific improvements are unwarranted.* This is evident in a variety of forms. Reduced budgetary slack in organizations implies that employees and organizational programs must produce more output per expenditure. For example, an investment in a non-revenue-generating program (e.g., staff development) must show a specific return on investment to justify the original expenditure; otherwise the investment should be reduced or terminated.

4. *Staff members need a new vocabulary and new skills to respond effectively to the new environment described above.* Consider some of the terms accompanying recent changes in this environment: competition, productivity, cost containment, marginal costs and benefits, prospective payment, efficiency, marketing, multi-institutional arrangements, profitability, and corporate infrastructure. For many health care professionals these are new terms. The related concepts are equally foreign to many health care staff members. Due to training in basic sciences, or lengthy exposure to the minimal demands of the traditional health care environment, staff members are uncertain about these changes or unable to respond to them in the most effective manner. They vitally need a new worldview. They must understand how to see the changes in terms of possible impacts on their areas of operation. They must know how to respond to such impacts for the benefit of their work unit, the department, and the organization.

The incentives mentioned above have placed staff development programs at a critical juncture. These programs can either respond in helping their organizations to meet new constraints or they can continue in the traditional mode of complacency and mediocrity. The choice is one of becoming involved in strategic management issues or of remaining a supporting program with little or no strategic importance.

The incentive for upgrading staff development programs is that without a specific contribution to organizational goals, such programs should be terminated. The resources should be reallocated to other programs managed by those who are interested in demonstrating a reasonable return on investment. This is a fairly threatening posture, but it is nonetheless a realistic one. Organizations in the health system simply cannot afford to fund programs that do not generate the results that allow goal accomplishment. The only catch to this posture is the licensing requirements of health facilities and professionals. At issue is the accreditation of a facility, which enables it to qualify for reimbursement. Hence, staff development (i.e., in-service education and continuing education) given to providers on the staff is essential for achieving other goals. This may be the salvation of staff development programs that have no intention of contributing to the strategic performance of their organizations. They must be retained to meet other needs.

In any event, the prognosis for health care organizations and staff development programs is certainly clear. They must attain high performance (Medearis & Popiel, 1975). The incentives are numerous and infallible. Without a timely and sufficient response from staff to these constraints, more organizations will face an uncertain future characterized by threatened financial solvency and inability to compete. Properly orchestrated staff development programs can play a significant role in strategically responding to these threats and incentives.

COMPONENTS OF EFFECTIVE STAFF DEVELOPMENT PROGRAMS

Given that health care organizations need to upgrade their staff development programs, what components should be managed in this endeavor? Figure 13.3 provides an overview of the primary components underlying an effective staff development program. Health care executives can use this model from two perspectives: first, to ensure that the content or programmatic infrastructure of their staff development effort includes each of these components, and second, to determine that the components have adequate resources for implementation.

Needs Assessment

Staff development begins and ends with needs assessment (Kirkpatrick, 1977; Moore & Dutton, 1978). Health care executives must adopt the philosophy that programmatic efforts are driven by need. There are at least two primary sources of need as suggested in Figure 13.3. Environmental assessment may identify relevant factors that force an organization to adopt a staff development program or to alter the content of an existing program.

For example, a chain of nursing homes faced with new licensing requirements for administrators should prepare to offer its existing and future administrators a method

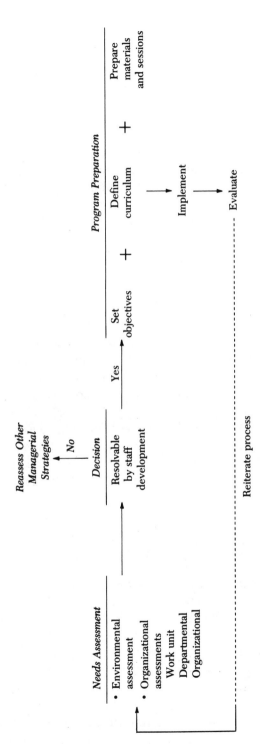

FIGURE 13.3. A visual model of staff development. (Smith, H.L. & Ebert, N.F. (1986). *The health care supervisor's guide to staff development.* Gaithersburg, MD: Aspen; reprinted with permission of Aspen Publishers, Inc., copyright © 1986).

for meeting these requirements. Thus an internal staff development program would be driven by the external regulatory licensing constraints. Or, suppose that a third-party payer proposes to introduce more stringent reviews of patient qualification for reimbursement of home health nursing services. A home health care agency would respond through a staff development program that teaches nurses to identify reimbursable patients. The point of these two illustrations is that external factors—legislation, reimbursement, technology, the marketplace, labor trends, or any other relevant environmental pressures—may force an organization to alter its staff development efforts. Creation of a staff development program's content should begin by assessing these external factors.

In addition to environmental assessment, organizational assessment is vital to health care organizations that are interested in creating effective staff development programs. This form of assessment is multidimensional and incorporates the work unit, departmental, and organizational levels. The differences in assessment at each of these levels can be summarized as follows:

1. *Work unit level.* Every work unit or team needs to determine the skills, knowledge, abilities, and attitudes that must be acquired or strengthened. Then the specific employees who need particular training must be identified so that the gap between actual and desired performance is reduced. There are numerous ways to collect such data, including advisory committees, assessment centers, attitude surveys, group discussions, employee interviews, exit interviews, management requests, observations of behavior, performance appraisals, performance documents, questionnaires, skills tests, and new strategic thrusts (Newstrom & Lilyquist, 1979; Ulschak, 1983). The specification of objectives facilitates needs assessment if the objectives are defined in terms of measurable end results that must be accomplished during a specific time period. When these objectives (i.e., patient satisfaction) are not being met, the supervisor can determine why (i.e., whether the problem is a lack of training). Problems amenable to training can then form the basis for training program content.

2. *Departmental level.* Every department should be guided by a set of specific goals or objectives, just as work units are meant to follow specific guidelines. The measures may be different at the departmental level compared to work units but the principle is the same. Having measurable standards facilitates the identification of substandard or deviant performance. After deviations have been identified, staff development curricula can be formulated to help resolve the causal factors that are amenable to training, education, mentoring, or other learning methodologies. Positive deviations (e.g., remaining under budget) can also be examined to ascertain the causal factor and, where appropriate, generalized through staff development to other department heads.

3. *Organizational level.* Just as every work unit and department should be guided by preset goals and objectives, so too should the entire organization. Obviously, if such standards are not available, an executive will experience great difficulty in defining problems in performance. At the organizational level, there is a greater departure in the intention of staff development than at the work unit or departmental levels. The causes of performance deficiencies at the organiza-

tional level may be result of the cumulative problems at the other levels. Furthermore, there are fewer managers responsible for performance at the organizational level. This means that staff development will have to focus on a few recipients. Moreover, the type of staff development needed at the organizational level will probably be at the most complex end of the continuum—career development or management development. Only in large multiorganizational firms does staff development at the organizational level approximate that for the work unit and departmental levels. Whatever the case may be, it is important that needs be assessed to guide program context.

In sum, organizational assessment attempts to explain why individuals or components of an organization are unable to perform at desired levels. Where those factors are amenable to staff development, it is possible to conceive a program for resolution.

The Decision to Institute or Modify a Program

The next major component of the staff development model in Figure 13.3 is the decision to institute or modify a staff development program. As the preceding discussion suggests, not every problem in a work unit, department, or organization can be rectified through staff development. The many determinants of effective performance include, but are not limited to, the following:

- Organizational structure
- Rewards and compensation
- Leadership style
- Extent of resource support
- Available technology

- Extent of planning (i.e., specification of goals and objectives)
- Control
- Impact of external forces (e.g., market competition)

These are only a few of the categories of variables that might produce an undesired impact on staff attempts to provide products or services. For example, an organization will not want to invest substantial money in altering its staff development program if poor performance is due to inadequate rewards, rather than inability on the part of personnel.

Program Preparation

Assuming that the performance problem of personnel is treatable through staff development, the next step is to prepare the program. Depending on the scope of previous staff development efforts, the degree of fine-tuning required may be limited. In other cases extensive modification in the staff development program may be needed. In any case, the preparation of a staff development program centers on three activities (Kirkpatrick, 1978; Newell, 1976).

1. *Setting objectives.* A staff development program should incorporate a specific set of measurable objectives that it will attempt to achieve during a specified time period. This is difficult because in the past there have been few expectations for employee training programs in health care organizations. Hence, there has been neither goal specification nor measurement of goal accomplishment. Consequently, there may be considerable work to be completed in setting measurable objectives. Remember that staff

development is often a rather abstract effort. It is difficult to measure skill or educational (i.e., knowledge) attainment precisely. Furthermore, there is the issue of knowledge decay, which may moderate the measurable results achieved in a training program. The best staff development programs will set objectives that relate not only to individual improvement (i.e., skill or knowledge development) but also to improvement in departmental and organizational performance.

2. *Defining curriculum.* The curriculum of a staff development program should be associated with identified needs and specified objectives. After these basic guidelines have been clarified, it is possible to determine the feasible alternatives for resolving a staff development deficit. At this point the issue of using inhouse or external trainers is vital to curriculum development. Inhouse resources are valuable in adapting a program to specific needs. However, the training skills may not exist in the organization, or those who have the knowledge may not be available to conduct the training. For example, assume that a group of physician executives vitally needs training on preparing and using budgets but the chief financial officer or the financial staff are too busy to provide sessions on budgeting. The organization may have to go outside to procure the needed training skills. There are many options and costs associated with using external sources.

3. *Preparing materials.* The final step in program preparation is to accumulate necessary training materials and to schedule the sessions in an environment that facilitates, rather than hinders, effective training. To a large extent these details depend on the specific instructor or trainer and the methods of instruction chosen to accomplish the objectives.

Program preparation is obviously a significant element in staff development. Entire books have been written on the three phases of program preparation mentioned above (Smith & Elbert, 1986). Interested readers should turn to these resources to clarify any of the programmatic stages.

Implementation

After a program has been defined it must be implemented, and implementation calls for a satisfactory budget to support the program. This is a critical premise that is not fulfilled automatically in today's health care environment. Although health care organizations have traditionally supported staff development, mainly in the form of inservice education, there is no certainty that such support will continue as it has in the past. In fact, the second step in Figure 13.3 assumes that if the employee performance problem is resolvable through staff development, resources will be available to fund the proper programmatic response. This assumption may be unwarranted in health care organizations that are encountering extreme difficulty in meeting budget targets. More often than not the slack has already been cut out of health organization budgets; hence, there are few resources available to expand staff development programs. Therefore, staff development programs must become more efficient and effective in their own stewardship of budgeted allocations.

In addition to economic resources, the implementation stage requires health care organizations to choose among the various types of on-the-job and off-the-job training techniques. On-the-job training is job instruction normally given by an employees' supervisor or an experienced employee. The Bureau of National Affairs (1975) reports that

90% or more of all training is performed on the job. Some common techniques include orientation training, apprenticeship, job rotation, enlarged job responsibilities, job instruction, learner-controlled instruction, committee assignments, understudy assignments, on-the-job coaching, and performance appraisal. The widespread use of on-the-job training is due to the many benefits it offers, including the following:

- Employees are doing the actual work rather than hypothetical or simulated tasks.
- Employees receive instructions from an experienced employee or supervisor who has performed the task successfully.
- The training is performed in the actual work environment under normal working conditions and requires no special training facilities.
- The training is informal, relatively inexpensive, and easy to schedule.
- The training may build cooperative relationships between the employee and the trainer.

Among the potential liabilities of on-the-job training are the following:

- The trainer may not be motivated to train or to accept the responsibility for training.
- The trainer may perform the job well but lack the ability to teach others how to do so.
- The trainer may not have the time to train and may omit important elements of the training process.
- Although the employee is learning on the job, resources may be used inefficiently, initial performance will be low, and costly errors may be made.

Off-the-job training is any form of training performed away from the employees' work area. Two categories of off-the-job training programs exist: 1) inhouse programs that are conducted within that company's training facility; and 2) off-site programs that are held away from the organization and sponsored by a professional association, educational institution, or independent training firm.

A variety of training methods are employed to train employees off the job including lectures, conferences, discussions, correspondence courses, audiovisual techniques (i.e., videotape, closed-circuit television, films, slides, and flipcharts), sensitivity training, vestibule training, organizational development (i.e., systematic, long-range programs of organizational improvement), programmed instruction, computer-assisted instruction, and simulation methods (i.e., case method, role-playing, in-booklet technique, and business games). The potential benefits of off-the-job training include the following:

- This training is cost-efficient because groups, rather than individuals, are usually trained.
- Trainers are likely to be more competent than on-the-job trainers who normally spend only a fraction of their time training.
- More planning and organization often go into on-the-job training.
- The trainees learn in an environment free from the normal pressures and interruptions of the work place.
- Off-site courses and seminars enable small organizations with limited resources to train employees without the formidable expenses of a large training staff and training facilities.

Potential disadvantages include the following:

- Off-the-job training is typically more expensive than on-the-job training.
- Because employees attending off-the-job training are not performing their jobs, there is a greater opportunity cost of lost production.
- Off-the-job training often has problems of transfer of learning. Because it is impossible for the trainer to customize training for each participant, such programs normally contain limited applications for a trainees' specific problems and situations.

To choose the training method or combination of methods that best fits a given situation, what is to be taught must first be defined carefully in the needs assessment phase. Only then can the method be chosen that best fits these requirements. To be useful, the chosen method should do the following:

- Motivate the employee to improve his or her performance
- Clearly illustrate desired skills
- Provide for active participation by the participant
- Provide an opportunity to practice
- Provide timely feedback on the trainees' performance
- Provide some means for reinforcement during learning
- Be structured from simple to complex tasks
- Be adaptable to specific problems
- Encourage positive transfer from the training to the job

Evaluation and Control

The final, but certainly not the least important, step in the visual model of staff development is evaluation and control of program performance. This is undoubtedly the most abused step in the model. Few executives have been concerned about the ability of staff development programs to produce proper results. These attitudes are rapidly changing, however, as health care organizations confront tighter budgets and as they begin to envision the capacity of staff development programs to offer strategic capabilities.

Many methods and measures are available for evaluating the impact of staff development programs. Among the more frequent measures are the following:

1. *Participant reaction,* in which the participants' feelings about the program are usually measured by participant questionnaires
2. *Participant learning,* in which the degree to which participants have mastered the concepts, information, and skills that the training tried to impose is usually assessed by testing the participant both before and after a program
3. *Participant on-the-job behavior and performance,* in which positive change in job behavior based on information gathered from peers, supervisors, subordinates, and customers is usually measured by performance appraisals before and after training
4. *Organizational goal attainment,* in which the impact on organizational goals such as cost savings, profits, productivity, turnover, absenteeism,

accidents, grievances, job satisfaction, and other employee attitudes is usually measured through comparing data in organizational records and questionnaires before and after training

Most organizations utilize some combination of the four methods listed above, with an emphasis on the first. Assuming that an organization has an active planning and control system in which goals are restated continually, performance is measured, and actions are taken to rectify deviations from preestablished standards, the best measure of staff development centers on changes in goal attainment. However, this is also the most difficult means by which to measure.

A working knowledge of evaluation methodologies is the fundamental basis for prudent assessment of staff development program efforts. An overview of such methodologies is beyond the scope of this chapter. Nonetheless, health care managers should recognize that the acid test of a staff development program is the ability to change—to improve—performance toward goals. Without documentation that relies on proper methodology for its conclusions, staff development will remain an expendable activity. Therefore, it is essential that evaluation methodologies be invoked to promote a clear understanding of the relevant accomplishments that justify continued resources allocations to staff development.

TRENDS IN STAFF DEVELOPMENT

What are the future trends in staff development in health care services? As noted in Chapters 1, 2, and 8, both economic and demographic trends suggest radical changes in the future composition of the work force. Other factors affecting the number, types, and requirements of available jobs include technological change and continuing worker displacement as a function of mergers, acquisitions, and downsizing (Cascio & Zammurto, 1989; Fiske, 1989).

These environmental trends suggest several reasons that the time and money budgeted for training will increase during the remainder of the 1990s (Goldstein & Gilliam, 1990):

1. The number of unskilled and undereducated youth who will be needed for entry-level jobs
2. Increasingly sophisticated technological systems that will impose training and retraining requirements on the existing work force
3. The need to train currently underutilized minorities, women, and older workers

These changes suggest a dual responsibility: the organization is responsible for growth and change, and the individual is responsible for deriving maximum benefits from these opportunities.

As this chapter has tried to convey, there is a new attitude developing among personnel directors, human resources managers, staff development directors, directors of inservice education, and health care executives in general. This new attitude indicates that a revolution has beset employee training and development. The revolution has already occurred as a result of the forces and incentives mentioned throughout this chapter. The only question remaining is the extent to which each health care organization and its managerial staff will build on these changes to significantly upgrade the content and expectations of staff development programs. A significant challenge is to reshape such programs to make a viable contribution to the strategic management of an organization. In all practicality, this process of reshaping will begin with the program content suggested in Table 13.2 (Odiorne, 1980; Von Glinow, Driver, Brousseau, & Prince, 1980; Wehrenberg, 1983).

There is a major philosophical trend conveyed in Table 13.2 that before the early 1980s would not have been evident. Until the rise of corporate involvement, competition, prospective pricing, marketing, deregulation, and multi-institutional arrangements in the early 1980s, staff development programs tended to differentiate between the content and orientation of employee training for clinical and for nonclinical personnel. For example, physicians and nurses would receive one orientation, and supervisors, operating personnel, and management staff would receive another. In many cases, the clinical program content was viewed as rigorous and a significant contribution to professional growth. The nonclinical program content was often

seen as less demanding and more oriented to less relevant finishing touches on employee development.

Although the curricula of staff development programs in health care organizations continue to be structured around the clinical-nonclinical difference, it is apparent that the health services sector has experienced changes that dramatically influence the entire approach to staff development. Hence, the programmatic content of staff development programs is also changing. This is conveyed in Table 13.2.

A significant problem for staff development programs in the future is the need to differentiate among categories of personnel. The most prevalent distinction has been between clinical and nonclinical personnel. This differentiating mechanism has been useful because of the professional licensing requirements often existing for medical practitioners and ancillary medical services personnel. However, this method of distinguishing personnel is beginning to break down as nonclinical staff pursue their own credentials and as clinical personnel seek skills formerly not related to clinical training. The end result of this trend, which is likely to

TABLE 13.2. Trends Reshaping the Content of Staff Development Programs in Health Care

From	To
Past Orientation of Program Content in Staff Development	Future Orientation of Program Content in Staff Development
Clinical staff requires complex training; nonclinicians require less complex development	All staff require complex program context; distinction between clinical and nonclinical staff must become less meaningful
Clinicians do not cross over into nonclinical areas; nonclinicians do not cross over into clinical areas	Clinicians and nonclinicians frequently share in the delivery of services
Personnel are narrowly focused on one profession or vocation	Personnel are well-educated and may be interested in pursuing several careers
Knowledge base is relatively stable except in clinical areas	The half-life of knowledge is rapidly decreasing for many health care vocations

continue, is that staff development programs must fill a greater diversity of needs. In short, the staff development program of the future is challenged to incorporate a variety of curricula and plans for development or training.

A case in point is clearly seen in many administrative positions, such as nursing home administrators. The professional licensure requirements have been raised gradually, and today's licensed nursing home administrator is well-educated. Many of these professionals have a continuing need to expand their knowledge and skills. Fortunately, they are given excellent motivation to pursue additional development from licensure requirements for continuing education. Certainly, many professionals, whether nursing home administrators, hospital administrators, or clinicians, may perceive that they do not require further education or training. For them, the issue is to ascertain the easiest way of fulfilling such requirements. But others are conscientious and concerned about obtaining the highest possible return on their time invested.

The preceding illustration demonstrates that staff development programs will increasingly need to address the career development of professionals—whether clinical or nonclinical. This trend must be integrated with the rising education level of staff in general. The evidence clearly suggests that workers are more highly educated today than ever before. A more highly educated work force is likely to remain interested in developing skills and knowledge during an entire career rather than acquiring just enough information and credentialing to permit their learning to terminate on employment.

To these trends must be added the decreasing half-life of knowledge in many vocations and professions. It is a blessing but also a problem that knowledge in the health professions is expanding at a phenomenal rate. For staff, the implication is that their knowledge will become obsolete more quickly. Hence, they must continually and conveniently upgrade their knowledge base. It should be clear to all who enter a highly technical field that they are accepting a significant responsibility for remaining current in the future. If there are no licensure requirements, this responsibility is a personal one. But in any environment in which knowledge changes rapidly (e.g., computer specialties), to forego continuing development because there are no licensing requirements would seriously undermine potential job effectiveness.

The implications of these trends for staff development planning are numerous. Above all, staff development programs will certainly be forced to grow in their scope of operations. Very simply, staff needs will be much more comprehensive and complex than before. As a result, these programs must begin to develop a more realistic array of options for filling staff development needs from both internal and external means. It is likely that greater emphasis will be given to continuing education and career development. Yet, at the present time, these components of staff development are managed on an ad hoc and very rudimentary level by health care organizations. More often than not there is no plan other than possibly reimbursing professionals when they obtain external training (e.g., college credits). There is little or no control over where, how, or from whom the education is obtained. The inference is that something must be better than nothing.

Staff development programs will also witness the problem of multiple careers among personnel. Increasingly, professionals and nonprofessionals are trying several careers. This is a distinct challenge to staff development programs that have been built on the traditional concept of one person remaining with one vocation. For example, some physicians and nurses are being attracted to the managerial ranks. How will they perform these administrative, managerial, and executive responsibilities effectively unless they are prepared with appropriate knowledge? There no longer is a guarantee that clinicians will remain clinicians. Nurse and physician executives are increasingly prevalent; to contribute effectively to an organization in a managerial capacity, they must be trained in the basics of management theory and practice, and their skills must be fine-tuned as they gain experience. Again, this presents a unique and challenging future to staff development.

Tom Peters (1987) claims that American investment in training is a "disgrace" (pp. 391–394) and offers the following 10 critical ingredients of successful training in the future:

1. Focus extensive entry-level training on those skills that "overemphasize" the company's uniqueness.
2. Treat all employees as potential career employees and train them in the context of career development.
3. Require regular retraining for all employees.
4. Spend time and money generously on training that is of a high quality and is effective.
5. Make sure managers are good coaches and evaluate them on their effectiveness as trainers.
6. Understand that there is no limit to the skills that can be taught.
7. Consider training an important part of the organization's strategic thrust.
8. Emphasize training during times of crisis.
9. Involve line managers fully in planning the content of training and teaching.
10. Use training to teach organizational vision and values.

One survey of corporate staff development practices found that several characteristics seem to distinguish companies with the most effective practices (Sirota, Alper, & Pfau, Inc., 1989):

- Top management is committed to training and development.
- Training is part of the corporate culture.
- Training is tied to business strategy, objectives, and bottom-line results.
- A comprehensive and systematic approach to training exists.
- Training and retraining are done at all levels on a continuous, ongoing basis.
- There is a commitment to invest the necessary resources in terms of time and money.

These characteristics, in conjunction with Tom Peters' (1987) 10 success factors, might constitute a model for future staff development programs.

A STRATEGIC POSTURE

Many pressures are confronting health care organizations. To the extent that these pressures are addressed adequately, it is likely that most organizations will thrive and prosper. Perhaps more than any other variable, it is going to be people—staff—who make or break health care organizations. To this point, however, health care organizations have done little to help prepare their human resources for the present and future challenges. The result is that many organizations cope with their internal and external demands inefficiently and ineffectively.

To be effective, staff development must be tied to the overall strategic objectives of the organization. To many in the health care field, the proposition that staff development programs should become a strategic factor in responding to these challenges would seem ludicrous. After all, staff development programs have occupied the backwaters of most health care organizations. They have been poorly planned and underfunded and more an ornament than a strategic resource for organizations. If a staff development program maintains this reputation, serious consideration should be given to paring it to the bone. Health care organizations do not have slack resources to waste. However, it is possible with sufficiently rigorous thinking to transform a staff development program into the sort of strategic tool that supports a vibrant response to present and future challenges presented in the health care environment.

Perhaps more than any other factor, health care managers will have to battle the stereotype that surrounds staff development programs before the strategic relevance of these programs will be understood. Commitment to staff development by top management echelons is a necessary ingredient. Throwing more money into programmatic efforts is only a partial answer. Top managers must reinforce the priority of staff development in the distribution of rewards and incentives (e.g., for participation and subsequent improvement in performance) to personnel as well as by their rhetoric. Through such postures, staff eventually will recognize that training and development are not superfluous extras, but prime ingredients underlying an organization's effort to remain competitive in the challenging environment confronting health care organizations.

Three caveats regarding staff development are in order. First, the process of staff development is both costly and time-consuming. Moreover, in times of fast growth or rapidly changing technology, hiring skilled employees from the outside may be the only way to acquire the needed expertise. Staff development may take too much time. Finally, staff development efforts may be counterproductive unless promotional opportunities are available. Otherwise, the best employees will leave.

SUMMARY

Inservice education, training, staff development, and employee orientation are all elements that may comprise an employee training or staff development program. This chapter defines and differentiates each of these programmatic activities to provide managers a better understanding of their role in health care organizations. An effective training or staff development program is predicated on using each of these elements to accomplish specific predetermined objectives.

Training and development programs have seldom lived up to their expectations because health care managers have not envisioned the programs in a strategic sense. For example, inservice education has been viewed as a mechanism to maintain accreditation and professional licensure. Yet, inservice education has seldom been incorporated within the strategic plans of health care organizations. This tendency has developed because managers believe that inservice education, orientation, training, and development are activities that contribute in a minor way to accomplishment or organizational goals such as quality of care or cost control. Consequently, training and development programs are seen as expendable programmatic efforts with a low priority.

Prudent use of training and development programs can promote attainment of individual, work unit, departmental, and organizational goals if they incorporate a number of specific components discussed in this chapter, namely the following:

1. Needs assessment to identify threats, opportunities, strengths, and weaknesses
2. Consideration of the relevance of staff development in resolving problems identified in the needs assessment
3. Program formulation including setting objectives, defining curriculum, and preparing sessions
4. Implementation of the program
5. Evaluation and control to improve programmatic efforts

These components represent the basic framework for strengthening the contribution made by training and development programs.

There are many factors that stimulate the need for more effective staff development programs in health care. These include greater competition, tighter operating margins, an emphasis on performance, and new concepts of health delivery. Health care organizations vitally need their employees to be more productive in delivering quality services at reasonable cost. Staff development programs can facilitate attainment of these goals when they have a comprehensive scope, are designed to address internal and external goals, are directly linked to performance, and receive a strategic emphasis because they help employees perform better. This chapter provides several guidelines for improving the structure and use of staff development programs.

Discussion Questions

1. What are the major purposes of training and staff development? What environmental forces have made staff development even more important than in the past?
2. Describe the activities involved in each phase of the training process.
3. Describe the various levels for evaluating training effectiveness. How would you evaluate the effectiveness of a program to train supervisors to appraise employee performance better?
4. If you were a newly appointed training director for a medium-size hospital (500 employees and 200 beds), how would you communicate the importance of training to top management?
5. Describe the various types of on-the-job and off-the-job training. What are the advantages and disadvantages of on-the-job versus off-the-job training?
6. What are the future trends in training development? How would you structure

a staff development program to reflect these trends?

CASE: RIO GRANDE MEDICAL GROUP

Rio Grande Medical Group (RGMG) is a multispeciality group practice of 35 physicians located in southwestern Texas in a city with a 325,000 population. The metropolitan area has a population to physician ratio of 330 to 1. Furthermore, the level of overt advertising from health providers is quite significant. Hospitals, prepaid health plans, medical groups, small group practices, and even solo practitioners are competing for patients.

RGMG has always been managed by physicians. The original founder of the group practice in 1935 was Dr. William Thomas. Currently, the chief executive officer is Dr. Geremy Thomas, the son of the founder. The group started with three physicians who were general practitioners and has prospered due to the high-quality care and personalized service given to patients. However, since the number of physicians on the medical staff reached 20, the organization has increasingly encountered significant management problems in cost control, patient relations, and personnel interaction (particularly between physicians and nursing staff). In order to rectify these problems, the group has departmentalized around the following clinical areas (The number of physicians in each department is noted in parentheses.):

- Obstetrics and gynecology (7)
- Pediatrics (9)
- General practice (10)
- Urology (3)
- Orthopedics (6)

Each department is headed by a clinical department head.

Dr. Thomas has observed that the clinical department heads have great difficulty in establishing productivity goals for staff, in controlling costs (i.e., remaining within budgets), and in mentoring staff to respect patient expectations. Considering these problems as well as those mentioned above, Dr. Thomas has decided that the clinical department heads need to receive managerial training.

Case Discussion Question

1. Outline a proposal (including objectives, curriculum, budget, and faculty skills required) for a 10-session (4 hours each) training program to be presented to Dr. Thomas. Be certain to provide Dr. Thomas with a compelling rationale regarding why this proposed program would not merely be throwing money at the problem.

REFERENCES

Berger, S., & Huchendorf, K. (1989). Ongoing orientation at Metropolitan Life. *Personnel Journal, 68*, 28–35.

Bureau of National Affairs. (1975). On-the-job training. *Personnel Management,* Washington, DC: Author.

Cascio, W.F., & Zammurto, R.F. (1989). Societal trends and staffing policies. In W.F. Cascio (Ed.), *Human resource planning, employment, and placement* (pp. 2–1 to 2–33). Washington, DC: Bureau of National Affairs.

Culbert, S.A., & McDonough, J.J. (1980). *The invisible war.* New York: Wiley.

Fiske, E.B. (1989, September 25). Impending U.S. jobs disaster: Work force unqualified to work. *The New York Times,* p. A1, B6.

Fottler, M.D. (1992). The evolution of manpower utilization patterns in health services and American industry. In K.D. Blayney (Ed.), *Healing hands: Customizing your health team for institutional survival* (pp. 1–23). Battle Creek, MI: Kellogg Foundation.

Geromsi, G. (1989). A good start for new hires. *Nations Business,* 21–22.

Goldstein, I.L., & Gilliam, P. (1990). Training system issues in the year 2000. *American Psychologist, 45,* 134–143.

Gomersall, E.R., & Myers, M.S. (1966). Breakthrough in on-the-job training. *Harvard Business Review, 44*(1), 62–71.

Hofer, C.W. (1975). Toward contingency theory of business strategy. *Academy of Management Journal, 18,* 784–810.

Jones, G.R. (1986). Socialization tactics, self-efficiency, and newcomers. *Academy of Management Journal, 29,* 262–279.

Kirkpatrick, D.L. (1977). Determining training needs: Four simple and effective approaches. *Training and Development Journal, 31,* 22–25.

Kirkpatrick, D.L. (1978). Developing an in-house program. *Training and Development Journal, 32,* 40–43.

Leibowitz, Z.B., Farren, C., & Kaye, B.L. (1986). *Designing career development systems.* San Francisco: Jossey-Bass.

Levine, H.Z. (1981). Consensus: Employee training programs. *Personnel, 58,* 4–11.

MacStravic, R.E.S. (1984). Performance auditing for health care supervisors. *Health Care Supervisors, 2,* 29–38.

Marion, B.W., & Frieb, S.E. (1969). Job orientation: A factor in employee performance and turnover. *Personnel Journal, 48,* 799–804.

McConnell, C.R. (1984). Employee training: The shape of things to come. *Health Care Supervisor, 2,* 29–38.

McGehee, W., & Thayer, P.W. (1961). *Training in business and industry.* New York: Wiley.

Medearis, N.D., & Popiel, E.S. (1975). Guidelines for organizing inservice education. In *Staff development* (pp. 2–8). Wakefield, MA: Contemporary Publishing.

Moore, M.L., & Dutton, P. (1978). Training

needs analysis: Review and critique. *Academy of Management Review, 3,* 532–545.

Morrow-Winn, G. (1983). Staff development—More management than training. *Nursing Homes, 32,* 6–11.

Newell, G.E. (1976). How to plan a training program. *Personnel Journal, 55,* 220–225.

Newstrom, J.W., & Lilyquist, J.M. (1979). Selecting needs analysis methods. *Training and Development Journal, 33,* 178–182.

Odiorne, G.S. (1980). Training to be ready for the 90s. *Training and Development Journal, 34,* 12–20.

Pascale, R.T., & Athos, A.G. (1981). *The art of Japanese management: Applications for American executives.* New York: Warner.

Peters, T.J. (1987). *Thriving on chaos.* New York: Harper & Row.

Peters, T.J., & Waterman, R.H. (1982). *In search of excellence.* New York: Harper & Row.

Sirota, Alper, & Pfau, Inc. (1989). *Report on respondents: Survey of views toward education and training practices.* New York: Author.

Smith, H.L., & Elbert, E.F. (1986). *The health care supervisor's guide to staff development.* Rockville, MD: Aspen.

Smith, H.L., & Fottler, M.D. (1985). *Prospective payment.* Rockville, MD: Aspen.

Smith, H.L., & Reid, R.A. (1986). *Competitive hospitals.* Rockville, MD: Aspen.

Snow, C.C., & Grant, J.T. (1980). Answers to questions about management development programs. *Hospitals and Health Services Administration Quarterly, 25,* 36–53.

Solomon, C.M. (1989). How does Disney do it? *Personnel Journal, 68,* 50–57.

Swansburg, R.C. (1968). *Inservice education.* New York: G.P. Putnam's Sons.

Ulschak, F.L. (1983). *Human resources development: The theory and practice of need assessment.* Reston, VA: Reston.

Von Glinow, M.A., Driver, M.J., Brousseau, K., & Prince, J.B. (1980). The design of a career-oriented human resource system. *Academy of Management Review, 5,* 23–32.

Wehrenberg, S.B. (1983). Training megatrends. *Personnel Journal, 62,* 279–280.

CHAPTER

PERFORMANCE APPRAISAL

Charles L. Joiner

John C. Hyde

LEARNING OBJECTIVES

Upon completing this chapter, the reader should be able to . . .

- Explain in detail and evaluate the various forms of performance appraisal systems and determine which systems are best suited for individual departments in the health care setting.
- Understand the linkage between performance appraisal and health care management, visualize this connection, and develop management plans that address this vital linkage.
- Describe the legal constraints that apply to performance appraisal based on actual job-related criteria.
- Place performance appraisal in the overall scheme of total quality management (TQM) and continuous quality improvement (CQI) within the organizational environment; relate the various aspects of performance appraisal with mandated Joint Commission on the Accreditation of Healthcare Organizations (JCAHO) quality standards and how organizations must incorporate these criteria in performance appraisal development.

INTRODUCTION

It continues to remain a mandate that today's health managers are under extreme pressure to contain costs and improve efficiency of operations. They may be the most constrained of all corporate executives. To be competitive in the health industry, these managers must develop and adopt new methods and techniques to improve the performance of their organizations. Before pro-spective reimbursement systems were implemented, many health executives generally ignored industrial models of management practice. However, much has occurred in recent years to push the management of for-profit and not-for-profit health care organizations into positions of strength regarding the transfer of management knowledge and technology to health care organizations.

One area of management not yet developed to its potential in the health care field is performance appraisal (PA). Interestingly, this field holds great opportunity for improving management of health care organizations and yielding sizable dividends at both the individual and organizational level. Through proper design, implementation, and maintenance of a dynamic performance appraisal system, individual and organizational performance may be monitored and enhanced, resulting in a more efficient and effective organization.

The need to develop a superior and effective performance appraisal system (PAS) in a health care organization can be described in clear and simple terms. Indeed, health care organizations are so "employee intense" that salaries and wages that comprise as much as 60% to 70% of their operating costs are not unusual. Such data reveal the clear linkage between the successful operation of the organization and the effective and efficient performance of its employees. A good performance appraisal system can help the organization to attract and retain highly qualified employees. Health administrators should understand the reasons for implementing a performance appraisal system that is effective in promoting organizational goals as well as in developing human resources.

The development of a performance appraisal system should be a key part of management's responsibility for a variety of reasons. These reasons include the following:

1. Evaluation of employees is an important management task because management must be able to make administrative decisions that cause changes in employee status.
2. Management must have current information on the performance of individual units and departments. Through the evaluation of individual performance, management can obtain information about the unit of which the individual is a part.
3. Performance appraisal systems provide managers with information about employees' skills and abilities. These data help to validate or change the organization's selection procedures, and they provide the basis for recommendations regarding employee training programs.
4. The performance appraisal system provides valuable information on the quality of supervision.
5. The performance appraisal system, if successfully implemented, provides useful information for analyzing the role of management in effecting changes in the performance and development of employees.

Performance appraisal is one of the most important processes in any organization. However, from the employee perspective, all too often organizations implement performance appraisal systems as a punishment rather than to assist the employees. If this attitude pervades an organization, it is difficult to realize the positive outcomes possible for both the employees and the organization. How, then, can an organization establish a performance appraisal system that will yield desirable results for all? Admittedly, an answer to this question is easy to prescribe but difficult to implement with consistency. In any system, special emphasis should be given to the human side of appraisal because, in the final analysis, the best system may be only as effective as it is perceived to be by the employees. If the system is to be perceived by employees as effective, all responsible levels of management must implement it fairly and consistently.

This chapter addresses the physical, mental, and organizational parameters that the management team must address in the construction of a performance appraisal system. For a performance appraisal system to be deemed successful, management and employees must understand its development and embrace it as an organizational necessity for long-term survival. Given the rapid changes in the health care industry, an effective and proactive performance appraisal system provides the health care employer with flexibility in dealing with the uncertain environment and future we face. Also in this chapter is a brief overview of history, methods, evaluation, and problems that provide background for discussion concerning strategic performance appraisal, application of management by objectives (MBO) and total quality management (TQM) for health care organizations, and linking rewards to performance (e.g., performance-based pay).

HISTORICAL DEVELOPMENT

The first recorded performance appraisal system in industry was developed by Robert

Owens in Scotland around 1800 (Harr & Hicks, 1976). Owens placed a colored block at each worker's place to designate how well the worker had performed the previous day. Different colors indicated various levels of performance.

Formal appraisal systems were first utilized in the United States by the federal government and by certain city administrators in the middle to late 1800s. Frederick Taylor and his work measurement program laid the groundwork for performance appraisal in business, which began shortly before World War I. Soon, in 1916, Walter Dell Scott began the development of the man-to-man rating chart that was widely used to identify and evaluate military leaders during World War I. These early appraisal systems were related to various numerical efficiency factors developed from both work simplification studies and time and motion studies popularized by the work of industrial engineers (Harr & Hicks, 1976).

The graphic rating scale approach was developed in the 1920s. It required the rater to evaluate an individual on a continuum of "poor" to "excellent" for several characteristics. Human relations were strongly emphasized by management in the 1930s and 1940s, as evidenced by appraisal systems that focused on rating employees' personality and behavior traits.

During the 1950s, the concept of management by objectives began to emerge when firms such as the General Electric Company began to focus on detailed planning processes for their organizations. General Electric first identified the elements of management by objectives in its extensive planning for reorganization in the period from 1952 to 1954. Peter Drucker (1954) emphasized the need for establishing objectives both for the entire organization and for its individual managers, and for then measuring performance against the objectives.

In 1971, the Supreme Court mandated that any form of testing procedure for a specific job must relate directly to the job tasks to be performed (*Griggs v. Duke Power Company, 1971*). This decision contained major implications for the construction of performance appraisal tools and the use of performance appraisal results. For example, using a test of mental ability for purposes of selection or promotion is illegal if no correlation can be established between the test and the performance of a specific job. When used as tools for selection, transfer, or promotion, performance appraisals are considered tests and the 1971 Supreme Court decision applies (Harr & Hicks, 1976).

Reinforcing the Supreme Court decision in *Griggs v. Duke* are the guidelines outlining employee selection procedures issued by the Equal Employment Opportunity Commission (EEOC) in 1970. These guidelines require employers using tests to have available data demonstrating that the tests are predictive of, or significantly correlated with, important elements of work behavior.

The topic of performance appraisal is now receiving considerable attention in many organizational settings. This attention has evolved from new demands for performance accountability brought about by cost containment efforts and reduced revenues during times of economic downturn in which expectations of high performance have continued. Additionally, recent EEOC rulings and court decisions have alerted employers to possible discriminatory effects of their performance appraisal systems (Rosen, 1992). Court judgments against employers reflect performance appraisal deficiencies that include: 1) no consistency of past performance problems, 2) no formal appraisals documenting substandard performance received by the employee, and 3) an employer's system inherently biased against protected categories of workers. As a result, managers today are examining performance appraisal systems to determine the degree to which the objectives of the appraisal systems are met to ascertain whether any discriminatory effects may be present.

The assessment of employee performance has become an essential component of health care management (Timmreck, 1989). All levels of management must be aware of the importance of a good mechanism for performance appraisal. One reason for this concern is that federal courts increasingly are hearing cases in which plaintiffs argue on behalf of management that EEOC guidelines and those of other agencies actually have contributed to unfair and illegal employment practices. The alleged unfair practices include promotions, demotions, transfers, and terminations based on performance appraisal data.

These developments and others should be considered in any organization's evaluation of its performance appraisal system. It also is important that management have a comprehensive understanding of the most commonly used methods of appraisal. A summary of such methods follows.

COMMON PERFORMANCE APPRAISAL METHODS

Numerous methods exist for evaluating performance; these generally are classified as comparative methods and absolute standards. An organization should choose a method based on two criteria: 1) the factors the organization desires to measure, and 2) the method that applies best to the nature of the organization.

Comparative Methods

As their name suggests, *comparative methods* compare one employee to another in order to determine performance ranking. *Straight ranking* merely asks the rater to list employees, beginning with the best employee and ending with the weakest employee. This method utilizes overall job proficiency on predetermined job dimensions or characteristics (Timmreck, 1989). In *alternative ranking,* the most common ranking method, the rater repeatedly chooses the best and weakest employees, each time choosing from the names remaining. The process is continued until all employees have been placed on the ranking list, with the last two ranked in the middle (Ivancevich & Glueck, 1986; Timmreck, 1989).

In *paired comparison,* one employee at a time is compared to all other employees. Each time an employee is ranked higher than another employee, a tally is placed by the higher-ranking person's name. The employee with the most tallies is considered to be the most valuable, and the others are placed in order according to the number of tallies by their name. *Forced distribution* asks the rater to assign a certain proportion of the employees to one category on each criterion. For example, 10% of employees might be in the "superior" category, 20% in the "good," 20% in the "average," continuing to "poor" (Ivancevich & Glueck, 1986).

Comparison methods are useful in making decisions regarding promotion and selection from within a work unit, and this is their major advantage. However, the use of more than one rater is advisable to obtain more accurate ratings.

Comparison methods are problematic in that they are time-consuming and useful only for relatively small groups of employees. Also, an employee's performance rating is based on other employee's work, rather than on desired outcomes. Comparisons can lead to judgment of personality rather than of performance. Finally, ranking assumes equal distance between employees' ranks, an assumption research shows to be unwarranted.

Absolute Standards

Through the use of standards, each individual is evaluated against written standards, and several factors of performance are measured. In one such method, the *weighted checklists* method (Fig. 14.1), the rater identifies and assigns a weight to each of the tasks to be evaluated. The employee is then scored on each task to determine overall performance. The major disadvantage of the use of a weighted (or nonweighted) checklist is that it does not reveal the degree with which

a specific behavior occurs, requiring only a mere yes or no judgment.

In the *forced-choice* method, the rater selects statements that best fit the performance characteristics of the individual employee. The rater does not know the value assigned to each characteristic, and consequently forced choice can reduce bias. However, this advantage can become a disadvantage if the rater is offended by the confidential weights assigned to the statements.

Graphic rating is the most commonly used method for performance appraisal. The scale requires the rater to choose a value or statement along a continuum that best fits the employee for each criterion being reviewed. The advantage of a graphic scale is that it shows the degree to which an employee performs a job or task (Douglas, Klien, & Hunt, 1985).

The *critical incidents technique* was developed in response to the faults of essay and behavioral trait methods. The rater records critical behaviors of employees that are related to both good and poor performance. This method, however, does not indicate the frequency with which a particular behavior

	Delivery of Patient Care	Yes	No	N/A
60%	A. Evaluate and intervene when necessary in nursing care delivered by other non-RN personnel in his or her unit.			
40%	B. Provide skillful and safe care to patients as indicated in patient chart and nursing care plan.			

FIGURE 14.1. Example of weighted checklists.

is performed, nor the degree to which it is performed (Douglas et al., 1985).

As a result of the shortcomings of the critical incidents method, the *behaviorally anchored rating scale* (BARS) was developed. BARS uses characteristics judged to be critical to job performance and rates the degree to which each characteristic is attained by the employee. The employee's performance is determined by summing the values assigned to each of the critical indicators and/or characteristics.

The main disadvantage of BARS is that its development is time-consuming because separate scales are needed for each job. BARS, however, offers objectivity, which is lacking in such clearly subjective appraisal methods as comparative methods and essays. BARS has been used effectively in hospital work units of nurses and ancillary personnel; such successful usage is due to the dimensionality of the BARS scale, which permits identification of separate components of complex job behaviors. BARS demonstrates a necessary movement toward evaluations that are developmental, rather than merely evaluative. Such developmental evaluations, being behaviorally based, then provide the basis for changes in behavior.

A system developed from the BARS model, the *behavioral observations scale* (BOS), attempts to eliminate some of the disadvantages of BARS. The development of BOS also begins with the identification of critical incidents, which are then categorized according to behavioral dimensions. The behavioral dimensions usually contain five to eight items each, and these are used to rate employee performance. A frequency format is developed in which the highest number corresponds with "almost never." A comparison of BOS with BARS reveals that BOS does not require the appraiser to record the occurrence of critical incidents regularly. Instead, BOS asks the rater to evaluate the employee on a variety of behaviors that have been determined to be critical to good or poor performance (Douglas et al., 1985).

Management by objectives (MBO) is a result-based evaluative program in which goals are mutually determined by supervisors and subordinates, and employees are rated on the degree to which these goals are accomplished. MBO stresses the value and importance of employee involvement and encourages discussion of employees' strengths and weaknesses. In a clinical health care setting for example, these patient-oriented treatment goals represent performance standards that may be extremely difficult to determine in advance. Given the variable nature of patient care, these performance goals must be flexible enough to allow the caregiver latitude in resources consumption while stressing cost containment measures. This obviously presents a potential dilemma in the health care environment.

MBO has become popular for several reasons. First, it promotes better communication and interaction between the superior and subordinate. Additionally, the process of MBO development forces the organization and individual units to recognize and coordinate goals. Also, employees gain understanding of work objectives and learn what is expected of them. This goal-setting emphasis provides the opportunity to integrate MBO with the performance appraisal by connecting standards and objectives to subsequent performance levels (Beck, 1990). Tables 14.1 and 14.2 may assist managers in reviewing various organizational performance appraisal techniques in terms of cost and applicability (Ivancevich & Glueck, 1986).

TABLE 14.1. Criteria for Choice of Performance Evaluation Techniques

Evaluative Base	Graphic Rating Scale	Forced Choice	MBO	Essay	Critical Incidents	Weighted Checklist	BARS	Ranking	Paired Comparison	Forced Distribution	Forced Test	Field Review
Developmental cost	Moderate	High	Moderate	Low	Moderate	Moderate	High	Low	Low	Low	High	Moderate
Usage costs	Low	Low	High	High supervisory costs	High	Low	Low	Low	Low	Low	High	High
Ease of use by evaluators	Easy	Moderately difficult	Moderate	Difficult	Difficult	Easy	Easy	Easy	Easy	Easy	Moderately difficult	Easy
Ease of understanding by those evaluated	Easy	Difficult	Moderate	Easy	Easy	Easy	Moderate	Easy	Easy	Easy	Easy	Easy
Useful in promotion decisions	Yes	Yes	Yes	Not easily	Yes	Moderate	Yes	Yes	Yes	Yes	Yes	Yes
Useful in compensation and reward decisions	Yes	Moderate	Yes	Not easily	Yes	Moderate	Yes	Not easily	Not easily	Yes	Yes	Yes
Useful in counseling and development of employees	Moderate	Moderate	Yes	Yes	Yes	Moderate	Yes	No	No	No	Moderate	Yes

Source: Ivancevich, J. M., & Glueck, W. F. (1989). *Foundations of personnel: human resource management* (4th ed.). Homewood, IL: BPI/Irwin. Copyright © 1989. Reprinted with permission.

TABLE 14.2. Recommendations on Evaluation Techniques for Model Organizations

Type of Organization	Graphic Rating Scale	Forced Choice	MBO	Essay	Critical Incident	Weighted Checklist	BARS	Ranking	Paired Comparison	Forced Distribution	Performance Test	Field Review	Assessment Center
Large size, low complexity, high stability	×	×	×		×	×	×	×	×	×	×	×	×
Medium size, low complexity, high stability	×		×	×	×	×	×	×	×	×		×	×
Small size, low complexity, high stability	×		×	×	×			×	×	×			
Medium size, moderate complexity, moderate stability	×		×	×	×	×		×	×	×			×
Large size, high complexity, low stability	×		×	×	×			×	×	×		×	×
Medium size, high complexity, low stability	×		×	×	×			×	×	×			

Source: Ivancevich, J.M., & Glueck, W.F. (1989). Foundations of personnel: Human resource management (4th ed.). Homewood, IL: BPI/Irwin. Copyright © 1989. Reprinted with permission.

The concept of performance-based pay is a mechanism whereby individual employees or work groups are rewarded according to their achievement of predetermined standards of performance. Terms such as gain-sharing, profit-sharing, and pay-for-performance are commonly utilized to market and define this concept internally. With the current emphasis on cost-containment measures, and almost assuredly greater future cost-containment directives, this concept has gained momentum and widespread management interest (Browdy, 1989; Eubanks, 1992; Eyes, 1993; Ross & Hatcher, 1992). A 1992 project funded by the U. S. Department of Labor found that a majority of surveyed hospitals are considering, or have implemented, some form of performance-based compensation as a viable option for evaluating performance (Eubanks, 1992). These findings suggest that all levels of employee (rank and file to executive management) are candidates for this system.

Total quality management (TQM) and its various permutations such as continuous quality improvement (CQI) have been adopted recently by the Joint Commission on the Accreditation of Healthcare Organizations (JCAHO) (1991). The concept of quality is not a new concept to health care. Professional standards review organizations (PSROs), which were then peer review organizations (PROs), legislation was established during the early 1970s and early 1980s by the federal government to provide retrospective quality monitoring. Although these programs addressed quality standards, the review and analysis was conducted on an outcomes basis. TQM approaches the quality equation from process and structure.

Health care providers, such as Hospital Corporation of America, have begun to use these TQM principles in an attempt to change their corporate thinking and adopt a focus on constancy purpose and process of continuing improvement (Koska, 1990). The health care industry has been quick to adopt TQM/CQI performance directives in an effort to counteract various economic and public opinion problems. Although the results of TQM/CQI improvements are mixed, it appears that the concept is one that deserves further analysis and consideration (Leibman, 1992). Given the tremendous pressures that confront health care, this concept theoretically offers many advantages.

The historical development of TQM began with W. E. Deming's introduction of American-related quality measures on levels of production. The success of many Japanese companies can be attributed to these production quality standards. Deming (1986) identified 14 points for quality management:

1. Create constancy of purpose.
2. Set a philosophy that focuses on quality.
3. Eliminate dependence on mass inspection.
4. Eliminate the practice of awarding business on the basis of price.
5. Find problems.
6. Institute modern methods of training on the job.
7. Institute modern methods of supervision.
8. Drive out fear to enhance work effectiveness.
9. Break down barriers among departments.
10. Eliminate numerical goals, posters, and slogans for the staff, asking for new levels of productivity without providing methods to accomplish them.

11. Eliminate work standards that prescribe numerical standards.
12. Remove the barriers between staff and individual rights to pride of workmanship.
13. Institute planned educational programs designed to prepare staff to acquire knowledge and skills needed to function in the future.
14. Create a structure in top management that will maintain constant awareness and accomplishment of the foregoing points.

The connection of TQM to performance appraisal is obvious. Under the theoretical application of TQM, employee performance appraisals are scrapped! This would be a theoretical approach, but one that is quite impractical. A modified approach would entail incorporation of traditional performance appraisal techniques along with tenets of TQM. The JCAHO (1991) has proposed that, by 1994, "the organization's leaders [shall] set expectations, develop plans, and implement procedures to assess and improve the quality of the organization's governance, management, clinical and support services."

Although an understanding of the most commonly used methods of performance appraisal is helpful, equally important is a review of significant theoretical and philosophical differences in evaluating methods of performance to date.

EVALUATION OF PERFORMANCE APPRAISAL

Performance appraisals are organizational instruments that facilitate increased employee communications and individual job performance (McGee, 1992). The problem that most organizations face is one of motivating employees to understand and accept the process of performance appraisal. The level to which each employee accepts this evaluative process and the need for optimal job performance becomes the main purpose of management. To solve this problem, organizations must devise ways to influence and handle the behavior of their members—correcting deviation and rewarding good performance. Performance appraisals constitute one of the major tools used in the organizational control process. In a practical sense, performance appraisals can be viewed as the means by which management defines and rationalizes corporate goals and sanctions desired job performance. The issues to address in designing an effective performance appraisal system include: 1) clear, measurable goals for each job; 2) regular appraisals and feedback; 3) linkage of the process to employee development; and 4) education of raters about its purposes and practices.

Therefore, it is important to assess objectively the process of performance appraisal, both in theory and in practice. This assessment includes a review of the purpose of performance appraisal, a review of the task characteristics important for the performance appraisal process, and a summary of performance appraisal system problems.

Purpose of Performance Appraisal

Performance appraisal serves multiple purposes: 1) analysis of employee progress, 2) problem identification in meeting job requirements, 3) opportunities to improve performance, 4) long-range career planning, and 5) overall tie-in to long-range corporate goals (Meyer, 1991). The goal accomplishment purpose of performance appraisal is historically oriented; past performance is reviewed in light of results or outcomes. Historically performance appraisal for evaluation has served as the basis for decision making regarding promotions, transfers, and salary adjustments. It also can be used as a basis for allocating terminations, particularly in an organization that has decided to reduce its work force.

The developmental function of performance appraisal is forward-looking, aimed at enhancing the future capacity of organization members to be more productive, effective, and/or satisfied (Brinkerhoff & Kanter, 1980). For developmental purposes, performance appraisal facilitates appraisee improvement in job skills and motivation, as well as career planning and effective coaching between managers and subordinates.

An assumption of this chapter is that all managers are involved in performance appraisal, regardless of whether it is properly organized and whether it is judgmental or developmental. All managers should be involved actively in organizationwide appraisal systems that are strategically focused and developmental. The role of performance appraisal in health care organizations is becoming increasingly crucial to institutional effectiveness and mere survival. Therefore, it seems reasonable that management should spend an appropriate amount of time analyzing its performance appraisal needs and developing a system that can be effective in meeting those needs.

Tasks Characteristics

Brinkerhoff and Kanter (1980) stress three characteristics of tasks that have strong impact on the performance appraisal pro-

cess. These characteristics are complexity, clarity, and predictability; each is discussed here.

Complexity

As pointed out by Dornbusch and Scott (1975):

> The more complex the task, the more complex is the evaluation process required. If the task entails many activities and there are numerous properties of interest in connection with the activities or outcome, then the process of arriving at a valid and reliable performance evaluation is likely to be complicated. (p. 145)

Therefore, the most technically accurate evaluations generally have been limited to jobs that have relatively simple content and unambiguous measures of performance.

Clarity

Clarity concerning tasks and goals is another characteristic that influences the performance appraisal process. In other words, knowledge of and/or agreement on what is to be done must be clear both to management and to the employee. Tasks with specific objectives on which organizational members can agree lend themselves to implementation and subsequent measurement that forms a good basis for relatively straightforward performance evaluation.

However, tasks characterized as ambiguous pose problems for performance appraisal. Diffused goals, moreover, provide little help in determining what to measure and/or what standards should be employed in the evaluation process. Conflicts and disagreements commonly occur when goals and tasks are vague and ambiguous.

Predictability

Predictability is another factor particularly relevant for evaluations based on outcomes. If the tasks are predictable, the relationships between quality of performance and amount and/or quality of outcome are relatively constant. Typing a letter is a good example of a predictable task in which examination of the outcome provides an accurate picture of performance.

However, unpredictable tasks do not allow accurate assessments of performance based on outcomes. Such ambiguous tasks are common in the health care environment where knowledge and direction of the casual relation is not readily known or discernable (Beck, 1990; Thompson, 1967). Brinkerhoff and Kanter (1980) have stated that as uncertainty in jobs increases (e.g., difficulties of measuring results, time lag between action and results), so does the tendency to use social characteristics in making decisions about who should occupy those jobs. Therefore, it is precisely the difficulty of doing objective appraisals of performance in areas high in uncertainty (e.g., risky ventures) and higher-level management strategic decisions that results in the appearance of bias through reliance on subjective factors such as trust and loyalty.

Brinkerhoff and Kanter (1980) also point out that the performance appraisal process is not an independent one but is structurally linked to a variety of other features and processes of the organization. The structural characteristics that have a direct impact on performance appraisal systems include task interdependence, observability of task performance, the structuring of the authority system, power differentials, and the nature of communicated appraisals.

In summary, what develops from a given performance appraisal system depends largely on purpose, task features, and characteristics of the organizational structure. Basically, performance appraisal data may tend to be unreliable or misleading from the standpoint of the organizational and social-psychological issues. However, most of the appraisal literature, with its technical focus on scientifically developed rating systems, fails to recognize the realities of practice that contribute to this unreliability. Brinkerhoff and Kanter (1980) conclude that data from formal performance measures tend to be most reliable when the following conditions exist:

1. The purpose of the appraisal is clear.
2. Tasks are simple.
3. Goals for the tasks are clear.
4. Outcomes are predictable.
5. Tasks are relatively independent.
6. Task performance is observable.
7. Criteria of performance are set by those later assessing performance.
8. Appraisers feel secure in their own jobs and have no personal stake in hurting the performers.

This conclusion suggests that single measurement systems based on formal checklists and ratings by the supervisor should be used only for the more routine tasks in organizations, which are likely to meet these criteria. However, as uncertainty grows (or as complexity, interdependence, power concerns, and/or multiple appraisal purposes grow), so should the number of additional features and sources of data used for the appraisal system.

Sashkin (1981) developed a brief questionnaire (Table 14.3) to elicit a rough evaluation

TABLE 14.3. Organizational Performance Appraisal Questionnaire Evaluation (OPAQUE)

Instructions

Respond to the six statements that follow by indicating the extent to which you agree (or disagree) that the statements accurately describe performance appraisal in your organization. Some statements refer to your experiences in appraising your subordinates' performance: others refer to your experiences in being appraised yourself. Try to reflect as accurately as you can the current conditions in your organization based on your experiences.

SA = Strongly agree   A = Agree   ? = Neither agree nor disagree
D = Disagree   SD = Strongly disagree

1. I have found my boss's appraisals to be very helpful in guiding my own career development progress.	SA	A	?	D	SD
2. The appraisal system we have here is of no use to me in my efforts toward developing my subordinates to the fullest extent of their capabilities.	SA	A	?	D	SD
3. Our performance appraisal system generally leaves me even more uncertain about where I stand after my appraisal than beforehand.	SA	A	?	D	SD
4. The appraisal system we use is very useful in helping me to clearly communicate to my subordinates exactly where they stand.	SA	A	?	D	SD
5. When higher levels of management around here are making major decisions about management positions and promotions, they have access to and make use of performance appraisal records.	SA	A	?	D	SD
6. In making pay, promotion, transfer, and other administrative personnel decisions, I am not able to obtain past performance appraisal records that could help me to make good decisions.	SA	A	?	D	SD

Source: Sashkin, M. (1981). *Assessing performance appraisal.* San Diego, CA: University Associates, Inc.

of an organization's appraisal system. The questionnaire is based on the following three basic objectives of performance appraisal:

1. Performance appraisal systems should generate information needed for short- and long-range administrative actions, such as salary decisions, promotions, and transfers (all short-range) or human resources planning and managerial succession (long-range).
2. Appraisal systems should let subordinates know where they stand and how well they are doing, as well as any changes in their behavior the superior wants.
3. Appraisal systems should provide a means for coaching and counseling

subordinates, to train and develop them to their full potential.

It is evident that no single system is appropriate or effective for every organization or category of employees. To further assist in the evaluation of an organization's appraisal system, Sashkin (1981) has developed the following 10 questions or rules of thumb:

1. Are managers rewarded for developing their subordinates?
2. Do mangers receive skill training and assistance in using the system and, specifically, in being helpers or counselors?
3. Are job descriptions or specific job goal documents based on behavioral characteristics or job-relevant performance?

4. Are employees actively involved in the appraisal process?
5. Does mutual goal setting take place?
6. Do the appraisal sessions have a problem-solving focus?
7. Is the judge role clearly separated from helper-counselor role?
8. Does the paperwork and technical assistance required by the appraisal system place an unreasonable work load on managers?
9. Are peer comparisons a central feature of the appraisal system?
10. Is information that is needed for administrative action accessible and effectively used?

Managers should be equipped with some understanding of the purpose and complexity of valid performance appraisal. They also should be aware of the variety of problems that may be encountered in the development, implementation, and operation of a performance appraisal system.

Performance Appraisal System Problems

The development, implementation, and operation of a performance appraisal system are major undertakings. Such a system may fail to bring the organization the desired results for a variety of reasons, ranging from problems in the development stage to the problem of reviewing the system.

Developmental Problems

Several problem areas may be encountered when an organization attempts to implement a performance appraisal program. One is designing the best possible system to meet the needs of the organization. The

design of the "best" system should comprise an objective program that will evaluate employees on the basis of behavior that can be observed and easily measured. Use of the essay format or a comparative method probably will not result in an objective, accurate evaluation of performance.

Second, a performance appraisal system ideally should be equally effective in evaluating employees at all levels in the organization. However, use of the same approach to evaluate everyone may not yield the desired result. In a hospital, for example, use of a critical incidents method for housekeeping staff may be appropriate; but for managers and top-level executives, this technique would not measure adequately such qualities as goal attainment and leadership ability.

A third factor crucial to the developmental stage is that of ownership of the performance appraisal system; those who will use the system—*the employees*—should own it. Studies show that a system seen as the personnel department's project is less likely to be accepted and to survive in the organization. Therefore, the employees must be involved in the developmental stage.

Finally, the goals and objectives to be measured must be tied into the organization's strategic plan. This linkage ensures coordination of different units, with each working for the long-term advancement of the organization. Unless the organization considers the strategic long-range plan, its work to obtain short-term performance improvements may at the same time be sabotaging future success in reaching long-range goals.

Implementation Problems

Several problems may arise in the implementation stage. For example, a lack of commitment from the organization will cause employees to lose faith in the system, believing that it will be short-lived. Management should show commitment by implementing the system throughout the entire organization, or from top management down, as evidence of top-level and managerial support.

A second possible problem area is training and education. Those who will be using the system should be educated thoroughly in its purpose and process. Such education includes training raters on evaluating employees. Training reduces evaluator resistance to the system while aiding in getting the most accurate information on performance. All raters should get practical, hands-on experience during the training sessions.

Even the most careful construction of an appraisal tool will not eliminate the need for training raters. Training is necessary to minimize rating errors because a biased, distorted, or inaccurate evaluation diminishes employees' motivation and allows management to make inaccurate personnel decisions, which in turn defeat the purposes of the system. To be successful at reducing rater errors, management should recognize the importance of training sessions in which the future evaluators can practice skills taught and receive immediate feedback.

Operational Problems

One of the most common problems in operation of a system is rater error. Identifying rater error can be very difficult if an employee is evaluated solely by one supervisor. Common rater errors include the following:

1. Central tendency and leniency, which occurs when the rater evaluates all employees as average, excellent, or poor. A rater who has this tendency should be made aware that such information is not very valuable and should be asked to rate employees from best to worst for each element of the job. This exercise will aid the evaluator in revealing more accurately the performance of those being evaluated (Lowe, 1986).

2. Halo effect, which occurs when some raters judge all performance based on one area in which performance is good or poor (Lowe, 1986) (i.e., the evaluator gives similar ratings for all performance areas even though the performance varies from area to area). This is possibly the most common rater error.

3. Contrast effects, in which the rater evaluates the individual relative to other employees, rather than on the requirements of the job. A rater who is tempted to change an individual's rating after rating others is probably making a contrast error. Most people assume that performance in a work unit should follow a normal curve; this is incorrect and can lead to a violation of EEOC regulations.

4. Similar-to-me ratings, or the tendency to judge more favorably people perceived as similar to the rater, should be avoided (Ivancevich & Glueck, 1986).

Crucial to the operation of a performance appraisal system are prompt feedback and guidance for the evaluated employee. Feedback allows the system to move from merely being evaluative to being also developmental (Ivancevich & Glueck, 1986). For example, if feedback is provided 3 months after the evaluation, performance may have changed and the postevaluation may praise correct behavior that no longer exists. Prompt feedback, when directly associated with the period under evaluation, can help to maintain good performance or to change poor performance. Prompt feedback in the form of a face-to-face meeting between the supervisor and subordinate is crucial to the operation of a performance appraisal system. The rater counsels the employee to help him or her reach their full potential.

Finally, the operation of a system must include periodic review. A rigid performance appraisal system cannot survive successfully in a dynamic organization. The system will require periodic alterations; a yearly review is advisable. The review should gather input from participants at all levels to accomplish a dual purpose: to assess the participant's level of satisfaction in the system and to determine changes that can be made to improve system effectiveness.

Crucial to the building of a strategic human resources management system is the recognition that the functions of performance appraisal comprise a significant part of the overall strategic human resources management process. These ideas are discussed in the sections that follow, along with the application of management by objectives.

STRATEGIC ROLE OF PERFORMANCE APPRAISAL

Latham (1984) defines strategic planning as the process through which the organization's basic need is identified, its objectives are set, and the allocations of resources to achieve these objectives are specified. La-

tham further notes that performance appraisals often are viewed as retrospective because they emphasize what occurred in the past. Yet, the success or failure of strategic plans rests, in large part, with management's ability to identify the key actions that must be performed to formulate and use the steps that will lead to the attainment of the organization's long-range goals. Therefore, performance appraisal must be the process through which the critical job behaviors of management are identified, the specific objectives of each individual manager are set, and the steps or resources needed to obtain them are agreed on.

A few organizations have formal appraisal systems to evaluate top-level managers on how well they perform against the organization's strategic plan. The prevailing attitude seems to be that good measurement indicators simply do not exist. Frequently, emphasis is placed on managerial style or charisma rather than substance, and/or on whether a given result was achieved, with little or no questioning as to how it was achieved. For example, a chief executive officer may appraise a senior vice president primarily on whether a set of objectives was pursued in a manner similar to the way in which the CEO would have pursued them. Creativity and divergence of thinking are consequently stifled. Quite common are appraisal measures that reward managers for attending the bottom line of their respective functions, without taking note of how their actions or those of their subordinates affected the operation of other departments. No formal assessment is made to determine whether they and their subordinates behaved in a unifying or integrated way with colleagues so that the organization's overall mission could be achieved. Fundamental to the understanding of the strategic role of performance appraisal is the recognition of the dual nature or purpose of the process.

Dual Nature of Strategic Performance Appraisal

The purpose of strategic performance appraisal is twofold (Latham, 1984). First, the performance appraisal instrument defines what is meant by implementation and adherence to a strategic plan related to the individual employee. Therefore, when the strategic plan changes, the evaluation instrument should be reviewed for necessary modification and revision. It is through the use of the evaluation instrument that the second objective of performance appraisal is attained—namely, to bring about and sustain effective and/or efficient job performance. This can be done either through self-management or through coaching and counseling other people.

Performance appraisal is the *sine qua non* of a strategic human resources management system. This is because a performance appraisal system should make explicit what effective and efficient behavior is required of an individual employee for the organization to implement its strategic plan. Just as a nursing services department is concerned with the quality of patient care, the maintenance department is concerned with the operation of equipment, and housekeeping is concerned with maintaining a sanitary environment, the human resources system should be concerned with identification of what people in nursing services, in maintenance, and in housekeeping must do to implement the strategic plan after it has been formulated (Latham, 1984). The outcomes of these analyses translate into an appraisal instrument that is valid in that people are being evaluated on areas that are important to the attainment of their departmental and/or organizational objectives. To the extent that valid performance appraisals are done, valid decisions can be made regarding which employee should be rewarded. To the extent that valid performance appraisals are not made, it is impossible to make valid selection and reward decisions.

Valid performance appraisals are also critical to health care training programs because they identify people who lack the ability to perform effectively in their jobs. Use of a valid appraisal instrument makes it possible to identify not only those who need training but also the type of training that is needed.

The strategic purpose of performance appraisal cannot be achieved without the implementation of a performance appraisal system designed to assist in blending organizational goals with those of individual employee goals, to assist in the strategic planning process and in the accomplishment of organizational mission. When a properly designed performance appraisal system is implemented with consistency, it becomes the cornerstone of an effective human resources management system. As such, the performance appraisal system serves a number of strategic functions, some of which are as follows.

Strategic Functions of the Performance Appraisal System

Douglas et al. (1985) list the following five strategic functions of the performance appraisal system:

1. To provide a major source of human resources planning information
2. To provide a control mechanism for management

3. To activate and support the motivation system
4. To provide a means of employee development
5. To provide a basis for justifying personnel actions

Human Resources Planning

If done properly, a performance appraisal system should form the basis for important records, including data on each employee's special abilities. This information can be particularly important in identifying managerial talent. The human resources planning aspect of the performance appraisal system is significant in terms of strategic plans as well. Each employee's permanent personnel records should include a complete evaluation of his or her background, ability, and potential. The records should also include a summary of work history, education, and training, as well as assessments of factors such as motivation, leadership skills, and potential for assuming greater organizational responsibilities.

Control and Motivation of Personnel

Performance appraisal systems, which contain the justification for distributing the rewards and punishments that organizations have to offer, should be the heart of any motivation system. In concept or theory, any organization should strive to distribute its available resources so that "excellent" or "good" performers are rewarded more than "average" or "poor" performers. Accomplishing this objective depends largely on the ability of the institution to develop reasonably objective appraisal measures and methods, and then to relate the rewards directly to these objectives and measurements.

If success is achieved in these areas, the problems or perceptions of inequity will be reduced, although probably not eliminated.

An extremely important aspect of motivation is setting goals. Much evidence points out that people with explicit performance goals do better than people with vague performance objectives, such as "Do the very best you can." Many studies also indicate that difficult goals produce higher performance than easy goals, although some work suggests that the goals must be limited to what is realistically possible. Unrealistic goals may simply cause people to become discouraged and unproductive.

The idea of control is also related to motivation. Key components of control are goals, measurement, and feedback. Good appraisal systems are supported by measurement, progress is noted according to those measures, and feedback occurs regarding areas in which changes can be made. Control is necessary to enable both management and employees to make associations between behavior and output. The same measures also can be useful in determining rewards.

Personnel Development

One of the primary reasons for performance appraisal in any organization should be to assist employees in developing their skills to their maximum potential. The control aspect of performance appraisal can help employees to make adjustments through better performance. In addition, objective appraisal can help in identifying the weaknesses, as well as the strengths, of each employee. Such weaknesses may be dealt with through planning recommendations communicated to the employee at the time of the appraisal interview.

Justification of Personnel Actions

The performance appraisal process is extremely important in providing information. It requires justification for promotion, transfer, and demotion or termination. This is particularly true in view of civil rights legislation and EEOC regulations. However, any good performance appraisal system must have a carefully considered plan of objective measurement and documentation process. Although judgment is extremely important in many aspects of management, a performance appraisal system that relies almost exclusively on supervisor's judgment will be very difficult to defend. Documentation of objective measurement is essential. If a record of well-designed and properly conducted appraisals is available and indicates consistency, important personnel actions such as promotions or terminations can be justified on the basis of objective, documented information.

To serve the purpose and functions of strategic performance appraisal, the organization must establish and effect a performance appraisal system that has application and acceptability throughout the organization. One system with this potential is management by objectives, presented as a strategic appraisal system for health care organizations.

MODIFIED MANAGEMENT BY OBJECTIVES: A STRATEGIC APPRAISAL SYSTEM

Although no performance appraisal system that exists will meet all of the needs of a given organization, the MBO concept is more broadly applicable and fundamentally sound than most other systems. Of particular relevance to this chapter is the possible linkage of the MBO concept to management's strategic planning functions and its linkage to TQM concepts.

The term "management by objectives" was first used by Peter Drucker (1954) almost 40 years ago. Drucker (1954) pointed out that in this system, each manager should have clear objectives that are identified with and support those of high levels of management. Individuals thus can develop an understanding of their own objectives, as well as those of their managers and the organization. Many authors have supported the MBO concept developed by Drucker. Douglas McGregor (1960) brought the concept into the performance appraisal arena by advocating that MBO be used to encourage the discussion of employee strengths and potential, making the supervisor more a counselor than a judge. Whereas Drucker (1954) first viewed MBO as a method of integrating the activities of an organization, McGregor (1960) developed the idea of applying MBO as a performance appraisal technique. In recent years, the MBO approach has been recommended as an appraisal technique that should be linked to management's strategic planning process.

Definitions

Although a variety of definitions of MBO programs exist, some common elements are present (Cummings & Schwab, 1973); these include the following:

1. Goal setting
2. Involvement of managers in participation in the formulation of personal goals and methods to accomplish these goals

3. Periodic reviews of progress toward the accomplishment of these goals
4. Evaluation of performance
5. Self-appraisal
6. Evaluation and feedback
7. Suggestions for development and training

As demonstrated by the common elements listed above, the real process may be viewed as a cycle of events that includes planning, setting objectives and goals, negotiation, performance, review of performance, and evaluation and feedback.

Figure 14.2 shows a model objective set-ting process, and Figure 14.3 presents an overview of the MBO cycles.

According to Kost (1986), MBO provides three functions to the health care organization in terms of employee performance-related evaluations: 1) objective setting of goals, 2) use/acceptance of these objectively set goals, and 3) employee involvement in the process leading to increased employee performance. The utilization of clinical staff members to develop MBO-guided departmental and clinical philosophy and objectives allows the tracking of individual progress (Gousse et al., 1990). It appears that with the linkage of MBO to performance appraisal

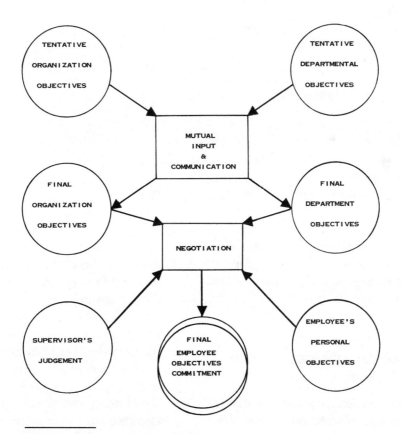

FIGURE 14.2. The objective-setting process.

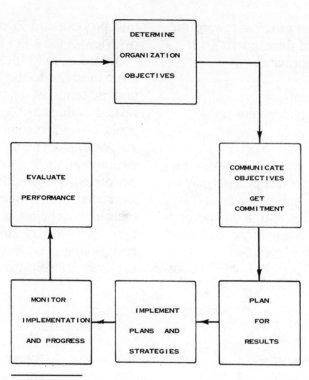

FIGURE 14.3. The MBO cycle.

to establish an effective system that provides a setting for managers and subordinates to set objectives against which performance is measured, management receives better data than are obtained from other traditional methods. It is important to note that the key areas of management involvement that contribute to the success of MBO programs relate to administration's understanding of and commitment to the various features of the system.

Management by Objectives as an Appraisal System

Migliore (1979) describes a frame of reference for the implementation of the MBO program that is based on identifying purposes, objectives, and desired results, and in evaluating performance in the following nine-step process:

1. Defining the organization's purpose and reason for being
2. Monitoring the environment in which it operates
3. Assessing the organization's strengths and weaknesses realistically
4. Making assumptions about unpredictable future events
5. Prescribing written, specific, and measurable objectives in principal results areas that contribute to the organization's purpose
6. Developing strategies on how to use available resources to meet objectives
7. Making long-range and short-range plans to meet objectives

8. Appraising performance constantly to determine whether it is meeting the desired pace and remaining consistent with the defined purposes
9. Reevaluating purpose, environment, strengths, weaknesses, and assumptions before setting objectives for the next performance year.

This system clearly reflects the intent to match the program to organizational goals, and this is particularly important for strategic planning. However, it is sometimes difficult to bring together organizational units in a way that takes advantage of the existence of such interdependencies.

Health care organizations present numerous examples of interdependencies. Most, for example, bring together persons from different disciplines to perform specific functions that contribute to the overall quality and efficiency of patient treatment or service. However, a successful treatment program, in terms of both health outcome and cost, generally requires a high degree of coordination among employees in different departments. These personnel represent very different backgrounds, training, and understandings of what activities or tasks need to be performed and in what order. Therefore, the treatment program must be linked to the total management perspective so that individual objectives are developed within the frame of reference of the contributions made by other departments and other individuals.

Management by Objectives and Health Organizations

Research shows that MBO programs often do not succeed in health care environments because of the lack of management support and lack of proper development of the concept (Radcliffe, 1989). However, properly developed, MBO affords the organization many benefits. "Incorporation of an MBO approach to [performance] appraisal facilitates identification of individual performance objectives for the next evaluative period (Beck, 1990). It is important that systems of performance appraisal, including MBO, reflect an interest in interdepartmental and, where applicable, interorganizational management and that health managers understand the many benefits that can accrue from their approach to performance appraisal.

Performance appraisal is not yet widely accepted by individuals in health care settings. Health care employees often feel that evaluation should be performed by peers and not be linked necessarily to the operation or management of an organization. Although such feelings may stem from years of professional training, management of health organizations must have appropriate methods to appraise employees and evaluate the effectiveness of the organization.

In terms of strategic human resources planning and overall management needs, it seems suitable for health care organizations to strive for systems that will contribute to individual growth and development. Some of the traditional methods of evaluation (which are composed of subjective or trait evaluations, requiring choices on numerical scales or markings on checklists) are not appropriate appraisal tools for many health care employees. Employees simply need an evaluation process in which they participate, one that provides an opportunity to enhance professional skills and will assist workers in making greater contributions to the organization.

An effective evaluation system must be based on observation of skills and performance, not on a laundry list of personal attributes. Job analysis procedures may lead to the development of objective criteria, which then may be used in performance evaluation. These criteria must address both the quality and the quantity of work performed.

Guidelines for Implementing Management by Objectives

When an organization is considering implementation of performance evaluation systems such as MBO, management and employees alike should be aware of the total process from its inception. Through this communication, management and employees can develop an understanding of the commitment needed and the length of time required for a successful program. Listed below are the guidelines Levitz (1981) offers for implementation of an MBO program:

1. Management and employees should be committed to the MBO program and supportive of it. A survey may be necessary to determine how open the organization's climate is.
2. Everyone involved in the process should develop an understanding of the purpose and objectives of the program.
3. Management and other personnel should meet to develop common goals.
4. Departmental objectives should be developed that are consistent with those of the health organization.
5. Job descriptions should be written in result-oriented form, with statements on the measurement of satisfactory performance.
6. Subordinate-superior goal setting should occur at regular meetings.

7. Clear, valid, and measurable objectives for individuals meet to be set and agreed upon.
8. Superiors should be trained in evaluation methods, developmental methods, and performance interviewing.
9. Developmental feedback sessions should be scheduled based on individual needs.
10. Employees should view the MBO program as being linked to the reward system.
11. Continual monitoring of the system should occur through a linkage with other management functions.

From the perspective of strategic human resources management, several benefits appear to accrue from the operation of MBO programs, and these make it worthwhile for the management team to invest the resources required for implementation and maintenance of such a system. Levitz (1981) lists the following advantages that may result from a successful program:

1. Improved direction and planning of activities toward the accomplishment of organizational goals
2. The linking of institutional management functions to control systems through the development of appropriate work standards
3. A reduction in role conflict
4. A better understanding of how performance is linked to rewards
5. Increased employee satisfaction through the use of objective data
6. The career development of personnel

Through an understanding of the total MBO program and its necessary linkage to performance appraisal, compensation, and other managerial functions, health care managers can exert better and broader control over performance. The end result will be a more effective and efficient health services organization.

Developing and consistently implementing a strategic performance appraisal system to meet the needs of a particular organization can be a very rewarding process. For the performance appraisal system to be effective, however, it must be linked properly to a strategically designed reward system. A brief discussion of this relationship between extrinsic rewards and job performance follows.

EXTRINSIC REWARDS AND JOB PERFORMANCE

The findings of management studies vary substantially in rating such factors as pay and other extrinsic rewards in their relationship to job performance. However, many advantages are obvious when rewards are tied to performance, and this section advances strong support for this position. A variety of other rewards such as recognition and praise are equally important and should be used to complement the basic extrinsic rewards.

Mohrman, Resnick-West, and Lawler (1989) emphasized that the relationship between extrinsic reward level and performance has a crucial influence on organizational effectiveness. When extrinsic rewards are related to performance, the results are higher motivation and a tendency for turnover to be concentrated among the poor performers. Despite the obvious advantages of having rewards tied to performance, many organizations do not adopt this practice. Although there are some situations in which tying rewards to performance is dysfunc-

tional, some organizations do no relate rewards to performance even when doing so would be highly functional.

Lawler's (1973) discussion of extrinsic rewards stresses the importance of who receives the extrinsic rewards given out by an organization. Each organization has a limited quantity of rewards to give. How they are distributed determines who will continue to work for an organization, how hard people will work, and the attitudes of employees toward the organization. Extrinsic rewards represent an investment in people, and such enhancements should be a crucial issue in any organization. Indeed, one effective way to understand an organization is to look at the actual distribution of its extrinsic rewards and how the arrangement is perceived by the employees. Determination of the relationship between extrinsic reward satisfaction and performance in an organization also can provide important information about the eventual impact of an organization's reward distribution system. A strong positive relationship between satisfaction and performance usually indicates a reward system that is functioning well and is rewarding for good performance.

However, a negative relationship between satisfaction and performance indicates a poorly functioning reward system and should be taken as a warning. Specifically, such relationships mean that motivation is likely to be low because rewards are not clearly tied to performance. They also mean that turnover in the organization is likely to be centered among the high performers, a costly and extremely negative result for an organization attempting to improve its effectiveness or market share. Therefore, a performance appraisal system not linked to extrinsic rewards will not be as successful in motivating employees as one that is linked to these rewards appropriately. Generally, when performance incentives are used, productivity can be expected to increase more significantly. A positive relationship between extrinsic rewards and a good performance appraisal system should yield large motivational dividends within the organization, laying a solid foundation for other complementary awards within the organization.

SUMMARY

This chapter has advanced the case of performance appraisal as one of the most important processes in any organization. In some manner, all organizations do it, but the results may be either positive or negative.

Performance appraisal is not new, nor is there a single system appropriate for all organizations. This is particularly true in health care organizations, which employ a multiplicity of highly trained individuals with diverse backgrounds, skills, and developmental needs.

A review of methods and theories concerning the evaluation of performance appraisal provides background for discussion focused on the strategic role of performance appraisal within the human resources management system. The MBO method is selected as the performance appraisal system with the most comprehensive application for health care organizations, and guidelines for the implementation of such a system are available.

The importance of tying rewards to job performance, although not the primary focus of this chapter, is discussed briefly. If the performance appraisal system is to be a positive motivational force, it must be administered consistently by all levels of management and linked directly to the organization's reward system.

Any organization should seek to develop the performance appraisal system that best meets it needs. Special emphasis should be given to the human side of appraisal because, in the final analysis, the best system may be only as effective as it is perceived to be by its employees.

Discussion Questions

1. Design a set of goals or objectives for a clinical department within a community hospital according to principles of MBO and TQM. Are these two concepts incompatible or are they basically addressing the same goals?
2. With JCAHO's continued emphasis toward TQM and CQI, how would you as a "quality consultant" plan to implement this philosophy in a new start-up facility or a facility that has just decided that quality is a necessary evil?
3. Formulate a plan of action that will establish an ongoing performance appraisal workshop with a facility that has traditionally been accused of EEOC violations and is under the gun to establish fair appraisal methods. Specify steps that are necessary to address this problem.
4. Discuss pay-for-performance issues that relate to clinical areas that are relatively new. Therefore optimal performance levels are presently unknown. How does this lack of performance benchmark hamper your efforts? What if these professionals are prone to unionization and demand that pay benchmarks be established?
5. What method(s) appears best in

establishing a performance appraisal system? Should you consider jumping on the TQM bandwagon without analyses because the JCAHO requires it anyway?

REFERENCES

Beck, S. (1990). Developing a primary nursing performance appraisal tool. *Nursing Management, 21*(1), 36–42.

Browdy, J.D. (1989). Performance appraisal and pay-for-performance start at the top. *Health Care Supervisor, 7*(3), 31–41.

Brinkerhoff, D.W., & Kanter, R.M. (1980). Appraising the performance of performance appraisal. *Sloan Management Review, 21*(3), 3–16.

Cummings, L.L., & Schwab, D.P. (1973). *Performance in organizations: Determinants and appraisal.* Glenview, IL: Scott, Foresman.

Deming, W.E. (1986). *Out of the crisis.* Cambridge, MA: MIT Press.

Dornbusch, S.M., & Scott, R.W. (1975). *Evaluation and the exercise of authority.* San Francisco: Jossey-Bass.

Douglas, J., Klein S., & Hunt, D. (1985). *The strategic managing of human resources.* New York: Wiley.

Drucker, P.F. (1954). *The practice of management.* New York: Harper & Row.

Eubanks, P. (1992). Work redesign calls for new pay and performance plans. *Hospitals, 66*(19), 56–60.

Eyes, P.R. (1993). Realignment ties pay to performance. *Personnel Journal, 72*(1), 74–77.

Gousse, G., Platt, D., Gannon, R., Walters, K., Chow, M., & Nightingale, C.H. (1990). Developing staff into clinical practitioners. *Topics in Hospital Pharmacy Management, 9*(4), 50–57.

Griggs v. Duke Power Company. (1975). 3 FEP 175.

Haar, L.P., & Hicks, J.R. (1976). Performance appraisal: Derivation of effective assessment tools. *Journal of Nursing Administration, 6*(7), 20–29, 37.

Ivancevich, J.M., & Glueck, W.F. (1986). *Foundations of personnel/human resource management* (3rd ed.). Plano, TX: Business Publications.

Joint Commission on the Accreditation of Healthcare Organizations (1991). *Quality improvement standards* (draft). Chicago, IL: Author.

Koska, M. (1990). Adopting Deming's quality improvements. *Hospitals, 64*(13), 58–62.

Kost, G.J. (1986). Management by objectives for the academic medical center. *American Journal of Clinical Pathology, 86*(6), 738–744.

Latham, G.P. (1984). The appraisal system as a strategic control. In C. Fombrun, N. Tichy, & M.A. Devanna (Eds.) *Strategic Human Resource Management* (pp. 87–100). New York: Wiley.

Lawler, E.E. (1973). *Motivation in work organizations.* Pacific Grove, CA: Brooks/Cole.

Levitz, G.S. (1981). Performance appraisal in health organizations. In N. Metzger (Ed.), *Handbook of health care human resources management* (pp. 225–238). Rockville, MD: Aspen.

Liebman, M.S. (1992). Getting results from TQM. *HR Magazine, 37*(9), 34–38.

Lowe, T.R. (1986). Eight ways to run a performance review. *Personnel Journal, 65*(1), 60–62.

McGee, K.G. (1992). Making performance appraisals a positive experience. *Nursing Management, 23*(8), 36–37.

McGregor, D. (1960). *The human side of enterprise.* New York: McGraw-Hill.

Meyer, H.H. (1991). A solution to the performance appraisal feedback enigma. *Academy of Management Review 5*(1), 68–75.

Migliore, R.H. (1979). The use of long-range planning/MBO for hospital administrators. *Health Care Management Review, 4*(3), 23–28.

Mohrman, A.M., Resnick-West, S.M., & Lawler, E.E. (1989). *Designing performance appraisal systems.* San Francisco: Jossey-Bass.

Radcliffe, M. (1989). MBO: an approach to quality assurance. *Dimensions in Health Service, 66*(1), 14–16.

Rosen, D.I. (1992). Appraisals can make or break your court case. *Personnel Journal, 57*(11), 113–116.

Ross, T.L., & Hatcher, L. (1992). Gainsharing drives quality improvement. *Personnel Journal, 57*(11), 81–85.

Sashkin, M. (1981). Appraising appraisal: Ten lessons for research for practice. *Assessing performance appraisal.* San Diego, CA: University Associates.

Thompson, J.D. (1967). *Organizations in action.* New York: McGraw-Hill.

Timmreck, T.C. (1989). Performance appraisal systems in rural western hospitals. *Health Care Management Review, 14*(2), 31–43.

CHAPTER

COMPENSATION MANAGEMENT

Charles L. Joiner

Kerma N. Jones

Carson F. Dye

LEARNING OBJECTIVES

Upon completing this chapter, the reader should be able to . . .

- Outline various compensation issues within the health care environment, map a strategy that addresses these industry-specific problems, and design a compensation program to be implemented facility-wide.
- Discuss the components involved in compensation management and factors that are instrumental in construction of a compensation system.
- Outline various management activities (i.e., long-range planning, budgeting, physician recruitment/retention) and their relationships to compensation management.

INTRODUCTION

Compensation management is the process whereby organizations arrange and structure the pay provided to employees. Although it has a number of scientific measurement-oriented aspects to it, it also includes an element that is less easy to measure (i.e., the dynamic human element that affects each individual who is paid a salary). Although effective compensation management is necessary in all businesses, it is of particular importance for health organizations. A changing (and aging) American society, shifting reimbursement and insurance systems, increasing consumerism, and rising costs have combined to exert mounting pressures on health care organizations. The presence of managed care also has placed a tremendous challenge for health care leaders to constrain costs. More than ever before, ad-ministrators of health organizations face a mandate for cost containment. Moreover, compensation represents a major portion of the total operating budget for a health organization. Although there are increasing pressures to cut costs through the reduction of staff, there will be an expanded call to manage compensation costs as well. In such a setting, effective compensation management becomes essential if the organization is to survive.

Compensation management incorporates three primary objectives: distributive justice (i.e., equity), incentives for employees to improve performance and productivity, and cost control. Equity is feasible only if the management system includes procedures for such consideration as job analysis, job evaluation, and job pricing. Incentive systems involve rewards dependent on performance, but these systems also must be clearly defined components of the total compensation program. There also must be some systematic control over the pay system that is designed to contain costs appropriately. A final aspect of total compensation management should be the consideration of benefits. The high costs of benefit programs makes this a necessary factor in overall cost management.

A comprehensive program for compensation management must address each of the foregoing areas. Additionally, success for such programs requires attention to internal (i.e., employee) pressures and concerns, as well as to external pressures from the general public, third-party payers, managed care contractors, governmental agencies, and at times, stockholders. If the portion of the total operating budget devoted to compensation increases, the validity of the compensation management plan grows in importance.

STRATEGIC PLANNING AND COMPENSATION

The various components of compensation management (e.g., wages, salaries, various differential, benefits, incentives, bonuses) are familiar to human resources and compensation management specialists, as well as to most health care administrators. However, the philosophy that compensation management strategy should be an integral part of the organization's strategic planning process is not so familiar.

Traditionally, human resources specialists have handled the compensation and benefits functions but were not involved in the strategic decision-making process. During the next few years, human resources personnel will need to be more directly involved in both developing and implementing the strategic plans of the organization. Performance appraisal and compensation management are two of the specific functions that need careful evaluation in terms of their mutual relationships and integration into the strategic management formulas of the organization.

Chapter 14 presents the case for the strategic nature of performance appraisal, and this chapter summarizes the significant functions of compensation management for health care managers. Specifically, compensation and benefit systems must be strategically related to the overall mission of the organization, as well as to its cost-efficiency objectives. Furthermore, compensation programs must be integrally related to any organizational efforts toward continuous quality improvement (CQI). It is also important to note the variety of environmental forces that influence the compensation of workers, including the following (Douglas, Klein, & Hunt, 1985):

1. Tax laws
2. Changes in mandatory retirement laws
3. Social Security retirement plans versus private pension plans
4. Employee attitudes toward work time flexibility
5. Individual benefit choices
6. The entry of more women into the work force
7. The presence of more dual-income, dual-career couples who want child care benefits
8. Changing values and norms regarding career mobility

These environmental factors, along with competitive market forces controlling market share and profits, are considerations that necessitate the continuous design, implementation, and evaluation of compensation management systems.

It is vitally important that health care executives and human resources managers understand the purpose of compensation management and its role in strategic management of human resources. In addition to such traditional issues as job evaluation, salary surveys, and compensation systems, this chapter addresses the key issues of merit-based pay, executive incentive programs, physician compensation, exceptional performance awards, and benefits.

A Strategic Compensation Model

Because so many compensation issues have an effect on productivity goals and the quality of work life, strategy-oriented compensation specialists will probably become an integral part of future strategic management teams. It is helpful to define a strategic model approach to the compensation process, given the relationships of compensation to internal and external environments, as well as to other management systems. Douglas et al. (1985) developed a three-stage model for this process, as shown in Figure 15.1. Various components of this model are developed in this and related chapters.

Compensation of Health Care Personnel

Certain principles of compensation management apply to all organizations; however, unique aspects of the health care industry require special consideration in the development and implementation of a strategic compensation management plan. For example, consumers expect availability of health care regardless of the extent of the problem, the time of day or night, or geographic location. In very few segments of the service industry does one find such a high degree of consumer expectation, and this places distinct requirements on health care organizations and their personnel. Moreover, the types of personnel involved in health care delivery vary from those involved in housekeeping and maintenance to physicians and top-level managers. When one also considers the federal, state, and local regulations within which such organizations operate, it is easy to see that the complex environment of health care organizations requires a detailed, yet flexible plan, for compensation management. Additionally, because of these very factors, the necessity for inclusion of human resources management specialists in the development

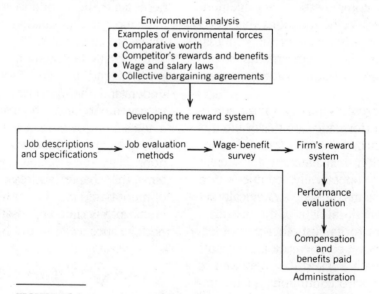

FIGURE 15.1. A strategic model for the study of compensation systems. (From Douglas, J., Klein, S., & Hunt, D. (1985). *The strategic managing of human resources.* New York: Wiley; Copyright © John Douglas; reprinted with permission.)

of the total strategic management plan becomes obvious.

Base Components of the Compensation Management System

In developing a comprehensive compensation plan, various factors must be considered. For each position, there should be a systematic process for developing a written job design, analysis, and description. Such specifics are essential in evaluating the job and in establishing equitable job pricing. Moreover, the existence of specific job design and analysis is essential to objective and equitable employee performance evaluations and determination of which employees merit consideration for bonuses or special rewards. Job designs and analyses for health care organizations also must incorporate such concerns as comparable worth and physician compensation, topics discussed later in this chapter.

Job Design

Job design encompasses the manner in which a given job is defined and how it will be conducted. This involves such decisions as whether the job will be handled by an individual or by a team of employees, as well as the determination of where the job fits into the overall organization. If properly implemented, job design requires a conscious effort for the organizing of tasks, duties, and responsibilities into a unit of work to achieve a certain objective. From the detailed information incorporated into the job design, a specific job description can be produced, and this will form the basis for recruiting and hiring an employee to fill that position, as well as the foundation for future employee evaluations and compensation schedules. In terms of strategic planning, each separate job design must be formulated to meet the organization's overall objectives. Where appropriate, each job design also must acknowledge any unique skills possessed by members of a given profession and must incorporate appropriate professional guidelines or limitations for tasks to be performed.

In stressing the need for compensation management to be incorporated into the total strategic management plan, it should be noted that job design is one of the single most important considerations. If each job within a given organization is well-defined and well-designed, the necessary basis exists for job analysis, job description, and job evaluation, as well as for equitable compensation, performance evaluation, and employee satisfaction. As indicated in Figure 15.1, development of job descriptions and specifications is the first step in developing the reward system. If specific requirements for each job are not defined clearly initially, there can be virtually no basis for assessing the value of a given position or the expertise of the employee who holds it.

Considerations to be included here extend far beyond the organization itself. Obviously, job designs in popular use in comparable businesses should be reviewed, and general satisfaction of both organizations and employees with these definitions should be determined. For a growing number of health care organizations, job design must involve union guidelines, whether they are contracted or informally outlined. In addition, each job design must allow for the concept of employee status. Employees with high skill levels can be expected to object if assigned the same job titles as employees with little or no skill.

It would not overstate the case to say that the long-term success of a given organization requires that each of these factors be considered. An excellent example of the importance of sometimes subtle distinctions can be seen in the design of nursing positions. Within the health care industry, the most prominent group of employees is nursing personnel, and specializations within nursing have changed dramatically during the past few decades, resulting in an increased need for precise job design and description. As suggested above, the graduate of a baccalaureate nursing program is likely to object to being given the same title and duties as a graduate of a certificate or associate degree program. A nurse with specialty training in emergency and trauma care has acquired skills that should be differentiated from the skills required of the nurse in a long-term care facility or an ambulatory diagnostic center. To disregard these differences in development of job designs (and resulting job descriptions and titles) is to set the stage for employee dissatisfaction, regardless of differentials in compensation.

Precision in job design is indispensable to the organization for even more obviously self-serving reasons. If an organization is to hire and retain only those employees who are essential to the organization's success, there must be a clear understanding of which employees will be needed and what their functions will be. As discussed later, employee compensation constitutes an enormous investment by service industries. To ensure that compensation dollars are being spent wisely, top-level managers must have an accurate view of each employee's role. It is during the job design stage of strategic planning that duplication of responsibilities must be eliminated to be sure that all necessary duties will be performed and to determine the actual skill level that will be required in each position. Care in this endeavor will make an important contribution to future employee job satisfaction and performance, as well as to the financial well-being of the organization.

Job Analysis

Closely linked to job design, job analysis involves the compiling of information about various jobs, their components, and the desired qualifications of persons performing those jobs. It is part of the process to develop concise job descriptions and specifications and to provide a sound basis for job evaluation. Douglas et al. (1985) note that job analysis is essential to the development and recruitment of highly productive and quality-oriented personnel. The necessity for thorough and expert job analysis in meeting the goals of the strategic management plan for any organization is apparent. It is also an intricate part of the development of equitable compensation in that it involves analysis of jobs within the given organization, as well as comparable jobs at other organizations within the field.

To return to the example of nursing personnel, analysis of nursing jobs within the health care industry indicates that different organizations specify varying duties for nurses, with accompanying pay differentials. Although the title "registered nurse" seems to be a definite choice for many people thinking about future career plans, job analysis could show it to be an inadequate and inappropriate job title for some organizations. During this phase of strategic planning, assessment of external organizations takes on renewed importance. Planners must review job descriptions and compensation scales at comparable organizations across the country, as well as those for similar positions in organizations within the community, even if the local organizations differ in product or service.

For example, maintenance personnel in a tertiary care facility are likely to confront equipment and standards that are more complex and demanding than those found in primary or general health care settings. Thus, comparing job descriptions for maintenance workers in the tertiary setting to job descriptions for similar workers at a walk-in diagnostic facility or a general hospital would not be as valid as a comparison with similar workers in the computer chip manufacturing industry, which also has exacting standards for sanitation and a complex high-technology environment. As with job design, the emphasis must be on the realistic needs of the organization and the actual work that will be required of a person in this position.

Job Evaluation

Job evaluation involves assigning a *relative* value to each job within the organization. Whether the jobs are within the health care field or in a manufacturing plant, the same requirements apply. As Strauss and Sayles (1980) have pointed out, job evaluation is a *system* for exercising judgment—a system that incorporates the value of each job in relation to other jobs. The value assigned to a given job must be equitable in terms of other jobs within the same organization, but it also must be in keeping with comparable jobs in the local job market. For health care organizations with facilities scattered across several states or even the entire country, an equitable evaluation for the entire system will throw some job values (and, as a result,

the pay scale) out of line with local standards if overall pay scales and the cost of living in certain communities are below the national or dominant levels. In such instances, managers must analyze and evaluate specific jobs even more minutely to avoid both internal and external problems.

Objective and consistent assignment of value is essential (see Strauss & Sayles [1980] for a more detailed discussion of specific job evaluation methods). One of the most common approaches to job evaluation is the development of a point system. This allows compensation managers to assign relative worth to numerous positions without discussing specific pay or benefit costs. It also allows managers to distinguish, when necessary, among positions that may appear to be equal. For example, maintenance positions that require personnel to work in excessively noisy conditions, in extremely hot or cold environments, or at unusual times may legitimately be allocated additional points to compensate for the hardships. Support personnel positions that require job holders to maintain budget figures or personnel records would be assigned more points than comparable positions without such requirements.

Importantly, a point system, when properly developed and managed, eliminates bias from the determination of job evaluation. Job evaluation is of greater significance for new organizations or businesses, but, to some extent, the changing nature of the entire health care industry calls for renewed attention to existing job designs and descriptions. Current employees may hold with traditional ideas of the relative values of given jobs, but the evolving role of professionals within the health care field—and the most recently educated professionals rushing to fill the newly created vacancies—will place new demands on strategic planners in health care organizations in coming years.

Strauss and Sayles (1980) note, for example, that sex discrimination has, to some extent, been traditional insofar as jobs more often held by women have been assigned lower relative values. Thus, nurses, who must complete training beyond the high school level, may be paid less than truck drivers. Such a system gained acceptance during a time when nurses were most likely to be women and truck drivers were most likely to be men. In keeping with changing social opinion and federal legislation, few such disparities will be acceptable in the future. In particular, the concept of comparable worth can be expected to be applied in more areas of health care. It is reasonable to assume that strategic planners for tomorrow's health care organizations will face even greater burdens to assess comparable worth in the absence of work similarities. Although this will represent quite a challenge, it is an area that offers future planners vast opportunities to develop compensation systems with greater equity than has been feasible in the past.

As will be seen when job pricing is discussed, the value placed on a given position by an individual employee does not always conform to the relative value assigned that position by strategic planners who must evaluate all positions within a given organization. For example, a clerical employee with minimal skills may view his or her position as infinitely "better" than that of an expert plumber. Because the traditional blue-collar jobs have often been held to be inferior to white-collar jobs, such self-assigned status may offset differences in compensation that would belie such a view. In other words, the minimally skilled clerical worker may be entirely satisfied with a wage below that of a highly skilled plumber as long as the perceived status of the clerical position is not challenged.

Another important area of job evaluation concerns the extent to which the evaluation is centralized. Should a job be evaluated in terms of an entire, possibly nationwide, company, or should the evaluation focus on a single facility? If a job is to be evaluated nationally (and the resulting job price tied to the result), should that position incorporate duties not routinely assigned to it in comparable, local companies? As health care organizations expand into regional and national chains, such questions will assume added significance.

Job Pricing

Job pricing is the final planning stage in establishing a staffing and compensation system for a given organization, and it involves exactly what the name implies. After each job has been designed, analyzed, described, and evaluated, it is assigned a specific financial value, a wage scale, and a range. Because equality across and within the system is vital, job pricing depends on the careful completion of the preliminary stages.

Interestingly, however, in this one area, the appearance of fairness is at least as important as the reality, if not more so. Perception is more important than reality. For example, employees are most likely to compare their wages with those of persons holding positions they deem comparable, regardless of the organization's formal job evaluations results. Employees who consider themselves to be skilled labor rarely compare their compensation with those they consider to be unskilled; clerical employees are more likely to compare their pay rates with other clerical workers, not with line workers or top-level managers. To return to the example of the minimally skilled clerical worker, the assigned price for the job must be in keeping with that assigned to other, probably more skillful, clerical workers. Thus, equality (or the appearance of equality) within broad categories of workers is often the determining factor in employee satisfaction with pay. The same is true for fringe benefits and other factors in the total compensation package. Workers in any general category will probably compare their paid holidays to those offered similar workers, even if some workers in other categories receive different holidays.

Job pricing comes under particular scrutiny in the provision of pay differentials for unusual requirements. Just as a point system gives added value for environmental factors, the job pricing system must acknowledge such differences as night or weekend shifts or assignment to a particularly demanding area. Although such differences are addressed during the evaluation stage, care must be taken to implement these distinctions when assigning job prices.

After relative values have been assigned during the evaluation process, it would seem that the assignment of an actual price to each position would be a relatively simple matter. However, the reality of job pricing is a far more complicated undertaking. First of all, the entire compensation investment cannot exceed the organization's income. This simple concept involves complex income projections, realistic assessment of the external environment, and a comprehensive understanding of regulations and professional standards governing the organization's operation. Before a total compensation plan can be developed and implemented, the organization must account for all factors that will influence its income and its ability to remain in business.

For example, the diagnosis-related groups (DRG) payment system recently implemented by the Medicare program establishes limits for Medicare coverage based on the primary diagnosis at the time of hospital admission. A hospital that habitually expends greater resources for these patients than can be recouped through the DRG system could face financial disaster, regardless of the care with which jobs were priced originally. To provide another example, a health care organization serving walk-in clients would be foolhardy to locate in an isolated area, where the likelihood of heavy usage could not be anticipated.

These are but a few indications of the factors to be considered by compensation managers. Another concern is the labor market in the area of operation. A definition of "labor market" usually incorporates the extent to which qualified workers are available for, and interested in, employment in a given field of endeavor and a given geographic region. Differences in the number and qualifications of workers usually vary with time and by location; nevertheless, such an assessment must be made when determining the fair market value of a given service and the jobs involved in providing it. Thus, the entire exercise of job pricing must assume that such homework has already been completed as thoroughly and accurately as possible.

In setting up the job pricing system, compensation managers must define such concepts as a base salary that is hourly, weekly, or monthly and whether to use salary ranges or a flat rate (i.e., a single amount paid to all incumbents regardless of longevity, experience, or special training). The advantages of such a system are the ease of communication of the wage, simplicity of salary planning, ease of cost analysis, and the defensibility of equal treatment by position and job title. The most obvious and problematic aspect of such an approach is that each employee with the same title receives the same base pay, regardless of justifications for differences.

A pay-range system involves setting minimum and maximum pay levels for each job title. Such a system has several advantages: No qualified incumbent will fall below a specified level of pay; better-qualified employees can justifiably be paid high wages; a maximum is established beyond which the organization will not go, thus helping to control costs; and the range can accommodate fluctuations in the job market, whether within a specific geographic region or with time due to a changing economy. One major disadvantage of the pay-range system is that it may, in practice, make some positions more difficult to fill. For example, if an organization usually fills positions at the lowest level of a pay range, a shortage of qualified personnel may make those positions more difficult to fill. If long-range planning has been based on filling those positions at the lower end of the pay range, the organization could be forced to choose between meeting staffing needs or meeting budget constraints.

When coming to the actual pricing of jobs, external factors again enter the picture. As with the evaluation process, job rates paid by comparable businesses and by competing businesses in the same area must be reviewed and considered. If one organization consistently sets job prices below comparable rates in the same area, that company will face ongoing employee dissatisfaction and personnel turnover. However, a company whose overall wage scale is far above the local market rate may be constantly challenged to meet its payroll commitment. As Strauss and Sayles (1980) point out, the burden is on the job evaluation system to include sufficient flexibility to accommodate internal variances and external standards.

MARKET PRICING

A newly developing approach to compensation management is called the *market pricing method*. A market pricing program is one in which all or most of the pay ranges within an organization are set according to how they fall within the external market. Using this system, an organization must first determine and articulate its desired compensation philosophy. To do this, it must do the following:

1. Define its market (e.g., who are the competitors for pay in terms of recruitment and retention)
2. Define where it wishes to be placed within the market (e.g., in the top third)
3. Determine which primary measure of compensation it will use in placing its jobs (i.e., the minimum, the maximum, or the average rate paid)

After the organization has specified its compensation philosophy, it then must conduct regular surveys to assess its market and make the needed adjustments to its pay ranges. This means that employees will receive increases that may be different according to where their positions fall within the market survey. As an example, an organization might articulate the following market-based compensation philosophy:

Our pay ranges are designed to fall within the top 5% of the local area hospital market. This market includes the other three local hospitals, and our market guide will focus primary attention on the minimum rates paid. Surveys will be conducted each spring and adjustments, if needed, will be made in July.

Based on this philosophy, if this hospital found during its spring salary survey that the average minimum rate paid for a staff nurse at the three local hospitals was $14.00 per hour, its minimum rate should be no less than $13.30 per hour (the target philosophy is to be in the top 5%, thus the average minimum of $14.00 × 0.95 = $13.30). If its minimum rate during the spring survey was $13.00 per hour, the minimum market adjustment for the summer should be one that takes the minimum up to at least $13.30 per hour. It could be more than the $13.30 based on factors such as turnover, degree of difficulty in recruiting, or past precedent.

Similarly, this hospital might find that its minimum rate for dietary assistant is $6.50 per hour, and the salary survey shows an average minimum rate of $6.55 per hour. Given this situation, the hospital might decide to provide no market-based salary increase to employees in that particular job title.

One major decision that must be made is whether all positions will be singularly market priced (which ultimately means that every single position within the organization must have its own pay range) or whether certain key jobs within each pay range are market priced and those anchor jobs drive the market-based adjustment for that particular pay range. The key variables involved in addressing this question are the size of the organization and the degree of complexity involved within the compensation system. Smaller organizations with smaller gross numbers of job titles may wish to consider single ranges for each position; larger organizations will probably opt for anchor positions that will drive each market-based, pay-range change. Also, the more pay ranges involved, the more complex and difficult to administer the pay system.

The market pricing approach to setting pay rates is becoming popular within health care. This has occurred because of the following factors:

1. Market pricing has historically been the primary factor in setting pay rates for health care workers, particularly those in high demand (e.g., nursing, physical therapy). Internal job evaluation systems are often set aside to allow the market to dictate the rates that have to be paid.

2. Market pricing is rather fair, or at least as fair as the market. Employees easily understand the concept and are able to personally relate their own rates to this method. There is little debate over issues of compensable factors that exist within most internal job evaluation systems.

3. Market pricing is an excellent system in today's reimbursement restricted environment to allocate needed dollars to those positions that are most critical in that they are in short supply or have market pay, which experiences strong upward spiral. Market pricing creates a fair scenario in which dollars are not wasted in "across-the-board" increase as in the past.

BASE PAY

The steps leading to job pricing are designed to establish equitable pay scales within a given organization, but base pay is just the beginning of employee compensation. As discussed later in this chapter, reward systems beyond the base pay are often of greater importance to employees. However, the base pay is the employee's initial primary concern. As is the case with job pricing, the perception of the relative ranking of one's base pay may be more important to an individual employee than the pay itself.

For example, a dietician who feels that his or her pay is in keeping with professional standards probably will not be concerned with the base pay of a truck driver or an administrative assistant. However, the same dietician may be content to work for a base pay below the national average in the field if he or she is aware of regional or organizational differences in pay across the board. Furthermore, an employee with several years of applicable experience will expect a base pay higher than that given beginning employees with the same job title.

The complex relationships that led to job pricing and the establishment of base pay for a specific employee do not go away after the job has been priced and an employee hired to fill the position. Thus, it is worthwhile to look briefly at the issue of pay over time.

Just as society changes, so do the jobs within an organization. This may be particularly true for certain areas of the health care industry. As increased technology alters the responsibilities of some employees, the very nature of the work day and its requirements may undergo drastic change. As Strauss and Sayles (1980) note, employees who feel that their jobs have become more difficult probably will ask for new evaluations of their positions. Employers, aware of the changes and the new demands on the employees, are likely to agree. At this point, the whole process of design, analysis, evaluation, and pricing may begin again. But such a reevaluation does not happen in isolation. If changes in the job evaluation and the relative value for one job place its value above others, a new group of employees is likely to request review, beginning the process again in a different area of the organization. It should be apparent that a payment system cannot remain static; at best, it can provide functional guidelines for relative values.

It should also be noted that actual management and implementation of the compensation system are of greater long-term benefit or damage than the system itself. A system with certain inequities may never be challenged (or may never generate employee dissatisfaction) if skilled managers apply it in a way that compensates for the problem areas. Conversely, an excellent system poorly applied or mishandled by inexperienced or inept administrators might just as well be flawed itself. As with each aspect of strategic management, the talents and judgment of top-level administrators must be oriented toward equitable standards that are fairly applied.

INCENTIVE COMPENSATION PROGRAMS

We now turn to the issue of compensation over and beyond the base. In recent years, numerous approaches have been developed to deal with motivating and rewarding employees who make significant contributions to an organization's success. Such programs are commonly referred to as *incentive programs.*

Incentive programs exist to serve two primary purposes: to motivate employees and to reward those who exceed certain, defined guidelines. Because of the potential expense involved, as well as the potential for increased productivity, such programs must be developed within the total strategic management plan. Bonus systems have existed for many years, but these have applied most traditionally to hourly paid employees or to those producing directly measurable piece goods. Recently, however, increasing attention has been paid to incentive programs for executives, top-level managers, and (within the health care industry) physicians. Because of the relative newness of these programs, additional care is necessary when incorporating them into the strategic management plan.

Executive Incentive Program

Executive incentive programs, which have been among the fastest growing, fastest changing forms of compensation in American business, are emerging rapidly in the health care field. More than ever before, health care organizations and their managers are involved in variable compensation plans. Because of the dynamic environment in health care, incentive plans in health care organizations are being developed or are being changed to link them more effectively with the organization's particular business requirements.

Until recently, the health care industry has lagged behind other industries in the area of executive compensation. However, these organizations now find that they must follow the lead of other industries and adopt more sophisticated approaches to executive compensation if they are to be successful. Health care institutions across the country are competing for the highest caliber executives. The health care organization cannot afford mediocre executives, particularly in an environment of changing reimbursement systems, declining census rates, and diversification. Increasingly, the health care industry is competing with other industries for the best executives, and—like the industries with which it must compete—health care is using compensation as a powerful recruitment tool. As the emphasis shifts to performance and leverage costs, the fixed costs of base salaries and benefits are giving way to a variety of incentive and bonus programs.

Executive incentive programs, when designed and administered properly, can reward outstanding performance appropriately and can be an effective management tool in achieving targeted results. When discussing incentive programs, it is important to understand the difference between an incentive and a bonus. An *incentive* is designed to motivate individual workers and to improve the economy and efficiency of organizational operations. A *bonus* is any compensation in addition to regular wages and salary. Bonuses are often related to the performance of a corporation or organization rather than to individual performance. If the corporation exceeds expectations, bonuses may be awarded to all employees, or to all employees within certain classifications. However, incentives are tied directly to executive performance, and rewards are related directly to preestablished individual performance targets. Incentives are developed to motivate executives to actions that accomplish organizational results.

Executive Benefits and Perquisites

Generally speaking, health care organizations provide fewer benefits and perquisites for management than do other industries. Perquisites are employee benefits applicable only to executives. "Perks" may supplement employee benefit coverage, or they may provide coverage that does not exist in the standard employee benefit program. The most common perquisites in health care organizations include company cars, country and lunch club memberships, physical examinations, and liability insurance.

Annual Executive Incentive Programs

Annual executive incentive programs in health care organizations often consist of measuring financial targets for operating revenue, operating income, receivable days, and productivity measures. In addition to financial goals, emphasis is placed on measures ensuring high-quality standards, as well as on personal, strategic, and innovative goals requiring attention.

Meeting well-established targets and standards of performance provides a return that is greater than the incentive payout. If the executive targets are not met, there is no obligation for the organization to reward the executive with the incentive pay. For example, assume the total operation revenue for a hospital is $100 million. A financial target is established to increase net operating income by $800,000, and in return the hospital's top six executives could receive 20% of their base salaries as incentives if the target is achieved. The return on investment would be as shown in Table 15.1.

For best results, incentive payouts should vary with the level of achievement. In the example shown in Table 15.1, the incentive program established could pay 10% to executives if they achieve an increase in income

TABLE 15.1. Effectiveness of Incentive Programs as Return on Investment

Position	Base Salary	Incentive Level		
		20%	10%	5%
CEO/ Administrator	$155,000	$31,000	$15,500	$7750
COO	$120,000	$24,000	$12,000	$6000
CFO	$115,000	$22,500	$11,250	$5625
Vice presidents				
Personnel	$85,000	$17,000	$8500	$4250
Marketing	$70,000	$14,000	$7000	$3500
Operations	$90,000	$18,000	$9000	$4500
Additional operating income	$800,000	$400,000	$200,000
Additional compensation		$126,500	$63,250	$31,625
Return on investment		$673,500	$336,750	$168,375
Percentage return on investment		632%	632%	632%

of $400,000 (or 5% if they achieve an increase in income of $200,000, and so forth). Financial "windfalls," representing an increase in revenue due to such factors as a technological improvement, should be excluded from the incentive agreement.

The measurement targets in executive incentive plans can be of three major types. They can be based on the following:

1. Group or team goals
2. Individual goals
3. A combination of group/team and individual goals

Most plans presently being developed include a combination of group and individual goals. Those that are solely based on group or team goals often give rise to charges from some members of the group that others did not carry their fair share of the effort toward the end-goal achievement. However, those plans that are based solely on individual goals create the possibility that some team members may see their goal challenges as more difficult than others and create some dissention as a result. Furthermore, there is the loss of the team feeling and synergy when there are no team goals.

It is also important that the targets and standards be "stretch" goals, (i.e., ones that are not easily achieved). Executives should not be rewarded with additional incentive compensation for doing a job that is ordinarily expected as a routine course of everyday work.

One final note is in order regarding executive incentive compensation. With the recent scrutiny by the Internal Revenue Service (IRS) of health care organizations, it is important that executives ensure that their total compensation (i.e., base plus incentive pay plus benefits) is in line with comparable organizations. Frequent executive salary surveys, a philosophy that sets executive pay and incentives in line with industry standards, and appropriate board of trustees oversight can assist in this endeavor. Without full awareness and attention to this issue, some organizations may risk losing their tax-exempt status.

Long-Term Executive Incentive Program

Another trend in incentive programs for health care administrators is the inclusion of top management personnel in both annual and long-term incentive plans. This ensures that management does not maximize short-term objectives at the expense of long-term goals. Long-term incentives for top executives have already become standard practice in other industries, as well as for-profit health care companies. However, they are just now gaining acceptance among not-for-profit

organizations, hence are still limited in number.

The specific purposes of long-term incentive programs are to direct the focus on strategic goals of the health care organization, to build a balance between short-term and long-term goals, to create among executives a sense of belonging and ownership, to assist in attracting good executives, to provide retention interest for outstanding executives, and to provide long-term, tax-efficient, capital-building opportunities for executives.

There has also been an increase in the use and formality of special incentive programs. Special incentives targeted for selected groups—exceptional performers, physicians, salespersons, and nonmanagement employees—also have begun to emerge in both for-profit and not-for-profit health care companies (Douglas, Klein, & Hunt, 1986).

Benefits from Executive Incentive Programs

Well-developed incentive programs can provide opportunities for added value and other significant benefits to any health care organization. These benefits include the following:

- Documentation of improved quality of care
- Early identification of key targets
- Development of a strong sense of managerial direction
- Development of a better balance between high-quality care and financial results
- Establishment of a tracking system for targets on at least a monthly basis so

early action can be taken when required

- Promotion of a team spirit and the understanding by executives that each must play a role in achieving group targets
- Focus of managers' attention on organizational, as well as functional or professional, goals
- Identification of outstanding performers for future executive openings

A properly planned and supported executive incentive program can pay dividends for the executives and the health care organization alike.

Group or Team Incentives

Today, more emphasis is being placed on programs that motivate and reward financially groups of employees for productivity improvement. Organizations accomplish this by sharing a portion of the savings with the employees directly responsible for the improved productivity. The concept is relatively new in the service industries, including health care. However, several very successful group incentive programs have been developed recently and are drawing attention and focus from other health care organizations.

With the present environment and challenges requiring maximum productivity, it can be expected that group incentive programs will receive much more attention in the health care industry. Such programs are typically very formal, incorporating eligibility and performance measures that are clearly specified in advance. In addition to design issues, the challenge is for management to assess employee attitudes and readiness carefully. This will take on added importance as programs planned and designed to focus activities on improved health care and unit productivity become more prevalent.

For some time, the industrial sector has experimented with variable compensation plans designed to increase productivity. Most of these efforts have tied the reward to the traditional profit-sharing or after-the-fact bonus concept. Others have been more ambitious, approaching productivity improvement through an integrated economic system that links all human resources to a previously defined business objective. Group incentives constitute a similar approach, with incentives available to all employees in a unit or even in the company. The overriding premise of such an incentive program is that the business must produce a measured improvement in performance before any such bonus or profit-sharing takes place. After this economic reality has been recognized and achieved, team incentives provide a way to increase the personal income of everyone involved.

The programs typically target improvements in defined areas, such as quality, profits, service, or cost reductions. Everyone in the organization is committed to a set of common objectives to increase productivity and, ultimately, profitability. The return received by the company is shared with all of the employees who made it happen. In addition to the shared reward, two other traits are common in successful group incentive programs. First, management philosophy and practices must create a positive climate for excellence and must encourage a high degree of employee commitment and participation. Second, a system and structure must be developed that enable all employees to become more deeply involved in solving problems of productivity, quality, and service. It has been demonstrated that all three factors—management practices, shared reward, and employee participation—have the potential of significantly improving productivity.

Trends in Incentive/ Bonus Compensation

All forms of incentive compensation plans are becoming more common in all segments of the health care industry, with slower growth found among organizations with religious affiliations. The plans are more prevalent in for-profit health care organizations, but they are continuing to increase at a significant pace in not-for-profit, secular health care organizations. The formality of these plans varies considerably—from being totally discretionary to incorporating strict, formal criteria for eligibility, performance measures, and award size. However, the overall trends are toward increasing formality and toward extending incentive programs to lower echelons within organizations, making such reward available to greater numbers and classifications of employees (Hay Management Consultants, 1986).

Physician Compensation

The entire area of physician compensation is one that is on the rise. Although most physicians have traditionally used health care organizations under the "workshop" model and were not under any form of employer-employee relationship, this is a trend that is rapidly changing.

A number of factors have given rise to an increase in the number of employed physicians. First, as a result of increasing competitiveness, an increasing number of health care organizations has begun to employ staff physicians to cover certain types of services, such as family care services, pediatric clinics, or ambulatory surgery services. These are programs that are run by the health care organization, which captures all of the billed revenue for these services. The physicians are paid a set salary and provide benefits.

Second, a larger number of new physicians who are entering practice have chosen a lifestyle that is different than their predecessors. They have made the decision that they do not wish to set up their own office practices and that they would prefer having set work hours.

Third, the introduction of the Medicare Resource Based Relative Value System (RBRVS) method of physician payment has changed the way different specialists are paid. As a result, many physicians are looking toward hospitals to help equalize their incomes. Many will become salaried as a result.

Finally, as more health care organizations have increased their physician recruitment efforts, various types of physician payments have surfaced. Income guarantees and other kinds of financial support have created more situations in which physicians are paid some kind of salary payments.

One of the most important aspects of physician compensation involves the accurate surveying of market rates. Internal equity is set by the market. The rates that different specialists receive has long been set within the external market. As a result, there is not that much of a focus on internal equity issues. Market surveys for physicians are still in the developing stages. Although some consulting firms have begun to develop national databases that can be helpful in determining going rates for physician compensation, there are still some concerns that make the analysis of this data difficult. First, it is difficult to determine the precise number of hours worked during a regular work week. Although most surveys figure full time at 40 hours per week, many organizations have physicians who provide service at longer work weeks. Second, some surveys do not provide information on which physicians are able to bill privately for services. In some cases, this private practice income is added to their base income and in other cases, the health care organization keeps this revenue. Finally, some rates are reported for physicians who have been in their communities for a long time and thus have developed a strong private practice (and thus receive a substantive amount of money from this source); others represent physicians new to their communities with no practice established. Typically, the former will have a much lower salary amount reported on the survey than the latter. This must be factored into the analysis when setting rates.

At a minimum, there should be some salary system established for employed physicians with established ranges based on appropriate survey data. A determination of starting salary can also be developed using guidelines similar to the one shown in Table 15.1 with performance-based practice incentives established. This method provides needed flexibility in recruiting and retaining key employed physicians.

A final consideration pertains to the development of quality and productivity measures in physician compensation. Both must be balanced so that payment made on an employed basis can recognize the need for some appropriate level of productivity as well as the provision and maintenance of quality care.

Exceptional Performance Awards

Many companies have begun to use incentives to motivate individuals who are particularly crucial to the long-term success of the organization. Special compensation approaches, particularly exceptional performance awards, are gradually increasing in the health care industry because of the usefulness of this method of eliciting high commitment and performance from selected employees. Health care organizations are experimenting with these plans to recognize outstanding contributions made by any employee. Incentives may be appropriate, for example, in projects with major cost-savings implications or in those that in some way increase the organization's ability to compete in today's rapidly diversifying marketplace. Special incentives are also being used to reward true entrepreneurial successes. Such plans are designed to acknowledge, motivate, and retain critical employees who are not adequately covered through existing compensation programs. These plans typically provide a limited number of awards for outstanding achievements, and they often include employees who would be very difficult to replace. These employees with ongoing records of significant contributions may have knowledge of a proprietary nature or may be involved in special projects. The award is usually sizable and varies considerably depending on the type of program, the significance of the accomplishment, or the importance of the individual to the organization (Douglas, Klein, & Hunt, 1986).

Traditional compensation components (i.e., base pay and benefits) are designed to meet broad human resources objectives. These, however, often fall short of meeting the demands of a health care business attempting to deal effectively with exceptional performers. Base salaries, even when administered under a merit-based system, typically reflect little difference between average performers and those who are outstanding. Annual merit increases tend to be only slightly greater for the best performers, and these increases are generally much smaller than the value received by the organization from a truly exceptional performer. Annual salary increases are rarely tied to specific outcomes. Furthermore, salaries usually are of limited value in retaining key individual high performers. Substantial salary increases are often offered by competitors to attract or recruit key talents. This situation, coupled with the industry's critical need for innovation and diversification, has caused health care organizations to begin to examine and adopt less conventional compensation techniques aimed at dealing with recognition and rewards based on an equitable remuneration scheme for key performers.

As the health care industry becomes more aware of effective ways to create and implement special compensation plans, it is likely that exceptional performance programs will grow in popularity. Pressure to protect the people and the ideas on which a given organization depends will lead to an increase in both the number and types of formal programs, and the pressure for such action also can be expected to increase. Group incentive plans offer significant leverage in targeting goals and objectives, but plans to recognize and reward exceptional performance are likely to receive greater acceptance.

BENEFITS

One might assume that benefits have been a part of health care employee compensation for many years. In reality, however, benefit programs in all industries are an occurrence of the mid twentieth century. The first major national development in benefits came in 1934. The Great Depression had made people overtly aware of financial problems associated with illness, old age, disability, and death, and the federal government responded with the Social Security program to provide a basic level of retirement protection. Until after World War II, there was little voluntary employer action. Because wages were frozen during the war, interest grew in the benefits area. After the war, however, in 1948, the National Labor Relations Board ruled that benefits were subject to collective bargaining, and employee pressure for benefits began to increase. The strong postwar American economy, coupled with substantial employee, union, and employer interest in benefits, resulted in a 30-year boom in employee benefits. Competing favorably with other employers or being the first to develop or implement a new benefit program was a primary objective for many businesses in the 1960s and 1970s. Another major turning point came in 1974 with the enactment of the Employee Retirement Income Security Act (ERISA). This act set guidelines for pension plans and required disclosure of information concerning welfare benefits. The ERISA provided increased assurance that employees would actually receive a retirement benefit and set the stage for even more government regulations. Although the ERISA added substantially to administrative burdens and to the costs of benefit programs, benefit plans continued to grow and improve throughout the 1970s. Indeed, there was virtually a benefits race that resulted in most major companies and industries offering a full package of benefits by the middle of the decade (Hay Management Consultants, 1986).

The health care industry was no exception. Although health care organizations tend to spend less on benefits than firms in other industries, the cost is still substantial. For example, among hospitals, the current average cost of so-called fringe benefits is nearly

36% of total payroll costs. In 1991, the average hospital investment in fringe benefits was $9398 per employee, compared with an all-firms average of $13,136. The investment of hospitals in fringe benefits may lag behind the national average, but it should be remembered that given the figures above, the total expected expenditure for a hospital with 1000 employees would exceed $9 million!

Data released by the U.S. Chamber of Commerce (1992) illustrate both the relative and the absolute cost of employee benefits in our economy. Table 15.2 summarizes some of these data. Note that the single largest expenditures category is for time-off benefits such as sick leave, vacation, and holidays. Annually the average hospital spends about $2555 per employee for these items. The true cost is much greater, however, because many absent employees in hospitals

must be replaced by other employees, often at overtime rates.

Legally, required benefits, such as Social Security, unemployment compensation, and worker's compensation, have increased dramatically over time and now constitute 23% of the cost of benefit programs. Further increases are expected in the future, and health care executives can do little to control expenditures in this area. Therefore, it will become even more important for health care organizations to integrate new legally required benefits with existing benefits coverage.

Pension expenditures for the hospital industry average $773 per employee in 1991, compared to $1370 spent per employee for all firms. Hospitals, like all health care organizations, are likely to face growing pressure in the future to increase their pension benefits. Careful restructuring of retirement and

TABLE 15.2. Employee Benefits in U.S. Economy Compared with Hospitals

	All Firms		Hospitals	
	Amount	Percent	Amount	Percent
Legally required	$ 2978	22.7	$2173	23.1
Social Security/railroad	$ 2363	18.0	$1858	19.8
Unemployment compensation	$ 179	1.4	$ 33	.4
Worker's compensation	$ 418	3.2	$ 277	2.9
Tax exempt	$ 3683	28.1	2436	25.9
Life/medical insurance	$ 3429	26.1	$2241	23.8
Dental insurance	$ 197	1.5	$ 110	1.2
Education	$ 57	.4	$ 85	.1
Tax deferred	$ 1670	12.7	$ 765	8.1
Pension	$ 1370	10.4	$ 733	7.8
Profit sharing	$ 169	1.3	$ 29	.3
Thrift plans	$ 131	1.0	$ 3	.1
Time not worked	$ 4217	32.1	$3662	39.0
Breaks, wash-up, etc.	$ 752	5.7	$1107	11.8
Vacation, holidays, sick	$ 3465	26.4	$2555	27.2
All other	$ 578	4.4	$ 362	3.9
Total	$13,126	100.0	$9398	100.0

Source: U.S. Chamber of Commerce. (1992). p. 20.

annuity benefits and integration with Social Security benefits may be helpful in this regard. Another important strategy is to terminate existing defined benefit plans and replace them with defined contribution plans. This trend, which is already becoming common in other industries, also could be beneficial to the health care industry. Sponsored tax-deferred programs, matching savings programs, and other sound investment strategies can also pay large dividends in the efforts of health care organizations to reduce total pension costs.

Referring again to Table 15.2, it is obvious that expenditures for insurance, especially health insurance, constitute the largest benefit cost that is not required by law. The average hospital spent $2241 per employee for insurance in 1991, compared with the average of $3429 for all firms. However, many hospitals write off as unmeasured costs to their employees or provide free medical services, so the amounts actually expended are probably much greater than they appear.

With expenditures by hospitals as examples, it is clear that benefits have become increasingly expensive for employers in the health care field. However, the benefits race slowed during the economic recession of the early 1980s when cost containment became the watchword and, for many organizations, the key to survival. Today, benefits are clearly no longer "fringe" compensation. Benefit programs, rather than base salary, often keep employees from changing employers. Over the years, the proportion of the compensation dollar allocated for benefits has grown so that today's benefits consume more than a third of the total compensation dollar. As a result of this growth, top-level executives share a great deal of interest in containing benefit costs.

One of the trends already evident in these years of reckoning is the increasing level of benefits costs that appeared to level off during the mid 1980s. The late 1980s to early 1990s has seen a reversal in this leveling trend. Direct pay and benefits escalated more rapidly than the cost of living in the twentieth century, but benefits grew at a faster rate than direct pay until the 1970s. A U.S. Chamber of Commerce (1992) survey (Figure 15.2) illustrates this pattern.

Cost containment continues to be the dominant trend in benefit planning and is considered by many employers as one of their top planning priorities. Top management is becoming more involved in benefits cost containment, but there is equal interest in the quality of what is purchased with the benefits dollar.

As health care organizations in all parts of the United States emerge from the recession of the mid 1980s, most continue to hold the line on benefits. Components of the health care industry continue to be challenged with changes in reimbursement systems and guidelines, a growing consumerism, and greater competition. Ambulatory clinics and freestanding diagnostic centers, as well as a range of entities of other types, now compete with traditional office-based medical practices or provide functions formerly carried out by hospitals. All of the factors exert pressure on the more traditional health care organizations to effect cost-savings measures. With the high price tag on benefits, savings in this area take on added importance.

Cost containment is unquestionably the dominant trend in benefits. Now that the quality of benefits is basically under control, renewed attention will be directed to cost containment. Instead of increasing the level of benefits, health care organizations are al-

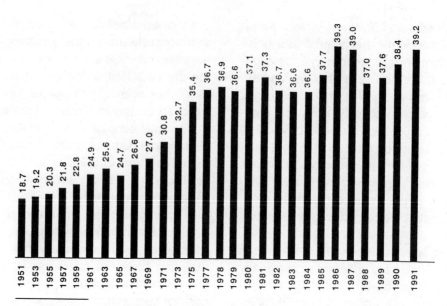

FIGURE 15.2. Benefits as a percentage of payroll, 1951 to 1991 (Source: U.S. Chamber of Commerce, 1992).

ready redesigning benefit programs to meet employee needs better while holding the line on costs. It is worth noting that efforts to contain rapidly escalating costs of health care benefits apparently have been successful. Previously skyrocketing costs are beginning to stabilize as premium increases slow, dropping from earlier rises between 18% and 26% in the first half of the 1980s to increase rates closer to the rate of inflation. This slowdown has been effected by increased use of cost-sharing measures, encouragement of the use of alternative services, and implementation of peer review programs. Plans designed to share more costs with employees are becoming more common as employers raise deductibles and copayments while increasing the employee's share of the premium.

In conjunction with the efforts of health care organizations to reduce the relative level of benefits, more benefit programs will feature choice-making options. More

cafeteria-style selections of benefits and perquisites will be offered so that individual employees can choose the options that best fit personal and family needs. Pressure for such flexibility can be expected to increase in the health care industry. The field is already dominated by female employees, and the growing trend of dual-income families can be expected to alter drastically the benefits deemed most desirable by one partner in a dual-income family. As health care organizations continue to emphasize limiting the quantity of benefits and stressing the quality of what can be purchased with each benefits dollar, they will most likely be joined in their efforts by employees with similar goals.

FLEXIBLE BENEFITS

A flexible benefits system is one under which employees have some choice in the form of their total compensation. As a cost-containment strategy, flexible compensation helps employers to control costs in several ways. First, it redefines the employer's obligation in terms of overall level of expenditure rather than locking an employer into paying for a specific package of benefits regardless of costs. Additionally, flexible plans enable the employer to control the benefits allowance for each employee (i.e., the employer is no longer at the mercy of inflation or other factors beyond the organization's control).

A positive side effect of flexible plans is that by giving an employee a choice, an employer can offset the negative effects of benefit cutbacks. This is particularly true with respect to health benefits. Surveys show that employees like flexible plans, even when fewer benefits are provided. Flex plans provide the opportunity for employees to tailor their benefits coverage to meet individual situations. In the past, most benefit programs were designed around the idea of the traditional family (in which the father works and the mother stays home), but patterns of family life have changed dramatically during the past few decades. There is now a significant need for benefits designed around the various stages of an employee's career and around the diversity of each employee's individual needs.

Because flex plans provide individual choices, they have been popular with employees, who can decide, for example, whether to contribute toward extensive coverage or to accept smaller benefits, paid for entirely by the employer. The presence of individual choice makes cost containment more acceptable while offering a wider menu of benefits from which to choose. And when cost containment involves added costs to employees, the workers show a greater willingness to help finance the benefits they most desire.

An example of the advantages of a flex plan is found in the area of medical insurance coverage. When employees are given a choice of medical options, the majority of employees select health coverage different from that originally offered. This usually results in cost savings due to decreased plan utilization. Moreover, since employees must choose their benefits under such a plan, they learn more about the various components, leading to increased employee understanding of the true value and cost of the programs. An additional asset is that certain benefits (e.g., child care, uncovered medical expenses, legal expenses) can be designed into a flex plan in a way that brings tax savings to both the employer and the employees.

Because of the various positive aspects of flexible benefit programs, the movement toward flex plans is anticipated to continue at a rapid pace in companies of all sizes. By the end of 1992, more than 1500 major U.S. companies were estimated to have implemented a formal flexible compensation program in employee benefits (Figure 15.3). As

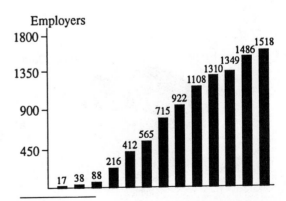

FIGURE 15.3. Prevalence of flexible compensation programs among major U.S. employers (Source: Hewitt Associates, 1993 Survey of Flexible Compensation Programs).

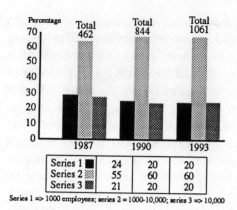

FIGURE 15.4. Full flexible compensation programs by employer size (Source: Hewitt Associates, 1993 Survey of Flexible Compensation Programs).

illustrated in Figure 15.4, flexible compensation programs have been implemented by companies in all size categories. Much of the recent growth has been fueled by medium-size organizations—those with 1000 to 10,000 employees. By industry, flexible programs are well-represented across industry lines. Figure 15.5, which gives the concentration of flexible programs by industry, indicates that the health care industry has been

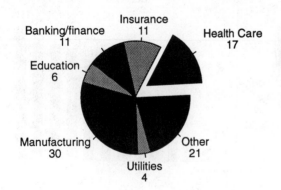

FIGURE 15.5. Flexible programs by industry (Source: Hewitt Associates, 1993 Survey of Flexible Compensation Programs).

a leader in the introduction of flexible compensation programs.

TAXING BENEFITS

When benefit programs started, several tax rulings established the "nontaxability" of most employee benefits. That philosophy was rarely attacked until recently. Strong movements are now underway to tax employee benefits. Aside from the need to obtain more tax dollars, the pressures for taxation of benefits appear to stem from the perception that it is not fair for employees who work for companies that provide benefits to receive those benefits tax-free while employees of companies that do not provide such benefits must purchase them with after-tax dollars. The opposing philosophy is that families with financial protection in the event of illness, disability, death, and retirement, employee benefits serve an important social goal and, in the long run, will save the government money. As more benefits become taxable, it is likely that many health care organizations will be pressured by employees to cut back on benefits and raise base pay. It can be expected, however, that many employees would not use such a salary increase to replace the protection they have lost, and many employees who eventually needed the protection would not have it. It can be argued that in addition to the potentially devastating impact on employees and their dependents, such a scenario would place additional burdens and pressures on social and government programs (Hay Management Consultants, 1986).

Future Benefit Trends

There will continue to be strong pressure from the consumer, the public in general, and the government for health care organizations to hold the line on costs. Health maintenance organizations and preferred provider organizations can be expected to increase in popularity, as can such alternatives to inpatient hospitalization as home health care, walk-in care centers, and surgery centers. Medical and hospital pre-admission authorization programs are likely to become more prevalent, as are employee fitness and wellness programs. Medical plans will continue to be redesigned to shift more cost to employees, and choice-making of benefits packages by employees will be more critical as the dollars available for benefits become more limited. Flexible benefit programs will be even more popular as their value and positive acceptance become more apparent. As health care organizations grow more determined to gain more control over the cost of benefit programs, defined benefit pension programs will continue to give way to defined contribution plans, profit sharing, or savings programs, or some combination of the three.

It will also be critical in the future for health care organizations to improve the manner in which they communicate with employees about benefits. Current benefit issues—redesign of the medical plan, 401K programs, and flexible benefits—are even more complex than traditional programs. In such a setting, employees must better understand both the actual cost of benefits and the significance of their total compensation plan.

SUMMARY

Effective compensation management has come to incorporate a multitude of human and environmental factors. From the establishment of specific jobs and their requirements to the formulation of a company-wide compensation program, decisions made by strategic planners determine the satisfaction of employees and the ultimate success of the organization. Compensation packages that motivate and reward the administrators and other employees responsible for the organization's success can be expected to increase in number and scope as governmental mandates for cost containment and cost-effectiveness add to consumer pressure for fiscal restraints.

Discussion Questions

1. Outline the process of job pricing and develop a compensation system for emergency room physicians that is determined by this concept. What incentives or disincentives should this compensation system incorporate?

2. Discuss the future of taxing employer-paid health insurance premiums and what impact it will have on your hospital employees? On your level of utilization? What steps should be undertaken now to prepare the employees and yourself for this potential?

3. Develop an executive compensation package for your facility that addresses base salary, perks, and performance-based pay. With this package, develop criteria that should be adopted to gauge executive performance—both economic and noneconomic guidelines.

4. Given the trend toward managed care and less inpatient utilization, how should the presently inpatient-oriented compensation system be developed to address this shift in patient care? What might you do as the human resources executive to prepare your institution for this eventuality?

5. Develop an institutionwide compensation plan designed to involve both professional and nonprofessional employees. What criteria are common to both groups and what criteria are specific to each group?

REFERENCES

Douglas, J., Klein, S., Hunt, D. (1985). *The strategic managing of human resources.* New York: Wiley.

Douglas J., Klein, S., & Hunt, D. (1986). Compensation and benefits. In Hay Management Consultants (Eds.), *1986 health care management company total compensation survey.* San Francisco: Hay Management Consultants.

Hewitt Associates. (1993). *Flexible compensation.* Chicago: Author.

Strauss, G., & Sayles, L.R. (1980). Wage and salary administration. In G. Strauss & L.R. Sayles, *Personnel* (4th ed.) (pp. 562–595). Englewood Cliffs, NJ: Prentice Hall.

U.S. Chamber of Commerce. (1992). *Employee benefits: 1992 edition.* Washington, DC: Author.

U.S. Chamber of Commerce. (1986). *Ideas and trends, issue 111.* Washington, DC: Commerce Clearing House.

CHAPTER

16

PREVENTIVE LABOR RELATIONS

Charles L. Joiner

John C. Hyde

LEARNING OBJECTIVES

Upon completing this chapter, the reader should be able to . . .

- Develop a management plan to maintain a "union-free" environment, if possible, and identify potential problem areas and specific management activities that should be implemented to counter such pro-union sentiment.
- Understand the issues surrounding union activities among employees and how these perceptions are dictated by management policies.
- Chronicle the rise of unionization within the health care industry and what future events or trends might arise and view management as a catalyst in the unionization equation and understand how management actions are perceived by the ordinary employee.
- Develop an anti-union management campaign that is specific in the course of events necessary for management to pro-actively address this issue and that describes what management can and cannot do in labor activities.
- Link the concept of anti-union environment to other management functions and explain how this affects other management activities.

INTRODUCTION

The concept of strategic labor management relations is concerned with the application and maintenance of positive labor relations within the organization. This employee-positive environment is utilized regardless of the presence or absence of organized labor. This chapter serves as a guide to the practitioner in developing a preventive labor management strategy, based on the premise of a management policy to maintain nonunion status. These fundamental principles are applicable, however, even if simply focused on maintaining good relations between management and organized labor.

Chapter 17, which assumes that employees are in an organized labor environment, is written from the perspective of management's need to understand the total framework and process of negotiating and administering contracts with a union. It was developed in the belief that good acumen of both cognitive and behavioral requirements can lead to a relationship that minimizes the adversarial factors and enhances the probability of mutual trust and respect. Many strategic decisions must be made during the negotiation process either for an initial contract or for a replacement contract. Also, administering the contract fairly and consistently requires a high level of attention from management to yield a productive and positive labor management relationship.

With more than 3.5 million workers, the health care industry represents one of the largest work force population groups in the United States. The health care industry also represents one of the largest pools of non-union employees, and, therefore, is a prime target for union organizers. This situation is particularly true in times of economic stress when management decisions must be made concerning the employment status of many employees, both professional and nonprofessional. The 1991 National Labor Relation Board regulation, upheld by the U.S. Supreme Court, increased the number of allowable bargaining units within the hospital environment from three to eight. This is a change that has the potential to result in an increasing number of unionization attempts in the health care industry. This seemingly prounion stance must be incorporated into management's preventive labor relations strategy to maintain a nonunion environment.

DEVELOPING AN EMPLOYEE RELATIONS PHILOSOPHY AND STRATEGY

Management strategies, specifically those regarding desired relationships to labor organizations, should be formulated as part of overall policy development. This strategy formulation must, of course, take into consideration the geographic, demographic, and historical factors pertinent to the setting. For example, an organization that is located in an area where unionization is prevalent may find it extremely difficult to prevent unionization of groups of its employees even with the best preventive plan. Nonetheless, it is management's responsibility to develop and communicate to its employees the organization's employee relations philosophy.

The organization's employee relations philosophy should be developed on the basis of its objectives regarding such factors as communication with employees, management rights, and union preferences. If an organization is not unionized, management should consider the array of environmental and organizational issues in the process of determining its policy relating to unions. Specifically, management should consider the available strategic options for developing and maintaining a positive employee relations climate.

One option is to adopt a nonunion policy and to begin to implement a preventive management program. This option is explored in detail in this chapter. A second option is for management to implement essentially the same program without communicating a formal nonunion policy, depending on its analysis of circumstances and objectives. Regardless of the strategic option chosen, it is essential for management to do the necessary analysis and adopt an appropriate employee relations program focused on maintaining good communication and positive relations.

MAINTAINING NONUNION STATUS

Maintaining nonunion status depends largely on what managers do to prevent the need for a union. This view is based on the philosophy that unionization is preventable if management is doing enough of the "right things." When management actions do not support a positive employee relations climate, workers may find it necessary to seek external help; in some situations, workers deserve help from union representation.

This argument may be supported further by noting that union organizers typically do not attempt to organize an employee group until workers themselves have sought union assistance. Union certification elections seem to suggest that employees really are voting for or against management instead of for or against a particular union. Based on these premises, this chapter seeks to help health care managers by identifying issues important to good personnel relations and the maintenance of nonunion status. *Avoidance* of a union election is preferable to *winning an election* (Goodfellow, 1991).

To provide a sound basis for prevention

of unnecessary problems, it is essential to understand the historical perspective of the underlying issues, including employee perceptions of the need for unionization. The purpose of this chapter, therefore, is accomplished through a review of labor law history and trends, an overview of the fundamental causes of friction between management and labor, a summary of reasons health care employees give for joining unions, an analysis of criteria used by union organizers to evaluate health care institutions, and finally specific recommendations for establishing a preventive management program and for maintaining nonunion status. Because knowledge of the legal framework is essential to any manager who desires to avoid foolish mistakes in the implementation of a well-conceived program, it is appropriate to review labor law history and trends first.

LABOR LAW HISTORY AND TRENDS

The National Labor Relations Act (NRLA) is the foundation for the labor laws of the United States. The NLRA, or so-called Wagner Act, was adopted in 1935 and has been amended by the Taft-Hartley Act of 1947, the Landrum-Griffin Act of 1959, and Public Law 93-360 (the Health Care Amendments) in 1974.

The Wagner Act authorized the formation of the National Labor Relations Board (NLRB) to administer the provisions of the Act. The Wagner Act encompassed all institutions that had an impact on interstate commerce. The status of nonprofit health care institutions was left to the interpretation of the courts. Proprietary institutions and nursing homes were considered within the jurisdiction of

the Act. Under terms of the Act, federal, state, and municipal hospitals were specifically exempted from legislating jurisdiction.

Under the protection of the Wagner Act, unions flourished in industries of virtually all types, creating a host of problems regarding the regulation of union-management relations. Industries had to contend with many jurisdictional strikes caused by disputes between competing unions. The Wagner Act proved inadequate in curbing these and other abuses of the bargaining process. Therefore, in 1947, Congress passed the Labor Management Relations (Taft-Hartley) Act.

The Taft-Hartley Act amended the Wagner Act by listing specific unfair labor practices. In addition, it specifically exempted nonprofit health care institutions from coverage under the Act. The status of other types of health care institutions did not change.

In 1959, the Taft-Hartley Act was amended by the Labor-Management Reporting and Disclosure (Landrum-Griffin) Act. Among its many provisions, this act requires employers, including voluntary nonprofit health care facilities, to submit a report to the U.S. Secretary of Labor detailing the nature of any financial transactions and/or arrangements that are intended to improve or retard the unionization process (Rakich, 1973).

Until 1967, the courts determined on a case-by-case basis which proprietary health care institutions and nursing homes had an impact on interstate commerce and thus were subject to the NLRA. As a result of several court cases, in 1967, the NLRB determined that proprietary health care institutions with an annual gross revenue of at least $250,000 and nursing homes, regardless of ownership, with an annual gross revenue of at least $100,000 were covered by the Act.

With voluntary hospitals comprising the largest sector of the health care industry, it was only a matter of time until they, too, fell under federal legislation. Their shift in status occurred in 1974, when Congress passed Public Law 93-360 to amend the Labor Relations Act. These amendments, which extended the coverage of the labor laws to include all health care institutions under nonpublic ownership and control, defined a health care institution as any "hospital, convalescent hospital, health maintenance organization, health clinic, nursing home, extended care facility, or other institution devoted to the care of sick, infirm, or aged persons" (Public Law 93-360). This legislation specifically addressed the health care industry and, as such, provided special considerations due to the nature of patient care concerns. These considerations included requirement of a 10-day advance strike or picketing notification, longer periods of intention to modify existing agreements, and mandatory mediation (Zimmerman & King, 1990).

As of 1990, approximately 20% of the total number of American hospitals were unionized (Kazemek & Candrilli, 1990). In the 1950s, one of every three American workers belonged to a union; now, less than 16% of the work force is organized (Stickler, 1991). Because of the declining rate of growth among blue-collar workers, labor unions are renewing their interest in the organizable group of white-collar employees in the health care industry (Fennell, 1987). During a recent 5-year period, between 1984 and 1988, unions won more health care elections than non-health care elections—55.3% versus 42.8% (Imberman, 1989). This trend should be viewed as potentially disturbing to health care managers.

Since the 1974 Amendment, the NLRB has used various methods to establish the number and scope of bargaining units. Initially a community-of-interest (resulting in narrow units) was utilized. Then a disparity-of-interest (resulting in wide groupings) was the model employed, and recently the NLRB has determined that eight units are appropriate for health care facilities (Gullett & Kroll, 1990). An April 1991 Supreme Court ruling (*AHA v. the National Labor Relations Board, No. 90-97 __U.S.__* [April 23, 1991]) upheld the NLRB determination, appealed to the U.S. Supreme Court by the American Hospital Association, that expanded the number of allowable bargaining within the hospital environment to eight specified groups. These eight groups are physicians; registered nurses; all professionals except physicians and nurses; all guards; all nonprofessional service workers except technical, skilled maintenance, business office clerical employees, and guards; technical workers; maintenance personnel, and clerical employees. Because union organizing activities are more successful with smaller bargaining units (as this creates a more homogenous voting unit with more work-related commonalities), this new criterion is viewed as a major victory for organized labor (Goodfellow, 1991; Gullett & Kroll, 1990; Hepner & Zinner, 1991; Stickler, 1990, 1991; Zimmerman & King, 1990). This decision has far-ranging labor management implications for the health care manager.

The legislative background and prospects certainly point to difficult times for health care managers seeking to stay nonunion. For a realistic perspective on maintaining nonunion status, management should have a good understanding of the fundamental causes of labor problems. Reasons for labor-management friction are summarized next.

CAUSES OF LABOR-MANAGEMENT PROBLEMS

Fundamental differences between the goals and objectives of management and labor create friction that cannot be totally explained in terms of desires for higher wages, shorter working hours, or better working conditions. Two fundamental causes of such friction are the issue of management rights and the issue of efficiency versus human value. Management will always assert its right to prescribe certain modes of action or levels of desired productivity to justify its existence or that of the organization. Yet labor unions question whether management should have complete power over the work force. This is a point of conflict. Organized labor attempts to shift the locus of control by seeking to obtain a voice for employees about working conditions and terms of employment.

The question of management's right to govern is paralleled by the question of human value versus efficiency. If management is to achieve its stated goals and objectives, it must maintain efficiency through increased productivity and cost containment. However, the union seeks to improve its members' standards of living. Neither side may be totally right or totally wrong in its demands, and unfortunate circumstances often trigger open conflict. For example, management that wishes to improve the existing fringe benefits package for employees may be prevented from doing so by pressures to contain costs. Evidence of this type of conflict in health services organizations is mounting almost daily, especially as new crises (e.g., malpractice insurance rate hikes, continued third-party cost containment efforts, restrictive reimbursement policies) arise and cause even greater cost constraints on management.

With an understanding of the fundamental causes of labor problems, administration can begin developing its philosophy for a preventive management program by reviewing research on employee reasons for joining unions. This research provides insight into employee relations and subsequent unionization activities. The analysis that follows summarizes findings from a selected number of such studies.

Why Employees Join Unions

The desire to unionize is thought to be centered on three issues—wages, employees' dissatisfaction with work benefits, and employees' perceptions about the organization as a place to work that could reflect perceptions about management or employer. However, other factors have contributed to increased union activity in the health care industry. During the past three decades, social turmoil has precipitated Civil Rights legislation and stimulated changes in the attitudes and social consciences of many individuals. The idea of being represented by a union is not considered as unprofessional as it once was (Fennell, 1987; Fenner, 1991; Hepner & Zinner, 1991; Zimmerman & King, 1990). The health care industry is just beginning to feel the effects of this turmoil, and passage of Public Law 93-360 served only to release the pent-up emotions of the industry's workers and union leaders. Recent labor reform efforts are further evidence of labor's continuing struggle to swing the pendulum in its favor.

In a study pertaining to why employees want unions, Goodfellow (1991) found the following three errors made by hospital administrators that lead to employee unionization:

1. Acceptance of the notion that low wages and poor fringe benefits cause most employee dissatisfaction (This is fallacy because the real reason for unionization is related to how the employees perceive management treatment as being fair and respectful.)
2. The assumption that interviewing of supervisors is a true barometer of employee feelings (The supervisors may not be trained in the identification of employee morale or may feel threatened by the revelation of morale problems within their departments.)
3. Ignorance of what is troubling the employees (This is a function of not listening to the employees'

understanding of the situation and not allowing communication to flow from the bottom to the top. Employees may feel that administration is indifferent to their welfare and unconcerned with their work environment.)

Table 16.1 shows that nonunion members report higher overall job satisfaction, more interesting work, increased task freedom, more pleasant surroundings, increased chances of job promotions, and increased ability to influence work decisions. Union workers reported higher feelings of job security and increased satisfaction with pay level.

Although the rationale for union-seeking activities by workers varies, Table 16.2 analyzes 10 articles to determine commonalities in the attitudes of workers who desire union representation. The results suggest that work conditions, grievances, poor communica-

TABLE 16.1. The Correlation Between Job Satisfaction and Voting for Union Representation[a]

	Correlation with Vote[a]
1. Are you satisfied or not satisfied with your wages?	−.40
2. Do supervisors in this company play favorites or do they treat all employees alike?	−.34
3. Are you satisfied or not satisfied with the type of work you are doing?	−.14
4. Do your supervisors show appreciation when you do a good job or do they just take it for granted?	−.30
5. Are you satisfied or not satisfied with your fringe benefits, such as pensions, vacations, holiday pay, insurance, and sick leave?	−.31
6. Do you think there is a good chance or not much chance for you to get promoted in this company?	−.30
7. Are you satisfied or not satisfied with the job security at this company?	−.42
8. Taking everything into consideration, would you say you were satisfied or not satisfied with this company as a place to work?	−.36

$^a p < 0.1; r = .08; N = 1004$

Source: Reprinted, by permission of publisher, from ORGANIZATIONAL DYNAMICS, Spring/1980 © 1980. American Management Association, New York. All rights reserved.
[a] The negative correlations indicate that employees who were satisfied tended to vote against union representation.

TABLE 16.2. Reasons Health Care Employees Join Unions: Derived from a Sampling of Studies in 10 Publications

Issue	Publication									
	1[a]	2[b]	3[c]	4[d]	5[e]	6[f]	7[g]	8[h]	9[i]	10[j]
Poor communication	X	X	X	X	X	X	X	X	X	X
Personnel policies	X	X	X	X	X	X	X	X	X	X
Supervision	X	X	X	X	X	X	X	X	X	X
Fringe benefits	X	X			X	X				X
Work conditions	X	X		X			X			X
Grievances		X	X	X				X	X	
Job security	X	X		X	X	X	X	X	X	X
Human dignity		X	X	X				X	X	X
Shift differentials	X	X			X	X				
Wages	X				X	X	X			

[a] Becker & Rowe (1989)
[b] Fennell (1987)
[c] Fenner (1991)
[d] Goodfellow (1991)
[e] Hepner & Zinner (1991)
[f] Hoffman (1989)
[g] Meng (1990)
[h] Powills (1989)
[i] Stickler (1991)
[j] Stickler (1990)

tions, personnel policies, quality of supervision, and job security are the most important considerations in why employees seek union representation. Issues concerned with wages, fringe benefits, shift differentials, and other human dignity factors are somewhat less important factors in those who consider unionization. This finding should convince the health care manager that employees are apparently looking for nonpay related conditions of work.

What the Union Organizer Looks For

Employees usually try to resolve their problems internally before seeking outside help. Typically, union organizers appear on the scene only if they have been invited. In other words, if a union organizer is involved,

it is likely that prolabor activity has progressed to a serious level (Eubanks, 1990a; Imberman, 1989; Powills, 1989).

There is no blueprint the health care manager can use to determine how a union organizer will evaluate a given situation. The method of evaluation depends on the organizing team sent into the area and its previous experience or success. Tactics may vary considerably, depending on the contacts from employees and management's response to the situation. However, the organizer may concentrate in certain areas, including the following.

Employee Loyalty by Work Shift

Normally, the first shift is the most loyal to the organization, the second shift less loyal than the first, and the third shift the least loyal. This probably is because new employees usually start on the second or third shift. They see top management seldom or never, and the supervisory force is usually smaller. Thus, there is no one who can provide consistent supervision (e.g., answering employee questions about personnel policies or benefits). These employees tend to feel overlooked and forgotten. They are more susceptible to the pleas of the union organizer, who usually is available on the later shifts (Goodfellow, 1991).

Female-Male Employee Ratio

Women historically have been less interested in unions than have men. In the past, many women worked to supplement the family income, but this has changed rapidly. Today, women are prevalent in the work force and frequently earn a primary or major part of the family income. Pay inequities are being addressed by unions as the number of female-related health care occupations increase (Fennell, 1987). This increase in the number and scope of health care occupations has opened additional avenues to union organizers in their efforts to establish a health care beachhead.

Nursing personnel, a majority of whom are women, are increasingly recognizing the need to organize to improve their status. Numerous professional organizations, such as the American Nurses Association and the American Society of Medical Technologists, are attempting to upgrade and negotiate conditions of employment for their memberships. Unions are currently capitalizing on the issue of gender-based pay inequities at the bargaining tables and through legislative and legal actions (Fennell, 1987).

Work Environment and Job Safety

Employees expect management to provide clean and safe working environments. If the health care institution allows the work environment to deteriorate, employees may think that the institution does not care much about them (Goodfellow, 1991). Work place hazards and related fears about such issues as AIDS and hepatitis B will be cultivated by union organizers as major organizing issues (Becker & Rowe, 1989; Fennell, 1987).

Wage Rates

Traditionally, the health care employee has subsidized health care institutions with low wages. This is an injustice to the employee, who must compete daily in the retail market for goods and services. In addition, the institution must have fair and regular wage differentials. Failure to update these differentials will cause a compression effect between the new employees' base pay and the tenured employees' level. Additional avenues of employment of various health care professionals (i.e., alternate care facilities, insurance companies, and general industry) has further affected the need for the health care industry to reward their employees adequately (Goodfellow, 1991; Stickler, 1991).

Incentive Pay

In areas in which an incentive pay program has been implemented, employees may complain that some of the performance expectations are too high. High expectations obviously breed dissatisfaction if management does not respond by reexamining these thresholds periodically. Wage differentials as a means of incentive pay must remain competitive and should not be adjusted arbitrarily (Goodfellow, 1991).

Overtime Practices

Problems arise when overtime is scheduled without the employee's consent. Management assumes that the worker will not object to the extra hours spent because of the overtime pay, but this often is not a valid assumption. Overtime can be very disruptive to the employee's family life and leisure time. The union organizer will exploit this point of dissatisfaction and force management to hire additional workers. Inequities in the distribution of overtime represent another aspect of this problem (Goodfellow, 1991). Mandatory overtime requirements of health personnel in shortage professions, such as registered nurses, has lead to increased pro-union feelings (Becker & Rowe, 1989).

Seniority/Job Security

Although management may prefer to recognize the skills and health of a worker in assigning a new job, it must not overlook the employee's view of seniority (Goodfellow, 1991; Hepner & Zinner, 1991). Seniority to them is job security. If management takes the time-honored seniority concept away completely, it is asking for employee dissatisfaction and unionization, particularly in geographic areas where unionization already is well-entrenched (Fennell, 1987). Cost containment efforts precipitated by changes in the reimbursement system and mandates from third-party payers have further added to the employees' feelings of job insecurity (Becker & Rowe, 1989).

Promotion Policy

When a new job becomes available or an employee leaves, present personnel should be given an opportunity to apply for the position. A good job-posting policy can be extremely helpful. Health care institutions also should have education and training programs available to assist employees' vertical or lateral career movements (Goodfellow, 1991).

Fringe Benefits

Research has revealed that most managements underrate the value of fringe benefits to the employee. Also, as employers continue to increase the benefits portion of total compensation, the benefits package is likely to increase in relative importance to employees (Hoffman, 1989). With the news media and the next door neighbor discussing the benefits of union representation, it is foolish for health care management to neglect to establish a good benefits program and to explain adequately to employees the benefits offered by the institution. A mechanism of providing this benefit information is through the employee benefits fair. This allows management to graphically display the value of the benefits package to the employees and to secure employee feedback on desired new benefits. With the development of various benefits packages resulting from cafeteria-style benefits programs, the benefits fair is an ideal management concept.

Discipline and Grievance Procedures

If the institution does not provide employees with written rules covering what is not allowed and what is and to what degree, some supervisors may abuse their authority to reprimand. The grievance procedure serves as a safety valve for employees to release their frustrations about supervisors or other major problems (Fenner, 1991; Hoffman, 1989). Management should develop and implement an internal procedure that employees will use instead of resorting to an outside agency to settle disputes. Management also should review the procedures periodically to make sure they are serving the worker's needs. Employees who have the opportunity to address their complaints or concerns about working conditions through the grievance procedure are less likely to feel the need for unionization (Becker & Rowe, 1989; Eubanks, 1990).

Multi-Unit Systems

As the American health care system undergoes reorganizations, mergers, and acquisitions, the hospital workplace has experienced dramatic changes. Increased centralized decision making, management systems developed to minimize costs and overheads, and increased employee production standards have all added to employee stresses. These factors are being viewed by organized labor as prime issues toward increased unionization potentials within the health care industry. Multi-unit systems are facing the prospects of multifacility bargaining units (Fries, 1986; Zimmerman & King, 1990). This condition coupled with the narrowing in definition of bargaining units should alert hospital administrators within the multi-unit system of increased unionization activity.

A PREVENTIVE MANAGEMENT PROGRAM

Assessing an institution's employee relations climate and implementing a program to prevent unionization is a process for which a myriad of management responses are possible. Each institution must carefully design a strategy that is both practical and suited to its situation. Recognizing the significant relationship between the reasons given by employees for joining unions and what a union organizer looks for, there is a substantial reason to believe that the primary causes of unionization include "communication problems" and the perception by employees of "unfair treatment."

Therefore, a preventive management program should be designed with a primary emphasis on improving in an honest and fair manner. This emphasis is detailed in several ways in the following recommendations for establishing a preventive management program. These recommendations are an outgrowth of previously described employee-related issues and could serve as the general framework within which each management team builds its own strategy.

Nonunion Policy

If a health care institution intends to be nonunion, it should give careful consideration to the development and publication of such a policy. Good labor counsel should be consulted to assist in the development of an up-front nonunion policy and to advise the best alternatives for communicating the policy to all who wish to work at the institution. All prospective employees should be informed in the screening process and given written evidence of the institutional position regarding union, along with other significant policies. The prospective employee then has the choice of whether to work for a non-union institution. This, in itself, should be an indication of fair treatment. Management also should consider publishing the non-union policy in the employee handbook for reference during orientation and other worker group meetings. This policy should include the following key resolutions (Rutkowski & Rutkowski, 1984):

1. Commitment of the administration to provide equitable treatment to all employees in their wages, benefits, hours, and conditions of employment
2. Commitment of adequate funds and time to provide all managers with the information that they need to be effective in employee relations and knowledgeable in ways of avoiding unionization
3. Commitment of administrators to the philosophy that each employee is important as an individual vital to the optimal functioning of the entire hospital team
4. Commitment to oppose efforts of outside organizations to unionize employees

Personnel Selection

Management must have effective policies and procedures regarding selection of new employees. Prevention of labor-management problems begins with the proper matching of personnel to specific jobs. A good wage and salary program including job analyses, job descriptions (with per-

formance objectives), and job evaluation is essential. If good procedures are used for selecting on the basis of both the individual's qualifications and the requirements of a specific job, the result is likely to be a better fit for the institution and the employee. Concurrently, the institution is likely to avoid many communication and morale problems. A fair wage and salary system provides at least a basis for establishing an objective employee evaluation system.

Employee Attitude Assessment

Employee attitude surveys, when conducted properly, can provide valuable management information at nominal costs. The method chosen should be simple to implement and should elicit concise employee responses. The result should be an accurate assessment of the topics surveyed, clearly differentiating between positive and negative attitudes.

Attitude surveying should be done on a planned, periodic basis so that employees perceive continual concern for their needs and management keeps abreast of fluctuations in worker attitudes. If this procedure is combined with efforts to obtain upward communication through formal and informal channels at all levels of the institution, the result should be a positive change in employees' attitudes and the development of management systems for dealing with personnel problems before they become sore spots. After attitudes have been assessed and problems identified, management should be ready to take corrective action, including an appropriate training program. Probably the single most important part of the attitude measurement analysis process is communication with the employees about the following:

- Purpose
- How data will be analyzed and used
- Confidentiality of individual responses
- Feedback concerning findings
- What changes, if any, they can expect as a result of survey findings

Management should be careful not to make promises that cannot be fulfilled, but should make a strong effort to do whatever is possible to improve employee relations. In summary, when management asks employees to take valuable time to participate in a survey, it is extremely important for them to feel that the administration values their input and is doing what it can to meet their needs.

Employee Training

Administration should examine its role and responsibilities in training employees as a function of management, rather than as a staff function. If this self-examination indicates that management is assuming little, if any, responsibility for employee training, such abdication is very likely to be related directly to workers' perceptions of poor treatment. For employees to perceive fair, honest, or decent treatment, top-level management must make the commitment to assume responsibility for training and must transmit it down through all levels to first-line supervisors. This is necessary, for example, before management can develop an adequate performance appraisal and reward system that employees will consider equitable.

After management has made the commitment to assume its training responsibility, it

must determine what type of training program to implement. The following questions may provide evaluative insight into employee needs:

1. Are employee functions and responsibilities agreed on and clear?
2. Do employees have the ability (i.e., technical training and experience) to do what is expected?
3. Do job descriptions contain specific performance objectives?
4. Do employees know what performance standards are being used to evaluate their work?
5. Is there a positive relationship between employee performance and reward?

Management implementation of an appropriate training program should have positive effects on employee attitudes and productivity and should be a major asset in eradicating the dead-end job syndrome.

Employee Value Systems

Management should recognize the different types of value systems that exist among various employee groups in both professional and nonprofessional categories. Research has identified as many as seven different employee value systems, varying from tribalistic to existentialist (Hughes, 1976). Some examples of responses to the myriad of value systems and needs include flexible work scheduling, earned time programs, methods of job enrichment, and a cafeteria-style approach to fringe benefits. Management must develop a variety of imaginative ways to respond to the needs of multiple employee families.

First-Line Supervisors

Management must recognize the importance of first-line supervisors in preventing serious labor problems. Supervisors become management's first line defense against unionization by determining how policies are implemented, serving as liaisons between top-level management, and being strong nonunion advocates (Eubanks, 1990a). If these supervisors do not have good management skills, the institution is inviting unionization. Frequently, a problem with first-line supervisors is manifested by the number of grievances filed involving situations that are either about or under the direct control of such persons. Management should evaluate the effectiveness of first-line supervisors' employee relations skills carefully and regularly. When deficiencies are found, management should either assist the supervisor through training or terminate the person, depending on his or her past record and potential.

Performance Appraisal

The institution should establish a performance appraisal policy that reflects management's desire to develop employees to their optimal potential. If management behavior indicates anything else, workers are likely to perceive treatment by supervisors as poor or unfair. To be effective in improving morale and productivity of all employees, performance appraisal must be done honestly and on a regular basis.

Management's avoidance of an honest appraisal of the nonproductive employee simply demonstrates to all workers that the reward is inequitable or that the laggards receive the same rewards as those who are productive. This can be interpreted logically by productive employees as evidence that the nonproductive actually are rewarded more than the productive in relation to their effort. If this attitude prevails, management is very likely to "teach" employees to move toward mediocrity and union thinking. The implementation of a good performance appraisal system depends largely on the management skills of the first-line supervisors. In other words, the appraisal system used is not nearly as important as the people (i.e., managers) who implement it. The best system is as weak as the people who operate it.

Disciplinary Policies and Procedures

Management must take great care in applying disciplinary policies and procedures consistently. Consistent and fair application normally can prevent unnecessary employee relations problems and grievances. One basic principle is that management should have "just cause" for imposing discipline. The definition may vary from case to case, but several basic tests can be applied to determine whether "just cause" exists for disciplining employees. These basic tests include the following:

1. Was the disciplinary rule reasonably related to efficient and safe operations?
2. Were the employees properly warned of potential consequences of violating the rule?
3. Did management conduct a fair investigation before applying the discipline?
4. Did the investigation produce substantial evidence of guilt?

5. Were the policies and procedures implemented consistently and without discrimination?
6. If a penalty resulted, was it related to the seriousness of the event as well as the past record of the employee? (i.e., Did the punishment fit the crime?)

Some form of grievance procedure should be viewed as a part of any prevention program because employees should be able to complain about perceived problems formally without fear of subjective reprisal. Although any grievance procedure is open to problems of interpretation and application, some basic factors can be applied equally in evaluating the system from the employees' perspective. These factors include the following:

1. All employees should be able to understand the mechanics of filing a grievance and should know where they can go to ask questions about any step of the system. Thus, the procedure should be written.
2. When employees file grievances, they expect prompt action. Promptness is one of the most important aspects of a grievance settlement, and failure to resolve the problem with reasonable speed is likely to lead to adverse feelings.
3. The first-line supervisor typically is the first step in a grievance procedure. When that individual is perceived to be the problem, however, employees must know they can access the grievance machinery without going through the first-line supervisor. However, the employees should take every reasonable step to solve the problem with the immediate supervisor before going to someone else with the grievance.

When employees realize that a fair grievance procedure is available and when management is doing what it can to prevent unnecessary problems, the result should be a decreased number of complaints, fair and objective processing of those that are filed, and an employee feeling that management is concerned about employee needs.

Wages

The health care institution should be very careful to stay competitive with regard to wages and should compare its rates at least annually to similar institutions in the same geographical area. Frequently, wage survey data can be found that apply to the local area, but if this is not the case, management should conduct its own survey. Even a sample survey of representative jobs will help to keep the institution abreast of trend information. Of course, certain shortage points will have to be dealt with on a case-by-case basis and possibly more frequently than every year. Competitive wages are a necessary condition in any preventive management program, but it should not be concluded that being competitive in wages is sufficient for maintaining nonunion status.

As has been indicated, wages is only one of the many factors that may enter into employees' decisions to seek union help. Health care is no longer as far behind other industries in wages as it was 15 to 20 years ago, and indeed, wages are probably not the major motivating factor for a significant portion of employees in a given institution. Although there may not be a great deal that management can conclude definitely from research regarding wages as a motivating factor, the folly of relying totally on competitive wages to prevent unionization can be illustrated best by review of wage structures in institutions that have had union elections recently.

In summary, the absence of competitive wage levels (particularly in times of double-digit inflation) is a potentially severe problem, but the presence of good wage levels is not sufficient, in itself, to prevent unionization. This is particularly true in multidimensioned institutions that employ a diverse group of employees with a variety of value systems.

MANAGEMENT STRATEGY FOR REACTIONS DURING UNION-ORGANIZING CAMPAIGNS

Although many "prevention" steps have been implemented, managers should not be so naive as to believe that a union organization attempt cannot happen. An extremely important part of a preventive management program is to have a well-planned strategy for reacting if such an attempt does occur.

Brett's (1980) two-point conceptualization of employee reactions during a union organizing campaign holds the following important implications for both employers and unions:

1. An employer's antiunion campaign that attempts to persuade employees by emphasizing economic control over them and using fear tactics is unlikely to be successful.
2. The employer's most effective antiunion campaign stresses the desire to remain

nonunion; provides factual information pertaining to working conditions, benefits, and so forth; and indicates that a labor organization cannot guarantee conditions that will exist under union representation.

SUMMARY

Maintaining nonunion status is an attainable goal. Whether it will be achieved is related directly to the behavioral dedication of management in demonstrating its concern for meeting employees' needs fairly and equitably. Although the material in this chapter is not all-inclusive and does not offer a formula to guarantee nonunion status, it is suggestive of management practices necessary to prevent communication problems and to avoid employees' perceptions of unfair treatment.

The unionization process is highly situational and in some locations may be essentially inevitable. Nevertheless, a positive nonunion philosophy and a preventive management program usually should obviate the need for a labor organization. When employees do not perceive a need for union assistance, the probability is slim that they will elect to begin paying union dues.

Discussion Questions

1. Develop a management anti-union strategy to deal with perceived union sentiments among the professional nursing staff in one of the critical care units in the hospital. This plan should address activities to be considered and who to involve in the development of this plan.
2. Discuss the future trends of hospital

unionization efforts and how the hospital should be prepared to confront these issues. What departments are the most vulnerable to union attack and what can the organization do to manage these areas?

3. Relate the concept of union-free work environment to professionalism and how professionals can accept the concept of unionization. What might you do as a senior health care executive to address this professional inconsistency?

4. Poll the health care providers in your area to determine the prevalence of unionization and what they think about future union potentials. Map a strategy that might incorporate these issues.

REFERENCES

AHA v. the National Labor Relations Board, No 90-97. (April 23, 1991).

Becker, W.L., & Rowe, A.M. (1989). Update on union organizing in health care. *Review of Federation of American Health Systems, 22*(5), 11–2, 14–6.

Brett, J.M. (1980). Why employees want unions. *Organizational Dynamics, 8*(4), 47–59.

Eubanks, P. (1990a). Avoiding unions: Supervisors are the first line of defense. *Hospitals, 64*(22), 40, 42.

Eubanks, P. (1990b). Employee grievance policy: Don't discourage complaints. *Hospitals, 64*(24), 36–37.

Fennell, K.S. (1987). The unionization of the health care industry: General trends and emerging issues. *Journal of Health in Human Resource Administration, 10*(1), 66–81.

Fenner, K.M. (1991). Unionization: Boon or bane?. *Journal of Nursing Administration, 21*(6), 7–8.

Goodfellow, M. (1991). Study shows ways to win, avoid union elections. *Healthcare Financial Management, 45*(9), 48, 50, 52.

Gullet, C.R., & Kroll, M.J. (1990). Rule making and the National Labor Relations Board: Implications for the health care industry. *Health Care Management Review, 15*(2), 61–65.

Hepner, J.O., & Zinner, S.E. (1991). Nurses and the new NLRB rules. *Health Progress, 72*(8), 20–22.

Hoffman, H.L. (1989). Personnel practices can help discourage unionization. *Healthcare Financial Management, 43*(9), 48, 50, 52.

Hughes, C.L. (1976). *Making unions unnecessary*. New York: Enterprise Publications.

Imberman, W. (1989). Rx: Strike prevention in hospitals. *Hospital and Health Services Administration, 34*(2), 195–211.

Kazemek, E.A., & Candrilli, A.J. (1990). New labor rules pose unionization threat. *Healthcare Financial Management, 43*(6), 126.

Meng, R. (1990). The relationship between unions and job satisfaction. *Applied Economics, 22*(12), 1635–1648.

Powills, S. (1989). Hospitals learn to deal with unionization. *Hospitals, 63*(13), 44–49.

Rakich, J.S. (1973). Hospital unionization: Causes and effects. *Hospital Administration, 18*(1), 7–18.

Rutkowski, A.D., & Rutkowski, B.L. (1984). *Labor relations in hospitals*. Rockville, MD: Aspen.

Stickler, K.B. (1990). Union organizing will be divisive and costly. *Hospitals, 64*(13), 68–70.

Stickler, K.B. (1991). Preparing for increased union organizing. *Health Progress, 72*(8), 18–19, 23.

Zimmerman, D.A., & King, G.R. (1990). Union elections and the NLRB. *Health Progress, 71*(1), 96–101.

NEGOTIATING AND ADMINISTERING THE LABOR RELATIONS CONTRACT

Norman Metzger

Donna M. Malvey

LEARNING OBJECTIVES

Upon completing this chapter, the reader should be able to . . .

- Understand and manage the processes of negotiating and administering the labor relations agreement
- Describe and implement all aspects of the preparation for collective bargaining
- Understand collective bargaining strategy and the importance of "good faith" bargaining
- Understand the differences between voluntary and mandatory bargaining topics
- Describe the typical grievance procedure and arbitration process under a union contract

INTRODUCTION

This chapter examines the process of negotiating and administering the labor relations agreement. Negotiators of collective bargaining agreements are skilled practitioners of an art that is little understood. Indeed, collective bargaining is an art, in which personalities play a far more important role than any theoretical or academic formats that may be suggested by numerous writers. The art of negotiating has been called a neglected one, and it is far more complex than the mere resolution of the terms of an agreement (Cook, 1972).

Collective bargaining has been described as a poker game that combines deception, bluff, and luck; as an exercise in power politics; as a debating society marked by both rhetoric and name calling; and as a "rational process" with both sides remaining completely flexible (Dunlop & Healy, 1955). Probably all of these characteristics at one time or another, in various combinations, are typical of collective bargaining and of negotiating any contract. The hallmarks of successful bargaining are more complex than trite descriptions of the process. In the final analysis, the charade itself is not as critical as the personalities involved in the bargaining, the realistic planning of strategy, and the commitment of top administration and trustees of an organization. These, then, are the hallmarks of successful bargaining.

Successful bargaining is built around and on the following cornerstones:

1. Advance planning of strategies with pragmatism and minimal subjectivity
2. Selection of a principal spokesperson who is experienced in labor relations and has been delegated full responsibility for presenting management's position in the bargaining
3. Full authorization of management's principal spokesperson to bind management and to make a "deal"

LEGAL DEFINITION OF BARGAINING

Moving from the unilateral determination of policy into the arena of collective bargaining, administrations are faced with the need for a new lifestyle. The National Labor Relations Act (NLRA) of 1935, amended as described in Chapter 16, requires an employer to recognize and bargain in good faith with a certified union, but it does not force the employer to agree with the union. You may, indeed, yield to the union's persuasions, but you may also resist, provided you have given the union an opportunity to persuade you. The Taft-Hartley Act definition of collective bargaining is pertinent to further discussion of the mutual obligations:

> To bargain collectively is the performance of the mutual obligation of the employer and the representative of the employees to meet at reasonable times and confer in good faith with respect to wages, hours and terms and conditions of employment or the negotiation of an agreement, or any question arising thereunder, and the execution of a written contract incorporating any agreement reached requested by either party, but such obligation does not compel either party to agree to a proposal or require the making of a concession. [Section 8(d), 1935]

To participate in "good faith" bargaining, the employer must be prepared to receive the proposals of the union and to meet with the union from time to time to discuss such proposals. After an election has been held and a union has been certified as the bargaining agent for a specific bargaining unit, a request to meet is most often presented in a formal letter to the institution. Management of the health care institution is then obligated under federal law to bargain with the union, and to bargain in good faith. This duty, under the NLRA, to meet and negotiate with the representatives of a majority of one's employees, has been interpreted over the years in decisions of the National Labor Relations Board (NLRB) and of the courts. For example, it has been determined that management may not require a union to give rights it possesses as a condition of meeting with management to bargain (*LLR*, 3130, p. 7909).* An express intention not to agree at the onset of negotiations violates the Act. This does not preclude "hard bargaining,"

---

* Throughout this section, references to paragraphs in interpretations found in the *Labor Law Reporter* (*LLR*) are given in the form shown above.

which is considered to be bargaining in good faith. Except for an outright refusal to negotiate, bad faith is the strongest evidence of a refusal to bargain; indeed, factors indicative of bad faith of themselves frequently constitute refusals to bargain (*LLR*, 3085). It is unlawful to insist that the collective bargaining contract be subordinated to individual contracts or to demand the right to make unilateral changes (*LLR*, 3130.16, p. 7915). Management does not fulfill its obligation to bargain by bargaining individually with employees or by offering them individual contracts when bargaining has been requested by the majority representative (*LLR*, 3130.6). It is also unlawful to fail to have a representative of management available for conferences with the union at reasonable times and places or to neglect to appoint representatives with power to reach agreements. Both failures are a violation of the collective bargaining agreements of the Act (*LLR*, 3105, p. 7874; 3110, p. 7881). In rejecting union proposals, the employer must submit counterproposals and attempt to reconcile the differences; to act otherwise is considered to be bad faith. If an understanding is reached, it is an unfair labor practice to refuse to reduce its terms to a written agreement (*LLR*, 3095, p. 7850).

The key then to satisfying the duty to bargain in good faith is approaching the bargaining table with an open mind, negotiating in good faith with the intention of reaching final agreement (*LLR*, 3115, p. 7888). The NLRB determines whether bargaining has been in good faith by the employer's *entire* conduct during the negotiations. A "take it or leave it" approach, a refusal to furnish information requested by the union during the negotiations, and an intensive communications campaign designed to discredit the union with employees during the negotiations are considered unfair labor practices (*Guidebook to Labor Relations,* 1985). When responding to a union demand, the institution must be prepared to back up a rejection by providing relevant information to the union or by agreeing to be audited (*LLR,* 3135.70, p. 7941). The U.S. Supreme Court has held that unilateral changes during talks with the union are, in themselves, unlawful without proof of bad faith by the employer (*LLR,* 3143.38, p. 7959).

MANDATORY BARGAINING SUBJECTS

The NLRA states that when a request for negotiation is made by a union representing a majority of employees in an appropriate unit, the employer must bargain collectively with respect to rates of pay, wages, hours, or other conditions of employment and with respect to questions arising under existing agreements [Sections 8(d) and 9(a)] (National Labor Relations Act; Sections 8(d) and 9(a), 1935). The National Labor Relations Board has interpreted the term "wages" to include such items of value that may accrue to employees out of their employment relationship as wage rates, hours of employment, overtime, and work requirements. In addition, such mandatory items include procedures and practices relating to discharge, suspension, layoff, recall, seniority, discipline, promotion, demotion, transfer, and assignment within the bargaining unit. It also includes conditions, procedures, and practices governing safety, sanitation, and protection of health in the place of employment. Indeed, vacations, holidays, leaves of absence, and sick leaves are mandatory subjects of bargaining.

The category of mandatory subjects of bargaining has developed from a long line of NLRB and court decisions. Included below are some of these subjects and references to decisions establishing their mandatory nature:

1. Discharge of employees (*NLRB v. Baj Chelder,* 120F2d574, 8LRRM723 (7th Cir. 1941))
2. Seniority grievances and working schedules (*NLRB v. U.S. Gypsum Co.,* 94NLRB112, 28LRMM1015 (1951))
3. Union security and checkoff (*NLRB v. Andrew Jergens,* 175F2d130, 24LRRM2096 (CA9, 1949) cert. denied, 338US827, 24LRRM2596 (1949))
4. Vacations and individual merit raises (*NLRB v. Singer Manufacturing Company,* 24NLRB444, 6LRMM405 (1940))
5. Retirement and pension and group insurance plans (*NLRB v. Inland Steel Co.,* 77NLRB1, 21LRRM1310, enforced, 170F2d247, 22LRRM2505 (CA7, 1948))
6. Christmas bonuses and profit sharing retirement plans (*NLRB v. Niles-Bemont-Pond Co.,* 199F2d713, 31LRRM2057 (CA2, 1952) and *NLRB v. Dicten & Marsch Manufacturing,* 29NLRB112, 46LRRM1516 (1960))
7. A nondiscriminatory union hiring hall (*NLRB v. Tom Joyce Floors Inc.,* 353F2d768, 60LRRM2334 (CA9, 1965))
8. Plant rules on rest or lunch period (*NLRB v. Miller Brewing Co.,* 166NLRB90, 65LRRM1649 (1967))
9. Safety rules, even though the employer may be under legal obligation to provide safe and healthful conditions of employment (*NLRB v. Gulf Power Co.,* 384F2d822, 66LRRM2501 (CA5, 1967))
10. Institution-owned houses occupied by employees, as well as the rent paid for

the houses (*NLRB v. Hart Cotton Mills Inc.,* 190F2d964, 28LRRM2434 (CA4, 1951))

11. No-strike clauses binding on all employees in the bargaining unit (*NLRB v. Shell Oil Co.,* 77NLRB1306, 22LRRM1158 (1948))

12. Insurance plans, even though the employer proposed to improve the insurance programs and the expiring agreement contained no provisions concerning the plans (*General Motors Corp. v. NLRB,* 81NLRB779, 23LRRM1422 (1949))

13. "Most favored nation" clauses (Dolly Madison Industries decision of NLRB 74LRRM1230, Dolly Madison Industries, Inc., Richmond Diary Division, Richmond, Va. and Truck Drivers and Helpers Local 592, International Brotherhood of Teamsters, Chauffeurs, Warehousemen and Helpers of America, Case #5-CA-3475, June 2, 1970, 182NLRB147)

14. A "zipper clause" closing out bargaining during the term of the contract and making the contract the exclusive statement of the parties' rights and obligations (*NLRB v. Tomco Communications Inc.,* U.S. Court of Appeals, 9th Cir., San Francisco, 97LRRM2660; National Labor Relations Board v. Tomco Communications Inc. 76-2178, January 16, 1978)

15. Inplant food services and prices, even where inplant food services are managed by an independent caterer (441US488, 101LRRM2222 (1979))

16. Subcontracting unit bargaining work (Timken Roller Bearing Co. 70NLRB500, 18LRRM1370 (1946) enf. denied on other grounds, 161F2d949, 20LRRM2204 (CA6, 1947))

VOLUNTARY (PERMISSIVE) BARGAINING SUBJECTS

The NLRB has distinguished between mandatory and voluntary bargaining subjects. Bargaining subjects of the latter type (i.e., those that may be proposed but not insisted on as a condition to an agreement) include the following:

1. A clause making the local union the exclusive bargaining agent, even though the international union was the certifying agent (*42NLRB2034 v. Wooster Division of Borg-Warner,* 356US342 (1985))

2. A clause requiring a secret ballot vote among the employees on the employer's last offer before a strike could be called (*42NLRB2034 v. Wooster Division of Borg-Warner,* 356US342 (1985))

3. A clause fixing the size and membership of the employer or union bargaining team (*31LRRM2422 American Newspaper Publishers v. NLRB,* 73 Supreme Court 552)

4. A requirement that a contract must be ratified by a secret employee ballot (*38LRRM2574 NLRB v. Darlington Veneer Co.,* 236F2d85 Court of Appeals, 4th Cir.), though the method of ratification is an internal union concern (*73LRRM2097 Lear Siegler Inc. v. UAW,* Court of Appeals, 6th Cir. 19134).

5. A clause providing that a contract will become void whenever more than 50% of the employees fail to authorize dues checkoff (*38LRRM2574 NLRB v. Darlington Veneer Company,* 236F2d85 Court of Appeals, 4th Cir.)

6. A requirement that the union post a performance bond or an indemnity bond to compensate the employer for losses caused by picketing by other unions (*32LRRM3684, NLRB v. Local 264, Laborers (D&G Construction Co.), 529F2d778*) (49LRRM1831 Arlington Asphalt Company, decision of NLRB 136NLRB67 (1962))

7. A requirement fixing terms and conditions of employment for workers hired to replace strikers (19LRRM1199 Times Publishing Co., decision of NLRB 72NLRB128)

8. Benefits for retirees (*78LRRM2974 Chemical Workers v. Pittsburgh Plateglass Co.* 404US157)

9. Interest-arbitration clauses calling for arbitration of disputes over terms of a new contract (93LRRM3055 *NLRB v. Columbus Printing Pressmen,* Court of Appeals, 5th Cir. (1976))

IMPORTANT CONSIDERATIONS THAT AFFECT THE BARGAINING MILIEU

Warschaw (1980) helps us to identify certain negotiating styles. The win-lose negotiators, or the "jungle fighters," are perhaps the most dangerous type of negotiators that you can confront in collective bargaining. They are abrasive, impatient personalities who resent being kept waiting. Because patience, as is discussed later, is a criterion for successful negotiators, these individuals attempt to rush the proceedings to closure and force agreements out of concern for expediting the process. "Dictators" constitute another win-lose negotiating style. These individuals

hold that knowledge is bargaining power, and they will share with you only information that they believe is appropriate for you to know. They believe that they can win by withholding information from you. Lose-lose negotiators can be characterized as "silhouettes." These are remote individuals who withdraw into silence because they are fearful of revealing their true sentiments to you. They avoid conflict at the bargaining table by ignoring it so there is no opportunity for conflict resolution. "Big Daddies and big Mamas" use a manipulative negotiating style. They are basically nurturing individuals, but they expect their investment in you to be returned by your agreeing with their positions. They will help you only until their control over you is threatened.

Truly successful negotiators are win-win negotiators. Winning is not a one-sided equation for these individuals. They recognize the value of how much the loss will affect not only the other party but the long-term relationship between management and labor. Because their outlook is focused on the long-run perspective of the negotiations, they tend to be objective in assessing the needs and expectations of their opponents.

Personalities remain a critical factor and can influence the bargaining outcome positively or negatively. Metzger (1990a) cited the selection of the principal negotiator as a threshold decision. Management should be fully cognizant of their counterparts on the union negotiating team and attempts should be made to have an intellectual meeting of the minds among negotiators. Although it is not a requirement for negotiators to become "friends," it is essential that they have mutual respect for one another and a mutual appreciation of each other's integrity.

Labor-management relations in an institution is a continuously evolving process. The collective bargaining environment brings together past, present, and future aspects of the labor management relationship. Economic conditions and competition in the health care industry will be a backdrop for contract bargaining for some time. Past history is a shared history for the parties to an agreement. As such, the negotiating process as well as the implementation of the contract will affect both present and future relationships between the two parties. A climate will be developed during the term of the present climate through the mechanisms of grievance and arbitration processes. Administering the contract requires constant evaluation and reinterpretation of the agreement through these processes and involves interaction between labor and management on a recurring basis. Thus, the collective bargaining environment should be viewed not only in terms of the current negotiations, but also in regard to future outcomes that result from the product of these negotiations.

Also of consequence is identifying new and emerging issues that will affect both the future of the contract and the future of negotiations. A skilled and experienced negotiator anticipates issues that might not yet have reached the bargaining table, but are growing in importance nevertheless. AIDS is an example of one such issue. Hospitals are confronting a multitude of dilemmas, not to mention lawsuits, because there is no specific agreement on testing, confidentiality, and hiring policies with regard to HIV status. In today's environment, drug testing and sexual harassment have assumed an importance that could not have been predicted a few years ago. It is incumbent on the bargaining team to address these issues in a proactive manner.

The advance in information technologies has also affected the collective bargaining process. Sethi (1990) reported that changes in these technologies may signal changes in power relations between the parties. Computers, for example, have already caused a shift in the balance of power during a strike. When the Professional Air Traffic Controllers Organization (PATCO) walked off the job in August 1981, the government was able to use computer technology to keep air traffic moving and thus decrease the strikers' leverage.

Technological advancements have complicated an already complex health care environment. Both management and unions must demonstrate strategic understanding of the ways in which the work place is influenced by technology. Furthermore, the collective bargaining process must evidence a concern for technology issues and provide measures for dealing with the uncertainties that accompany automation and computerization. Consequently, negotiating technology provisions requires the competence and skills to formulate and make strategy decisions.

Sethi (1990) also identified what he regarded as a trend in job security issues. Management and unions have expanded the job security of younger workers who, presumably, are capable of acquiring the skills demanded by new technologies. Older workers, however, are presumed to be less able to adapt to technological changes and are being phased out with various types of severance packages.

Ornati's (1985) study of contract clauses that provide workers protection from new technologies (cited in Sethi, 1990) revealed that in the industrial setting, the major developments were the expansion of workers' rights to job retraining coupled with an increased use of severance pay. However, he also noted that there was an increase in the number of contracts that contained no job security clauses relating to technological changes. Given the increase in automation and computerization that has occurred in the health care industry, it is highly likely that technological issues will appear increasingly on the bargaining agenda. It is uncertain, however, if health care organizations will follow the trends reported in industrial settings.

SELECTING A NEGOTIATING TEAM

Management must make certain decisions *before* selecting the members of its negotiating team. One of the first and most important decisions is the character of the approach to the union at the bargaining table. Will the hospital take a "hard-nosed" approach? Will it attempt to contain the union at each turn? Will it attempt to discredit the union during the bargaining sessions? Will it attempt to change major provisions in the collective bargaining agreement?

The decisive factor in determining the eventual settlement is the makeup of the negotiating team. Much depends on the individual skills and judgments brought into the bargaining arena by the negotiators. Logically the major responsibility for negotiating a contract should be with the management executive who has day-to-day responsibility for labor relations. In most institutions this is the director of personnel or labor relations. This person should be familiar with the bargaining unit (its longevity, its wage structure, its grievances and arbitrations over the years)

and should understand and appreciate the needs of employees and the needs of the institution. Very often institutions do not employ experienced labor relations executives and, therefore, use labor attorneys to represent the institution in collective bargaining. Such attorneys are well-versed in labor law and the realities of collective bargaining. The presence of an experienced labor attorney to direct, guide and, perhaps, plan the strategy for the administrators' position at the bargaining table is truly an asset. Many institutions use both a labor relations or personnel executive and a labor attorney, placing the latter in the role of adviser to the principal spokesperson. In any case, it is essential to have a labor attorney to review the proposed language of the contract before it is signed, whether this specialist is the institution's chief negotiator.

Line administrators normally offer advice and ideas before the negotiations begin. Some are included as members of the negotiating team. The chief executive officer or chief operating officer of the institution does not usually serve on the negotiating committee. It is well to note that the introduction of critical demands and arguments by the union may require the management negotiating team to confer with its principals (i.e., the chief executive officer, the chief operating officer, or the chief financial officer).

It is not unusual to have a key department head on the negotiating team. The smaller the number of members on the negotiating team, the more effective the negotiating.

Most union negotiators are skilled practitioners of their art—at the very least, the union officials. They are well-versed in negotiating techniques. The union negotiating team may include the president of the local, vice presidents, and employees of the institution who have been elected by their fellow workers to represent them in the negotiations. This committee is often composed of the delegates who have been elected to handle the day-to-day problems and, therefore, are well-versed in the grievances and arbitrations of preceding years. More often than not, they are the institution's most outspoken and militant proponents of the union, and more often than not they were instrumental in bringing the union into the institution. Many union negotiating teams include a labor attorney, who represents the union. In most instances, the principal spokesperson for the union is the local president.

STRATEGIES FOR BARGAINING

At the outset the institution must decide on the issues that cannot be compromised. Strategy must be planned in advance, and experienced labor relations practitioners must supervise strategic planning and actual conduct of the negotiations.

The preparation for bargaining begins long in advance of the actual face-to-face sessions. Management must gather and organize material obtained both from within the institution and from similar institutions and other firms in the community. Such information should include the following:

1. The present wage rates operative in the institution, classification by classification
2. Job descriptions, when available
3. A complete review of the fringe benefits program, showing costs and areas amenable to savings
4. The total number of employees, by classification, in the bargaining unit
5. Hourly schedules for each classification
6. Average amount of overtime by classification
7. Average straight time hourly wage rates
8. Rates of employee turnover by department
9. Seniority lists (i.e., number of employees with length of service in the 5-, 10-, 15-, and 25-year classes)
10. Analysis of experience with grievances and arbitrations

It is also essential to assemble collective bargaining agreements in effect in other institutions in and out of the area, which may be used by either party to the negotiations. Most important are contracts recently negotiated by the same union.

Bade and Stone[1] (1951) provide an excellent list of dos and don't's:

1. Strategy must be planned in advance. Do not play it entirely by ear. Clear-cut decisions must be made as to those issues that (a) cannot be compromised, (b) can be compromised (and to what extent and in exchange for what), and (c) merely represent an antidote to anticipated overreaching in union demands, which one recognizes will be dropped when the union does the same thing with its extreme demands. As part of the preparations, a pragmatic anticipation of union demands should be completed.
2. Do not start with the hard issues and leave the easy ones for the end. It is

[1] *Source:* Bade, W.J., and Stone, M. (1951). *Management Strategy in Collective Bargaining Negotiations.* New London, CT: National Foreman's Institute, Copyrighted material reprinted with permission of Bureau of Business Practice, 24 Rope Ferry Road, Waterford, CT 06386.

best to set a mood of compromise. Do not emphasize technicalities and legalisms at the onset. Develop a mood that is conducive to give and take (the hallmark of successful negotiators is the understanding that for every take there may need to be a give).

3. Do not be subtle, pedantic, threatening, or hesitant. Use the right language. Be direct, clear, *calm,* patient, and tolerant. Of course, it may be necessary to play to the bleachers; if so, do not get lost in the feigned emotion.

4. Do not exaggerate or misrepresent the facts. A fact is a fact, and there is no substitute for honesty. It has been said many times that although a union might be able to get away with deception, management cannot. Management's position must always be factually defensible. It may not be the one the union wants management to have, but if it is supported by facts and is rational, it is the only one that should be taken.

5. When responding to the other side's positions, give reasons. A reasoned "no" includes the sharing of how decisions were reached.

6. Do not make commitments at the table that you do not intend to keep. Do not hide behind tricky, vague, or inconclusive language. If making a commitment is not possible, do not gloss over it with murky language.

7. Keep control of the negotiations. It is always best to make proposals or counterproposals the basis of future negotiations. If an issue gets too difficult, too hot to handle, put it aside for the time being.

8. When there is agreement on a clause or issue, translate the agreement into actual words that both parties can agree on.

9. Do not agree on anything until *everything* has been agreed on. Until the entire contract is negotiated and signed, make sure the union understands that agreement on anything before the entire contract settlement should be considered tentative.

10. Thinking of quid quo pro as the order of the day may well be the backbone of successful bargaining. A granting of a concession by management should be related to the granting of an equal concession by the union. Withdrawals of proposals should be mutual. If one party will not listen to the needs of the other it should be made clear that the party's needs will not be listened to.

11. The myth of "final offers" must be debunked. Never describe a position as the final offer *unless it is.* Never take the position that "this is as far as management will go," then go forward while the pronouncement is still clear in the minds of the union.

Raiffa (1982) offers the following checklist for negotiators:

- First, know yourself.
- Know your adversary.
- Give thought to the negotiating conventions in each context.
- Consider the logistics of the situation.
- Remember that simulated role playing can be of value in preparing your strategy.
- Iterate and set your aspiration levels.

Knowing the style of the negotiator is critical, but it is also of fundamental importance to know how that individual has negotiated in the past. You must also be aware of your negotiating style and anticipate how it will influence the negotiations. Furthermore, to be a truly successful negotiator, it is imperative that you consider the alternatives. Entering collective bargaining with an all-or-nothing attitude will reduce your possibilities for crafting an agreement that will meet the needs of both parties. Ultimately, the success not only of the negotiations, but also the administration of the contract, will depend on how useful the contract is in sustaining the day-to-day working relationships of both management and labor. Being able to offer alternative recommendations for consideration enhances the possibilities for finding the contract acceptable to both sides.

Bazerman (1986) identifies a common failure in negotiations when individuals offer extreme demands expecting to obtain a compromise somewhere in the middle. This bargaining stance promotes competitive behavior in which the parties can become involved in a struggle to hold on to their positions. Instead of problem solving, they expend their energies defending their demands.

Fisher and Ury (1981) support the concept of principled negotiations or negotiations on the merits. The following four basic points are involved:

1. People: Separate the people from the problem.
2. Interests: Focus on interests, not positions.
3. Options: Generate a variety of possibilities before deciding what to do.
4. Criteria: Insist that the results be based on some objective standards.

They emphasize the essential importance of understanding the other party's position and reasons supporting that position. Understanding, however, should not be misinterpreted as agreeing with the other party's position. Understanding involves attempting to identify what motivates the other side's interests in supporting its position in order that the negotiations can concentrate on the actual needs and expectations of both sides and not on what each side speculates the other wants from the negotiations. Subsequently, listening to the other party becomes a crucial element of the negotiations, but there is another element that transcends hearing what is being said. The truly successful negotiator makes the effort to understand the emotional forces that underlie the words

and position so he or she listens to the other party with all senses open and is receptive to the emotions that are being transmitted. This would include body language and other signs that interpret the degree of feeling the speaker attaches to the message.

Metzger (1990a) identified typical styles that fail in negotiations. One is the "macho" or "cowboy/cowgirl" style that is demonstrated by negotiators who essentially pit their strength against the strength of the other party. This action is reminiscent of the dramatic high-noon confrontation. Someone will be forced to give way, thus promoting a win-lose result with the loser most likely harboring resentment and animosity toward the opponent who overpowered him or her. Another negotiating style that is destined to failure is the "bottom-line approach." This, by its very nature, is a rigid approach that sets extremely high expectations that are unlikely to be met. There are no options or alternatives in this approach and consequently no room for failure.

Clearly, the win-win negotiating style creates opportunities for successful negotiations because the negotiator is open to new possibilities and opportunities for resolving conflicting positions. The win-lose negotiating strategy that preoccupies so many negotiators is basically counterproductive. Negotiating the contract is about resolving the differences between the parties relative to the rules of the work place. The real measure of successful negotiations is when these differences have been settled to the satisfaction of both parties. Both sides believe they have gained through the process. No one is a loser, and all are winners.

Jandt (1985) comments on "positional bargainers," those individuals who measure their success in terms of how often the other side capitulates to their demands. This is a very destructive bargaining strategy because the bargaining position, and not the resolution of conflicting differences, becomes the objective of the negotiating process. Successful negotiators know that resolving conflicts also involves identifying similarities between the two parties' positions. By examining similarities and dissimilarities, the negotiator expands his or her view of the negotiations and considers the full range the parties' interests. He or she creates room for mutually beneficial agreements. Instead of being locked into and focused on a position or demands, he or she is free to explore all possibilities.

The negotiator must be aware of the pressure to conclude negotiations. Collective bargaining negotiations are laborious and time-consuming. The negotiator can become tired and desirous of closing the deal. There are a lot of group dynamics occurring throughout the negotiations that can be especially emotionally draining. It is not easy to listen completely and fully and maintain an objective position throughout the process. There will be emotional outbursts, and the negotiator may feel pressured to keep the process moving along to prevent it from stalling. The truly successful negotiator will have invested considerable physical and emotional energy in the process and must resist the temptation to agree simply to check an item off the bargaining agenda. Illiche (1980) refers to the "It's a shame to" technique in which the other side pressures you to continue because you have already accomplished so much. It would be a shame to stop now. The successful negotiator will realize when enough is enough and when there is a need for a recess in the proceedings. Patience is clearly a virtue among negotiators. Don't accede to arbitrary deadlines of the other side. They are usually counterpro-

ductive. Exploring all of the options and alternatives requires time. Be prepared for lengthy negotiations, and, although you should keep an eye on concluding negotiations, realize that the road to agreement often is replete with detours. You should not eliminate consideration of options simply because they require more time.

Successful bargaining strategies require the negotiator to consider alternative positions before the bargaining even begins. A key element in preparing your negotiation strategy is considering the possibility of not reaching agreement on an issue. You must evaluate whether the type of agreement that can be reached is better than no agreement at all. By considering mutual options for resolving differences, you develop a more flexible approach toward bargaining. Your flexibility extends toward the other side because you are able to offer alternatives to their positions. However, you must weigh the outcome of having a one-sided position adopted to avoid nonagreement on an issue. Sometimes a one-sided position, because it does not satisfy both parties, can be more detrimental in the long run to the labor-management relationship.

Metzger (1990a) offers some caveats, or dos and don'ts, that may be helpful. They come from his own exposure to top-flight negotiators as well as from his own extensive negotiation experiences:

- Do not think of negotiations as a Roman gladiator's battle—as a test of strength.
- Preconceived notions of the other party's responses, which bring you into the bargaining with a chip on your shoulder, are to be discouraged.
- Prepare! Prepare! Prepare! Make the hard choices of positions and a realistic analysis of interests before you start.

- Success in negotiating involves an informed awareness and understanding of the compulsions that are operating on the other party. Keep your eye on the whys of the other party's positions.
- Assumptions of your opponent's understanding of what he or she can gain in a settlement should not be made lightly.
- Do not make the fatal error of underestimating your opponent.
- Personal integrity and courage are the pervasive traits of successful negotiators.
- Talk less. Listen more.

It cannot be emphasized enough how critical the element of personalities is to the negotiating process. Peck (1980) has written on the psychodynamics of negotiations. Clearly, one of the most valuable traits of a negotiator is an intuitive understanding of the process of negotiations. Understanding the personalities involved cannot be overestimated. Peck has emphasized certain personality traits of which you should be aware in formulating your bargaining strategy. There is transference that occurs when you attribute to another in the negotiations values, expectations, and motivations that you derived outside of the process from past experience. Transference can be dangerous, and the negotiator should be careful to analyze the person across the table based on the reality of the situation. Nonverbal communication of the other party may be the most important indicator of the possibility of obtaining agreement. As was discussed earlier, a successful negotiator must listen with all of his or her senses. Physical movements can convey information that is often more accurate than the spoken word. Uncertainty, ambiguity, silence, and delay are expected in negotiations. If you are easily frustrated or impatient, your chances of being successful are low.

An important part of planning the strategy for negotiations is a clear, objective estimate of strike issues. Are there issues that are likely to be critical for the union, thus becoming instigators for a strike? By identifying such issues, an institution need not change its position. Reality-based negotiations are productive ones.

It is essential to forecast the impact of a possible strike. In any industry, strikes put economic pressure on both parties: The workers lose wages while the employers lose revenue. The key to a successful strike from a union's viewpoint is to inflict inordinate discomfort, expense, and pressure on the employer to effect a compromise or a move toward the union's position. An institution must evaluate carefully the "discomfort," the "expense," and the "pressure" it will be called on to withstand if it takes a strike. The real losers in strikes of health care institutions are the patients, their families, and prospective patients. The patients may well be deprived of services; they may need to be moved from a struck hospital or nursing home; they may be discharged prematurely. Prospective patients will be troubled by the limited beds available; operations will be delayed, and outpatient care discontinued. It is well to state at the onset of discussions of the impact of a strike that such action at a health care facility is the most severe form of labor-management dispute. Many strikes produce mass picketing and still more produce violence.

There are, in any discussion of the impact of a strike, critical factors: the ability of the health care institution to withstand the strike, and the willingness to take a strike. There are at least eight critical indicators that must be evaluated when estimating the impact of a strike in a health care institution; these are the following:

1. What effect will it have on revenue? Will lost revenue be recoverable in the poststrike period?
2. How long will a strike be acceptable? Is there a critical point at which pressure on the institution will be unbearable?
3. What support will be available to the institution to make up for the employees who are withholding their services (supervisors, non-bargaining-unit employees, temporaries, bargaining-unit employees who will cross the picket line)?
4. Can strikers be replaced? A policy of whether the economic strikers are to be replaced with permanent new hires must be decided.
5. Will striking employees be able to augment or replace their lost income by finding temporary employment elsewhere?
6. What is the union's policy on strike benefits?
7. What is the hospital's policy on discontinuing benefits coverage for strikers? Health benefits may be covered under a union plan or under the institution's own plan. What is the policy on discontinuing coverage for striking employees?
8. What outside forces may be brought to bear on the institution to avoid or settle a strike?

One other consideration is the use of employees from nonstruck hospitals. The Allied doctrine is a legal doctrine developed from the National Labor Relations Board case law. It defines the rights of third parties who provide assistance to the employer involved in a labor dispute. The Allied doctrine affects a secondary employer who, during the course of a labor dispute, performs work that would have been performed by striking employees of the primary employer. In doing such work, the secondary employer loses neutral status and, therefore, is subject to the labor organization involved in the dispute, thus extending its economic activity to the secondary employer. As the reports of both houses of Congress (U.S. Congress, 1974) in the deliberation regarding the Health Care Amendments to the NLRA stated:

> It is the sense of the Committee that where such secondary institutions *accept the patients of the primary employer,* or otherwise provide life-sustaining services to the primary employer, by *providing the primary employer with an employee or employees who possess critical skills such as EKG technician,* such conflict shall not be sufficient to cause the secondary employer to lose its neutral status . . . (*Emphasis added*)

In effect, Congress intended to affirm that a neutral hospital accepting patients of a primary employer will not lose its status as a neutral. Such a neutral hospital will, however, lose its status if it supplies *noncritical* personnel to a hospital that is experiencing a strike, or if it not only accepts patients from such a hospital but also greatly expands its noncritical staff in the process. Gradually, the NLRB's exception to the Allied doctrine for the health care industry has come to depend on the *urgency* of the medical needs of the patients who were transferred from the primary hospital to the neutral hospital (Metzger, Ferentino, & Kruger, 1984).

RELEVANT LEGISLATION AND REGULATIONS

The 1974 Health Care Amendments

The Taft-Hartley Act of 1947 excluded from the definition of "employer" private, not-for-profit hospitals, and health care institutions. The NLRB asserted jurisdiction over proprietary hospitals and nursing homes, but it was not until the so-called Health Care Amendments of 1974 that Congress, through Public Law 93-360, brought the private, not-for-profit health industry within the jurisdiction of federal labor law. The 1974 amendments enacted the following changes.

1. The exemption contained in Section 2(2) of the federal statute that excluded non-for-profit hospitals from the definition of "employer" was removed.
2. A new Section 2(14) was added to define the term "health care institution." It included any "hospital, convalescent hospital, health maintenance organization, health clinic, nursing home, extended care facility or other institutions devoted to the care of sick, infirm, or aged persons." This definition is essential in the determination of which employees fall under the special health care provisions and within the scope of the act.
3. A new series of special notices applicable to the health care industry and unions representing employees in that industry was enacted. This Section 8(d) notice period for notices of disputes, which one party is legally obliged to give to the other, was extended from the normal 60 days

before contract expiration to 90 days, and notices filed with the Federal Mediation and Conciliation Service (FMCS) from the normal 30 days to 60 days. In the case of initial contract disputes notice must be given 30 days before any strike notice.

4. A new Subsection 8(g) was added. It requires that a union representing employees in a health care institution must give 10 days' written notice to the employer and to the FMCS of its intent to engage in a strike, picketing, or other concerted refusal to work.
5. Broader sanctions under Section 8(d) provide that employees who are represented by labor organizations and do not comply with the requirements of the 90- and 60-day dispute notices or with Section 8(g), Strike Notices, lose their protected status under the Act.
6. Mandatory mediation of disputes in the health care industry was provided under Section 8(d). The FMCS must mediate health care disputes, and the parties involved in such disputes are compelled to participate in that mediation process. It is an unfair labor practice for a party to refuse to participate in such mediation.
7. Section 213, the second special dispute resolution provision, provides that when substantial interruptions of delivery of health care in a community are threatened, the director of FMCS may appoint a special board of inquiry to investigate the issues in the dispute and to issue publicly a written report on the dispute.
8. A new Section 19 provides for an alternate to the payment of union dues

by persons with religious convictions against making such payments. It allows contribution to designated 501(C)(3) charities in lieu of dues.

In an interpretation by the Office of the General Counsel of the NLRB, the following guidelines have been established regarding Section 8(g) notices.

1. The notice should be served on someone designated to receive such notice, or through whom the institution will actually be notified.
2. The notice should be personally delivered or sent by mail or telegram.
3. The 10-day period begins on receipt by the employer and the FMCS of the notice.
4. The notice should specify the dates and times of the strike and picketing, if both are are being considered.
5. The notice should indicate which units will be involved in the planned action.

As with Section 8(d) notices, workers engaged in work stoppage in violation of the 10-day strike notice lose their status as employees. The NLRB will probably interpret violations of the Section 8(g) notice requirement as a separate and distinct unfair labor practice.

In drafting the 1974 amendments to the NLRA, the congressional committee included the 10-day strike and picket notice provision [Section 8(g)] to ensure that health care institutions would have sufficient advance notice of a strike. The committee realized, however, that it would be unreasonable to expect a labor organization to commence job action at the precise time specified in a notice provided to the employer. However, if a labor organization failed to act within a reasonable period after the time specified in the notice, such action would not be in accordance with the intent of the provision. Therefore, the committee report of the amendments provided that:

> It would be unreasonable, in the committee's judgment, if a strike or picketing commenced more than 72 hours after the time specified in the notice. In addition, since the purpose of the notice was to give a health care institution advance notice of the actual commencement of a strike or picketing, if a labor organization does not strike at the time specified in the notice, at least 12 hours notice would be given of the actual time for commencing of the action.

Thus, absent unusual circumstances, a union would violate Section 8(g) if it struck a facility more than 72 hours after the designated notice time unless the parties agreed to a new time or the union gave a new 10-day notice. Additionally, if the union does not start the job action at the time designated in the initial 10-day notice, it must provide the health care facility at least 12 hours' notice before actual commencement of the action. The 12-hour warning must fall totally within the 72-hour notice period.

The committee report notes that "repeatedly serving 10-day notices upon the employer is to be construed as constituting evidence of a refusal to bargain in good faith by a labor organization," that is, a violation of Section 8(b) of the NLRA. What constitutes "repeatedly serving notice" will have to be defined and interpreted by the NLRB in individual cases. In a memorandum, the board's general counsel provided the following guidelines to regional offices regarding the handling of intermittent strikes or picketing situations:

1. Where the facts and circumstances of the labor organization strike or picketing hiatus support the reasonable conclusion that the activity has not indefinitely ceased and that it is reasonable to assume that it will commence again, no new notice will be required if the activity recommences within 72 hours of the start of the hiatus; but 12 hours' notice to the institution will be required if the activity is to recommence more than 72 hours from the start of the hiatus.

2. Where the facts and circumstances of the hiatus support the reasonable conclusion that the activity has ceased indefinitely and that it will not be resumed in the near future, 12 hours' notice to the institution will be required if the activity is to resume within 72 hours of the start of the hiatus, but a new 10-day notice meeting all the requirements of Section 8(g) will be required if the activity is to resume more than 72 hours from the start of the hiatus.

Exceptions to the requirements that labor organizations provide Section 8(g) notices are indicated in two situations. First, if the employer has committed serious or flagrantly unfair labor practices, notice would not be required before the initiation of the job action. Second, the employer is not allowed to use the 10-day notice period to "undermine the bargaining relationship that would otherwise exist." The facility would be free to receive supplies, but it would not be "free to stock up on the ordinary supplies for an unduly extended period" or to "bring in large numbers of supervisory help, nurses, staff and other personnel from other facilities for replacement purposes." The committee reports held that employer violation of the foregoing principles would release the union from its obligation not to engage in a job action during the Section 8(g) notice period (Metzger & Kruger, 1984).

The 1989 NLRB Rule on Bargaining Units

On April 21, 1989, the NLRB published its final rule, hereinafter referred to as "the NLRB Rule," establishing eight units for the purposes of collective bargaining in acute care hospitals. The units are physicians; nurses; all other professionals; technical employees; business office clericals; skilled maintenance employees; guards; and all other nonprofessionals. The rule was promulgated through Section 6 of the National Labor Relations Act and Section 553 of the Administrative Procedure Act (Miller, 1990). Subsequent to publication of the final rule, the American Hospital Association (AHA) sought and obtained injunctive relief through the courts. Ultimately, the AHA was unsuccessful in its opposition to the NLRB Rule, and on April 23, 1991, the U.S. Supreme Court ruled that the NLRB had acted within its legal authority in establishing the bargaining unit rules affecting acute care hospitals.

From a practical and operational perspective, it was anticipated that the NLRB Rule would promote a proliferation of bargaining units in the hospital that, in turn, would lead to fragmentation of health care collective bargaining. Proliferation of bargaining units, research has shown, increases the likelihood of unions winning elections. There is an inverse relationship between unit size and election outcomes. As the size of the bargaining unit decreases, unions are more likely to win (Redle & Rakich, 1991; Scott & Beadles, in press). Furthermore, it was assumed that the resulting multiple bargaining units would increase overall hospital costs along with the administrative costs of collective bargaining and create difficulties for hospitals in implementing hospitalwide policies. Hospitals also would be expected to confront multiple unions, and the nature and formidability of these unions would be an issue.

Unions who announced an intent to organize hospital employees included the following:

- Service Employees International Union
- American Federation of State, County and Municipal Employees
- International Union of Operating Engineers
- American Federation of Teachers
- Federation of Nurses and Health Care Professionals
- The Retail, Wholesale and Department Store Union (includes New York District 1199 of the National Union of Hospital and Health Care Employees)
- The United Food and Commercial Workers International Union
- The International Association of Machinists and Aerospace Workers
- The International Brotherhood of Teamsters
- United Automobile, Aerospace and Agricultural Implement Workers of America (American Hospital Association, 1991)

Furthermore, the NLRB Rule does not require unions to limit their organizing efforts to only one type of bargaining unit. The teamsters, for example, indicated that they would attempt to unionize any and all classifications of workers (American Hospital Association, 1991).

Multiple Units

Because health care organizations are labor intensive and employ a variety of professions and occupations, there is a high degree of interdependence and teamwork. Simultaneously, jobs tend to be segregated by education, training, and often legal requirements of certification and licensing. The situation that results from the diversity and subsequent segregation increases the possibility for a large number of different bargaining units within a hospital (Kilgour, 1989). Moreover, multiple units have the potential to further segment the hospital work force as each unit supports its own special interest issues and demands. Special premium pay demands, job security provisions, and staffing ratios will reflect the single interest of each bargaining unit. The opportunity for conflict and rivalry among multiple units will increase as each unit advances its own self-interest and economic position. Hospital employees' loyalty will be determined by the unit to which they belong. It will not be unusual for a department within a hospital to find its workers' loyalties lie outside the department and the hospital. Communication, teamwork, and morale all will be affected by the advent of multiple bargaining units within the hospital (Stickler, 1990). In addition, hospitals can expect that multiple bargaining units will increase the likelihood of strikes (Schwarz & Koziara, 1992).

As it happens, the expected proliferation of bargaining units has yet to occur. Schwarz and Koziara (1992) reported that most unionized hospitals have four or fewer bargaining units. Moreover, only two unions have demonstrated increased activity, the Union of Operating Engineers and state affiliates of the American Nurses Associations. Similarly, the greatest level of organizing activity has occurred in skilled maintenance units and registered nurse units (Bureau of National Affairs, 1991).

Organizing and the Election Process

In the aftermath of the U.S. Supreme Court decision, attention has been focused on the changes in the process of organizing workers. The NLRB Rule was expected to facilitate union organizing and accelerate both the organization and representation election processes in acute care hospitals. It was anticipated that unions would win more elections through bargaining unit proliferation and also because the NLRB Rule effectively eliminated management's ability to challenge the appropriateness of the bargaining unit and thereby incur lengthy delays between petition filing and elections. These delays had allowed management time to conduct anti-union information campaigns (Bazerman, 1986; Burda, 1989). However, since the U.S. Supreme Court upheld the NLRB Rule, union organizing has not gotten any easier. Management has continued to use delay tactics, only now it relies on unit placement issues as a mechanism for launching legal chal-

lenges to bargain unit composition. Scott and Beadles (in press) explain that although the NLRB Rule greatly reduced the number of cases hospitals could contest based on appropriateness of the bargaining unit, the hospital still has opportunities to challenge specific employee classifications.

The NLRB Rule caused hospitals to take a proactive stance in regard to union organizing. Many hospitals engaged consultants to help them in efforts to keep unions out of the work place. Hospitals expected that unions seeking to represent hospital workers would be experienced in contract negotiations and would rely on sophisticated computer systems and researchers to gain access to a variety of information about the hospital. For example, reports on uncompensated care that report the amount of bad debt incurred for charity could be misinterpreted to show that the hospital is mismanaged. The Hospital's IRS Form 990, which contains information on the salaries of the 5 most highly paid executives, could be used to support union claims that management is overpaid at the expense of the workers. OSHA safety records could help the union make safety an issue. Certificate of Need (CON) applications that provide information on hospital spending for equipment and renovations, usually substantial amunts, could be used by the union to further exploit the employee wage issue (American Hospital Association, 1991).

Subsequent to enactment of the NLRB Rule, much of the attention has focused on the bargaining unit as it relates to the organizing campaign and the representation election. At this time, the precise impact the NLRB Rule will have on contract negotiations is unknown. From the hospital perspective, few of the anticipated negative side effects of the rule making have been felt (Schwarz

& Koziara, 1992). What is known, however, and what is discussed here, are some of the implications for the future of collective bargaining.

IMPLICATIONS FOR THE FUTURE OF COLLECTIVE BARGAINING

Because 90% of contract issues and demands are similar, bargaining with multiple units over the same issues of wages, pensions, health insurance, hours of work, seniority, layoffs, safety issues, sick pay, premium pay, vacations, holidays, overtime, time-off, and grievances and arbitration will result in costly, repetitive, and duplicative negotiations. It has been projected that one round of contract negotiations for eight bargaining units would cost approximately $360,000 (Stickler, 1990). Contract costs also can be expected to escalate as competing labor unions attempt to secure terms more favorable than those secured by other bargaining units. Management will clearly have greater incentive to coordinate collective bargaining in order to achieve comparable agreements on similar issues across bargaining units (Redle & Rakich, 1990/1991). Furthermore, the NLRB Rule furnishes management with an incentive to work with labor to minimize the number of bargaining units by allowing for fewer units on agreement between management and labor. However neither party can be coerced into forming units that conflict with the rule making (Scott & Beadles, in press).

Clearly, management will face a complex agenda of bargaining issues when confronting multiple unions and multiple units. Gourley (1990) has identified two mecha-

nisms to facilitate the negotiation process. The "accept/reject" test allows both parties to identify particular issues for collective bargaining and helps to structure expectations about the outcome of the process. "Force field analysis" is another suggested means for considering issues in a systematic way and highlighting key concerns that deserve priority attention.

According to Savage and Blair (1989), relationship outcomes should be considered in conjunction with substantive outcomes in the development of negotiation strategies. Relationship outcomes involve not only what occurs during the process of negotiation, but also the long-term effect of relationships on future negotiations. Each episode of the negotiation process has the potential to influence not only subsequent negotiations with that particular union, but also negotiations with other bargaining units in the hospital. If a union represents more than one bargaining unit, relationship outcomes assume even greater significance. Savage and Blair (1989) explain that the negotiation process itself can induce changes in the relative power and level of conflict between the parties. Relative power of the relationship is determined by the nature of the association (i.e., whether management has an independent, dependent, or interdependent relationship with the union). The level of conflict refers to the context of the negotiations and the degree of hostility or supportiveness espoused by the parties. By including relationship outcomes in the development of negotiation strategies, the process becomes interactive and more likely to result in effective negotiations.

The creation of a bargaining unit for physicians could have serious implications for future collective bargaining activity. Unit placement issues will undoubtedly arise because the NLRB has not distinguished among medical doctors and other types of doctors such as chiropractors, podiatrists, and osteopaths. Furthermore, in teaching and research facilities, there is a question of physicians who also hold Ph.Ds and function as research scientists. Many physicians may be excluded from the bargaining unit because they are technically not employees of the hospital, but independent contractors, students, supervisors, or managerial employees. Although the NLRB will be resolving unit placement issues in the years to come, hospitals must also acknowledge that more physicians are beginning to resemble employees. Approximately 30% of physicians (excluding students) are currently practicing in salaried positions, and as many as 50% of physicians earn a substantial portion of their income from salaried arrangements. Moreover, there is a growing trend among younger physicians toward salaried employment, with 47% of physicians 35 years and younger employed in salaried positions (Hepner & Sobal, 1990). Although interns and residents are not covered by the NLRA (Cedars-Sinai Medical Center, 1976), they are actively seeking union representation. The AFL-CIO recently announced that it had charted its first association of residents and interns in California representing 2000 members statewide. Furthermore, Holland (1990) reported that in some hospitals there are consensual units that include interns and residents.

Although physician unions are not common, Holland (1990) suggests that there is probably not that much difference between their negotiations and those of other professional unions. He recommends that professional issues be separated from administrative and economic issues and referred to committees and task forces that will function outside of collective bargaining. In addition, Holland (1990) advises that physicians include their legal counsel in the collective bargaining process. Too often, physicians waive legal counsel during the bargaining, and on completion of the agreement, announce that they require the legal opinion of counsel before they can agree to the terms. Inevitably, the inclusion of the physician's attorney means reopening the negotiation process.

Since the Supreme Court upheld the NLRB Rule, there has been no significant increase in the willingness of health care employees to join unions and to engage in collective bargaining. Unions have been largely unsuccessful, according to a preliminary report of the Bureau of National Affairs (1991) in organizing health care workers or in achieving election victories. Although the number of election petitions filed since the NLRB Rule was upheld has been higher than before the court decision, the unionization growth rate is slower than was anticipated by the hospital industry. Many health care labor analysts believe that health care workers have no more interest in joining a union than other U.S. workers and that this indifference reflects the overall decline in union growth across other industries. The NLRB may have changed the rules, but not the sentiment of health care workers.

In addition, it has been suggested that hospital management is generally more sophisticated today and better prepared to manage employee relations as the result of extensive education and training in human resources management. Rakich, Longest, and Darr (1992) have identified the important proactive steps that management has followed in its efforts to remain union free: 1) following

AHA guidelines on human resources management, 2) assuring effective first line supervision, 3) increasing two-way communication between workers and management, and 4) establishing a formal grievance procedure in nonunion hospitals.

According to Metzger (1990b), the key components of the union's power base—the detailed contract, narrow job designs, and emphasis on stability—are now being challenged by management with new forms of employee participation, more flexible forms of work organization, and technological changes in the work processes. Given the increases in computerization and the competitive economic situation, there are radical changes going on in today's work place. Management appears to be better at addressing these changes than unions. The challenge to unions is whether they can find a way to meet the needs of new work groups for whom the traditional package of union services has little appeal and is often irrelevant.

Schwarz and Koziara (1992) examined the union wage effect on hospital employees to determine whether the higher wages paid to unionized hospital employees was influenced by the number of bargaining units in the hospital. They found that the number of bargaining units did not lead to higher wages. In fact, wage levels in hospitals tended to differ by occupation and not by the number of bargaining units, with the exception of nurses and stationary engineers. An 8% to 10% wage effect was reported for nurses, and a 17% wage effect was identified for stationary engineers. The wages paid to X-ray technicians and food service workers seemed to depend more on bargaining unit specification than on number of units. Licensed practical nurses and pharmacists actually showed no difference in wages with

hospitals that had only one bargaining unit and hospitals with any number of bargaining units.

Fottler (1987) cited the degree of management resistance to unions as a significant organizational factor affecting the future of health care collective bargaining. When the NLFB Rule was upheld, unions anticipated that hospital management's resistance would be diminished. What has occurred demonstrates that management does not intend to give the unions any ground. Positive labor-management relations programs and court challenges to unit placement classifications give evidence that management will continue to resist union organization and collective bargaining. Unions insist that they are committed to organizing health care workers on a large scale and stipulate that many of their organizing efforts have as yet to reach the election petition state. Survey data from the Bureau of National Affairs (1991) indicate that although union activity is occurring nationwide, most of the efforts have been concentrated in traditional union stronghold states such as Ohio, Michigan, and Pennsylvania. Unions are also hopeful that the election of a Democratic president will mean a more union-responsive NLRB.

The future of union efforts to organize health care workers is unclear. What is certain is that the challenges of collective bargaining continue to provide hospital managers with the impetus to focus considerable effort and resources on human resources management.

KEY CONTRACT CLAUSES

Among the many clauses that will be included in a collective bargaining agreement with the union, four have specific interest to any practitioner (for a full list of clauses, see Appendix A). These clauses are the following:

1. Union security
2. Management rights
3. Seniority
4. No-strike

Union Security

After a union has been certified as the collective bargaining agent for the employees in a hospital, one of its primary aims is to get a contractual provision that gives it (the union) maximum protection in its continued existence in that hospital Therefore, the union attempts to secure by bargaining some form of compulsory union membership. Six forms of union security will be defined: an open shop, a maintenance of membership shop, a union shop, a modified union shop, a closed shop, and an agency shop.

The *open shop* offers a maximum choice to employees in the bargaining unit. They can join or not join the union, and they can remain in the union or drop out of the union without losing their jobs.

In the *maintenance of membership shop*, members of the bargaining unit are not required to become members of the union to keep their jobs, but employees who do decide to join the union must maintain membership for a specific length of time: either 1 year or for the duration of the contract. Such a union security arrangement often includes an escape clause that clarifies the times at which union members may drop out of the union without losing their jobs. The following is a typical maintenance of membership clause:

> Any employee who is a member in good standing of the union at the end of thirty (30) days from the date the provision becomes effective or who thereafter joins the union during the term of this agreement shall remain a member of the union in good standing as a condition of employment with the hospital.

Another form of union security is the *union shop*. It is found in the majority of collective bargaining agreements and provides that all employees in the bargaining unit must join the union within a specified period of time after hire, usually at the end of a probationary period. In addition, these employees must remain members in good standing during their employment in the hospital. A sample union shop provision follows.

> All employees on the active payroll at the time of the signing of the contract who are members of the union shall maintain their membership in the union in good standing as a condition of continued employment. All employees on the active payroll as of the time of the signing of the contract who are not members of the union shall become members of the union within thirty (30) days after the effective date of the contract. All employees hired after the effective date of the contract shall become members of the union no later than the thirtieth day following the beginning of such employment and shall thereafter maintain their membership in the union in good standing as a condition of continued employment.

A *modified union shop* provides an option to employees presently on the payroll. Those who are members of the union must maintain their membership, but those who have not joined the union need not join. New employees, however, must join the union within a specified period after hire, again usually after the probationary period. This form of union security is a compromise that protects present employees who do not wish to join the union. The movement from a modified union shop is sometimes affected by a clause stating that after a certain percentage of employees have joined the union, all those remaining out must join the union.

The *closed shop* (which was largely outlawed by the Labor-Management Relations Act of 1947 but is permissible under certain state laws for hospitals that are so covered) requires applicants for employment to be members of the union before they can be hired. This form of union security is usually accompanied by a union hiring hall provision. The union is notified of employment needs and sends applicants to fill the jobs. A sample closed-shop clause follows.

> The hospital shall hire only applicants for employment who are members of the union. The union shall furnish such applicants for employment provided that, however, if the union is unable to fill such request, the hospital may hire applicants who are not members of the union, but such applicants must become members of the union immediately upon being hired.

The *agency shop* was a comparatively rare form of union security that had a rebirth as a counterposition of unions to right-to-work laws (operative in several states), which outlaw mandatory or compulsory union membership. In an agency shop, the employee can join or not join the union and remain a member or drop out, but all employees in the bargaining unit that is serviced and represented by the union must pay a service fee to support the union as a condition of employment.

In all forms of union security, whether they are partial or total in compelling employees of the bargaining unit to join the union, such employees are covered by all conditions of the contract if they are indeed part of the bargaining unit. If the employ-ees are given the option to remain out of the union, they are nonetheless covered by all provisions of the collective bargaining agreement including the grievance procedure; however, they may not attend meetings and they may not vote on union issues.

Labor leaders argue in favor of compulsory union membership, and their principal argument revolves about the "free rider" inequity. A "free rider" is a worker who refuses to join the union and is permitted to maintain this position based on a union security clause. This worker, the labor leaders argue, reaps all the advantages hard won by the union in its negotiations with management. The union leaders maintain that the philosophy of compulsory union membership is rooted in a basic democratic principle, the rule of the majority. It is their position that given free choice, the employees will join the union, but usually remain out because of fear of reprisal or promise of reward from the employer. Management defends its position for optional membership on the basis of the inherent right of the individual to make choices and to withhold membership from any organization. Actually agreement to a compulsory union security provision offers some advantages to management. Often when employees are given the option of joining or not joining a union, only the most outspoken critics of management join immediately. In a modified union security arrangement, however, the union continues its drive to enroll employees, often undertaking this activity during the normal workday and throughout the year. A compulsory agreement, of course, not only finesses such militance, but may also mollify the extremists, who are unlikely to be influenced by more conservative employees in any event.

Management Rights

Management and labor have usually agreed that any rights not restricted by the collective bargaining agreement reside in management. The question of whether management rights clauses should be expressly included in a contract has been hotly debated over the years. Most managements feel that the right to manage the business or administer the hospital is solely theirs. *But it should be clear that when the administration enters into a collective bargaining agreement with a union, it no longer has the sole authority to administer the hospital.* There are limitations clearly outlined in each of the contract clauses.

The U.S. Supreme Court has ruled that management prerogatives can be exercised only in the cases "over which the contract gives management complete control and unfettered discretion." The court's decision points out that management retains only those rights specifically outlined in the labor agreement. Almost three-quarters of all collective bargaining agreements contain a management rights clause. For years, many practitioners presumed that the employer could exercise the right to manage the enterprise and that such a clause was unnecessary. They further warned that in an effort to construct a management rights clause that would outline those rights reserved for management, it was impossible to anticipate all of the contingencies that should be included. In supporting their position against the inclusion of the management rights clause, some practitioners felt that in negotiating such a clause, which was indeed the prerogative of managements in any case, they would have to grant certain concessions to the union. Yet, the majority of labor negotiators were convinced by the arguments for inclusion. They felt that the institution needs as much protection as it can get and that the clause outlining management prerogatives is most helpful in adjudicating day-to-day grievances. The battle over the pros and cons of including a management rights clause in a collective bargaining agreement has become an academic one in light of the decisions of the U.S. Supreme Court.

The collective bargaining agreement does indeed limit management's action in the cases outlined in each of its clauses. Management does well to define those areas in which union rights are waived, because most arbitration awards and court decisions have indicated that any management decision or action that affects the employment relationship and is not clearly reserved to management should be discussed with the union representing the employees. If management wishes to retain its freedom to act in specific areas without recourse to the grievance and arbitration procedure, the management rights clause is the proper place to define those areas.

There are two major categories of management rights clauses. One is a brief clause dealing not with specific rights but with the principle of management rights in general. The other is a detailed clause that clearly lists areas of authority that are reserved to the management. The key areas of authority that would be included in such a clause involve the rights to do the following:

1. Manage and administer the hospital and direct the work force
2. Hire, discipline, and transfer
3. Introduce new or improved methods or facilities
4. Promulgate rules of conduct

5. Set quality standards
6. Discontinue jobs
7. Decide employee qualifications
8. Subcontract work

An example of a brief encompassing clause follows.

> The management of the hospital and the direction of the work forces are vested exclusively with the administration, subject only to the restrictions and regulations governing the exercise of such rights as are expressly provided in this contract.

Seniority

One of the most important clauses in the collective bargaining agreement and one that often cuts deepest into management prerogatives is the seniority provision. The principle of seniority should no longer be at issue between management and the union. Unilateral interpretation and application of seniority, on the part of management, is no longer possible. Under the seniority principle, the employee with the longest service is given preference in such areas as promotions, transfers, layoffs, rehirings, choice of shifts, and choices of vacation periods. Unions tend to seek straight seniority, recognizing no factor other than period of service in gaining preference. To them, strict seniority means job security and the basic protection against the possible biases or acts of favoritism on the part of the administration. They maintain that with the application of strict seniority measures, a more stable, experienced, efficient, and loyal work force will develop. Of course the administration argues that operating efficiency requires compromise on the position of straight seniority. Management would prefer more emphasis on merit

and ability. In its earliest application, the National Railroad Adjustment Board held that seniority is a personal right and "the keystone upon which many rights of individuals under collective bargaining agreements are based."

The right to preference on the basis of seniority exists only by virtue of contractual clauses contained in the collective bargaining agreement. Hospital negotiators focus on two main areas when bargaining a seniority provision, namely: the role of ability as it modifies the strict application of seniority, and the definition of the seniority unit. The first area has dramatic implications in instances of promotions, layoffs, and rehires. Many agreements provide for a qualifying clause, either the "seniority plus ability test" or the "relative ability test." The *seniority plus ability test* provides preference in promotions or other job rights on the basis of seniority, but the most senior employee must be able to do the work involved: Just being able to do the job—not necessarily better than other employees—will suffice under this provision. The *relative ability test* provides for a comparison of the abilities and skills of the employees claiming rights to a job on the basis of seniority. Here, in instances of layoffs, recalls, promotions, or demotions, ability and seniority will be considered, and where ability is relatively equal, seniority will be the governing factor. If ability is not relatively equal, however, the more able employee will be granted preference.

The definition of the seniority unit is key to the application of the provisions of the seniority system. The broader the unit, the more difficult for the administration to maintain its control over the efficient operation of the hospital. The narrower the unit, the more strict is the limitation on the exercise of an employee's seniority rights. Where there is a wide variation in skill requirements for jobs (such as is evident in a hospital), it is more practical to negotiate a departmental or occupational unit. Departmental seniority, for example, sets up separate seniority units for each department and is applied within an employee's specific department. Because the unit is smaller and contains many interchangeable jobs, the advantages are obvious.

The most efficient seniority unit for a hospital is occupational seniority (i.e., separate units for employees performing the same type of job). This is far more practical for departments that contain a broad spectrum of noninterchangeable occupations. Hospital unions will usually agree to a compromise between the limited occupational seniority unit and the broader departmental system. This approach is sometimes called "noninterchangeable occupation groups." When the occupational groups to which seniority may be applied have been defined, the groups are broadened to include occupations that are clearly interchangeable and, therefore, should form one occupational family.

No-Strike and No-Lockout Clauses

A no-strike clause is probably one of the most important provisions of the agreement for the hospital. It is the administration's assurance of peaceful and uninterrupted operation during the life of the contract. No-strike clauses fall into two categories: unconditional clauses and conditional or contingent clauses. An *unconditional no-strike clause* elicits a firm pledge from the union and its rank-and-file members that they will in no circumstances be involved in a work stoppage or slowdown during the life of the agreement. A *conditional or contingent no-strike clause* prohibits stoppages or slowdowns unless certain clearly defined conditions have been met, such as the exhausting of the grievance procedure including arbitration and the refusal of either party to abide by the decision of an arbitrator. These clauses often provide that strikes or slowdowns are prohibited in matters subject to arbitration and that the union must take certain positive action against any unauthorized (wildcat) strikes if it is to avoid any liability. Such actions may include informing its membership in writing that they must return to work and posting notices on union bulletin boards or taking ads in local newspapers stating that the strike is unauthorized and workers should return to work. A union that calls workers out in violation of a no-strike pledge in a contract may be sued for damages the employer suffers as a result. Nearly all no-strike clauses in collective bargaining agreements contain a quid pro quo for the union, a comparable ban against lockouts by the company.

Additional key contract clauses may emerge in response to changes in the health care environment. Job security has been increasingly cited as a critical clause in today's contract negotiations because workers are apprehensive about layoffs and other effects of financial problems in the hospital industry.

Unarguably, DRGs have brought about dramatic changes in health care industry employment. Prior to DRGs, health care employees enjoyed relative job security, and layoffs were virtually unknown in the industry. Today's hospitals have experienced dramatic staffing changes due to the impact of DRGs. Declining occupancy rates have resulted in massive layoffs, and hospitals have shifted many full-time positions to part-time employment. Given these employment setbacks, contract negotiations are focusing more intently on issues of job security and staffing (Metzger, 1987). Resolution of these issues will necessarily involve negotiation over issues of job assignment and job content (Holley & Jennings, 1991).

ADMINISTERING THE CONTRACT

After a collective bargaining agreement has been completed and negotiations concluded, breathing life into the agreement is a key responsibility of the parties. This includes the disciplinary, grievance, and arbitration procedures.

Discipline

The collective bargaining agreement imposes limitations on the disciplinary powers the administration may exercise. However, any limitations of a management right may be counterproductive to the primary goal of establishing an efficient work force. To minimize such limitations, an effective and constructive approach to discipline must be designed and implemented. The limitations imposed on management's right to discipline do not, in themselves, remove from management the right to impose discipline on its employees. The key point about such limitations is that management *may* discipline up through discharge only for sufficient and appropriate reasons. This requires the development of a sound procedure based on due process in the application of discipline toward unionized employees. The right to discharge, suspend, or discipline is clearly enunciated in contractual clauses and in the adoption of rules and procedures, which may or may not be incorporated in the collective bargaining agreement.

The union's role in the disciplinary process is to defend vigorously the employee in the face of what could be considered unfair management actions. Employees expect the union to come to their assistance. It is the heart of the disciplinary process to ascertain the propriety of the management action. The best way to judge the propriety of a management action in a disciplinary case is to "program" the case to its ultimate conclusion in arbitration. Arbitrators will normally support a management action if they find progressive discipline, which includes verbal reprimands, full explanation of what is necessary to remedy the situation, followed by a written reprimand for a second infraction with a clear warning of future penalties that may be imposed. Suspensions may precede the final disciplinary action of termination. In essence, the review of a disciplinary action, which terminates in arbitration, should be directed to ascertaining whether the employee was fully aware of the standards against which his or her behavior was to be measured. These standards include basic rules and regulations outlining offenses that will subject employees to disciplinary action, and the extent of such disciplinary action. The critical question in all disciplinary actions is: Is there sufficient reason for such action? Frequently supervisors find themselves on the defensive after having administered discipline, and often such actions are overturned because of insufficient evidence or improper remedies, which do not fit into the concept of progressive disciplining. To the arbitrator, discharge is economic death; therefore, the burden of proof lies with the management that such action was the only proper avenue of recourse.

Discipline to be effective—to be fair—must be corrective in nature. Justin (1969) lists the following basic rules of proper disciplinary procedures.

1. Discipline to be meaningful must be corrective, not punitive. Corrective discipline encourages the wrongdoer to correct him- or herself and leads to self-discipline.
2. When you discipline one, you discipline all.
3. Corrective discipline satisfies the rule of equality of treatment by enforcing equally among all employees established plant rules, safety practices, and the responsibility of the job.
4. It is the supervisor's job to make the workers toe the line, or to increase efficiency, not the shop steward.
5. Just cause or any other comparable standard for justifying disciplinary action under the labor contract consists of three parts:
   a. Did the employee breech the rule or commit the offense charged against him or her?
   b. Did the employee's act or misconduct warrant corrective action or punishment?
   c. Is the penalty just and appropriate to the act or offense as corrective punishment?
6. The burden of proof rests on the supervisor to justify each of the three parts that make up the standard of just cause under the labor contract.
7. Prove the misconduct or offense charge by sensory facts. Avoid opinions, feelings, or conclusions.

8. In drafting rules or writing disciplinary letters, avoid stating opinions, inferences, or conclusions. Base your rule on neglect of job; support your disciplinary action by giving the facts of how, when and where the employee neglected his job.
9. To prove cause for disciplinary action, the circumstantial evidence must permit two reasonable inferences or inescapable conclusions to be drawn:
   a. Does the circumstantial evidence point to or compel one reasonable finding or conclusion?
   b. Does the circumstantial evidence exclude all other reasonable findings or conclusions? (pp. 294–295)

It is imperative that management keep a record of each reprimand, warning, layoff, and discharge. Annotations of verbal warnings should be maintained by the supervisors in the department. The procedure for written warnings should include the writing of warnings as soon as possible after the incident. It is important to note on the warning notice the rule violated, or the specific provision of the union contract in question. Explanations should be specific and comprehensive. One helpful device on a warning notice is a special notation, where indicated, that immediate satisfactory improvement must be shown and maintained, or further disciplinary action will be taken. The specific action to be taken by management in the event of further violations should be clearly noted on the form.

The right to discipline or discharge for proper cause and the right to make rules and regulations governing the conduct of the employees are primary management prerogatives. These rights notwithstanding, the union will attempt to protect the disciplined employee. In the main, collective bargaining agreements permit the employer to discipline or discharge for cause, but they also permit the union to protest such actions through the grievance and arbitration procedure. Therefore, it is essential that "just cause" be established, that the reasonableness of the action be clear, and that the documentation be complete.

Administering the Grievance Procedure

The grievance procedure is the real heart of the collective bargaining agreement. It is a useful and productive management tool when it makes use of the finding of facts, objective evaluations, and equity. Consistent and fair adjudication of grievances is the hallmark of sound employee-employer relations.

Most grievance procedures contain four steps. The first step always involves the presentation of the grievance by the employee and/or his or her representative to the immediate, first-line supervisor. This is an essential cornerstone of a grievance procedure. Because most grievances refer to actions by first-line supervisors, a second step must be taken outside the department or at a higher level in the department. The second step involves the employee, his or her representative where indicated, and a department head or an administrator from outside the department. The underlying rationale for the third step is the final inhouse review of the management decision by an individual outside the department with the twofold responsibility of ensuring objectivity and evaluating the need for consistency. The third step involves the employee and/or his or her representa-

tive and a union official and, in most instances, a labor relations representative of the personnel department. To ensure each objectivity and the evaluation of the need for consistency, it is important to understand the following caveats.

1. Objectivity and consistency cannot be achieved if the last step remains at the same operating department from which the grievance arose.
2. Objectivity and consistency cannot be achieved if the management representative at the third step has neither the power nor the inclination to overrule an improper decision.
3. Objectivity and consistency cannot be achieved if anyone representing management is perceived as other than neutral.

The following six basic areas make up the manager's responsibility for the grievance procedure:

1. Hearing the complaint
2. Getting the facts
3. Making the decision
4. Communicating the decision
5. Preparing a written record
6. Minimizing grievances

The management hearing officer should be guided by the following general principles for effective grievance handling:

1. A strong desire to resolve dissatisfaction and conflicts
2. An empathy toward employees, an understanding of their problems, and an ability and willingness to listen and probe for hidden agendas

3. A complete knowledge and understanding of personnel policies, procedures, and practices, and the union contract
4. A personal commitment to the interest of the institution, side by side with a sense of fair play on behalf of the employees

Very few grievances can be adjudicated as soon as they arise. Indeed, the critical nature of sound administration of the grievance procedure is a thorough investigation rather than a quick evaluation. It is essential in dealing with employees' grievances that management gain employee commitment and reduce employee dissatisfaction. Therefore, the facts are the key. By uncovering the facts it is possible to discover the underlying causes of grievances, rather than their surface appearances.

Rules for Grievance Administration

The following checklist is provided as a guide for managers involved in administering the grievance procedure (Metzger, 1979):

1. *Listen.* Permit the presentation of the full story by the employee and/or the delegate.
2. *Try to understand.* Uncover the how, who, what, when, where, and why of the grievance.
3. *Separate fact from emotion.* This requires painstaking investigation.
4. *Refer to policy and contract provisions.* These are the rules of the road. Do not attempt to rewrite policy and the bargaining agreement at this stage of the game. The role of the supervisor is to interpret such policy and contract provisions as they pertain to the grievance at hand.
5. *Remember that your decision may set a precedent.* A decision in one case has a direct bearing on subsequent cases.
6. *Consult with others.* It is not a sign of weakness to check with other supervisors who may have had similar grievances, and to check with the personnel department.
7. *Explain your decision fully.* It is essential to get employee commitment and understanding. Therefore, be explicit and honest in communicating your decision. (p. 265)

Along with the foregoing checklist are the following key points to effective handling of grievances (Metzger, 1978):

1. Employees deserve a complete and an empathetic hearing of grievances they present.
2. The most important job in the handling of grievances is getting at the facts.
3. Look for the hidden agenda.
4. Hasty decisions often backfire.
5. While you are investigating a grievance, try to separate fact from opinion or impression.
6. After you have come to your decision, promptly communicate that decision to the employee.
7. Remember that you have to sell your decision.
8. There is no substitute for common sense in arriving at a decision.
9. Written records are most important.
10. Follow-up is essential. (pp. 91–92)

Arbitration

Provisions for the use of arbitration to resolve contract interpretation disputes during the life of the contract appear in more than 90% of all collective bargaining agreements. Arbitration is the final step in the grievance procedure.

A voluntary arbitration is judicial in nature. When two parties are unable to resolve a dispute by mutual agreement, they submit the particular issue to an impartial person for solution.

There are several types of voluntary arbitration clause dealing with contract administration disputes. The most common provides for both parties to select an arbitrator each time a dispute arises. Many contracts state that the arbitrator shall be selected through the American Arbitration Association (AAA). When an issue is in dispute, the aggrieved party petitions the AAA, which, in turn, submits a list of arbitrators to both parties. If the two parties cannot agree on which arbitrator to select, the AAA designates the arbitrator. The selection of a separate arbitrator for each issue has the marked advantage of securing a qualified individual to rule on a particular type of dispute (Metzger, 1970).

A less widely used voluntary arbitration clause provides for a permanent arbitrator system (i.e., the parties agree on the identity of an impartial arbitrator, who will handle *all* arbitrations during the life of a specific agreement). This has the distinct advantage of providing the parties with a carefully selected individual, who has earned the respect of both labor and management and who, because of repeated experiences with the parties, can develop a thorough understanding of the problems and unique difficulties of a particular institution.

An arbitrator's award is binding on both parties. The arbitrator's decision is final. The first principle of effective arbitration in contract administration is joint agreement between management and the union on the type of arbitration desired: Will it be the ad hoc arrangement (i.e., selecting a different arbitrator for each case), or will a permanent arbitrator be selected for the life of the contract? Even more critical is the question of the limits or nonlimits on what matters shall be submitted to the arbitrator. In deciding which matters should be submitted to the arbitrator and the arbitrator's authority, contractual definitions must be considered. The arbitrator's authority is limited by the agreement. Typically, he or she is responsible for interpreting or applying a specific clause in the contract. The arbitrator is precluded from adding to or deleting from any clause contained in that agreement. Some contracts limit the arbitration process to specific issues and not to all clauses contained in the collective bargaining agreement.

In submitting contract interpretation disputes to an arbitrator, both parties risk losing the decision on matters they deem to be important, but this is a small price to pay for uninterrupted service. The advantages of continuing operations while deciding disputed claims arising from interpretation of the contract are obvious. Arbitration neither diminishes nor detracts from the collective bargaining process. Rather, it is an extension of the bargain arrived at during the negotiations. It is an administrative tool for living with the contract. Having adopted the arbitration process voluntarily, both parties are more likely to accept the decision which emanates from the arbitrator.

The AAA (1981) provides us with a good 50-word arbitration clause.

Any dispute, claim, or grievance arising out of or relating to the interpretation or the application of this agreement shall be submitted to arbitration under the Voluntary Labor Arbitration Rules of the American Arbitration Association. The parties further agree to accept the arbitrator's award as final and binding upon them. (p. 11)

A grievance procedure without voluntary arbitration at its terminal step is ineffective. All grievances should be heard regardless of whether they are covered by the definition in the contract. When grievances cannot be settled internally, the disputed matter should be submitted to a disinterested party. In this way, both the union and the aggrieved employee understand that management's decision can be questioned or reviewed by a disinterested and unbiased tribunal.

SUMMARY

Successful bargaining requires advance planning of strategies. Such planning can only be successful with a pragmatic and minimally subjective view. Good faith bargaining is a requirement indelibly inscribed in the National Labor Relations Act. The key to satisfying the duty to bargain in good faith is entering the bargaining arena with an open mind and with the full intention of reaching a final agreement.

This chapter reviews the mandatory and voluntary subjects of collective bargaining, it addresses the critical decision of selecting a negotiating team, and thoroughly outlines strategies for bargaining. A most useful section includes key contract clauses with sample language.

After the contract is negotiated its administration, which is breathing life into the words so negotiated, is critical. A review of the disciplinary mechanism, the grievance procedures, and the arbitration process follows. The appendix provides a checklist of items to be included in the first collective bargaining contract.

We have entered a new era, an era of human capital where the spotlight will be on human resources programs. The challenge to managers will be to establish new rules and approaches for positive employee relations programs. The emphasis on human capital provides us with a new definition of labor relations in which employees are considered as partners and not adversaries.

Discussion Questions

1. Discuss the current and potential impact in the position of the NLRB regarding the number of bargaining units in a hospital.

2. Discuss the importance of the management rights clause and how management rights could be eroded. How can these rights be compromised by a contract's seniority provisions?

3. Prescribe a "dos" and "don'ts" list for negotiators of collective bargaining agreements. How can management improve communications during collective bargaining? Why is the element of personality so pivotal in the collective bargaining process?

4. Why should labor and management aspire to a collaborative relationship as partners in the work place instead of remaining adversaries?

5. Describe the relationships and

responsibilities that characterize the grievance process.

6. Supervisors play a key role in the disciplinary process. What should they know about dispute resolution?

REFERENCES

American Arbitration Association. (1981). *Labor arbitration, procedures and techniques.* New York: Author.

American Hospital Association. (1991, July). *Legal Memorandum Number 16, Collective Bargaining in the Health Care Industry.*

Bade, W.J., & Stone, M. (1951). *Management strategy in collective bargaining negotiations.* New London, CT: National Foreman's Institute.

Beyond unions. (1985, July). *Business Week,* pp. 56–63.

Bazerman, M.H. (1986, June). Why negotiations go wrong. *Psychology Today, 20(6),* p. 54–58.

Burda, D. (1989, June). Hospitals expect more union activity. *Modern Healthcare,* pp. 44, 46.

Bureau of National Affairs, Inc. (1991). *Daily labor report* (Vol. 196). Author.

Cedars-Sinai Medical Center. (1976). 223 N.L.R.B. No. 251. Reconsideration denied, 224 N.L.R.B. No. 90 (1976).

Cook, S.A. (1972, January 19). The neglected art of negotiation. *The Daily Record,* Baltimore, p. 1.

Dunlop, J.T., & Healy, J.J. (1955). *Collective bargaining* (rev. ed.). Homewood, IL: Irwin.

Fisher, R., & Ury, W. (1981). Getting to yes—Negotiating an agreement without giving in. In B. Patton (Ed.), *Harvard Negotiation Project* (pp. 21–53). Boston: Houghton Mifflin.

Fottler, M.D. (1987). Health care collective bargaining: Future dynamics and their impact. *Journal of Health and Human Resources Administration, 10,* 22–52.

Guidebook to labor relations (1985). Chicago: Commerce Clearing House.

Gourley, R. (1990). Negotiations for managers. In N. Metzger (Ed.), *Handbook of health care human resources management* (2nd ed.) (pp. 245–266). Rockville, MD: Aspen.

Hepner, J.A., & Sobal, L.V. (1990). Physician unions: Any doctor can join, but who can bargain collectively? *Hospital and Health Services Administration, 35,* 327–340.

Holland, E.J., Jr. (1990). Dealing with physicians as employees. In N. Metzger (Ed.), *Handbook of health care human resources management* (2nd ed.) (pp. 429–440). Rockville, MD: Aspen.

Holley, W.H., & Jennings, K.M. (1991). *The labor relations process* (4th ed.). Chicago: Dryden Press.

Illiche, J. (1980). *Power negotiating.* Reading, MA: Wiley.

Jandt, F.E. (1985). *Win-win negotiating.* Toronto: Wiley.

Justin, J.J. (1969). *How to manage with a union.* New York: Industrial Relations Workshop Seminars, Inc.

Kilgour, J.G. (1989). The health-care bargaining unit controversy: Community of interest versus disparity of interest. *Labor Law Journal, 40,* 81–93.

Metzger, N. (1970). Voluntary arbitration in contract administration disputes. *Hospital Progress, 51(9).*

Metzger, N. (1978). *The health care supervisor's handbook.* Rockville, MD: Aspen.

Metzger, N. (1979). *Personnel administration in the health service industry* (2nd ed.). New York: Spectrum.

Metzger, N. (1987). The changing marketplace. *Journal of Health and Human Resources Administration, 10,* 53–65.

Metzger, N. (1990a). Negotiating and administering the contract. In N. Metzger (Ed.), *Handbook of health care human resources management* (2nd ed.) (pp. 441–464). Rockville, MD: Aspen.

Metzger, N. (1990b). The union movement: Dead or alive. In N. Metzger (Ed.), *Handbook of health care human resources management* (2nd ed.) (pp. 383–399). Rockville, MD: Aspen.

Metzger, N., Ferentino, J., & Kruger, K. (1984).

When health care employees strike. Rockville, MD: Aspen Systems.

Miller, L.S. (1990). The NLRB and rule making: Determining bargaining units in the health care industry. *Labor Law Journal, 41,* 711–724.

Ornati, O. (1985). *Rights arbitration and technological change* (Working paper no. 85-38). New York: New York University.

Peck, C.J. (1980). *Cases and materials on negotiations* (2nd ed.) (pp. 226–236). Washington, DC: Bureau of National Affairs.

Raiffa, H. (1982). *The art and science of negotiation* (pp. 14, 126–127). Cambridge: Beltnap Press of Harvard University Press.

Rakich, J.S., Longest, B.B., & Darr, K. (1992). *Managing health services organizations* (3rd ed.). Baltimore: Health Professions Press.

Redle, D.A. & Rakich, J.S. (1990/1991). Judicial review of NLRB rulemakings in the health care industry: Implications for labor and management. *Employee Relations Law Journal, 16,* 333–346.

Redle, D.A., & Rakich, J.S. (1991). Bargaining units in acute care hospitals: The Supreme Court upholds NLRB rulemaking. *Employee Relations Law Journal, 17,* 307–315.

Savage, G.T., & Blair, J.D. (1989). The importance of relationships in hospital negotiation strategies. *Hospital and Health Services Administration, 34,* 231–253.

Scott, C., & Beadles, N. (in press). Unit placement decisions in acute care hospitals. *Labor Law Journal, 44*(3), 143–152.

Schwarz, J.L., & Koziara, K. (1992). The effect of hospital bargaining unit structure on industrial relations outcomes. *Industrial and Labor Relations Review, 45,* 573–590.

Sethi, A.S. (1990). Information technology and collective bargaining. In N. Metzger (Ed.), *Handbook of health care human resources management* (2nd ed.) (pp. 411–428). Rockville, MD: Aspen.

Stickler, K.B. (1990). Union organizing will be divisive and costly. *Hospitals, 64*(13), 68–70.

U.S. Congress: S. Rep. #93-766, 93rd Cong., 2d Sess. 5 (1974); H.R. Rep. #93-1051, 93rd Cong., 2d Sess. 7 (1974).

Warschaw, T.A. (1980). *Winning by negotiation.* New York: McGraw-Hill.

APPENDIX

Checklist for a Collective Bargaining Contract

I. RECOGNITION. This clause defines the employees who will be covered by the collective bargaining agreement. It usually contains those jobs to be represented by the union and those to be excluded from the bargaining unit.

SAMPLE

Bargaining Unit Recognition

Section A: The Hospital recognizes the Union as the sole and exclusive representative of the employees of the Hospital as hereinafter defined for the purposes of collective bargaining with respect to rates of pay, hours of employment, and other conditions of employment within said bargaining unit.

Section B. Except as hereinafter limited, the term "employee" as used herein shall apply to and include the following classifications:

ALL OTHER PROFESSIONAL UNITS

Audiologists
Physical and occupational therapists
Dieticians
Chemists
Teachers
Counselors

Nuclear physicists
Pharmacists
Psychologists
Recreational therapists (if college degree required)
Medical technologists
Medical artists (if related college degree)
Social workers
Educational programmers (teacher degrees)

Section C. Exception as hereinafter limited, the term "employee" when used in this agreement shall exclude all other classifications not so included in Section B.

II. UNION SECURITY. This clause states the extent to which employees are required to join, maintain their membership, and pay union dues.

SAMPLE

Union Security

1. All Employees on the active payroll as of July 1, 1988, who are members of the Union shall maintain their membership in the Union in good standing as a condition of continued employment.
2. All Employees on the active payroll as of July 1, 1985, who are not members of the Union shall become members of the Union within thirty (30) days after the effective date of this Agreement, except those who were required to become members sooner under the expired Agreement who shall become members on the earlier applicable date, and shall thereafter maintain their

membership in the Union in good standing as a condition of continued employment.
3. All Employees hired after July 1, 1985, shall become members of the Union no later than the thirtieth (30th) day following the beginning of such employment and shall thereafter maintain their membership in the Union in good standing as a condition of continued employment.
4. For the purposes of this Article, an Employee shall be considered a member of the Union in good standing if he or she tenders his or her periodic dues and initiation fee uniformly required as a condition of membership.
5. Subject to Article XXVII [not given in this appendix], an Employee who has failed to maintain membership in good standing as required by this Article, shall, within twenty (20) calendar days following receipt of a written demand from the Union requesting his or her discharge, be discharged if, during such period, the required dues and initiation fee have not been tendered.

III. CHECK-OFF. This clause will outline management's obligation to deduct dues and initiation fees from union members and remit them to the union.

SAMPLE

Check-Off

1. Upon receipt of a written authorization from an Employee, the Hospital shall, pursuant to such authorization, deduct from the wages due said Employee each month, starting not earlier than

the first pay period following the completion of the Employee's first thirty (30) days of employment, and remit to the Union regular monthly dues and initiation fee, as fixed by the Union. The initiation fee shall be paid in two (2) consecutive monthly installments beginning the month following the completion of the probationary period.

2. Employees who do not sign written authorization for deductions must adhere to the same payment procedure by making payments directly to the Union.

3. Upon receipt of a written authorization from an Employee, the Hospital shall, pursuant to such authorization, deduct from the wages due said Employee each pay period, starting not earlier than the first period following the completion of the Employee's first thirty (30) days of employment, the sum specified in said authorization and remit same to the [Local] Credit Union to the credit or account of said Employee. It is understood that such check-off and remittance shall be made by the Hospital wherever feasible.

4. Upon receipt of a written authorization, the Hospital shall, pursuant to such authorization, deduct from the wages due said Employee once a year the sum specified in said authorization and remit same to [the Local] Fund as the Employee's voluntary contribution to said Fund. It is understood that such check-off and remittance shall be made by the Hospital wherever feasible.

5. The Hospital shall be relieved from making such "check-off" deductions upon (a) termination of employment, or (b) transfer to a job other than one covered by the bargaining unit, or (c) layoff from work, or (d) an agreed leave of absence, or (e) revocation of the check-off authorization in accordance with its terms or with applicable law. Notwithstanding the foregoing, upon the return of an Employee to work from any of the foregoing enumerated absences, the Hospital will immediately resume the obligation of making said deductions, except that deductions for terminated Employees shall be governed by paragraph 1 hereof. This provision, however, shall not relieve any Employee of the obligation to make the required dues and initiation payment pursuant to the Union constitution in order to remain in good standing.

6. The Hospital shall not be obliged to make dues deductions of any kind from any Employee who, during the dues month involved, shall have failed to receive sufficient wages to equal the dues deduction.

7. Each month, the Hospital shall remit to the Union all deductions for dues and initiation fees made from the wages of Employees for the preceding month, together with a list of all Employees from whom dues and/or initiation fees have been deducted.

8. The Hospital agrees to furnish the Union each month with the names of newly hired Employees, their addresses, Social Security numbers, classifications of work, their dates of hire, and names of terminated Employees, together with their dates of termination and names of Employees on leave of absence.

9. It is specifically agreed that the Hospital

assumes no obligation, financial or otherwise, arising out of the provisions of this Article, and the Union hereby agrees that it will indemnify and hold the Hospital harmless from any claims, actions, or proceedings by an Employee arising from deductions made by the Hospital hereunder. Once the funds are remitted to the Union, their disposition thereafter shall be the sole and exclusive obligation and responsibility of the Union.

IV. PROBATIONARY PERIOD.

This clause defines the period of time a newly hired employee shall be considered to be on probation.

SAMPLE

Probationary Employees

1. Newly hired Employees shall be considered probationary for a period of two (2) months from the date of employment, excluding time lost for sickness and other leaves of absence.
2. Where a new Employee being trained for a job spends less than twenty-five percent (25%) of his or her time on the job, only such time on the job shall be counted as employment for purposes of computing the probationary period.
3. The probationary period for part-time Employees whose regularly scheduled hours are fifteen (15) or less shall be twice the length of the probationary period of full-time Employees.
4. Notwithstanding the foregoing, the probationary period for social workers including part-time social workers,

according to custom, shall be six (6) months.
5. During or at the end of the probationary period, the Hospital may discharge any such Employee at will and such discharge shall not be subject to the grievance and arbitration provisions of this Agreement.

V. SENIORITY.

This clause outlines the application of seniority to eligibility for holidays, vacations, promotions, transfers, overtime, layoffs, shift and shift preferences.

SAMPLE

Section A. Bargaining Unit Seniority is defined as the length of time an Employee has been continuously employed in the Hospital. An Employee shall have no seniority for the first three (3) months of employment, or for the probationary period whichever is longer; but upon successful completion of this probationary period, seniority shall be retroactive to the date of hire. Bargaining Unit Seniority shall apply in the computation of vacation eligibility, holiday eligibility, free day eligibility, sick leave eligibility, and pension eligibility.

Section B. An Employee shall have seniority to be known as Classification Seniority, in each classification in which he or she has completed a probationary period of 3 months retroactive to the date of his or her employment in that classification.

1. An Employee's Classification Seniority shall be used for the purposes of transfers, promotions, demotions, shift preferences, vacation scheduling, lay offs, recalls, and rehires.

Section C. In case of an indefinite layoff, Employees shall be laid off and recalled by classification within their Department.

1. In the event of a layoff, recall, or a promotion within the Bargaining Unit, the following factors shall govern:
   a. Ability to do the work
   b. Classification Seniority
2. Where factor (a) above is relatively equal, factor (b) shall be the governing factor.
3. The Hospital shall be the sole judge of the ability of an Employee to do the work.

Section D. The Hospital may make any transfer deemed by it to be expedient, either within the Department, to another department, or to another shift. When an Employee is transferred to another classification or to another shift, he or she shall maintain seniority in his or her original classification until that Employee has completed the three-(3)-month probationary period in his or her new job. Thereafter his or her Classification Seniority shall be retroactive to his or her date of transfer.

Section E. Seniority shall be broken when an Employee:

1. Terminates voluntarily.
2. Is discharged for cause.
3. Exceeeds an official leave of absence.
4. Is absent for three (3) consecutive working days without properly notifying the Hospital, unless proper excuse is shown.
5. Fails to report for work within three (3) working days after being notified by telegram or mail to do so, unless proper excuse is shown.

6. Is laid off for six (6) consecutive months.

Section F. Bargaining Unit and Classification Seniority shall not accumulate during the period of an official leave of absence exceeding one month.

Section G. Employees whose pay is charged to a special or nonbudgetary Fund, and who are informed at the time of their hire or at the time of transfer that their employment is for a special nonbudgetary or research project, shall be excluded from the provisions of this Article. Such Employees may be laid off or transferred without regard to seniority.

Section H. Proper notification of absence for purposes of this Article shall be by telephone call to the Employee's supervisor immediately at the start of the work shift.

Section I. Notification of recall from layoff for purposes of this Section shall be by a telegram or a registered letter to the Employee's last known address, as shown by the Hospital's records.

VI. HOURS. This clause states the hours of work, time for lunch, rest periods, and number of days in a regular work week.

SAMPLE

Hours

1. The regular work week for all full-time Employees shall consist of the number of hours per week regularly worked by such employees as at June 30, 1988. The regular work week for part-time Employees shall not exceed five (5) days. Such hours, not to exceed forty (40) per week, shall be specified in a

Stipulation (Stipulation H) between the Union and each Hospital, to be annexed hereto. Employees shall receive two (2) days off in each full calendar week except in the event of overtime.

2. The regular work day for all full-time Employees covered by this Agreement shall consist of the number of hours in the regular work week as above defined, divided by five (5), exclusive of an unpaid lunch period, except for those Employees who received a paid lunch period as of June 30, 1988.

3. The scheduling of weekends off shall be negotiated on a Hospital by Hospital basis.

VII. OVERTIME. This clause states when overtime premium pay shall be paid and in what amount. It also covers how overtime hours are to be distributed and the requirements for working such overtime.

SAMPLE

Overtime

1. Employees shall be paid one and one-half times their regular pay for authorized time worked in excess of the regular full-time work week for their classification as set forth in Article I, Section B.

2. The following paid absences shall be considered as time worked for the purposes of computing overtime: holidays, vacations, jury duty days, condolence days, paternity day, marriage days, and sick leave days. Unpaid absences shall not be considered as time worked.

3. The Hospital will assign on an equitable basis, "on call" duty and required prescheduled overtime among qualified Employees. Employees shall be required to work overtime when necessary for the proper administration of the Hospital.

4. There shall be no pyramiding of overtime.

VIII. SHIFT AND SHIFT DIFFEREN-TIALS. This clause includes any provisions for special premium pay for work performed outside the regular day shift.

SAMPLE

Shifts and Shift Differentials

1. Employees working on shifts whose straight time hours end after seven (7:00) P.M. or begin prior to six (6:00) A.M. shall receive the following differentials:
   a. Licensed Practical Nurses. An amount equal to three-fourths (3/4ths) of the dollar amount of shift differential paid to Registered Nurses working at the same institution on the same shifts.
   b. All other Employees. A shift differential of ten percent (10%) of salary, including speciality differential.

2. Employees shall work on the shift, shifts, or shift arrangements for which they were hired. The Hospital may change an Employee's shift only for good and sufficient reason, and any such change shall apply to the Employee with the least classification seniority qualified to do the work.

Whenever the Employee requests a change of shift, approval of such request shall not be unreasonably withheld if a vacancy exists in the classification in which he or she is then working and if more than one Employee applies, such change shall apply to the Employee with the most classification seniority qualified to do the work. Notwithstanding the foregoing, Employees shall have preference in filling vacancies on another shift in the classification in which he or she is then working over new Employees.

IX. DISCIPLINE. This clause may include work rules, the mechanism for discharging or suspending Employees.

SAMPLE

Discharge and Penalties

1. The Hospital shall have the right to discharge, suspend, or discipline any Employee for cause.
2. The Hospital will notify the Union in writing of any discharge or suspension within twenty-four (24) hours from the time of discharge or suspension. If the Union desires to contest the discharge or suspension, it shall give written notice thereof to the Hospital within five (5) working days, but no later than ten (10) working days from the date of receipt of notice of discharge or suspension. In such event, the dispute shall be submitted and determined under the grievance and arbitration procedure [set forth in the full agreement].

3. If the discharge of an Employee results from conduct relating to a patient and the patient does not appear at the arbitration, the arbitrator shall not consider the failure of the patient to appear as prejudicial.
4. The term "patient" for the purposes of this Agreement shall include those seeking admission and those seeking care of treatment in clinics or emergency rooms, as well as those already admitted.
5. All time limits herein specified shall be deemed exclusive of Saturdays, Sundays, and Holidays.

X. MANAGEMENT RIGHTS. This clause outlines those activities where management is free to act subject only to the limitations of the contract.

SAMPLE

Management Rights

Section A. The management of the Hospital and the direction of the working forces are vested exclusively with the Hospital. The Hospital retains the sole right to hire, discipline, discharge, lay off, assign, and promote, and to determine or change the starting and quitting time and the number of hours to be worked; to promulgate rules and regulations; to assign duties to the work force; to reorganize, discontinue, or enlarge any department or division; to transfer Employees within departments, to other departments, to other classifications, and to other shifts; to introduce new or improved methods or facilities; to reclassify positions and carry out the ordinary and customary functions of management whether or not possessed or exercised by the Hospital prior to the execution of this Agreement, subject only to the restrictions and regulations governing the exercise of these rights as are expressly provided in this Agreement.

Section B. The Union recognizes that the Hospital has introduced a revision in the methods of feeding patients, which has and will provide a revision in job duties and a reduction in personnel in the Food Service Department. The Union agrees that nothing in this Agreement contained shall prevent the implementation of this program and of the specific reductions or of any other similar program to be hereafter undertaken by the Hospital.

Section C. The Union, on behalf of the Employees, agrees to cooperate with the Hospital to attain and maintain full efficiency and maximum patient care and the Hospital agrees to receive and consider constructive suggestions submitted by the Union toward these objectives.

XI. SEPARABILITY CLAUSE. This clause, sometimes referred to as a savings clause, protects the agreement from the possibility that any part of it is found to be contrary to the law.

SAMPLE

Effect of Legislation—Separability

It is understood and agreed that all agreements herein are subject to all applicable laws now or hereafter in effect; and to the lawful regulations, rulings, and orders of regulatory commissions or agencies having jurisdiction. If any provision of this Agreement is in contravention of the laws or regulations of the United States or of [the state of this agreement], such provision shall be superseded by the appropriate provision of such law or regulation, so long as same is in force and effect; but all other provisions of the Agreement shall continue in full force and effect.

XII. ENTIRE AGREEMENT CLAUSE. This clause, sometimes referred to as a zipper, provides that once negotiations have been completed, no further negotiations are necessary. Both parties mutually waive the right to negotiate on any further subject during the term of the Agreement.

SAMPLE

Duration

Section E. The Union, in consideration of the benefits, privileges, and advantages provided in this Agreement and as a condition of the execution of this Agreement, suspends meetings in collective bargaining negotiations with the Hospital during the term of this Agreement with respect to any further demands except as may be dealt with as a grievance . . . or except as may be dealt with under [a section not given here].

XIII. SICK LEAVE. This clause states the eligibility requirements for and amount of sick leave negotiated by the parties.

SAMPLE

Sick Leave

1. Employees, after thirty (30) days employment, shall be entitled to paid sick leave earned at the rate of one (1) day for each month of employment,

retroactive to date of hire, up to a maximum of twelve (12) days per year. Employees, after one (1) or more years of employment with the Hospital, shall be entitled to a total of twelve (12) additional days of sick leave as of the beginning of his or her (sic) second and each subsequent year of employment, provided that at no time will an Employee be entitled to accumulate more than thirty-six (36) working days of sick leave during any one year, including the days earned or to be earned in the current sick leave year.

2. Pay for any day of sick leave shall be at the Employee's regular pay.
3. To be eligible for benefits under the Article, an Employee who is absent due to illness or injury must notify his or her supervisor at least one (1) hour before the start of his or her regularly scheduled work day, unless proper excuse is presented for the Employee's inability to call. The hospital may require proof of illness hereunder.
4. Employees who have been on sick leave may be required to be examined by the Hospital's Health Service physician before being permitted to return to duty.
5. If an Employee resigns or is dismissed or laid off and has exceeded his or her allowable sick leave, the excess sick leave paid shall be deducted from any moneys due him or her from the Employer at the time of resignation, layoff, or dismissal.

XIV. HOLIDAYS. This clause will include the requirements for eligibility for holiday pay, the number of holidays granted, and method of payment for such holidays.

SAMPLE

Holidays

Section A. Employees shall be entitled to eight (8) paid Holidays each year as follows:

1. New Year's Day
2. Martin Luther King's Birthday
3. Washington's Birthday
4. Memorial Day
5. Independence Day
6. Labor Day
7. Thanksgiving Day
8. Christmas Day

Section B. To be paid for a Holiday, an Employee must have worked that last complete scheduled shift prior to and the next complete shift after such Holiday unless the absence is authorized or excused.

Section C. Recognizing that the Hospital works every day of the year, and that it is not possible for all Employees to be off duty on the same day, the Hospital shall have the right, at its sole discretion, to require any Employee to work on any of the Holidays, provided however that such Employee shall be given a day off in lieu of such Holiday at the convenience of the Department. Employees who work on a Holiday and cannot be scheduled for a compensatory day off, at the discretion and option of the Hospital shall in lieu thereof be paid an additional day's pay at straight time, in addition to time and one-half their regular straight time rate of pay for all hours worked on the Holiday.

Section D. Employees shall be entitled to four (4) "free days" with pay in the course of a calendar year in addition to the eight (8) paid Holidays listed above. Free days shall be scheduled at the convenience of the Hospital and shall not be taken immediately preceding or immediately following vacation time or a Holiday. Request for scheduling a "free day" must be made by the Employee at least two (2) weeks prior to the date requested.

Section E. For the purposes of computation of pay for Holidays and "free days" under this Article, an Employee will be paid for his or her regular scheduled work day at his or her regular straight time hourly rate.

Section F. Employees will be entitled to time off with pay to vote at regularly scheduled city, state, or federal elections, in accordance with applicable state laws. Such time off will be granted only if the employee does not have at least four (4) hours time between the time the polling places open and the start of his or her work schedule or between the close of his or her work schedule and the time the polling places close. Such time off shall not exceed two (2) hours and shall be granted only if the Employee notifies his or her supervisor not more than ten (10) nor less than two (2) days before the day of election.

New series of clauses will be included in the new contract covering wages and minimums, vacation provisions, paid leave provisions, no-discrimination requirements, severance pay, uniform allowance, and any agreement on past practices.

PART FOUR

HUMAN RESOURCES OUTCOMES

CHAPTER

ASSESSMENT OF HUMAN RESOURCES OUTCOMES

Stephen Strasser

Kathryn Dansky

LEARNING OBJECTIVES

Upon completing this chapter, the reader should be able to . . .

- Understand the concepts critical to measuring human resources management (HRM) effectiveness in health care organizations.
- Recognize some of the benefits and costs of developing HRM effectiveness models.
- Understand how HRM effectiveness models must be integrated with the organization's overall strategic plan.
- Understand the importance of creating reliable and valid measures of HRM effectiveness.
- Understand how the principles of continuous quality improvement can be integrated into a system designed to measure HRM effectiveness.
- Begin the development of an HRM effectiveness model for a health care organization.

INTRODUCTION

This chapter is about developing methods of evaluating, monitoring, and improving the quality of human resources management (HRM) services in health care organizations. There are three primary goals.

First, we want health care management students to understand the benefits and risks of developing and implementing quality monitoring methodologies that assess human resources management effectiveness. Although internal evaluation systems can contribute to managerial control and effectiveness, they also can create sociotechnical chaos.

Second, we want health care management

students to learn a conceptual approach to developing HRM effectiveness models and implementation methods. Our approach finds its roots in three places: 1) the early work conducted in the 1960s regarding program evaluation (e.g., Deniston, Rosenstock, & Getting, 1968; Knutson, 1969; Weiss, 1972); 2) work conducted in the 1980s regarding strategic planning; and 3) work done in the 1980s regarding the development of quality assurance and continuous quality improvement[1] (e.g., Crosby, 1984, 1989; Deming, 1982, 1986; Juran, 1986, 1988).

Our conceptual approach is not intended to suggest that there is only one correct methodology for developing HRM effectiveness models. Certainly, there are many effective and appropriate ways of developing HRM quality monitoring systems. However, the model described herein may serve as a catalyst for developing a hybrid model that best fits the reader's organization's strategic and operational purposes.

Third, we hope that health care management students will learn to use the data generated by HRM effectiveness models to improve managerial practices. Based on our experiences with other quality control processes, this may be the most challenging objective of all.

Throughout the chapter, we have provided examples and case studies. There also is an exercise to help students understand and internalize the concepts presented.

---

[1] The terms *total quality management* (*TQM*) and *continuous quality improvement* (*CQI*) are used interchangeably in this chapter.

DEFINING HUMAN RESOURCES MANAGEMENT EFFECTIVENESS

HRM effectiveness is defined as the extent to which the activities, programs, attitudes, and behaviors of the human resources management department contribute to the strategic objectives of the health care organization.[2] There are three characteristics of this definition that we wish to highlight: 1) a contingency perspective, 2) a fluid definition, and 3) definitional integration.

A Contingency Perspective on HRM Effectiveness

Because the needs of health care organizations differ, the criteria for measuring HRM quality vary from setting to setting. The above definition provides for this flexibility. For one health care organization, HRM effectiveness may depend in part on the success its staff has in recruiting physicians. In an ambulatory care setting, the critical determinant of HRM effectiveness may be defined by the speed with which vacant positions in occupational and physical therapy are filled. In a freestanding primary care center, HRM effectiveness may be defined by how well administrative support staff are intrinsically motivated in their jobs. The key learning point is that there is *no* single, universal definition of HRM quality or effectiveness. Like contingency theories of leadership or motivation (e.g., Vroom, 1964; Vroom & Yetton, 1973), the forms HRM effectiveness can take are

[2] Throughout this chapter, the phrases *quality of HRM* and *HRM effectiveness* are used synonymously.

contingent on the situation the health care organization faces.

A Fluid Definition

Health care organizations are constantly adapting to a rapidly changing external environment. Sometimes changes originate within the organization; at other times, changes are thrust on the organization from its environment. Consequently, the organization's strategic mission is often changing or at the very least being fine-tuned and adjusted. The definition of HRM effectiveness must be commensurately fluid. Although constantly changing goals and objectives should be avoided, an overly rigid definition of HRM effectiveness would probably create the same outcome.

Definitional Integration

Although at times it may appear otherwise, the HRM department is not a semi-autonomous business unit operating independently of the health care organization. Instead, the HRM department is perhaps the most highly integrated staff function within the health care setting. As noted in earlier chapters, most HRM activities and programs affect every employee in the organization. At times HRM staff are designing ways to optimize the relationship between costs and benefits on a new health care insurance program; at other times, HRM staff are settling disputes among employees and managers; and at still other times, HRM staff are developing new staffing models to meet the demands of the hospital's expansion in women's health care services. These events, although ostensibly independent, may still relate to one another and to the strategic mission of most organizations in a systems theory sense (see Georgopolous and Matejko, 1967). As a result, an understanding of, and consideration for, the strategic objectives of the organization become *necessary conditions* for development of a conceptual and operationally meaningful definition of HRM effectiveness. If the two are not predicated on one another, organizational entropy (i.e., chaos) (Katz & Kahn, 1966) is more likely to emerge.

In sum, our definition of HRM effectiveness focuses on three objectives. First, the definition must reflect the wide variance in strategic objectives that characterize health care organizations. Second, the definition must be responsive to changing strategic initiatives. Third, the definition must integrate the activities of the HRM department into the health care organization's overall strategic mission.

THE BENEFITS OF MEASURING HRM EFFECTIVENESS

As incredible as it may seem, many HRM departments cannot tell you precisely how well or poorly they are performing. Although bits and bytes of anecdotal information abound, a systematic method for evaluating HRM effectiveness is probably lacking in many health care organizations. This creates a variety of managerial and operational problems.

Diagnosing for Continuous Quality Improvement (CQI)

Without a conceptual and operational model for HRM effectiveness, it is very difficult for an HRM department to identify where it is performing well and where continuous improvement efforts should be directed. Using a medical model as a metaphor, we are much further along in our ability to identify how well the immensely complex and differentiated human body is performing than we are in our ability to measure HRM quality. Actually, we can even better diagnose how our automobiles are performing than how our HRM departments are. Without diagnostic information, we are unable to identify where managerial activity is successful and where ameliorative intervention is necessary. Moreover, without diagnostic capability, it becomes difficult to know which prevention programs designed to ensure HRM effectiveness should be implemented.

Contingent Reward Programs

There is evidence which shows that employees will perform better and be more satisfied with their work if they perceive that their supervisors reward them for good performance (Greenberger, Strasser, & Lee, 1988; Podsakoff, Todor, & Skov, 1981). Without having diagnostic or evaluative information on HRM performance, it becomes virtually impossible to implement contingent reward programs.

Decision-Making Quality

Health care managers' ability to make appropriate resource allocation decisions is hampered without information on HRM effectiveness. For instance, you may need to be allocating money into improved employee relations programs. However, if you do not possess reliable and valid data that employee relations need resources support, then you would have no idea that this *in actuality* is a critical problem area. Similarly, without systematic evaluation systems, we might be more prone to making inaccurate managerial judgments (see Nisbett & Rosh, 1980). For instance, a board member may call and indicate dissatisfaction with how a job search for a clinical department head was conducted. Even though this might be an anomaly in your HRM department (i.e., the vast majority are well-conducted and this is an aberrant case), without adequate supporting documentation you may be prone to putting together a resources task force to "clean up" the job search protocols, when staff time, money, and energy might be better spent elsewhere.

Accountability

Health care managers and academics alike bemoan the difficulty of holding HRM staff accountable for the contributions they make and the problems they may cause. One reason for this is the relative "softness" of its outcomes or effectiveness criteria. Specifically, it can be difficult to translate HRM activities and programs into well-defined "hard" outcomes such as dollars saved or made, census increase or decrease, or morale improvement or decrement. Although Cascio (1990) has made great progress in beginning to resolve this dilemma, the problem remains. This may be a mixed blessing for HRM departments. At one level, it is difficult to hold them accountable for their actions because it is difficult to attribute cause or to measure their efficacy; this is the "ignorance is managerial bliss" argument. At a second level, it is one of many reasons that HRM is sometimes relegated second-class citizenship in some health care organizations; this is the "ignorance equates with organizational anonymity" argument.

Without accountability, demonstrating the positive role HRM can play in facilitating strategic goal attainment is hampered. Without accountability, HRM will not be perceived as a major force in the organization. Without accountability, HRM will have difficulty taking itself seriously and moving toward continuous quality improvement.

We are not suggesting that being able to measure HRM effectiveness will solve the majority of problems HRM managers face. As we discussed later in this chapter, there are substantial risks and problems with developing and implementing models of HRM effectiveness. However, we believe that the consequences of maintaining the status quo are more negative than the problems associated with trying to construct and implement an HRM effectiveness model.

CONCEPTUAL PROBLEMS IN DESIGNING AN HRM EFFECTIVENESS PROGRAM

There are three categories of problems in designing an HRM effectiveness program: conceptual, methodological, and implementational. In this section, we discuss only conceptual problems. In later sections, we examine methodological and implementation problems.

Content Validity

Content validity is a term that has particular relevance for answering the question, "What *is* HRM effectiveness for my health care organization?" Content validity is defined as the extent to which a measure captures the totality of the construct being measured. The more of a construct that is captured in a measure, the more content valid the measure is. Consider the following example. A measure of quality of patient care services for Get Well Memorial Hospital that is based *solely* on age-adjusted mortality rates is *not* as content valid a measure as one that includes age-adjusted mortality rates, unplanned recidivism rates within 30 and 60 days, and the frequency of nosocomial infection rates within the hospital. A measure of employee satisfaction based on the answer to the question, "How satisfied are you with your pay," is not as content valid as one that is based on the multiple facets or indicators of staff satisfaction such as pay, benefits, supervision, coworkers, task, scheduling, physical working conditions, opportunities for advancement, and intrinsic motivation.

Thus the problem faced by HRM staff in developing an effectiveness model is to develop a model that relies on a *comprehensive set of effectiveness criteria and measures*. As just noted, a model that defines effectiveness using employee turnover as the sole criteria will not be as content valid as one that uses multiple indicators. However, selecting these indicators is not easy. Sometimes necessary criteria may be omitted because the HRM department lacks the data to measure them. In fact, Etzioni (1964) argues that we tend to measure only what we believe we can measure, not what we *should* measure. Sometimes necessary indicators are omitted for political reasons—staff and/or management know they are doing poorly in a given area and choose not to measure their performance in order to ensure that others in the organization do not discover their less than perfect performance. At other times, HRM staff may not know which indicators are the focal criteria to measure. Although organizationwide strategic objectives should help to guide HRM staff in the selection of HRM effectiveness criteria, some strategic plans lack

content validity themselves or they are simply too vague.

Who Defines the Effectiveness Model's Content/Criteria?

If we were to ask all HRM staff to describe their definition of HRM effectiveness, we would guess that different effectiveness criteria would emerge. There are many reasons for this. One is that staff in different HRM jobs might define HRM effectiveness from their unique, job-related, perceptual orientations. For instance, payroll staff may define their role in HRM effectiveness in terms of the fewest numbers of errors made in processing paychecks. In contrast, employee relations staff may define HRM effectiveness in terms of how long the disputes they resolve stay resolved. A second reason is that HRM senior managerial staff, who are more likely to be exposed to strategic objectives, may be more influenced by these than other managerial and nonmanagerial staff. Finally, the HRM staff itself are likely to possess differential work and life experiences. These may be reflected in substantial variance (and disagreement) over what the HRM effectiveness criteria should be.

Because no single perspective on HRM effectiveness will be right or wrong, management faces the challenging, although necessary, task of synthesizing these honest differences into a cohesive and integrated HRM effectiveness model.

Do We Measure Processes or Outcomes?

Processes are defined as activities, programs, and staff behaviors and attitudes that the health care organization must undertake or possess to attain desired outcomes. They are the means to a desired end. Outcomes are the ends necessary for HRM to attain in order to support the organization's strategic goals. In theory, they are the causal result of process (see Campbell, 1977; Strasser, Eveland, Cummins, Deniston, & Romani, 1981). For example, HRM may define an outcome as reducing controllable turnover among nursing aides at the Happy Stay Continuous Care Retirement Center by 25% within 6 months. The means or processes to this end may be multiple: collect data to identify reasons for turnover, be open to criticism nursing aides may have of management, study salary patterns and dollar shift differentials, and so forth.

The question for the HRM manager now becomes is HRM effectiveness measured in terms of the processes that lead to desired outcomes or in terms of outcomes alone? At a more macro organizational level, this question captures the essence of the debate held in the 1970s and 1980s in the organizational effectiveness literature between the system model school (i.e., process) (e.g., Georgopolous, 1972, 1980) and the goal model school (i.e., outcomes) (Deniston et al., 1968; Weiss, 1972) of organizational effectiveness. Theoretical work primarily conducted by Campbell (1977) and secondarily by Strasser et al. (1981) suggest that both should be measured. The basic argument posed is a reciprocal one. If you are going to understand outcomes (e.g., high turnover rates), you need to have measures of work process that may be causally related to these (e.g., underpaid staff, poor supervisory practices). On the other side of the equation, if you are going to understand work processes (i.e., poor supervisory practices), you will want to know how these manifest as outcomes. Figure 18.1 displays this relationship.

By now you may be wondering whether establishing an effectiveness model/program for human resources is worth all the trouble. The answer despite these conceptual problems is still yes. One key reason is that the alternative—no effectiveness modeling—is probably a greater evil. A manager driving without any map will be a clear and present danger to the well-being of his or her staff and the health care organization's patients. A manager driving with an even partially valid map is less likely to do harm and may in fact do much good.

DESIGNING MODELS OF HRM EFFECTIVENESS

Designing models of HRM effectiveness can be accomplished in a variety of ways. As noted previously, the approach we suggest is not the *only* way managers can accomplish this task. Health care managers must recognize that their unique situations may make it necessary for them to use a modified version of this model or to develop their own hybrid models using only some of the ideas contained herein.

Our approach focuses on five critical steps: identification, integration, patterning, implementation, and monitoring and evaluation through continuous quality improvement. These are displayed in Figure 18.2.

Identification—Analyzing the Health Care Organization's Strategic Plan

Identification is defined as the study and understanding of the health care organization's strategic plan and related objectives. This is where HRM staff begin developing

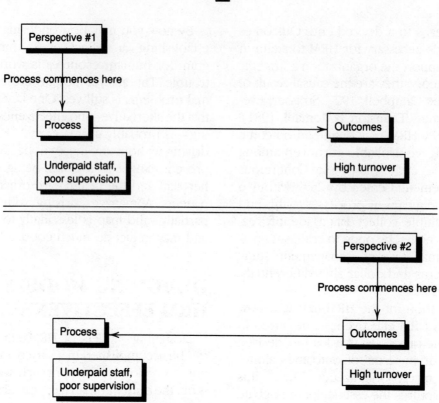

FIGURE 18.1. The relationship between analyzing process and outcomes. In Perspective #1, when starting with process data only, it is important to know the consequences. In Perspective #2, when starting conceptually and operationally with outcome data, it is important to look retrospectively at contributory processes.

their own effectiveness model. Identification is an important process for many reasons. Most important is that it helps ensure goal congruence and goal integration. Goal congruency is defined as the extent to which departmental, hierarchical, and sociotechnical subsystems within the health care organization are trying to accomplish similar objectives. Goal integration is defined as the extent to which goal-directed activities of one subsystem help support the goal-directed activities of another. There are both *within* subsystem and *among* subsystem dimensions to these concepts. *Among* the traditional subunits of HRM (e.g., employee relations, training, recruitment, employee benefits), goals must be congruent or complementary in the same way that goal congruency is necessary among HRM and other departments of the health care organization. By the same token, integration must occur *within* HRM amongst its various subsystems in the same way that it occurs among HRM and other departments or hierarchical levels in the organization. If

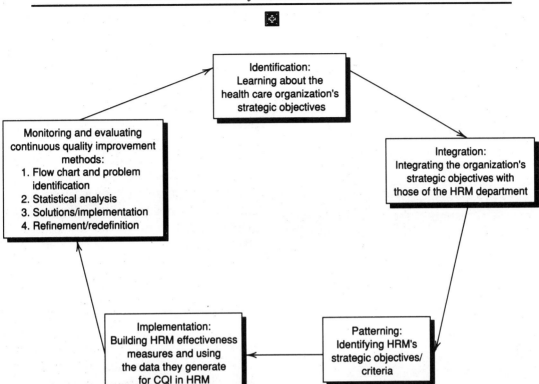

FIGURE 18.2. Five steps of human resources effectiveness modeling and implementation.

the HRM effectiveness model's criteria are not congruent with and integrated into the overall organization's strategic plan, subsystems within the organization will be more likely to work at cross purposes. Goal conflicts, dysfunctional competition for scarce resources, poor communication, and nonresponsive decision-making structures are likely sequelae.

Health care organizations are almost perfectly designed to have difficulty integrating their goal-directed activities. One reason is their high levels of functional, technical, and sociodemographic differentiation that result from different value orientations of stakeholders. Therefore, it becomes even more critical for the HRM's objectives to be integrated with the total organization's objectives

from the start. This takes on more meaning in light of today's effort to implement a total quality management philosophy and strategy. The success of TQM programs is partly based on the organization's ability to implement cross-functional teams that work well internally and with other units in the organization (see Fargason & Haddock, 1992). If goal congruency and integration are lacking it becomes extremely difficult for these teams to work effectively internally and with others.

Ideally, the vice president of HRM is intimately involved in organizational strategic planning and the objective-setting process. Theoretically, he or she should be cognizant of and understand the organization's strategic objectives. Unfortunately, this is not al-

CASE: NO ONE ASKED ME WHAT *I* THOUGHT!

In one hospital, a Director of Human Resources arrived at her office one morning and was greeted with a rather informative memo. The contents of the memo indicated that senior management with the majority support of the hospital's board had decided to commence an aggressive physician-recruiting program. The Director of Human Resources also learned for the first time from this memo that it was her job to offer staff and logistical support for the recruiting effort. Specifically, she was to interface with hospital administration, medical staff, and physician recruitment firms if necessary. The goal was to complete the recruiting effort successfully within a 6-month period.

No one had considered to ask the Director of Human Resources if she had the staff resources, time, skills, and staff expertise to carry out this assignment. No one had considered to include her in the organization's strategic planning process.

As incredible as this may sound, it really did occur. What is so important for the health care management student to understand are the reasons that human resources managers may be omitted from the strategic planning and implementation loop.

One reason is that the CEO and perhaps other members of the senior management team do not understand or fully appreciate the potential contribution HRM staff can make to strategic planning and implementation. In health care management, the field of finance has been a dominant managerial discipline for many managers and scholars. As a result, senior management is sometimes not as well-versed on HRM issues as they are on others. This is one reason, for example, that the American College of Health Care Executives is making a concerted effort to increase their constituencies' exposure to HRM issues (personal communication, Anne Schwarzwaelder). A second and related reason alluded to earlier is that it can be difficult to attribute better quality care or improved financial performance specifically to the success of HRM programs and activities. For example, HRM training staff may run excellent basic supervisory training programs for all newly promoted managers. However, how this actually contributes to better financial performance or patient care, for example, is difficult to assess. In contrast, finance can implement a more comprehensive, thorough, and faster billing procedure. When evaluated, finance staff will be able to document more directly how these resulted in new dollars found (or saved) for the organization. A third reason is that HRM programs sometimes are their own worst enemies. Rather than being viewed as programs facilitating the success of clinical and other administrative units, they may be viewed as obstacles. How often have we heard health care managers say, "HRM won't allow me to:

- hire the person I really like for the job."
- fire the person who is making everyone crazy in my department."
- fill the position I so desperately need."

ways the case as the following actual case study illustrates.[3]

---

[3] Facts within cases presented in this chapter have been altered to protect the confidentiality and anonymity of those involved. However, the substance and major issues pertaining to these cases remain unaltered.

- issue an emergency paycheck to my new employee on everyone else's payday."
- ask what I really need to ask in job interviews."

The learning points from these comments and the above case study are not complex. HRM has little chance of successfully developing and implementing its own effectiveness model if it is not intimately part of developing and implementing the health care organization's overall strategic plan. A second learning point is that HRM will have difficulty developing an effectiveness model if other subsystems in the organization do not *understand* and, as importantly, *value* the contribution it makes.

Integrating the Organization's Strategic Plan with the Design of an HRM Effectiveness Model

We have already defined goal integration as the extent to which the goal-directed activities of one subsystem help support those of another. After the organization's strategic objectives are identified and understood, HRM staff can develop the substance of their own organizational effectiveness model.

The integration process begins by identifying how HRM can *contribute to* the successful attainment of overall organizational strategic objectives. To better understand the *integration* process, please participate in the following exercise.

EXERCISE 1

Below are two strategic objectives the board of directors of the Hospital for the

Sick and Getting Better (HSGB, Inc.) have targeted for the next 24 months. Please review these carefully. Then define specific actions HRM can take to *help* this hospital meet its objectives.

- *Strategic Objective #1:* Within 24 months, same-day surgery visits will increase by 10% annually from 6000 procedures per year to 7260.
- *Strategic Objective #2:* Within 24 months, patient admitting time will be reduced for nonemergency room admissions by 20%—from 55 minutes to 44 minutes.

Strategic Objective #1: List *specific actions* HRM staff at HSGB, Inc. can take to help the organization attain this objective.

Strategic Objective #2: List specific actions HRM staff at HSGB, Inc. can take to help the organization attain this objective.

For *Strategic Objective #1,* you may have listed some of the following ideas:

- HRM can develop staffing models for the expected growth in same-day surgery visits and procedures.
- HRM can help in the recruitment of the additional staff that same-day surgery will need to meet the increased patient volume.
- HRM can help identify pools of internal staff who may wish to make job or career development transfers to the same-day surgery. These staff may come from areas in which planned cutbacks or downsizing will occur.
- HRM can alter its new employee orientation program so that it better explains the role same-day surgery plays in the organization.
- HRM can conduct interview training

with line staff who will be hiring new same-day surgery staff.

• HRM can encourage the hospital's staff and family members to use the new and expanded same-day surgery services.

For *Strategic Objective #2,* you may have listed the following ways in which HRM can contribute to reducing nonemergency room visits:

• HRM can conduct a job analysis of admitting department staff positions to assess if staff are assigned tasks that ensure smooth and expedient patient flow.
• HRM can assess whether admitting is understaffed and therefore not able to process new patients efficiently through the system.
• HRM (with management engineering's help) can conduct a patient flow analysis to identify why admitting times

are not shorter. For instance, HRM staff may be able to conduct separate focus groups with patients and admitting staff to gather pertinent information.

• HRM (with the assistance of the patient relations department) might be able to conduct patient/customer relations training for admitting staff. This may help to buffer some of the annoyances waiting patients experience.

Figure 18.3 displays the conceptual framework for the process of meeting strategic objectives.

The purpose of the exercise is to demonstrate how HRM's programs and activities can support strategic goal attainment at the macro-organizational level. *These activities and programs ultimately form the substance of HRM's effectiveness model.* Because these programs are in response to the organization's strategic objectives, the HRM's effectiveness model will possess *criteria* that are

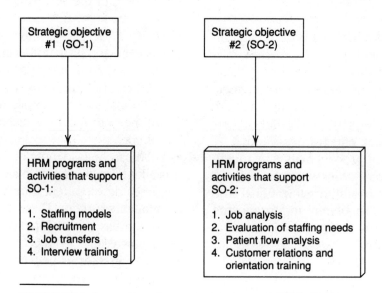

FIGURE 18.3. Integration of strategic objectives with HRM effectiveness criteria.

congruent and integrally linked to the organization's strategic mission.

Patterning—Identifying the Criteria of the HRM Effectiveness Model

Patterning is defined as the identification of similar or overlapping activities and programs HRM staff must conduct to assist in macro-organizationwide strategic goal attainment. These ultimately will form the criteria of effectiveness for the model. Consider Exercise #1 to better understand the patterning process.

If your HRM staff were to carry through Exercise #1 for each strategic objective in the organization, a long list of activities and programs would likely emerge. If this list were scrutinized closely, patterns or themes of activities and programs could be identified. In the above example, one pattern that emerges revolves around *training*—training line managers in how to interview, training new employees during orientation programs, and training staff in customer relations skills and techniques. It is these patterns that form the substance for selecting criteria of HRM effectiveness. Again, using the above example, one criteria of HRM effectiveness might revolve around training programs, and a second might revolve around staffing and recruitment activities. Within each HRM effectiveness criterion (e.g., training and staffing), each of the programs and activities HRM is able to provide will be listed as the means to attain the end. For each HRM effectiveness criterion (e.g., training), the appropriate data must be collected and analyzed in conjunction with its corresponding strategic objective.

What if certain activities and programs are

unique and do not fit into a definable pattern or strategic category? Obviously, these are not ignored. They can form a miscellaneous category called *HRM special strategic objectives*. Given their uniqueness, HRM staff might also choose to reconsider whether they are the appropriate functional area to implement these programs successfully. Figure 18.4 displays the outcome of the above patterning process.

Although our model facilitates goal congruency and integration with the overall organization's strategic mission, attention also should be focused *inward* toward the identification of additional *maintenance and developmental* objectives for HRM itself (see Figure 18.4). Maintenance and developmental objectives are defined as goals that are primarily unique to HRM and that HRM needs to attain internally in order to support the attainment of the organization's macro strategic objectives. For instance, if HRM is going to develop a staffing plan for the new ambulatory surgery initiative, it may need to send two of its own staff to other facilities throughout the United States, Canada, and Europe to learn more about staffing issues.[4] Or, if HRM is going to conduct more training for the health care organization, it may need to establish a maintenance and developmental goal of hiring an additional training and development staff person. If budget neutral breaks (e.g. budgetary controls on spending) are being applied, then HRM may decide to deploy existing staff in this capacity while cutting back time commitments to other activities. A third example may be HRM's objective to serve its internal customers better—other subsystems of the health

---

[4] This is a difficult job that someone must do!

HRM first-level objectives

Strategic objectives	HRM objective #1	HRM objective #2	HRM objective #3	HRM objective #4	HRM objective #6
	Training	Staffing/ recruiting	Benefits	Management information systems for HR	Maintenance and developmental systems

HRM second-level objectives

SO#1					
Increase same-day surgery	Provide interview training.	Provide staffing models. Recruit new staff. Build applicant pool.	Improve benefits for re-cruitment purposes.	Develop database on employees interested in working in same-day surgery.	Site visit others to assess optimal volume.
SO#2					
Reduce admitting waiting time.	Provide customer relations training.	Conduct job analysis.		Download data on patient waiting times from patient satisfaction surveys for within department analysis.	Hire new training and development staff. Increase internal customer service quality: a. Develop automated payroll b. Conduct survey Measure client satisfaction with HR. Develop more automated payroll systems.
SO#n					

* * * * *

FIGURE 18.4. Developing HRM effectiveness criteria—patterns leading to HRM effectiveness and criteria.

care organization. An example of how this can be accomplished is to conduct an internal customer satisfcation survey for the department heads HRM staff serve.

Maintenance and developmental objectives may have only a tangential relationship to the organization's strategic objectives. For example, although there may be no organizationwide strategic concern over the performance of the hospital payroll systems, HRM management still may feel a need to target this area for continuous quality improvement (e.g., implementing a faster and more automated accounting and check-writing system). Maintenance and developmental objectives, therefore, give HRM the flexibility needed to integrate its own unique strategic needs with those of the overall organization.

The Political Process of Model-Buliding

As important as the HRM effectiveness criteria are to a successful model, *how* HRM staff go about building the model is just as important. One critical issue is consensus-building. HRM staff must recognize that their role is to *serve* the organization and to *facilitate* the success of other subsystems within the larger health care organization. As such, it is critical for HRM not to design the effectiveness model in a void, but in coalescence with other units in the organization. Although the organization's strategic objectives will serve as a guiding force in effectiveness model development, HRM should get input from a variety of consumers as to what *they* believe HRM should be and what HRM should be doing. This means HRM staff will need to receive specific strategic input from each of the following consumers:

- Nonmanagerial staff (clinical and administrative)
- First-line supervisory staff
- Middle management/department heads
- Senior management
- The board (in particular, the personnel and executive committees)
- Certain community groups

Input from these consumer groups can be gathered through informal meetings, focus groups, and sending out a brief and anonymous self-administered survey. Another approach that may be operationally easier is to convene an HRM effectiveness advisory group that comprises a cross-section of the above constituencies.

If HRM staff is to be perceived as credible and responsive, it is crucial that these constituencies be listened to and involved in the model development and implementation process. Moreover, they should be involved on an ongoing basis—from model development to analysis of effectiveness data to implementation of CQI programs on HRM's behalf. If they are not, HRM runs the risk of designing an elegant effectiveness model that has little organizational acceptance or approval.

Health care organizations are process sensitive. *How* things are done matters as much as, or even more than, *what* is actually done. The strong ethic of "professionalism" that continues to characterize many health care settings is one reason. A second reason is the diversity of constituents that comprise the organization itself. Increasingly strong legal and sociopolitical trends toward greater egalitarianism and participation in the work place is a third factor. Last, basic organizational development principles that focus on building constituency investment, consensus, and support are vital for effective implementation.

Implementation—Operationalizing the HRM Model Effectiveness

Thus far, we have focused on developing a conceptual model of HRM effectiveness. We know what general criteria we will use to evaluate effectiveness, however, we do not know how we will *measure* them. The process of defining specific measures—turning an effectiveness criterion concept into a measurable process—is called *operationalization*. Unless we can operationalize reliable and valid measures of HRM effectiveness, the measurement process is reduced to subjectivity.

Conceptually defining HRM effectiveness is a difficult and time-consuming task. Measuring it can be extremely demanding as well. Key attributes that your HRM measures should possess are discussed below.

Translating Conceptual Goals into Operational Goals[5]

In Figure 18.4, we outlined three types of goals: 1) strategic or organizationwide objectives; 2) HRM first-level objectives; and 3) specific programs and activities (i.e., second-level HRM objectives) that are necessary to accomplish first-level HRM and ultimately strategic level objectives. The challenge is to translate first- and second-level HRM goals into measurable goals. Doing this with second-level goals (i.e., the programs and activities to attain first-level HRM objectives) may be easier than doing this with first-level goals because the level of specificity is explicitly narrower and conceptually more consistent with the former. For instance,

[5] See Organ and Bateman (1991) for a summary of the organizational development literature.

when we focus on providing interview training (a second-level HRM objective), we know that we will be measuring dimensions of effectiveness, such as whether all managers were trained, how quickly they were trained, whether trainees gained new knowledge, and whether they are implementing this knowledge in job interviews. Developing measures for first-level HRM objectives may be more challenging because these objectives represent the *totality* of all of the second-level objectives that may comprise less conceptually consistent criteria. To better understand this argument, refer again to Figure 18.4 and consider its simplest mathematical expression:

First-Level HRM Objective #1:

$$\text{Training} = \text{Interview Training} + \text{Customer Relations Training}$$

The close reader will immediately see at least two problems with this formulation. First, who is to say that interview training should be valued equally (i.e., weighted) to customer relations training? Moreover, is it meaningful to add numerical effectiveness rating of the second-level HRM objectives into one number that expresses the totality of the first-level HRM training objective?

In terms of the first question, we strongly recommend that HRM management weight the importance of each second-level objective, such as in the following equation:

First-Level HRM Objective #1:

$$\text{Training} = (.3)\,(\text{Interview Training}) + (.7)\,(\text{Customer Relations Training})$$

Naturally, the weighting scheme should reflect the relative importance of each first- and second-level HRM objective. In terms of the second question, we think that a single numerical score can be deceiving *unless* the components or dimensions that went into the derivation of the single score are reported as well. This also applies to the measurement of second-level HRM objectives. It is much more useful and methodologically sound to measure the effectiveness of, for example, the interview training program, in terms of multiple dimensions (e.g., knowledge gained, number of attendees, length of training). Although a single effectiveness score can be computed, it is not meaningful unless the dimensions comprising the single score are reported as well.

Components of HRM Effectiveness Goals

The first- and second-level HRM goals developed in the HRM effectiveness model should have the following characteristics that are consistent with research on goal-setting theory (Locke & Latham, 1990). As just noted, the criteria should be definable and measurable. Examples include, "Hire five new cardiac catherization technicians," and "Give all HRM staff at least 6 hours of customer relations training." Goals of this nature usually generate better productivity among staff than vague goals such as, "Do your best," or, "Give it a real try, and we'll see what happens." Second, there should be a temporal component to goals (i.e., a time when the objective should be met). Examples include, "Give all 264 managers customer relations training within 12 months."

Third, goals or objectives should be challenging but attainable. To give recruiting staff only 1 week to hire five cardiac catherization support staff is obviously too little time, and staff will feel helpless. If given 2 years to attain this goal, it may become so simple that it is perceived as boring and unchallenging. This could engender a lackadaisical or indifferent effort. Fourth, staff must receive knowledge of results. They must receive feedback regarding their goal progress from the HRM effectiveness system through reports and verbal communications. For example, if the objective is to reduce employee grievances about harassment by 20% over a 3-month period, a staff member must collect these data and feed them back to staff working toward this end. The data are a beacon that HRM staff can follow to stay on course toward goal attainment. Last, the criteria must be valuatively acceptable by HRM staff. They must believe in the criteria and the goal they are trying to attain. Without this, there will be little psychological investment in and motivation toward goal attainment.

Measurement Reliability and Validity

Reliability is defined as the extent to which the measure being used generates similar results when used repeatedly to measure an unchanging phenomenon. For example, it is more reliable to measure employee morale through a psychometrically validated attitude survey than to simply interview five employees and ask them, "How do you feel about your job?" Reliable measures are critical because they are a necessary condition for developing valid measures of HRM effectiveness.[6]

Measurement validity is defined as the extent to which we are measuring what we believe we are measuring. For instance, confidentially asking employees how satisfied they are with their pay is a far more valid

---

[6] There are many forms of measurement reliability and viability, and space does not permit us to go into a detailed discussion and explanation of each. The interested reader should refer to Kerlinger (1986).

measure of pay satisfaction than simply comparing annual salaries broken out by job classification against other employer groups in the same area. Confidentially asking employees about their pay satisfaction is said to be a relatively more valid measure of pay satisfaction. It is wrong to think of reliability and validity in bipolar terms (i.e., "Yes, it's valid"; "No, it is not valid"). Instead, one should view these ideas as if they are on a continuum ranging from totally unreliable (or invalid) to totally reliable (or valid). It is rare that researchers ever develop measures that are 100% reliable and valid.

The reliability and validity of your HRM effectiveness measures are important not only for the obvious reason of being honest and accurate. If your measures are not considered valid, it will be easy for other constituencies in the organization to discount the meaningfulness of your measures if it suits their political purposes.

Revisiting Process and Outcomes Measurement

This topic was discussed previously (see Figure 18.1), but it merits further attention here. Suppose a hospital establishes a strategic objective of effectively training all employees in the values and philosophy of the institution. In response, HRM develops an integrated effectiveness objective of conducting value and philosophy training seminars for the total organization and implements a program to attain this end. What should HRM measure?

If HRM simply measures how many staff attended the seminars and the number of seminars conducted, process is being measured—the extent to which the steps along the way to the final outcome were comp-

leted. This is acceptable except that it does not indicate how effective the process was. There could have been 100% attendance and 50 programs could have been implemented; however, this does not tell us if anybody learned anything. If we go ahead and measure how much employees felt they learned in these workshops, then we are a step closer to measuring outcomes. If we go even a step further and measure the average number of times employees allude to appropriate hospital values and philosophy in their decision making, then we are even closer to measuring outcome. The health care manager's job is to attempt to measure both—the process that leads to the desired outcome and the outcome itself. As Campbell (1977) has argued, to learn if the process has been effective, one begins by measuring outcome. To learn *why* a successful or unsuccessful outcome occurred, one must assess whether the process succeeded.

Unit of Analysis

For HR effectiveness data to be effectively utilized it is almost always desirable to measure it at the smallest unit of analysis possible. Unit of analysis is defined as the level at which data are grouped or aggregated. The smallest level is usually at the individual employee or activity level. The objective is to be able to group/aggregate your data in as many ways as possible. Consider the following example: Suppose you conduct a wage and benefit satisfaction survey of non-physician employees in a large hospital-based outpatient clinic and you do *not* ask employees their age or the department in which they work. The result would be that you could not analyze your data broken out by age or department. This could lead to erroneous conclusions. The overall satisfaction with pay and benefits across 250 employees, for example (the total clinic), may be very high. However, you would never know if extreme pay dissatisfaction is experienced by nine radiological technologists unless you knew the department in which they work. Or, consider turnover data. Which is more valuable to you—turnover data rates for the hospital as a whole or turnover rates for the total hospital *in addition to* rates broken out by departments? Better yet, which kind of data would you prefer to have: 1) turnover rates broken out by department; or 2) turnover rates broken out by department and then *further broken out* into desirable turnover (i.e., percentage of low performers leaving) and undesirable turnover (i.e., percentage of high performers leaving) (Dalton & Todor, 1979).

Longitudinal Measurement

Longitudinal measurement is defined as monitoring HRM effectiveness goal performance over time. It is desirable that HRM measures of effectiveness be monitored longitudinally so that *trends* and *patterns* in HRM quality are monitored. In today's total quality management environment where continuous improvement is so focal, it is critical to measure effectiveness longitudinally. Moreover, longitudinal measures offer you at least one other benefit. They permit you to become your own "control group." It is far more meaningful in a continuous quality improvement environment to compare yourself to yourself over time versus comparing your organization to others no matter how similar the organizations appear. This is not to say that comparisons among like health care organizations are not useful. They are.

However, more emphasis must be placed on longitudinal self-comparison and improvement.

Monitoring and Evaluating HRM Performance Effectiveness through CQI

To this point we have developed an operational HRM effectiveness model. Criteria—first- and second-level outcomes—of effectiveness are defined and measures to assess these criteria are developed.

The conceptual framework for the final stage of our model is based on principles of quality improvement. These principles are employed to assess why specific HRM effectiveness criteria are being attained and why others are not. Some background information on this subject is necessary to further clarify the notion of HRM effectiveness.

Continuous Quality Improvement (CQI)

The concept of quality improvement is not new. In the 1950s, W. Edwards Deming proposed to Japanese automobile makers that the way to improve production was to focus on the process. His philosophy was that management must create a work environment that promotes continuous improvement aggressively in all of its processes (Deming, 1982, 1986). His ideas are summarized in the following 14 points that became the foundation of the TQM movement in Japan and, 30 years later, in the United States:

1. Create constancy of purpose for improvement of products and service.
2. Adopt the new philosophy.
3. Create dependence on inspection to achieve quality.

4. Don't award business on the basis of price tag alone.
5. Improve constantly and forever every process for planning, production, and service.
6. Institute training on the job.
7. Institute leadership.
8. Drive out fear.
9. Break down barriers between staff areas.
10. Eliminate slogans, exhortations, and targets for the work force.
11. Eliminate numerical quotas for the work force and numerical goals for management.[7]
12. Remove barriers that rob people of pride of workmanship.
13. Institute a vigorous program of

---

[7] The careful reader may note a potential contradiction between our goal-based strategy and Deming's eleventh principle, which argues *against* goal-setting. We believe that goals and a CQI philosophy are not contradictory as long as two principles are maintained by HRM management: 1) Goal-setting programs as a positive (as opposed to punitive) managerial strategy. No doubt, under "rule by objective" managerial practices, goal-setting will undermine the creativity, freedom, and problem-solving culture TQM demands. Yet, goal-setting programs do not have to function in this harmful way. 2) Management ensures that new goals for continuous improvement are established on an ongoing basis. We have already seen this done in a number of health care organizations. Our use of goals to achieve HRM effectiveness is analagous to the CQI benchmarking process. Benchmarks are quantitative indicators that reflect levels of performance toward which the unit or organization is striving. Both goals and benchmarks are futuristic in the sense that efforts are directed toward continuous improvement.

education and self-improvement for everyone.
14. Put everyone in the company to work to accomplish the transformation.

During the last decade, Joseph M. Juran (1986, 1988) and Philip B. Crosby (1984, 1989) have refined the TQM concept to underscore the need for a quality "culture" and to reflect the ongoing nature of striving for quality—hence the name, "Continuous Quality Improvement." Although their methods differ, Deming, Juran, and Crosby have the same goal: quality improvement with an emphasis on the process. Their principles have been applied to the health care industry in a variety of settings (Green, 1990; Lynn & Osborn, 1991). In the contemporary health care environment, CQI is now defined as *an ongoing, organizationwide framework in which health services organizations and their employees are committed to and involved in monitoring and evaluating all aspects of the HSO's activities (i.e., inputs and processes) and outputs in order to improve them continuously* (American Hospital Association, 1990).

One common denominator in all CQI programs is the use of statistical techniques (e.g., Pareto diagrams and control charts) to understand the production process. A discussion of these techniques is beyond the scope of this chapter. A number of excellent works are available for this purpose (Lowe & Mazzeo, 1986; Re & Krousel-Wood, 1990; Vonderembse & White, 1991), and the reader is encouraged to explore this methodology. The point we wish to make is that *data are critical* for understanding the variables in a process, a prerequisite to improvement.

Monitoring the Work Flow Process

When analyzing the efficacy of the HRM activities and programs that are necessary to achieve strategic goal attainment, it is necessary to consider the following questions, both borrowed from the CQI approach, which form the basis of the monitoring and evaluation process:

- Are we doing the right things?
- Are we doing things right?

The first question relates to the outcome of the HRM activity. Output quality is a cornerstone of CQI. Output that is consistent with internal or external stakeholders' expectations means that the organization is doing the right thing. As an example, consider *Strategic Objective 1* (i.e., to increase same-day surgery visits). If management is reasonably confident that the HRM objectives have resulted in an increase in same-day surgeries, this first criterion is met. Realize, of course, that other factors may be responsible for the results. Regardless of the cause of the increase in same-day surgeries, it would be impossible to observe patterns and correlations without data. Thus, monitoring is crucial to determine if the right things are being done.

Continuing with this same exercise, what if same-day surgeries do *not* increase? We must then ask the question, "Are we doing things right?" The following two responses are possible:

1. We are doing the right things, but we are doing them the wrong way.
2. We are not doing the right things to accomplish our objective.

In order to answer the question, "Are we doing things right?", it is necessary to develop a flow chart for the process of how the HRM activity is conducted in order to influence the strategic objective. A flow chart gives a visual display of the total process. It also shows the relationships among steps and departments involved in the process. In CQI language, flow charts show where the process begins (i.e., input), activities, decision points, places at which the process stops until another activity is completed, and where the process ends (i.e., output) (Crosby, 1984). The following list explains how to construct a flow chart:

- *Step 1:* Identify what begins the process and what ends it.
- *Step 2:* List all of the steps in the process from the input to the output.
- *Step 3:* Arrange the steps in the order in which they are completed.
- *Step 4:* Draw a diagram, using appropriate symbols for each step.
- *Step 5:* Use arrows to show the direction of the process flow from step to step.
- *Step 6:* Show points in the process at which steps are delayed due to actions outside of the process; these are called "wait states."
- *Step 7:* Label all symbols. Title and date the flow chart.
- *Step 8:* Check your work and correct the flow chart as necessary.
- *Step 9:* Get consensus from the team. Ask, "Is this how it really is?"

By constructing a flow chart for each strategic objective, it is possible to visualize the contribution made by each HRM activity and its supporting objective. There are many other tools you can use in conjunction with flow charting. Data can be gathered through interviews, archival retrieval of records, surveys, interviews, and observation.

Problem Analysis

Flow charts will help to identify problems that occur in a process. Different factors can affect a process and the people doing the work; these differences create variation. A certain amount of variation is to be expected, but reducing variation is the first step in process improvement. One of the principles of Pareto analysis is that 80% of the problems are caused by 20% of the variables. The key is to determine the vital few causes of the problem(s). A Pareto diagram is a useful tool for understanding and prioritizing problems because it shows the relative importance of variables that contribute to a result. For example, in Figure 18.4, HRM Objective #2 is to recruit new staff in order to increase same-day surgery volume (i.e., Strategic Objective #1). Suppose that a flow chart of the recruiting and staffing process indicates that the orientation phase lasts 10 days. Pareto analysis of same-day surgery volume indicates that surgeries are down when staffing is low. The problem may be inadequate staffing, possibly caused by a lengthy orientation stage.

Flow charts help to identify obvious problems. They also identify those points at which additional information is needed. In some cases, it may be necessary to collect additional data to zero in on a problem.

Select and Implement Solutions

After problems have been broadly identified through the HRM effectiveness system, they must be clearly articulated: *What exactly* is occurring, *when* does it happen, and *who* are the key actors? When these questions are answered, solutions begin to emerge. The single most important element of this step is to include employees when developing solutions to problems. Worker involvement is essential because workers are most knowledgeable about the process. CQI theorists and practitioners, Deming, Juran, and Crosby, all advocate giving employees authority to identify and solve quality problems (Crosby, 1989; Deming, 1986; Juran, 1986). The advantages of participative management (Miller & Monge, 1986; Sashkin, 1984) and group problem solving (Hill, 1982) have been well-documented. Whether CQI is a function of quality circles, project groups, or self-managed teams, it is safe to say that teams are no longer an option in contemporary health care organizations, they are absolutely essential!

A number of techniques, such as brainstorming and nominal group technique (see Delbecq, Van de Ven, & Gustafson [1975]; Van de Ven & Delbecq [1974] for a review of these techniques), are available to improve the team's ability to generate solutions. Creativity is critical at this step; the team should generate as many solutions as possible and then select the final solution(s).

Refinement and Redefinition

Results of the CQI monitoring and evaluation stage serve as inputs that help us to reformulate our strategies for attaining HRM and strategic objectives or to redefine these objectives for improved HRM effectiveness model (and operational) utility. The HRM effectiveness model can be assessed along a number of dimensions. For instance, goal redefinition may be called for; or new measures to assess goal attainment can be developed. If the utility of the HRM effectiveness model is not assessed on an ongoing basis, chances increase that it will atrophy.

RISKS AND PROBLEMS IN HRM EFFECTIVENESS MEASUREMENT

HRM quality assessment is nothing more than developing systems of evaluation, accountability, control, and benchmarks for continuous improvement. They exist to facilitate the sociotechnical components of the organization, not to inhibit it. However, as the adage goes, "the road to hell is paved with good intentions."

Means/Ends Displacement[8]

Management can become so "intense" about measuring quality, that it may forget that its primary mission is to deliver quality services; not measure it. Excessive paperwork stands as a good example. In theory, HRM effectiveness systems can be so extensive that staff spend too much of their time gathering, recording, processing, entering, re-entering, and analyzing data (i.e., the "means") and insufficient time on using the data for the purposes of delivering better quality services. For instances, nurses often bemoan the extensive paperwork requirements of their jobs, wishing they could spend more time delivering point-of-service patient care. HRM can easily get caught in this quagmire of data as well. Management must make sure that *they* "drive" their evaluation process, rather than having their evaluation process drive them.

"Ruling by Objective"[9]

Information is emerging as one of the most powerful resources of the late twentieth century. It is a relatively newer resource that can help to identify problems for ameliorative intervention or strengths for management to build on and perpetuate. However, like all powerful resources, information can be and is badly misused. Instead of using it to monitor HRM performance effectiveness and continuous improvement initiatives, it can be used to attribute blame and failure. Instead of using it to learn more about delivering high-quality services, it can be altered, re-interpreted, and reconfigured to support the self-serving political purposes of its users. Many politicians have used information in this way for years. Health care managers perhaps, are known to do this as well. Last, information often is threatening to staff. They perceive it as something that will "rule" or ultimately hurt them. When the word "evaluation" is used within organizational settings it usually triggers an avalanche of anxiety and resistance.

Developing an HRM effectiveness system runs the risk of having all of these problems. It is critical that the chief of human resources and his or her staff anticipate and manage them. Here are seven steps managers can take to ensure that these risks are mitigated:

1. Train staff in what the data from the HRM effectiveness system mean. Lack of understanding is often the reason staff feel threatened by information.
2. Create organizational readiness for information use. This means not only training, but an understanding that HRM

---

[8] See Etzioni (1960).

[9] This phrase is from French (1988).

effectiveness information is available to help improve HRM services, not to attribute blame or to get people fired.

3. Reward the positive use of information. Staff who use the information gleaned from the HR effectiveness systems appropriately should receive visible rewards. Those who do not should be counseled initially and punished ultimately.

4. Recognize and be open to the weaknesses in your HRM effectiveness system's data-gathering and analysis capabilities. Honesty begets trust with your staff. Honesty about the system's weakness also will help to keep the system in proper perspective.

5. Share the data generated from your HRM effectiveness model as much as possible without breaching the performance and personal confidentiality of any staff. If the data are not shared, staff will lose touch with the system and be more likely to view its outputs with suspicion.

6. Build your system with consensus. Include in the system design process the multiple constituencies identified previously.

7. Keep your system flexible. Without altering it on a daily basis, it should be evaluated and altered when necessary over time.

Using the Data

The biggest risk to developing and implementing an HRM effectiveness model is *not* using the data for the purposes of service delivery improvements. If reliable and valid measurement systems are put in place but their output lays buried on someone's desk,

the usefulness of HRM effectiveness modeling and measurement is undermined. This is especially true if the results are buried because they are less positive than desired.[10] If HRM management choose to build and implement an HRM effectiveness model, it must also *commit* itself to using the data in concrete and highly visible ways. If not, HRM will lose enormous amounts of credibility and trust with their staff and the organization at large.

Managerial Implications

1. *Leadership* Evaluation of HRM effectiveness is moving from the personnel department to the board room. The notion that human resources objectives can be integrated into the organization's strategic plan presumes *top-down leadership:* support and direction from the CEO and board, as well as a senior-level executive who is committed to the mission of the organization. "The human resources executive must do his or her best to understand the vision of the institution and articulate that vision to the rank and file," states Darryl Lippman, President and CEO of St. Vincent Medical Center in Toledo, Ohio (quoted in Wachel, 1993). We might add that encouraging the "rank and file" to develop the vision is important as well.

2. *TQM environment* The contemporary focus on quality increases the

---

[10] This is akin to asking a colleague how he or she "honestly" feels about your work performance and then discounting his or her comments if the feedback is negative.

likelihood that any HRM effectiveness model will be heavily influenced by TQM/CQI principles. However, the HRM department cannot march to a different drummer; the whole organization must reflect the spirit of quality improvement, as evidenced by its culture. Thus, the health organization's reward systems, policies, and procedures must reflect practices that contribute to quality improvement endeavors. Implicit in a TQM culture is the goal of *exceeding customer expectations.* For the health care organization, the primary customers are *patients, employees,* and *physicians.* To be truly effective, HRM practices must be focused not just on meeting, but also on exceeding the needs and expectations of these customers.

3. *Information*   Traditionally, data collection and analysis have been the domain of the MIS specialist. No more. Effective HRM practices are in part data-driven. *Every health care manager must be willing and able to use information effectively.* He or she must be comfortable with new computer technologies, such as E-mail, networking and groupware, as well as the more traditional "number-crunching" mechanisms. Earlier in this chapter, we suggested several ways to smooth the transition to the age of information. Creating organizational readiness, training staff, rewarding the positive uses of information, and sharing data foster an environment of trust and enable staff to *act with the data, rather than react to the data.*

4. *Ethics*   We have stressed that HR managers must work within the context

of the organization's strategic plan. Unfortunately, the HR manager is frequently caught in the cross-fire of objectives, presenting ethical dilemmas. For example, a health system that is redirecting its mission to include rehabilitation services may need to downsize its acute care staff. Leadership that is sensitive to multiple outcomes will place a high value on shared, deliberate decision making. Organizations with structures (i.e., codes, procedures, committees, etc.) for consideration of ethical issues will be one step ahead. Professional organizations such as the American College of Healthcare Executives (ACHE) and the American Hospital Association (AHA) publish guidelines to assist health care managers in decision making.

5. *HRM effectiveness in small organizations*   Moving HRM into the twenty-first century will require a new *modus operandus.* We have emphasized the importance of strategic thinking, cultural rewards, and structured decision making. At first glance, it would appear that larger organizations, with their economies of scale, are more capable of making these adaptations. Smaller organizations, such as rural hospitals, independent nursing homes, and home health agencies, often do not have the people, technology, or funds to make significant changes in management practices. Their strength, however, is their smallness. They have fewer levels of bureaucracy to interfere with change. Their managers are more likely to be generalists rather than specialists, which

often means that they are not tied to specific disciplines. Most important, smaller organizations often have very different climates, which may translate to greater flexibility and *esprit de corps*. Small organizations can capitalize on these assets to promote effective change.

Clearly, this list is not comprehensive. However, it should help you anticipate some of the major problems and risks you will face when developing and implementing an effective HRM effectiveness model.

SUMMARY

The contemporary view of HRM is that its objectives and activities are interrelated parts of a management system. HR managers are responsible for determining how effectively components of the system are functioning. This chapter focuses on HRM effectiveness—how to conceptualize effectiveness and how to develop tools to achieve this purpose.

We began by defining HRM effectiveness and noting its three characteristics: (1) it must denote a contingency perspective; (2) it must be fluid (i.e., responsive to changing directives); and, (3) most important, it must emphasize integration with the organization's strategic objectives. The benefits of measuring HRM effectiveness were discussed, with emphasis on enhancing accountability of HRM activities.

Developing and monitoring an HRM effectiveness model was conceptualized as a series of five steps: (1) identify organizational strategic objectives; (2) integrate strategic objectives with HRM objectives and activities; (3) pattern objectives; (4) implementation

through the formulation of measures; and (5) monitor and evaluate the data the model generates using a CQI framework. Each step was described and illustrated.

Methodological issues were reviewed in the context of building an HRM effectiveness model. Content validity as well as measurement reliability and validity were discussed. Finally, risks such as means/end displacement, ruling by objective, and not using the data are presented as pitfalls to be avoided.

Clearly, this chapter is not a comprehensive, how-to manual. It offers an initial theoretical and pragmatic approach to developing and using a model for improving HRM effectiveness continuously. To this end, it should help you to anticipate some of the major challenges, problems, and risks you will face when developing and using your own HRM effectiveness model.

Discussion Questions

1. Given the importance of integrating HRM's strategic objectives with organizationwide strategic objectives, what role must HRM senior management play in the development and implementation of the organization's overall strategic plan?

2. Sophisticated database management systems are needed to drive the implementation of an HRM effectiveness model. How do you see such a system taking shape? What implications might this have for how HRM departments are currently staffed in health care settings? What new skills and abilities must HRM staff possess to implement an HRM effectiveness model successfully?

3. One could argue that that the development of "maintenance criteria"

represent in part, HRM's departmental level strategic plan. Why might this argument be made?

4. Is the proposed HRM effectiveness modeling system a classic example of an academic approach that has no basis in operational reality (i.e., acceptable theory that has no chance of being operationally implemented effectively)? Do you believe the application of continuous quality improvement theory will play a critical role in turning an HRM effectiveness model into an operational reality?

5. What do you see as the top five obstacles to implementing an HRM effectiveness model successfully?

CASE: HRM AT PLEASANT VALLEY HOME HEALTH

Margaret Ford, the Supervisor of Nurses at Pleasant Valley Home Health Services, Inc. was concerned. Pleasant Valley needed to hire a nurse quickly. One of the staff nurses had just handed in her resignation because her husband was being transferred out of state. The nurse who was leaving gave Pleasant Valley 2 weeks notice, which complied with the agency policy; however, it still left the agency in a bind. Margaret knew that recruiting and interviewing of home health nurses was a time-consuming process, and even after a nurse was hired, several weeks of orientation were usually required before the nurse could perform independently. She knew that all of the regular staff were working to capacity and that the loss of even one nurse at this time would have major implications. She walked over to Lee Sullivan's office to discuss the situation. Lee was the Executive Director of the agency.

Margaret knocked on the door, saw that Lee was sitting at her desk, and walked in. "Sue is leaving. She sure picked a bad time to move!" She laughed halfheartedly, and said, "We need to replace her quickly. Do you have any brilliant ideas?" Lee sighed, and responded, more in the form of a statement than a question, "We don't have any decent applications on file, do we?

"Nope," replied Margaret.

"Great. Well, let's get our ad into the local paper today. Maybe something will turn up," said Lee.

Pleasant Valley Home Health Services, Inc. is a private, not-for-profit home health agency, located in a rural area of a midwestern state. The stated purpose of Pleasant Valley is to provide high-quality health care services at home to elderly and disabled individuals and to persons with short-term, specific health care needs that can be handled at home.

Most of Pleasant Valley's clients are elderly. Frequently, they have a chronic illness that requires monitoring or have need for rehabilitation therapy following an acute episode, such as a stroke or hip fracture. Some patients are disabled and require ongoing therapy at home. Some are convalescing from a hospital stay and need short-term care (e.g., dressing changes). Others have a special type of medical need that does not require hospitalization (e.g., intravenous antibiotics, chemotherapy).

Pleasant Valley is a fee-for-service health care organization; it provides in-home services and then bills for the services, either to a public or private insurance carrier (e.g., Medicare, Medicaid, Blue-Cross/Blue Shield) or to the patient directly. Pleasant Valley receives all of its revenue from billed services. As a private organization, it does not receive government subsidies or tax support. Because it is a small agency, economies of scale are difficult to maintain and the budget is often in the "red." One of its current goals is increase the number of patient visits, in order to maintain a large enough caseload of patients to generate revenues sufficient to provide a small profit margin.

Competition for Pleasant Valley comes primarily from Chestnut Home Health (CHH), a multicounty operation that has been established in the area for more than 10 years. Pleasant Valley surpassed CHH in total number of visits after its second year of operation and has been steadily growing. Many of the physicians in the area, however, continue to use CHH. Chestnut also receives more referrals from non-local hospitals than does Pleasant Valley. A second objective for the current fiscal year is to increase the number of referrals it receives from out-of-town hospitals.

Pleasant Valley currently has 30 employees: 15 registered nurses (full-time and part-time), eight nursing aides, one physical therapist, one speech therapist, one social worker, and four administrative staff.

The Role of the Home Health Nurse

The registered nurse is the central caregiver in the home health field. The nurse must be able to function independently in the patient's home and must be capable of performing a variety of clinical procedures (e.g., injections, inserting catheters, obtaining specimens). Furthermore, the RN is considered both a "case manager" and a "gatekeeper" in coordinating medical, health, and social services with physicians and area social service agencies (Figure

18.5). This position requires high-level skills in nursing and communications. Nurses with a B.S.N. (Bachelor of Science in Nursing) plus experience in home health or community nursing are usually sought for these positions.

JOB DESCRIPTION

Registered Nurse

Definition
The registered nurse administers skilled nursing services to patients in accordance with a written plan of treatment established by the patient's physician. The incumbent is directly responsible to the Nursing Supervisor and ultimately to the Executive Director.

Qualifications
1. Graduate of an approved school of professional nursing
2. Current license to practice as a registered nurse in Ohio

Responsibilities
1. Conducts initial patient assessment and evaluation
2. Evaluates the ongoing needs of patients on a regular basis
3. Initiates the patient's plan of treatment and any necessary revisions
4. Provides services that require substantial specialized nursing skills
5. Initiates appropriate preventative and rehabilitative nursing procedures
6. Prepares and maintains clinical notes
7. Coordinates care with allied health professionals
8. Informs the physician and other personnel of changes in the patient's conditions
9. Counsels the patient and family in meeting nursing and related health needs
10. Participates in inservice and continuing education programs
11. Supervises and teaches other nursing personnel

FIGURE 18.5. Job description for registered nurses at Pleasant Valley Home Health Services, Inc.

After Margaret left, Lee asked the office manager to run off a copy of their standard classified advertisement for a home health nurse, and to take it to the local newspaper's office. The next day, the newspaper carried the ad in the classified section. (Figure 18.6) The advertisement ran for 3 consecutive days. Applicants were requested to send resumes to the nursing supervisor.

Pleasant Valley received three responses to the advertisement. One was a resume from a student at a nearby technical college. The college had a 2-year associate degree, registered nurse program, and the applicant was in the last quarter of her second year. Margaret read over the resume. She knew from past experience that RNs from 2-year programs lacked many of the skills for this type of work. Furthermore, the applicant was not available until the end of the quarter (a month away). She decided not to interview this applicant. The second resume was from a nurse who had retired from her job at the local hospital, and wanted to "fill-in" somewhere to keep herself busy. She stipulated that she would be unavailable during the winter months, as she travels to Florida with her husband every year.

The third applicant, Ann Jones, sent a letter to express interest in this position. In her letter she stated that she had been working for the last 10 years for a local obstetrician who was retiring. She had not held any other positions. Ann was a registered nurse with a B.S.N. from the local university. References from her past employers indicated that she was hard-working, responsible, professional, and got along well with patients, staff, and physicians.

The Interview

Because of Ann's good work record and the fact that no other suitable applicants were available, Margaret asked Ann to come in for an interview and set up an appointment for the next day. The procedure at Pleasant Valley was for all RN applicants to be interviewed first by the nursing supervisor, then by the executive director, Lee Sullivan.

Ann Jones walked in to the Pleasant Valley office and greeted everyone warmly. She was on time, was dressed appropriately, and looked a little nervous. Margaret introduced herself and led her into the conference room for the first interview. Margaret explained the role of a home health nurse and provided details of the job. A half hour later, Margaret brought Ann to Lee's office for the second interview. Margaret went in first and briefly summarized her interview. Although she had a positive overall impression, she was concerned about Ann's lack of experience with home health procedures, particularly interviewing and assessment skills. (Because this part of the job was so important to the overall plan of care, it was essential that RNs have experience in this area.) Margaret then left the office, and Ann went in.

Ann sat down with Lee. The two women discussed Pleasant Valley policies and general personnel issues, including benefits. It

---

Registered nurse in Home Health Agency.
State license required. Must have own
transportation. Prefer candidate with
home health/community health experience. Call Pleasant Valley, 1-614-555-
1212 or send resume to Box 163, Anywhere,
U.S.A. E.O.E.

FIGURE 18.6. Advertisement for registered nurse run in local newspaper by Pleasant Valley Home Health Services, Inc.

was clear that Ann had some of the abilities and skills needed, that she knew the geographical area well, and that she could communicate effectively with area physicians. Her major weakness was that she did not have home health experience. At the end of the interview, Lee thanked her for coming, and said, "You do meet many of the qualifications, but I'm not sure if you're the right person for this job." Ann smiled at her and said, "I'm not sure I could handle this job anyway."

After she left, Margaret and Lee looked at each other. "I don't know what to do," Lee said.

"I don't know either!" responded Margaret. Despite the urgency of the situation, neither was sure whether they should hire Ann Jones.

Case Discussion Questions

1. What strategic objectives of the organization have been identified in this case?
2. How can HRM objectives contribute to these strategic objectives? For each strategic objective that you have identified, list one HRM objective. For each HRM objective, list three HRM activities.
3. Make a flow chart (from the facts presented in this case as well as your own knowledge regarding HRM practices) outlining the staffing process, from recruiting to assignment of a nurse to a caseload of patients. Where are problems likely to occur? Do you need to collect more data?
4. How can an HRM effectiveness model improve HRM decision making at Pleasant Valley Home Health?

REFERENCES

American Hospital Association. (1990). *Quality management: A management advisory.* Chicago: American Management Association.

Campbell, J.P. (1977). On the nature of organizational effectiveness. In P.S. Goodman, J.M. Pennings, & Associates (Eds.), *New perspectives on organizational effectiveness.* San Francisco: Jossey-Bass.

Cascio, W. (1990). *Human resources accounting* (2nd ed.). New York: Kent.

Crosby, P.B. (1984). *Quality without tears.* New York: McGraw Hill.

Crosby, P.B. (1989). *Let's talk quality.* New York: McGraw Hill.

Dalton, D.R., & Todor, W.D. (1979). Turnover turned over: An expanded and positive perspective. *Academy of Management Review, 4*(2), 225–235.

Delbecq, A.L., Van de Ven, A.H., & Gustafson, D. (1975). *Group techniques for program planning: A guide to nominal group and delphi processes.* Glenview, IL: Scott, Foresman.

Deming, W.E. (1982). *Quality, productivity and competitive position.* Cambridge, MA: MIT Press.

Deming, W.E. (1986). *Out of the crisis.* Cambridge, MA: MIT Press.

Deniston, O.L., Rosenstock, L.M., & Getting, V.A. (1968). Evaluation of program effectiveness. *Public Health Reports, 83*(4), 323–335.

Etzioni, A. (1960). Two approaches to organizational analysis: A critique and a suggestion. *Administrative Science Quarterly, 5,* 257–278.

Etzioni, A. (1964). *Modern organizations.* Englewood Cliffs, NJ: Prentice Hall.

Fargason, C.A.. & Haddock, C. (1992). Cross functional integrative team decision making: Essential for effective QI in health care. *Quality Review Bulletin. 18*(5), 157–164.

French, W. (1988). *Personnel management* (4th ed.). Boston: Houghton-Mifflin, 1988.

Georgopolous, B.S. (1972). Organization

research on health. Ann Arbor: Institute for Social Research, University of Michigan.

Georgopolous, B.S., & Matejko, A. (1967). The American general hospital as a complex social system. *Health Services Research, 2,* 76–111.

Green, D.K. (1990). Implementing a corporate quality management program: The AMI experience. *Topics in Health Records Management,* 10(3), 23–31.

Greenberger, D.S., Strasser, S., & Lee, S. (1988). Personal control as a mediator between perceptions of supervisory behaviors and employee reactions. *Academy of Management Journal, 31,* 2.

Hill, G.W. (1982). Group versus individual performance: Are N + 1 heads better than one? *Psychological Bulletin,* 535–562.

Juran, J.M. (1986). The quality trilogy. *Quality Progress, 19,* 19–24.

Juran, J.M. (1988). *Juran on planning for quality.* New York: Free Press.

Katz, D., & Kahn, R.L. (1966). *The social psychology of organizations.* New York: Wiley.

Kerlinger, F. (1986). *The foundations of behavioral research* (3rd ed.). New York: Holt, Rinehart, & Winston.

Knutson, A.L. (1969). Evaluation of what? In H.C. Schulberg, A. Sheldon, & F. Baker (Eds.), *Program evaluation in the health fields* (pp. 221–242). New York: Behavioral Publications.

Linder, J.C. (1985). Computers, corporate culture and change. *Personnel Journal, 64,* 49–55.

Locke, E.A., & Latham, G.P. (1950). *A theory of goal setting and task performance* Englewood Cliffs, NJ: Prentice Hall.

Lowe, T.A., & Mazzeo, D.P. (1986). Crosby, Deming, Juran: Three preachers, one religion. *Quality, 25,* 22–25.

Lynn, M., & Osborn, D.P. (1991). Deming's quality principles: A health care application. *Hospital & Health Services Administration, 36,* 111–120.

Miller, K.I., & Monge, P.R. (1986). Participation, satisfaction and productivity: A meta-analytic review. *Academy of Management Journal, 29,* 727–753.

Nisbett, R., & Rosh, M. (1980). *Human inference: Strategies and shortcomings of social judgment.* Englewood Cliffs, NJ: Prentice Hall.

Organ, D., & Bateman, T.S. (1991). *Organizational behavior* (4th ed.). Homewood, IL: Irwin.

Podsakoff, P.M., Todor, W.D., & Skov, R. (1981). Effects of leader reward and punishment behaviors on subordinate performance and attitudes. *Proceedings: Academy of Management, 41st Annual National Meetings,* 151–155.

Re, R.N., & Krousel-Wood, M. (1990). How to use continuous quality improvement theory and statistical quality control tools in a multi-specialty clinic. *Quality Review Bulletin, 16,* 391–397.

Sashkin, M. (1984). Participative management is an ethical imperative. *Organizational Dynamics, 12*(1) 4–22.

Strasser, S., Eveland, J.D., Cummins, G., Deniston, O.L., & Romani, J.H. (1981). Conceptualizing the goal and system models of organizational effectiveness—Implications for comparative evaluation research. *Journal of Management Studies, 18,* 321–340.

Van de Ven, A.H., & Delbecq, A.L. (1974). The effectiveness of nominal and delphi techniques in interacting group decision making processes. *Academy of Management Journal, 17.*

Vonderembse, M.A., & White, G.P. (1991). *Operations management: Concepts, methods and strategies* (2nd ed.). St. Paul, MN: West Publishing.

Vroom, V.H. (1964). *Work and motivation.* New York: Wiley.

Vroom, V.H., & Yetton, P. (1973). *Leadership and decision making.* Pittsburgh: University of Pittsburgh Press.

Wachel, W. (1993). Beyond personnel: Human resources comes to grips with its leadership role. *Healthcare Executive, 8,*(2), 16–19.

Weiss, C.H. (1972). *Evaluation research: Methods of assessing program effectiveness.* Englewood Cliffs, NJ: Prentice Hall.

CHAPTER

19

CONTEMPORARY AND FUTURE HUMAN RESOURCES CHALLENGES

Myron D. Fottler

John D. Blair

Elizabeth W. Michael

Grant T. Savage

LEARNING OBJECTIVES

Upon completing this chapter, the reader should be able to . . .

- Understand and appreciate the internal and external human resources challenges facing the health care industry now and in the future.
- Understand, describe, and implement a process for integrating strategic and human resources planning and management.
- Understand and describe the role of human resources in productivity enhancement, implementation of total quality management programs, and corporate restructuring.
- Recommend improved or optimal human resources strategies and tactics for responding to the above challenges.

INTRODUCTION

This chapter integrates material found throughout the book while examining the future of human resources management in health care organizations. To predict likely changes in human resources management, we first consider likely changes in the external and internal environment of health care organizations. Then we discuss the major human resources challenges that will confront health care executives in the future, including the integration of strategic planning and human resources planning, enhancement of employee performance and productivity, total quality management, and managing corporate restructuring.

To illustrate the integration of strategic and human resources management we examine the human resources practices in three community hospitals and the impact that different strategic planning and human resources planning linkages have on those practices. Through a set of qualitative interviews, we will explore generic business strategies the organizations were pursuing, the degree to which human resources practices were integrated with business strategies, and the present and future human resources challenges identified by the participants. The reader should remember that *all* health care managers are human resources managers, because all are responsible for recruiting, training, evaluating, and rewarding their subordinates.

ENVIRONMENTAL CHANGE

Recent

The external environment of the health care industry has shifted dramatically during the past decade. Among the more important changes have been the active encouragement of competition by the federal government; the shifting balance of power between managers and physicians; increasing cost-consciousness on the part of government, employers, and third-party payers; the implementation of a prospective pricing system for reimbursing hospitals under Medicare; and the growth and increasing dominance of multihospital systems (Arthur Andersen and Company and the American College of Hospital Administrators, 1984; Fottler & Malvey, 1994).

The increased competition stems from the efforts by all third-party payers to encourage greater utilization of less expensive alternatives to acute inpatient hospital care. This change in attitude toward competition is manifested by a greater willingness to provide reimbursement for services received in such alternative settings and fewer restrictions on their entry into the marketplace. Among the major alternatives that have grown rapidly during this decade are health maintenance organizations (HMOs), emergicenters, surgicenters, wellness centers, outpatient clinics, employee assistance programs, and preferred provider organizations (PPOs) (Ermann & Gabel, 1985).

The environmental changes listed above as well as the growing surplus of physicians have reduced the power of physicians vis-à-vis health care managers (Fuchs, 1982; Morone & Dunham, 1984). The pressures for institutional survival and cost containment have caused managers to attempt to gain firmer control over what doctors do. This has created inevitable manager-physician conflict in many situations. Among the reasons for the increasing relative power and control of managers have been the need for capital to finance growth, the growth of government regulation, and the ability of managers to integrate technology and human resources (Fuchs, 1982).

In addition to the federal government's attempts to contain health costs, major employers have been active in aggressively promoting health care cost containment (Fox, Goldbeck, & Spies, 1984). These activities have included regulatory approaches to cost containment (Egdahl, 1984), as well as promotion of incentive approaches such as cost sharing by employees, wellness programs, employee rewards, healthful behavior, and health maintenance organizations (Fottler & Lanning, 1986).

Since hospital reimbursement is now based heavily on payment *per case* (rather than *per day*), there is no longer any incentive to lengthen the patient stay to maximize revenues. The previous reimbursement system emphasized retrospective reimburse-

ment (i.e., payment after service delivery based on costs); consequently, there was no incentive to provide cost-efficient or cost-effective service. Now there are incentives to minimize patient stay as well as the resources devoted to patient care. Prospective payment has affected all areas of health care management in ways that are just beginning to be understood (Boerma, 1983; Crawford & Fottler, 1985; Smith & Fottler, 1985).

The growth of multihospital systems has been both a response to environmental changes and a major environmental change in and of itself. Such systems represent the ultimate outcome of the "corporatization" of health care. The reasons for the development of systems are similar to reasons for development of large, multiunit national and international corporations in other industries: greater access to capital, easier response to government regulation, economies of scale in the provision of some services, and easier implementation of sophisticated management practices (Ermann & Gabel, 1984).

Emphasis in the health-care system has shifted to ambulatory services, less expensive alternatives to inpatient hospital care, and alternative delivery systems. Both multihospital systems and investor-owned hospitals continue to grow. Hospitals have created new corporate structures and business ventures to compete in the service and capital markets.

In addition, the anticipated oversupply of physicians and the continued trend toward practicing in hospital-based positions and alternative delivery systems will mean for these professionals a continued decline in influence. Indicators of such a decline will include prescribed patient care protocols and increased fiscal restraints on physician expenditures. There will be increased potential for both conflict and collaboration (Arthur Andersen and Company and the American College of Hospital Administrators, 1984).

With the implementation of a prospective pricing system for reimbursing hospitals under Medicare, the active encouragement of competition by the federal government, a growing surplus of physicians, and increasing cost-consciousness on the part of government, employers, and third-party payers, the health care industry has been forced during the last 15 years to reevaluate and redesign missions, delivery systems, and management practices (Arthur Anderson and Company and the American College of Hospital Administrators, 1984; Fottler & Malvey, 1994).

Attempts to address these environmental pressures have led to such outcomes as the following:

- An increase in numbers of HMOs from 175 in 1976 to 575 in 1990 with enrollment in such organizations increasing from 6 million in 1976 to 36.5 million at the end of 1990 (Gold, 1991)
- The numbers of federal hospitals and nonfederal, nonprofit community hospitals decreasing while the number of for-profit hospitals increased by 22% (Sear, 1992; U.S. Bureau of the Census, 1991)
- Occupancy rates for all types of hospitals decreasing, with the exception of those providing long-term and psychiatric care (U.S. Bureau of the Census, 1991)
- Hospital admissions per thousand population dropping from 154 in 1980 to 124 in 1988 while outpatient visits increased by 27.8% (Arthur Anderson and Company and the American College

of Healthcare Executives, 1991; U.S. Bureau of the Census, 1991)
- An increase in membership in multihospital systems from 38.3% in 1984 to 45.7% of total hospitals in 1989 (American Hospital Association, 1991)
- The percentage of physicians in group practices, the number of group practices, and the number of physicians practicing in hospital-based positions increasing steadily since 1980 (Arthur Andersen and Company and the American College of Healthcare Executives, 1991)

All of these changes indicate an understanding of the need for health care organizations to be more entrepreneurial in order to achieve simultaneously both the higher quality and the lower costs necessary to compete in increasingly competitive markets. The achievement of these partially incompatible objectives requires the utmost care in the recruitment, selection, development, appraisal, and compensation of human resources.

Despite the magnitude of these efforts, the positive effects that were hoped for have yet to materialize. The percentage of gross domestic product spent on health care has continued to rise from 9.1% in 1980 to 14% in 1993 (Rublee & Schneider, 1991; Schieber, Poullier, & Greenwald, 1991; U.S. Bureau of the Census, 1991); 37 million people have no health insurance of any kind (Himmelstein, Woolhandler, & Wolfe, 1992; Rakich, 1991); and only a fraction of Americans think the health care system is functioning well (Smith, Altman, Leitman, Moloney, & Taylor, 1992).

Adding to the difficulties is the projection by the Health Care 2000 Commission (American Society for Healthcare and Human Resources Administration, 1992) of a very rapid growth in demand during the next decade that will necessitate further expansion of the health care industry due to continued population growth, the creation and utilization of new technologies, the aging of the population, and the growth of the AIDS epidemic. That forecasted expansion, in an industry already burdened with shortages of some key personnel and demands from all quarters for cost-containment, will be further impeded by national work force predictions of an aging work force, a national labor shortage, and a work force whose level of skills will not match the skills needed in the work place (Bureau of Labor Statistics, 1987). For labor intensive health care organizations to meet these additional demands (as well as to counter present shortages) and to achieve the previously mentioned objectives of higher quality and lower costs will require the utmost care in the recruitment, selection, development, appraisal, and compensation of human resources. Such efforts may prove futile, however, without careful reconsideration of the assumptions and theories that drive present human resources practices.

HUMAN RESOURCES IMPLICATIONS

Early observers of these environmental changes described what managerial changes and human resources challenges might face health care organizations in the new environment. For example, the Delphi studies of health care managers by Arthur Andersen and Company and the American College of Healthcare Executives (1984, 1987) predicted that the 1990s would be an era requiring considerable managerial ability to har-

ness the talent and skill of human resources in health care. They discussed such challenges as developing compensation programs to attract and retain competent managerial and ancillary staffs and achieving greater employee productivity. Pointer (1985) recommended an internal incentive system that encourages creativity and Robbins and Rakich (1986) also mention a participative and competitive internal environment. All of these observers identified some of the coming changes in our society (e.g., the aging of the population) and offered good, generic suggestions for managing human resources in health care. Yet their suggestions were based on the assumptions that: 1) human resources would be available to be managed, and 2) those resources would not differ significantly from the resources with which they were familiar. More recent observers would challenge those assumptions.

The New Work Force

Beginning with the Hudson Institute's 1987 study, *Workforce 2000,* and continuing through the American Society for Healthcare and Human Resources Administration's 1992 study, *Health Care 2000: A World of Human Resource Differences,* researchers have projected a work force that will be dramatically different and perhaps woefully inadequate to meet the needs of the health care industry. We have touched on some of these differences earlier and elaborate on them as follows:

1. *Work force availability:* One-quarter (3.4 million) of all new jobs will be in health care, and health care has been growing twice as fast as the economy as

a whole. The labor force, however, is growing at a slower rate than at any time since the 1930s (Hudson Institute, 1987; Bureau of Labor Statistics, 1987).

2. *Work force composition:* Forty-two percent of new work force entrants during this decade will be Causacian women, 22% will be immigrants, and 22% will be minorities, including Asians, Hispanics, and African Americans. Single parents will be present in significant numbers as well as employees who are caring for aging parents. By 2000, the average worker will be more than 39 years old (Hudson Institute, 1987; National Alliance of Business, 1985).

3. *Work place needs:* The health care industry, as noted earlier, will require not just more workers, but higher skilled workers. Yet even today, business organizations are finding it necessary to provide basic skills education programs in reading and math because new entrants cannot meet minimum standards (Massachusetts Hospital Association, 1989; National Alliance of Business, 1985).

Managing the New Work Force

What does all of this mean for health care organizations? The *Health Care 2000* study (American Society for Healthcare and Human Resources Administration, 1992) emphasizes that the profound changes in the work force will require not only redesign of internal policies governing human resources management but a reexamination of both public and private sector relationships and government regulations. Specific examples based on the *Health Care 2000* study include such external items as the following:

- Formulation of partnerships between community business leaders, local government, educators, and the health care industry to design and implement programs to increase both enrollment in and numbers of educational programs for health care professionals
- Active participation by the health care industry in the public and private partnership that is attempting to set educational standards that will raise the educational level of the work force and press for additional human capital investments by states, communities, individuals, businesses, and the federal government

Examples of internal items include the following:

- Health care organizations must succeed in attracting and retaining more women, minorities and immigrants. To do so will require creating multicultural work communities in which each individual's contribution is valued and installation of new programs and practices that enhance the employment, development, and upward mobility of women and minorities.
- Internal environments must become more participative and encouraging of innovative thinking and creative problem solving to meet both the expectations of the work force and the requirements of such concepts as continuous quality improvement.
- In an industry such as health care, in which labor costs represent 45% to 55%

of operating expenses and there is a great diversity of personnel requirements, the role of human resources cannot be relegated to record keeping and simple functional tasks.

- Health care employers must take steps to support employee's family responsibilities in such areas as day care, sick child care, elder care, and schooling.

The environmental changes discussed above further highlight the need for human resources to be involved in the strategic processes of the organization if the desired outcome is not only success, but perhaps survival. In the next section, we discuss ways in which linkages between strategic planning and human resources planning might be configured.

INTEGRATION OF STRATEGIC AND HUMAN RESOURCES PLANNING

Strategic planning is described earlier in this book as a management philosophy designed to provide the organization with a long-term collective purpose and direction (Zallocco, Joseph, & Furey, 1984). The purposes of strategic planning are to assess and respond to the opportunities and threats in the external environment, to provide for appropriate allocations of resources, and to develop methods for evaluating organizational performance. A study conducted by Zallocco et al. (1984) of midwestern hospitals indicated that 60% use a formal strategic planning process. It also reported, however, that designing methods for implementing and monitoring the resulting strategic plans was

rarely considered. Perhaps this is a result of other findings, which suggest that strategic planning is a top-level administrative function with exclusion of middle-level or upper-level management personnel or staff representation (including the human resources function). In other words, as conceptualized in Chapter 1, health care executives have failed to assess and manage the various external, interface, and internal stakeholders whose cooperation and support are necessary to implement any business strategy successfully (Blair & Fottler, 1990). However, as one writer has commented:

> Strategic planning is generally geared to the gaining of systematic advantage over competitors. If human resource strategy is to be maximally useful to the corporation, it must share the corporation's plan. Too often, the linkage is missing. But without it, the human resource plan cannot be truly strategic. (Goodmeasure, Inc., 1982, p. 1)

Golden and Ramanujam (1985) proposed four possible linkages between human resources strategy and strategic planning—administrative, one-way, two-way, and integrative. Buller (1988) provided the following characterizations of four CEO orientations to correspond with each:

- *Administrative*—"We are primarily concerned about the product, the market, and the bottom line. We can always get the right people when we need them. That's personnel's job."
- *One-way*—"After we have established the business strategy, we make sure the human resources people understand our needs. It's up to them to respond to those needs with the appropriate programs and services."
- *Two-way*. "We work closely with the

human resources function in exploring the human resources implications of various business strategies. Our human resources experts point out some possible blind spots and show us how we can strategically attract, position, and develop our people."

• *Integrative*—"We don't make financial, marketing, technical, or human resources decisions, we make business decisions. We routinely involve all of the functions, including human resources, in important decisions. [Human resources] is just as much a part of the team as anybody else."

Each of these linkages, along with probable human resources strategy outcomes and competitive impact, was modeled by Fottler, Phillips, Blair, and Duran (1990) in Table 19.1.

As Table 19.1 illustrates, only the integrative approach allows for constant, mutual reinforcement of human resources strategy and strategic planning that can, in turn, lead

to competitive advantage. Lengnick-Hall and Lengnick-Hall (1988) point out, however, that an integration approach does have the potential to generate many costs and difficulties unless the relationship between human resources management and strategic management is designed to be one of reciprocal interdependence. If so, the benefits of such an integration can overcome and/or outweigh costs and difficulties by performing the following functions:

• Providing a broader range of solutions for solving complex organizational problems
• Ensuring that human, financial, and technological resources are given consideration in setting goals and assessing implementation capabilities
• Having organizations explicitly consider the individuals who comprise them and must implement policies
• Limiting the subordination of strategic considerations to human resources preferences and the neglect of human

TABLE 19.1. Probable Outcomes of Different Types of Human Resources Strategy/Strategic Planning Linkages on Business Strategy and Competitive Advantage

	Types of Linkage Between Human Resources Strategy and Strategic Planning			
	Administrative	One-Way	Two-Way	Integrative
Probable outcome of human resources practices on business strategy	Counteracting or unrelated	Partially reinforcing	High degree of reinforcement	Constant reinforcement
Probable impact of human resources practices on competitive advantage	Human resources practices decrease competitive advantage	Little impact of human resources practices on competitive advantage	Improved use of human resources practices to gain competitive advantage	Maximized use of human resources practices to improve competitive advantage

Source: Fottler, M. D., Phillips, R. L., Blair, J. D., and Duran, C. A. (1990). Achieving Competitive Advantage Through Strategic Human Resources Management. *Hospitals & Health Services Administration, 35*(3), 352.

resources as a vital source of organizational competence and competitive advantage (Lengnick-Hall & Lengnick-Hall, 1988).

However, assuming the organization is convinced that such an approach would be beneficial and is ready to adopt it, how can integration be accomplished? Miles and Snow (1984) suggest that the human resources department needs a comprehensive understanding of the language and practice of strategic planning. Moreover, appropriate human resources representatives must continually participate in the planning process to assess the probable demand for their unit's services and to help line executives trace the human resources implications of their strategic decisions. The department also should pursue appropriate strategies on its own to match the organization's business strategies.

Chapter 2 mentioned several generic categories of strategies that health care organizations might use to gain competitive advantage. These strategies, together with strategy implementation emphases and key human resources practices, are outlined in Table 19.2. Note that organizations can simultaneously pursue different strtegies, particularly in different subunits.

Different human resource strategies, as shown in Table 19.2, should be used with various business strategies because the expected role behaviors of employees are different. For example, innovative strategies require that employees exhibit a high degree of creative behavior, a longer-term focus, a relatively high level of cooperative behavior, a greater degree of risk-taking behavior, and a higher tolerance for ambiguity and unpredictability as compared to quality-enhancement or cost-reduction strategies (DePree, 1986). A quality-enhancement strategy requires that employees exhibit relatively repetitive and predictable behaviors, a high concern for quality, and a high concern for how services are delivered. Finally, the cost-reduction strategy requires a short-term focus on results, low risk-taking activity, and a high concern with quantity of output (Schuler & Jackson, 1987). All components of a human resources management system—employee planning, recruitment, selection, development, appraisal, and compensation—must work together to stimulate and reinforce the employee behaviors that support the broader strategic posture of the organization. If human resources strategies are not planned and implemented in conjunction with business strategies, behavior opposite of that desired may be reinforced causing employee frustration and subsequent strategy failure.

BUSINESS STRATEGY AND HUMAN RESOURCES PRACTICES

To illustrate actual organizational practices and strategic linkages, we examined three large tertiary care hospitals in a community in the southwestern United States. Because the three hospitals compete in the same area and each has chosen some differing strategies, they provide a microcosm for examining the matters we have been discussing. Interviews were conducted with chief executive officers (CEOs), personnel directors, nurse recruiters, and vice presidents for human resources and for nursing. Table 19.3 describes the organizations, the overall strategies being pursued, and types

TABLE 19.2. The Linkage of Strategies, Implementation Emphasis, and Key Human Resources

Generic Strategy	Implementation Emphasis	Key Human Resources Practices
1. *Diversification into new health-related or nonhealth-related markets:* achieve competitive advantage through service/market development	1. New product or service development; entrepreneurship	1. Recruit and select experienced clinical and executive personnel; reward both based on incentive comprehension and/or indirect compensation
2. *Technical quality leadership:* achieve competitive advantage through clinical and technological sophistication	2. Clinical quality; technological sophistication; clinical research evaluating new protocols	2. Recruit and select and retain top physicians and medical researcher; design compensation packages to attract and retain "superstars"; provide high staffing levels
3. *Functional quality leaderhip:* achieve competitive advantage through responsiveness to patients needs and demands	3. Patient service	3. Provide above-average staffing; implement sophisticated career counseling and promotion career system; monitor employee attitudes; train all staff in guest relations; appraise and reward based on interpersonal skills and responsiveness to patients
4. *Cost leadership:* achieve competitive advantage through being the low-cost provider	4. Economies of scale; cost control; productivity	4. Provide lean staffing related to patient acuity levels; develop measurable performance standards for all positions; appraise based on performance standards; compensate for good attendance and money-saving innovations; redesign jobs for maximum utilization and productivity
5. *Focus (i.e., specification):* achieve competitive advantage through dominance of a limited market	5. Varies by specific market niche	5. Recruit and select specialist physicians and other professionals to serve specific market niche; supplemental use of nonemployee professionals; other practices depend on how the organization intends to pursue the specialized market (i.e., cost of leadership)

Source: Fottler, M. D., Phillips, R. L., Blair, J. D., and Duran, C. A. (1990). Achieving Competitive Advantage Through Strategic Human Resources Management. *Hospital & Health Services Administration, 35*(3), 345.

TABLE 19.3. Hospital Types and Strategies

	Type	Major Strategy	Human Resources Strategy-Planning Linkage
Hospital A	Academic medical center	Cost leadership	Administrative
Hospital B	Independent not-for-profit	Diversification/ vertical integration	One-way
Hospital C	Religious not-for-profit	Functional quality leadership	Integrative

of human resources linkages that were discovered during these interviews.

The emergence of the range of strategies and linkages across the organizations is a relatively recent occurrence. In the mid to late 1980s, the three hospitals engaged in a flurry of one-upmanship at great expense that resulted in an oversupply of some types of facilities and services and did not produce the "front-runner" status each organization had sought. Subsequently, according to the various CEOs, each hospital reevaluated its mission and goals and the key strategies listed in Table 19.3 evolved.

In addition to Hospital A's overall cost leadership strategy, it is also attempting a technical quality leadership strategy in the area of trauma care. The director of personnel stated that his department is not involved in top-level strategic planning at all and that it "doesn't deserve to be." He has begun a total revamping program, however, that he believes will elevate his unit to a level of functioning congruent with such planning. He recognized the difficulties involved and reported the main problem to be "a focus on results/lack of concern with methods" by upper-level management.

Hospital B's diversification/vertical integration strategy has evolved along several different paths. Within the main hospital it has built a children's hospital and a heart transplant center. A day care center for employees' children and a home health unit have been constructed near the hospital, and geographic diversity has been undertaken through the purchase of several small hospitals in surrounding communities. The strategy/human resources linkage is one-way, but the human resources vice president noted that executives are always careful to include in their planning the funding necessary for his unit to respond to project needs.

Hospital C is part of a multi-institutional system, all of whose members are following a functional quality leadership strategy through a policy of commitment to their four "core values" or "guiding principles" of dignity, service, excellence and justice. All units within the hospital, including human resources, are directly involved in strategic planning. Human resources plays an integral part through design and implementation of training programs, performance appraisal systems, and satisfaction surveys that reinforce the quality strategy. That the success of a functional quality leadership strategy is dependent on total commitment at all levels of an organization appears to be well understood by Hospital C. For example, the plans for its new intensive care and coronary care units were designed by the nursing department with input from other inhouse units and local physicians.

It is too soon to determine if one hospital's strategies and methods will afford it a significant competitive advantage over the other two, but in terms of human resources, it was interesting to find that Hospital C had the lowest turnover and absenteeism rates of the three organizations. Indeed, at the time the interviews took place, Hospital C had no (zero) job openings in any department.

Finally, interviews with human resources executives pinpointed the following present and future challenges for their area similar to those identified earlier in this chapter:

- Recruitment and retention of professional and technical staff, especially nurses
- A need for people with a service mentality
- A need for people who can work in groups
- Development of compensation

programs to attract and retain competent managerial and ancillary staffs

• Further integration and development of human resources management as a strategic function

ENHANCEMENT OF EMPLOYEE PRODUCTIVITY

The Delphi study of Arthur Andersen and Company and the American College of Hospital Administrators (1984) identified a number of CEO skills critical to success in the increasingly competitive health care environment. In addition to strategic planning skills, leaders of vision are needed to maximize institutional productivity.

Several of the guidelines identified by Shortell (1985) in his analysis of high-performing health care organizations relate to various methods of enhancing employee productivity. For example, such organizations tend to stretch themselves, to maximize learning, to manage ambiguity and uncertainty, and to exhibit a well-defined culture. Organizations can stretch themselves only if they allow employer participation in jointly setting ambitious goals for individual and/or work group performance. To maximize learning, the organization has to have a very well-developed training and development function. The management of ambiguity and development of a well-defined culture requires implementation through appropriate recruitment, selection, and compensation policies.

Health care executives have become increasingly concerned with productivity as cost containment, prospective payment systems, and increasing competition have become environmental realities. The public has become convinced it is spending too much for health care and receiving too little. The era of "open-ended" funding is past. One method of dealing with this new situation is to generate more output from existing resources (i.e., to increase productivity).

The principal difficulty encountered by health care organizations in addressing the question of productivity is that productivity analysis stands as a relatively underdeveloped management tool (Fottler & Maloney, 1979; Margulies & Duval, 1984). Most health care institutions have not established productivity tracking systems or methods for measuring and analyzing productivity improvement (Mannisto, 1980). However, several recent publications have provided guidelines and systems for such measurement (Eastaugh, 1985; Margulies & Duval, 1984; Williams, 1973).

Specific management approaches to raising employee productivity fall into two general categories: technical and human resources. The technical approaches include changes with respect to capital investment, new technology, and subcontracting. Human resources approaches include changes in work organization, work scheduling, work rules, and participation processes.

A recent review article (Fottler, 1987) has examined a number of structure and process variables related to productivity. Some are related to human resources and some are not. Among the structural factors related to human resources that seem to be associated with higher employee productivity were the use of contract management in the provision of certain services, little or no unionization of the labor force, structural mechanisms to involve physicians in decision making, use of physician extenders, and a close fit between structure and technology.

Process variables associated with higher employee productivity included significant physician, nurse, and department head participation in strategy development and implementation; an emphasis on inter- and intradepartmental communication and coordination; use of incentive compensation; use of many indicators of employee performance; efforts to reward creativity and innovation; use of quality circles and other employee participation programs; development of data to measure and enhance employee satisfaction; active efforts to modify physician behavior through a conbination of strategies; use of flex time and flexible staffing; provision of many opportunities for employees to voice dissatisfaction; organizationwide development efforts; development of physician protocols in which process/outcome relationships are fairly certain; and the recruitment and selection of managers who emphasize outcomes and the constant necessity to adapt to environmental change (Fottler, 1987).

Not all of these structural and process human resources variables will necessarily be appropriate or productivity enhancing in all situations. Clearly, there are contingencies that will make some more appropriate than others in a given situation. From the viewpoint of the health care executive, the key is to keep up with research results that provide guidelines to productivity improvement in both the human resources and the technical areas. Then the approaches that seem to be most appropriate should be adapted to the particular circumstances of the particular organization.

One particularly promising approach to productivity enhancement is to achieve greater flexibility in the utilization of health manpower (Fottler, 1992). The rapid advancement of technology in the health services has been accompanied by a rapid proliferation of allied health specialties, each of which has identified its own unique role. Specialty training programs have tended to be modeled on whatever the members of the specialty desired. Consequently, an elongation of curriculum with associated increases in expected salaries has occurred.

Financial limitations and a limited pool of trained specialists in rural areas have made it impossible for every physician's office, clinic, or hospital to recruit and hire specialists in major areas of need. Consequently, many individuals perform as generalist health technicians in small and rural facilities. However, one result is a lower quality of health services as a result of these employees' lack of formal training for such roles. Even in facilities that can afford the specialist technicians, the inevitable result is higher than necessary costs due to idle time and high wages.

The training of a new health worker variously labeled "multiskilled workers," "multiple-competency clinical technician," or "expanded-skill health practitioner" represents one approach to solving the cost/quality problem identified above. Interest in this concept is growing rapidly, not only in the United States, but in foreign countries as well (W. K. Kellogg Foundation, 1986). In fact, progress in implementing the concept is much greater abroad.

There is a growing interest in the multiskilled movement in the United States, due mainly to cost-containment pressures, competition, and the emergence of outpatient alternative delivery settings. However, relatively few formal educational programs exist here to provide training for the multiskilled health worker. In 1987, the two major programs were at the University of Alabama at Birmingham and Southern Illinois University.

For health organization, the multiskilled worker can provide cost benefits by reducing the idle or "down" time of employees and the number of employees needed. (Vaughan, Fottler, Bamberg, & Blayney, 1991). Productivity can also be enhanced as a result of the greater versatility of the multiskilled worker. Shortages of labor are reduced as individuals assume new functions. Cost effectiveness is enhanced by a reduction in the number of required workers. In addition, the multiskilled workers should benefit as a result of job enrichment, higher job satisfaction, a potential for increased pay, increased job security, and increased marketability.

If the idea of multiple competency is so timely, why is it not more widespread? Among the obstacles are human nature's resistance to change; established disciplines that oppose encroachment; allied health and nursing schools, which have been encouraged by federal grants and accreditation bodies to train only specialized technicians; and accreditation. No established multiple-competency associations exist to accredit programs (Blayney, 1986). Legal restrictions and liability issues associated with the use of multiskilled personnel also limit utilization.

Health care executives have a vested interest in working for multiple-skilled technician programs and other approaches that make the manpower credentialing process more flexible. Otherwise they will continue to have little control over their staffing, particularly in terms of matching credentials to institutional needs. Calls for reevaluation are becoming increasingly common in the health care literature (Hofmann, 1984).

The issue of flexibility applies not only to human resources, but to all areas of management. As Peter Drucker (1992) has noted: "Every organization has to prepare for the abandonment of everything it does. . . . Indeed organizations increasingly will have to plan abandonment rather than try to prolong the life of a successful product, policy, or practice" (p. 102).

TOTAL QUALITY MANAGEMENT

The continuous improvement in all facets of health and medical services quality has received attention recently as a result of increased competition, changing expectations of the Joint Commission on Accreditation of Healthcare Organizations, and rising expectations of consumers, payers, and regulators. All health care organizations now face considerable pressure to increase their current levels of efficiency (i.e., cost containment) and effectiveness (i.e., quality/appropriateness of care) (Casalou, 1991; Counte, Glandon, Oleske, & Hill, 1992; McLaughlin & Kaluzney, 1990; Shortell, 1990).

One of the most promising managerial innovations introduced within the health services industry during the past 5 years is the total quality management (TQM) program. Initially developed in the United States and later implemented successfully in Japanese manufacturing, this approach to quality management offers considerable promise to health services managers confronted with the challenge of simultaneously increasing the efficiency and effectiveness of their services. Thus, TQM offers substantial potential in health services (Deming, 1986; Merry, 1991) because it views cost containment and quality enhancement as compatible. According to McLaughlin and Kaluzney (1990):

> Total quality management is a conceptual approach different from quality assurance (QA) and quality inspection and runs counter to many underlying assumptions of professional bureaucracies. It calls for continuous and relentless improvement in the total process that provides care, not simply in the improved actions of individual professionals. Improvement is thus based on both outcome and process. (p. 7)

Among the major characteristics of TQM are a focus on multiple customers, the continuous improvement of quality, development of teams, the statistical monitoring of results, and appropriate management follow-up actions.

TQM requires that change be based on the needs of the customer rather than the values of the provider, meaningful participation by all personnel, and a rapid and thoughtful response from top management to suggestions made by participating personnel. In contrast to the bureaucratic model, management no longer can stifle employees' suggestions by requiring additional study or approval by higher levels of management. Moreover, TQM does not respect existing professional standards because it is continually demanding new ones. Finally, under TQM the focus is on improving the system rather than the individual employee.

From a human resources perspective, there are differences in emphasis between TQM and the traditional model of health care delivery. These differences include empowerment, teams, training, and performance appraisal. Empowerment includes all managerial and nonmanagerial personnel as well as patients. All are empowered to work with others to achieve desired results with minimal managerial controls and constraints. Obviously, managers and professionals lose some of their power to control others while maintaining their power to lead. Rigid professional boundaries are reduced. Patient improvement means providing them with information to make choices between competing quality alternatives. Examples include mortality, other quality indices, and prices.

The TQM process also brings people together in teams that focus on meeting patients' needs. Members of the team attempt to develop a deep understanding of what other members are doing in order to better communicate and coordinate their services. Corporations with successful TQM programs are more likely than their less successful counterparts to have pushed responsibility for quality down to lower-level workers, flattened their organizational structures, and broken down departmental barriers (Port, Carey, Kelly, & Forest, 1992). The teams emphasize the criteria selected by the patients and other "customers" and all team members are equally respected.

Obviously, all employees need to be trained in the principles and practices of TQM. Such training needs to be long-term because successful TQM programs involve changing the culture of the organization. It needs to focus not only on definitions and measurement of quality improvement, but also on processes of communication and team building.

Most performance appraisal systems are based on setting goals and then meeting them. TQM appraisals focus on demonstrating skills to contribute to the process of quality improvement. Thus, the appraisal system is based on contribution to a team effort to improve outcomes rather than on whether a specific set of objectives are met. Input from team members and subordinates may be considered rather than simply an appraisal by the immediate supervisor. With TQM, the objectives will change continually. When some objectives are met, new objectives are set.

What has been the impact of TQM in industry and health services? Arthur D. Little did a survey of 500 manufacturing and service companies that used TQM and found that only 36% felt it was significantly boosting their competitiveness (Port et al., 1992). TQM is not a substitute for structural change. It will not fix poor strategic planning, excess administrative overhead, poorly executed diversification, and resistance from managerial employees or physicians. Finally, larger organizations have more bureaucratic and professional inertia to overcome. It therefore takes longer to implement a TQM program. In very small organizations, various hallmarks of total quality such as employee empowerment and teamwork come more naturally.

Despite these problems, TQM represents an approach with a great deal of potential. Yet, it presents some basic conflicts with underlying norms and cultural values that guide all professional bureaucracies. The challenge for health care executives is to overcome these barriers in order to achieve the potential benefits of successful implementation of TQM.

MANAGING CORPORATE RESTRUCTURING

The 1980s were characterized by corporate restructuring (in the form of acquisitions, mergers, and downsizing) in both American industry in general and in the health care industry in particular (Tomasko, 1987). This restructuring continues in to the 1990s as increased competition is forcing organizations to cut layers of managers and restructure work forces (The age of consolidation, 1991).

It is difficult to imagine circumstances that pose a greater challenge for human resources management than the restructuring that has characterized the last decade (Fisher, 1989). Such restructuring inevitably affects many organization levels and employees. As a result of restructuring, employees may face the following potential changes: 1) loss of job, pay, and benefits; 2) new job roles and job assignments; 3) transfer to a new geographic location; 4) changes in compensation and benefits; 5) changes in career possibilities; 6) changes in organizational power, status, and prestige; 7) staff changes; and 8) changes in corporate culture.

There is little indication that the pace of corporate restructuring will slacken in the near future and a recent survey of nearly 600 organizations showed that between 60% and 70% of the respondents were evaluating downsizing and/or restructuring (HR Strategies, 1991). To a greater extent than ever before, health care organizations consider restructuring as routine business transactions. The pressures from health care reform make such restructuring almost a necessity. For example, University Hospital in Birmingham planned to drop 350 jobs in 1993 through attrition, early retirements, and layoffs (Botgereit, 1993). The reduction in force is part of the hospital's efforts to trim $20 million from its $497 million budget and better position itself for health care reform efforts. In a city in which health care is the main industry and UAB is the largest employer, most health care organizations have been examining personnel's role in costs.

Downsizing refers to the planned elimination of positions or jobs. Proponents of downsizing cite the following six potential organizational benefits (Heeman, 1989):

- Lower overhead
- Less bureaucracy
- Faster decision making
- Smoother communications
- Greater entrepreneurship
- Increased productivity

Yet critics note that these benefits are rarely achieved because most employers are not well-prepared for downsizing, have no retraining or redeployment policies in place, and fail to anticipate the kinds of human resources problems that subsequently develop (Cascio, 1993). Strategic planning suffers and the remaining employees exhibit "survivor's syndrome" (Brockner, 1988). The latter refers to a tendency to be narrow-minded, self-absorbed, risk-adverse, less-productive, unmotivated, distrustful of management, and dispirited. Productivity and quality often suffer because there is no change in the way work is done. The same amount of work is simply loaded onto the backs of fewer workers.

The long-term implications of reduced employee morale and commitment are extremely negative. For example, a key ingredient that is necessary to sustain programs of total quality management/continuous quality improvement is high morale. Employees must "buy in" to the management strategy for improving quality; they must align their interests with those of management; and they must become involved and committed to bring about genuine, lasting improvements

in this area (U.S. General Accounting Office, 1991).

Employers who execute downsizing well (i.e., to experience productivity increases) seem to share the following management characteristics (Cameron, Freeman & Mishra, 1991):

- Downsizing is planned with employees instead of springing it on them unannounced based on job analyses of how work is currently organized.
- Both short-term (workforce reduction) and long-term (organization redesign and cultural change) are used together with targeted downsizing.
- Special attention is paid both to those employees who lost their jobs (through outplacement, severance pay, retraining, family counseling) and to those who did not (by increasing information exchange among top-level managers and employees).
- Employees identify precisely where redundancy, excess cost, and inefficiency exist through internal data gathering and data monitoring. They then attack these areas specifically whether they are internal or external (i.e., suppliers) to the organization.
- Reorganizations often produce smaller, semiautonomous organizations within large, integrated organizations.
- Downsizing is viewed as a means to an end (i.e., to enhance competitiveness) as well as the targeted end.

Planning is the crucial element in managing downsizing. It is crucial that the organization develop plans for coping with an over-supply of labor *before* the need arises. Decisions made hastily under economic pressure may be poor ones. Yet a 1988 survey found that 50% of human resources managers responding indicated their organizations were unprepared for reducing their work force (Bunning, 1990). Layoffs should be a last resort. Polls of 1204 and 909 companies found only 6% had tried cutting pay, 9% had shortened work weeks, 9% used vacation without pay, and 14% had developed job sharing plans (Greenberg, 1991).

General policies and procedures for handling downsizing should include: 1) viable methods of reducing the work force, including both layoffs and other alternatives; 2) procedures for identifying candidates for layoffs and for dealing with them at the time of layoff; and 3) procedures for managing people who remain with the organization. All of these decisions must be considered as a coordinated whole rather than as separate and isolated decisions. They also need to be made with the strategic goals and strategic implementation plan of the health care organization in mind. The knowledge, skills, and abilities of some individuals and groups will be more valuable for achieving these goals than will those of others. The layoff of individuals and groups whose contributions are crucial to the implementation of the strategic plans would obviously adversely affect the achievement of strategic goals.

Finally, management should use the opportunity of downsizing to consider *why* the cost-reduction program was necessary in the first place. What could be done strategically to solve the underlying problems? Unless this is done, further cost-cutting programs, including downsizing, may be necessary in the future.

SUMMARY

Present and future environmental changes will require health care organizations to collaborate with other organizations in both the public and private sectors in new and innovative ways. These environmental changes will also lead to significant increases in competition within the health care industry. Strategies to gain competitive advantage have little hope of succeeding, however, without integration of human resouces planning into the strategic planning process.

Then a continual search for productivity improvement should utilize a variety of human resources approaches such as continuous quality improvement, incentive compensation, and flexible use of human resources. In particular, the trend toward extreme specialization of human resources in health services has become dysfunctional. The use of multiskilled health practitioners offers a promising option for the future as does the implementation of total quality management systems. The management of corporate restructuring and downsizing poses a continuing challenge as a result of health reform efforts and the increasingly competitive environment.

Discussion Questions

1. What is the present role and influence of the human resources in those health care organizations with which you are familiar? Why? What factors will affect the *future* roles and influence of the human resource management function in health care organizations? Why?

2. What environmental changes do you expect to occur in the health care industry during the next decade? Select one major environmental change and indicate how it might affect each of the human resource functions identified in this book (i.e., human resources planning, recruitment, selection,

training, performance appraisal, and compensation).

3. What are the benefits of integrating human resources planning and strategic planning in health care organizations? Why is such an integration relatively rare?
4. How can improvements in employee productivity enhance both quality and cost containment? Give specific examples.
5. What are the major impediments to the more flexible use of manpower in the health services industry? How does this situation affect the health care executive? How can constructive change be accomplished?
6. Discuss the relevance and importance of human resources management in the implementation of total quality management programs.
7. Why is downsizing so prevalent in the health care industry today? What are its costs? How can the process be managed so as to minimize negative outcomes?

CASE: THE CAREER OPPORTUNITY

You are a 30-year-old M.H.A. graduate currently working as an Assistant Administrator in the human resources department of a large metropolitan hospital. You have initiated several innovative projects on your job, including quality circles, but you do not always feel you have the support of the "higher-ups." As an active member of the American Society for Personnel Administrators (ASPA) chapter, you have given several talks to that group as well as other local groups. Your basic contention is that human resources managers need to take a more

proactive role in helping their organizations survive and prosper in an increasingly competitive environment.

Perhaps as a result of your activity, you have been asked to interview for a position as vice president of human resources at the University Medical Center in the largest city in your state. If you are offered this position, it would represent a significant step up in terms of position, status responsibility, and salary. On the basis of materials sent to you as well as telephone conversations, it appears the medical center now has a very traditional personnel function with an emphasis on processing paper.

The search committee for the position has asked you to come for an interview in the following week and be prepared to analyze, evaluate, and make recommendations concerning its present personnel system. They also want you to discuss your own philosophy and what you would do to turn this function into a "state-of-the-art human resources function for the 1990s."

Case Discussion Questions

1. Prepare an outline for what you would present to the search committee and be prepared to justify each element.
2. Select students to form a search committee, to play the role of job applicant, and to role play the interview.

REFERENCES

The age of consolidation. (1991, October 14). *Business Week,* pp. 86–94.
American Hospital Association. (1991). *Hospital Statistics.* Chicago: Author.
American Society for Healthcare and Human Resources Administration. (1992). *Health*

care 2000: A world of human resource differences. Chicago: American Hospital Association.

Arthur Andersen and Company and the American College of Healthcare Executives. (1987). *The future of healthcare: Changes and choices.* Chicago: Author.

Arthur Andersen and Company and the American College of Healthcare Executives. (1991). *The future of healthcare: Physician and hospital relationships.* Chicago: Author.

Arthur Andersen and Company and the American College of Hospital Administrators. (1984). *Health care in the 1990s: Trends and strategies.* Chicago: Author.

Blair, J.D., & Fottler, M.D. (1990). *Challenges in health care management.* San Francisco: Jossey-Bass.

Blayney, K.D. (1986). Restructuring the health care labor force: The use of the multiskilled allied health practitioner. *Alabama Journal of Medical Sciences, 23*(3), 277–278.

Boerma, H. (1983). *The organizational impact of DRGs: DRG evaluation.* Princeton, NJ: Center for Health Affairs, Health Research and Educational Trust of New Jersey.

Botgereit, B. (1993, May 13). University cutting 350 jobs. *Birmingham News,* pp. 1A, 8A.

Brockner, J. (1988). The effects of work lay offs on survivors: Research, theory, and practice. In B.M. Staw & L.L. Cummings (Eds.), *Research in organizational behavior* (pp. 213–255). Greenwich, CT: JAI Press.

Buller, P.F. (1988). Successful partnerships: HR and strategic planning at eight top firms. *Organizational Dynamics, 17,* 27–43.

Bunning, R.M. (1990). The dynamics of downsizing. *Personnel Journal, 69*(9), 68–75.

Bureau of Labor Statistics. (1987). *Projections 2000.* Washington, DC: Office of Economic Growth and Employment Projections.

Cameron, K.S., Freeman, S.J., & Mishra, A.K. (1991). Best practices in white collar downsizing: Managing contradictions. *Academy of Management Executive, 5*(3), 57–73.

Casalou, R.F. (1991). Total quality management in health care. *Hospital and Health Services Administration, 36*(1), 134–146.

Cascio, W.R. (1993). Downsizing: What do we know? What have we learned? *The Executive, 7*(1), 95–104.

Counte, M.A., Glandon, G.L., Oleske, D.M., Hill, J.P. (1992). Total duality management in a health care environment: How are employees affected? *Hospital and Health Services Administration, 37*(4), 503–518.

Crawford, M., & Fottler, M.D. (1985). The impact of diagnosis-related groups and prospective payment on health care management. *Health Care Management Review, 10,* 73–84.

Deming, W.E. (1986). *Out of Crisis.* Cambridge: MIT Press.

DePree, H. (1986). *Business as usual.* Zeeland, MI: Herman Miller.

Drucker, P.F. (1992). The new society of organizations. *Harvard Business Review, 70*(5), 95–104.

Eastaugh, S.R. (1985). Improving hospital productivity under PPS. *Hospital and Health Services Administration, 30,* 97–111.

Egdahl, R.H. (1984). Should we shrink the health care system? *Harvard Business Review, 62,* 125–132.

Ermann, D., & Gabel, J. (1984). Multihospital systems: Issues and empirical findings. *Health Affairs, 3*(1), 50–64.

Ermann, D., & Gabel, J. (1985). The changing face of the American health care: Multihospital systems, emergicenters, and surgery centers. *Medical Care, 23*(5), 401–420.

Fisher, C.D. (1989). Current and recurrent challenges in HRM. *Journal of Management, 15*(1), 157–180.

Fottler, M.D. (1987). Health care organizational performance: Present and future research. *Journal of Management, 13*(2), 179–203.

Fottler, M.D. (1992). The evolution of manpower utilization patterns in health services and American industry. In K.D. Brayney (Ed.), *Healing hands: Customizing your health team for institutional survival* (pp. 1–23). Battle Creek, MI: W.K. Kellog Foundation.

Fottler, M.D., & Lanning, A. (1986). A comprehensive incentive approach to employee health care cost containment. *California Management Review, 29*(1), 75–94.

Fottler, M.D., & Maloney, W.F. (1979). Guidelines to productivity bargaining in the healthy care industry. *Health Care Management Review, 3,* 59–70.

Fottler, M.D., Phillips, R.L., Blair, J.D., & Duran, C.A. (1990). Achieving competitive advantage through strategic human resource management. *Hospital and Health Service Administration, 35,* 341–363.

Fottler, M.D., & Malvey, D. M. (1994). Multiprovider systems. In L.F. Wolper & J.J. Pena (Eds.), *Health care administration: Principles and practice.* Rockville, MD: Aspen.

Fox, P.D., Goldbeck, W.B., & Spies, J. (1984), *Health care cost management: Private sector initiatives.* Ann Arbor, MI: Health Administration Press.

Fuchs, V.R. (1982). The battle for control of health care. *Health Affairs, 1,* 5–13.

Gold, M.R. (1991). HMOs and managed care. *Health Affairs, 10*(4), 189–206.

Golden, K.A., & Ramanujam, C. (1985). Between a dream and a nightmare: On the integration of the human resource management and strategic business planning processes. *Human Resource Management, 24*(4), 429–452.

Goodmeasure, Inc. (1982). *Strategic planning for human resources.* Cambridge: Author.

Greenberg, E.R. (1991). Downsizing: AMA survey results. *Compensation and Benefits Review, 23*(4), 33–38.

Heenan, D.A. (1989). The downside of downsizing. *The Journal of Business Strategy, 9*(6), 18–23.

Himmelstein, D.V., Woolhandler, S., & Wolfe, S.M. (1992). The vanishing health care safety net: New data on uninsured Americans. *International Journal of Health Services, 22*(3), 381–396.

Hofmann, P.B. (1984). Healthcare credentialing issues demand increased attention. *Hospital and Health Services Administration, 29*(3), 86–93.

HR Strategies. (1991). *Survey of human resources trends.* Gross Point, MI: Author.

Hudson Institute. (1987). *Workforce 2000.* Washington, DC: U.S. Government Printing Office.

Lengnick-Hall, C.A., & Lengnick-Hall, M.L. (1988). Strategic human resource management: A review of the literature and a proposed typology. *Academy of Management Review, 13*(3), 454–470.

Margulies, N., & Duval, J. (1984). Productivity management: A model for participative management in health care organizations. *Health Care Management Review, 9*(1), 61–70.

Massachusetts Hospital Association. (1989). *Health care personnel: Avoiding a crisis in the 1990s.* Report of the health personnel task force. Burlington, MA: Author.

McLaughlin, C.P., & Kaluzny, A.D. (1990). Total quality management in health: Making it work. *Health Care Management Review, 15*(3), 7–14.

Merry, M.D. (1991). Illusion and reality: Tom beyond the yellow brick road. *Healthcare Executive, 6*(2), 18–21.

Miles, R.E., & Snow, C.C. (1984). Designing strategic human resource systems. *Organizational Dynamics, 13*(2), 36–52.

Morone, J.A., & Dunham, A.B. (1984). The waning of professional dominance: DRGs and the hospitals. *Health Affairs, 3,* 73–84.

National Alliance of Business. (1985). *Responding to the entry-level hiring crisis.* Washington, DC: Author.

Pointer, D.D. (1985). Responding to the challenges of the new healthcare marketplace: Organizing for creativity and innovation. *Hospitals and Health Services Administration, 30,* 10–25.

Port, O., Carey, J., Kelly, K., & Forest, S.A., (1992, November 30). Quality. *Business Week,* 66–72.

Rakich, J.S. (1991). The Canadian and U.S. health care systems: Profiles and policies. *Hospital and Health Services Administration, 36,* 25–42.

Robbins, S.A., & Rakich, J.S. (1986). Hospital personnel management in the late 1980s: A direction for the future. *Hospital and Health Service Administration, 31,* 18–33.

Rublee, D.A., & Schneider, M. (1991). International health spending comparisons. *Health Affairs, 10*(3), 22–38.

Schieber, G.J., Poullier, J.P., & Greenwald, L.M. (1991). Health care systems in twenty-four countries. *Health Affairs, 10*(3), 22–38.

Schuler, R.S., & Jackson, S.E. (1987). Linking competitive strategies with human resources management practices. *Academy of Management Executive, 1*(3), 207–219.

Sear, A.M. (1992). Operating characteristics and comparative performance of investor-owned multihospital systems. *Hospital and Health Services Administration, 37,* 403–415.

Shortell, S.M. (1985). A more total approach to productivity improvement. *Hospital and Health Services Administration, 30*(4), 7–35.

Shortell, S.M. (1990). Adding value is a must for survivors and thrivers. *Healthcare Executives, 5*(3), 17–19.

Smith, H.L., & Fottler, M.D. (1985). *Prospective payment: Managing for operational effectiveness.* Rockville, MD: Aspen.

Smith, M.D., Altman, D.E., Leitman, R., Moloney, T.W., & Taylor, H. (1992). Taking the public's pulse on health system reform. *Health Affairs, 11*(2), 125–133.

Tomasko, R.M. (1987). *Downsizing: Restructuring the corporation for the future.* New York: American Management Association.

U.S. Bureau of the Census. (1991). *Statistical abstract of the United States: 1991.* Washington, DC: U.S. Government Printing Office.

U.S. General Accounting Office. (1991). *Management practices: U.S. companies improve performance through quality effort.* Washington, DC: U.S. Government Printing Office.

Vaughan, D.G., Fottler, M.D., Bamberg, R., & Blayney, K.D. (1991). Utilization and management of the multiskilled health practitioners in U.S. hospitals. *Hospital and Health Service Administration, 36*(3), 397–419.

W.G. Kellogg Foundation. (1986). *Restructuring the health care labor force: The rise of the multiskilled health practitioner.* International Conference, Birmingham, Alabama.

Williams, N. (1973). *The management of hospital employee productivity.* Chicago: American Hospital Association.

Zallocco, R., Joseph, B., & Furey, N. (1984). Do hospitals practice strategic planning? An empirical study. *Health Care Strategic Management, 2*(2), 16–20.

INDEX

Q

R